*Production
and
Operations
Management*

By the same author

The Techniques of Production Management (1971)
Management and Production (1972) *(2nd ed. 1980)*
Women in the Factory
   (with A. B. Hill and C. C. Ridgeway) (1970)
Mass Production Management (1972)
Principles of Modern Management
   (with B. Lowes) (1972)
Work Organization (1975)
Concepts for Operations Management (1977)
Operations Management—A Policy Framework (1980)
Essentials of Production and Operations Management (1980)
Management and Production—Readings (1981)
How to Manage (1983)
Four children's books comprising the 'Read and Explain' series (1982)

Production and Operations Management

Principles and Techniques

Third Edition

Ray Wild

*The Management College, Henley
and
Brunel University*

Holt, Rinehart and Winston
London·New York·Sydney·Toronto

Holt, Rinehart and Winston Ltd: 1 St Anne's Road,
Eastbourne, East Sussex BN21 3UN

Printed in Great Britain by Mackays of Chatham Ltd

British Library Cataloguing in Publication Data

Wild, Ray
    Production and operations management—3rd ed
    1. Production management
    I. Title
    658.5   TS156

ISBN 0-03-910480-X

Last digit is print no: 9 8 7 6 5 4 3 2 1

Contents

Preface

This is a book about production and operations management. The production and operating functions within business are concerned with the processes which provide goods and/or 'services'. Production and operations managers are responsible for these processes. This book is concerned with the management of both goods-producing and service-producing processes.

The definitions and ideas presented later in this book are based on a wide view of production and operations management. This approach views the production/operations function as the core—the essential part—of *any* business. Furthermore, taking this view it will be shown that we are all production and operations managers. All types of business depend on production or operating systems and therefore require good production/operations management. Our subject, therefore, is of importance to all managers whatever their title and whatever their job.

The book introduces some theories, ideas and concepts. It deals also with principles, procedures and techniques. It is intended as a teaching text.

The book is intended as an economic, straightforward volume. Unnecessary words have been kept to a minimum and 'padding' has been avoided. The result, I hope, provides maximum value for minimum effort, for both student and teacher. From Chapter 5 the book is structured in a 'life-cycle' form since (from Part 3) it deals, in order, with the types of problems which would be encountered in establishing, designing, planning, running and maintaining a production and operating system.

This, in effect, is a new edition of *Production and Operations Management—Principles and Techniques* (Wild, 1979), which in turn was the second edition of *The Techniques of Production Management* (Wild, 1971). In this book the overall structure and style of the 1979 book has been retained; however, I have added several new features, including the chapter on operations economics (Chapter 4). I have strengthened Part 2 of the book, in which the broader business context of production and operations management is discussed, and I have substantially changed several other chapters. New features in this edition include a checklist at the end of each chapter. Throughout I have attempted to make reference to computer-based methods, and I have added new examples to those chapters which have undergone significant changes.

The book deals with both goods-producing and service-producing systems. I have attempted to deal in a realistic manner with this broad field, and have sought to avoid any camouflaging of material. For example, I have tried wherever possible to deal with topics in a manner relevant to both goods-producing and service-producing systems, but where topics relate to one or the other I have treated them in that manner rather than pretend that they have some broader relevance.

Chapter 1 is the main foundation of the book. It provides definitions and identifies the critical production/operations management problem areas. Chapters 2 and 3 relate operations management to the other business functions. Together these chapters provide a framework for the study of operations management. I hope, therefore, that the book provides an economical treatment of the broad subject area of production and operations management, with an approach which offers not only details of specific problem areas and decision-making techniques but also a framework and set of ideas on which to build a better understanding of the relevance and importance of these problem areas and decision-making techniques.

ACKNOWLEDGEMENTS

I am grateful to several companies and publishers for their permission to reproduce certain material in either original or modified form within the book. I am grateful to the United Kingdom Universities at Bradford, Lancaster, Salford, London, Sussex and Warwick and to the Cranfield Institute of Technology for the reproduction of examination questions (often in modified form). My thanks are also due to numerous colleagues and friends, too numerous to mention by name, who have made useful comments on several chapters of the book in both original and revised form, and to the typists and secretaries (paid and unpaid) who prepared the manuscript.

Finally, I am grateful to the numerous users of this textbook in educational establishments throughout the world who over the past few years have written to me with comments, suggestions, criticisms and encouraging remarks. It is due to their efforts, as much as mine, that the previous edition of this book was so widely adopted. I hope that they, above all, find this new version equally acceptable.

Henley-on-Thames   Ray Wild
England
March 1983

PART 1

OPERATING SYSTEMS AND OPERATIONS MANAGEMENT

INTRODUCTION TO PART 1

This part of the book is the principal foundation for subsequent chapters. Here we take a broad view of operations management. Definitions are developed and a categorization of types of operating systems is provided. The major problem areas, or decisions required of operations managers, are considered and three principal problem areas are identified. A model is presented to identify the factors influencing the operations manager's decision-making and role. And finally we consider the operations management decision-making process.

The chapter introduces several new concepts and ideas, and aims to encourage the reader to think about the fundamental nature of operating systems and the role of the operations manager.

CHAPTER ONE

The Nature of Operating Systems and Operations Management

We must, necessarily, begin by tackling one of the more controversial aspects of our subject. We must provide definitions. Since the structure of this book to some extent reflects a particular view of the nature of operating systems and operations management, that view must be explained. Bookshop browsers are advised to scan this chapter before deciding whether to buy. Those who have omitted this simple precaution are advised to reconsider their decision when they have read this chapter. All serious readers, including those who have no choice but to use this book, are advised to study this chapter before plunging into the remainder of the book.

Throughout this book we will, for brevity, use the terms 'operations management' and 'operating systems'. They will be defined below.

THE NATURE OF OPERATING SYSTEMS[1]

Definition

> *An operating system is a configuration of resources combined for the provision of goods or services.*

Bus and taxi services, motels and dentists, tailors and mines, fire services and refuse collectors, retail organizations, hospitals and builders are all operating systems. They all, in effect, convert inputs in order to provide outputs which are required by a customer. Physical inputs will normally predominate, hence operating systems convert physical *resources* into outputs, the *function* of which is to satisfy customer wants, i.e. to provide some utility for the customer.

---

[1] The ideas introduced in this section are developed in more detail in Wild, R. (1977) *Concepts for Operations Management*. Wiley: New York.

Resources in operating systems

Operations managers are principally concerned with the use of physical resources; therefore we shall take a physical view of operating systems and concentrate on the physical resources used by the system, which for convenience will be categorized as follows:

1. *Materials*, i.e. the physical items consumed or converted by the system, e.g. raw materials, fuel, indirect materials.
2. *Machines*, i.e. the physical items used by the system, e.g. plant, tools, vehicles, buildings.
3. *Labour*, i.e. the people who provide or contribute to the operation of the system, without whom neither machines nor materials are effectively used.

Function of operating systems

Given this definition a large range and variety of systems may be considered as operating systems. The examples above illustrate this variety. Some form of categorization of such systems would be of value, if only for descriptive purposes. If we distinguish between goods-producing and service-producing systems we have a simple categorization of operating systems. However, a more useful categorization is afforded by a consideration of system function.

The function of an operating system is a reflection of the purpose it serves for its customer, i.e. the utility of its output to the customer. Four principal functions can be identified:

1. *Manufacture*, in which the principal common characteristic is that something is physically created, i.e. the output consists of goods which differ physically, e.g. in form or content, from those materials input to the system. Manufacture therefore requires some physical transformation, or a change in *form utility* of resources.
2. *Transport*, in which the principal common characteristic is that a customer, or something belonging to the customer, is moved from place to place, i.e. the location of someone or something is changed. The system uses its resources primarily to this end, and such resources will not normally be substantially physically changed. There is no major change in the form of resources, and the system provides primarily a change in *place utility*.
3. *Supply*, in which the principal common characteristic is that the ownership or possession of goods is changed. Unlike manufacture, goods output from the system are physically the same as those input. There is no physical transformation and the system function is primarily one of change in *possession utility* of a resource.
4. *Service*, in which the principal common characteristic is the treatment or accommodation of something or someone. There is primarily a change in *state utility* of a resource. Unlike in supply systems, the state or condition of physical outputs will differ from inputs by virtue of having been treated in some way. (NB. It should be noted that this definition is somewhat narrower than that normally implied by this term.)

Many organizations comprise several systems with different functions. For example, an airline will depend on operating systems the purposes of which are transport, supply and service, and a typical manufacturing organization will have internal transport and service systems. In fact, except in very small organizations, we are likely to be able to identify all four functions providing we consider small enough parts of the total system. For this reason the description of a complex organization as a manufacturing system, or transport system, etc., provides only a very general indication of its *overall* or principal purpose. A more detailed description necessitates the consideration of parts, or sub-systems, of the whole. These four principal functions can together be used in describing all operating systems and their sub-systems. They provide a basic language for operations management and permit the development of a slightly more detailed definition of an operating system.

Redefinition[2]

> *An operating system is a configuration of resources combined for the function of manufacture, transport, supply or service.*

Each of these four basic functions is considered briefly, with examples, below.

Manufacture

This is perhaps the principal functional category of operating systems. Most texts on operations management focus implicitly on manufacture, and, while we shall try to avoid undue bias, it is pertinent here to consider the nature of manufacture and, in particular, the types of manufacturing system which might be encountered.

Considering businesses or organizations as a whole, a tailor, coal mine and builder would be categorized as manufacturing systems since their *overall* purpose is that of creating goods. Manufacture is the principal purpose of motor-vehicle firms such as Ford, and within such an organization most factories will be involved primarily in manufacture. Whether we consider large systems and therefore describe their function in overall terms, or whether we consider much smaller systems and therefore take account of more detail, will depend on our purpose. However, whatever our level of description, in general it should be possible to identify different types of manufacturing system, such categorization again being of value mainly for description. We can divide manufacture in two traditional ways.

Firstly we can identify continuous, repetitive and intermittent manufacture. Theoretically a *continuous* process will run for 24 hours per day, seven days per week and 52 weeks per year. In practice, however, while this degree of continuity is often the objective, it is rarely achieved. Examples of this type of manufacture are steelmaking and petrochemicals. A *repetitive* process is one in which the product (or products) is processed in lots, each item of production passing through the same sequence of operations, as, for example, in the assembly of motor vehicles. An *intermittent* process is one in which very small lots, or even single products, are made in response to separate customer orders.

The second and similar classification divides manufacturing into process (or mass), batch and jobbing. *Process* manufacture involves the continuous production of a commodity in bulk, often by chemical rather than mechanical means. *Mass* production (or manufacture) is conceptually similar to process manufacture except that discrete items

---

[2] This, deliberately, is a wide definition. The approach employed throughout this book is equally wide. It derives from the belief that operating systems are at the centre of all types of enterprise and that running all types of enterprise can be seen to be the task of operations management.

such as cars and domestic appliances are usually involved. A single item or a very small range of similar items is manufactured in very large numbers. *Batch* production occurs where the number of discrete items to be manufactured in a period is too small to enable mass production to be used. Wherever possible, similar items are manufactured together in batches. Finally, *jobbing* manufacture, although strictly consisting of the manufacture of different products in unit quantities, in practice corresponds to the intermittent process mentioned above.

Each of these types of manufacture is characteristic of several different industries, but nevertheless no industry consists exclusively of any one type of manufacture. Increasing demand for products at present manufactured by means of a jobbing-type arrangement may enable a form of batch production to be introduced; and, similarly, increased demand for products at present manufactured in batches may indicate the desirability of mass production. It is, however, quite unrealistic to consider these types of manufacture in a strict or absolute sense, since they are only parts of a production continuum the ends of which do not, except in theory, exist.

Transport

The principal function of transport systems is that of changing the location of someone or something. Taxi or bus services, ambulance services, furniture removers and refuse disposal systems can be categorized as transport systems. Within manufacturing organizations, transport systems may be employed for moving work-in-progress between manufacturing departments, removing waste materials, etc.

Supply

The principal function of supply systems is to change the ownership or possession of item(s) which are otherwise physically unchanged. At an organization level, a retail shop, warehouse, petrol station and broker may be seen to have the principal function of supply. Within organizations, supply systems may be evident as internal stores, etc.

Service

Dentists, fire services, launderettes, hospital wards and motels may be considered to have the principal function of service, i.e. the function of treating or accommodating something or someone. Within organizations a similar function may be performed by systems such as welfare departments and rest rooms.

No such categorization can be watertight: inevitably there will be overlap, and such an approach is of value only for descriptive purposes. Such descriptions indicate something about the purpose of and reason for systems, but we must develop a somewhat different approach if we are to explore the nature of operating systems from an operations management viewpoint.

THE STRUCTURE OF OPERATING SYSTEMS

The above categorization by function identifies the scope of operations systems but tells us little about their nature. The nature of the operations manager's job will to some extent depend on the nature of the system being managed. His or her role is partly influenced by the characteristics of the system. Not only what must be done, but the way in which it can be done, is influenced by the nature of the system. To explore the nature of operating systems we shall examine their structure or 'shape'.

Using simple systems terminology all operating systems may be seen to comprise inputs, processes and outputs in the manner of Figure 1.1. This simple system structure can represent any operating system at any level of detail, e.g., an organization as a whole, or some part of it. As a descriptive device it is limited, so we must examine system structure in slightly more detail. The terminology of Figure 1.2 will be used for this purpose. With this simple approach we can identify four simple structures for manufacturing systems:

(a) '*Make from stock, to stock, to customer*', i.e. all input resources are stocked and the customer is served from a stock of finished goods.
(b) '*Make from source, to stock, to customer*', i.e. no input resource stocks are held, but goods are produced to stock.
(c) '*Make from stock, direct to customer*', i.e. all input resources are stocked but goods are made only against and on receipt of customers' orders.

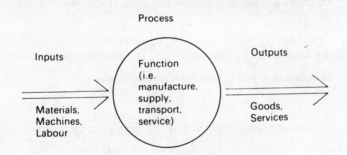

Figure 1.1 *A simple system model.*

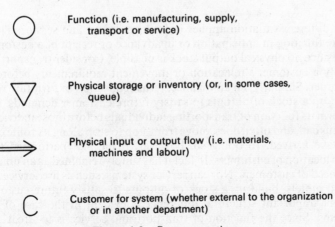

Figure 1.2 *System notation.*

(d)   '*Make from source, direct to customer*', i.e. no input resource stocks are held and all goods are made only against and on receipt of customers' orders.

Each structure shows how a system will provide for future output. Structure (d), for example, indicates that, in order to provide the next output for a customer, resources must first be acquired, whereas in (c) the next customer order will be satisfied through the use of already existing resources.

Now considering supply systems in a similar manner, by substituting 'supply' for 'make' in the above list, we may recognize the validity of these four simple structures. Both structures (a) and (b) require function in anticipation of order, i.e. structure (a) depicts 'supply from stock, to stock, to customer' and structure (b) depicts 'supply from source, to stock, to customer'. Neither case is common in supply operations, but both can exist. More commonly structures (c) and (d) will exist. Structure (c) depicts 'supply from stock direct to customer'. These four basic structures for manufacture and supply systems are shown in Figure 1.3.

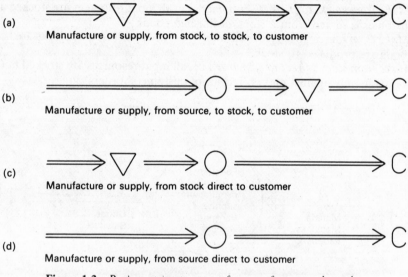

(a)   Manufacture or supply, from stock, to stock, to customer

(b)   Manufacture or supply, from source, to stock, to customer

(c)   Manufacture or supply, from stock direct to customer

(d)   Manufacture or supply, from source direct to customer

Figure 1.3   *Basic system structures for manufacture and supply.*

A slightly different situation applies in both transport and service. Those structures which require function in anticipation or in advance of receipt of a customer's order are not feasible, since no physical output stock is possible. Consider transport. A taxi service cannot satisfy a customer's relocation or movement requirements before receiving the customer's order. Similarly, an ambulance, refuse collection or furniture removal service cannot build up a stock of outputs to satisfy future customer demands. Nor can a bus service perform its function of transporting individuals before those individual customers arrive. The bus can, and often does, move from stop to stop along its route even though no customers have arrived. In doing so, however, it has not performed its function of changing the location of customers. In fact it has simply remained as an unutilized stocked resource, in need of customers. Nor can service systems, such as fire services, launderettes, hospitals and motels, build up a stock of outputs to satisfy future customer orders.

One further important structural difference is evident in the case of transport and service systems. Since the function of transport and service is to 'treat' the customers (whether a thing or a person), the customer is a resource input to the system, i.e. *the beneficiary of the function is or provides a major physical resource input to the function.* Thus transport and service systems are dependent on customers not only taking their output and in some cases specifying what that output shall be, but also for the supply of a major physical input(s) to the function without which the function would not be achieved. For example, in transport, a taxi, ambulance or bus service moves customers or something supplied by them, e.g. pieces of luggage. In service systems, e.g. hospitals or motels, the customer is treated in person, while launderettes and fire services treat items which might themselves be considered as customers (e.g. burning houses) or whose supply is controlled by the customer.

In other words, unlike manufacture and supply, transport and service systems are activated or 'triggered' by an input or supply. The customers exert some 'push' on the system. In manufacture and supply the customers act directly on output: they 'pull' the system, in that they pull goods out of the system whether direct from the function (structures (c) and (d)) or from output stock (structures (a) and (b)). In transport and service the customers push the system: they act directly on input. In such systems, therefore, some part of the resource input is not directly under the control of operations management. In these 'push' systems the customers control an input channel, and we must therefore distinguish this channel when developing models of systems.

Somewhat different structures are therefore required to represent transport and service systems. Three structures would seem to exist, as illustrated in Figure 1.4:

(e) *'Function from stock, and from customer'*, i.e. input resources are stocked, except in the case of customer inputs where no *queuing* exists.
(f) *'Function from source, and from customer queue'*, i.e. no input resources are stocked although customer inputs accumulate in a queue (or stock).
(g) *'Function from stock, and from customer queue'*, in which all inputs are stocked and/or allowed to accumulate in stocks.

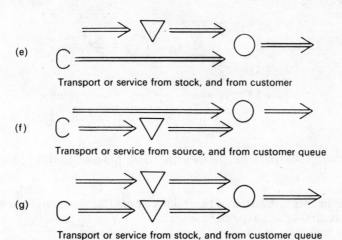

(e) Transport or service from stock, and from customer

(f) Transport or service from source, and from customer queue

(g) Transport or service from stock, and from customer queue

Figure 1.4 *Basic system structures for transport and service.*

Customer queues are physical stocks in the customer input channel, although they cannot be utilized by operations management in the same way as other resource stocks, for they are usually beyond their direct control. Queues comprise those customers who have 'arrived' at the system and await service or transport. They are the customers who at any one time have asked to be 'treated' by the system. The queue therefore represents known and committed future demand.

In total, therefore, we have seven basic structures for operating systems. They are listed in Figure 1.5. They are simple system descriptions. For example, they deal only with single channels for outputs and only with physical flows. However, this type of approach can be used to describe more complex systems. Furthermore, these basic system models can be used to describe operating systems at any level of detail—the organization, a division, a department, a section, etc.—depending on our particular focus.

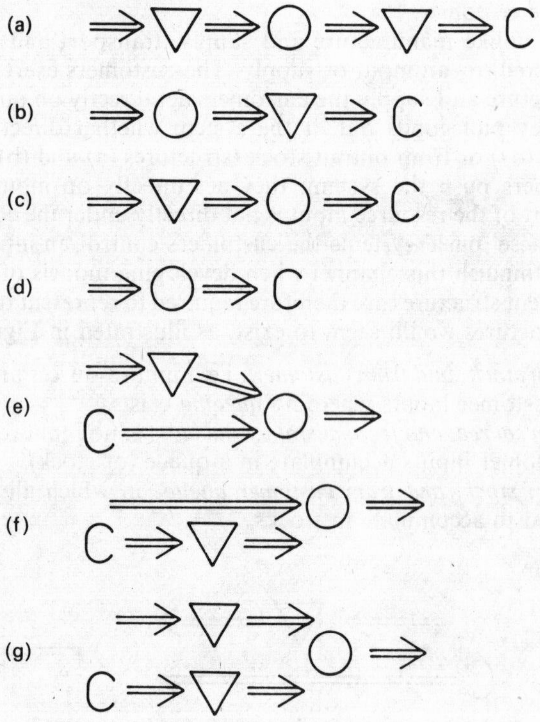

Figure 1.5 *Seven basic operating system structures.*

THE NATURE OF OPERATIONS MANAGEMENT

Again, it must be emphasized that we are taking a broad view of operations management. We see it as central to any type of enterprise.

Definition

> *Operations management is concerned with the design and the operation of systems for manufacture, transport, supply or service.*

We are all operations managers, but the nature of an operations manager's job will be different in different circumstances. An operations manager in a taxi company will have quite a different job from one in a bus company, and one in shipbuilding will have quite a different job from one in mass car production. They will tackle their jobs in different ways, i.e. their *strategies*, or the ways in which they tackle problems, will differ. Their jobs will 'feel' quite different, i.e. they will have different *roles*. It is important that we understand the reasons for these differences.

The nature of the operations manager's job is to some extent a function of the nature of the system he or she is required to manage. In fact the nature of certain of the problems which face operations management can be shown to be influenced by operating system *structure*; hence the operations manager's strategies and role are in part also influenced by the structure of the operating system. Thus, for example, an operations manager responsible for a system in which output stocks exist will face a different task if he or she moves to a situation in which there are no such stocks.

Additionally, the role of operations management is influenced by the objectives which are adopted by or prescribed for operations management, since these, together with the characteristics of the system, necessitate the use of particular operations management strategies, i.e. the general approaches adopted for tackling problems.

Figure 1.6 outlines these types of relationships. This simple model or framework is the foundation for the approach employed in this book. The model indicates that, because of the nature of a small number of principal operations management problem areas, particular operating system structures have distinctive problem characteristics. These

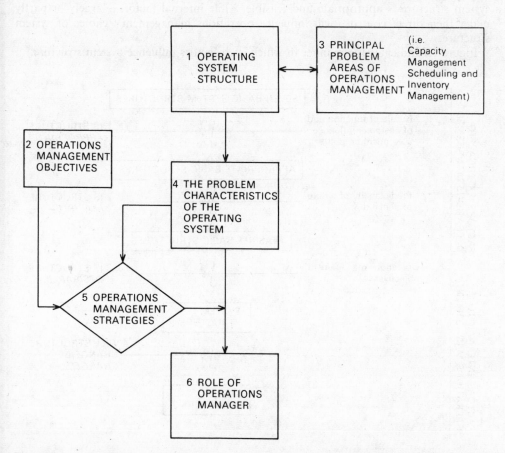

Figure 1.6 *A framework of concepts for operations management. From Wild, R. (1977) Concepts for Operations Management. New York: Wiley. Reproduced with permission.*

problem characteristics, together with operations management's objectives, influence the strategies or general approaches which are adopted by operations management in tackling problems, and in turn the nature of the strategies employed and the circumstances in which they are employed influence the role of the operations manager.

We shall now consider each of these topics, i.e. each of the 'boxes' of Figure 1.6, and then use a simple example to illustrate the relationships shown in the figure.

1. The choice of operating system structure

The seven basic operating system structures were identified earlier in this chapter. Given the influence of the basic operating system structure on the operations manager's job (shown in Figure 1.6), one aim of operations management will be to try to select the system structure which is to be employed or, failing that, to influence its selection.

Operations managers may have some choice of system structure or be able to change structures, but only within certain constraints. The system structure which exists at a particular time is determined by both internal and external factors. External factors—largely beyond the direct control of operations management—will determine whether a system structure is appropriate and feasible, while internal factors—largely or partly under their direct control—will influence operations management's choice of system structure.

Figure 1.7 indicates the manner in which such factors influence system structure:

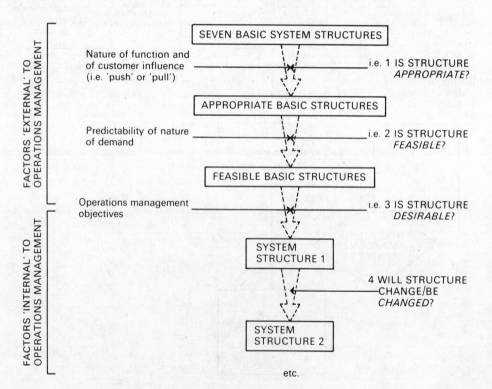

Figure 1.7   *Factors influencing system structure. From Wild, R. (1977) Concepts for Operations Management. New York: Wiley. Reproduced with permission.*

1. *Appropriateness*. The function of the system and the nature of customer influence (i.e. whether customers 'push' or 'pull') will determine the appropriateness of the structure. (For example there will be only four appropriate structures for manufacture and supply situations and only three for transport and service situations.)

2. *Feasibility*. Given appropriateness, feasibility will be determined by the nature of customer demand, in particular the predictability of the nature of the demand. Unless the nature of the product which will be required by future customers is certain, it will not be possible to operate in anticipation of demand and to provide output stocks. Unless there is some knowledge of the nature of the items which will be required by customers, it may even be impossible to stock resources. Similarly, unless the general nature of the service or transport required by customers is known, certain structures may not be feasible.

3. *Desirability*. The function of the system, the influence of customers on the system, and the predictability of the nature of demand are all factors which are normally beyond the direct control of operations managers, so we can consider these to be the *external* influences on system structure (Figure 1.7). Operations management may choose only from feasible system structures. This choice will reflect the desirability of each of the feasible system structures, desirability in turn being influenced by objectives which are partly influenced by operations management. One particular structure may be desirable given the relative importance of customer service vis-à-vis resource productivity. For a different balance of importance between these two objectives a different structure may be considered to be more desirable.

4. *Change*. Once adopted, a system structure may be changed by operations management usually through changes in capacity, schedules or inventories. The question of structure change leads us to consider the influence of *time*. System structure can change over a period of time, and for this reason we should consider the structure of systems at a given point in time. If a system is designed to have, or if it must normally have, a certain structure, the strategies adopted by management should reflect the needs and constraints of that system structure. If the structure changes, for whatever reason, either the approach to the management of the system will remain basically unchanged or the approach will be changed. It is likely that in the case of temporary structure changes the approach to management will not change, but in the case of long-term change a corresponding management change will be desirable. Clearly a system may not always exist or work as it is intended to. For example, all customers must ultimately be prepared to wait or queue in a 'push' system. Even an emergency ambulance service may on occasion require customers to wait. However, it may be inappropriate or unnecessary to consider changing the system structure every time such a queue forms. The length of time customers are prepared to wait may be too short to permit the system to be run or managed in a different way. The way the system is managed, therefore, may not change at all, despite a temporary structure change. In practice the manner in which a dentist manages will not change simply because the non-arrival of a few patients causes the system structure to change temporarily. Short-term structure changes may affect customer service or resource productivity, but little else.

In certain cases different 'parties' may see systems in different ways. Customers may consider queues to exist, while operations managers may perceive a different structure. It is the latter which is of importance for us. The operations manager's perception of a system will influence his or her behaviour. We must therefore consider the normal, intended or actual system structure—whichever is appropriate—and consider system structure from the operations manager's viewpoint.

2. Operations management objectives *(see also Chapter 21)*

Given the relationships shown in Figure 1.6, the operations manager will also seek to influence operations management objectives. In most cases these objectives will be influenced by those responsible for establishing the objectives for the business as a whole, but in all cases the operations manager must have some influence over their formulation.

The objective of operating systems is the conversion of inputs for the satisfaction of customer wants. Customer satisfaction is therefore a key objective of operations management. Table 1.1 identifies the main aspects of customer satisfaction for each function. Customers will want the outputs of the operating system; this is the primary condition for their being customers. Secondary considerations, however, will exist and for simplicity these can be considered in terms of costs and timing. Thus, using the classic marketing phrase, one objective of operations management is to ensure customer satisfaction by providing the 'right thing at the right price and at the right time'. We shall refer to this as the objective of *customer service*.

Table 1.1 *Aspects of customer satisfaction (From Wild, R. (1977) Concepts for Operations Management. New York: Wiley. Reproduced with permission.)*

Principal function	Principal customer wants	
	Primary considerations	Secondary considerations
Manufacture	Goods of a given, requested or acceptable specification	Cost, i.e. purchase price or cost of obtaining goods Timing, i.e. delivery delay from order or request to receipt of goods
Transport	Movement of a given, requested or acceptable specification	Cost, i.e. cost of movement Timing, i.e. (1) duration or time to move (2) wait, or delay from requesting to its commencement
Supply	Goods of a given, requested or acceptable specificiation	Cost, i.e. purchase price or cost of obtaining goods Timing, i.e. delivery delay from order or request to supply, to receipt of goods
Service	Treatment of a given, requested or acceptable specification	Cost, i.e. cost of treatment Timing, i.e. (1) duration or time required for treatment (2) wait, or delay from requesting treatment to its commencement

Given infinite resources any system, however badly managed, might provide adequate customer service. Many organizations have gone bankrupt despite having loyal and satisfied customers. The problem for operations management arises from the fact that operating systems must satisfy multiple objectives. Customer service must be provided simultaneously with the achievement of efficient operation, i.e. efficient use of resources. Either inefficient use of resources or inadequate customer service is sufficient to give rise to the 'commercial' failure of the operating system.

Using conventional definitions, i.e. 'the ratio of useful output to input', efficiency would take a value between 0 and 1. Although this measure might be of relevance in essentially physical activities, it is inappropriate for organizations as a whole, since in many cases the objective will be to output *more* than is input, i.e. the concept of profit or 'value added'. For this reason the term 'effectiveness' might be preferred, since it suggests perhaps the extent or degree of success in the achievement of given ends. Operations management is concerned essentially with the utilization of resources, i.e. obtaining maximum effect from resources or minimizing their loss, under-utilization or waste. The extent of the utilization of the resources' potential might be expressed in terms of the proportion of available time used or occupied, space utilization, levels of activity, etc. Each measure indicates the extent to which the potential or capacity of such resources is utilized. We shall refer to this as the objective of *resource utilization*.

Figure 1.8 summarizes the twin objectives of operations management. Operations management is concerned with the achievement of both satisfactory customer service and resource utilization. Operations managers must attempt to balance these two basic objectives. They will be judged against both, and the relative importance attached to each will in part be influenced by them. An improvement in one will often give rise to a deterioration in the other. Often both cannot be maximized, hence a satisfactory performance must be achieved on both and sub-optimization must be avoided. All of the activities of operations management must be tackled with these twin objectives in mind.

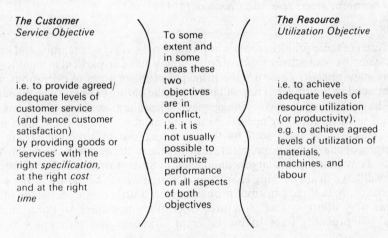

Figure 1.8 *The twin (often conflicting) objectives of operations management.*

3. Operations managers' problems

The scope of the operations manager's job is indicated by the list of problem areas or fields of activity given in 'life-cycle' order in Table 1.2. Operations management will normally be responsible for the management of inventories, quality, the maintenance and replacement of facilities, and the scheduling of activities. Such responsibilities will be discharged in respect of an operating system, the nature, location, layout, capacity and staffing of which will have been determined largely by operations management. Managers working in this function will also normally have some influence on the design or specification of the goods or services,[3] processes, staffing policies and performance measurement.

---

[3] Throughout we shall use the term 'goods and services' to include all outputs from operating systems, i.e. items, transports and the services defined at the beginning of the chapter.

Table 1.2 *The scope of operations management*

	Problem areas
Design and planning	Involvement in design/specification of the goods/service Design/specification of process/system Location of facilities Layout of facilities/resources and materials handling Determination of capacity/capability Design of work or jobs Involvement in determination of remuneration system and work standards
Operation and control	Planning and scheduling of activities Control and planning of inventories Control of quality Scheduling and control of maintenance Replacement of facilities Involvement in performance measurement

Principal problem areas *(see also Chapters 11–17)*

Although each of these problem areas is important in the effective planning and operation of the system, we can identify *three areas* which have a particular significance for operations management. These are the principal problem areas of operations management mentioned in Figure 1.6. They will influence the nature of operations management. They are the problems of capacity management, scheduling, and inventory management. The type of problem faced by operations management in each of these three principal problem areas will be influenced by the operating system structure. These are the distinguishing or characteristic problem areas; in others, the nature of the problems faced by operations management is largely unaffected by system structure. Each basic system structure will have distinguishing characteristics because of the nature of the problems which occur in these three principal problem areas. Furthermore, decisions in each of these areas may affect system structure. Operations managers working in different situations will probably have to use different strategies and techniques in tackling

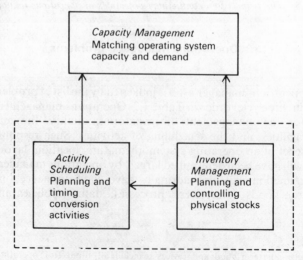

Figure 1.9 *The relationship of the three principal operations management problem areas.*

problems in the three principal problem areas. In contrast, when making decisions in other areas, operations managers may be able to rely on the same types of strategy and technique in different situations. For this reason, in discussing decision-making techniques in the remainder of this book we must, when considering the principal problem areas, ensure that we consider the appropriateness of techniques, while in considering other problem areas the matter of appropriateness is less of an issue.

These three principal problem areas are closely related. Indeed it might be argued that the major problem is that of capacity management, and that inventory and scheduling decisions are subordinate to that decision and provide means of implementing capacity management plans. (See Figure 1.9).

Inventory management

The problem of managing physical stocks or inventories is influenced by the system structure, if only because certain structures provide for the existence of stocks while others do not. The location of inventories is a function of structure, as is the nature of the inventory management problem. Defining inventory management as the planning and control of physical stocks, both aspects of the problem may be affected by structure and may also affect structure. The structure of an operating system will largely reflect the nature and location of inventories, and the management of such inventories will influence both resource productivity and customer service. The existence of output stocks may facilitate the provision of high customer service, at least in terms of availability or 'timing'. However, their existence may be costly. The provision of input resource stocks may benefit customer service, yet resource productivity may be adversely affected because more resources are idle. Few organizations can exist entirely without stocks of raw materials, work in progress or, where appropriate, output goods. The planning of inventory levels, the control of inventories and the maintenance of such stocks are expensive but necessary. Inventories will normally tie up considerable amounts of capital, so there is a balance to be struck between obtaining the benefits of inventories, such as flexibility, high customer service and insulation against demand fluctuations, on the one hand, and minimizing the costs of such stocks on the other.

Scheduling

The nature of some aspects of scheduling in operations management is influenced by the system structure, and decisions made in scheduling can affect the structure. Scheduling is concerned with the timing of occurrences. *Operations scheduling* in its widest sense may therefore be considered to be concerned with the specification in advance or the timing of occurrences within the system, arrivals to and departures from the system including arrivals to and departures from inventories within the system. Thus we can consider the inventory management problem to be a part of a wider operations scheduling problem. The nature and extent of this overall scheduling problem will therefore be influenced by the presence and location of inventories and the relationship between the customer and the system, all of which are characteristic of system structure. As with all characteristic problems, the procedures and methods deployed in scheduling may be influenced by structure, and the effectiveness of scheduling may in turn affect structure. If we consider operations scheduling to relate to the physical flow or transfer of resources or goods, then the nature or extent of the overall scheduling problem is clearly influenced by the number of stages involved in the system, and therefore by structure. Where output stocks exist, customer demand will be met by scheduled output from stock, such stocks being replenished by scheduled inputs. In the absence of such stocks customer demand will be met by scheduling output from the function, which in turn will necessitate the scheduling of resource inputs either from input stock or direct suppliers. Conventionally we take a narrower view of the scheduling problem. We normally focus on *activity scheduling*, which is concerned only with activities directly related to the function.

Capacity management

The determination and adjustment of *capacity* in an operating system is an important problem area, since decisions made here may intentionally or inadvertently change the structure of the system and/or affect the efficiency of operation of a particular system. Equally, decisions not made, or wrong decisions, may also result in structure changes and/or loss of efficiency, as for example following the failure to adjust system capacity to match customer demand changes. The planning and control of capacity is both important and complex, and furthermore the nature of the problem will often be affected by structure. In other words, for a given system structure the capacity management problem may differ from that facing management in a different structure. Since structure affects the nature and complexity of the capacity planning problem, the methods, procedures and techniques appropriate for tackling the problem may also be influenced by structure. In all respects, therefore, we can consider capacity management to be a principal problem area, the nature of which is characteristic of system structure. The management of system capacity is of crucial importance in operations management. The determination of capacity is the key system planning or design problem and the adjustment of capacity is the key problem area in system control. Capacity decisions will have a direct influence on system performance in respect of both criteria, i.e. resource productivity and customer service. It is difficult to see how any organization can operate effectively without good capacity management. Excess capacity inevitably gives rise to low resource productivity, while inadequate capacity may mean poor customer service. Decisions made in other areas are unlikely to offset errors in this area. The capacity problem is often of a medium-to long-term nature. Since system capacity is a reflection of the nature and amount of resources available in the system, short-term adjustments are often impossible. Capacity management is concerned primarily with the matching of resources to demand. It is concerned, therefore, with the levels of resources and demand.

One factor adding considerably to the complexity of inventory, capacity and scheduling problems is their close interdependence. Decisions made in one will have a direct impact on performance in the others. Such interdependence is less evident in the other problem areas, a fact which tends to 'underline' the central importance of these three problem areas in the management of operations. In many respects the problems of inventory management and scheduling are subsidiary to the problem of capacity management. Capacity management decisions will determine how the operating system accommodates customer demand level fluctuations. Capacity management decisions will provide a context within which inventories and activities will be both planned and controlled. They will to some extent reflect operating policy decisions, while inventory and scheduling problems might be considered as more tactical issues.

Common problem areas *(see also Chapters 4–10 and 17–21)*

Certain problems which face operations managers have much the same 'appearance' and require much the same approach in each type of operating system. They are also important, but they do not differentiate different types of operating system in the manner shown in Figure 1.6. Since we are dealing here specifically with the relationships of Figure 1.6, our description of these 'common problem areas' (taken from Table 1.2) should be regarded as parenthetical.

Goods/services design and specification

The design of the goods/services will often be the responsibility of a separate function within the company or even a separate company. A major contribution will often be made by both operations and marketing functions, since it is their responsibility to provide the offering. In all the cases the nature and specification of the goods/services will reflect the policy or strategic objectives of the organization, and thus those responsible within the organization for determining the detailed goods/services specification will, in most cases, be working within fairly clearly defined terms of reference and towards clearly specified objectives.

Process/system design and specification

Operations managers will have considerable influence in determining or influencing the nature, i.e. the structure, of the system which they are to manage. Additionally they will in most situations be largely responsible for specifying the 'hardware' of that system. In many large organizations this process/system design responsibility will be allocated to a separate department, but in some organizations, including some large organizations, the responsibility for system design will lie with those responsible for the operation of the system, i.e. the operations managers.

Location of facilities

The location of the organization, or the static parts of the organization, must be determined internationally, nationally, and locally. In some cases the international location question will be of relatively minor importance. However, in most cases, locational choice within a country or within a particular area will constitute a real problem, and of course the solution to this problem will influence the subsequent operation of all aspects of the organization and its operating systems.

Layout of facilities resources and materials handling

Decisions on the arrangement of departments and the resources within these departments must be made with the objective of enabling given goods or services to be provided at minimum total costs. The nature of the layout of the system and within the system will determine the extent of movement, handling, materials flow, etc.

The design of work and of jobs

Effective methods of working are essential for the efficient design of an operating system and some control of work is necessary in order for adequate use of resources to be achieved and in order for management to determine the times necessary for all operations. The development and implementation of 'optimum' work methods frequently necessitates the study and design of workplaces and work equipment, the consideration of ergonomic factors, and the training of workers, all of which will often be regarded as a principal responsibility of operations management. Control is achieved by means of performance standards, which are obtained after exhaustive investigation of work methods and are subsequently used for the planning of operations and as a basis for incentive payment systems and other remuneration schemes.

Remuneration system design

Deriving from the above, the operations manager has some direct responsibility in the operation, if not the design, of the remuneration system, especially where a payment-by-results scheme is used and where work standards are obtained through, for example, work measurement or similar calculations. In most cases the nature of the remuneration system will be closely related to the nature of the work undertaken by workers, their job designs and the work organization. In this area, therefore, operations managers are likely to share responsibility with functions such as personnel management and industrial relations.

Operations control

Operations control is the complementary activity to operations and activity scheduling and, simply stated, involves the implementation of operations schedules. The problem is most severe in intermittent activities, where, because of the variety of jobs undertaken and services provided, accurate planning is frequently impossible. In repetitive situations, whether in manufacture, transport, supply or service, the planning process is likely to be a good deal more precise simply because of the availability of more accurate information, and thus the problem of control is minimized.

Quality control and reliability

Rarely, if ever, are the resources employed in operating systems likely to be capable of operating continually at a specified level and in a specified fashion without breakdown or failure, and the need for replacement, repair or adjustment. Thus variations in the quality of the goods or services provided, such as changes in dimension, content, appearance, duration, performance and so on, will result either from assignable causes, such as wear or loss of efficiency in operating resources, or for reasons of pure chance. The ability of resources to operate at a desired level of accuracy in a specified fashion must be established and procedures installed to minimize the number of faulty operations and to ensure that sub-standard goods produced are identified and not passed on to the customer.

Maintenance and replacement

None of the resources used within operating systems, whether human or inanimate, can work continually and effectively without maintenance and repair. Some of the problems and decisions involved in the maintenance and repair of equipment are as follows:

1. Should maintenance consist of service or repair or both?
2. What should be the timing of service or preventive work in order to involve minimum effort and cost, yet minimize the probability of breakdown of resources?
3. How should repair work be conducted?
4. What should be the size of maintenance teams?
5. How should information be gathered to enable the above questions to be answered?

Performance measurement

Some measurement and monitoring of performance within organizations is essential. Since the operating systems are likely to be a major component of any organization, the measurement of the performance of such systems is an essential aspect of any total performance measurement. Measurement of the extent to which resources are utilized and the level of service provided are ingredients of such performance measurement. They are, if not the principal responsibilities of operations managers, the means by which the performance of operations managers is assessed by others, and thus are matters of considerable importance to such managers.

4. Problem characteristics of operating systems

A manager responsible for managing a system which 'functions from stock to output stock' will be faced with somewhat different capacity, scheduling and inventory problems from those of a manager responsible for operating a system without such output stocks. Similarly, a manager responsible for operating a transport system with an input queue of customers, e.g. a bus service, will face somewhat different types of problems in managing capacity, in scheduling activities, and in controlling inventories, from those facing a manager responsible for the operation of a system without input stocks. The problem characteristics of the system which is being managed and the objectives which must be achieved will be the two principal considerations of operations managers. In viewing their job, operations managers will see themselves as having the responsibility of achieving certain objectives while managing systems with certain characteristics. The problem characteristics of the operating system are a direct result of the existence of a particular structure, together with the fact that the principal problem areas take on different forms in different types of structures.

5. Operations management strategies

Given what we have said above it must follow that operations managers in different circumstances will tackle problems in different ways. For each of the three principal problem areas there will be different alternative strategies. For example, in managing the capacity of a system, in some circumstances operations managers will choose to vary the capacity of the system to match varying customer demand. This might be achieved through the use of overtime working, subcontracting, etc. In other circumstances a different strategy may be employed, e.g. the decision to avoid varying capacity. This might be achieved through the provision of excess capacity, the use of output stocks, the necessity of turning customers away at times of excess demand, etc.

The choice from among these strategies will be influenced by the problem characteristics of the system and the objectives which are being pursued. Similarly, in the two other principal problem areas (activity scheduling and the management of inventories), alternative strategies will exist and the operations manager will choose those which are most appropriate given the type of system which is being managed and the objectives which are to be pursued.

6. Role of the operations manager

Given all of the above it must follow that the role of the operations manager will be quite different in different situations. The nature of the operating system structure will affect the problem characteristics of the system. The objectives which must be pursued, together with the characteristics of the system, will influence the choice of strategies, and these strategies, together with the nature of the system, will influence the role of the operations manager or the nature of the job which he or she must do. In certain situations the operations manager's role will be a particularly difficult one. He or she will have few alternatives available, but will be required to pursue complex and perhaps even conflicting objectives. In other circumstances the choice will be great, and the demands placed on the operations manager will be fewer. In those circumstances the job will be less demanding.

EXAMPLE: A DENTIST

In setting up a new dental practice the dentist, as operations manager, will be influenced by the following factors:

1. The *operating system structure* will probably be of type (e) (Figure 1.5) in which the resources required for the dental practice are in stock, but where customers are able to gain direct access to those resources without queuing. This situation will be the direct result of the fact that, as yet, the dentist has been unable to create sufficient demand to necessitate customer queuing or the use of a customer appointments system.

2. The *operations management objectives* must provide for some emphasis on high customer service. Thus the operations manager (i.e. the dentist) will wish to ensure that, even when demand increases, customer waiting times are not excessive either when waiting for an appointment or when waiting for attention after arriving at the surgery at the time required by the appointment.
3. The nature of the operating system will give rise to certain *system problem characteristics* as regards: (a) the management of capacity; (b) the scheduling of activities; and (c) the management of inventories. For example in managing capacity it will not be possible to rely on the use of output stocks. In scheduling activities, because of the existence of the queue of customers in the appointments book, it will be possible to some extent to schedule activities in order to ensure a fairly high resource utilization. (For example it may be possible to ensure that customers with particular types of problems or in need of particular types of treatments are timetabled to arrive sequentially on the same day.)

The objectives being pursued and the problem characteristics of the system will necessitate the use of particular *strategies*. For example in managing capacity it will not be possible, in the short term, to vary capacity to match demand changes, e.g. those caused by the effects of holidays. It will be necessary, therefore, to tolerate some under-utilization of capacity at times of relatively low demand, and some temporary increases in the size of the customer waiting list at times of high demand.

The use of such strategies, together with the type of operating system being employed, will influence the *role* of the operations manager. In these circumstances the operations manager, attempting to provide customer service and relatively high resource utilization, will find it necessary to work to a strict timetable. Since a dentist is unable to subcontract work easily, he or she must try to ensure that facilities are continually available, with no breakdowns, illness, etc. The job will be a somewhat 'relentless' one, with relatively little opportunity for interruptions and little scope for changes in routine.

OPERATIONS MANAGEMENT DECISION-MAKING

Operations managers must solve problems in the areas identified above on a regular or 'as required' basis. Not only will it be necessary to decide on the problem-solving procedure, but also in many cases it will be necessary to decide between alternative solutions. We have made a distinction between what has been called the 'principal' or 'characteristic' problems, which necessitate the problem-solving procedure being tailored to the particular circumstances, and the 'common' problems, which may yield to the same type of problem-solving approach each time they are encountered. Much of the remainder of this book is about problem-solving in these areas and therefore about operations management decision-making. Before beginning to discuss the problem-solving strategies, procedures, techniques, etc., we can pull together some of the points made in the previous sections, and develop an overview of the operations manager's decision-making process. This will give a foundation for our discussion in the next part of the book, where we shall deal with operations management in the business policy context and the relationships between operations management and other functions within the organization.

For the purposes of this discussion we define the *operations management decision-making process* as 'the formulation of overall strategies for operations, typically involving interrelated areas of responsibility within operations management, and the making of decisions in these areas in pursuit of these strategies within the broader business context'.

Figure 1.10 provides a simple model of the operations management decision-making process. It is derived from our discussion above, in particular from Figure 1.6 and 1.7 and Table 1.1. The figure shows the decision-making process as a 'contingency' model. It

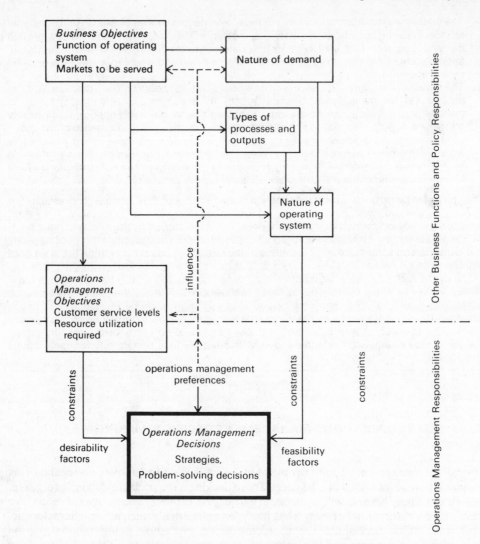

Figure 1.10 *A model of the operations management decision-making process.*

suggests that operations managers' decision about: (a) the formulation of strategies for the solution of problems; and (b) particular problem-solving procedures is not a free, unconstrained process. It suggests, naturally, that operations managers' decisions are contingent upon other factors, and, deriving from our discussion above, suggests that the three sets of *contingent factors* or constraints might be categorized as follows:

1. *Feasibility*. The feasibility of choosing a particular course of action in the principal decision-making areas of operations management (i.e. capacity management, scheduling and inventory) will be influenced largely by the nature of the operating system, which in turn will be a function of the demand situation, the processes and outputs involved and the systems function. (See Figure 1.6 and 1.7.)

   We have seen that the predictability of the nature of demand (i.e. whether or not it is known what future customers want) will influence the feasibility of the existence of output stocks created in anticipation of demand, and ultimately the use of input stocks of particular resources. For example, an operating system established to satisfy demand which is totally unpredictable in nature will contain neither output stocks of finished (unsold) goods or services nor stocks of specialized input resources, e.g. specialized materials, equipment, etc.

The types of processes and outputs involved may influence the nature of the system. For example, in electrical power generation, even though the nature of future demand is known (i.e. for electricity of a particular voltage, etc.), it will not normally be possible to provide substantial output stocks.

The function of the system will also influence its nature, since the configuration of transport and service systems will differ from that of supply and manufacturing systems, as in both the former cases the customers or some physical item provided by the customers will be a direct input to the process.

Thus the nature of demand, process and outputs, and system function, and their relationship with the customer influence the nature of the system, which in turn will have a major feasibility influence on the approaches adopted by operations management for the management of such systems.

2. *Desirability*. The desirability of pursuing a particular approach in managing the system will be influenced largely by the operations manager's perceptions of desired outcomes, which in turn will be associated with explicit or implicit business objectives (see Table 1.1). Thus, considering the twin operations management objectives of providing customer service and achieving high resource utilization, an emphasis on the former will possibly encourage the adoption of particular strategies in capacity management, scheduling, etc., while an emphasis on resource utilization may encourage a different approach. For example, given feasibility, an emphasis on customer service will encourage the use of output stocks and possibly the maintenance of excess capacity, while an emphasis on resource utilization may mitigate against the use of output stocks and lead to a reduction in capacity. Although in general the operations manager's basic strategies may be seen as a function of the given or required balance between customer service and resource utilization, other objectives, e.g. labour policies and pricing policies, will also have some influence. Most of these factors will be beyond the direct and total control of the operations manager. We can consider them to be policy-level decisions to which the operations manager will make some contribution.

3. *Preference*. Given feasibility and desirability, we would expect operations managers to have certain preferences. For example, the operations manager may prefer a situation in which his or her activities are in some way 'buffered' or protected from demand uncertainties. This, for example through the use of output inventories, permits the 'core' of the operating system to be in some way protected from uncertainties and thus to be run in a steady and efficient manner. In a labour-intensive situation the operations manager may prefer to minimize the amount of change in the labour force, hours worked, etc., thus minimizing the risk of labour/industrial relations problems. Or the operations manager may prefer to schedule work in such a way as to avoid the need to schedule each activity against a particular customer's 'requirement' date. All such approaches provide the operations manager with a far greater choice of strategies, etc, but the extent to which this approach might be employed is of course a function of both feasibility and desirability.

The operations manager who, for whatever reason, has greater 'power' within the organization is likely to be able to exercise his or her preferences to a greater extent than might otherwise be the case. Such power may be informal or formal. It may have been acquired, have evolved, or simply exist because of the broader circumstances, e.g. the existence of minimum feasibility and desirability constraints. This view associates 'power' with the scope, freedom of action and breadth of choice of the operations manager given certain feasibility and desirability constraints. This, however, is largely an internal perspective. We must recognize that such power, perhaps rather more broadly defined, may be exercised by the operations manager in seeking to influence both feasibility and desirability constraints which operate on him or her. Thus in certain circumstances the operations manager may be able to influence product/service design and/or marketing policy in order to make feasible the provision of output stocks of uncommitted goods. Further, he or she may seek to retain an overriding commitment to customer service and a tolerance of low resource utilization. Thus the extent to which the operations manager contributes to and influences these policy-level decisions will at least ensure that such decision-making takes into account the needs, constraints and abilities of the operations function, and at best ensure that constraints are minimized, thus enabling maximization of preference. This mechanism ensures that operations managers who are unable, or unwilling, to influence their policy-level decisions within the organization can be required to operate in highly undesirable situations, seemingly having to meet conflicting objectives while using resources in a diverse range of activities in a continually changing situation. In such circumstances the power of the operations manager clearly approaches zero: no preference is exercised, and the operations manager's decision-making process is entirely constrained by 'external factors'.

Summarizing, we can view the operations management decision-making process as a contingent/constrained process where outcomes are influenced by feasibility, desirability and preference factors. Such a view is presented in the simple model in Figure 1.10. The recognition of these relationships and the adoption of a suitable decision-making process are the prerequisites for effective operations management, and the solution of particular operations management problems must be seen as a subsidiary part of this decision-making process. The operations manager's responsibility within the broader business context must include the recognition of the fact that decisions in other functions will limit his or her own decisions, but, equally important, the operations manager must also seek to influence those factors which give rise to feasibility and desirability constraints on his or her decisions in the light of, and in order to exercise, his or her particular preferences.

   In the next part of the book we shall look more closely at the policy decision-making context for operations management and the relationships of operations managers with those in other functions within the business.

CHECKLIST FOR CHAPTER 1

The nature of operating systems
   Definition: operating system
   Resources in operating systems
      Materials
      Machines
      Labour
   Functions of operating system
      Manufacture
      Transport
      Supply
      Service
   Redefinition: operating system
The structure of operating systems
   Manufacture and supply
      Function from stock to stock to customer

Function from source to customer
Function from stock direct to customer
Function from source direct to customer
Service and transport
Function from stock and from customer
Function from source and from customer
      queue
Function from stock and from customer queue
The nature of operations management
   Definition: operations management
   Choice of system structure
      Appropriateness
      Feasibility
      Desirability
      Change

Operations management objectives
  Customer service
  Resource utilization
Operations managers' problems
  Principal problem areas
    Capacity management
    Scheduling
    Inventory management
  Common problem areas
    Goods/service specification
    Process design
    Location ⎫ of facilities
    Layout ⎭
    Work and job design

Remuneration
Operations control
Quality control and reliability
Maintenance and replacement
Performance measurement
Problem characteristics of the operating system
Operations management strategies
Role of the operations managers
Operations management decision-making
  Process
    Feasibility factors
    Desirability factors
    Preferences
  Power

FURTHER READING

Pegels, C. C. (1976) *Systems Analysis for Production Operations*. London: Gordon and Breach. For comparison: a different systems type of approach to production and operations management.

Schoderbek, P. P., Kefalos, A. G. and Schoderbek, G. C. G. (1975) *Management Systems—Conceptual Considerations*. Dallas, Texas: Business Publications. A general treatment of systems theory from a management/business viewpoint. Good complementary reading to this chapter.

Wild, R. (1977) *Concepts for Operations Management*. New York: Wiley, A detailed treatment (with examples and cases) of the ideas and concepts introduced in this chapter.

Wild, R. (1983) Decision making in operations management. *Management Decision*, **21** (1), pp. 9–21.

QUESTIONS

1.1 'Operations management is the "heart" of any business, and we are all operations managers.' Discuss.

1.2 How far is it possible for the operations function within the firm to operate independently of the other main functional areas? Which functions, in particular, must have a close relationship with operations management, and why?

1.3 Describe the principal types of manufacture. What are the prerequisites for each of these types of manufacture and what are the principal operations management problems associated with each type? Illustrate your answers by describing actual cases with which you are familiar.

1.4 Identify seven basic operating system structures and give examples of each, making the simplifying assumption, if necessary, of single-channel outputs.

1.5 Using the basic operating structures, in series and /or in parallel, with multiple input and output channels if necessary, describe (i.e. model) the following operating systems:
  (a) a typical 'take-away' or 'fast food' shop (e.g. a hamburger house);
  (b) a restaurant;
  (c) a taxi service.
Identify and explain any assumptions you make.

1.6 The table below identifies the main resources, customers, objectives and activities associated with an ambulance service. Prepare similar tables containing appropriate details for:
  (a) a motel;
  (b) a 'take-away' Chinese food shop.

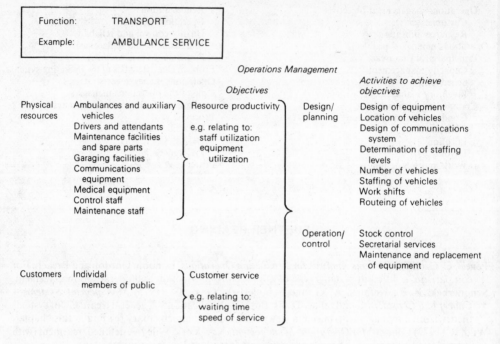

Operations Management

1.7 Using the concepts summarized in Figure 1.10 illustrate, using hypothetical or real examples, how and why the decisions of an operations manager in a service organization (e.g. a hotel, hospital or entertainment centre) are influenced by 'feasibility' and desirability' factors and 'preference' considerations.

1.8 To what extent is predictability of the nature of demand a prerequisite for the existence of each of the seven basic structures shown in Figure 1.5?

PART 2

THE CONTEXT OF OPERATIONS MANAGEMENT

INTRODUCTION TO PART 2

Here we consider the business context of operations management. If we take the view that the operating system and operations management are the heart of any enterprise, we must recognize that there must be relationships with other functions in the business. Here we look at business policy decision-making, the nature of its influence on operations management, and the nature of the influence of operations management on it. We then consider the nature of the relationships between operations management and marketing, organizational, financial control and design decisions. Throughout we shall concentrate on basic concepts and ideas, so that the nature of and reasons for these relationships are clear. Similarly in Chapter 4 we shall look at some basic aspects of operations economics and costs.

CHAPTER TWO

Business Policy and Operations Management

The importance of the business context to operations managers was discussed in Chapter 1. Although operations managers will have a considerable degree of control over decisions within their own area of responsibility, they will not, in general, be able to ignore the actions of others. There exists an external 'framework' for their actions, and marketing, financial, personnel and other decisions are the components of this framework. In a small organization most of these areas will be the sole and direct responsibility of one person, and so co-ordination is easy. In larger organizations, however, some formal co-ordination is necessary. Procedurally this is provided through the hierarchical or pyramid-type structure of most organizations; thus, ultimately, at the apex of the pyramid someone has some knowledge of, and responsibility for, all areas. At this level decision-making will be long-term, strategic and concerned with the business as a whole. This business policy decision-making provides purpose and co-ordination throughout the organization and therefore largely creates the framework within which each function works. Before considering operations management decision-making we must consider the manner in which this policy mechanism works, for it is essential that we are aware of those factors which influence operations decisions and the manner in which this influence is exerted. This chapter will therefore consider business policy and its influence on operations management, while Chapter 3 will examine some particularly important components of the framework for operations management decisions. Here we shall take a fairly conceptual approach, since the principal objective is to indicate the *nature* of the relationship between business policy and operations management decision-making.

BUSINESS POLICY[1]

Planning occurs in all functions of an organization, but, alone, such plans are an inadequate basis for decisions about the future of the organization. The effectiveness of

---

[1] Also referred to as business or corporate strategy

each function within the organization is dependent on effective planning, but all such planning must start and end with business policy, which is long-term, takes an organization-wide perspective and is concerned with the role, purpose and success of the business as a whole, and thus with the *total* resources of the organization.

Business policy planning is a continuous and systematic activity aimed not only at identifying purposes for the organization but also at defining procedures and organizing efforts to achieve these purposes and measuring results against expectations through systematic feedba^k of information. It is a systematic approach to both the formulation and the implementation of total business plans.

Formal systematic planning is essential, since detailed forecasts and action plans are required to allow co-ordinated action throughout the organization and adequate evaluation of performance. Such planning necessitates co-operation between functional specialists, subdivisions, etc., and therefore brings about a degree of co-ordination and a perspective which might not otherwise have existed within the organization. The existence of detailed plans facilitates delegation and permits the establishment of relatively autonomous divisions, while ensuring that overall control remains. It provides a set of goals and criteria for assessing the merits of new opportunities and proposals, whether for concentration or diversification of the business.

Business policy formulation and implementation

Two important and interrelated aspects are evident in the business policy process: formulation (or planning) and implementation.

Formulation of business policy

Classically, four steps must be taken in formulating a business policy:

1. the identification of opportunities for, and threats to, the organization, together with the estimation of the degree of risk associated with each;
2. the assessment of the organization's present and potential strengths and weaknesses, particularly in respect of its material, financial, technical and personnel resources, i.e. its potential capacity to pursue identified opportunities and/or to deal with threats;
3. consideration of the personal values and aspirations of the organization's major stakeholders and its managers;
4. clarification and acknowledgement of the major social responsibilities and objectives of the organization.

Consideration of (1) and (2) above can give rise to the development of a rational *economic policy* for an organization through the matching of opportunities to capabilities. This is rarely the total perspective for the development of business policy, for it will often be necessary to consider personal aspirations and preferences (3). It will be necessary to identify what an organization will 'want to do' as distinct from, or as a sub-set of, what it 'can or might do'. Finally, the inclusion of (4) above—a largely non-economic dimension—raises the question of what the organization 'should do', i.e. having regard to its responsibilities and social objectives. This four-part perspective is illustrated in Figure 2.1, which identifies the economic and non-economic aspects of the process.

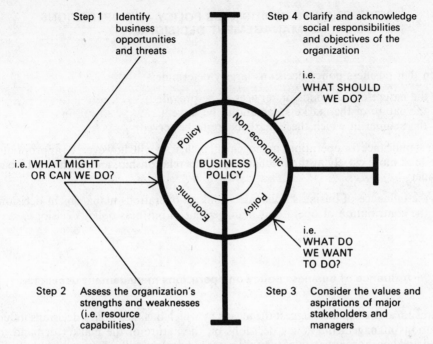

Step 1 Identify business opportunities and threats

Step 4 Clarify and acknowledge social responsibilities and objectives of the organization

i.e. WHAT SHOULD WE DO?

i.e. WHAT MIGHT OR CAN WE DO?

BUSINESS POLICY

Policy

Non-economic

Economic

Policy

i.e. WHAT DO WE WANT TO DO?

Step 2 Assess the organization's strengths and weaknesses (i.e. resource capabilities)

Step 3 Consider the values and aspirations of major stakeholders and managers

Figure 2.1 *The formulation of business policy. From Wild, R. (1979) Operations Management – A Policy Framework. Oxford: Pergamon. Reproduced with permission.*

The culmination of this policy formulation stage is the statement of policies on:

(a) the nature of the goods or services to be provided by the organization;
(b) the nature of the markets/demand to be served;
(c) the manner in which these markets are to be served.

These are all aspects of considerable direct significance to operations management.

Implementation of business policy

Implementation of an agreed policy is concerned with the acquisition and mobilization of resources, the creation of appropriate structures and processes, and monitoring and control. Again four aspects can be identified:

(a) use of physical resources, e.g. equipment, machinery and labour, and the development of appropriate technology;
(b) the creation of appropriate organization structures and relationships, e.g. the roles and responsibilities of individuals, departments and functions, and the use of appropriate information systems, etc.;
(c) organizational processes and behaviour, e.g. the development of individuals, their motivation and rewards, performance measurement, and the establishment of standards;
(d) top leadership, i.e. the provision, monitoring and updating of overall objectives, inter-function and inter-division co-ordination, overall resource allocation, etc.

RELAT ONSHIPS OF BUSINESS POLICY AND OPERATIONS MANAGEMENT DECISIONS[2]

Given that business policy decisions largely determine:

(a)   the nature of the goods or services to be provided;
(b)   the nature of the markets/demand to be served;
(c)   the manner in which these markets are to be served;

Their significance for operations management is clear. It will, however, be appropriate for us to look more closely at the mechanism of this relationship, and to this end we must consider:

(a)   the influence of business policy decisions on operations management decisions;
(b)   the contribution of operations management to business policy decisions.

Influence of business policy on operations management decisions

Figures 1.6 and 1.7 in fact suggest the means by which business policy decisions influence operations management. Policy decisions on the nature of the market/demand to be served and hence the *predictability of the nature of demand* will influence system structure feasibility (Figure 1.7). The manner in which markets are to be served influences *operations management objectives*, which in turn must influence the choice or desirability of system structure (Figure 1.7) and the choice of management strategies (Figure 1.6).

   Thus policy decisions on the nature of the goods or services to be provided, the nature of the markets/demand to be served, and the manner in which these markets are to be served, will influence:

(a)   operations management's choice of operating structure;
(b)   the formulation of operations management objectives;
(c)   operations management's choice of strategies.

The way in which these influences are exerted is shown diagrammatically in Figure 2.2 and is discussed below.

Business policy influences on operating system structure decisions and the formulation of operations management objectives

The structure of the operating system influences the role and problems of operations management; however, operations managers are unlikely to have a free *choice of system structure*, since the nature of the function and the customers' influence on the system are major external factors influencing the appropriateness of a system structure (Figure 1.7). For example, we have indicated that one fundamental feature of transport and service systems is their dependence on inputs controlled by the customer. In practice an organization may have some scope for influencing the customer, and thus the 'pull' or

---

[2]   The ideas introduced in this section are developed in more detail in Wild, R. (1979) *Operations Management— A Policy Framework*. Oxford: Pergamon.

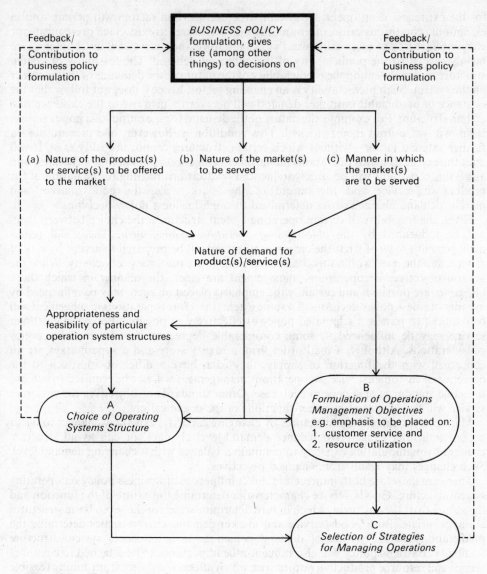

Figure 2.2 *The principal influences of business policy on operations management decisions.*

'push' on the operating system. Such influence may derive from advertising and marketing activities, pricing, product policies, etc. An organization may therefore have some influence on the structure of the operating system, but such influence will normally be external to the operations manager. From the operations manager's point of view the nature of the function and the customer influence on the system are constraints, deriving in part from decisions relating to the nature of the product or service and the nature of the market, i.e. the goods/services and market/demand characteristics determined through business policy decisions.

Taking a slightly different viewpoint, the operations manager will recognize that in some circumstances certain system structures cannot be adopted, i.e. they are infeasible, since the factors which permit their existence are absent. There are certain prerequisites for the existence of an operating system structure. Certain factors will permit, and in exceptional conditions cause, one or more of the structures to exist. Such prerequisites or enabling factors are essentially of an external nature and, as we saw in Chapter 1, are mainly related to the predictability of the nature of demand. The feasibility of system structures is dependent on the predictability of the nature of the demands of the customer on the system. Such predictability is an enabling factor, hence it does not follow that the existence of predictable customer demand will necessarily give rise to the existence of a certain structure. For example, the nature of the demand for the output of a power station is known, yet output is not stocked. This condition is, however, one prerequisite—a further external factor—without which certain structures cannot in reality exist. It will limit the extent to which operations management can choose, or change, structures, and again this constraint will be largely influenced by decisions relating to the nature of the product or service and the nature of the market, i.e. the goods/market and market/demand characteristics determined through business policy decisions.

Given the feasibility of certain operating system structures, the choice between them will be influenced by the *objectives of operations management*. These will reflect management's view of what the customer wants or will be prepared to accept by way of service, and the need within this constraint to maximize resource productivity. While the general objectives of operations management are clear, the manner in which those objectives are pursued, and certainly the emphasis placed on each, may be influenced by broader business policy decisions. To some extent, therefore, operations management will be required to pursue a stipulated policy as effectively as possible. Policy on customer service may be influenced to some considerable degree by broader business policy considerations. Although a mail order firm, a luxury store and a supermarket are all concerned with the function of supply, they each have a different approach to the objective of customer service, so operations management will not be required to achieve the same standards of service in each case. Often standards or objectives for customer service will be influenced by other functions in the organization.

Management can change structures by changing capacity, can allow changes to occur by not adjusting capacity to balance demand-level changes, or can avoid structure changes by manipulating capacity to maintain a balance with a changing demand level. Such changes may result from changed objectives.

There are therefore both indirect and direct influences of business policy on operating system structure. Goods/service characteristics determine the nature of the function and the influence of the customer, which in turn determine which of the seven basic structures are appropriate. Both goods/service and market/demand characteristics determine the predictability of the nature of demand, which in turn influences system structure feasibility. Business policy will also influence the importance to be attached to customer service and resource productivity objectives, which affects the choice from among feasible structures.

Business policy influences on the choice of operations management strategies

In Chapter 1 we considered how system structure and operations management objectives influence the strategies and role of operations management (see Figure 1.6). Each system structure is likely to have different problem characteristics in each of the three principal problem areas. The nature of the problems to be tackled by operations management is therefore influenced by system structure. The manner in which these, and other problems, are tackled will also be influenced by the objectives which exist. In other words, a problem may be tackled in a particular manner in order to achieve a particular outcome given one set of objectives, and in a different manner for a different end given a different set of objectives. Thus the strategies adopted for the management of a given system, i.e. the general approaches employed, will be influenced by the nature of the problems which exist and the objectives which are to be pursued. The selection of strategies is therefore influenced by business policy decisions in two ways: through the influences on the selection of system structure in the manner discussed above, and through the influence on operations management objectives.

Contribution of operations management to business policy decisions

The principal means by which operations management contributes to or influences business policy decisions is through the provision of information on:

(a)   the existing operating system structure, objectives and strategies;
(b)   the implications for operations management of the goods/service and market/demand characteristics which are proposed or being considered by the business policy makers.

In 'change' situations, both (a) and (b) are relevant, whereas in the establishment of entirely 'new' systems only (b) is appropriate. Change situations may occur when a change or modification of the existing goods or service(s) is under consideration and/or when new markets are being investigated. In such situations an operating system is in existence and changes are being considered which might affect or necessitate a change of system objectives and strategies. Clearly some knowledge of the nature of the existing system, its characteristics and performance will be of value in making business policy considerations in such circumstances. The alternative is the 'greenfield' situation, in which business policy decisions will lead to the establishment of new operating systems. Here operations management must interpret alternative goods/services and market/demand strategies into implications for operations management, since the nature of the system structure, operations management objectives and strategies required to meet given goods/service and market/demand characteristics will influence the choice between alternatives.

Whatever the situation, operations management is, in effect, using the same type of information in seeking to influence business policy decisions. The main factor in both cases is the need to match operating system structures, operations management objectives and strategies to given goods or service and demand conditions, or vice versa. If it is intended to change goods or service and/or demand specifications, then a knowledge of the characteristics and capabilities of the existing operating system, existing operations management objectives and strategies, and the effectiveness of existing systems and strategies, is important. Equally, it is important when considering alternative goods or service and/or demand specifications to know what system structures, objectives and strategies will be required for effective operation.

OPERATIONS POLICY

We have seen that three major operations management decisions are influenced by prior business policy decisions, i.e.

(a) selection/choice of system structure;
(b) selection/formulation of operations management objectives;
(c) selection/formulation of strategies for the management of the operating system.

These are key operations management decision areas. They are all concerned with planning. Operations management must determine system structure and objectives and contribute to the determination of objectives before anything can be manufactured, supplied, transported or serviced. They are key decisions, since wrong decisions in these areas will inevitably affect the performance of the system and the organization. Together they will determine the nature and character of the operating system. They are in fact operations management *policy* decisions. The choice of operating system structure, the objectives of the system, and the strategies which will be employed in the management of the system are the principal ingredients in the formulation of an operations management policy.

We have seen that operations management contributes to business policy decisions by providing information on:

(a) the existing system structure, objectives and strategy, in order that the characteristics and capabilities of the system might be considered in the selection/change of goods or service and demand characteristics;
(b) the implications of proposed or alternative goods or service and demand characteristics for system structure, objectives and strategy.

This contribution of operations management to business policy decision-making therefore derives from the three operations management policy decision areas. In fact, therefore, as would have been expected, it is principally the policy decisions of operations management which both are influenced by and contribute to business policy decisions.

EXAMPLE: A RESTAURANT

An example of the manner and nature of the influence of business policy decisions on operations management is shown in Figure 2.3. Here the major policy decision—to establish a 'take-away' and 'rapid food' restaurant—gives rise to decisions on the nature of the product, the markets to be served and the manner in which the organization is to deal with its customers. These decisions, in turn, give rise to the need for operations management decisions in the three key operations policy areas, which in turn will give rise to decisions on labour and staffing, the layout of the system, quality control, the maintenance of equipment, etc. Any problems anticipated in the implementation of the operations policies will encourage operations managers to feed back views to the business policy decision-makers with the intention if necessary, of modifying the business policy and/or modifying objectives of the operations function.

BUSINESS GROWTH AND DEVELOPMENT

Business policy formulation often reflects certain beliefs about the growth and development of an organization. The tacit objective of growth may be questioned or qualified, yet it must be a legitimate and major consideration in business policy formulation.[3] The formulation of an appropriate policy for an organization requires an

---

[3] See, for example, Ansoff, H. I. (1970) *Corporate Strategy*. Harmondsworth: Penguin.

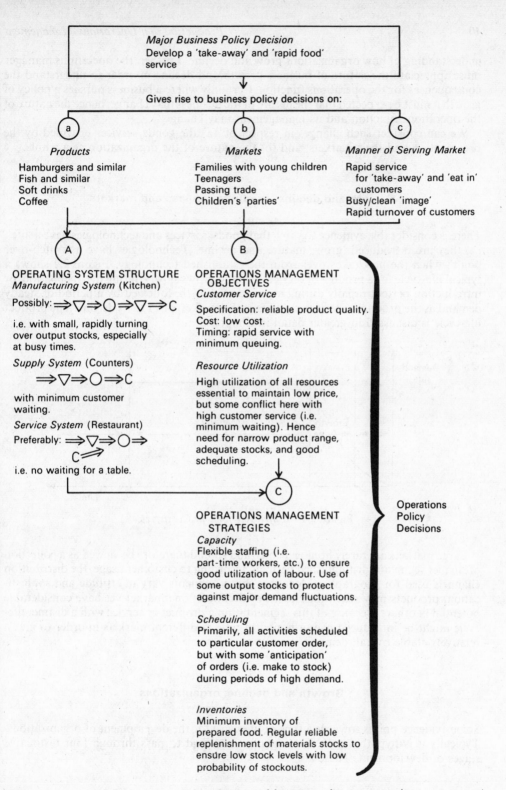

Major Business Policy Decision
Develop a 'take-away' and 'rapid food' service

Gives rise to business policy decisions on:

a

Products
Hamburgers and similar
Fish and similar
Soft drinks
Coffee

b

Markets
Families with young children
Teenagers
Passing trade
Children's 'parties'

c

Manner of Serving Market
Rapid service
   for 'take-away' and 'eat in'
   customers
Busy/clean 'image'
Rapid turnover of customers

A

OPERATING SYSTEM STRUCTURE
Manufacturing System (Kitchen)

Possibly: $\Rightarrow\triangledown\Rightarrow\bigcirc\Rightarrow\triangledown\Rightarrow C$

i.e. with small, rapidly turning over output stocks, especially at busy times.

Supply System (Counters)

$\Rightarrow\triangledown\Rightarrow\bigcirc\Rightarrow C$

with minimum customer waiting.

Service System (Restaurant)

Preferably: $\Rightarrow\triangledown\Rightarrow\bigcirc\Rightarrow$
$C\Rightarrow$

i.e. no waiting for a table.

B

OPERATIONS MANAGEMENT OBJECTIVES
Customer Service

Specification: reliable product quality.
Cost: low cost.
Timing: rapid service with minimum queuing.

Resource Utilization

High utilization of all resources essential to maintain low price, but some conflict here with high customer service (i.e. minimum waiting). Hence need for narrow product range, adequate stocks, and good scheduling.

C

OPERATIONS MANAGEMENT STRATEGIES
Capacity
Flexible staffing (i.e. part-time workers, etc.) to ensure good utilization of labour. Use of some output stocks to protect against major demand fluctuations.

Scheduling
Primarily, all activities scheduled to particular customer order, but with some 'anticipation' of orders (i.e. make to stock) during periods of high demand.

Inventories
Minimum inventory of prepared food. Regular reliable replenishment of materials stocks to ensure low stock levels with low probability of stockouts.

Operations Policy Decisions

Figure 2.3 *An example of the major influences of business policy on operations management decisions: a restaurant.*

understanding of how organizations grow and decline. Further, the operations manager must appreciate the nature of business growth and decline in order to understand the consequences for the operations function. Certainly where a business pursues a policy of growth it must be expected that the nature of the business may change, hence the nature of the operations function and its management may change.

We can consider such changes in respect of: (a) the goods/services provided by the organization and their markets; and (b) the nature of the organization as a whole.

Growth and decline: products/services and markets

There is considerable evidence to show that goods, services and technologies have a 'life', i.e. they are introduced, grow, mature and decline. Technologies have a 'switch-over point', when the new takes over from the established technology. Figure 2.4 shows a typical life-cycle for a product or service: demand grows slowly during the 'incubation' or introduction period, rapidly during a period of growth, followed by a period of steady demand as the product or service matures in the market, prior to its decline. The product life-cycle is discussed in greater detail in Chapter 3.

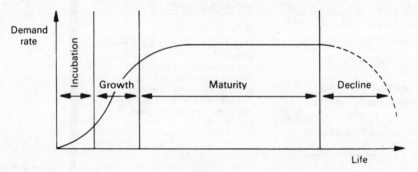

Figure 2.4 *A life-cycle for a product/service.*

Large markets are rarely homogeneous, and should therefore be viewed as a collection of smaller segments, distinguished perhaps according to customer usage, the distribution channels used for geographical location. Since segments vary in attitude and sophistication, products may reach their point of decline in one market yet have considerable potential in others. Because of this segmentation a product or service with a distinct life-cycle might be introduced over a period of time in different markets in order to give a relatively stable overall demand.

Growth and decline: organizations

Some evidence points towards a type of life-cycle for the development of organizations. Typically it is hypothesized[4] that organizations tend to pass through four distinctive stages of development. These are:

---

[4] Chandler, A. D. (1962) *Strategy and Structure*. Cambridge, Massachusetts: MIT Press.
Salter, M. S. (1970) Stages of corporate development. *Journal of Business Policy*, **1** (1).
Channon, D. F. (1973) *Strategy and Structure of British Enterprise*. London: Macmillan.

(a) the owner-entrepreneur with a single product/service and an informal organization;
(b) a single unit with delegated control to departmental managers, e.g. engineering, production, sales and service;
(c) a divisional organization with a number of semi-autonomous businesses based on different goods/services;
(d) a diversified organization with central management working through an industrial holding company and regarding the business largely as investments.

Table 2.1 summarizes these four stages of corporate development, and identifies their characteristics. Growth, as a means of avoiding goods/service obsolescence, is implicit in these stages, and is indeed a central concept in business policy. Consideration of growth needs and opportunities gives rise to the concept of the 'business of the firm'. Increased market penetration, the development of new markets, the development of new products or services, and diversification are therefore principal directions for growth. These are illustrated in the manner of a product/service and market/demand matrix shown in Figure 2.5.

Table 2.1 *Four possible stages in corporate development*

Stage	Organization structures	Goods/service and market characteristics	Management	Measurement of performance
1	Single unit managed by a sole proprietor	Small scale, single line of related goods/service for one market, one distribution channel	One person operation, very little task differentiation	Very few, personalized, not based on formal criteria
2	Single unit managed by a team	Large scale, single line of related goods/service for one market, one distribution channel	Responsible for single functions, e.g. operations, sales, finance	Operating budgets for each function
3	Several regional units reporting to a corporate HQ each with structure 1 or 2	Each region produces same line for single market, multiple channels	Regional units performing several functions	Operating budget, return on sales, return on investment
4	Several semi-autonomous units reporting to corporate HQ each with structure 1, 2 or 3	Each unit produces different lines for separate markets, multiple channels	Divisions performing all major functions	Return on sales, return on investment

Implications for operations management

Clearly, if product/service life-cycles are evident, the level of demand for a particular product/service will change over time. For operating systems which provide few products/services, such demand changes will have particular importance. Systems

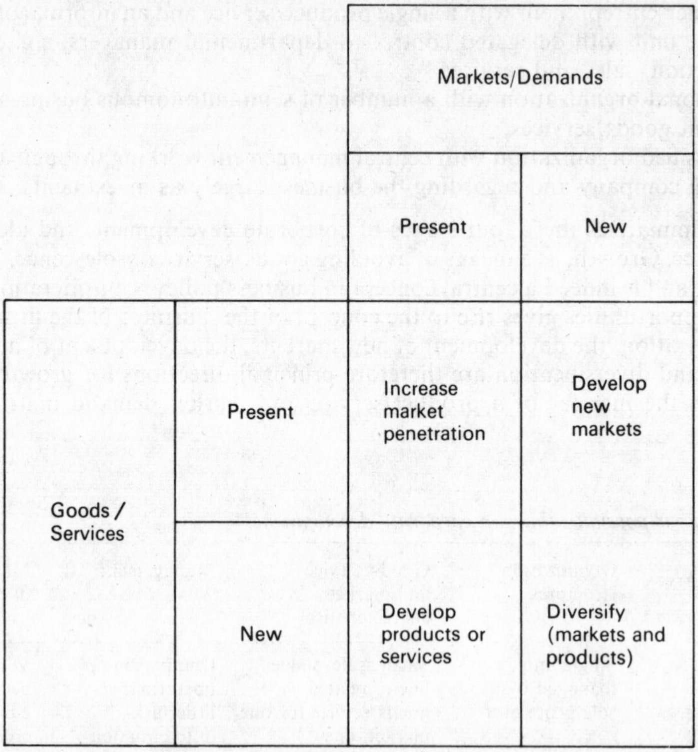

		Markets/Demands	
		Present	New
Goods / Services	Present	Increase market penetration	Develop new markets
	New	Develop products or services	Diversify (markets and products)

Figure 2.5 *Directions for growth. Adapted with permission from Ansoff, H. I. (1970) Corporate Strategy. Harmondsworth: Penguin.*

providing a range of products/services, perhaps launched at different times with different life-cycle patterns, may benefit from a relatively smooth aggregate demand. The development and provision of a set of products/services with complementary product life-cycles, and perhaps also complementary seasonal demand patterns may be a major objective in both business and operations policy.

If a pattern of corporate development exists, whether growth (as in Table 2.1) or decline, then it will be reasonable to suppose that these 'structural changes' within the organization will be matched by structural changes within the operating system. Certainly it can be argued[5] that the structure of operating systems may change in some predictable fashion during business growth, and equally during business decline. Similarly, it can be argued that the strategies employed in the management of operations must also change to reflect the changing nature of the organization during growth or decline, and of course the objectives of the operations manager will be affected by the 'state' of the business, i.e. differing where business is in a state of positive growth from where the business is in a defensive contraction state.

It will not be appropriate to speculate on these notions at this stage, but we must note that as business policy formulation is an ongoing process, often designed to achieve growth, it follows that both the policies and the nature of the organization in which they are to be implemented will change; hence operations managers' policies must also change and constantly be under review.

---

[5] Wild, R. (1979) *Operations management—A Policy Framework*, Oxford: Pergamon. Chapter 6.

CHECKLIST FOR CHAPTER 2

The importance of the business context to operations management
Business policy
  Business policy planning and implementation
    Formulation of business policy
    Implementation of business policy
Relationships of business policy and operations management decisions
  1. Influence of business policy on operations management decisions
    Choice of system structure
    Formulation of objectives
    Choice of strategies
  2. Contribution of operations management to business policy
Operations management policy decisions
Growth and development of businesses
  1. Growth and decline: products and services
    Product/service life-cycle
  2. Growth and decline: organizations
Implications for operations management
  1. Product/service life-cycle
  2. Business growth and decline

FURTHER READING

Hayes, R. H. and Schmenner, R. W. (1978) How should you organise manufacturing. *Harvard Business Review*, Jan.—Feb., pp. 105–118. Primarily concerned with manufacture.

Skinner, W. (1978) *Manufacturing in the Corporate Strategy*. Chichester: Wiley. Deals specifically with manufacture but, broadly, is of relevance to other types of organization.

Wheelwright, S. C. (1978) Reflecting corporate strategy in manufacturing decisions. *Business Horizons*, Feb., pp. 57–66. Again, primarily concerned with manufacture.

Wild, R. (1979) *Operations Management—A Policy Framework*. Oxford: Pergamon. A conceptual/theoretical treatment of operating systems and operations management in a business policy context. The text develops in detail many of the points raised in this chapter.

QUESTIONS

2.1 Show, by modifying and developing Figures 1.6 and 1.7, how business policy decisions might influence the principal decision areas of operations management.

2.2 Discuss the relationships of operating system structure and:
  (a) the characteristics of the goods or services provided by the system;
  (b) the nature of demand for those products or goods.
Show, by reference to examples, how changes in (a) and/or (b) give rise to changes in the operating system structure.

2.3 Show by means of a diagram similar to that in Figure 2.3 how the following business policy decision might affect the operations manager's decisions.

  Organization: A large hotel adjacent to city airport.
  Major policy decision: in addition to airline passenger and airport staff trade, to develop trade associated with business conferences, seminars, exhibitions, etc.

2.4 Discuss how the growth of an organization in the manner described in Table 2.1 might affect the job of the most senior person responsible for managing the operating system. If appropriate use a hypothetical case study on which to base /to illustrate your answer.

2.5 In what circumstances might an operations manager wish to seek to reverse, or promote further discussion on, recent business policy decisions? How might that influence be exercised, and what would be an appropriate role for the operations manager in such discussions with colleagues of equal status from other functional areas?

CHAPTER THREE

Operations Management and Other Business Functions

Following our examination of the business policy context of operations management in Chapter 2, we can now look more closely at the relationships of the operations function with other functions in the business. We shall consider relationships with marketing, personnel, finance and design, but concentrate on marketing, which is perhaps the most important relationship for operations management. We shall look for the nature of these relationships at *basic factors*, in order that the reader might apply this approach in his or her own particular situation. Detailed descriptions of the other business functions cannot be given here. Readers may wish to obtain more information by consulting the references marked with an asterisk in 'Further Reading' at the end of the chapter.

OPERATIONS MANAGEMENT AND MARKETING

Chapter 2 showed that certain decisions which are largely 'external' to the operations function have a considerable influence on decisions within the function. These external, policy-related decisions are largely concerned with the organization's relationship with its market(s).

Three market-related policy decisions have been shown to be of particular importance, i.e.

(a) the nature of the goods or services to be provided by the organization, i.e. the goods/service(s) characteristics;
(b) the nature of the markets to be served, i.e. the market demand characteristics;
(c) the manner in which these markets are to be served.

The marketing function

Marketing managers will have a major influence on these policy decisions, since the marketing function is primarily concerned with decisions on the nature of the 'offering' (i.e. the good or service(s) to be provided to customers) and the methods by which the 'offering' is made. These marketing decisions are usually referred to as the four aspects of the *marketing mix*, i.e. goods or services, cost, distribution, and promotion. Although all businesses must make decisions on each of these four elements of the marketing mix, different types of businesses will employ different mixes, since they will attach different relative importance to each element. For example, companies involved in providing consumer goods might emphasize promotion (e.g. advertising), while companies providing a specialist service might emphasize cost or price. Decisions on these four factors, outlined below, may be considered to be the deliberate *market decisions* of the organization.

(a) *goods/service*, i.e. goods/service characteristics—the actual item, transport or service provided to the customer, its attributes and characteristics, the features and provisions surrounding it and the essential benefits it provides;
(b) *cost*, i.e. the purchase price of the goods or service and any additional costs or allowances;
(c) *distribution*, i.e. the location of the market, channels of distribution, outlets, territories, etc., involved in the provision of the offering to the customer;
(d) *promotion*, i.e. the publicity, selling and advertising practices employed to bring the goods or services to the notice of the intended customer.

These market decisions influence, but do not determine, the nature of the demand faced by the organization, i.e. the demand felt by the operating system. In addition, other factors only partially influenced by the organization will influence demand, i.e.

(a) *environmental variables*—factors (largely beyond the control of the enterprise) that have broad effects on demand, e.g. the economic situation, public policy and culture;
(b) *competitive variables*—factors under the control of competitors.

Figure 3.1 indicates the manner in which environmental, competitive and market decision factors influence demand. The introduction of a new product or service may affect the total actual demand for products or services of that type and will also attract a part of that total. Environmental variables, the action of competitors and the market decisions of the enterprise may all affect the total potential size and the actual market. Certain actions of competitors, e.g. advertising, price changes, etc., may affect the size of the actual market, and of course market decisions by an organization, particularly promotion decisions, will directly affect actual market share. The nature of the environment will be known and therefore may influence market decisions. The actions of competitors will be uncertain but nevertheless may be considered by an enterprise when making decisions on goods/services, cost, promotion and distribution.

Within this framework we shall focus on the market decision factors, i.e. those decisions required of the business. In so doing we shall be looking more closely at the three market-related policy decisions identified at the beginning of this section in order to try to identify how these decisions, which directly influence operations management, are made, and thus to identify the means by which operations managers might influence them.

Decisions on goods/service characteristics

The nature of the 'offering' is, from the operations manager's viewpoint, perhaps the most important market decision. (See also the section on design later in this chapter.) We shall identify some of the factors that influence this decision.

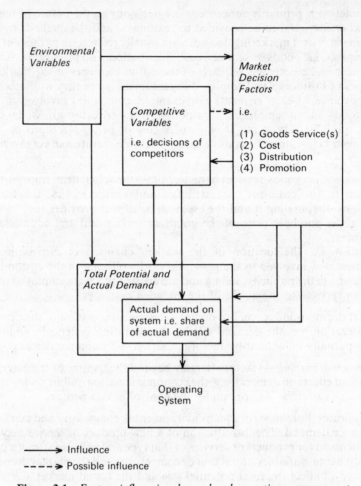

Figure 3.1 *Factors influencing demand and operations management.*

Growth is a common if not universal corporate objective. Goods/service(s) decisions are an important ingredient in the formulation and implementation of each of the four policies for growth identified in Chapter 2, i.e.

1. *Market penetration* is the expansion of sales of existing offerings in existing markets by selling more to existing customers, and/or gaining new customers in existing markets.
2. *Market development* is the creation of new markets by discovering new applications for existing offerings.
3. *Product development* is the launching of new offerings onto existing markets.
4. *Diversification* or lateral integration is the development of new offerings for new markets.

For reasons of diversification and goods/service development, most enterprises will offer a range of goods and/or services. This market decision may therefore require consideration of the characteristics of a particular offering or the number and mix of the whole range of offerings. It may be concerned with the addition, change or abandonment of one offering or one group of offerings from the whole range, and/or the nature, consistency and mix of the whole range. Three notions are of importance in this context:

1. A small part of the range often provides a relatively large part of the profits of the enterprise. It follows, therefore, that this group of offerings must be closely managed and monitored.
2. The upper limit of revenue is influenced by the nature of the range of offerings. Eight categories of offering have been identified for most ranges:
   (a) yesterday's 'breadwinners' (or yesterday's profit-makers)
   (b) today's 'breadwinners'
   (c) tomorrow's 'breadwinners'
   (d) products needing too many repairs
   (e) unnecessary specialities
   (f) undesired specialities
   (g) investments in management ego
   (h) 'Cinderellas'
   An enterprise's profit capacity can be improved by regularly abandoning those offerings which cost more to retain than to drop (e.g. (d) and (h)).
3. Most offerings have a sales curve or life-cycle. In the course of this cycle the offering progresses through a number of logically interrelated stages in which sales and profitability vary. For most enterprises, since offerings must pass through a distribution channel (see below), the maximum sales level is reached before the maximum consumption level. Furthermore, profits tend to reach their maximum level while sales are still increasing.

Life-cycles

Four stages in the life-cycle of offerings can be identified, i.e. 'incubation', 'growth', 'maturity' and 'decline'. Life-cycles may be practically unnoticeable for some offerings and very obvious for others, such as consumer durables. The span of the life-cycle may be determined by such factors as:

(a) the degree of technological progress;
(b) changes in customer habits;
(c) ease of entry to the market.

Different actions or market decisions may be required at each stage of a life-cycle. Price decisions will be required before or at the launch time, while during the incubation period the emphasis will be on promotion. Distribution is all-important during the growth period. The maturity period may see the introduction of price changes or changes in specifications to prevent decline and/or the introduction of new offerings.

The development process

Goods/service development involves the search for new offerings as well as the improvement of the existing. Since the number of entirely new offerings is normally small, development is largely concerned with the introduction of variants through adaptations and improvements.

At least six stages of development can be identified. These are:

(a)   exploration, including research, i.e. the continual search for new ideas;
(b)   systematic, rapid screening to eliminate less promising ideas;
(c)   business analysis, including market research and cost analysis;
(d)   development of the remaining possibilities;
(e)   testing the offerings developed;
(f)   launching on a commercial scale.

Development, testing and launching (d, e and f) are the most time-consuming and most costly stages. Few new ideas are eventually launched, and of these only a small proportion succeed. For these reasons enterprises may adopt contrasting *philosophies on development*, resulting in:

(a)   some enterprises assuming market leadership because of their strong research and development base; or
(b)   some enterprises seeking to react quickly to the innovations of others and therefore joining the competition during the growth stage; or
(c)   some enterprises joining in at a later stage, just before market saturation sets in, by adapting the offerings to the needs of special market segments; or
(d)   some enterprises not wishing to be excluded from new markets but relying on their ability to produce on a mass scale and offer very competitive prices.

Market policies

Three main methods are available to the enterprise to exploit the market: market aggregation, market segmentation and production differentiation.

Market aggregation is the penetration of the market to the greatest possible width and depth with a single offering or a very limited range. This approach relies on a uniform pattern of consumption and an appeal to the needs which customers have in common in order to win sales.

Market segmentation is concerned with placing an extensive range of offerings each of which is suited to the needs of a different submarket or market segment. Here a conscious search is made to determine the essential differences between buyer groups so that they can be clearly separated into different segments, each varying in size, buying power and buyer behaviour.

Production differentiation is the deliberate attempt to encourage demand to adjust itself to the manner in which supply has been segmented. Unlike market segmentation, product differentiation may be employed where segments are not clearly defined and where segments must therefore be created by emphasizing the presence of product differences between the enterprise's own offerings and those of competitors, in particular by emphasizing product differences which promote a social—psychological segmentation of the market favouring the product concerned.

Quality, brand and brand policy

Quality is the extent to which an offering satisfies a need. Improving the quality of an offering or a line is known as 'trading up', and the reverse as 'trading down'. Quality may be changed. For example, it may be appropriate to adjust the range in response to economic developments such as the trade cycle and/or to raise or lower both the quality and the price of offerings in the range. Trading up or down in the long term may help the enterprise to gain access, from its traditional market position, to other higher or lower segments of the market.

A brand is used to identify and distinguish offerings from those of competitors. For brand policy to be successful the offering must lend itself to differentiation, to facilitate advertising and promotion. The aim of branding is to facilitate, improve and simplify control of the market process. A successful brand image will help to secure a market. A brand suggests consistency in the quality and origin of the offering.

Decisions on cost, distribution and promotion

Here we shall consider the three remaining market decision variables, since all three directly influence market and demand characteristics. The operations manager will, of course, have some interest in these decisions and will wish to make some contribution to them. He or she will wish to influence decisions on the market which is to be pursued, to measure or estimate demand, and to predict future demand, in order to facilitate his or her own decision-making on capacity, schedules and inventories.

Cost

We shall concentrate on the *price* of the product/service, which is normally the most important but not the only cost factor.

Price is clearly important as a regulator of demand and a component of customer service. It:

(a) regulates sales volume;
(b) determines revenue;
(c) influences the rate of return on investment through its influence on sales profitability;
(d) has an impact on unit costs.

Thus price policy has several major objectives:

(a) a sales target;
(b) a profit target;
(c) a liquidity target;
(d) meeting competition;
(e) maintaining price and margin stability in the distribution chain;
(f) discouraging potential competitors;
(g) eliminating existing competitors.

Reactions to pricing decisions can be expected from:

(a) resellers, i.e. intermediaries in the distribution channel;
(b) final customers.

The principal decisions in pricing derive from four main problems, discussed in order below.

1. How should the relative importance and the relative emphasis of price and non-price variables within marketing decisions be determined?

2. To which pricing policy is a particular price geared? Pricing policy, in a broad sense, should answer two questions:
    (a) What are the objectives for pricing?
    (b) How will these objectives be attained?
3. How should prices (i.e. price levels) for offerings be determined (and redetermined)?
4. How should pricing policy, e.g. the timing and extent of price changes and deviations such as discounts, be implemented?

Relative importance of price and non-price variables

Competition on price may be an attractive proposition to an enterprise provided:

1. total demand for the offering in the market as a whole is price elastic (or sensitive to price);
2. the enterprise's (lower) price is based on a more or less lasting advantage, e.g. a cost advantage based on a technological lead.

Without these conditions any enterprise relying on the price variable may discover that the price of its offerings will never be low enough, hence competitive advantages derived from one of the other marketing decisions will probably be preferred.

Pricing policy

Two main pricing policy alternatives are available in marketing policy, i.e.

1. an *active* pricing policy in the case of
    (a) a new product service
    (b) changes in cost levels (inflation)
    (c) changes in the level of demand (product cycle)
    (d) discounts;
2. A *passive* pricing policy in the case of
    (a) non-price competition
    (b) pricing agreements
    (c) price cartels
    (d) leasing
    (e) price leadership.

An active pricing policy may take any one of a broad spectrum of different forms:

(a) skimming the market—a skimming price, often temporary in nature, followed by (2);
(b) sliding gradually down the demand curve;
(c) maintaining a margin above the current market price—a price premium;
(d) setting a price fractionally below the current market price;
(e) a penetration price for penetrating the market quickly and within a short period;
(f) an expansion price for accelerating the penetration process;
(g) stay-out pricing—a warning to potential competitors;
(h) put-out pricing—the elimination of competitors.

In the case of a new offering, the enterprise may choose between a skimming price and a penetration price. A skimming price may be used:

(a) if sales are insensitive to price changes;
(b) if the offering is difficult to imitate;
(c) if the market is gradually expanding—with the aid of successive price reductions, more new, lower market/income segments are tapped;
(d) if competition is expected to increase considerably and the enterprise wants to build funds for promotional activities in the later phases of the life-cycle;
(e) if it is suspected that a new offering's life span is likely to be short.

A penetration price may be used:

(a) if, from the beginning, sales are price sensitive;
(b) if a large market share is essential to compete in the market;
(c) if the enterprise expects to achieve short-term economies of scale.

Implementing pricing policy involves:

(a) timing price changes to coincide with various factors such as a particular stage of the life-cycle;
(b) defining a policy on price variations, i.e. where there should be departures from pricing policy.

Objectives of price variations include:

(a) encouraging customers to better their performance by granting performance discounts for reaching certain targets, e.g. quantity rebates, turnover bonuses, discounts for prompt payment, etc.;
(b) keeping certain distribution channels open long-term by means of functional discounts, e.g. to wholesalers;
(c) meeting competition in the short run;
(d) offsetting short-run fluctuations in demand;
(e) promotional objectives such as sharing the costs of dealer campaigns, supplying advertising material, etc.;
(f) ensuring operations at a high level of plant capacity.

Distribution

Two aspects of decision-making for distribution can be identified: distribution channel decisions and physical distribution management decisions. The latter are more likely to influence operations management directly. The former will be described briefly in the interests of comprehensiveness, and a more detailed treatment of the subject will be provided in Chapter 16.

The channels through which items flow to the customer or through which the customer flows to the organization will range from the simplest, i.e. a system dealing directly with the final customer, to the complex, in which several intermediaries intervene in the distribution process. The nature of the channel(s) employed will depend largely on the nature of the organization and on the number and location of final customers. The more diverse the points of contact with customers the longer and more complex the distribution channel.

The management of physical distribution or customer channels is normally termed physical distribution management (PDM). Three principal PDM decision areas can be identified, the last two of which are of particular relevance to operations management as sources of influence on customer service and demand:

(a) channel design;
(b) service-level decisions;
(c) inventory decisions.

High customer service, in terms of short delivery delays or a lower probability of stock-outs, incurs higher cost through the need for a larger number of stock holdings, higher stock levels, more and frequent stock replenishments, etc. Distribution service levels conflict with distribution costs, hence enterprises must determine economic service or delivery levels for distribution systems.

Service-level decisions are intimately related to inventory decisions.[1] There are two basic approaches to inventory control:

(a) the re-order level system, in which stock is replenished (usually with a fixed quantity) or a replenishment order is made when stock falls to a fixed re-order level;
(b) the re-order interval system, in which stock is replenished, or a replenishment order is made such that the stock level returns to a fixed maximum level at fixed intervals.

Whichever approach is adopted, the variable rate of stock depletion which normally exists, plus possibly the uncertain delays between placing a replenishment order and receiving items into stock, necessitates the use of a buffer or safety stock designed to ensure a required customer service level. For example, use of the re-order level system will normally necessitate the adoption of a re-order level which is high enough to ensure that in most, if not all, cases a replenishment order is received into stock before the stock level falls to zero. Given information on the variability of both demand and replenishment lead time, a re-order level can be established to provide a required service level (e.g. a maximum probability of stock-out).

Decisions on re-order levels or intervals, re-order quantities, etc., at various stages in the distribution channel affect both customer service and the nature of demand, and are therefore of some importance to operations management.

Promotion

Promotion is concerned primarily with persuasion, aimed largely at securing and increasing the share of the market. Four promotional activities can be identified.

(a) *advertising*—any paid form of non-personal presentation and promotion of products or services by an identified sponsor;
(b) *personal selling*—oral presentation to one or more prospective purchasers for the purpose of making sales;
(c) *publicity*—non-personal stimulation of demand for a product or service, by planting commercially significant news about it in a published medium or obtaining favourable presentation of it that is not paid for by the sponsor;
(d) *sales promotion*—those marketing activities, other than personal selling, advertising and publicity, that stimulate consumer purchasing and dealer effectiveness, such as displays, shows and exhibitions, demonstrations and various non-recurrent selling efforts not in the ordinary routine.

An enterprise must decide how much promotional effort to make and the relative mix or importance of each of the above within that total effort. The importance of promotion

---

[1] Discussed in detail in Chapter 17.

will depend, among other things, on the merits of alternative non-promotional expenditure, the nature of the product or service offered by the enterprise and its competitors, and the stage in the product or service life-cycle.

Promotion is one way to secure and stimulate demand. Given limited resources, promotion competes for funds with the other three market decision variables. The more impersonal the method of distribution and the greater the similarity to the products or services offered by competitors, the greater is the need for promotional effort. Products and services which are at an early stage in their life-cycle, where exposure and customer awareness are important, may also need relatively high promotion.

Figure 3.2 suggests the relative importance of the four elements of the promotional mix in respect of the four stages of promotion, i.e. customer awareness of, interest in, desire for, and acquisition of the offering. We shall concentrate on advertising and personal selling, which are normally the most important elements of the promotional mix.

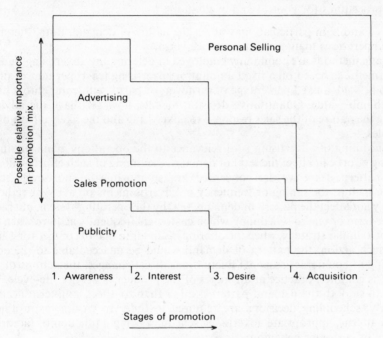

Figure 3.2 *Promotion mix and the 'stages' of promotion.*

Advertising

In general, the demand-related objectives of advertising are to attract new customers both from the actual market (i.e. competitors' customers) and from the potential market (i.e. previously 'non-users'), to increase the existing customers' rate of consumption and to control demand patterns. The persuasion process through which these objectives are pursued involves the enterprise sending 'messages' (or ideas) via various 'media' to a 'target group' (or audience), the effectiveness of the whole being subject to some form of assessment through feedback.

Ultimately enterprises require some positive net effect of advertising on revenues and profits. Simply to increase demand is not enough if the additional sales increase is more than offset by the cost of attracting it. Advertising at the beginning of a life-cycle may enable an enterprise to gain time by achieving quicker market penetration and an earlier break-even. In the longer term, advertising may be used to secure a market share to combat the effects of any external influences on demand (e.g. environmental and competitive variables), to combat seasonal variations, etc., the latter being concerned more with the control of demand patterns than with the change of long-term demand levels.

The major decisions required in advertising are:

(a)   the amount of advertising (the advertising budget);
(b)   the scheduling of advertising effort;
(c)   the advertising message(s);
(d)   the advertising media;
(e)   the procedures for control and evaluations.

Decisions a and b, in particular, may affect the nature of demand. Both, therefore, may influence operations management, and vice versa.

Pragmatic methods are commonly employed in determining advertising budgets. For example, methods based on a fixed amount of advertising (cost) per unit of product or service to be sold, a fixed percentage of turnover, or parity with competitors have some 'rule of thumb' value. Quantitative decision models, however, have the advantage of indicating the nature of the sales response to advertising and the likely effects of changes in variables.

The scheduling of advertising is of relevance to the operations manager since, if the advertising effort can affect the level of demand, the timing of such efforts will affect the demand pattern. Here we are concerned not so much with short-cycle scheduling problems, such as the timing or frequency of advertisements on a TV or radio station, which may not affect the pattern of demand 'felt' by the operating system, but rather with the longer-term or macro scheduling which customers frequently acquire when competitors adopt a similar strategy, when the offering is similar to that of competitors, and when, without such action, the pattern of demand would be unacceptable to the enterprise. Advertising to counteract seasonal fluctuations, fiscal changes, the actions of competitors, etc., is common practice at all stages of the product or service life-cycle. They are attempts to smooth the demand patterns rather than to affect long-term needs.

Similarly, scheduling decisions are required in order to ensure favourable overall demand patterns, appropriate advertising schedules being a function of factors such as the nature of customer behaviour.

Selling

Personal selling, with advertising, is the normal form of promotion, at least for consumer offerings. Personal selling is directed at individuals. It involves direct contact, offers direct feedback, is time-effective, flexible and adaptable, but time-consuming and expensive.

The major decisions affecting the nature and extent of personal selling as a promotional activity are:

(a)   the size of the sales force;
(b)   the sales force design (e.g. territories);
(c)   the management of sales staff (e.g. recruitment, training, remuneration);
(d)   the evaluation of selling.

The relationships of operations management and marketing decisions

Marketing managers are primarily responsible for the four 'marketing mix' decisions discussed above. These decisions are of substantial interest to operations managers, for they will determine the products/services to be provided by the operating system and the nature of demand for those outputs. Operations managers will, at least, wish to monitor all the decisions which influence them. In most cases they will wish to exercise some influence on these decisions, and in some cases they may need to ensure that marketing managers do not make decisions which give rise to circumstances which operations managers cannot adequately accommodate. For example, they will wish to avoid situations in which, as a result of decisions over which they had no influence, they feel obliged to deal with a great diversity of products/services, each with too small quantities, with unacceptable deadlines or delivery dates, too high a quality and too low a cost. This is an extreme situation, but operations managers must seek to avoid the impossible by emphasizing the feasible. It would be appropriate for them, therefore, to have in mind a 'checklist' of those decisions which influence the nature of the product/service, the market for that 'offering' and the manner in which that market is to be satisfied. Table 3.1 provides such a checklist.

Table 3.1 *A checklist of some marketing decisions which influence operations management*

Product/service characteristics
   the development philosophy
   market policy
   the nature and quality of the product/service

Cost
   pricing policy
   the price of the offering
   price variations

Distribution
   level of service
   inventory decisions

Promotion
   advertising—amount
            —scheduling
   selling—size of sales force

Operations managers will also need to measure, estimate or forecast demand. We saw in Chapter 1 that, in certain types of operating systems, resources are stocked in anticipation of their being needed at a future date. Similarly, some systems rely on the provision of output stocks from which customers are supplied direct.

In all such systems the level of both resource and output stocks provided must be influenced by the level of demand which is expected to exist at some future date. In such cases, therefore, the estimation or prediction of demand is of importance.

Existing demand levels can be measured, and this is of significance in the management of operating systems which require resources to be obtained directly to meet demand from particular customers. It should be noted, however, that even given this need, and given the ability to measure demand levels, errors may be introduced. Rarely is it possible to measure directly the amount of resources required to satisfy particular customer orders. Normally, since orders will probably differ (otherwise resources will probably have been stocked), it will be necessary to estimate the resource requirements of a particular customer order. Thus for all types of operating systems the translation of either known or expected demand into required resources will be susceptible to error through:

(a)   demand estimation/forecasting errors; and/or
(b)   errors in the estimation of the resource requirements associated with customer orders/demand.

Procedures appropriate for demand estimation and forecasting are discussed in some detail in Appendix II, hence our purpose here is simply to note that operations management must employ such procedures in order adequately to accommodate this externally influenced factor and ensure realistic internal decision-making on problems such as capacity and inventory management and activity scheduling.

In demand forecasting, the length of the forecast period will depend largely on the nature of system resources and the nature of the market. For example, capacity planning may involve periods in excess of five years where there is sufficient stability or predictability of the nature of demand. A long-term view may be essential where there is a long lead time on the provision or replacement of resources. Examples might include:

(a)   manufacture—steel manufacture, electricity generation and supply, oil production;
(b)   transport—airlines, rail systems;
(c)   service—hospitals, telephone service.

In contrast, a shorter-term view would be appropriate where the nature of demand is less stable or less predictable, and where resources are more readily provided or replaced, or where the manner in which the function is accomplished may change, for example through technological change. Examples might include:

(a)   manufacture—fashion goods, consumer durables;
(b)   supply—retail shops, mail order;
(c)   transport—bus service, taxi service, road delivery service;
(d)   service—secretarial services, security service.

OPERATIONS MANAGEMENT AND PERSONNEL/ORGANIZATIONAL FACTORS

The 'technology' in an organization will inevitably have some impact on its employees. For example, the type of equipment used will inevitably affect the nature of the jobs and the working conditions of employees. Further, the type of technology employed within an organization may affect its structure or shape. Here we shall consider briefly the relationship between technology and job/organizational factors, with particular reference to the role of the operations manager. We shall in effect be looking at some aspects of the relationship between operations management decisions and the decisions of those responsible for personnel/organizational matters.

Technology and organization

Early research by Woodward[2] suggested a relationship between technology and the nature (or shape) of the organization. In considering different types of production systems

---

[2] See 'Further Reading' at end of chapter.

Woodward found relationships between the type of technology employed and organizational factors such as the length of the chain of command, the span of managerial control, and the ratio of direct to indirect labour. This research gave rise to a considerable amount of study aimed at clarifying the relationships between technology and such organizational factors. Over a period of time new definitions emerged, and eventually the research began to focus on the relationships of the types of factors defined in Table 3.2. This research resulted in a series of general conclusions which can be summarized as follows:

1. *Task uncertainty.* The greater the routineness or repetitiveness of tasks and the less the task variability, complexity and uncertainty, then the less the degree of participation in organization decision-making and the greater the formalization of roles, procedures and practices.
2. *Task interdependence.* The greater the interdependence of tasks, roles and activities and the less the rigidity of workflows, then the greater the participation in decision-making and the less formalized the authority structures, procedures, etc.
3. *Workflow uncertainty.* The less the variability, complexity or uncertainty of workflow, and the greater the standardization of inputs and outputs, then the more formalized and centralized the management, the greater the vertical integration and departmentalization, and the more sophisticated the control procedures.
4. *External uncertainty.* The less the rate of change in products/service specifications and ranges, the less the rate of programme/demand change, the less the market uncertainty and the greater its homogeneity, then the more mechanistic the management of the organization, the greater the formalization and centralization of management, and the more structured the organization.

Taken together these conclusions suggest a negative relationship between the extent of uncertainty in and around an organization and the degree of structuring and concentration of authority and decision-making of that organization. We might expect this type of relationship to exist at different levels within the organization. For example, the uncertainty of tasks, their interdependence, the uncertainty of workflows and the demands placed on a department and the workgroups within that department will be reflected in the organization of both the department and its workgroups. At the organizational level, a high degree of structuring and concentration may be evident through functional divisions, staff/line relationships, reporting and control mechanisms, etc., while at the workgroup level a similar organizational structure or style may be evident through detailed job descriptions, work procedures, closeness of supervision and high division of labour. At the organizational level, low structuring and concentration may be evident through the use of 'matrix'-type structures, project or task group arrangement, working parties, an emphasis on informal communications, frequent role or job changes and transfers. At the workgroup level such an approach may be evident as job rotation, worker control of workflow, absence of formal supervision, the use of semi-autonomous workgroup arrangements, informal training procedures, broadly defined jobs, and absence of specialist and technical functions.

Technology factors and operations management

The existence of a particular technology (as defined above) can, as we have seen, influence the nature of people's work. It follows, therefore, that if operations managers, through their decisions, influence the nature of this 'technology' then their decisions can influence

Table 3.2   *'Technology' and 'organization' factors or measures*

Technology factors (relating mainly to the nature of the work or tasks performed within the organization)		Organizational factors (relating to the nature and shape of the organization and the manner in which decisions are made)
Task uncertainty, comprising (a) task difficulty, as indicated by the extent to which there are known and adequate procedures for performance, and the amount of time required for solving task problems (b) task non-routineness, indicated by the amount of variety in and/or the number of changes in the task over a period of time (c) task unmanageability, as indicated by the extent to which the task and any changes in it are understood by the worker *Task interdependence* as indicated by the need for active self-initiated collaboration and co-operation between workers *Workflow uncertainty*, comprising (a) workflow variability, as indicated by the number of possible or alternative sequences of activities available for each item (b) workflow complexity, as indicated by the difficulty of determining the appropriate sequence or next stage of activity for each item *External uncertainty* as indicated by the rate of change of product or service characteristics, or demand, and the heterogeneity of demand	? Relationships between these factors	*Specialization* refers to the division of labour within the organization. One aspect is the number of specialisms as indicated by a count of those functions that are performed by specialists. The degree of 'role' specialization is a further aspect and is concerned with the differentiation of activities within each function. It refers to the specificity of the tasks assigned to any particular role. Other relevant aspects are the level of specialist operation in terms of technical complexity and the relative status and influence of particular specialisms as exemplified by their level in the line hierarchy for which the top person in the function is responsible. *Standardization* can be considered as two aspects. Standardization of procedures is a basic aspect of organizational structure and may cover decision-making procedures, information-conveying procedures and procedures for operating or carrying out decisions. Procedures are standardized when there are rules or definitions that cover all circumstances and that apply invariably. Standardization of roles is concerned with the degree to which the organization prescribes the standardization of role definition and qualifications for office, role performance measurement, titles for offices, symbols of role status, and rewards for role performance. *Centralization* concerns the focus of authority to make decisions affecting the organization. Two types of authority can be identified: formal or institutional authority stemming essentially from ownership, and real or personal authority stemming from knowledge and experience. Factors affecting centralization include: the location of the actual decision-making function at particular points in the authority structure, the promulgation of rules for decisions which limit the discretion of subordinates, the frequency and thoroughness of review procedures and control systems, and the legitimate availability of relevant information. *Configuration.* The relationships between positions or jobs, described in terms of the authority of superiors and the responsibility of subordinates, are commonly expressed in the form of an organization chart. Various aspects may be distinguished, including vertical and lateral spans of control and numbers of positions (or jobs) in various segments.

the nature of individuals' work, and the structure of the organization. (Equally, if the existence of a particular organizational structure and particular job arrangements obliges or encourages the adoption of a particular technology, this is of interest to operations managers, since it may affect their decisions or limit their courses of action.)

Operations managers do influence 'technology', both indirectly and directly.

All organizations must deal with some uncertainties in the external environment, e.g. uncertainties in demand. Operations managers, perhaps working with marketing personnel, are largely responsible for determining the extent to which these external uncertainties are allowed to give rise to internal uncertainties. For example, an organization might protect itself against uncertainties in demand by the use of output stock etc., but if it chooses to operate directly in response to individual customer orders then external uncertainties will be communicated directly into the organization. Thus decisions about the way in which capacity is managed, the way in which activities are scheduled and the deployment of inventories will affect the extent to which uncertainties external to the organization are reflected in internal uncertainties. It will be appreciated that operations managers, therefore, through their decisions, can mediate the effect of external uncertainties on the organization. In this manner, therefore, *indirectly* their decisions may affect the 'technology' (as defined above) within the organization and thus the nature of the work which must be undertaken and the nature of the organization, which will be appropriate to such circumstances.

Equally, operations managers may choose *directly* to use their resources, including their workers, in a particular way. We shall see in Chapters 7 to 10 that they are responsible for the design of the jobs and the tasks undertaken by workers. It is for these reasons that operations managers' decisions have some relevance to those concerned with the management of labour, the design of jobs, and the design and structuring of the organization. For just these reasons operations managers must be aware of any limitations on their actions resulting, perhaps, from the existence of a particular organizational structure.

These relationships are outlined in Figure 3.3 and illustrated by the following example.

EXAMPLE: A TAXI COMPANY

In this company the operations manager is responsible for obtaining, maintaining and deploying adequate resources for the company to operate an effective taxi service within an urban area. *Until recently* the company has operated in a fairly stable environment. There were few external (e.g. demand) uncertainties and much of the company's custom was regular and repeat business. The operations manager aimed to provide high customer service while also attempting to achieve at least 75 per cent utilization of the cars and drivers. His major decisions gave rise to the operation of a system with a 'function from stock, and from (a small) customer queue' structure, using a capacity management strategy which maintained a small quantity of excess resources (spare cars and drivers) and necessitated customer queuing during times when demand exceeded capacity. Wherever possible customers were asked to pre-book taxis, and special price discounts were given for pre-booked customers using regular services. The decisions by the operations manager, taken in the light of the external uncertainties facing the organization, gave rise to the existence of fairly repetitive, routine and predictable jobs within the company and therefore the opportunity to operate in a fairly centralized, routine and structured fashion.

Recently major changes have taken place which have now begun to affect this company. Other taxi companies have begun to compete and the nature of other local transport has changed, so that it is no longer possible to predict demand accurately or to be certain about the types of journeys likely to be made by the majority of customers. It has now become necessary, in order to retain an adequate part of a somewhat uncertain market, to place more emphasis on customer service, particularly in terms of minimizing delays etc., and to accept, hopefully for a short period only, a lower utilization of resources. This in turn has given rise to the operations manager adopting a somewhat different strategy for the management of the system, i.e. the use of more variable capacity through the use of part-time drivers and vehicles, subcontracting arrangements, etc., and trying to maintain an operating system structure which does not oblige customers to queue. These decisions in turn have given rise to the existence of quite different types of jobs within the organization. No longer is it possible for work to be organized on a routine and predictable basis. Drivers now have to be given far more discretion and the size of the labour force now varies. Much more initiative and authority has been delegated to drivers, and there is far less of a dependence on routines, rules and procedures. Thus the tasks and jobs of the drivers and maintenance crews are no longer quite so predictable, and the organizational structure is now more decentralized, with a far greater delegation of authority and decision-making.

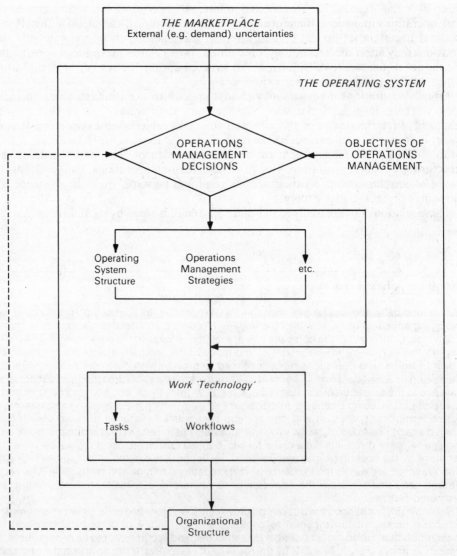

Figure 3.3   *Operations management decisions and their influence on work and organization structure.*

OPERATIONS MANAGEMENT AND THE FINANCE/ACCOUNTING FUNCTION

Many of the relationships between these two functions are obvious. For example, in the acquisition of capacity (e.g. physical facilities for the operating system) a capital investment will be required, so the finance manager will have some interest in the operations manager's decision. Also, the finance manager will have some interest in the operations manager's inventory decisions, since inventory represents tied-up capital. Equally, the relationship is clear in respect of the operations manager's decisions about facilities maintenance, the payment of incentives, etc. All these aspects are dealt with later in the book. Here we shall concentrate on one somewhat different aspect of the relationship between operations and finance managers, namely that involving financial control.

Managerial and financial controls *(see also Chapters 18 and 21)*

The top management of any organization will seek to exercise some control over the constituent parts of that organization and hence over the managers responsible for those parts. Such control will seek to measure progress and compare it with plans or intentions, in order to facilitate correction where necessary. Such controls may take several forms, but will often involve financial measures, and thus involve finance managers and accountants.

The purpose of such management controls on operations management must be to ensure that operations managers achieve agreed objectives. This, as will be clear from our discussion of objectives in Chapter 1, must recognize operations managers' objectives in respect of the achievement of adequate levels of customer service and resource productivity.

It has been pointed out that two basic types of control mechanism exist: (a) behaviour control and (b) output control. The differences are identified in Figure 3.4. Using a 'behaviour' control mechanism the behaviour of the system which is to be controlled is monitored and compared to a standard or objective in order that corrective action can be applied to the system if necessary. Using an 'output' control system the output from the system is observed and compared to a standard in order that the system itself can be adjusted if necessary. The distinction between the two types of control, therefore, is the point at which the system is monitored, i.e. the system itself or the output of the system.

In some cases the use of either of these two types of control will ensure adequately comprehensive control of the operating system for senior managers. In many cases, however, in order that the performance of the operating system can be monitored against *both* objectives, i.e. customer service objectives and resource utilization objectives, both types of control mechanism must be employed. It can be shown that the need to use both mechanisms in order to control performance against both objectives is mainly a function of operating system structure, the type of scheduling strategy, and the location of inventories.[3]

For example, if the scheduling of activities within an operating system is undertaken primarily to satisfy internal (e.g. machine-loading) requirements, and does not take direct account of individual customers' delivery-date requirements, then it will be difficult to monitor customer service solely by monitoring the internal working of the operating system. In these circumstances an 'output' control measure will be needed to check on

---

[3] See Wild, R. (1979) *Operations Management—A Policy Framework*. Oxford: Pergamon. Chapter 10.

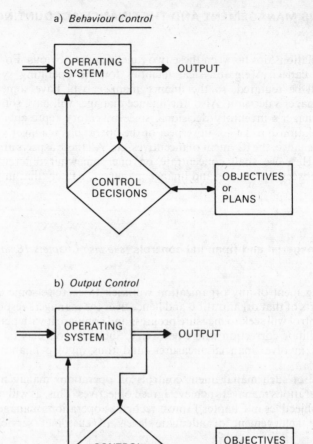

Figure 3.4　*Basic types of control.*

customer service, since a 'behaviour' control measure will monitor only resource utilization. Similarly, where an inventory or queue exists between the operating system and the customer, then what happens within the system is not necessarily directly linked to what happens for the customer at the same time. In these circumstances also, both types of control must be employed if the performance of the operating system against both objectives is to be controlled. It follows that operations managers must seek to ensure that appropriate and adequate controls are applied to them, otherwise they will be assessed only on the achievement of one of their twin objectives, which in time can lead to a distortion of their behaviour with too much emphasis on that objective and consequent neglect of the other.

It can be argued that, in general, financial/accounting controls are primarily of the 'behaviour control' type. For example, budgetary control methods based on the calculation of cost variances etc. are essentially a form of 'behaviour control'. It can be argued, therefore, that in many situations such controls in themselves are an inadequate means of providing management control over the operations function. In such circumstances, unless some other form of managerial control is employed, the operations manager's performance will be assessed largely in terms of productivity, with insufficient emphasis on customer service. It is for this reason that the operations manager must at least establish a close relationship with the finance manager, who will need to understand the nature, method of operation, strategies, etc., of the operating function in order to be able to implement comprehensive system managerial controls.

We shall look again at the use of management controls in dealing with performance measurements in Chapter 21.

EXAMPLE: A PRIVATE HOSPITAL

A small private hospital exists in an urban area. It is part of a larger company and it is run on a commercial basis. The hospital provides treatment and care for certain types of ailment. The operations manager is responsible for the administration of the entire hospital. She must achieve an annual profit, and her performance is monitored by the parent organization. The existing management controls monitor primarily the bed occupancy rates and length of patient stays in the hospital. The number of patient bed days per month is compared with the number of staff days worked, as a measure of labour productivity.

Patients are referred to the hospital by local doctors. They are placed on a waiting list and are admitted as soon as an appropriate bed becomes available in one of the small specialist wards. However, the admissions policy is not strictly on a 'first come first served' basis, since the hospital will often admit at the beginning of a week several patients who all need the same type of treatment, thus making it possible to schedule the work of the staff more easily. The lengths of waiting lists vary, but the hospital operations manager is anxious that they should not grow too long, as clearly one objective must be to satisfy the local doctors by ensuring that their patients are admitted without undue delay.

The operations manager is anxious that the management controls which are applied to her are adequate to measure her performance against her two objectives of resource utilization and customer service. She is aware that the present controls are largely of a 'behaviour control' type. She realizes that they focus on the 'internal' operations of the hospital, and is concerned that they over-emphasize performance related to productivity and resource utilization. She feels that in these circumstances such controls cannot monitor customer service, and intends therefore to persuade the parent organization that additional controls of the 'output control' type must be employed, aimed at collecting, directly from customers, information relating to customer service. She plans to put up specific proposals for additional measures which she hopes the parent company will use in controlling the hospital. (NB. This case is further developed in Chapter 21.)

OPERATIONS MANAGEMENT AND PRODUCT DESIGN DECISIONS

In most manufacturing organizations there will be a separate design department, and there must be an effective relationship between design, marketing and operations so that products will satisfy market and manufacturing requirements. In other types of organizations, i.e. in most service, supply and transport organizations, the responsibility for design may be less clearly identified. Nevertheless, in designing, i.e. in specifying, a service, as in designing or specifying a product, there must be effective relationships between design, marketing and operations decisions.

Our discussion of the relationship between marketing and operations decisions earlier in this chapter emphasized the manner in which design (or specification) decisions influence the operations manager, and vice versa, in service, supply and transport organizations. In this brief section we shall highlight some factors in this relationship which are specifically concerned with product design, and therefore which are of primary interest in manufacture. (The Appendix to this chapter provides further information on some specific topics relating to product design.)

Product design and operations management

Figure 3.5 outlines steps involved in product design. The following discussion considers certain of these steps and identifies other considerations and constraints.

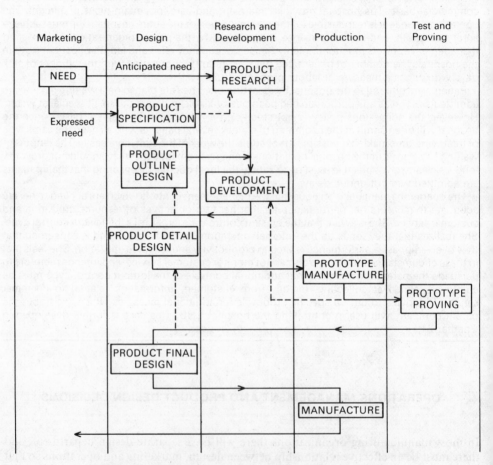

Figure 3.5   *Product design, development and manufacture.*

Research and development

Product research is seldom begun only in response to consumer demand. Indeed a great deal of research is conducted in most industries, the purpose of which is to make discoveries, establish new applications and interpret new findings, in the hope of anticipation that these will lead eventually to commercial application. Pure or fundamental research is not specifically oriented to commercial application or product design, but is encouraged by companies in anticipation of its future commercial worth. The same justification and motivation apply, but to a lesser extent, to fundamental research conducted on behalf of companies by co-operative research establishments or universities. Applied research is of more immediate worth and is often undertaken in order to provide answers to specific problems relating to either existing or proposed products.

It is often difficult to distinguish clearly between research and development; however, development is concerned with either a prototype pre-production product or a specified design for a product or part of a product.

Quality (see also Chapter 19)

In Chapter 19 we shall show that quality, and hence reliability, is invested in a product during two stages: design and manufacture. During the design stage quality is determined by the specification of appropriate standards and tolerances on dimensions, content, etc.

The quality level obtained is, of course, a function of cost. While no product can be designed to have perfect quality or perfect maintainability and reliability, the expenditure of more money on materials, testing, manufacture and control will, of course, improve quality levels. In practice, product quality will be determined not by the availability of suitable materials or production equipment, but by the quality of competitors' products, the elasticity of demand, and the planned product price. In many cases the use of standards such as those formulated by the British Standards Institute or the American Society for the Testing of Materials is obligatory or advisable.

Purchasing (see also Chapter 16)

Since no manufacturer is completely independent of suppliers, for direct materials, indirect materials, components, or sub-assemblies, the purchasing function will influence product design. Not only will the design of a new product depend on the ready availability of certain purchased items, but on the redesign, i.e. modification, replacement or improvement, of existing products. The purchasing department will play an important part because of its knowledge of such factors as the development of new materials and improved components. (Purchasing and supply will be discussed in Chapter 16.)

Make or buy decision (see also Chapter 16)

Theoretically, every item which is currently purchased from an outside supplier is a candidate for internal manufacture. Conversely, every item currently manufactured is a potential candidate for purchase. In reality the problem is not quite so extensive as this, since there will always be many items which it would just not be in our interest to make, such as raw materials, specialist parts and indirect items like stationery, ink, etc. Similarly, there will always be many items which it would not be in our interest to purchase.

The obvious question to ask is 'How can we determine whether it is or is not in our interest to buy or to make an item?' and the obvious but not very helpful answer is 'by determining which alternative involves least cost'. Inevitably this must be an economic decision, but the problem is how to determine what contributes to total cost.

Let us consider briefly some of the cost benefits which might accrue from our deciding to make an item ourselves rather than purchase it. By making an item we reduce our dependence on other companies and avoid the consequences of their labour disputes, we are able to determine our own quality levels and we preserve our trade secrets. Conversely, to purchase items rather than make them ourselves may enable us to obtain them more quickly, and to obtain the benefits of a continual development programme which we ourselves could not sustain. Additionally, purchase instead of self-manufacture may reduce costs such as those associated with storage, handling, paperwork, etc., as well as releasing our facilities for jobs on which they might be more suitably and profitably employed. Consequently, we can see that the apparently simple motto 'if it's cheaper to make than buy—make', and vice versa, is a little difficult to put into practice. We can usefully consider the make or buy decision as falling into two categories: first, as above, decisions about items already being manufactured or purchased; and second, decisions about new items. As regards current items, neglecting those factors which cannot readily be costed, we must ask ourselves the following questions.

If we choose to manufacture items which are currently purchased, what *additional* costs will necessarily be incurred, and how do these compare with the costs which will be saved?

If we choose to purchase items rather than make them, what costs will necessarily be *avoided* and how do these compare with the costs which will be incurred?

An analysis such as this is often referred to as *incremental cost* analysis. At the outset it is important to distinguish between fixed and variable costs. For example, the decision to cease purchasing an item does not necessarily result in a saving of a portion of purchasing department overheads, since many of the factors which contribute to overheads are, in the short term, fixed, e.g. purchasing department salaries. Similarly, the decision to cease manufacturing an item does not necessarily result in the saving of such costs as manufacturing overheads or even direct labour unless the released capacity can immediately be devoted to other jobs. It is normally easy to account for the direct cost associated with both manufacture and purchase but more difficult to account for, or even to identify, indirect cost. It should not be forgotten, however, that the cost of purchasing an item is not merely represented by the purchase price, but is also dependent on the cost of implementing the purchase, such items as inspection, receiving, etc often contributing significantly to total cost.

As regards projected or new items, the make or buy decision is often simpler, but rarely simple. The prospect of making an item on presently under-utilized equipment is a far more attractive one than if the present facilities are fully utilized and capital investment in equipment or recruitment of labour would be necessary. Nevertheless, even in the latter case it may be desirable to make items oneself if the quantity required is likely to increase considerably, or if the present manufacture of another item is due to cease, thus liberating capacity.

It is precisely because of complications such as these that we are unable to offer a definitive formulation of this problem or to define a general procedure for the solution. In those borderline cases which inevitably arise, nothing short of a comprehensive costing exercise will reveal enough data to make a truly objective decision, but, except in a few cases, such an extensive and costly exercise is unwarranted. Few companies will continually assess currently manufactured and currently purchased items, and rarely will changes in make/buy strategy be made unless a very clear economic benefit can be shown. A value analysis team may occasionally suggest that it would be beneficial to purchase rather than to continue to make an item, particularly when recent developments in technology or product developments result in the item offered by suppliers being either greatly improved or substantially cheaper. It may be beneficial also to subcontract or purchase items rather than acquire additional facilities when an additional product must be made, but apart from such clear-cut cases, decisions will inevitably be contentious. Because of the impracticability of considering all possible incremental costs, many companies make a policy of not reversing previous make/buy decisions unless a direct cost difference of at least 10 per cent can be shown.

CHECKLIST FOR CHAPTER 3

Operations management and marketing
  The marketing function
    Four market mix decisions
    Environmental variables
    Competitive variables
  Decisions on goods/service characteristics
    Growth policies and product/service
      decisions
    Life-cycles
    The development process
    Market policies
    Quality, brand and brand policy
  Decisions on cost
    Price decisions
    Relative importance of price and non-price
      variables
    Pricing policy
  Decisions on distribution
    Distribution channels
    Physical distribution management
  Decisions on promotion
    Advertising
    Selling
    Publicity
    Sales promotion
  The relationships of operations management
    and marketing decisions
    Demand considerations
    Forecasting
Operations management and personnel/organiz-
  ational factors
  Technology and organization
    Woodward research study
    Technology factors: definitions

Organization factors: definitions
  Relationships and technology and organiz-
    ation factors
Technology factors and operations
  management
  Influence of operations management deci-
    sions on work technology
  Influence of operations management on
    organization structure
Operations management and the finance/account-
  ing function
  Managerial and financial controls
    Types of control
      Behaviour control mechanism
      Output control mechanism
      Need for controls on operations
        management
      Financial control as a control mechanism
      Need for dual controls on operations
        management
Operations management and product design
  decisions
  Product design and operations management
    The relationships of marketing
      design
      research and
        development
      production
      test and proving
  Research and development
  Quality
  Purchasing
  Make or buy decisions

FURTHER READING

Anthony, R. N. (1965) *Planning and Control Systems—A Framework for Analysis*. London: Harvard University Press. Refers among other things to mechanisms for financial control.

*Khandwalla, P. N. (1977) *Design of Organisations*. London: Harcourt Brace Jovanovich. A comprehensive study and summary of material relating to the design of organizations including that referred to in this chapter.

Kotler, P. (1976) *Marketing Management—Analysis Planning and Control*, 3rd edition. Englewood Cliffs, NJ: Prentice-Hall. A comprehensive treatment of marketing. Chapters 12 to 17 are of particular relevance.

*Kuhlmeijer, H. J. (1975) *Managerial Marketing*. Leiden: Stenfert Kroese. A very concise marketing text giving more detail on all the topics covered in the marketing section of this chapter.

Ouchi, W. G. (1977) The relationship between organisational structure and organisational control. *Administrative Science Quarterly*, **22** (1), pp. 95–113. Identifies and demonstrates the distinction between 'behaviour' and 'output control'.

Wild, R. (1980) *Operations Management—A Policy Framework*. Oxford: Pergamon. The material covered in this chapter is dealt with in greater detail in Chapters 8, 9, and 10 of this book.

Woodward, J. (1965) *Industrial Organisation—Theory and Practice*. Oxford: Oxford University Press. A description of the research work which began the interest in the relationship between technology and organizational design.

QUESTIONS

3.1 In what way can 'marketing mix' decisions influence the customer demand on the operating system?

3.2 How does the performance of the operating system influence decisions on the 'marketing mix' variables? In other words, to what extent and in what way does the success with which the operations manager achieves his or her objective influence any one, or all four, of the marketing mix variables, i.e. product /service characteristics, cost, distribution and promotion?

3.3 Identify and discuss the principal considerations and factors which will be taken into account in determining the nature of the goods or services to be provided by the organization.

3.4 What factors or variables can be manipulated in order to create particular market /demand conditions and how might decisions on these factors /variables be made?

3.5 How might the operations manager's decisions on operating systems structure affect the nature of jobs within the organization and the manner in which the organization must operate?

3.6 A particular organization has a high degree of task uncertainty and workflow uncertainty. Comment on the manner in which decisions might be made within the organization, the nature of roles, procedures and practices within that organization, and the authority structures.

3.7 Appropriate management control procedures are to be introduced in order to ensure that the operating system achieves its twin, and equally important, objectives. For each of the seven basic types of system structure indicate whether an output control mechanism alone, or a behaviour control mechanism alone, or both mechanisms, will be necessary if performance of both objectives is to be monitored.

APPENDIX TO CHAPTER 3

Aspects of Product Design

Here we shall deal specifically with some topics relating to product design. These will be of particular relevance in operations management in manufacture and supply systems.

VALUE ANALYSIS AND VALUE ENGINEERING

Value analysis has been defined as 'an organized approach to get the same performance at lower cost without affecting quality', 'an organized and systematic effort to provide the required function at the lowest cost consistent with specified performance and reliability' and 'a functionally oriented scientific method for improving product value by relating the elements of product worth to their corresponding elements of product cost in order to accomplish the required function at least cost in resources'.

Often the term 'value engineering' is used synonymously with 'value analysis'. We shall use the latter only, but it is perhaps worth noting that 'value engineering' is normally used in relation to the design of new products and 'value analysis' in relation to existing products.

The principal objective of value analysis is to increase profit by means of a critical examination of areas of high cost. Such an objective can, of course, be pursued retrospectively by an examination of existing products and parts, or currently by involvement in the design of future products or parts. Although the cost breakdown varies between industries, it is common for direct materials to represent up to 50 per cent of total product cost (Figure A3.1).

Value is maximized when the cost associated with achieving the necessary function is minimized. Alternatively 'value' can be defined as the 'lowest cost reliably to accomplish the essential function'.

Two types of value can be identified: *esteem* value and *use* value. Use value is related entirely to function, i.e. the ability of an item to perform its specific purpose, while esteem value is not directly concerned with function but with the status or regard associated with

69

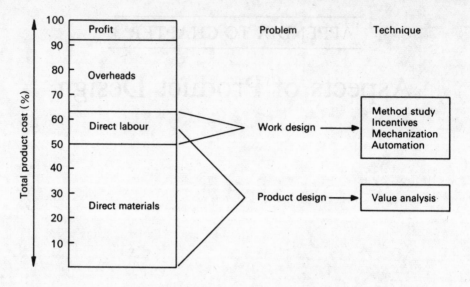

Figure A3.1 *Methods of reducing product cost.*

ownership. Value, for our purpose, is the sum of these two, use value normally being the principal component.

The result of properly applied value analysis is not, as is sometimes claimed, an inferior product but rather a product whose value/cost relationship is improved, a product which provides the necessary function with the essential qualities at a minimum cost.

Although other methods of conducting value analysis are available, it is usually found that the team approach is most appropriate and successful. Value analysis teams should consist of members with complementary skills drawn from the following departments within a company: design, purchasing, marketing, production and accounts.

Value analysis is therefore a common-sense approach to product design or redesign which involves the following steps:

1. Determine the function of the product, the customer requirements, etc.
2. Develop alternative designs.
3. Ascertain the costs and evaluate alternative designs.
4. Recommend and implement.

The relative importance placed by the customer on the following will determine design or redesign objectives:

(a) function;
(b) appearance;
(c) esteem associated with possession;
(d) intrinsic cost of materials or labour;
(e) replacement, exchange or disposal value.

As regards existing products the following questions will help to identify potential value improvements:

1. Which areas appear to offer largest savings?
2. What percentage of total cost is associated with bought-out items?
3. What percentage of total cost is associated with labour?
4. What percentage of total cost is associated with materials?

Often the maximum cost saving associated with existing products relates to bought-out parts or materials. The value of purchased parts and material can be investigated with a view to material or design changes by asking questions such as the following:

1. How does it contribute to the value of the product?
2. How much does it contribute to the total cost of the product?
3. Are all its features and its specification necessary?
4. Is it similar to any other part?
5. Can a standard part be used?
6. Will an alternative design provide the same function?

Generally four main steps are involved in a value analysis investigation, whether in relation to a new or an existing product.

The first step involves the collection of information. Information should be collected about costs, function, customer requirements, the history and possible future development of the product design, the manufacturing methods, and so on.

The second stage covers the development of alternative designs, i.e. alternative methods of achieving the required function. This is the creative, speculative stage during which use may be made of 'brainstorming' sessions, etc. No reasonable alternative or suggestion should be rejected during this stage, irrespective of apparent cost or practical disadvantages. It should be the objective during this stage to:

(a) eliminate parts or operations;
(b) simplify parts or operations;
(c) substitute alternative materials;
(d) use standard parts or materials;
(e) relax manufacturing tolerances;
(f) use standard manufacturing methods;
(g) eliminate unnecessary design features;
(h) change design to facilitate manufacture;
(i) buy rather than manufacture parts if cheaper;
(j) use prefinished materials;
(k) use prefabricated parts;
(l) rationalize product ranges;
(m) substitute low-cost manufacturing processes;
(n) rationalize range of purchased parts;
(o) eliminate material waste.

Use of checklists such as that shown in Table A3.1 may be of value during this stage.

The third stage involves the *evaluation of alternatives*. Alternative designs must be compared on a cost basis, cost information relating to all aspects of the designs being obtained from the purchasing, production and accounts departments. The temptation to dismiss alternatives perfunctorily should be resisted. Furthermore. whenever possible, ideas should be salvaged from eliminated alternatives.

The final stage involves *recommendation and implementation*.

STANDARDIZATION

Specifications provide details of product or component requirements in terms of materials, composition, dimensions, performance, and so on, while *standards* are rules, models or criteria against which comparisons can be made. *Standardization* is therefore concerned with the concept of variety, and, more specifically, with the control of *necessary*

Table A3.1 *Value analysis checklist*

Area	Questions
Production function	1. What are basic functions? 2. What are secondary functions? 3. Are all the functions necessary? 4. What else will perform the same function? 5. Can any of the functions be incorporated in other components?
Materials	1. What material is used? 2. What is the material specification? 3. Can any other material be used? 4. Can any other specification of the same material be used? 5. Can waste material be reduced? 6. Can raw material be standardized? 7. Can raw material be obtained in a different form? 8. What is the price of the material? 9. What indirect materials are used (e.g. packing, lubrication, etc.)? 10. Can pre-finished materials be used?
Size and specification	1. Can dimensions be reduced? 2. Is the part over size? 3. If less expensive material is used can size be increased? 4. What tolerances are specified? 5. Which tolerances are not critical? 6. Can tolerances be increased? 7. Can a standard part be used? 8. What finish is required? 9. Are the finish standards essential? 10. Can an alternative method of applying the finish be used?
Manufacture	1. Can any operations be eliminated? 2. Can any operations be combined? 3. Can any operations be simplified? 4. Would a different material simplify manufacture? 5. Can standard processes be used? 6. Can standard tools and jigs be used? 7. Can assembly operations be reduced? 8. Can prefabricated parts be used? 9. Would it be cheaper to buy the parts?

variety. Company standardization begins to operate once unnecessary variety has been eliminated. The elimination of unnecessary variety (variety reduction) can be defined as 'the process of eliminating the unnecessary diversity which frequently exists in the various stages from design to manufacture or selling' and is undertaken in anticipation of obtaining some or all of the following advantages:

1. There is increased interchangeability of parts, simpler stock-keeping and improved customer service.
2. Production of parts in larger quantities enables better machine utilization.
3. Production planning and control are facilitated.
4. Operator training is simplified.
5. Drawing office records, sales and service records are simplified.
6. There are lower stocks of raw materials, work in progress and finished products.
7. There are fewer jigs, tools and fixtures.
8. There are fewer set-ups and change-overs of machinery.

The principal prerequisite for successful standardization is an effective system of coding and classification which will enable component or part variety to be identified and controlled. An appropriate classification and coding method is invaluable during variety reduction, as well as during the design of new products, and such a coding and classification method should satisfy the following requirements:

1. It should enable items identical, or similar, to others to be identified and located.
2. It should enable existing items to be used in new designs where possible.
3. It should facilitate the reduction of necessary variety.
4. It should enable substitutes for 'out of stock' items to be identified.
5. It should enable groups of similar items to be located for production planning and production purposes.

CLASSIFICATION AND CODING

Clearly an adequate coding and classification system is beneficial to many departments in the company (see Table A3.2); indeed, one of the principal benefits of such a system is contained in requirement 5 above. (The manufacture of parts in groups or families rather than in small quantities makes increased machine utilization possible and often results in an entirely different plant layout. This method of manufacture, normally called *group technology*, depends entirely on effective coding and classification methods and will be discussed in more detail in Chapter 14.)

Table A3.2   *Use and benefits of parts coding and classification in certain departments*

Department	Design	Stores	Production
Use	Code similar parts under similar code numbers	Code similar parts under similar code numbers	Code similar parts, tools, jigs, etc., under similar code numbers
	Classify parts by shape and size	Classify parts according to type	Classify parts, tools, jigs, etc., by type
Benefits	Locate similar past designs	Lay out stores according to code numbers	Lay out facilities for group production
	Ensure use of existing designs when possible	Control variety by examining records	Ensure use of existing jigs, tools, etc.
	Control and reduce number of designs by variety reduction	Code together all purchase documents	Control variety of jigs, tools, fixtures, etc.
	Collect data for family formation	Provide for bulk buying of a smaller variety	Control variety of sub-assemblies
	Establish a preferred range of items		

Here we are concerned primarily with the design of products, and hence the principal benefit of an effective coding system is that it enables similar items to be classified together and thus facilitates the control of variety during design. In many cases, because of the lack of such a system, a great deal of time is wasted in designing items which are similar (often identical) to designs already in existence.

Methods of coding

Parts or components are often coded by one of the following methods (see Table A3.3).

Table A3.3   *Types of part coding*

Method of part coding	Nature and example	Extent of classification	Usefulness for			
			Variety reduction	Standard-ization	Group technology	Production planning
Sequential	Drawing or part numbers taken from register, e.g. 12345	None	None	None	None	None
Product	Usually two parts. First to identify product. Second is unique number, e.g. HD4–12345[a]	Little	None	None	None	Very little
Production	Usually two parts. First to identify product method or material. Second is unique number, e.g. F.MS–12345[b]	Some. Useless after changes in production methods	None	Very little	Useful	Useful
Design	Often identifies nature and principal character of product, e.g. S. 14–12345[c]	Useful	Useful	Useful	Some	Some

[a] Product type HD. Model 4.
[b] Forging (F) in Mild Steel (MS).
[c] Stud (S) overall length 14 inches (14).

Sequential coding

When drawings for new parts are coded sequentially, with numbers taken from a register, no useful classification results. Occasionally code letters are used in conjunction with sequential numbering, but even so, little useful classification is obtained.

Product coding

Parts are often coded in such a way as to indicate the product for which the part was originally designed. Alpha/numerical codes are often used, the numerical portion giving a unique identity to the part while the alphabetical part identifies the original product or even the original contract or customer.

Production process code

Less frequently, parts are coded according to their method of manufacture or their sequence of operations. For example, different codes will be used for cast, forged and welded items, for items produced from stock bar, plate, etc.

Design code

Often, where there is an effort to maintain variety control and standardization, parts coding is mainly on a design basis. Products of similar appearance or purpose are coded in a similar manner, thus facilitating the selection and adoption of suitable existing parts rather than the design of new ones. Clearly, if any useful classification of products or components is to result, some form of design coding must be adopted.

There have been basically two approaches to the problem: the overall or macro approach and the specific or micro approach.

Several research workers, adopting the macro approach, have attempted to develop universal component classification systems as a result of studies of statistics of the components most commonly found in certain industries. The first of these research projects was begun at the Aachen Machine Tool Laboratory in Germany in the early 1950s, and resulted in the Opitz method of coding and classification. The object of this research was to determine the statistics of the components commonly manufactured in the engineering industries. The Opitz method of classification, which is used for machined parts only, uses a five-digit code to describe the shape of the component and a four-digit supplementary code to specify the component size, material, raw material and accuracy.

The 'Vuoso' method of coding was developed at the Prague Machine Tool Research Institute and represents a more recent attempt to develop a universal system. The coding method is simpler than the Opitz method and is contained on only one piece of paper. The four-digit code is naturally less detailed than the Opitz code, but it offers a simple method of coding which is adequate for most small companies or manufacturing units.

Despite the relative popularity of universal classification systems, particularly the Opitz system, macro systems have recently been subject to a good deal of criticism. It is argued that the proportion of certain types of component, e.g. rotational components found in industry, is likely to vary with the nature of the industry concerned, and that the statistics or features of a particular class of components are likely to vary according to the type of industry concerned.

Several researchers have concluded, therefore, that there is no fixed pattern of components throughout industry and that the concept of a universal classification system is at worst mistaken and at best of very limited value.

In contrast to the overall or macro approach, the micro approach concentrates on the particular requirements and characteristics of an individual company. Perhaps the best example of this approach is the Brisch classification system.

The Brisch system is designed for the needs of each particular company—needs which can be established only after a survey of the types of components and methods of production. The method of coding is mainly design-oriented, but additional 'production' information can be added by means of a second code. The design information is contained in a *monocode*, e.g. shape, design, size, features, while a *polycode* contains information relevant to during-production planning. The micro system can therefore be designed specifically according to the requirement of the drawing office concerned and is therefore considered by many to be a superior approach to company standardization.

CHECKLIST FOR APPENDIX TO CHAPTER 3

Value analysis (VA): definitions
Value engineering: definitions
Objective of VA
    Definition of value

VA procedure
Standardization
    Benefits of product/part standardization
    Prerequisites for standardization

Classification and coding   Different approaches
  Use and benefits of coding   Macro
  Methods of coding and their uses   Micro
    Sequential   Systems
    Product   Opitz
    Production   Vuoso
    Design   Brisch
  Coding systems

FURTHER READING

Hayes, R. H. and Schmenner, R. W. (1978) How should you organize manufacturing? *Harvard Business Review*, January/February, pp. 105–118. The article and the Wheelwright one (below), while dealing specifically with manufacturing systems, are valuable reading, and complement the material covered in this chapter.

Holt, R. (1977) *Product Innovation*. Sevenoaks: Newnes-Butterworths. Covers all the stages and decisions from product concept through design to launch.

Wheelwright, S. C. (1978) Reflecting corporate strategy in manufacturing decisions, *Business Horizons*, February, pp. 57–66.

QUESTIONS

3.1 (a) What is value analysis?
        (b) What is value engineering?
        (c) How does value analysis differ from conventional cost reduction?
        (d) 'Value analysis is merely the application of the techniques of method study to the problems of product design.' Discuss.
        (e) 'There is no need for the existence of a value analysis department in a company which employs competent product designers.' Discuss.

3.2 Conduct a value analysis exercise on the product shown opposite, which is a three-pin unfused electric plug. Enumerate the principal steps involved in such an exercise and at each step provide the appropriate information or answers from your knowledge of this particular product, its use and its specification. As a result of this exercise suggest an alternative design if possible.

3.3 Discuss the advantages and disadvantages of employing a value analysis engineer working alone against the use of an organized value analysis team. What would you consider to be the best composition of the value analysis team, and to whom should the team leader report?

3.4 What are the requirements of an effective method of coding and classification? What are the benefits to a small jobbing engineering company of adopting such a method of coding and classification?

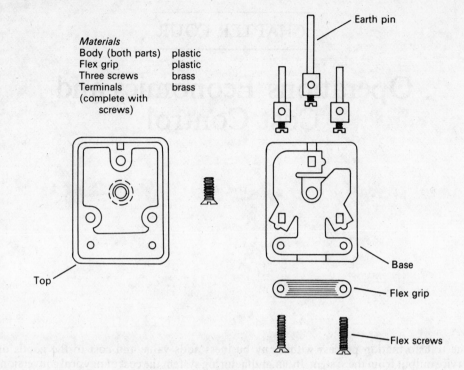

Materials

Body (both parts)	plastic
Flex grip	plastic
Three screws	brass
Terminals	brass
(complete with screws)	

Earth pin

Top

Base

Flex grip

Flex screws

CHAPTER FOUR

Operations Economics and Cost Control

The transformation process within any business adds value and cost to the goods or service output from the system. In a manufacturing system the cost of physical conversion, e.g. materials processing, assembly, will often represent a major part of the total cost of the products produced. In transport, the cost of moving the customer, comprising the cost of the equipment used (e.g. the vehicles and service equipment) and the cost of the labour employed, as well as any overheads, will often be a major ingredient determining the total cost of the transport to the customer. Similarly, in supply and service systems the operations function, which is the responsibility of the operations manager, will add significant cost to the total cost of the items or service provided for the eventual customer. Given this responsibility for 'cost contribution', the operations manager must be familiar with the factors contributing to the cost of operations, the factors influencing these costs, and the means available for the measurement and control of the cost of operations.

Without venturing into a detailed discussion of either microeconomics or cost accounting, we must here devote some time to a consideration of the nature of the costs associated with operations and the means available for the control of such costs.

OPERATIONS COSTS *(see also Chapter 21)*

The components of operations costs may be direct or indirect. *Direct costs* (or the prime cost) comprise those which may be identified separately for each good or service produced, e.g. the cost of the direct materials consumed or incorporated and the cost of the direct labour involved in the provision of output items or services.

Indirect costs (or operations overheads) are all other expenses which cannot be charged specifically to particular output items, services or transports. Indirect costs include the cost of indirect materials, indirect labour and all other charges involved in operating the system where such charges cannot be allocated realistically or accurately to particular goods or services, e.g. administration costs.

78

Together these costs might be seen, sequentially, to build up to the *total operations cost* and thus, with the general and administrative costs and the profit, to the total cost to the customer, i.e. the selling or purchase price, in the manner shown in Figure 4.1. It will be noticed that while the prime cost is normally considered to comprise the sum of direct labour and materials, no provision is made for direct costs associated with the third of the major resource inputs to the operating system, i.e. the machinery employed. The assumption here, as is usually the case in practice, is that machinery is used for multiple purposes and its costs therefore cannot normally be seen as a direct charge; they must be allocated as part of the overheads associated with the operation. Although in some cases expenses other than those associated with labour and materials can be charged directly to particular outputs, other expenses are normally seen as part of the operations overheads. The operations overheads can, in turn, be subdivided into material, labour and other expenses in the manner outlined in Table 4.1.

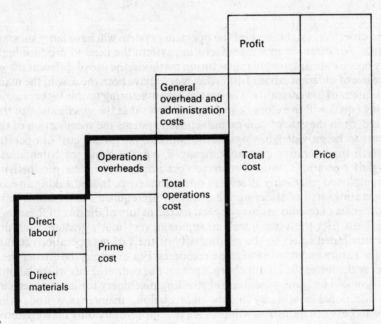

Figure 4.1 *Operations and total costs.*

Table 4.1 *Operations overheads*

Indirect materials	Indirect labour	Other expenses	
		Standing costs	General costs
Tools	Supervision	Rent	Management
Consumed materials	Technical services	Depreciation	Welfare costs
	Transport	Insurance	Planning
	Quality control	Rates	Services
	Operations control		Power Maintenance

Operations managers are responsible for the total operations cost. They will be interested in the components of this cost, and will also be interested in the distinction between *fixed* and *variable* costs. Over a fairly short period of time certain of the organization's costs, in particular those associated with the operating system, can be seen to be fixed; they will not be affected by changes in the scale of the operation, i.e. changes in the throughput rate or output rate. These fixed costs will include many of the operations overheads, e.g. rent and rates on premises, depreciation on significant items of equipment, and insurance. Certain other costs, e.g. direct costs, in particular wages and the cost of consumer materials, will vary in the short term in that they will increase roughly in proportion to increased throughput or output, and vice versa.

Factors influencing operations costs

Clearly the objectives established for the operating system will have fairly substantial cost implications. For example, in a manufacturing system the need to produce high-quality items may necessitate different manufacturing methods, the use of different materials and indeed the use of different labour from what would have been the case in the manufacture of a similar item of lower quality. The cost of manufacturing to this higher quality, other things being equal, will therefore be higher. It follows that the specification of the item to be produced, or in the case of non-manufacturing systems the specification of the service or transport to be provided, has significant implications for the cost of operations. The way in which the operating system is managed, e.g. the choice of batch sizes and the scheduling of operations, must also have cost implications. The productivity of the resources employed will clearly affect unit operations costs. Indeed, taking an economist's view of operations and considering the principal prerequisites to be 'land', 'capital' and 'labour', the costs of operations may depend on the nature of the mix of these ingredients. In certain industries the value added to inputs is very much greater. Such differences cannot be attributed solely to the productivity of the various operations resources, but rather to the nature and mixture of these resources. For example, the greater the quantity of machinery the lower the labour charges per unit of output. Thus where labour charges are high there will be some benefit in substituting machinery for labour, despite the fact that the additional machinery incurs depreciation, maintenance and other costs. Comparisons between industries will provide the opportunity only for long-term control and not enough opportunity for day-to-day control of costs within the operations function. For this reason certain budgeting and cost control systems must be employed (see below).

It should also be noted that certain scale factors are associated with the cost of operations, so that with increasing throughput or output rates unit costs might be reduced. These are discussed in the following section.

OPERATIONS ECONOMICS

Figure 4.2 illustrates some aspects of the relationship between operations cost and output (or throughput) rate. Over a short period certain of the operations costs can be seen to be fixed while others, the variable costs, will increase as output or the scale of operations increases. Initially this increase will be fairly rapid, then will become more stable, and eventually become rapid as the maximum possible output or throughput rate is reached, and as bottlenecks are experienced and overtime working/subcontracting, etc., become necessary. The sum of the fixed variable costs is shown in Figure 4.2 as the total operations costs.

Also shown in Figure 4.2 is a curve representing revenue, i.e. the income generated from customers in payment for the goods or services provided by the operating system, and a curve representing the profit associated with that output, i.e. revenue less total costs. Total revenue rises as the organization is able to expand its scale of operations and thus its sales, although eventually revenue will reach a maximum point as price is lowered in order to stimulate further sales. The profits are maximized at a point where the difference between the total revenue and total cost curve is greatest. Notice that in most cases this profit maximization point occurs at a lower level than the point of maximum revenue, which in turn occurs at less than maximum output/sales.

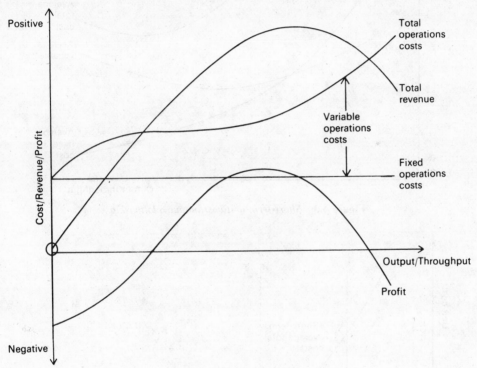

Figure 4.2 *Costs v. output.*

The relationship which will be of particular interest to the operations manager is that between the cost per unit throughput or output and the level or scale of throughput or output. In the short term the operations manager might seek to alter output by varying the amount of variable factors employed, e.g. materials and labour, whereas in the longer term all factors can be varied. In the short term the unit cost structure might appear as in Figure 4.3. As fixed costs remain the same the fixed cost per unit will fall as output or throughput increases. The variable cost per unit will fall at first and then rise as further variable factors are employed in order to expand output or throughput. Figure 4.4 shows the long-run average total cost/output relationship. Superimposed on this long-run average total cost curve is an average total cost curve for a short-run period. Thus while in the short term increasing output or throughput from Q_1 to Q_2 will give rise to a U-shaped curve representing falling unit total cost followed by increasing total costs, in the long run, since the 'fixed' factors can also be varied, the unit total cost curve should continue to fall.

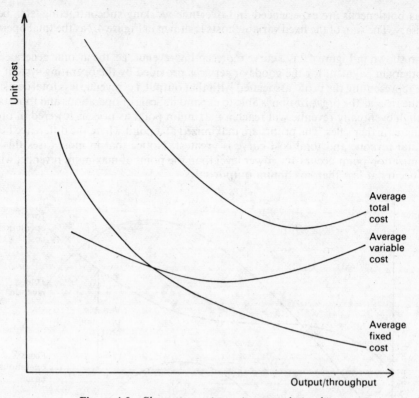

Figure 4.3   *Short-term unit cost/output relationship.*

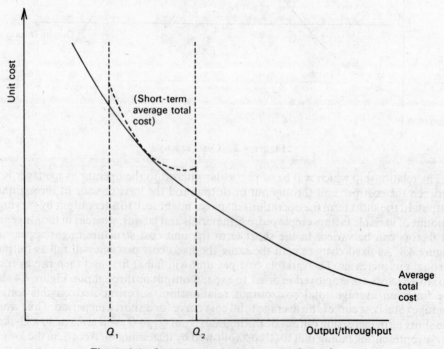

Figure 4.4   *Long-term unit cost/output relationship.*

Thus in the long term, since all the factors can be considered variable, increasing output should result in economies of scale reflected in reduced unit costs.

It follows that while the operations manager might, by clever combination of the resources at his or her disposal, effect a reduction in unit cost in the short term, continued increase in the scale of operations can be undertaken economically only by the manipulation of the mix of all of the factors involved, including those which in the short term are fixed.

Break-even point

A break-even point chart also shows the relationship between output or throughput on the one hand and cost on the other. Figure 4.5 shows two break-even charts. A chart for operating system A shows relatively low fixed costs but fairly substantial variable costs and thus a fairly steeply rising total cost curve, albeit one starting from a relatively low point. The cost structure for operating system B shows higher fixed costs with relatively low variable costs, thus a less steeply rising total cost curve, albeit one starting from a substantially higher initial total cost point than in system A. The cost structure for operating system B might reflect the higher capital investment of that system, whereas operating system A may be more dependent on the use of overtime work, double staffing,

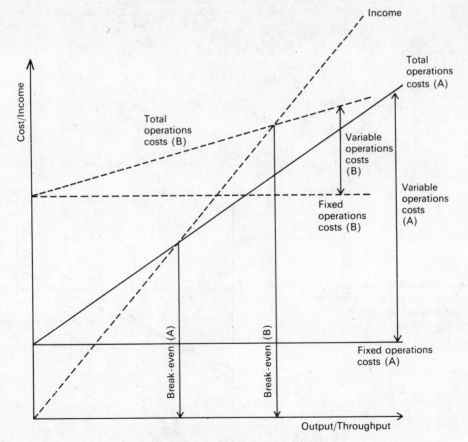

Figure 4.5 *Break-even charts.*

etc. to achieve increased outputs. Notice that because of the differing cost structures the break-even point, i.e. the point at which income begins to exceed total costs, is lower for operating system A than it is for B but that the excess of income over total cost increases less rapidly beyond the break-even point in the case of operating system B. A point worth noting, therefore, is that for systems dependent on greater fixed costs, greater output must be achieved before a break-even point is reached but that, thereafter, rewards are likely to increase at a greater rate.

EXAMPLE: BREAK-EVEN CALCULATION

Current costs and sales @ 100 per cent capacity:

Annual sales   = £200 000
Fixed costs   = £ 80 000
Variable costs = £100 000

What is current break-even capacity now, and how would this change if fixed costs increased to £90 000 while variable costs fell to £65 000?

		Percentage capacity used	
Calculations (£'000)		0%	100%
Present situation	Sales	—	200
	Fixed costs	80	80
	Variable costs	—	100
	Profit	−80	+20
New situation	Sales	—	200
	Fixed costs	90	90
	Variable costs	—	65
	Profit	−90	+45

From Figure 4.6: break-even capacity =
   Present situation, 80 per cent
   New situation, 68 per cent

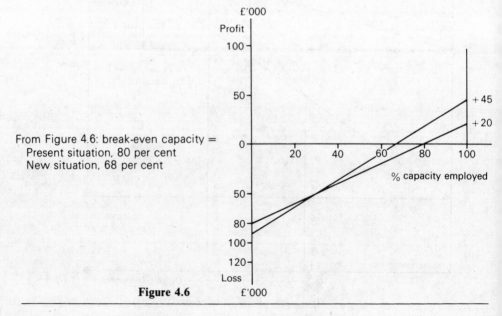

Figure 4.6

COST CONTROL SYSTEMS *(see also Chapters 3 and 21)*

Some form of cost accounting or cost control system will be essential within an organization and will be of considerable importance to the operations manager. As with all such managerial control systems the operations manager will seek to employ the cost control mechanisms to sustain and improve the efficiency of the operating system, whereas his or her superiors will use the same cost information, albeit analysed somewhat differently, as a means of establishing objectives for and maintaining control over the operations manager.

From the operations manager's viewpoint, therefore, the cost control mechanism provides a means of assessing the efficiency of the operating system, noting significant variations from normal or budgeted performance, assessing the efficiency of new operating methods, determining the relative allocation of resources, determining the capacity required, etc. The cost control or cost accounting system adopted by an organization, and thus by the operations manager, will depend largely on the scale and nature of the organization, in particular on the type of operating system employed and the type of goods/services provided. Basically, two types of costing system can be identified: job costing and process costing.

Job costing

Job costing is often employed by organizations which produce goods or provide services, transport, etc. to the specific requirements of the customer. In job costing, items or customers passing through the system remain identifiable and are associated with particular costs. All costs specific to particular jobs, items or customers will be accumulated, while all indirect costs will be apportioned or allocated to jobs so that on completion the total cost of each job is ascertained.

EXAMPLE: JOB COSTING CALCULATION

	Dept 1	*Dept 2*
Materials used	£6 000	£500
Direct labour	£3 000	£1 500
Operations overheads	£1 800	£1 200
Direct labour hours	12 000	5 000
Machine hours	10 000	2 000

The following information relates to job A:

	Dept 1	*Dept 2*
Materials used	£120	£10
Direct labour	£65	£25
Direct labour hours	265	70
Machine hours	255	25

We are to prepare a statement showing the cost for job A as a percentage of direct material.

The overhead absorption rates are as follows:

	Dept 1	Dept 2
Percentage of direct material	30%	240%

Cost of job A:

	Dept 1	Dept 2	Total
	£	£	£
Material	120	10	130
Direct labour	65	25	90
Prime cost	185	35	220
Operations overheads	36	24	60
Total cost	221	59	280

(Based on Sizer, J. (1979) *An Insight into Management Accounting*. Harmondsworth: Penguin.)

Process costing

Process costing is used by organizations engaged in more repetitive acitivities, i.e. where the operating system is devoted to the provision of a relatively small variety of goods, services or transport on a fairly repetitive basis. Since in such situations it is not practical to identify separate items of throughput, unit costs are determined by dividing the total costs of each process by the number of units, i.e. goods or customers output or throughput, making allowances for items partially completed or customers partially serviced at the beginning and the end of the costing period.

Budgeting

The long-range plans formulated for the organization must be translated into detailed short-term plans or budgets for individual departments. The performance of departments, including the operating system, will be evaluated against these departmental budgets. The operations budget will specify the output or throughput required as well as the planned direct and indirect costs, broken down into appropriate detail. Preparation of this budget will involve apportioning or allocating operations overheads on some equitable basis between departments and/or 'jobs'. Overheads might be apportioned in proportion to the direct wages or direct materials costs, etc. The budget will make a distinction between current costs and revenue items and capital expenditure items. The former comprises such things as wages, salaries and material costs. The latter group includes expenditure on equipment and building.

Once budgets have been established and the periods to which they relate have commenced, the actual costs incurred during each period must be collected for subsequent comparison.

Standard costing

Standard costing is widely used in industries where rapid cost feedback information is required, i.e. where operations take place on a relatively short cycle time. In such circumstances costs are estimated and compared with actual costs on a month-by-month basis. The estimate is referred to as the 'standard cost'. Standard costs for items or services are established by category, e.g. labour, materials and overheads, based on predicted prices, labour rates and other expenses for the given period. Variations from predicted costs can be assessed and the necessary action taken to prevent their recurrence without having to wait for the end of the costing period, e.g. one year, before the necessary cost control information is available.

Marginal costing

Accurate standard costs necessitate the use of realistic means and bases for the apportionment of overhead costs to departments, cost centres, jobs, etc. and accurate pre-estimation of throughput or output volumes as bases for establishing cost rates. The use of marginal costing avoids these problems. After distinguishing direct from overhead costs, marginal costing divides overheads into those which vary with output and those which are fixed. Direct costs are also divided into the categories 'variable' and 'fixed'. All variable costs are then related to units of throughput/output while fixed costs are not charged to separate units but kept as a single block to be set against revenues earned by the throughputs of the system. Thus with marginal costing the cost of unit throughput or output is considered to comprise direct material, direct labour and direct expenses plus their variable overheads only, the total being the variable cost per unit output/throughput. This variable cost is in fact the marginal cost, since it is the amount by which total cost would increase as a result of the processing of one extra unit. Marginal costing provides a convenient way of assessing the effects of volume on profits and can be used in conjunction with the break-even chart approach.

CHECKLIST FOR CHAPTER 4

Operations costs
  Price = Profit +
       Total cost = General and administration costs +
          Total operations costs   = Operations overheads +
                        Prime cost   = Direct labour +
                                                Direct materials

Factors influencing operations costs
  Quality
  Mix
  Volume
Operations economics
  Cost v. output, long term
  Cost v. output, short term

Break-even point
Cost control systems
Job costing
Process costing
Budgeting
Standard costing
Marginal costing

FURTHER READING

Horngren, C. T. (1977) *Cost Accounting*. Hemel Hempstead: Prentice-Hall.
Mare, R. F. de la (1982) *Manufacturing Systems Economics*. Eastbourne: Holt, Rinehart and Winston. A comprehensive study of life-cycle costs and benefits of industrial assets.
Sizer, J. (1979) *An Insight into Management Accounting*. Harmondsworth: Penguin.

QUESTIONS

4.1 Within organizations overheads are usually divided between operations overheads and general and administrative overheads and costs (including administrative overheads and selling and distribution overheads). Explain why this distinction is made and suggest methods by which each class of overhead can be absorbed or allocated to units of throughput/output.

4.2 The following data relate to a manufacturing company:

Total capacity, 75 000 units
Fixed costs, £12 000 per annum
Variable expenses, 75 p per unit
Sales prices, up to 4000 units £1.5 per unit and then over 4000 units £1.0 per unit

Draft a break-even chart incorporating these data.

4.3 Throughput volumes (or output volumes) can affect unit operating costs. In addition, batch volumes can affect unit costs. Both output/throughput volumes and costs are related to profits. Outline the nature of these relationships, illustrating your answer with simple graphs.

4.4 How, in the long term, might a transport organization seek to reduce unit total operations costs beyond the level available in the short term?

4.5 You plan to go into the 'mail-order' business. You will advertise and sell (cash with order) personal stationery. The following two alternatives are available to you depending on the quality of the product:

		£
Option 1	Cost, to you, of product	8.00
	Cost of processing each order	1.25
	Cost of advertising	220.00
	Overhead 100 per cent of product cost	
Option 2	Cost, to you, of product	6.75
	Cost of processing each order	1.20
	Cost of advertising	350.00
	Overhead 100 per cent of product cost	

Compare the two options on a break-even analysis. Which option would you employ if you expected sales of 30 products?

PART 3

THE ARRANGEMENT OF FACILITIES

INTRODUCTION TO PART 3

This section deals with locational and layout decisions. We deal with the relatively rare problem of locating internationally an entirely new facility. We also deal with the problem of locating an additional new facility for an organization, to provide access to existing facilities, suppliers and markets. In Chapter 6 we look at layout decisions—themselves a form of layout problem. We look at the fairly uncommon problem of arranging an entirely new layout for a facility, and consider also the modification of existing facilities and the addition of new departments or items of equipment to existing facilities. Throughout we consider the nature of the problems involved and introduce some relevant procedures and techniques. We emphasize computer-based techniques, for this is an area in which numerous alternative solutions exist and where there is considerable merit in obtaining some alternative solutions quickly and economically.

CHAPTER FIVE

Location of Facilities

NOTATION USED IN THIS CHAPTER

O_{i_m}	Cost, score, etc., associated with factors $1, 2, 3 \ldots m$, for location i
W_m	Weight attached to factors $1, 2, 3 \ldots m$
L	Total transport cost
T_i	Transport cost/unit distance/unit quantity between facility and location i
Q_i	Quantity to be transported between facility and location i
D_i	Distance between facility and location i
n	Number of locations ($i = 1 \ldots n$)

The facilities location problem is of major importance in all types of business. Whether we are concerned with manufacture, supply, transport or service we must consider the problem of where to base our operations. Certainly the location problem for a transport operation is slightly different, since, by definition, transport moves. However, even in such cases there will normally be a 'home base' or centre of operations at which certain facilities are provided. Throughout this chapter, when referring to facilities we mean the collection of *geographically static resources* required for the operation.

Having decided the nature and specification of the goods/services to be provided, the location of the business facilities is the next major problem to be considered. In most cases this will be the logical order of decisions, i.e. 'What?' and then 'Where?', since often the nature of the offering will suggest suitable locations and preclude others. At times, however, these decisions may occur in the reverse order, or the two decisions may be quite unconnected. For example, a company intending to manufacture ships will be restricted to comparatively few locations, unlike a company intending to manufacture scientific electronic instruments; the location of ferry services will be relatively restricted compared with the location of furniture removers; and the location of a holiday hotel or an airport hotel will be relatively limited compared with the location of a retail store.

91

THE NEED FOR LOCATIONAL CHOICE

We can consider the facility location problem as applying in two basic situations, i.e. the case of the entirely new business and the case of the existing business.

The choice of location is a vital decision for any new business; indeed, there are numerous examples of new businesses which have had brief and troubled lives solely because of their disadvantageous location. The existing firm will seek new facility locations either in order to expand capacity or to replace existing facilities. An increase in demand, if it is to be satisfied by the organization, gives rise to one or more of three decisions:

(a)   whether to expand the present capacity and facilities;
(b)   whether to seek locations for additional facilities;
(c)   whether to close down existing facilities in favour of larger premises elsewhere.

Replacement of existing facilities may be occasioned by one or more of the following occurrences:

(a)   the movement of markets, i.e. changes in the location of demand;
(b)   changes in the cost or availability of local labour;
(c)   changes in the availability of materials;
(d)   demolition or compulsory purchase of premises;
(e)   changes in the availability or effectiveness of transport;
(f)   relocation of associated industries or plants;
(g)   national legislation.

For our purposes in discussing the facility location problem, it makes little difference whether we consider the problem as applying to a new business or to an existing one. However, since the latter tends to be the more complex, we shall focus on it. An increase in demand will, unless associated with increased productivity, inevitably result in pressure for additional capacity; the only alternatives to an expansion of the existing facilities or the acquisition of additional facilities are a reduced share of the market or an increased amount of subcontracting. On the other hand, a reduction in demand will often result in the under-utilization of existing capacity and encourage a move to smaller premises. Figure 5.1 outlines some of the forces within a company which give rise to the pressure for either an increase or a decrease in the amount of space available. While the main forces are associated with demand, and hence with the operations and marketing functions, it is worth noting that both finance and labour management might also be instrumental. Changes in interest rates may affect the cost of holding stock and cause a change in stock-holding policy, which in turn may affect space requirements.

Legislation relating to investment allowances, employment tax, depreciation, etc., may influence company financial policy enough to affect the scale or the nature of the undertaking; similarly, legislation relating to labour may necessitate a change in the nature or extent of facilities, e.g. the addition of extensive training facilities and welfare facilities. Scientific discoveries or developments, new fields of technology, increasing competition, licensing or patent arrangements all may affect company research and development effort, which in turn will influence space requirements, as will changes in operations technology, the obsolescence of equipment, etc.

A change in space requirements is only one of several possible reasons for the need to consider the acquisition of an additional facility location. Figure 5.2 identifies other forces which may give rise to such a decision. The need to seek smaller or larger premises may arise without the occurrence of a change in demand and thus capacity. For example, the cost associated with the present location may change through increases in the cost of labour caused, perhaps, by increasing employment opportunities in the area. The price of

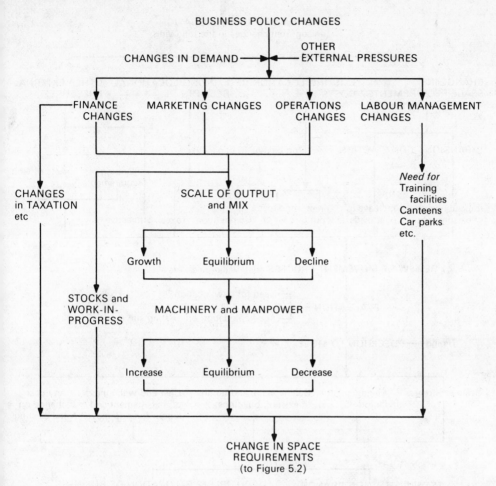

Figure 5.1 *Pressures for change in space (which must give rise to the need to select a facility location).*

raw materials or indirect materials may change through changes in the cost of transport or changes within associated industries. Indirect costs such as those associated with communications, education, housing, etc., may change. Also, new competition or changes in local taxation may prompt the decision to seek alternative premises, as may other external pressures such as labour disputes. Such forces may prompt the consideration of a complete move or the acquisition of an additional site(s).

FACTORS INFLUENCING LOCATIONAL CHOICE

Theoretically, both new and existing businesses have a vast range of alternative new facility locations. The selection of the site of the facility will be the final stage of a sequence of decisions which begins with the selection of an appropriate region, then involves the selection of an appropriate area in that region, etc. For an international organization, it is possible to identify at least four stages in this locational choice process, as outlined in

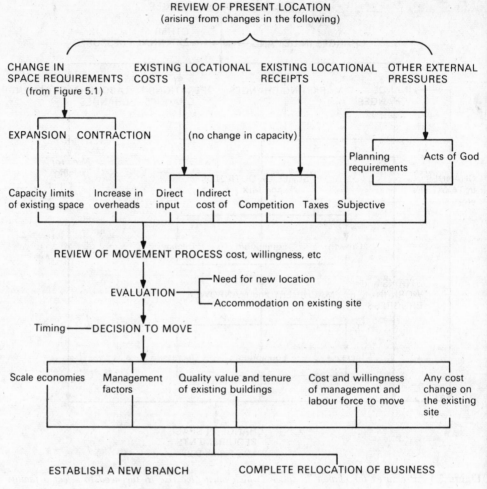

Figure 5.2 *Pressures for a new location.*

Figure 5.3. Different factors will influence decisions at each of these levels, and these also are outlined in Figure 5.3.

The relative importance of some of these factors will depend on the type of operation or business which is to be located. For example, proximity to customers is of crucial importance for a service or supply organization; efficient transport is essential for a manufacturer or a distributor; and proximity to sources of supply will be important for some types of manufacture. The principal factors which will be of importance in the location of different types of businesses are summarized in Table 5.1.

Figure 5.4 examines in more detail some of the factors which will generally be of importance in locational choice. These can be summarized as three sets of factors:

(a)   variable costs;
(b)   fixed costs;
(c)   subjective factors.

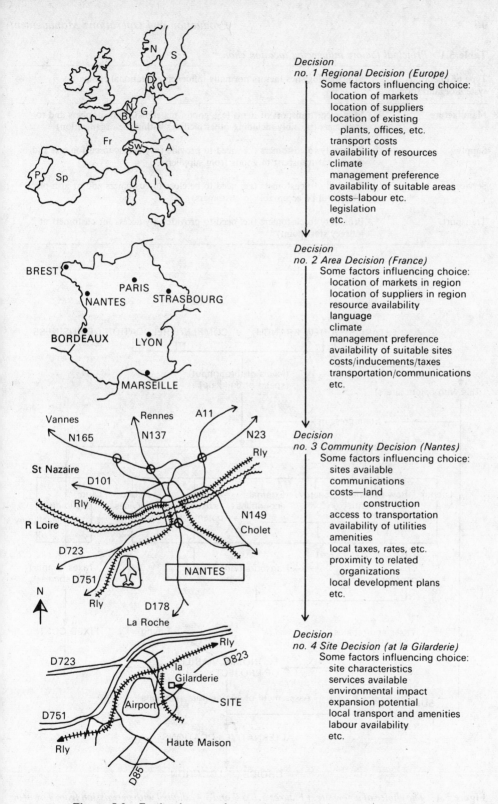

Figure 5.3 *Facility location decision levels (an international example).*

Table 5.1 *Principal factors influencing location choice*

Type of operating system/organization	Principal logistics factors normally influencing locational choice
Manufacture	Movement/transport of items (e.g. goods, materials) from suppliers and to customers (possibly including other facilities within the organization)
Supply	Proximity to customers (i.e. need to provide easy access to customers) and movement/transport of goods from suppliers
Service	Proximity to customers (i.e. need to be close to customers and/or at a place which will be acceptable to customers)
Transport	Proximity to customers (i.e. need to provide easy access for customers at journey start point)

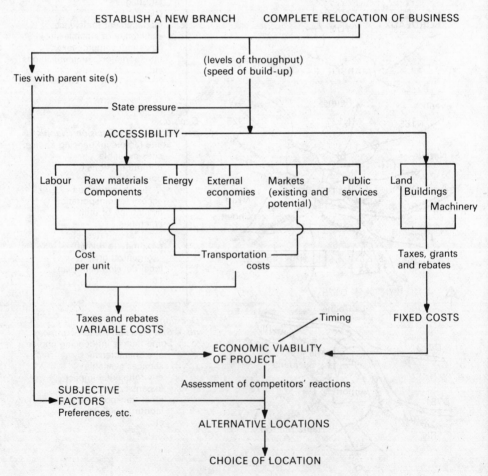

Figure 5.4 *The choice of a new site. (Figures 5.1, 5.2 and 5.4 adapted with permission from Townroe, P. M. (1969) Locational choice and the individual firm, Regional Studies, 3(1), pp. 15–24.)*

Variable costs

Perhaps the main factor here is the 'accessibility' of the proposed location in terms of both inputs and outputs. As regards input, accessibility to labour is important; not merely sufficient labour, but labour of the correct type and at a correct price. Accessibility of raw materials, sub-assemblies and components is important, the cost of such input being mainly a function of transport. Access to technical advice and to other services such as warehousing and maintenance is often essential. With regard to output, a location must clearly have easy access to adequate markets, as well as public services and associated industries.

Fixed costs

These are associated with the provision and maintenance of facilities. The design of buildings and the layout of facilities will influence such costs. The cost of erecting and maintaining buildings, the cost of access roads, the cost of transportation of machinery, rates, rent, and so on will all influence the choice of location. We should also consider as fixed costs the cost of inventories of materials and finished items which may depend on the plant location.

It will be seen from Figure 5.5, which compares fixed and variable costs for four possible new facility locations, that volume considerations can influence the selection of a site.

Subjective or largely non-quantitative assessments

These may also influence the decision. Individual preferences, congeniality of the district, attitudes of present employees, etc., will all be important. National and regional data relating to the various factors influencing the facility location decision are available from a variety of sources. Data on population change, average wage levels, unemployment, industrial disputes, absenteeism, labour turnover, etc., may be of relevance and will often be available.

A further factor which will influence the choice of location is the *time factor*, i.e. the urgency of acquiring the facility compared with the time required to make it available, the latter being influenced by the necessity for planning permission, preparation of plans, purchase of land, availability of building labour, provision of services, electricity, water, roads, etc.

The role of central and local government and the influence of legislation and incentives can be of importance in locational choice, especially for manufacturing organizations. There may be several reasons for government concern with the location of companies and industry, e.g. regional unemployment costs associated with the congestion of major conurbations, problems of environmental pollution, and population drift from rural areas.

In the UK, legislation such as the Special Areas (Development and Improvement) Acts 1934 and 1937, the Distribution of Industry Act 1945, the Town and Country Planning Acts 1947 onwards, the Distribution of Industry (Industrial Finance) Act 1958 and the Local Employment Act 1960 was the forerunner of a great deal of direct and indirect effort to influence the location of manufacturing industry, offices, etc. Currently there are very substantial incentives to encourage companies to establish plants in certain parts of

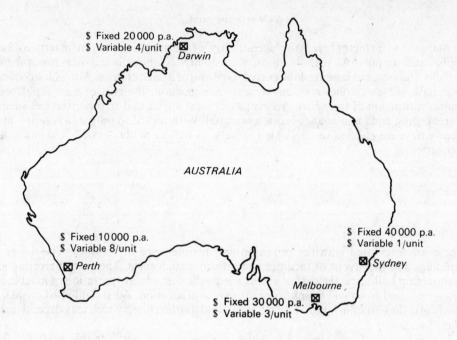

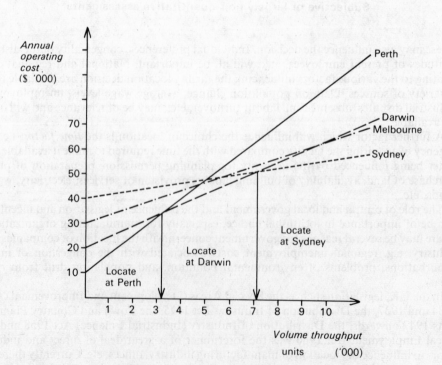

Figure 5.5 *Fixed and variable cost relationships for four possible new facility locations.*

the country designated for industrial and economic development. Similarly, in other countries, legislation and other devices provide incentives and obstacles in locational choice. Furthermore, with the growth of multinational firms and the increasing importance of the international dimension in locational choice, for example in industries such as motor vehicles and chemicals, similar factors at an international level (e.g. within the EEC the 'competitive' bidding of national governments) are of considerable significance.

TYPES OF LOCATION PROBLEMS

As we have seen, the need to select a location or site for a facility can arise for many reasons. The cause is perhaps less important to the operations manager than the nature of the locational choice problem. For example, if it is necessary to select the location of a new single-facility business which is entirely self-contained, with no dependence on suppliers, the problem will be relatively straightforward and the choice wide. In contrast, in the choice of a site of a new facility for a company which has several existing facilities which have some supply interdependence and which together supply a particular market, the problem will be more complex and the choice more limited.

In order to understand how best to try to solve locational choice problems we must first appreciate the range of types of problems which might be encountered. Some of the common types of locational choice problems are identified in Table 5.2, and of course combinations of these basic types can exist. In discussion procedures for tackling location problems in the remainder of this chapter we shall refer back to this simple classification of problem types.

The single-facility location problem *(Table 5.2, categories A1, 2, 3 and 4 and B1, with relevance also to B2, 3 and 4)*

Here we are concerned with the location of a single business facility, e.g. the new single plant firm or single-facility service organization, or the location of a new facility for a larger organization where the facility has no significant dependence on or relationship with the other facilities in the business (e.g. Table 5.2, category B1).

Unlike the multi-facility location problem, the existing or future locations of other facilities within the business will be of little relevance. Here, therefore, we are *not* concerned with the type of locational problems encountered in businesses with interdependent facilities (as in the car industry, in which different parts of final products are made in different facilities, or specialized hospitals and clinics in a regional health service). Procedures for tackling the single-facility location problem may, however, be of relevance in multi-facility organizations in which there is no specialization or interdependence of facilities, e.g. supply organizations comprising several similar outlets servicing different areas. Some procedures are discussed below.

Checklists

Given a choice of possible locations, perhaps the simplest but least rigorous means for decision-making involves their comparison against a checklist of relevant factors. Such a

Table 5.2 *Some types of location problems*

Type of problem		Example—location of:
A. *Single Facility*		
1. Single facility with *no* connections to other locations	Locate a self-contained facility to serve a local community	Single, new cinema for a small community
2. Single facility with connections *in* from other locations	Locate a facility to serve a local community taking into account the need for the facility to be supplied from elsewhere	Single new retail shop for a small community
3. Single facility with connections *out* to other locations	Locate a facility to serve customers elsewhere	Market garden to serve an area of several towns
4. Single facility with connections *in* from and *out* to other locations	Locate a facility to serve customers elsewhere, with supplies also being received from elsewhere	Single new manufacturing plant; single new wholesale distributor or warehouse
B. *Multi-facility*		
1. Addition(s) to an existing 'set' of facilities, with *no* connections to others in the set or to other locations	Effectively, as A1	Additional new cinema for a small community, but part of a national 'chain'
2. Addition(s) to an existing set of facilities, the 'set' having connections *in* from other locations	Effectively, as A2 (but possibly with the need to consider the distribution of capacity within the set)	Additional new retail shop for a small community, but part of a national 'chain'
3. Addition(s) to an existing set of facilities, the set having connections *out* to other locations	Effectively, as A3 (but with need to consider the distribution of capacity within the set)	Additional market garden for national organization
4. Addition(s) to an existing set of facilities, the set having connections *in* and *out* with other locations	Effectively, as A4 (but with the need to consider the distribution of capacity within the set)	Additional manufacturing plant for a company, where there is no flow between plants
5. Addition(s) to an existing set of facilities with connections *in* from within the set	Effectively, as B2	Retail shop for company to sell items supplied from elsewhere within the company
6. Addition(s) to an existing set of facilities with connections *out* to elsewhere in the set	Effectively, as B3	Additional market garden for a company to supply goods to other company locations, e.g. for packaging or processing
7. Addition(s) to an existing set of facilities with connections *in* and *out* within the set	Effectively, as B4	Additional manufacturing plant for a company, to be supplied from other plants in company, and to supply items for other company plants

Note. In many cases combinations will exist, particularly B2 and 5, B3 and 6, and B4 and 7.

checklist is shown in Table 5.3, which also gives some indication of the relevance of each factor at each of the four 'levels' of decision-making discussed earlier. If not an adequate means of decision-making, such a checklist at least provides a means of initially narrowing down the range of alternative regions and/or areas and/or communities and/or sites.

Table 5.3 *Checklist: some factors influencing locational choice*

	Of region (international)	Of area (national)	Of community (city)	Of site
Political stability	✓			
Relevant legislation, e.g. industrial relations	✓			
Unionization of labour	✓			
Industrial relations 'climate'	✓			
Feasibility of joint operations	✓			
Capital restrictions	✓			
Transfer of earnings restrictions	✓			
Taxation for foreign firms	✓			
Currency restrictions	✓			
GNP trends	✓			
Foreign investment trends	✓			
Restrictions on foreign labour/staff	✓			
Climate	✓			
Language	✓			
Management preference	✓		✓	?
Location of company's existing facilities	✓	✓	✓	?
Availability of 'suitable' areas	✓			
Cost of living	✓			
Standard of living	✓			
Location of markets	✓	✓	✓	
Location of suppliers	✓	✓	✓	
Proximity to related industries	✓	✓	✓	
Labour/staff availability and skills	✓	✓	✓	
Unemployment, turnover and absenteeism	?	✓	✓	
Pay levels and scales	?	✓	✓	
Planning and development restrictions	?	✓	✓	?
Tax structures and incentives	?	✓	?	
Environmental (e.g. pollution) controls	?	✓	?	
Communications: international	✓			
national		✓		
local			✓	
Transport: air	✓	✓	✓	
rail	✓	✓	✓	
road	✓	✓	✓	
other		✓	✓	
Availability of suitable communities		✓		
Land availability and costs		✓	✓	
Availability of premises		✓	✓	
Cost of land		✓	✓	
Cost of building			✓	
Rents for premises			✓	
Cost of services			✓	
Zoning and planning restrictions		✓	✓	
Availability of utilities		✓	✓	
Availability of amenities			✓	
Availability of education and training		✓	✓	
Community attitudes and culture			✓	
Energy availability		✓	✓	
Energy costs		✓	✓	
Impact on environment			✓	
Development plans			✓	
Availability of subcontractors			✓	
Availability of suitable sites			✓	
Site characteristics				✓
Availability of adjacent space				✓
Transport access				✓
Parking space				✓
Local transport provisions				✓
Facilities for waste disposal				✓

Location factor comparisons

Most locational decisions will at some stage involve the preparation of tabular comparisons of the type shown in Table 5.4. In some cases it will be possible and appropriate to draw up such comparisons entirely in cost terms, in which case addition of columns provides a means of comparing alternatives and therefore of choosing a location. Frequently, however, it will be necessary to consider cost and non-cost factors, and some of the latter may be represented only as 'yes' or 'no'. This ensures that the use of this type of approach, while providing a means of summarizing the factors to be considered, or providing a checklist against which to assess alternatives, must normally be employed along with more rigorous procedures of the type discussed below.

Table 5.4 *Comparison of factors for three possible locations for a retail shop*

Location factor	Location A	Location B	Location C
Site rental per year	£1000	£1200	£800
Car parking spaces within ½km	110	30	205
Shop frontage	4m	3m	4m
Cost of services per year	£750	£275	£800

Dimensional analysis

Even if we are able to identify the various factors influencing locational choice, the problem of quantification remains. How, for example, do we determine, for various potential locations, the cost of moving or the cost of labour? Furthermore, having quantified such factors, what weight or importance do we attach to each? Do we, for example, consider the subjective factors as being of equal importance to the fixed-cost factors? Indeed, we may even find that we are unable to attach cost figures to some of the important factors.

Consider a simple example in which we are faced with two possible locations. We have decided that the choice between these locations will be made on the basis of the following factors:

(a) the cost of land;
(b) the cost of buildings;
(c) the cost of labour (fixed investment, cost for the total required labour force for a location).

We have further found that the cost associated with each of these three factors for each of the possible locations is as shown in Table 5.5.

Table 5.5

Factor	Location A £	Location B £
Land	10 000	15 000
Buildings	25 000	30 000
Labour	15 000	10 000

We might compare the relative merits of the two locations merely by summing the relevant costs, i.e.

$$\text{Total for A} = £50\,000$$
$$\text{Total for B} = £55\,000$$

Using this method of comparison we would choose location A, since it is the cheaper of the two. This method assumes that each of the factors is of equal importance, which may be far from true. For example, suppose we decide that, while the costs of land and buildings are equally important to our decisions, the cost associated with labour is twice as important as the two other costs. Then we may assess the alternatives by introducing this weighting factor:

$$
\begin{array}{rl}
 & £ \\
\text{Location A:} & 10\,000 \\
 & 25\,000 \\
 & +2(15\,000) \\
\hline
 & = £65\,000
\end{array}
$$

$$
\begin{array}{rl}
 & £ \\
\text{Location B:} & 15\,000 \\
 & 30\,000 \\
 & +2(10\,000) \\
\hline
 & = £65\,000
\end{array}
$$

Now it appears that each location is equally attractive.

Let us take this type of argument a little further by introducing two more factors into our examination of the two locations. Now, as well as the costs associated with land, buildings and labour, we need to consider the influence of community relations and the cost of moving. We find it difficult to place an accurate cost on either of these factors for the two locations, so we settle for a system of rating using a scale of 1 to 100. A rating of 1 indicates that a location scores very highly, i.e. it is the best possible result, whereas a rating of 100 is the worst possible result.

Suppose the five factors for the two locations are quantified as shown in Table 5.6; then we might again compare locations by adding together the figures to obtain the totals shown in Table 5.6. This comparison would lead us to select location A.

Table 5.6

	Location A	Location B
Land (cost)	10 000	15 000
Buildings (cost)	25 000	30 000
Labour (cost)	15 000	10 000
Community relations (score)	60	30
Cost of moving (score)	80	40
Total	50 140	55 070

However, this type of analysis is quite wrong, because we have indiscriminately mixed together two dimensions: cost and ratings. To illustrate the inadequacies of the procedure, suppose we alter the scale of the first three factors and perform our calculations in £'000s rather than £s, i.e.

Location A	10	Location B	15
	25		30
	15		10
	60		30
	80		40
	190		125

Such an analysis would lead us to select location B, since the change of scale has distorted our analysis.

So that such an anomaly does not occur, we must take care to treat such multi-dimensional analysis in a more satisfactory manner. Such a method was developed by Bridgeman,[1] and is referred to as dimensional analysis. Using the following notation:

$$O_{i_1}, O_{i_2}, O_{i_3}, \ldots O_{i_m} = \text{costs, scores, etc., associated with factors} \\ 1, 2, 3, \ldots m, \text{for location } i$$

$$W_1, W_2, W_3, \ldots W_m = \text{the weight to be attached to factors} \\ 1, 2, 3, \ldots m$$

The merit of the various locations should be assessed as follows:

For location i, merit $= (O_{i_1})^{W_1} \times (O_{i_2})^{W_2} \times (O_{i_3})^{W_3} \ldots \times (O_{i_m})^{W_m}$

In the case of two possible locations the merit might be compared as follows:

$$\frac{\text{Merit of A}}{\text{Merit of B}} = \left(\frac{O_{A_1}}{O_{B_1}}\right)^{W_1} \times \left(\frac{O_{A_2}}{O_{B_2}}\right)^{W_2} \ldots \times \left(\frac{O_{A_n}}{O_{B_n}}\right)^{W_m}$$

If > 1, select B.
If < 1, select A.

EXAMPLE: A RETAIL SHOP

Several factors are identified as being important in choosing one of two available locations for a new retail shop. Wherever possible the factors have been costed; otherwise a score from 1 to 10 has been given, 1 representing the best possible result and 10 the worst possible. The factors are of different importance, so they have been weighted from 1 to 10 (weight of 1 indicating least importance and 10 most importance).

Table 5.7

Factor		Location A	Location B	Weight
Cost	=	£10 000	£15 000	1
Score	=	3	7	2
Score	=	6	2	3
Cost	=	£1 500 000	£1 000 000	4
Score	=	4	7	4
Score	=	5	5	3

The merit of location A is represented by:

$$(10\,000)^1 \times (3)^2 \times (6)^3 \times (1\,500\,000)^4 \times (4)^4 \times (5)^3$$

---

[1] Bridgeman, P. W. (1963) *Dimensional Analysis*. New Haven, Connecticut: Yale University Press.

and that of location B by:

$$(15\,000)^1 \times (7)^2 \times (2)^3 \times (1\,000\,000)^4 \times (7)^4 \times (5)^3$$

To simplify the calculations we can change the scales for the cost factors for both locations. Hence:

Merit of A: $(1)^1 \times (3)^2 \times (6)^3 \times (150)^4 \times (4)^4 \times (5)^3$

Merit of B: $(1.5)^1 \times (7)^2 \times (2)^3 \times (100)^4 \times (7)^4 \times (5)^3$

$$\therefore \frac{\text{Merit of A}}{\text{Merit of B}} = 1.79$$

Such an analysis indicates that location B is superior on the basis of the six factors considered.

In this example we have considered only factors which should be minimized, i.e. costs. Such an analysis might also be undertaken even where some factors are to be maximized (e.g. profits, revenue) while others are to be minimized. In such a case the powers would be positive for factors to be minimized and negative for factors to be maximized.

EXAMPLE: A CINEMA

Compare the merit of two locations X and Y on the basis of factors with different weights, i.e.

	Cinema Location X	Cinema Location Y	Weight
Costs (£)	10 000	12 000	4
Benefits (score, 1–10)	8	6	3

$$\frac{\text{Merit of X}}{\text{Merit of Y}} = \frac{(10\,000)^4 (8)^{-3}}{(12\,000)^4 (6)^{-3}}$$

$$= \frac{(10)^4 (8)^{-3}}{(12)^4 (6)^{-3}}$$

$$= 0.203$$

$$\therefore \text{ Select location X for the cinema}$$

Minimization of transport costs

It is clear from our previous discussion that many factors other than transport cost are likely to affect locational choice. Nevertheless, minimization of transport costs may provide a suitable first solution which might then form a basis for further discussion, analysis and modifications. Such an approach might be relevant in selecting the location of a warehouse relative to its principal customers or markets, or a manufacturing plant relative to its suppliers and customers.

Employing such an approach we would seek to minimize the sum of all transport costs, i.e. minimize:

$$L = \sum_{i=1}^{n} T_i Q_i D_i$$

where

L = Total transport cost to and from the facility to be located

T_i = Transport cost per unit distance per unit quantity for movement between the facility and existing location i

Q_i = Quantity to be transported between the facility and existing location i

D_i = Distance between the facility and existing location i for n locations

Considering movement between the facility and the supplier/customer locations to be in a rectangular pattern, and using Cartesian co-ordinates to indicate locations, distances D_i may be represented as follows:

$$D_i = |x - x_i| + |y - y_i|$$

where x_i and y_i indicate the existing location of a supplier or customer i, and x and y give the location of the facility. Hence:

$$L = \sum_{i=1}^{n} T_i Q_i |x - x_i| + \sum_{i=1}^{n} T_i Q_i |y - y_i|$$

Our task now is to develop a procedure to identify values for x and y which minimize L, and this can be done independently for the x and y dimensions. In fact the location required is given by the *median* point for each dimension.[2] A simple example will illustrate the procedure.

EXAMPLE: A WAREHOUSE

Square Deal Ltd wish to establish a new warehouse in the UK from which to supply a new line of building products to existing customers in Manchester, Liverpool, Birmingham and London. The locations of the customers are shown in Figure 5.6 and transport details are given in Table 5.8.

Table 5.8   *Transport details for Square Deal Ltd*

Customer	Q_i Annual delivery quantities (kg)	T_i Transport cost (per kg km)
Manchester	80 000	£0.0001
Liverpool	40 000	£0.0001
Birmingham	90 000	£0.0001
London	50 000	£0.0001

Multiplying T_i by Q_i and summing gives:

$$\sum_{i=1}^{4} T_i Q_i = (8 + 4 + 9 + 5)$$
$$= 26$$

In this situation the median point is taken as the value where the sum of the TQs below the point equals the sum of the TQs above the point.

Now to find the value of x which minimizes $\sum_{i=1}^{4} T_i Q_i |x - x_i|$ we work from west to east and find the existing location x_i which corresponds to the median value of $T_i Q_i$. With the sum of the TQs equal to 26 the median value occurs at the 13th unit. To find the value of x which minimizes L we calculate the cumulative TQ total from west to east as follows:

		Cumulative total	
Liverpool	$T_i Q_i = 4$	4	
Manchester	$T_i Q_i = 8$	12	
Birmingham	$T_i Q_i = 9$	21	Includes the 13th unit
London	$T_i Q_i = 5$	26	

Now the 13th unit is associated with Birmingham, so the value of x which minimizes L occurs at the Birmingham x co-ordinate.

---

[2] The median is the mid-point in a frequency distribution, i.e. the point below which 50 per cent of observations fall and above which the other 50 per cent fall.

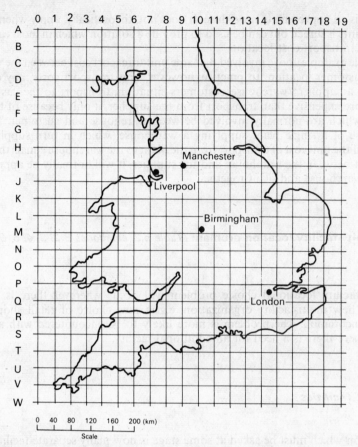

Figure 5.6 *Location of customers for warehouses for Square Deal Ltd (UK).*

Similarly, to find the value of y which minimizes $\sum_{i=1}^{4} T_i Q_i |y - y_i|$ we work from south to north and find the existing location which corresponds to the median value of $T_i Q_i$, as follows:

	Cumulative total	
London $T_i Q_i = 5$	5	
Birmingham $T_i Q_i = 9$	14	Includes the 13th unit
Liverpool $T_i Q_i = 4$	18	
Manchester $T_i Q_i = 8$	26	

Again, Birmingham corresponds to the median value. Hence the preferred location for the warehouse is to be found on the x co-ordinate corresponding to Birmingham and on the y co-ordinate corresponding to Birmingham, i.e. at Birmingham.

The total transport cost for this warehouse location can be found by substituting values of x, x_i, y and y_i into the equation for L, i.e. taking approximate distances from Figure 5.6:

	$T_i Q_i |x - x_i|$		$T_i Q_i |y - y_i|$
for Manchester	8(40)	+	8(140)
for Liverpool	4(120)	+	4(120)
for Birmingham	9(0)	+	9(0)
for London	5(150)	+	5(160)
	$L = £1550$	+	$£2400 = £3950$

In fact this is an approximate procedure. It does not, theoretically, apply when transport between points is direct, but can be used to provide a solution which in most cases is near to the least transport cost location.

The simple example above involved the same unit transport cost between the warehouse and each customer location. In practice, however, unit transport costs may differ. For example, in a suppliers/warehouse/customers situation, transport to the customer will often be more expensive than transport from the supplier, if only because of the smaller quantities which are normally involved between warehouse and customer. In the not unusual case of a single plant supplying a warehouse, which in turn supplies several customers, if the unit cost of transport from the plant to the warehouse equals the unit cost of transport between the warehouse and the supplier, it will normally be appropriate to locate the warehouse and plant together.

The multi-facility location problem *(Table 5.2, categories B 2, 3, 4, 5, 6 and 7)*

The multi-facility locational choice problem will occur wherever there is a need to establish a new multi-facility organization, e.g. a new choice of retail shops. This is relatively uncommon. The problem is more likely to be encountered with an existing business where there is a need for an additional facility.

Number of facilities

One question which must be asked at some stage is how many separate facilities should exist. Would it be better, for example, to have three separate facilities each capable of dealing with a throughput of 100 units per year, or two capable of dealing with 150 each. Consideration of economies of scale would suggest that fewer, larger facilities might be desirable, but consideration of transport costs, etc. might suggest that more facilities closer to their respective suppliers and/or markets might be more attractive. In fact, as is often the case, in this situation there are certain counter-directional costs to consider. One set of costs will increase as the number of facilities increases, e.g. cost of equipment, building, etc., while another set of costs will decrease as the number of facilities increases, e.g. transport costs. The point at which the total of these two sets of costs is minimized indicates the (least cost) number of facilities to employ.

Facility capacity

The need to decide on the distribution of capacity between facilities where several facilities are undertaking, or are able to undertake, similar activities is a related problem. If an organization currently has the capacity to deal with 1000 units per year, yet demand is sufficient to encourage the company to expand to a throughput of 1200 units per year, then this expansion in capacity can be provided by the addition of a new facility capable of dealing with 200 units per year, or the expansion of one or more of the existing sites, or the addition of a larger site coupled with the closure of or reduction in some of the existing facilities.

To consider locational choice and capacity simultaneously would necessitate the use of extremely complex procedures. In many cases, therefore, the two aspects are treated separately. Again, the procedures which are available apply equally to problems involving the location of manufacturing facilities, supply establishments, etc. We shall again consider the latter. We shall deal only with the simple case in which there are a finite number of locations with fixed and known capacities.

EXAMPLE: A DISTRIBUTION COMPANY

A company has two warehouses both handling the same range of goods. They are located in the United Kingdom at Cambridge and Bradford. Both distribute goods to five major centres: London, Bristol, Birmingham, Manchester and Hull. Because of an increase in demand the company is anxious to establish another warehouse, and the choice has been narrowed to two possible locations, Nottingham and Crewe, both of which are within easy reach of all major customer locations (Figure 5.7).

The unit distribution costs and the capacities of the existing warehouses are shown in Table 5.9. The forecast unit distribution cost and the capacities of warehouses at the two possible new locations, together with forecast demand for the five distribution centres, are shown in Table 5.10.

Clearly we are faced with the problem of selecting one of the two possible situations:

1.   Warehouses at Cambridge, Bradford and Nottingham;
2.   Warehouses at Cambridge, Bradford and Crewe.

In order to make this choice we must investigate the costs associated with each of the two situations. Considering situation 1, we can rearrange our data in the manner shown in Table 5.11. This table shows the total distribution cost/unit moved from each of the warehouses to each of the customer locations. The total capacity of the three warehouses is sufficient to satisfy the total demand, but in order to be able to evaluate the merit of this situation we must find the minimum cost allocation of goods between warehouses and customer locations.

This is now a straightforward linear programming problem which can be solved quite easily using the transportation method, or algorithm.[3] This method of obtaining an optimal solution to allocation problems of this type is described in detail in Appendix I. Using this technique, a minimum cost allocation of goods from warehouses to destinations as shown in Table 5.12 can quite easily be found.[4]

The total distribution cost associated with this situation and with the choice of this location is found as follows (referring to Tables 5.11 and 5.12):

$$9000 \times 1.6$$
$$1000 \times 1.7$$
$$2000 \times 1.7$$
$$4000 \times 1.7$$
$$8000 \times 1.6$$
$$7000 \times 1.4$$
$$6000 \times 1.5$$

$$\therefore \text{Total} = \pounds 57\,900$$

---

[3] An algorithm is an iterative solution procedure, i.e. a procedure which, by means of a defined sequence of steps or calculations, converges on a solution.

[4] You may wish to read Appendix I at this point. Having become familiar with the transportation method, you will be able to solve the problem shown in Table 5.11.

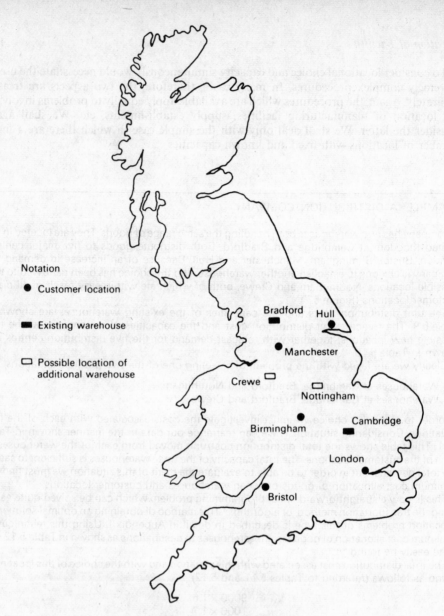

Notation

● Customer location

■ Existing warehouse

▢ Possible location of additional warehouse

Figure 5.7 *Location of facilities.*

Table 5.9 *Distribution cost data for existing warehouses*

Warehouse	Customer location London	Bristol	Birmingham	Manchester	Hull	Unit distribution cost	Monthly capacity
Cambridge	0.3[b]	0.4[b]	0.4[b]	0.5[b]	0.6[b]	1.3[a]	10 000
Bradford	0.5[b]	0.5[b]	0.4[b]	0.2[b]	0.3[b]	1.2[a]	15 000

[a] £/unit distributed from warehouse to any customer
[b] Additional £/unit distributed from warehouse to a particular customer

Table 5.10 *Forecast demand and distribution cost data for each of possible warehouses*

Warehouse	London	Bristol	Birmingham	Manchester	Hull	Unit distribution cost[a]	Monthly capacity
Nottingham	0.3[b]	0.3[b]	0.2[b]	0.2[b]	0.3[b]	0.4[a]	12 000
Crewe	0.4[b]	0.3[b]	0.2[b]	0.2[b]	0.4[b]	1.3[a]	12 000
Forecast monthly demand	9000	7000	8000	7000	6000		

[a] £/unit distributed from warehouse to any customer
[b] Additional £/unit distributed from warehouse to a particular customer

Table 5.11 *Total unit costs associated with situation 1 (£/unit)*

Warehouse	London	Bristol	Birmingham	Manchester	Hull	Capacity
Cambridge	1.6	1.7	1.7	1.8	1.9	10 000
Bradford	1.7	1.7	1.6	1.4	1.5	15 000
Nottingham	1.7	1.7	1.6	1.6	1.7	12 000
Requirements	9000	7000	8000	7000	6000	

Table 5.12 *Minimum cost allocation of goods for situation 1*

Warehouse	London	Bristol	Birmingham	Manchester	Hull	Capacity
Cambridge	9000	1000				10 000
Bradford		2000		7000	6000	15 000
Nottingham		4000	8000			12 000
Requirements	9000	7000	8000	7000	6000	

Now consider the alternative situation (2). Table 5.13 shows the total unit costs associated with the delivery of goods from each of the warehouses to each of the customer locations. (Only the third line, the costs associated with the additional location, differs from Table 5.11.) We can again use the transportation method of linear programming to obtain an optimum allocation of

Table 5.13 *Total unit costs associated with situation 2 (£/unit)*

Warehouse \ Customer location	London	Bristol	Birmingham	Manchester	Hull	Capacity
Cambridge	1.6	1.7	1.7	1.8	1.9	10 000
Bradford	1.7	1.7	1.6	1.4	1.5	15 000
Crewe	1.7	1.6	1.5	1.5	1.7	12 000
Requirements	9000	7000	8000	7000	6000	

goods as shown in Table 5.14. The quantities allocated from the three warehouses to the five centres are the same as in the previous case, but for this situation the total cost is as follows:

$$9000 \times 1.6$$
$$1000 \times 1.7$$
$$2000 \times 1.7$$
$$4000 \times 1.6$$
$$8000 \times 1.5$$
$$7000 \times 1.4$$
$$6000 \times 1.5$$

Total = £56 700

Table 5.14 *Minimum cost allocation of goods for situation 2*

Warehouse \ Customer	London	Bristol	Birmingham	Manchester	Hull	Capacity
Cambridge	9000	1000				10 000
Bradford		2000		7000	6000	15 000
Crewe		4000	8000			12 000
Requirements	9000	7000	8000	7000	6000	

Since this cost is less than the minimum obtained for situation 1, then on a basis of the criterion considered here, *i.e. cost of distribution*, we would select situation 2, i.e. Crewe, as the location of our additional warehouse. It should of course be remembered that distribution costs are rarely the sole criterion considered during the determination of plant locations; however, this type of analysis is often useful if only as a means of providing a first solution.

It should also be noted that the factors influencing location decisions are liable to change. The logical location at present may, at a later date, appear quite inferior because of change in one of the many factors which influenced the original choice.

Conceptually, the problem of the location of facilities abroad does not differ from the problems discussed in this chapter. In practice, however, such a problem will often be more complex and will assume greater proportions, if only because more investment may be involved. In such situations the identification and quantification of factors may be more difficult; nevertheless, the decision is amenable to the type of technique discussed earlier.

CHECKLIST FOR CHAPTER 5

The need for locational choice
  Expansion/contraction
  Replacement
  Pressures for change of space
  Pressures for a new location
Facilities location decisions
  Facility location decision levels
    Region
    Area
    Community
    Site
  Factors influencing decision at these levels
The choice of a new site
  Costs: fixed
  Costs: variable
  Volume considerations in location choice
  Timing
  Subjective assessments
Government inducements
Types of location problem
  Single-facility
    No connections
    Connections IN
    Connections OUT
    Connections IN and OUT
  Multi-facility

Set with no connections
Set with connections IN
Set with connections OUT
Set with connections IN and OUT
Addition to set with connections IN from other set locations
Addition to set with connections OUT
Addition to set with connections IN and OUT
Combinations
Single-facility location problems
  Checklists of factors
    Regional
    Area
    Community
    Site
  Location factor comparisons
  Dimensional analysis
    With weightings
  Minimization of transport costs
Multi-facility location problems
  Number of facilities
  Capacity of facilities
  Location decisions
  Capacity decisions
The transportation method

FURTHER READING

Bridgeman, P. W. (1963) *Dimensional Analysis*. New Haven, Connecticut: Yale University Press. Describes dimensional analysis.

Elon, S. et al. (1971) *Distribution Management: Mathematical Modelling and Practical Analysis*. London: Griffin.

Greenhut, M. (1956) *Plant Location in Theory and Practice*. Chapel Hill, North Carolina: University of North Carolina Press. Most textbooks devoted to this subject treat the problem from an economist's point of view; this book reviews economic location theory as well as plant location practice (although it is now rather dated).

Karaska, G. J. and Bramhall, D. F. (1969) *Location Analysis for Manufacturing*. Cambridge, Massachusetts: MIT Press. Deals with the plant location problem in the broader context.

Khumawala, B. M. and Whybark, D. C. (1971) A comparison of some recent warehouse location techniques, *Logistics Review*, **7** (31), pp. 3–19.

Schmenner, R. W. Look beyond the obvious plant location, *Harvard Business Review*, Jan–Feb., pp. 126–32.
Townrof, P. M. (1969) *Location Analysis for Manufacturing*. Cambridge, Massachusetts: MIT Press. Again, deals with the plant location problem in the broader context.
Weston, F. C. (1972) Quantitative analysis of plant location, *Industrial Engineering*, **4** (4), pp. 22–28.

QUESTIONS

5.1 Briefly, what changes might result in the need for additional space for a service operation (of your own choice)? Under what circumstances might such changes lead to the need for an entirely new site, and what would influence the choice of such a site?

5.2 Galvanated Decorations (Sales) Ltd is a family business situated in the heart of the UK midlands, i.e. at Birmingham. The company distribute ornamental lamp-posts to agents in London, Newcastle and Manchester. The lamp-posts are obtained from a manufacturer in Liverpool. The tables below show the annual quantities involved, the distances and the transport cost per item per 40 km travelled. What maximum total transportation cost benefit would Galvanated Decorations Ltd obtain by relinquishing their Birmingham premises for a warehouse elsewhere, and where should this new warehouse be located?

Product	Annual quantity	Transportation cost per unit per 40 km £
Lamp-posts from Liverpool	13 000	0.4
Lamp-posts for London	7 000	0.8
Lamp-posts for Newcastle	3 000	0.65
Lamp-posts for Manchester	2 400	0.65

Table of distances (km)

	London	Manchester	Birmingham	Liverpool	Newcastle
London	—				
Manchester	306	—			
Birmingham	177	129	—		
Liverpool	322	61	145	—	—
Newcastle	475	217	290	241	—

Note: See Figure 5.6. Birmingham, shown; Liverpool, shown; London, shown; Newcastle, Ref. 11D; Manchester, shown.

5.3 Incredible Chemicals Ltd intend to establish a plant solely for the blending of Formula X14, which is a composite of X9 and X5 and is used by the company in the manufacture of agricultural fertilizer.

X9 is imported by Incredible Chemicals and is to be transported from London docks, while X5 is obtained from a subsidiary company at Hull.

Formula X14 is to be used at three other Incredible Chemicals works at Manchester, Bristol and Newcastle, where the requirements are 40, 30 and 50 tonnes per week respectively. Equal quantities of X9 and X5 are required to blend Formula X14, but because of atmospheric contamination 15 per cent of the tonnage of Formula X14 is wasted and has to be burnt.

Incredible Chemicals transport all products and materials by road, the cost per tonne per kilometre being £0.016. There is, however, an additional charge associated with imported items which effectively increases transportation costs to £0.018 per tonne per kilometre. Considering only transportation costs, where should the new Incredible Chemicals blending plant be situated?

Table of distances (km)

	Manchester	Bristol	Newcastle	London	Hull
Manchester	—				
Bristol	257	—			
Newcastle	217	483	—		
London	306	193	475	—	
Hull	121	290	193	322	—

Note: See Figure 5.6. Manchester, shown; Bristol, Ref. P9; Newcastle, Ref. 11D; London, shown; Hull, Ref. H13.

5.4 In the interests of public health, Incredible Chemicals Ltd decide not to burn the 15 per cent of Formula X14 which is wasted by atmospheric contamination during blending. (See previous question.) After careful consideration and research they decide to sell this 'waste' product to a company in London who intend to use it in their patent weed-killer.

How does this decision affect the choice of site for the new Formula X14 blending plant, and what is the total weekly transportation cost difference between the previous choice of site and the new choice of site?

5.5 The British Confectionery Corporation are anxious to build a new factory for the manufacture of a range of export goods. Although in theory the choice of location for this factory is wide, in practice the choice is limited to two government-designated development areas centred on Sunderland and Birkenhead. One of the economists employed by the BCC has evaluated both of these locations and has completed the following information. Which location should the company choose?

Factor	Sunderland £	Birkenhead £	Weighting factor[b]
Cost of land	10 000	12 500	4
Cost of buildings	30 000	35 000	4
Cost of labour	7 500	10 000	3
Transport cost p.a.	6 000	2 000	3
Industrial relations[a]	50	80	5
Labour training needs[a]	75	60	2
Community benefits[a]	70	30	1

[a] Because of the difficulty of costing these factors, a score (1 to 100) has been given where 1 is equivalent to a low cost and 100 to a high cost.
[b] This weighting factor indicates the importance of each factor, 1 is of least importance and 10 is of most importance.

5.6 Space-age Transport Ltd is a British company and the world's only successful supplier of high-speed, three-wheeled, electric automobiles. After several years' successful trading in Europe the company has decided to establish a subsidiary company in North America. The possible locations for the American company have been reduced to three: Chicago, Seattle and Michigan.

The following information has been provided by the company's accountants and marketing people. All other things being equal, which location should the company adopt for its American distribution operations?

Factor	Chicago	Seattle	Michigan
1. Cost of buildings	$50 000	$45 000	$38 000
Cost of land	$ 9 000	$ 8 000	$ 7 000
Distribution costs	$ 7 000	$10 000	$12 000
2. Initial labour training and recruitment costs	$ 4 000	$ 6 000	$ 7 000
3. Percentage annual labour turnover expected	10%	20%	35%
4. Recreational attractions[a]	1	2	3
Availability of housing[a]	2	1	3
5. Suitability of site for subsequent expansion[b]	5 .	7	10

[a] *Ranking:* 1 = most attractive; 3 = least attractive.
[b] Rating on ten-point scale provided by managing director: 1 = most attractive; 10 = least attractive.

As a means of evaluating the alternatives, the managing director considers that factors 1 and 3 above have twice the importance of factors 2 and 4 and three times the importance of factor 5.

5.7 Company Z manufactures the same product at two existing factories located at A and B, and distributes them to three retail outlets at L, M and O. Because of an expected increase in demand for the product the company is considering opening an additional factory at *either* C or D. The tables below show:

(a) the unit production costs, the unit distribution costs and the monthly production capacity associated with the present situation, i.e. factories at A and B distributing to L, M and O;
(b) the unit production costs, the unit distribution costs and the monthly production capacities associated with each of the possible additional factories;
(c) the forecasted monthly product demands for each of the three retail outlets.

Where should the additional factory be established?

(a)	Outlet L	Outlet M	Outlet O	Unit production cost	Monthly production capacity
Factory A	0.2	0.4	0.3	1.0	4000
Factory B	0.3	0.3	0.2	1.2	6000

(b)	Outlet L	Outlet M	Outlet O	Unit production cost	Monthly production capacity
Factory C	0.3	0.2	0.4	1.2	3500
Factory D	0.2	0.3	0.5	1.0	3000

(c)

Outlet	Forecasted monthly demand
L	3800
M	4500
O	4500

5.8   Referring to the previous question, how does the inclusion of *both* of the following modifications affect the choice of location?

(a) The cost per unit associated with the under-utilization of production capacity is 0.1 for factories A and C and 0.12 for factories B and D. (For example, if the required output from factory A is 3500 units per month compared with its production capacity of 4000 units per month, a cost of $(4000 - 3500) \times 0.1$ is incurred.)

(b) The forecasted monthly demand for outlet L is 4000 units.

5.9   A company rents three warehouses at A, B and C, from which they supply timber to two builders, P and Q. The profit $(\pounds)$ per tonne of timber supplied, the annual demands of the builders and the supplies available from the warehouses are shown below.

	P	Q	Supply ('000 tonnes)
A	3	4	4
B	2	3	4
C	5	4	3
Demand ('000 tonnes)	6	6	

The company is unhappy at not being able to meet the total annual demand of the builders, and for this reason is considering replacing warehouse C with a warehouse rented at D whose annual supply capacity would be 5000 tonnes, the use of which would give a profit of $\pounds6$ and $\pounds5$ per tonne of timber distributed to P and Q respectively. The additional annual cost of renting warehouse D in place of C would be $\pounds5000$.

(a) Should the company replace warehouse C?

(b) If warehouse C were replaced, at which warehouse would the excess supply capacity by stored, assuming that storage is possible at A, B or D at negligible cost?

5.10   The map on p. 118 shows, to scale, the location of four cities in the Eastern United States of America. The Moonshine Corporation is to locate three new facilities at Cleveland, Memphis and Jacksonville. One facility is the primary process, which is to supply each of the two other facilities, both of which supply a single customer at Richmond. The total annual output from the two secondary processes is 10 000 units per year. The maximum size of either facility is 7000 units per year. The annual demand from Richmond is 10 000 units per year.

The primary process facility has sufficient capacity to satisfy the two secondary processes.

The transportation costs are shown on the next page. Assume direct movement between cities. Where should the three facilities be located, and what should the size of the two secondary process facilities be?

Eastern USA.

$movement cost/unit[a]/mile

From \ To	M	C	R	J
M		0.1	0.2	0.15
C	0.8		0.25	0.2
R	–	–		–
J	0.13	0.15	0.31	

[a] whether of 'primary' or 'secondary' outputs

CHAPTER SIX

The Layout of Facilities and Materials Handling

NOTATION USED IN THIS CHAPTER

n	Number of facilities
L	Cost value of a point (direct movement)
x_i	Ordinate of point i
y_i	Ordinate of point i
A	Closeness rating: essential
E	Closeness rating: very important
I	Closeness rating: important
O	Closeness rating: ordinary close
U	Closeness rating: unimportant
X	Closeness rating: undesirable

The facilities layout problem is common to every type of enterprise, but, unfortunately, there is no single meaningful goal, since objectives will vary from one situation to the next. Furthermore, there is no single acceptable and rigorous procedure by which to achieve our objectives. Even in seemingly straightforward situations where comparatively few items are to be arranged, a vast number of alternative acceptable solutions are available. For example, arranging six different departments in two adjacent rows of three produces 720 possible answers. Not surprisingly, therefore, people have relied heavily on intuition, experience and improvization. Recently, however, some progress has been made in the more scientific treatment of this problem, so in this chapter we discuss traditional methods, which have proved valuable and which are widely adopted, together with recent developments in the treatment of the same problems which either are of value now or promise well for the future.

119

THE NEED FOR LAYOUT PLANNING

We often tend to think in terms of *planning complete layouts* and designing entirely new *sets of departments*, but although such occasions undoubtedly do arise the following are the types of problems we are much more likely to encounter.

Enlarging or reducing existing departments

The addition or removal of facilities, the trading of areas between departments, or a complete relayout may be necessary because of increases or decreases in demand for goods or services, changes in the nature of goods and services, or changes in the scope or capability of processes.

Movement of a department

The need to move a department because of a change in the specification or nature of the goods or service, or because of changes in demand or operating processes, may constitute a simple exercise. Alternatively, if the existing layout is inadequate, it may present the opportunity for a major change, the extent of which bears little relationship to the primary cause.

Adding or removing a department

Adding a department may be the result of a desire to undertake work never before done on the site, or the desire to centralize work previously undertaken in several separate departments. Conversely, the removal of a department which is no longer required may facilitate or obviate the need for a rearrangement of other departments.

Replacing equipment and adding new equipment

Frequently, even equipment designed to perform exactly the same function as its predecessors is physically different and its installation necessitates a certain amount of reorganization. Occasionally new machines may be installed to replace or supplement existing machines.

OBJECTIVES IN LAYOUT PLANNING

Some of the advantages of good facilities layouts and hence some possible objectives in planning layouts are as follows.

Cost of materials handling and movement

In most operating systems there will be physical flows. The extent and cost of these flows will be affected by the layout of facilities. In manufacturing, the handling and movement of materials, components and the finished product, as well as the movement of labour, are primarily dependent on the location of the production and service facilities. The movement of customers in a retail store or in a service system such as a hotel or restaurant will be influenced by the layout of facilities. Improved layout will result in a reduction in the distance moved by items and/or customers and the time consumed, and hence in the cost of such movement whether to the organization or to the customer.

Congestion and delay

The objective of most operations is to add to the value of inputs. This is achieved by subjecting inputs to some form of processing. No value is added and nothing is contributed to profits by delays or storage during operations. Although the extent of work in progress is also determined by the effectiveness of operations scheduling and the nature of the production process, poor facilities layout may necessitate high work in progress and hence increase throughput time. Time spent by the customer waiting in a system generates no turnover, and the turnover of a supply system is adversely affected by delays in obtaining items for customers, so in all such cases an objective will be to minimize congestion and delay and thus provide for the more intensive use of facilities and the more efficient use of capacity.

Utilization of space, facilities and labour

The cost of space is high and wasted space may be eliminated and the total area necessary for an operating system minimized by adequate facilities layout. Effective arrangement of facilities may reduce idle time and cut down investment in both direct (e.g. plant) and indirect (e.g. support) equipment. Adequate layout also facilitates operation, maintenance, service and supervision, and therefore permits a better utilization of labour.

Our discussion above raises two issues which merit further comment at this stage. We have identified the importance of movement and flows and thus the handling of physical items and/or customers as factors or criteria in layout planning. Much of our discussion of layout planning techniques will reflect the importance of minimizing physical movement and handling. We have also referred to capacity, one objective of layout planning being the maximization of capacity utilization. When planning a new facilities layout we must know the extent or quantity of each type of facility to be provided; we must know what capacity is to be provided. Layout planning is therefore contingent capacity planning, which is discussed in Chapter 11.

FACILITIES LAYOUT PROBLEMS

We can recognize three levels of facilities layout planning problems. Layout planning begins after the solution of the site location problem and then moves through these three levels:

(a)   the layout of 'departments' within the site;
(b)   the layout of 'facilities' within the 'departments';
(c)   the layout of individual 'workplaces'.

In this chapter we are concerned explicitly with level (a) but implicitly the discussion relates to level (b) also, since they are the large-scale and small-scale levels of the same problem. Level c), being concerned with ergonomics and work study, is dealt with in Chapters 7 and 9. We shall use the term 'department' to mean an area containing several (perhaps interrelated) facilities. A 'facility' will be considered as a single (perhaps large and complex) piece of equipment, while a 'workplace' can be seen as the work area of one person or a work team.

Examples of the types of layout planning problems which might occur in different types of operating systems are given in Table 6.1.

Table 6.1   *Facilities layout problems: examples*

Type of operating system	Examples of operating system	Examples of a facilities layout planning problem	Basic type (or cause) of problem	Possible objectives
Manufacturing system	Kitchen of a large restaurant	Because of building changes elsewhere in the restaurant, the locations of drains have been changed, and it is now necessary to relocate dish washing and drying.	Movement of a department	1. Maximize space utilization 2. Minimize amount of movement of crockery and/or people in kitchen
Supply system	Supermarket	It has been decided to provide a petrol station in or adjacent to the car park, to provide fuel for customers' cars and for others who choose to call.	Adding a department	1. Ease of access (minimum distance for customers) 2. Space utilization 3. Prominence
Transport system	Passenger transport within an airport terminal building	The transport system comprises elevators (lifts), escalators and moving walkways. There is a need to replace the main set of four (adjacent) elevators with eight rapid elevators. They cannot be located in the present elevator area.	Enlarging a department	Minimum passenger congestion

Type of operating system	Examples of operating system	Examples of a facilities layout planning problem	Basic type (or cause) of problem	Possible objectives
Service system	Reception area in a large hotel	Information for residents (e.g. weather reports, local entertainments, bus, rail and flight times, etc.) was displayed on a notice-board. This is to be removed and a computer data terminal is to be installed to provide a complete information service for customers.	Replacing a facility	1. Minimize customer congestion 2. Maximize space utilization 3. Maximize utilization

BASIC TYPES OF LAYOUTS

Manufacture

There are, classically, three main systems of manufacturing plant layout, each with individual characteristics and each appropriate to some form of manufacture, depending on the output rate and the range of products involved. Although each system is normally associated with a particular type of production, none is exclusive to any one industry. We shall examine each of these basic systems in turn, identifying the nature of production and the characteristics of each.

Layout by process (or functional layout) (see Figures 6.1 and 6.4(a))

In a process or functional layout all operations of a similar nature are grouped together in the same department or part of the factory. For example, there may be separate areas for drilling operations, milling, grinding, fitting, and so on.

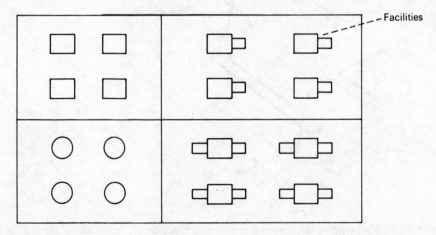

Figure 6.1 *Process or functional layout with four departments.*

Layout by process is appropriate where small quantities of a large range of products are to be manufactured, perhaps the best example being jobbing production. The nature of the layout permits flexibility in production, i.e. complex products requiring processing in every one of the functional departments may be made alongside simple products requiring processing in only a few departments. Such a situation would be difficult to accommodate in either of the other two systems of layout. This flexibility, however, brings disadvantages. Process layouts normally operate with a comparatively high level of work in progress, and throughput time is high. Specialist supervision is possible and the grouping of operatives of similar type and skill within the same department promotes cohesiveness and enables individual bonus schemes to be used. The provision of services, e.g. water, power, removal of scrap, is simpler than in other forms of layout, but the cost of materials handling is high.

Layout by product *(see Figure 6.2)*

Layout by product is appropriate for the production of a small range of products in very large quantities. Ideally, only one standardized product is involved and production should be continuous, as in mass production industries such as the car industry. Facilities are arranged according to the needs of the product and in the same sequence as the operations necessary for manufacture. Because this is a specialized production layout designed solely for the production of large quantities of one or a very small range of standardized products, it is relatively inflexible. Enough stable demand to ensure a high utilization of equipment is absolutely essential, as is a regular supply of the right quantities of raw materials and components. Failure in the supply of a piece of epuipment results in the

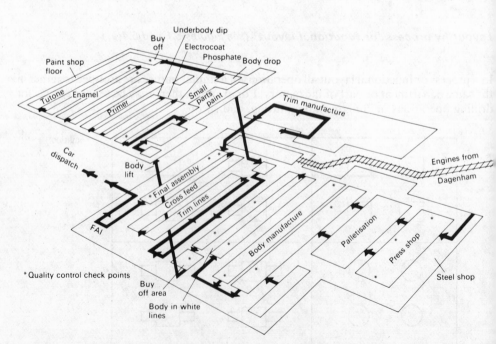

Figure 6.2 *Product-type layout: general arrangement of facilities at the Halewood plant of the Ford Motor Company. Reproduced with the permission of the Ford Motor Company Ltd.*

entire production line stopping, and apparently quite remote failures can reıult in disproportionately high losses.

The provision of services is difficult, since where particularly elaborate machinery is used quite different pieces of equipment with different characteristics and requirements may be located adjacent to one another. A mixture of skills and operations often occurs, resulting in difficulties in payment and supervision, but usually little specialized supervision is required, since the work performed is often highly rationalized. Minimum floor space is required, work in progress is minimized and the throughput is high. The requirements for handling materials are small and machine utilization is high.

Layout by fixed position *(see Figure 6.3)*

In the two previous layout systems the product moves past stationary production equipment. In this case the reverse applies. In the extreme case, e.g. civil engineering, neither the partly completed nor the finished product moves. Alternatively, as in ship building, the product remains stationary only until it is completed.

Unlike in the period prior to the Industrial Revolution, when a large proportion of production was undertaken by artisans in their own homes, layout by fixed position is now comparatively unimportant, except where civil engineering and large items such as ships and aircraft are concerned.

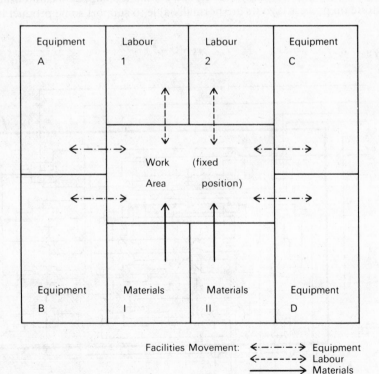

Figure 6.3 *Layout by fixed position.*

Group layout *(see Figure 6.4(b))*

Process, product and fixed-position layouts are the traditional forms in manufacturing industry. Recently, however, in batch production, configurations known as group layouts have begun to emerge as a distinctive facilities arrangement. In effect, group layout is a hybrid form which provides a type of product arrangement of facilities for the manufacture of similar items, each of which, if taken individually, would normally be manufactured through a process configuration. This approach is used as a means of achieving some of the benefits of layout by product in the batch manufacture of products. Groups of similar items are formed using group technology classification procedures of the type described in the Appendix to Chapter 3. Given a large enough group it is practical to arrange in one area all the facilities required for their production. Group layouts differ from layouts by product, therefore, in that they are used for the manufacture of similar (but not the same) items required for the batch manufacture of final products. In most cases all items passing through a group layout will not require the use of all facilities, so flow patterns will differ, but because of the similarity of items utilization will be high. Figures 6.4(a) and (b) show flow patterns for alternative arrangements, the group layout having been designed to accommodate items A to H as groups I to IV. The most advanced application of group-type layouts can be found in computer-controlled flexible manufacturing systems (see 'Further Reading' at the end of the chapter).

Most practical manufacturing layouts are combinations of process and product layouts. Rarely are companies in the enviable situation where they are able to produce continuously large quantities of an absolutely standard product. Similarly, even the largest range of products normally uses certain common components, and firms obliged to concentrate on process layouts are normally able to support some product layouts as well.

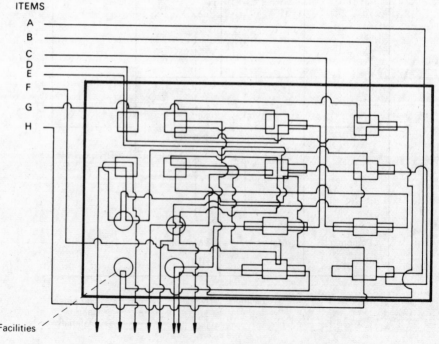

Figure 6.4 (a)   *Work flow in a functional layout (with four 'departments').*

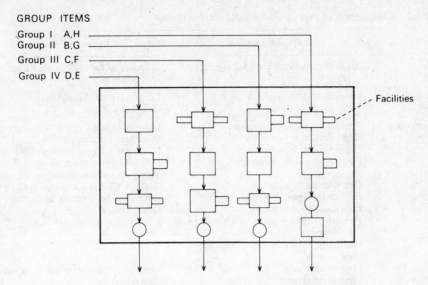

GROUP ITEMS

Group I A,H
Group II B,G
Group III C,F
Group IV D,E

Facilities

Figure 6.4 (b) *Work flow in a group layout.*

Comparison of layout types

The characteristics of layout by product and by process are listed and contrasted in Table 6.2. Figure 6.5 shows a break-even point analysis of three types of production, indicating the relative cost benefits first of process layout, then of product layout as output increases.

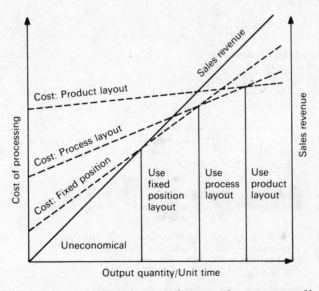

Sales revenue

Cost: Product layout

Cost: Process layout

Cost: Fixed position

Cost of processing

Use fixed position layout

Use process layout

Use product layout

Sales revenue

Uneconomical

Output quantity/Unit time

Figure 6.5 *Break-even analysis showing economic advantage of various types of layout for the same product at different output levels.*

Table 6.2 *Comparison of process and product layouts*

	Layout by process	Layout by product
Nature	All similar facilities grouped together	Sequence of facilities derived from needs of product
Application	Low quantity throughput Large range of items	Large quantity throughput Only a few items
Characteristics	Permits specialist supervision High work in progress High material handling cost Ease of provision of services Can tolerate breakdowns Easy to incorporate inspection Individual bonus possible Flexibility, variety and product changes possible Possibility of loss or neglect of some jobs/items Maintenance easy Control complex Planning simple Long throughput time	Little specialized supervision required Minimum work in progress Minimum material handling cost Difficult to provide services Minimum space required Single breakdown stops all machines Difficult to incorporate inspection Group bonus Little variety possible Maintenance out of production hours Control simple Planning complex Accurate work measurement essential Low throughput time

Non-manufacturing systems

The four types of layouts described above also exist in non-manufacturing situations. With the exception of transport systems, these four layout types encompass most of what will be encountered in planning the layout of non-manufacturing systems. Some examples are given in Table 6.3.

Table 6.3 *Types of layout: examples*

Type of operating system	Type of layout			
	Process layout	Product layout	Fixed-position layout	Group layout
Service systems	1. Hotel 2. Reference library	1. Automatic carwash 2. Medical screening and diagnosis	Hospital operating theatre	—
Supply systems	1. Supermarket 2. Warehouse	1. Restaurant self-service counter	Restaurant dinning-room	—
Manufacturing systems	1. Jobbing production 2. Small batch production	1. Motor-vehicle assembly line 2. Chemical process plant	1. Shipyard 2. Civil engineering	Batch production of components for a variety of products
Transport systems	See text	See text	—	—

Supply and service systems

Similar configurations can be identified in supply and service systems. In supply the principal flows and movements will resemble those of manufacturing systems, since again goods are involved. In service systems the principal flows may involve people, often customers. In a warehouse, for example, a functional layout may be employed in which particular areas are used for the storage of particular product lines or goods. In such situations flow patterns will be relatively simple in that goods will be received into the warehouse and placed into storage, from where eventually they will be transferred to customers. In such cases therefore there will be little flow or movement between areas, and thus the layout problem is considerably simplified. A similar situation may exist in a retail store. In these situations, however, the 'picking' problem will exist in that warehouse or counter staff may be required to collect together all items required for a particular customer by travelling between the appropriate areas within the facility. Thus movement problems are of importance and minimization of movement becomes a relevant criterion for layout planning. In service systems such as hospitals, the process or functional layout will often be found, since particular wards and particular parts of the hospital will be devoted to particular types of activity, e.g. general surgery, medicine, geriatrics. Here again there may be substantial movement between areas, since customers, i.e. patients, may need attention from several areas, and staff will have to move between and work in several of these areas. In certain medical facilities the layout by product or flow-type layout may be used. For example, in certain cases a series of fairly elaborate medical tests will be made on patients as part of screening or diagnosis procedure. These tests may be arranged sequentially and facilities provided to minimize throughput time and maximize resource utilization. In both these functions it is possible to envisage a layout by fixed position, particularly in the service sector, where facilities might be brought to a customer; e.g. in the case of a road accident, medical facilities would be brought to the injured patient.

Thus the three traditional layouts may exist in supply and service organizations and the movement and flows of items and people between areas within the layout may be a principal feature in determining the configuration.

Transport systems

The essential feature of transport systems is movement. In many such systems the principal facilities employed are mobile. In this chapter we are concerned with the arrangement of essentially static facilities, so a somewhat different situation applies as regards facilities layout for transport systems, since in this context we are concerned only with the arrangement of a portion (perhaps in a way the least important portion) of the facilities of the system, namely the fixed facilities, e.g. garage, service bays. Given this, however, much the same situation might be found, and again it will be possible to identify at least two of the three traditional configurations, namely layout by process and by product. As with manufacture, supply and service, movement and physical flows may again be seen to be the principal criteria in establishing the layout.

LAYOUT PLANNING PROCEDURE

The planning of an entirely new layout is the most comprehensive problem and although such occasions are comparatively rare we shall consider this case in detail in order to cover the subject adequately.

In practice, facilities layout planning procedures tend to be elaborate and complex; nevertheless, beneath this complexity a comparatively straightforward procedure exists and this is what we shall consider, despite the risk of over-simplification. We are proposing to establish a new set of facilities in one location. It is assumed that the precise nature of the goods or service to be provided from the facilities and the demand for them either are known or may be determined by appropriate market research. Given this information, the required capacity and hence the number and nature of facilities can be determined (see Chapter 11).

Nature of facilities = f(nature of goods or services and demand)

In addition to the principal facilities required, other equipment will be needed; hence additional space must be provided. Storage space will be required, depending on such factors as fluctuations in demand for goods or services and the supply of raw materials. Departments such as personnel, etc., must be accommodated.

Space required = f(nature of facilities and nature of additional facilities required)

Plant layout planning procedure therefore involves consideration of the following: demand, capacity, work methods and standards, resource requirements, handling and movement, and space requirements, among other factors.

Demand

Normally, an operation will be established to meet an existing demand. If we are building a new factory to increase the ouput of an existing product, then the extent of the demand for the product will be known. If we are building a new warehouse to supply a particular area with existing items we will again know something of expected demand. Otherwise we will rely on market research to establish the following:

(a) specification of the goods/services;
(b) selling price;
(c) demand for each goods/service;
(d) expected fluctuations in demand.

This information will help in the determination of the capacity required.

Capacity

The determination of capacity requires not only the estimation of steady state or average demand levels but also decisions on how best to deal with demand level fluctuations. In Chapter 11 it will be seen that the accommodation of demand fluctuations may necessitate the provision of storage space, over-capacity, etc.; thus detailed capacity planning is essential before facilities layout planning is begun.

Work methods and standards

Work study data should exist or be generated for each operation required in the manufacture and supply of goods and/or provision of services. Method study (see Chapter 7) will establish the sequence of operations to be performed and the types of equipment to be used. Given standard work methods, work measurement (see Chapter 8) will be used to establish operation times. Such information, which is a prerequisite for all operations planning, will be of relevance in determining the configuration of facilities.

Resource requirements

Given an estimate of the required capacity in terms of output and work standards, it will be possible to calculate resource requirements in terms of both labour and equipment. Some allowance must be made for breakdowns, holidays, stoppages, etc.

Handling and movement

Although in many cases the layout planning procedure will seek to minimize movement, distance or time, and/or handling cost, some knowledge of the nature of the movement and the manner in which it is to be achieved, i.e. the nature of any handling equipment, will be essential in planning the layout. The equipment required to provide movement and handling will itself require space both for operation and for maintenance, repair, etc. Furthermore, in certain industries movement and handling may be achieved only in particular ways because of the particular requirements of the process.

Space requirements

In addition to the space necessary to accommodate the machinery and materials required in the operation, allowances must be made for the movement of personnel and for service and repair, etc.

Other factors affecting layout

Normally additional, often obscure, factors affect layout, for example: the removal, reprocessing or use of scrap and waste materials; the characteristics of the materials used, e.g. stability, value, etc.; noise; safety legislation; customer areas; anticipated developments and the necessity for change. Consequently, the stages above can be considered only as a general procedure for the generation and collection of basic data which, along with other considerations peculiar to the particular circumstances, enable us to begin to plan the layout. Some of these considerations will be outlined later, with particular reference to supply and storage layouts.

Layout planning method

When we have considered the factors above we can begin to plan the layout. The method which we shall adopt will depend on our objectives and circumstances. Some common methods are outlined below.

LAYOUT PLANNING METHODS

In many fields of management current practice is far removed from current theory and research. Present practice is a reflection of previous research, and current research results from the inadequacies of present practice. Progress is continually being made in both practice and research, but the variance between the two levels rarely decreases. Nowhere is this more apparent than in layout planning. The conventional layout procedures appear quite mundane beside current theory, but nevertheless these procedures are proven, accepted and valuable.

Visual aids play an important part in layout planning. Some form of scale representation, e.g. scale drawing, templates, three-dimensional models, etc., is invariably used. Frequently movement patterns are shown on the drawings or models. String diagrams are a familiar method of showing movement, coloured cord being attached to diagrams or models to indicate the paths taken by different products.

The main criticism of these methods, about which little more need be said here, is that they are completely unstructured and depend entirely on the knowledge, experience and insight of the planner. This same fact, however, can be interpreted as their main advantage. If they are completely unstructured it is theoretically possible, while planning the layout, to take into account all relevant constraints. Their merit, therefore, is the breadth of their approach rather than their rigour.

If we attempt to develop analytical methods of layout planning we must determine precisely what our objective is, e.g. to maximize facilities utilization or to minimize movement, congestion, etc. Undoubtedly, the lowest common denominator of all layouts, whether in manufacturing, supply, service or transport, is the need for movement. Even in visual planning procedures the need to minimize movement is usually the first consideration, and only after an initial layout has been obtained are additional objectives allowed to intervene. In most situations there will be some need for movement, and the type of equipment used, the distance travelled and the time involved will affect the total cost. However, in planning layouts, particularly new layouts which exist only on paper, it is often possible to measure only the distance involved in movement. Each movement operation normally involves pick-up, movement and put-down, but the distance is the main variable factor.

It is reasonable, therefore, to adopt as our primary objective *the minimization of the total movement cost for items or people*, and as our main criterion the *total distance moved*. This approach will be taken in this and the following section. Situations in which this type of approach is not relevant will be examined later in the chapter.

We shall deal first with analytical and similar methods which can be used in the planning of entirely new layouts, and then we shall look at the modification of existing layouts.

PLANNING NEW LAYOUTS

Cross and relationship charts

The pattern and extent of movement or handling which is known to take place, or expected to exist, are often summarized on some form of chart, which can then be used to assist in layout planning.

The cross chart shown in Figure 6.6 indicates the pattern and amount of movement of items among ten departments in a small factory. In the case of a new layout the routeing will have been obtained from routeing instructions, e.g. flow process charts, and the quantities from production requirements. The figures in the matrix are the number of items or loads which in a given period of time must move from one department to another. In the case of the existing layouts this information may be obtained by sampling of the activity taking place within the factory.

FROM \ TO (Dept no.)	1	2	3	4	5	6	7	8	9	10	TOTAL
Dept no. 1		15				12	8	5			40
2			10	5							15
3				10							10
4					5	7		3			15
5						5					5
6							12				12
7								12	8		20
8									12	8	20
9										20	20
10											
TOTAL		15	10	15	5	24	20	20	20	28	

Figure 6.6 *Cross chart showing the nature and extent of the movement of items between departments over a given period of time.*

Notice that the row and the column totals are not necessarily equal. Where some of the items are consumed or combined, row totals may be less than column totals.

Absence of any figures below the diagonal means that none of the items backtracks between departments, but the scatter above the diagonal indicates a varied movement pattern characteristic of the production of several products. Some of the items follow a path through from department 1 to department 10, but, judging from this data alone, a 'product layout' seems impractical.

Various elaborations on the cross chart have been suggested, but the simple principle remains the same. For example, a *weighted cross chart* may on occasions offer sufficient advantages to justify the extra effort. Here, unlike the procedure of Figure 6.6, the movements of items between departments are not given equal weight, but each movement is weighted according to that item's importance, e.g. in terms of its contribution to profit, etc.

An alternative approach either with a weighted or with an unweighted cross chart is to consider only the principal goods or services.

Cross charts are a means of collecting and presenting information from which preferable departmental relationships can be obtained. This information can then be summarized on a relationship chart. For example, the relationship chart shown in Figure 6.7 is partly derived from the previous cross chart (Figure 6.6).

The required closeness of departments summarized by a relationship chart may reflect needs other than the minimization of movement; indeed, a relationship chart can be used to summarize proximity requirements where the minimization of movement is not of overriding importance.

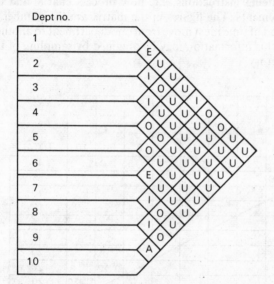

Figure 6.7 *A relationship chart (derived from the cross chart in Figure 6.6).*

General requirements of a layout planning procedure

To be of value, any procedure must:

1. take as its objective(s) something that we believe to be of overriding, if not sole, importance;

2. (a) be capable of producing several good layouts, from which we might choose the best or most appropriate, or which can be modified to take into account additional objectives and/or constraints; *or*

   (b) work in such a way that the development of one layout, or a set of alternative layouts, is undertaken interactively, with the layout designer being given the opportunity to modify, adapt or select alternatives at each stage in the development of the layout(s);

3. (a) be capable of dealing with the situation in which an entirely new layout, or a set of alternative layouts, are to be developed from a set of data; *or*

   (b) cope with the situation in which an existing layout is to be improved, modified or changed in some way.

Taking point (1) above, we have previously agreed that our primary objective will often be that of minimizing total movement cost. Additionally we also often need a procedure which can accommodate:

(a) different floor areas for departments;
(b) a wide variety of flow patterns among departments;
(c) different costs of movement;
(d) the fact that certain departments may need to remain in a given position;
(e) the fact that, in certain circumstances, certain departments must have a given relationship with one another;
(f) the use of more than one floor.

In respect of 2(a) above, it will be appreciated that no procedure which satisfies the above requirements is likely to be optimal. In practice a heuristic procedure will be used, and in these circumstances the procedure should, preferably, develop several alternative layouts, since the designer is more likely to want to choose between alternatives, and perhaps modify these alternatives, than simply take one layout as being the most appropriate.

In respect of 2(b) above it may, alternatively, be appropriate to develop layouts interactively, i.e. to employ a method which does not simply produce one or more given layouts for a set of data, but which provides a procedure for moving towards a solution, with the opportunity to input additional information or modify the layout at various stages.

In respect of 3(a) and (b) above, any layout planning procedure which is to be of value in practice must be able to cope with the situation in which a new layout is to be planned and/or the situation in which improvements or modifications are to be made to an existing layout.

Computer programs

It was not until 1963 that procedures were developed which began to comply with at least some of the above requirements. In 1963 the first of many computer programs for layout planning became available. From that date there has been considerable interest in the use of computers in layout planning, and at the present time twenty or more such programs are available commercially. These programs have in some cases been developed to deal with specific situations. For example, some are 'complete design' programs in that they are capable of providing a complete layout from a set of input data, while others are 'improvement' or 'modification' programs which in effect seek to modify, improve or change an existing layout in order to satisfy certain new or additional requirements. The majority of the programs which have been developed to date would satisfy 1, 2(a) and 3 above, but only recently have programs been developed which will satisfy requirements 1, 2(b) and 3. The early programs, which were designed for batch processing on mainframe computers with line printer output, were not interactive. More recently, however, there has been an emphasis on the development of interactive programs, and in particular on the use of computer graphics in facilities layouts, possibly as part of a comprehensive computer-aided design/computer-aided manufacturing approach.

So far computer programs for layout planning have not found widespread use. Where used they have tended to provide only marginally better layouts than might have been achieved by using a systematic manual method. There are several problems, the difficulty of preparing data and the restricted number of factors which can be taken into account being perhaps the most important. However, rapid progress is being made, and such methods, particularly interactive and graphics-based methods, will find widespread application.

Some programs are listed in Table 6.4. The source of the program is given where known. Further details on some of these programs are available from the sources listed in 'Further Reading' at the end of this chapter.

Table 6.4 *Some computer programs for facilities layout planning*

Program	Source (where known)	References at end of chapter
ALDEP	Program Number 360D–23.0.004 Share Program Library Agency Triangle Universities Computation Centre Post Office Box 12076 Research Triangle Park, North Carolina 27709	Seehof and Evans (1967)
COFAD	Program Number 360D–23.0.001 Share Program Library Agency Same address as ALDEP	Tompkins and Reed (1973)
COL COMP 2	Mr Eric Teicholz Laboratory for Computer Graphics Graduate School of Design Harvard University Cambridge, Massachusetts	Teicholz (1968)
COMPROPLAN and COMSBUL	Mr Kaiman Lee Perry, Dean & Steward 955 Park Square Building Boston, Massachusetts 02116	Lee (1971)
CORELAP	Program Number 360D–23.0.002 Share Program Library Agency Same address as ALDEP	Lee and Moore (1967)
Interactive CORELAP	Engineering Management Associates 590 UR c/o North Eastern University Boston, Massachusetts 02115 USA	Moore (1971)
	University of Nottingham, UK	O'Brien and Abdel Barr
COSFAD	Dr J. A. Tompkins Department of Industrial Engineering Box 5511 North Carolina State University Raleigh, North Carolina 27607	Tompkins (1976)
CRAFT	Program Number 360D–15.6.003 Share Program Library Agency Same address as ALDEP	Armour and Buffa (1963)
FATE (an extension of MAT)		Block (1978)
FRAT	—	—
GRASP	Mr Eric Teicholz Same address as COMP 2	—
HC. 66	—	—
IMAGE	Dr T. E. Johnson Department of Agriculture Massachusetts Institute of Technology	Johnson (1970)
LSP	—	—

Program	Source (where known)	References at end of chapter
MAT	Dr H. K. Edwards General Motors Institute Flint, Michigan, 48502	Edwards, Gillett and Hale (1970)
OFFICE	Dr T. E. Vollman Management Science Department College of Business Administration University of Rhode Island Kingston, Rhode Island	Vollman, Nugent and Zartler (1968)
PLANET	Program Number 360D–23.0.003 Same address as ALDEP	Apple and Deisenroth (1972)
PLOP (Modification of CRAFT)	ICL Ltd, UK	
PLANTAPT	Department of Production Management and Manufacturing Technology Strathclyde University Glasgow	Carrie (1980)
(Based on CRAFT)	F. R. Jacobs Department of Management University of Houston Houston, Texas 7004	Jacobs, Bradford and Ritzman (1980)
PREP	—	—
QUAINT	T. E. Block Department of Mechanical Engineering University of Melbourne Australia	Block (1976)
RMA COMP 1	Mr R. Muther Richard Muther and Associates, Inc. 6155 Oak Street Kansas City, Missouri 64113	Muther and McPherson (1970)
SUMI	Professor W. R. Spillers Civil Engineering Department Columbia University 116th and Broadway New York 10025	Spillers and Weidlinger (1970)

Non-interactive programs

In this section we shall describe the *original* versions of three programs. They were the first to become widely available and are described here not because they are the best or the most useful, but because they are indicative of the *type* of approach which can be employed when using a computer-based layout planning procedure.

CRAFT (Computerized Relative Allocation of Facilities Technique) (Armour and Buffa (1963))

CRAFT was developed in order to satisfy requirements 1, 2(a), 3(a) and 3(b) above and has as its objectives the minimization of total materials handling costs. The program requires an initial layout to be input at the beginning. It can therefore be considered as an 'improvement' or 'modification' *procedure*; however, it is in fact intended for the design of new layouts, since the initial layout can be an arbitrary one.

A simplified flow diagram for the program is shown in Figure 6.8.

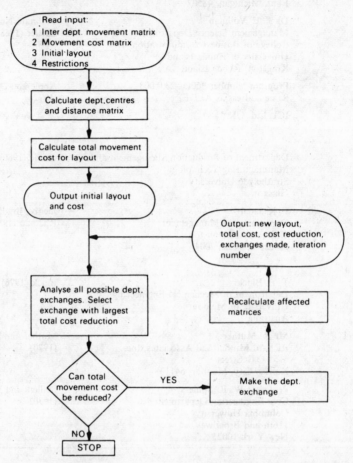

Figure 6.8 *Simplified flow chart for CRAFT program. From Armour, G. C. and Buffa, E. S. (1963) A heuristic algorithm and simulation approach to the relative location of facilities, Management Science, 9(2). Reproduced with permission.*

The necessary input is:

(a) interdepartmental flow matrix, which gives the number of unit loads moving between all departments over a given period of time (this matrix need not be symmetrical);

(b) interdepartmental movement cost matrix, giving the cost per unit distance of movement between all departments (this matrix need not be symmetrical);

(c) initial layout configuration showing the size of departments, arranged so that one line can be represented by an 80-column punch card (it may be an arbitrary or an existing layout);

(d) any restrictions, i.e. fixed departments which cannot be moved.

The program then attempts to improve on the initial layout by interchanging pairs of departments. Every pair of departments is examined and the effect of their interchange on the total movement cost for the layout is calculated. The pair change giving the greatest reduction in total movement cost is effected and the process is repeated until no further interchange of departments will provide any additional reduction in the total movement cost associated with the layout.

The algorithm by which the program operates is as follows:

1. Determine which pairs of departments may be interchanged. Departments are considered for interchange when they are adjacent, of equal area, or bordering on a common third department.
2. Calculate the distance between departments, the distances being taken as those between the centres of the departments.
3. Calculate the reduction in total movement costs resulting from the interchange of all possible pairs of departments.
4. Interchange the two departments which provide the greatest saving in total movement costs.
5. Calculate the total movement cost and print out the revised layout.

This procedure is repeated until no further cost saving is possible, and then the final layout is printed.

CORELAP (Computerized Relationship Layout Planning (Lee and Moore (1967))

CORELAP was developed about 1967 and adopts a quite different approach to layout planning. It satisfies requirements, 1, 2(a) and 3(a) and is intended for use in the design of new layouts. Unlike CRAFT, CORELAP concerns itself only with the latter part of the layout problem, i.e. developing an acceptable layout from given preferable departmental relationships. In fact a relationship chart of the type described previously (Figure 6.7) forms part of the input to this program, the rest of the input being: (a) departments and their required areas; and (b) a maximum building length to width ratio.

Lee and Moore, who developed this program, adopted the following rather unusual terminology:

Victor: a department which has earned the privilege of being next to be placed in layout.
Winner: a Victor which has been placed earlier in the layout.

Each of the closeness ratings used in the relationship chart, i.e. A, E, I, O, U, is given a numerical value, and the total closeness rating (TCR) for each department is calculated by adding together the values for that department's relationships with all other departments. Departments are listed in descending order of TCR, and the department with the highest TCR is the first to be placed in the layout, i.e. it becomes the first Winner. This department is placed in the middle of the layout and the program then asks, 'Which department is to be placed next?' and 'Where is this Victor to be placed in the layout?'. The program searches the relationship chart to determine if any departments have an A relationship (the highest relationship) with the first Winner. If there are any departments with A relationships then the one with the highest TCR becomes the first Victor and it is positioned in the layout as close as possible to the Winner. Other departments with A relationships with the Winner are then placed in the layout, those with the highest TCR first. They are placed as close as possible to the Winner, and also as close as possible to any other departments already in the layout with which they have a desired relationship. When all departments with an A relationship with the first Winner have been placed, the first Victor becomes the second Winner and the procedure is repeated until all departments with an A relationship with the second Winner have been placed. When all departments with an A relationship with the first and subsequent Winners have been placed, the complete procedure is repeated for E, I, O and finally U relationships. A simplified flow diagram for the programme is shown in Figure 6.9.

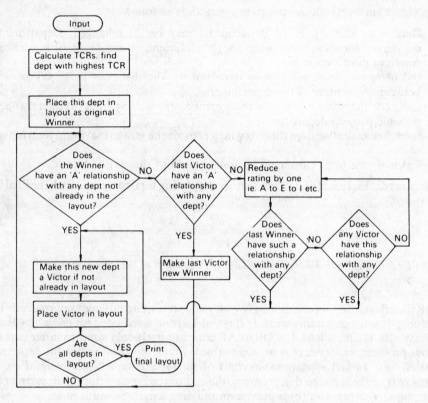

Figure 6.9   *Simplified flow diagram for CORELAP program.*

The advantage of this approach is that, since layouts are developed from stated, preferred relationships, all the necessary reasons for a desired relationship between departments can be taken into account in developing the layouts, unlike CRAFT, which depends solely on product flow.

A further advantage of CORELAP is that an initial layout is not required, the only constraint being the maximum building length to width ratio. This ratio is necessary to ensure that the program does not develop unrealistic layout configurations, e.g. very long, thin layouts.

ALDEP (Automated Layout Design Program (Seehof and Evans (1967))

ALDEP is similar to CORELAP in that it employs a preference ratings approach. The program either generates a series of random layouts and selects that with the best total performance score, or generates one random layout and then makes comparisons and exchanges between pairs of areas until no further improvement of the total preference score is possible.

Several detailed comparisons of these three programs have been made (e.g. Muther and MacPherson (1970)). Numerous other programs are available for the design of new layouts, and many authors have surveyed their use and made comparisons.[1]

Interactive programs and computer graphics

Interactive CORELAP (Moore (1971))

Interactive CORELAP was introduced around 1971, since when it has been further developed. The program is able to handle both new plant and existing plant problems. It permits certain departments to be placed in a fixed location, and scores any alternative layout. The program is designed to be run in an interactive manner from a terminal on a time-sharing computer. The designer, at the terminal, can interrupt the program to make adjustments, or the program might interrupt itself when it gets into a particularly difficult situation in order to seek further information and/or assistance from the designer. At any stage the designer can ask the program to cost alternative layouts, and he or she may move departments around in much the same way as moving templates around on a drawing board. The more recent developments of interactive CORELAP provide for graphical input and output of information. Data can be input through a keyboard, but in addition can be generated directly by the designer on the terminal screen, and alternative layouts can be displayed there for inspection and modification.

Other interactive programs are available specifically for use in non-manufacturing situations. For example, that described by Jacobs et al (1980) provides an interactive improvement procedure.

Computer-aided design (CAD)

The availability of powerful interactive computer *graphics* facilities has opened new possibilities for computer-aided facilities layout planning. In particular the introduction of Computer Aided Design (CAD) permits the development of layouts in an interactive fashion, with the possibility of storing layout information, modifying layouts, and printing out departmental and plant layouts using high speed plotters. In considering the use of CAD it is important to distinguish two applications.

---

[1] Moore, J. M. (1974) Computer aided facilities design: an international survey, *International Journal of Production Research*, **12**(1), pp. 21–44.
Moore, J. M. (1980) Computer methods in facilities layout, *Industrial Engineering*, September, pp. 82–93.
Schriabin, M. and Vergin, R. C. (1975) Comparison of computer algorithms and visual based methods for plant layout, *Management Science*, **22**, p. 172.

At the simplest level CAD provides for computer-assisted drafting. This is of some relevance in facilities layout planning, in that it provides an alternative to the use of the drawing board or the use of templates on a scale model, but it does not itself provide a procedure for the development of layout plans and therefore does not satisfy the requirements listed earlier. At a more sophisticated level, CAD also provides a procedure or algorithm for the design of layouts from certain input data, whether for an existing or for a modified layout, with the opportunity for the designer, seated at a graphics terminal, to interact directly with the computer. The computer develops a layout plan which is shown at each stage on the terminal screen. The designer may interrupt the program as required to impose particular requirements on the layout or to try out alternatives. This interruption can take the form of direct manipulation of the layout on the screen using either digitizing tablet and/or light pens, and may also involve the input of additional information through the terminal keyboard. Through this 'on-line interactive' procedure many alternative layouts will be developed for subsequent modification or choice, and ultimately the chosen layout will be printed out in full or in part, in detail. The CAD facility can be used in preparing details, e.g. for the location of services, pipe lines, services to the buildings, etc., all of which can be stored for subsequent reference or modification and provided as detailed drawings through a line plotter. At the time of writing such programs are becoming available and are of use in facilities layout planning in engineering, manufacture, architecture, the health services, etc.

MODIFYING EXISTING LAYOUTS

Many of the computer-based procedures described above will be of relevance when modifying existing layouts. For example, the CRAFT procedure requires the input of an initial layout which it then seeks to improve, given certain traffic information and movement cost. CRAFT is in effect an 'improvement' program. Other 'improvement' programs include COFAD, HC.66, COL and FRAT. The use of these programs may be of relevance where an existing layout is to be modified, e.g. the addition of a new department, the redistribution of space in existing departments, or the relocation of one of the existing departments.

Another approach concerned essentially with the addition of new facilities to existing facilities is described below.

Level curves

Suppose we wish to position one additional facility in an existing single-floor layout. Adopting the same movement cost objective, and knowing the facilities to and from which the new facility will send and receive material or customers, we can calculate for every point in the layout a numerical value which represents the total cost of movement to and from that point. For example, for an existing layout consisting of one facility, a position five metres away will be twice as attractive as one ten metres away. Where we can calculate the cost of several points in the layout and then join up these points of equal cost we can produce an isocost curve. These curves we shall call level curves, since they can be considered as analogous to contour lines on maps. For a single facility, straight-line movement example, the level curves are shown in Figure 6.10.

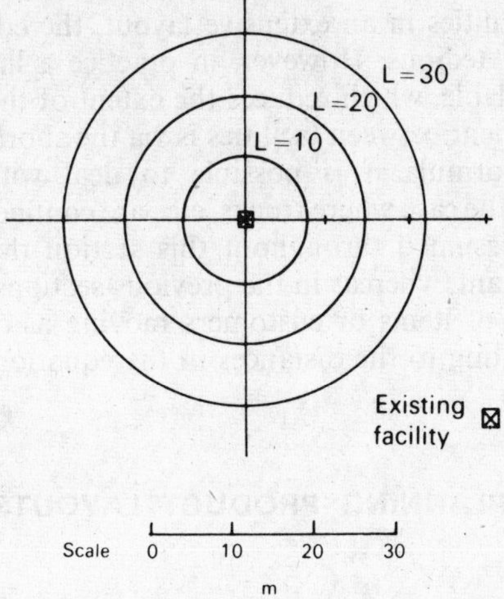

Figure 6.10 *Level curves for a single existing facility layout, assuming straight line movement.*

Where L equals the cost value of a point, and x and y = ordinates of existing facilities.[2]

$$L = \left| \sqrt{x^2 + y^2} \right|$$

In the case of n facilities existing at positions $x_1\, y_1; x_2\, y_2; x_3\, y_3; \ldots\, x_n\, y_n$, the L value for any point x, y is given by:

$$L = \sum_{i=1}^{n} \left| \sqrt{(x - x_i)^2 + (y - y_i)^2} \right|$$

For example, Figure 6.11 shows the level curves for a layout with four existing facilities.

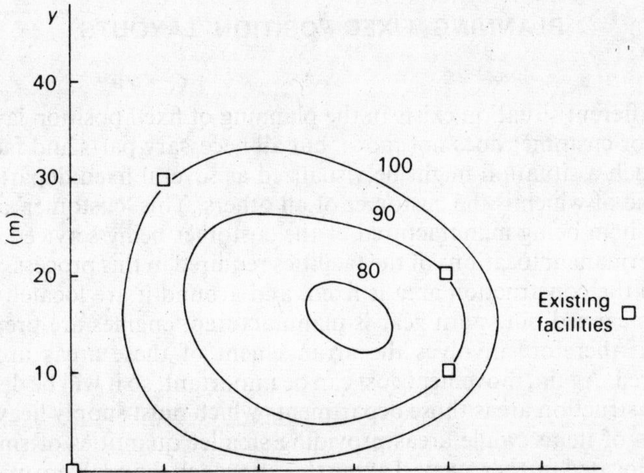

Figure 6.11 *Level curves for the location of one facility among four existing facilities.*

---

[2] || indicates that the value contained is taken to be a positive value only.

Two disadvantages of this method are evident. First, where the problem involves the positioning of several facilities in an extensive layout, the construction of level curves becomes rather long and tedious. However, in practice a limited number of possible locations are usually available, which reduces the extent of the calculations. Second, we have assumed that movement between facilities is via the shortest direct route. However, with a more complex formula it is possible to deal with movements which are 'rectangular', as would be the case where trucks, etc., are confined to a series of orthogonal aisles. We have further assumed throughout this section that movement between all facilities is equally important, whereas in the previous sections we used a product of the distance and the number of items or customers moving as our criteria; however, it is possible to apply a weighting to the distances in the equations.

PLANNING 'PRODUCT' LAYOUTS

The approaches discussed above are concerned primarily with minimizing movement, whether of materials or of people. They are of particular relevance in planning functional/ process layouts, and can be used for planning layouts in which facilities are organized on a product or, group basis. As such, therefore, they are relevant in certain types of manufacturing and non-manufacturing situations. The planning of product-type layouts, whether in manufacture or service systems (e.g. flow or assembly lines, or flow-processing customers through specialist service systems), may require a somewhat different approach, and this is discussed in some detail in Chapter 15, which deals solely with the design of flow processing systems. The approaches described there are concerned not only with the configuration of facilities but also with the balancing of the resources within each of those facilities. The problem is often referred to as that of 'line balancing'.

PLANNING 'FIXED POSITION' LAYOUTS

A somewhat different situation exists in the planning of fixed position layouts. Here the principal item or customer does not move, but all necessary parts and facilities move to and from it. Such a situation might be visualized as several fixed departments or areas within a site one of which is the customer of all others. This 'customer' area is the fixed location of the item being manufactured or the customer being serviced, while all other areas are the permanent locations of the facilities required in this process. For example in building a ship the construction area is fixed, and around it are located areas in which plating work is carried out, stern gear is manufactured, engines are prepared, etc. The layout problem therefore involves the arrangement of these areas around the main construction area. Again, movement cost can be important, so it will be desirable to place close to the construction areas those departments which must supply heavy items and/or large quantities of items, while areas providing smaller quantities of smaller or lighter items might be located further away. Taking this approach the problem may be tackled by one of the methods outlined above, since in effect we are planning a process-type layout in which the flow pattern is largely one in which all departments communicate with a supply department.

PLANNING SUPPLY AND STORAGE LAYOUTS

While the above methods, which focus primarily on movement, may be relevant in planning the layout of supply and storage systems, it is appropriate to consider such systems separately, since in these cases other factors may also be of some importance.

The facilities layout problem in supply systems often involves the location of display and/or storage areas to which customers have direct access. The arrangement of display and shelving areas in a supermarket is a good example of the type of problem often encountered. In such cases there will be a need to minimize total movement for most customers. Thus the procedures referred to above will be of relevance providing that those responsible for layout planning have some data concerning the average or typical customer's needs in terms of goods or items to be acquired. Given this information, shelving and passageways can be arranged so that, with a knowledge of the layout, customers may collect their goods with the minimum of movement. Other factors, however, are of relevance in the planning of the layout and should be introduced at this point. For example, the arrangement of displays and storage in supply systems such as supermarkets is also a function of display-type considerations. It is, for example, well known that 'traffic' patterns in supermarkets follow a particular form, with most customers preferring, initially at least, to travel around the edges of the area rather than along intermediate aisles and passageways. It is known that goods displayed at the end of the aisle tend to sell better than those placed in the middle of an aisle and that goods stored in such a way that they can be seen from the entrance or through windows attract the customer to the store. Thus it might be argued that the arrangement of such facilities must take into account certain customer-oriented factors rather than simply concentrating on retailer-oriented factors such as maximum use of space, minimum transport, etc.

The arrangement of storage areas such as warehouses also necessitates the consideration of factors other than movement. In such cases there is often a conflict between the need to obtain maximum space utilization and the need to minimize the cost of movement. For example, maximum space utilization often involves high stacking, whereas the storage of items in this manner often necessitates the use of expensive materials handling equipment and therefore gives rise to high movement costs. The arrangement of passageways is also of considerable importance, while the possibility of future expansion, the need to accommodate new items which may have different dimensions or different weight, the need to locate items associated with one another in the same area, the need to provide secure areas for other items, etc., are all of some importance in layout planning.

EVALUATION OF ALTERNATIVE LAYOUTS

The comparison of alternative layouts is a necessity in many of the procedures described above. The emphasis there was on movement criteria, and it will be appropriate here to look at this need from a broader perspective.

Determining which of many alternative layouts to adopt is often a very difficult problem. If we consider all the possible features and characteristics then our list is likely to be very long indeed. If, on the other hand, we consider only the problem of movement and evaluate the alternative layouts only in this light, we shall very probably neglect certain quite important considerations and be guilty of sub-optimization. One factor should be common to whatever considerations we adopt: cost. We must, as a rule, aim to minimize the total cost involved in establishing and using the layout. Muther, referring specifically to manufacturing systems, has suggested that layouts should be evaluated on the basis of the following costs:

1. Investment:
   (a) Initial cost of new facilities of all kinds:
       (i)   *buildings
       (ii) *construction
       (iii) *machinery
       (iv) *equipment
   (b) Accessory costs:
       (i)   tools, jigs, fixtures
       (ii)   *handling equipment
       (iii) *containers
       (iv)   benches and chairs
       (v)   timeclocks, water coolers, etc.
       (vi)   *shelves, bins, racks
       (vii) wiring and lighting
       (viii) piping and ducting
   (c) Installation costs:
       (i)   *building changes
       (ii)   *machinery and equipment
       (iii) *services and supporting facilities
       (iv)   *auxiliary service lines
   (d) Depreciation and obsolescence costs
2. Operating costs:
   (a) Material:
       (i)   production
       (ii)   scrap and waste
       (iii) supplies and packing
       (iv)   maintenance parts and materials
   (b) Labour:
       (i)   direct
       (ii)   overtime or extra-shift premium
       (iii) idle or waiting time
       (iv)   efficiency variation
       (v)   clerical
       (vi)   maintenance
       (vii) inspection
       (viii) *handling and storerooms
       (ix)   other indirect labour
       (x)   supervision
   (c) General:
       (i)   *floor space
       (ii)   power
       (iii) fuel
       (iv)   taxes
       (v)   insurance
       (vi)   rentals
       (vii) interest on investment

This is not the most comprehensive list that could be suggested, but even so it is a little difficult to appreciate how certain of these items will vary with different layouts, or to understand how some depend on layout at all. We would suggest that in the majority of cases cost items marked with an asterisk will be the most important. Nevertheless, in certain circumstances many of the other costs will merit consideration. The comparison and evaluation of designs for completely new layouts is a difficult problem, and, while such factors as movement, cost of equipment, space required, etc., are normally the principal components of comparison, they are by no means the only components.

The evaluation or rearrangement of parts of factories or departments constitutes an easier problem only because of the relative lack of size of the layouts, and not because fewer factors need be considered.

MATERIALS HANDLING

The fact that we have considered the minimization of total movement cost as one principal objective in planning facilities layout is sufficient evidence of the importance of efficient handling and the efficient management of movement in most operating systems. Although we have adopted the title 'Materials Handling' we should emphasize that the management, i.e. the efficient planning and control of movement in all types of systems, is of considerable importance, whether that movement relates to raw materials, finished goods, customers or indirect materials. Movement of materials, work in progress and finished goods is of crucial importance in all manufacturing operations. The movement of customers and goods is clearly of ultimate importance in transport systems, while the handling, i.e. the organization of the movement of customers and items, is of considerable importance also in supply and service systems. Here, therefore, we are concerned with the movement of customers or items (whether materials or finished goods) into or out of stores, during processing, into the operating system, and from the operating system to the final customer.

Efficient materials handling (i.e. the movement of items or customers) can bring considerable cost benefit to operating systems. Work in progress might be reduced; accidents or losses might be reduced; the capacity of the operating system might be increased; speed of processing, i.e. the throughout time, might be improved; level of service to the customer, e.g. the waiting time and the number of stock-out situations, might be improved; total space required by the operation might be reduced; etc. Naturally there are equally substantial costs involved in designing, installing, staffing and maintaining an efficient system, including both recurrent and capital costs, so the design and planning of the system must be undertaken with a full awareness of, and therefore after, detailed analysis of movement needs, conditions, requirements and constraints, both present and future.

Materials handling objectives

The principles of efficient materials handling are listed in Table 6.5, from which it will be seen that an early objective should be the elimination of the need for handling or movement, or, failing that, a reduction in the need for such handling or movement. This might be achieved by more appropriate layout of the operating facilities, by combining operations with movement, etc. The *necessary* handling/movement should be organized in as efficient a manner as possible. This will often involve the minimization of 'pick-up/put-down' movements, the use of unit loads and pallets, the use of straight line movement, the use of mechanical rather than manual movement, and the separation of items which require subsequent separate processing.

Table 6.5 *Principles of efficient materials handling*

1. Eliminate need for handling/movement (e.g. by eliminating unnecessary movement and by suitable arrangement of processes)
2. Combine processing and movement
3. Plan layout of operations together with planning of materials handling to minimize handling/movement
4. (In general) use mechanical handling where regular high volume movement is required or where safety hazards exist
5. Arrange handling/movement to minimize number of 'pick-up/put-down' movements
6. Use unit loads and use pallets and containers to avoid damage, reduce subsequent handling, etc.
7. Avoid mixing items/materials which subsequently need to be separated
8. Use straight line movement

Methods for materials handling

We cannot discuss the details of materials handling technology here, and it would be inappropriate to do so. However, some consideration of the *types* of handling equipment and their applications will be appropriate.

Table 6.6 identifies the principal classes of materials handling equipment and suggests some of the normal applications for such equipment. In this table the applications are considered in terms of the type of movement required, i.e. whether predominantly overhead, vertical, a combination of vertical or horizontal, or largely horizontal (having a fixed route, or with a variable, i.e. non-fixed, route). Certain types of equipment conventionally operate at a constant speed, although often on an intermittent basis. Conveyors normally fall into this category. Other equipment, e.g. trucks, cranes, is able to operate at variable speeds.

The selection of appropriate materials handling equipment will be determined by the types of applications required as well as by factors of the type listed in Table 6.6. Principal among these (see Table 6.7) are the types of materials/items/customers to be moved, their volume or weight, the frequency and regularity of movement and of course the extent to which this movement requirement is temporary or 'permanent'. The movement route, particularly whether fixed or variable, and the extent to which this route is influenced by existing constraints such as the location of equipment, the shape of buildings, etc., will be of considerable importance. In certain cases the speed of movement is determined; e.g. the handling of hot items may require a speed of movement differing from that needed for the handling of fragile items. In certain cases the speed of movement required is low, since some form of processing is associated with the movement; e.g. in the brewing industry, movement, storage and maturing often occur simultaneously. The type of storage employed, both before and after movement, will influence the type of materials handling equipment envisaged, as will considerations of safety and the needs of concurrent and subsequent processes.

A recent development in materials handling in industry is the use of 'unit load procedures'. The use of pallets, containers and other unit load handling is often associated with unit load storage procedures. Such an approach might be considered as a form of batch materials handling in situations in which larger quantities of identical or similar items are collected together into a container, pallet or other device for convenience in storing and handling. Alternatively, unit load procedures are used as a form of 'kit' handling and storage where a variety of different yet complementary items are collected together so that the entire unit or 'kit' contains all necessary items for a particular purpose, e.g. for the manufacture or assembly of a particular item.

Table 6.6 *Methods for materials handling and their applications*

Class of equipment	Type of equipment	Speed (v = variable; c = constant)	Overhead	Vertical	Vertical/horizontal	Horizontal fixed route	Horizontal non-fixed route
Cranes	Gantry	v	✓	✓	✓		
	Mobile (e.g. truck)	v	✓	✓	✓		
	Revolving	v	✓	✓	✓		
Lifts	Elevator	v		✓			
	Escalator	v		✓			
	Bucket	c		✓			
Trucks	Fork	v					✓
	Hand	v					✓
	Tractor	v					✓
	Sideloader	v					✓
	Platform	v					✓
	Pallet	v					✓
	Straddle	v					✓
Conveyor	Belt	c				✓	
	Roller	c				✓	
	Flight	c			✓	✓	
	Pneumatic	c			✓	✓	
	Screw	c				✓	
	Slatted	c				✓	
	Vibrating	c				✓	
	Drag chain	c				✓	
Towing	Overhead chain	c	✓			✓	
	Overhead monorail	v	✓			✓	
	Floor	c				✓	✓
Chute	Gravity	c		✓	✓		
	Spiral lift	c	✓				

Table 6.7 *Factors influencing selection of materials handling equipment*

Materials/items	to be moved i.e. size, weight, nature (e.g. fragility or hazards)

Volume/rate	of movement
	i.e. frequency of movement
	    volumes to be moved
	    regularity of movement
	    temporary or 'permanent' need

Route of movement	i.e. whether fixed or variable, or complex (or straight line) and whether influenced by building layouts, etc.
Speed of movement required	i.e. speed required/necessary (e.g. fast for hot items, slow for fragile items)
Storage	method employed (for storage before and after movement) i.e. how and where stored (e.g. pallets, unit loads, loose, packed, etc.)
Safety/hazards	involved e.g. fire hazards, spillage risks, etc.
Concurrent processing	involved or possible e.g. whether movement can be combined with processing

CHECKLIST FOR CHAPTER 6

The need for layout planning
  Enlarging/reducing departments
  Moving a department
  Adding a department
  Replacing/adding facilities
Objectives in layout planning
  Movement
  Turnover
  Space and resource utilization
Facilities layout problems
  (a) Departments
  (b) Facilities in departments
  (c) Workplaces
  Examples of (a)
Basic types of layout
  Manufacture
    (a) Process/functional
    (b) Product
    (c) Fixed position
    (d) Group
    Comparison of (a) and (b)
    Break-even comparison of (a), (b) and (c)
  Non-manufacturing
    Supply and service
    Transport
    Examples
Layout planning procedure
  Demand
  Capacity
  Work methods and standards
  Resource requirements
  Handling and movement
  Space requirements

  Other factors
  Layout planning method
Layout planning methods
  Movement criteria
Planning new layouts
  Cross and relationship charts
    Weighted cross chart
  Sequence analysis
  General requirement of a procedure
  Computer programs
    Non-interactive
      CRAFT
      CORELAP
      ALDEP
    Interactive and graphics
      Interactive CORELAP
      CAD
Modifying existing layouts
  Computer programs for 'improvement'
  Level curves
Planning 'product' layouts
  Line balancing
Planning 'fixed position' layouts
Planning supply and storage layouts
Evaluating alternative layouts
  Investment
  Operating cost
Materials handling
  Objectives
  Principles
  Methods
  Factors influencing selection of methods
  Automated handling and storage

FURTHER READING

Buffa, E. S. (1965) Sequence analysis for functional layout, *Journal of Industrial Engineering*, **6**, (2), pp. 12–15. A description of sequence analysis.

Francis, R. L. and White, J. A. (1974) *Facilities Layout and Location*. Hemel Hempstead: Prentice-Hall. Contains a detailed comparison of CRAFT, CORELAP and ALDEP.

Gunn, T. G. (1982) The mechanization of design and manufacture, *Scientific American*, **247** (3) (September), pp. 87–108. Discusses CAD, CAM and flexible manufacturing systems.

Muther, R. (1973) *Systematic Layout Planning*. Boston: Cahners.

Tomkins, J. A. and Moore, J. M. (1977) *Computer Aided Layout—A User's Guide*. Facilities Planning and Design Division of American Institute of Industrial Engineers, Publication No. 1.

Woodley, D. R. (1964) *Encylopaedia of Materials Handling*. Oxford: Pergamon.

Computer programs

Apple, J. M. and Deisenroth, M. P. (1972) A computerized plant layout analysis and evaluation technique (PLANET), Proceedings, American Institute of Industrial Engineers, 23rd Annual Conference, pp. 121–177.

Armour, G. C. and Buffa, E. S. (1963) A heuristic algorithm and computer simulation approach to the relative location of facilities, *Management Science*, **9** (1), pp. 294–309.

Block, T. E. (1978) A new construction algorithm for facilities layout, *Journal of Engineering Production*, **2**, p. 11.

Block, T. E. (1976) Users Guide: QUAINT Report No. DR2/76, Department of Mechanical Engineering, University of Melbourne, Australia.

Carrie, A. S. (1980) Computer-aided layout planning—the way ahead, *International Journal of Production Research*, **18** (3), pp. 283–294.

Edwards, H. K., Gillett, B. E. and Hale, M. E. (1970) Modular allocation technique (MAT), *Management Science*, **17** (3), pp. 161–169.

Jacobs, R. F., Bradford, J. W. and Ritzman, L. P. (1980) Computerized layout, *Industrial Engineering*, July, pp. 56–61

Johnson, T. E. (1970) IMAGE: An interactive graphics based computer system for multi-constrained spatial synthesis, MIT Department of Architecture.

Lee, K. (1971) Computer programs for architects and layout planners, Proceedings, 22nd AIIE National Conference.

Lee, R. C. and Moore, J. M. (1967) CORELAP—Computerized relationship layout planning, *Journal of Industrial Engineering*, **18** (3), pp. 195–200.

Moore, J. M. (1971) Computer program evaluates plant layout alternatives, *Industrial Engineering*, **3** (19).

Muther, R. and McPherson, K. (1970) Four approaches to computerized layout planning, *Journal of Industrial Engineering*, **2** (2), pp. 39–42.

O'Brien, C. and Abdel Barr, S. E. Z. *An Interactive Approach to Computer Aided Facility Design* (unpublished).

Seehof, J. M. and Evans, W. O. (1967) Automated layout design programme, *Journal of Industrial Engineering*, **18** (12), pp. 690–695.

Spillers, W. R. and Weidlinger, P. (1970) An algorithm for space allocation, *Proceedings, 5th Annual Association for Computing Machinery, Urban Symposium*, pp. 142–150.

Teicholz, E. D. (1968) Architecture and the computer, *Architecture Forum*, pp. 27–32.

Tompkins, A. (1976) Safety and facilities design, *Industrial Engineering*, **8** (1), pp. 38–42.

Tompkins, J. A. and Reed, R. (1973) Computerized facilities design, *Proceedings, American Institute of Industrial Engineers, 25th Anniversary Conference and Convention*, Chicago, pp. 75–84.

Tompkins, J. A. and Reed, R. (1975) Using the computer to solve your layout and handling problems, *Modern Materials Handling*, **30** (4), pp. 40–43.

Vollman, T. B., Nugent, C. E. and Zartler, R. L. (1968) A computerized model for office layout, *Journal of Industrial Engineering*, **19** (7), pp. 321–327.

QUESTIONS

6.1 The following cross chart has been constructed by means of observations of all movement between the seven production departments of a factory over a typical one-month period. In addition to these seven production departments, there are three other departments: the general office, the drawing office and the personnel department. The general office should preferably be close to the assembly department but not close to the test department. The drawing office should preferably be close to assembly, stores and the general office, but must not be close to the test area. The location of the personnel department is comparatively unimportant; however, it should not be too far away from any of the production departments. The relative location of the production departments depends on materials flow only, as shown in the figure.

Construct a relationship chart showing the desirable relative locations of each of these ten departments. Use an appropriate notation to indicate the desired proximities.

	R	S	T	M	G	A	T
Receiving	40					3	3
Stores		20	20				
Turning			18	2			
Milling				18	20		
Grinding					10	10	
Assembly						38	
Testing					5		

6.2 'Visual or graphical minimization is the only satisfactory and practical method of designing facility layouts, and the minimization of total movement costs is the most appropriate objective function during layout planning.' Discuss.

6.3 Determine a rectangular layout consisting of the eleven departments of a hospital included in the table below.

Department	Part					Department area (m²)
	A	B	C	D	E	
1	2	2	2	2	2	500
2	3	7	3	4	3	400
3	5		4		4	200
4			7	6	7, 7	600
5	7					200
6	9	9		10	4	500
7	6	8	8		8, 9	1000
8		6	9		6	500
9	10	10	10		10	800
10	11	11	11	11	11	500
11						

	A	B	C	D	E
Loads/month	50	100	250	100	100

6.4 What are the fundamental differences between the methods of layout planning adopted in the two computer programmes CRAFT (computerized relative allocation of facilities technique) and CORELAP (computerized relationship layout planning)?

Make a comparative evaluation of each of these programs in respect of each of the following:

(a) input requirements;
(b) limitations as regards departments and factory shape, size and configuration;
(c) the heuristic procedures used and the 'objective functions';
(d) the value of the program for planning layouts of non-industrial facilities.

6.5 What factors, other than the cost of movement, need to be considered during the planning of a new layout, and how is the consideration of these factors included in the whole layout planning procedure?

6.6 Evaluate the comparative merits of locating an additional facility at points A, B and C in the four existing facility layouts shown below. You may assume that all movement between

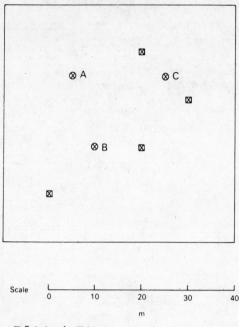

Scale

| 0 | 10 | 20 | 30 | 40 |

m

⊠ Existing facilities

the new facility and each existing facility is equally costly, and that movement is by the shortest direct route.

6.7 Discuss the requirements of the handling systems and identify appropriate types of handling equipment for the following applications:

(a) the handling of passengers' baggage (other than hand baggage) in an airport terminal;

(b) the movement of metal waste from the machine shop of a mass-production engineering company;

(c) the movement of goods from the goods receiving department through stores, onto shelves, and to customers in a large supermarket.

PART 4

WORK AND WORK SYSTEMS

INTRODUCTION TO PART 4

In this part of the book we shall concentrate on work systems. We shall focus on human work, i.e. the execution of tasks by people within the operating system, and in so doing we shall look at some traditional and established areas of responsibility of operations management as well as at some newer topics.

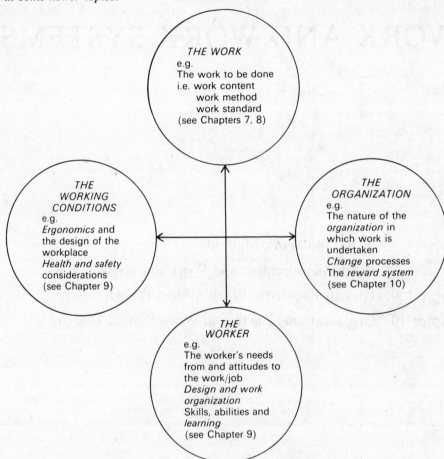

THE WORK
e.g.
The work to be done
i.e. work content
    work method
    work standard
(see Chapters 7, 8)

THE
WORKING
CONDITIONS
e.g.
Ergonomics and
the design of the
workplace
Health and safety
considerations
(see Chapter 9)

THE
ORGANIZATION
e.g.
The nature of the
organization in
which work is
undertaken
Change processes
The *reward system*
(see Chapter 10)

THE
WORKER
e.g.
The worker's needs
from and attitudes to
the work/job
*Design and work
organization*
Skills, abilities and
learning
(see Chapter 9)

Considerations in the design of work systems

Operations management decisions covered in other parts of the book will also affect the nature of the work which must be undertaken by people within the operating system. For example, the scheduling system (Chapters 12 to 15), the design of the product/service (Chapter 3) and the quality control system (Chapter 19) all have some influence on the nature of the tasks and work required within the system. The topics covered in this part, however, are concerned primarily with work. We shall look at work methods, work standards, the rewards for work, the problems of learning, people's attitudes to work, the design of the workplace, health and safety considerations, etc. All these topics are interrelated. For our purposes we can perhaps identify four sets of considerations which must be taken into account in the design of work systems. We might take as our focus the design of the work itself, i.e. the specification of the tasks to be performed—the work content, the determination of appropriate methods of executing these tasks and the establishment of standards of performance for this work. This work focus is a necessary but insufficient consideration in the design of work systems. We might take as our focus the conditions in which people work, that is the design of the workplace, the ergonomics of the workplace, and health and safety considerations. Again, this is a necessary but insufficient consideration. An important aspect to consider is the workers themselves: workers' needs, motives, expectations and attitudes, their skills, abilities, the need to learn, etc. This worker focus is a necessary but insufficient consideration. We might take an organizational focus and consider the nature and design of the organization in which the work is to be undertaken, the reward or payment system for such work, etc. Again this is a necessary but insufficient consideration. These four sets of considerations, outlined in the figure opposite, are each examined in the following chapters. No one set of considerations is more important than any other. All must be taken together.

CHAPTER 7

Work and Work Methods

NOTATION USED IN THIS CHAPTER

D	Delay
□	Inspection
O	Operation
▽	Storage (or hold)
⇨	Transportation
MTM	Methods time measurement
PMTS	Predetermined motion time system
SIMO	Simultaneous Motion

Certainly the situation is changing, but it is still very much the case that in most types of business human manual work is of considerable importance. The development and use of robotics, automation and information technology has influenced and will continue to influence the number of people employed and the nature of their work. The need for people to work in hazardous conditions, the need for manual work in information storage and retrieval, etc., is reducing, but people still work in large numbers in mines, at sea, in offices, in factories, etc. Production workers, dentists, surgeons, typists, agricultural workers, etc., spend a considerable part of their time in manual activities. Such human work must be specified and designed. Tools, equipment and workplaces must be designed. In many cases standards or estimates of the time required to undertake particular tasks must be obtained for scheduling, capacity planning, training or payment purposes. Even the work of a robot must be designed and measured.

In this chapter we shall look largely at the design of human manual work, i.e. the specification of work methods. This we shall refer to (using the European terminology) as method study. In Chapter 8 we shall deal with measurement of work, the establishment of work standards, etc., using the term work measurement. Chapters 7 and 8 deal with the subject which is generally referred to as work study. Elsewhere it is referred to as time and motion study or in some cases industrial engineering.

In this chapter, although the focus is on work methods, we shall begin by considering the nature, relevance and purpose of work study.

WORK STUDY

The nature of work study

Work study is concerned primarily with human manual work and therefore is relevant in all types of operating systems. Specifically, it is concerned with the efficient design and execution of manual work, and with the establishment of standards of performance. Work study is practised extensively in manufacturing, services, transport and supply industries and some of the major developments in the subject took place in the service sector, e.g. in hospitals, and in transport. It is a fairly controversial subject. The principles were laid down many years ago; they still exist and are applied, but not without criticism. The work study practitioner, in whatever industry, will now be concerned with applying the principles of method study and work measurement in a sensitive and adaptable way, in particular taking into account work conditions, the characteristics of workers, and behavioural and organizational factors.

The history of work study

There are many examples, particularly during the Industrial Revolution, of people being concerned with what has since become known as work study, but the most important contributions were made by three Americans: Taylor, Gilbreth and Bedeaux.[1]

F. W. Taylor (1856 to 1915) was concerned principally with the time factor in work. He realized that the overall time for jobs were of little value as standards of performance, and that times for 'elements' of jobs were more useful if methods were to be examined. Taylor believed that management should accept the responsibility for planning and organizing work. His main objective was to treat work and management in a 'scientific' manner and to replace subjective procedures. He was responsible for introducing the production planning function and for developing a bonus system based on time studies of jobs.

The work of the Gilbreths (Frank and Lilian) was contemporary with, and complementary to, that of Taylor. Frank Gilbreth (1868 to 1924) was concerned with the methods by which jobs were done, and believed that once optimum methods were established the time factor would look after itself. He was responsible for defining the 17 fundamental movements by which all manual work could be described, and helped to develop the 'principles of motion economy' by which better work methods could be developed.

---

[1] The work of Taylor and Gilbreth is described briefly in Urwick, L. (1956) *The Golden Book of Management*. Oxford: Newman Neame. Little has been written about Bedeaux; however, R. L. Currie devotes a little space to him in *Work Study*, Pitman, London, 1968.

Charles Bedeaux was responsible for introducing the concept of rating in order to determine how observed times differ from the times which should be required. He attempted to construct an objective system of time study by which work methods could be compared and on which incentive schemes could be based. In Bedeaux's system a common unit was used to describe work on any particular job; furthermore, the time unit included rest and relaxation allowances.

From the work of these pioneers developed what was later known as the scientific management movement, the first comprehensive 'theory' of management. The concept of the best way of doing a job was fundamental to this approach, and although workers tended to be regarded merely as extensions of machines, their increased earnings were regarded as adequate compensation for the repetitive work life they had to lead.

Contemporary work study sprang from this background. The historical association with repetitive work, in particular the belief that the practice of work study in a rigorous, traditional and narrow fashion has led to the establishment of repetitive, highly rationalized work, gave rise to the need to extend, if not modify, some of the traditional principles of work study. In the late 1960s and through the 1970s there developed subjects such as job design, work organization and the humanization of work. Here the emphasis was on the worker, his or her role, motivation, satisfaction, skills, abilities and rewards. This development, together with the further development of ergonomics, coming at a time of increasing technological change, e.g. the introduction of automated processes, robotics, etc., led to the establishment of a broader and more comprehensive framework for the design of work.

Chapter 9 will be devoted entirely to human, behavioural and organizational factors in the design and organization of work and work systems. That chapter is an essential aspect of this part of the book, since Chapters 7 and 8 will initially present a fairly straightforward description of 'conventional' work study principles and practices.

The applications of work study

Work study, as described above but practised under different titles, is of relevance wherever manual work is undertaken, and in particular where such work is of a fairly repetitive nature, i.e. where it is both possible and appropriate to seek to examine and establish appropriate work methods, and where it is appropriate and necessary to establish work standards. Work study, time and motion and such aspects of industrial engineering are well established in manufacturing industries, building and building services, the health services, transport, the military, etc. (See Table 7.1.)

In planning the layout of facilities and methods and procedures for the handling of materials, etc., it will often be necessary to conduct some form of work study investigation. Wherever it is necessary to obtain estimates for the duration of activities for the purposes of scheduling, capacity management, work/worker allocation, incentive payments, etc., some form of work measurement will be needed. The study of work methods will be necessary for the development of training plans, for the design of workplaces, for the design of equipment, and in satisfying health and safety requirements at the workplace. Whether undertaken as a particular discipline or profession by work study 'professionals' or undertaken by those involved in other aspects of operations management, the topics covered in this and the following chapters are of considerable importance and relevance.

Table 7.1 *Some examples of the applications of work study (method study and work measurement)*

Type of operation	Examples	Applications of method study	Applications of work measurement (other than to obtain standards for examples in previous column)
Transport systems	Road freight	Devise most appropriate method of loading and unloading vehicles	To obtain standard times for certain vehicle repair/service refuel operations
	Passenger bus	Devise best method of fare collection and ticket issuing for 'one-person' operated buses	To obtain standard journey times
	Passenger airline	Devise best method of emergency evacuation of airline on ground	To obtain standard times for flight deck pre-flight checks
Service systems	Hotel	Devise most appropriate procedure for customer check-in, registration, key issue, etc.	To obtain standard time for cleaning a bedroom
	Dentist	Devise best layout of equipment and work procedure for filling a tooth	To obtain standard time for a 'clean and polish'
	Hospital	Devise most appropriate procedure for routine patient screening/testing	To obtain standard time for specific medical activities, e.g. eye test, blood test, pathological analysis, etc.
Supply systems	Post office	Devise most appropriate allocation of different activities to tellers/counters (e.g. change, traveller's cheques, pensions, etc.)	To obtain standard time for opening a new account
	Supermarket	Devise most appropriate layout and work method at check-out desks	To obtain standard time for replenishing shelves
	Mail order	Devise most appropriate procedure for filling an order, e.g. 'picking and packing' goods	To obtain standard time for processing a telephoned order
Manufacturing systems	Motor vehicle production	Devise best method for an operation on an assembly line	To obtain standard time for the service of a piece of equipment
	Construction	Devise best method and layout of equipment for brick laying	To obtain standard time for tiling roofs (e.g. per square metre)
	Brewing	Devise most appropriate method of packing bottles into crates and/or stacking crates	To obtain standard time for a line change-over, i.e. from one product to another

The structure and purposes of work study

Throughout these two chapters we shall use the British terminology and, where possible, the British Standard definitions.[2] The British Standards Institution defines work study as

---

[2] BS 3138, *Glossary of Terms in Work Study*

'a generic term for those techniques, particularly method study and work measurement, which are used in the examination of human work in all its contexts, and which lead systematically to the investigation of all the factors which affect the efficiency and economy of the situations being reviewed, in order to effect improvements'.

The aims of work study are, by analysis of work methods and the materials and equipment used, to:

(a)   establish the most economical way of doing the work;
(b)   standardize this method, and the materials and equipment involved;
(c)   establish the time required by a qualified and adequately trained worker to do the job, while working at a defined level of performance;
(d)   install this work method as standard practice.

Work study, then, is a comparatively low-cost way of either designing work for high productivity or improving productivity in existing work by improving current work methods and reducing ineffective or wasted time. In each case the design or improvements are sought within the context of existing resources and equipment; consequently work study is an immediate tool and is not dependent on the redesign of goods or services, research and development of operating processes, or extensive rearrangement of facilities.

We must apply the technique in circumstances from which we expect maximum returns. The economic results of the study, whether they are increases in output, reduction in scrap, improved safety, reduction in training time, or better use of equipment or labour, should always outweigh the cost of the investigation, and to attempt to ensure this we should consider:

(a)   the anticipated life of the job;
(b)   whether manual work is an important part of the job, e.g. (1) the wage rate for the job, (2) the ratio of machine time to manual time in the work cycle;
(c)   utilization of equipment, machines, tools, etc., the cost of such equipment, and whether the utilization is dependent on the work method;
(d)   the importance of the job to the company, e.g. the output quantity, profit margin, and so on.

We should distinguish between work study of existing jobs and that of proposed or anticipated jobs. Whenever new products are to be made or new equipment used, jobs must be designed. Consequently the question is to what extent work study should be used and how much effort is justified by the importance of the job. Some investigation may be necessary on existing jobs, not necessarily because they were inadequately designed in the first place, but perhaps because there has been a slight change in the product, new equipment is being used, or wage rates or incentives are to be altered. Examinations of existing work methods could also result from low machine utilization, excessive labour overtime or idle time, complaints from the workers, inadequate quality, high scrap or wastage rate, etc.

Figure 7.1 shows the structure of work study. Two aspects exist: first, method study, concerned with establishing optimum work methods; and second, work measurement, concerned with establishing time standards for those methods. One can consider methods without considering time, although in practice this rarely occurs. Occasionally the reverse applies. i.e. work measurement is conducted without prior method study. Method study is normally conducted before work measurement. Apart from the possible need to compare the times for old work methods with the times for new methods, work measurement conducted before method study is poor practice.

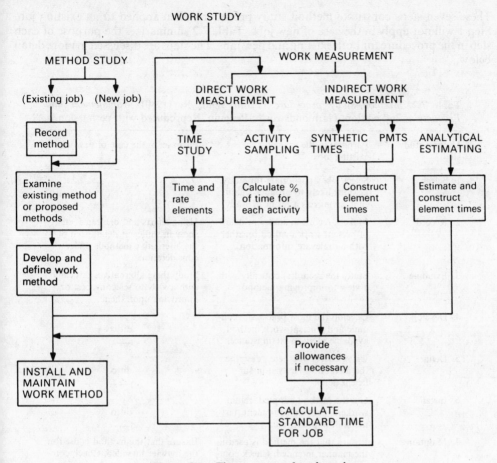

Figure 7.1 *The structure of work study.*

METHOD STUDY

'Method study is the systematic recording and critical examination of existing and proposed ways of doing work, as a means of developing and applying easier and more effective methods and reducing costs.'[3] The method study procedure consists of a maximum of seven steps:

1. Select the work to be studied.
2. Record the existing work method and all other relevant facts.
3. Examine the method.
4. Develop the most efficient or optimum method of doing the work.
5. Define the method.
6. Install this method as standard practice.
7. Maintain this practice.

---

[3] BS 3138

These seven steps constitute method study procedure when applied to an existing job. Step 1 will not apply in the case of new jobs. Table 7.2 summarizes the purpose of each step in the procedure for both existing and new jobs. The steps are discussed in more detail below.

Table 7.2 *Method study procedure* (From Wild, R. (1980) *Management and Production*, 2nd edition. Harmondsworth: Penguin. Reproduced with permission.)

Method study step	Purpose: in the case of existing jobs	Purpose: in the case of new jobs
1. Select	Select jobs appropriate for study, i.e. jobs likely to produce significant savings as a result of study	
2. Record	Make a record in sufficient detail of present work method together with all relevant information	Using charts and diagrams, etc., show in sufficient detail each of the alternative methods under consideration
3. Examine	Study the record(s) critically with a view to improving method	Study these alternatives critically with a view to selecting best or improving upon them
4. Develop	Develop the most practical, economic and efficient work method available in given circumstances	ditto ◁——
5. Define	Using charts, lists, etc., describe the method to be used in sufficient detail	ditto ◁——
6. Install	Get the method adopted, retain workers, provide equipment, test method, improve, etc.	ditto ◁——
7. Maintain	Ensure that the method is used in the manner intended. Check complaints and check improvements in productivity, etc.	Ensure that the method is used in the manner intended. Check complaints and measure productivity

Step 1: Select the job to be studied

The problem of selecting the work to be studied has been mentioned above. Maximum potential cost benefit is the normal objective. Direct cost of labour, materials and equipment is certainly the main component of total cost, but indirect cost, such as the cost of supervision, training, recruitment and welfare, is also relevant. Although work methods may affect each of these costs there is a tendency to emphasize direct costs, and to develop work methods which minimize the cost of labour, machinery and materials. This approach can be criticized by those who are concerned with the human or behavioural implications of work design (Chapter 9). They point out that factors such as labour absenteeism and labour turnover may result from the nature of the work, and that work design should be evaluated in a broad manner.

Step 2: Record the work method

The objective here is to obtain a record of the work method for subsequent examination. We must discuss two aspects:

(a) the type of record which is to be obtained (the principal distinction between the different types being the amount of detail provided);
(b) the procedure by which this record is to be obtained, e.g. by direct observation or subsequent examination of films, video tapes, etc.

These two aspects, of course, are interrelated. Certain procedures will be appropriate for obtaining records with a particular level of detail, whereas other procedures will be appropriate for obtaining a less detailed record of work methods.

Types of records

We shall first consider the type of record. We shall begin by considering records which provide relatively little detail of the work method: such records might be appropriate for a preliminary investigation of a work method. Later we shall look at more detailed records which might be appropriate for detailed critical examination of existing work methods with a view to improvement and/or where a subsequent objective is to establish a work standard for the method. In the latter context it is worth noting that the subsequent use of the record may determine the type of record and the type of notation which will be employed. For example, if a work standard is to be developed using a predetermined motion time system (PMTS) (e.g. MTM, see Chapter 8) then the record of the method must be in sufficient detail, and must employ the same terminology as the appropriate PMTS system.

The principal types of records are listed in Table 7.3.

1. *Diary*

Usually a self-recording of the work method by the worker himself or herself. Usually fairly little detail is obtained, and often the record is in the form of a diary of activities or movements. This method of recording might be appropriate as a first means of establishing the amount of time devoted to particular jobs, etc.

2. *Flow diagrams*

Three types of flow diagram are in general use. *A flow diagram* (see Figure 7.2) shows the location and sequence of the activities carried out by workers and the routes followed by materials, components, etc. A *string diagram* is a scale diagram (or model) on which coloured thread wrapped around pins or pegs is used to indicate the paths taken by workers, materials or equipment during a sequence of activities. String diagrams are a

Table 7.3 *Types of recording* (Based on Wild, R. (1980) *Management and Production*, 2nd edition. Harmondsworth: Penguin. Reproduced with permission.)

Type of record	Definition (where appropriate from BS 3138)	Amount of detail	Applications
1. Diary	A record of a work method, normally constructed by the worker himself or herself, in the form of a diary or list of activities	Usually very little, e.g. often just a diary of activites or movements	To establish amount of time devoted to particular jobs, etc.
2. Flow diagrams (a) Flow diagram	A diagram or model substantially to scale which shows the location of specific activities carried out and the routes followed by workers, materials or equipment in their execution	Shows location with respect to departments, etc. and sequence of principal activities	Particularly useful as a means of studying layout
(b) String diagram	A scale plan or model on which a thread is used to trace and measure the paths of workers, materials or equipment during a specified sequence of events	Shows only extent and nature of movement between areas	Particularly useful as a means of studying layout
(c) Travel chart	A tabular record for presenting quantitative data about the movement of workers, materials or equipment between any number of places over any given period of time	Gives in quantitative terms extent of movement between areas	Particularly useful as a means of studying layout
3. Multiple activity charts (activity analysis)	A chart on which the activities of more than one subject (worker, machine or equipment) are each recorded on a common timescale to show their interrelationship	Difficult to record more than a limited number of types of activity, e.g. working, idle, delay, etc.	As a preliminary investigation, or to study extent of occurrence of particular activities
4. Process charts (a) Outline	A process chart giving an overall picture by recording in sequence only the main operations and inspections	Shows principal elements only, i.e. operations and inspections	As a preliminary investigation
(b) Flow process chart for worker	A process chart setting out the sequence of the flow of a product or a procedure by recording all events under review using the appropriate process chart symbols. This chart gives a record of all events associated with the worker	Operations, inspections, movements and delays associated with the worker	Normally used as the principal means of recording work methods
(c) Flow process	A process chart setting out the sequence of the flow of a product or a procedure	Operations, inspections, movements, delays and storage of	ditto

	Description		
material	using the appropriate process chart symbols. This chart gives a record of all events associated with the material	Operations, inspections, movements, delays and storage	ditto
(d) Flow process chart for worker and material	A process chart setting out the sequence of the flow of a product or a procedure by recording all events under review using the appropriate process chart symbols. This chart gives a record of all events associated with worker and material		ditto
(e) Flow process chart for equipment	A process chart setting out the sequence of the flow of a product or a procedure by recording all events under review using the appropriate process chart symbols. This chart shows how equipment is used	ditto	
(f) Two-handed (or operator)	A process chart in which the activities of a worker's hands (or limbs) are recorded in relationship to one another	Shows work method in same detail as above for each hand of operator at a given workplace	Operations at a workplace. To provide greater detail than other types of process chart
5. SIMO (simultaneous motion chart)	A chart, often based on film analysis, used to record simultaneously on a common timescale the Therbligs or groups of Therbligs performed by different parts of the body of one or more workers	Equivalent to above but gives much more detail, i.e. in terms of 'work elements'	Where considerable detail is required, or as convenient record of film analysis
6. Memomotion	A form of time lapse filming which records activity frame by frame at longer intervals than normal. The time intervals usually lie between $\frac{1}{2}$ second and 4 seconds	Little detail but compacts activities occurring over a long period of time into shorter periods	For studying jobs with long cycle times, or jobs involving many people and movement over a large area
7. Cyclegraphic (a) Cyclegraph	A record of a path of movement, usually traced by a continuous source of light on a photograph, preferably stereoscopic	Paths of movement of limbs within a fixed area	Movement of limbs at workplace (infrequently used)
(a) Chrono-cyclegraph	A cyclegraph in which the light source is suitably interrupted so that the path appears as a series of pear-shaped spots, the pointed end indicating the direction of movement and the spacing indicating the speed of movement	Details of direction and speed of movement of limbs within a fixed area	Movement of limbs at a workplace with added timescale

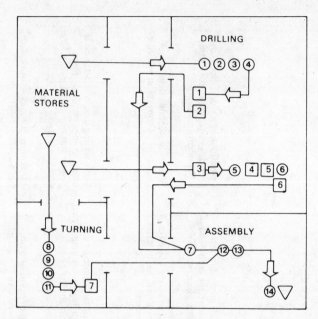

Figure 7.2   *Flow diagram (for the process shown in Figure 7.4).*

useful means of recording when complex movement patterns are involved and/or when the objective is to record and illustrate the movement of numerous items or workers. They can, like flow diagrams, be used to record movements throughout large areas, such as entire departments or buildings, or movement throughout smaller areas, such as individual workplaces. The *travel chart*, sometimes called the cross chart, is a slightly more sophisticated instrument for recording patterns of movement and the extent, e.g. volume, of movement between areas. Further details are given in the discussion of facilities layout planning in Chapter 6.

3. *Multiple activity charts*

These are also referred to as *activity analysis* or *worker and machine charts*. This type of record is of value where the activities of one or more workers and/or pieces of equipment are to be examined. The activities and their duration are represented by blocks or lines drawn against a timescale. It is not usually possible to include much detail on such charts, but colour or shading is often used to distinguish between:

(a)   independent work (worker working independently of equipment, e.g. reading instructions, preparing material, etc., or equipment working independently of worker);
(b)   combined work, where both worker and equipment work together, e.g. setting up, adjusting;
(c)   waiting time, by either worker or equipment.

Figure 7.3 shows a multiple activity chart for the operation of five identical pieces of equipment in a small office. The cycle of work consists of setting up the equipment,

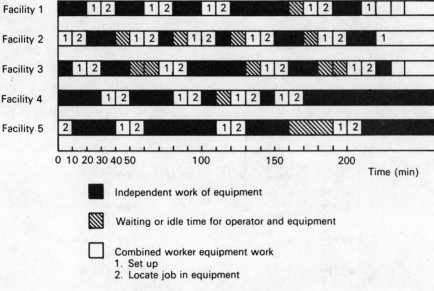

Figure 7.3 *Multiple activity chart.*

locating the job in it and finally performing an operation. A certain amount of idle or waiting time is also involved.

Multiple activity charts were used in a study of work methods in post offices. It had previously been the practice to allocate certain jobs to different counters in the post office, stamps and parcels being dealt with at one or more counters, and pensions, telegrams, licences, savings, etc., at others. Method study using multiple activity charts showed that the loads on the counters were by no means even. Certain items were dealt with throughout the day and throughout the week, whereas others were confined to particular periods. As result of the analysis it was possible to reallocate items to counters to provide a more even workload.

Multiple activity charts are also of value in studying maintenance jobs where work-loads are varied and uneven and where several products and machines are to be attended by one worker.

4. Process charts

The three types of process charts are certainly the most familiar of the method study recording procedures. The sequence of events is represented by a series of symbols which are basically the same for each type of chart. The symbols shown in Table 7.4 differ slightly from those originally developed by Gilbreth, but these are the ones currently used. The definitions are based on those suggested by the British Standards Institution.

An outline process chart (Figure 7.4) is a record of the main parts of the process only (i.e. the operations and the inspections). It is often used as a preliminary step in a method study investigation, prior to a more detailed study. Alternatively, outline process charts are often used to record basic information for use during the arrangement or layout of plant, during the design of the product, or even during the design of machinery for manufacturing the product. It is a simple record of the important 'constructive' and essential steps in a process, omitting all ancillary activities.

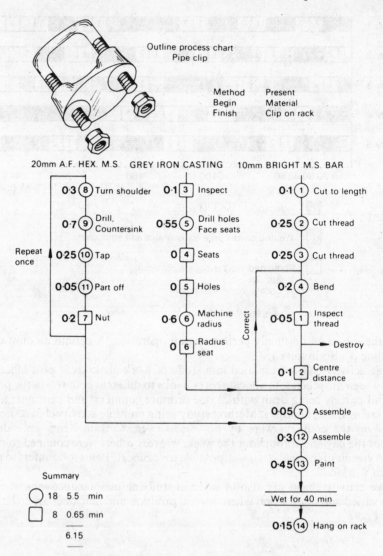

Figure 7.4 *Outline process chart.*

A flow process chart may be concerned with either materials (material flow process chart) or workers (worker flow process chart), or both. It is an amplification of the outline process chart and shows, in addition, the *transportations, storages* and *delays* which occur. In material flow process charts, *operations* occur when an object is intentionally changed in any way; *transportations* when an object is moved, except where such movement forms part of the operation; *inspections* when an object is examined; *storage* when an object is deliberately kept or protected against unauthorized removal; and *delay* when conditions do not permit the performance of the next activity. There is no storage symbol for worker flow process charts since it is assumed that the worker will never have cause deliberately to place himself or herself in confinement; otherwise the symbols for the two types of charts are the same. Figure 7.5 shows a simple worker-and-material flow process chart.

Table 7.4 *Process chart symbols*

Symbol	Process chart			Two-handed (or operator)
	Outline	Flow process chart		
		Worker type	Material type	
○	Operation	Operation	Operation	Operation
▷	—	Transportation	Transportation	Transportation
□	Inspection	Inspection	Inspection	—
▽	—	—	Storage	Hold
D	—	Delay	Delay	Delay

Note: Operation indicates the main steps in a process method or procedure. Usually the part, material or product concerned is modified or changed during the operation

Transportation indicates the movement of workers, materials or equipment from place to place

Storage indicates a controlled storage in which material is received into or issued from stores under some form of authorization, or an item is retained for reference purposes

Delay indicates a delay in the sequence of events, for example work waiting between consecutive operations, or any object laid aside temporarily without record until required

Inspection indicates an inspection for quality and/or a check for quantity

Hold indicates the retention of an object in one hand, normally so that the other hand may do something to it

A two-handed or operator process chart is the most detailed type of flow process chart, in which the activities of the worker's hands are recorded in relation to one another. Unlike the previous recording methods, the two-handed process chart is normally confined to work carried out at a single place. The ordinary symbols are used, except *inspection* is omitted since this can be represented by movements of the hands, and the *storage* symbol is now taken to mean *hold*.

Pre-printed charts are normally used, and the necessary comments, descriptions and explanations of activities are usually included in the record. The value of the chart is restricted by the rather broad meaning of the symbols, which prevent detailed descriptions of the movement of hands and arms from being shown. Furthermore, the paths and directions of movement are not shown on the chart. Nevertheless, this is certainly the most popular chart used to record movement when studying methods at a single location, and, while even more detailed recording methods are available, the occasions when the extra work involved is justified are infrequent. A two-handed process chart for a simple job is shown in Figure 7.6

5. *SIMO (simultaneous motion cycle) charts*

When it is necessary to study work in more detail than is possible using two-handed or flow process charts, a different notation and a different type of record is required. The recording method most frequently used is the SIMO chart which shows in detail the work method, usually for the worker's left and right hands. Two types of notations are available: 'Therbligs' and 'PMTS' notation.

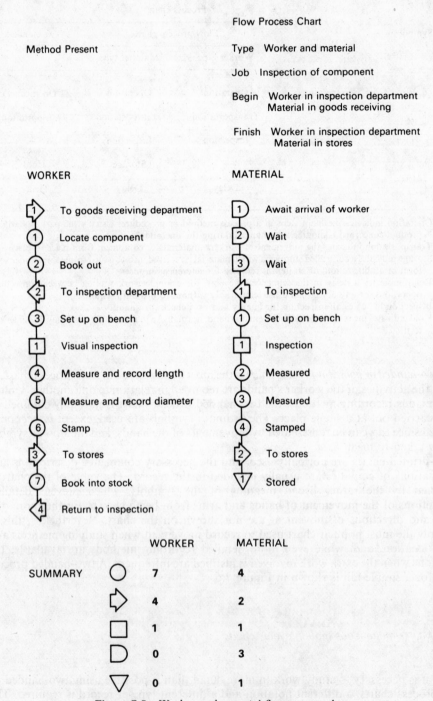

Flow Process Chart

Method Present

Type   Worker and material

Job   Inspection of component

Begin   Worker in inspection department
        Material in goods receiving

Finish Worker in inspection department
        Material in stores

WORKER		MATERIAL	
⟐ 1	To goods receiving department	1	Await arrival of worker
①	Locate component	2	Wait
②	Book out	3	Wait
◁ 2	To inspection department	◁ 1	To inspection
③	Set up on bench	1	Set up on bench
□ 1	Visual inspection	□ 1	Inspection
④	Measure and record length	2	Measured
⑤	Measure and record diameter	3	Measured
⑥	Stamp	4	Stamped
▷ 3	To stores	▷ 2	To stores
⑦	Book into stock	▽ 1	Stored
◁ 4	Return to inspection		

		WORKER	MATERIAL
SUMMARY	○	7	4
	▷	4	2
	□	1	1
	D	0	3
	▽	0	1

Figure 7.5 *Worker and material flow process chart.*

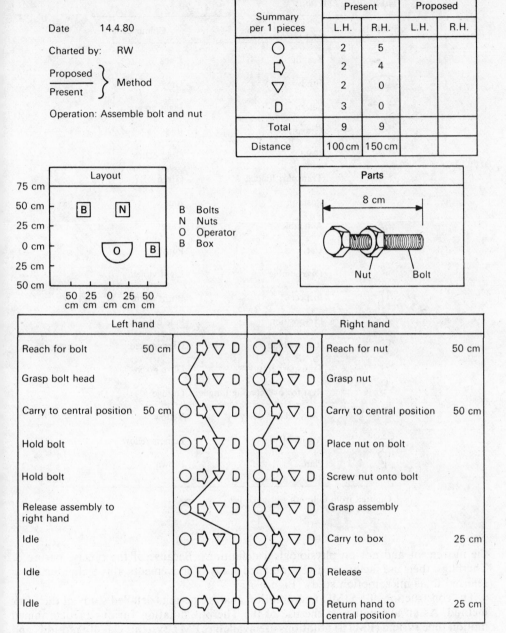

Figure 7.6 *Two-handed process chart.*

Frank Gilbreth was responsible for identifying and defining the 17 elementary or fundamental movements which together constitute all types of manual work. These Gilbreth called *Therbligs* (almost the reverse of his own name). Since Gilbreth's work (about 1924), one additional element has been added to the original list of 17 and the symbols have been altered. It is now conventional to use the symbols given in Table 7.5.

This classification of elementary movements is based on an analysis of the purpose of

Table 7.5 *Therbligs*

Symbol	Name	Colour code
 ⬭	Search	Black
 ⬭	Find	Grey
→	Select	Light grey
⌒	Grasp	Red
[a]  ⌓	Hold	Gold ochre
�	Transport loaded	Green
9	Position	Blue
#	Assemble	Violet
∪	Use	Purple
⫲	Disassemble	Light violet
0	Inspect	Burnt ochre
⌂	Pre-position	Pale blue
⟠	Release load	Carmine red
⌣	Transport empty	Olive green
⟒	Rest for overcoming fatigue	Orange
⌒o	Unavoidable delay	Yellow
 ⌣o	Avoidable delay	Lemon yellow
 ⟜	Plan	Brown

[a] Omitted from Gilbreth's original list

the movement and not on physiological definitions. Because of the precise nature of Therbligs, their use facilitates a very detailed study of movements, this technique being referred to as micromotion study (Figure 7.7).

The construction of a SIMO micromotion analysis permits detailed study of the work method. As an alternative to the use of the Therblig notation various predetermined motion time system (PMTS) notations are available. PMT systems classify motions and provide codes to identify each type and class of motion. They are of particular value in developing work standards, since each type and class of motion has a known standard time. The PMTS notion can be used in recording and describing the method, especially where it is intended to use the record subsequently to determine a standard time for the job. (See Chapter 8.)

In the methods of recording referred to previously, visual observation has been enough to obtain the data necessary to construct the charts. By contrast, in micromotion study, visual observation is often inadequate for identifying the detail required and consequently movie or cine photography is normally used. In this way work methods can be

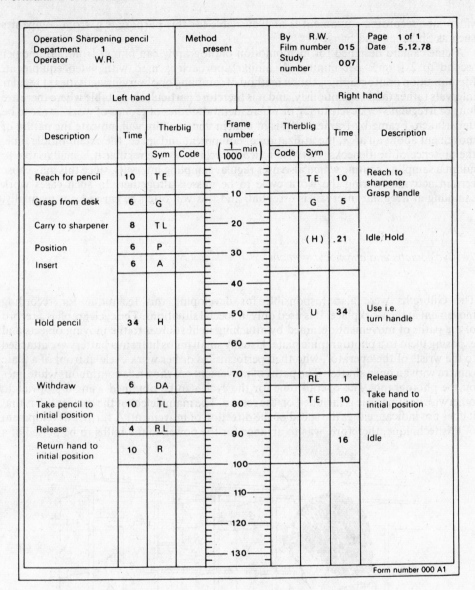

Operation Sharpening pencil Department 1 Operator W.R.			Method present			By R.W. Film number 015 Study number 007			Page 1 of 1 Date 5.12.78

Left hand				Right hand			

Description	Time	Therblig		Frame number $\left(\frac{1}{1000}\text{min}\right)$	Therblig		Time	Description
		Sym	Code		Code	Sym		
Reach for pencil	10	T E		— 10 —		T E	10	Reach to sharpener Grasp handle
Grasp from desk	6	G				G	5	
Carry to sharpener	8	TL		— 20 —		(H)	.21	Idle Hold
Position	6	P		— 30 —				
Insert	6	A						
				— 40 —				
Hold pencil	34	H		— 50 —		U	34	Use i.e. turn handle
				— 60 —				
				— 70 —		RL	1	Release
Withdraw	6	DA				T E	10	Take hand to initial position
Take pencil to initial position	10	TL		— 80 —				
Release	4	R L		— 90 —			16	Idle
Return hand to initial position	10	R		— 100 —				
				— 110 —				
				— 120 —				
				— 130 —				

Form number 000 A1

Figure 7.7 *SIMO (simultaneous motion) chart with Therblig notation.*

filmed and played back at various speeds, or even frame by frame, and from this the SIMO chart can be constructed.

6. *Memomotion filming and work sampling*

Memomotion filming is a technique for recording movements using equipment designed to take pictures at longer-than-normal intervals. Traditionally cine equipment is used, but video-tape recording equipment is now available for this purpose (e.g. from companies such as Shibaden and Sanyo).

A cine camera designed for memomotion photography can film at from 1 frame per second to 2 frames per minute. A similar approach is used with video equipment. Memomotion photography is thus a method of sampling or observing activities at regular intervals rather than continuously, and it is therefore particularly suitable where there are long or irregular work cycle times, or where method studies of groups of workers are to be undertaken. Frame-by-frame analysis of a memomotion film will indicate the nature of movement about an area, the utilization of equipment and space, the extent of idle time, the presence of bottlenecks, etc. Where work cycle times are regular it is inadvisable to adopt a sampling routine which also uses regular sampling intervals, since this may cause certain activities during the work cycle to be missed altogether. In such cases work sampling at irregular intervals is essential, and this will often be carried out manually.

7. Cyclegraphs and chronocyclegraphs

The Gilbreths were also responsible for developing this technique for recording movement at the workplace. It is used only in special situations. The cyclegraph is a record of the paths of movement obtained by attaching light sources to the moving objects and exposing them to a photographic plate. Usually small bulbs lit from a battery are attached to the wrists of the operator, who then performs his or her work cycle in front of a plate camera with an open shutter. The paths of movement are shown as continuous white lines on the photograph. The overall time for the cycle can be obtained using a stopwatch; otherwise no timescale is included on the record. The main defect of the cyclegraph is that it does not indicate either the speed or the direction of movement. A further development of this technique, therefore, was to arrange for the power to the bulbs to be pulsed at a

Figure 7.8 *Chronocyclegraph. From Larkin, J. A. (1969) Work Study – Theory and Practice. London: McGraw-Hill. Reproduced with permission.*

known frequency which could be adjusted according to the speed of movement. The record then appears as a dotted line, the spacing of the dots corresponding to the speed of movement and the pointed end of the pear-shaped dots indicating the direction of movement.

Figure 7.8 shows the type of pear-shaped dot that will appear on a photograph when a chronocyclegraph is taken.

Recording procedure

The type of record to be obtained, in particular the level of detail to be incorporated, will in part determine the recording procedure to be used. For example, a 'self-recording' procedure will be feasible for obtaining a diary-type record. The construction of a record of a work method by the worker himself or herself may also be feasible for some of the less detailed flow diagrams or process charts, but in general work method records will be obtained by an independent 'observer' adopting one or more of the procedures outlined below.

Direct visual observation

Direct observation of a work method will permit the development of any one of the records listed in 2 and 4 above, but when more detail is to be obtained, e.g. in two-handed and SIMO charts, the observer will need to watch several repetitions of the task. It may, therefore, take some considerable time to develop a process chart for even a short cycle-time task. Similarly, in developing a multiple activity chart several complete work cycles must be observed. Direct visual methods can be used without too much difficulty in developing outline process charts etc.

Recollection/memory

For simple tasks and for the development of records with little detail, it may be possible to describe a task, i.e. to prepare a method record directly from memory. The extent to which the recorder is familiar with the task will, of course, affect the accuracy and the level of detail which can be obtained.

Video and cine filming

Video (and less frequently, cine) filming is of considerable use in method study. A film or video record of a work method permits a permanent record to be held and also facilitates method analysis 'away from the job'. Such an approach has been found to be time saving, up to 30 per cent time saving being claimed in many cases for methods analysis of a job or subsequent development of the time standard for a method. If a video film of a method is obtained, process charts can subsequently be developed in any level of detail, or 'frame-by-frame' analysis can be undertaken to develop a micromotion record.

Electronic procedures

Increasingly, electronic portable 'data capture' terminals are used in work study. These are of particular use in time study, where the objective is to record the times for the elements of a job in order to determine the time required. The terminals will store such information and then transmit it to a computer for analysis. Some such terminals allow the type of work elements to be recorded as well as the elapsed time. Using an alpha/numeric code the keys on the terminal can be used to record the sequence of (predefined) work elements in a job for subsequent examination. (See Chapter 8 'Computers in Work Study'.)

Techniques have also been developed to enable the observer to dictate information about the job to be recorded into a tape recorder. *Tape data analysis* provides a 'terminology' and set of codes for this purpose, the tape subsequently being transposed/interpreted to provide a detailed work method record.

Step 3: Examine the method

The third stage of method study begins the constructive procedure. The purpose of recording the existing method is to enable subsequent examination and criticism. The recording method used should be sufficient to show all the relevant information, but of course not until we examine the record are we likely to know exactly how much information is needed. Therefore it may occasionally be necessary to repeat the second stage, either to obtain more detail of the entire work method or to enlarge upon certain areas.

Many procedures for examining and criticizing existing work methods have been suggested and adopted, but basically they simply involve asking six basic questions: Why? What? Where? When? Who? How?

Examine the process as a whole. The purpose of this is to define what is accomplished, how and why.

> Why was the process undertaken?
> What purpose does it serve?
> Where is it accomplished and why?
> When is it accomplished and why?
> Who is involved and why?
> How is it accomplished and why?

The answer to these primary questions will serve as a means of determining the effectiveness of the process as a whole, and should indicate whether or not any of the following major changes would be beneficial:

(a)   changes in material used;
(b)   changes in the design of the product;
(c)   changes in the nature or design of the process.

Examine aspects and parts of the process. The various activities in the process belong in one of two categories. Activities in each category must be examined and considered for elimination or change. First are those in which something is happening to the material or the product, i.e. it is being moved, inspected or worked on. Second are those in which nothing constructive is happening to the material or the product, i.e. it is being delayed or stored.

The first category can be further divided into *make ready, do,* and *put away. Make ready* activities are required to prepare the material or workpiece and set it in position ready to be worked on; *do* activities occur whenever the material or product is changed in shape, condition or composition; and *put away* activities occur when the material or product is moved away from the machine or workshop. (This may also constitute the subsequent *make ready* activity.) It is obviously beneficial to have a high proportion of *do* activities during the process and a low proportion of the others, since it is only *do* activities which carry the product towards completion, and it is only during these activities that value is added to the raw material.

Examination of these activities will question purpose, place and sequence, the person undertaking the activity and the means by which it is performed, in order to establish useful alternatives which subsequently can be examined and perhaps incorporated in an improved work method.

Step 4: Develop and improved work method

The device specifically designed for improving work methods is known as the *process improvement formula*. The formula, which consists of four steps—eliminate, combine, sequence, simplify—is applied to each separate activity in the job, i.e. to each meaningful group of work elements.

Complete *elimination* of unnecessary activities is clearly the most important step that can be taken in developing an improved work method. An activity may have been retained because of custom, history, inertia, inadequate communications, or even ignorance. Changes in materials, product design, process design, tools or the workplace may facilitate the elimination of activities. If elimination is not possible, then combination of activities should be considered. In many processes two or more activities may be usefully *combined*, e.g. drilling and facing holes, or drilling and countersinking holes. Changes in the *sequence* of activities is the next possibility, and this may then facilitate elimination or combination. Should none of these three steps succeed in eliminating or combining the activity then the last, more expensive step should be considered, i.e. attempting to *simplify* the activity by reducing the number of operations, reducing or eliminating delays and storage, or minimizing transportation. It may become necessary to conduct a more detailed motion study to obtain enough information to enable activities to be simplified, and again consideration should be given to changes in materials and to product and process design. The object of simplifying the activity is to permit the worker to complete the job more quickly and easily. The principles of motion economy shown in Table 7.6 provide a means of developing efficient work methods.

Step 5: Define the new method

It will be necessary to describe the work method to be adopted in sufficient detail for others to be able to install it or for subsequent use in training and instructions, etc. This definition comprises a statement of the nature of the work method and may be used

Table 7.6   *Principles of motion economy: use of the worker's body and design of the workplace, tools and equipment*

Use of the worker's body

1.   It is easier and more natural to work with two hands rather than one.
2.   The two hands should begin and complete their movements at the same time.
3.   The motion of the arms should be in opposite directions and should be made simultaneously and symmetrically.
4.   Hands and arms naturally move smoothly in arcs, and this is preferable to straight-line movement.
5.   Hand, arm and body movements should be confined to the lowest classification with which it is possible to perform the work satisfactorily, e.g. Gilbreth's classification of hand movements:
     (a) fingers
     (b) fingers and wrists
     (c) fingers, wrists and forearm
     (d) fingers, wrists, forearm and upper arm
     (e) fingers, wrists, forearm, upper arm and shoulder.
6.   Work should be arranged to permit natural and habitual movements.
7.   Movements should be continuous and smooth with no sharp changes in direction or speed.
8.   The two hands should not, except during rest periods, be idle at the same time.
9.   Whenever possible, momentum should be employed to assist the work and minimized if it must be overcome by the worker.
10. Ballistic movements are faster, easier and more accurate than controlled (fixation) movements.
11. The need to fix and focus the eyes on an object should be minimized and, when this is necessary, the occasions should occur as close together as possible.

Arrangement of the workplace

1.   There should be a definite and fixed position for all tools, equipment and materials.
2.   All tools, equipment and materials should be located as near as possible to the workplace.
3.   Drop deliveries of materials (and even tools and equipment) should be used whenever possible.
4.   Tools, equipment and materials should be conveniently located in order to provide the best sequence of operations.
5.   Illumination levels and brightness ratios between objects and surroundings should be arranged to avoid or alleviate visual fatigue.
6.   The height of the workplace and the seating should enable comfortable sitting or standing during work.
7.   Seating should permit a good posture and adequate 'coverage' of the work area.
8.   The workplace should be clean and adequately ventilated and heated.
9.   Noise and vibration, both local and general, should be minimized.

Design of tools and equipment

1.   Wherever possible, clamps, jugs or fixtures rather than hands should be used to hold work.
2.   Wherever possible, two or more tools should be combined.
3.   Wherever possible, tools and equipment should be pre-positioned.
4.   The loads should be distributed among the limbs according to their capacities.
5.   Wheels, levers, switches, etc., should be positioned to enable manipulation with the minimum movement of the body.

subsequently in the case of any disputes or misunderstandings. It may be referred to when work method changes are contemplated or when changes are considered to have taken place.

Steps 6 and 7: Install and maintain the new method

Clearly the first stage is to gain acceptance of the method from management, supervisors and workers. Then a programme for the installation of the method should be developed showing the main steps, those responsible for carrying them out, and the timetable involved. This will include time for training and the rearrangement of equipment, tools, workplaces, etc.

Finally, once the method is installed, a period of maintenance will be needed. Unless necessary or beneficial, deliberate or accidental alterations in the new work method should not be allowed, and periodic reviews should be conducted to ensure that the work method is satisfactory, that disputes do not arise, that earnings are maintained, and that complications in associated departments or with suppliers do not jeopardize the benefits of the new work method.

Computers in method study *(see also pp. 205–213)*

Increasingly, computers are being used in work study. They permit the rapid recording and analysis of data, storage of data for subsequent use, etc., and such applications benefit all aspects of work study, i.e. method study and work measurement. We shall look at some of these applications in the next chapter, but here we consider some uses of computers and computing *specifically related to method study*. Such applications can be seen to fall into one of three categories: methods development and analysis; methods description; and data storage and retrieval. In all cases the use of computers in method study will be justified more easily if computer-based work measurement is also to be employed. (See Chapter 8 'Computers in Work Study'.)

Methods development and analysis

Several computer programs or suites of programs are available to the work study engineer to assist in the development or analysis of work methods. A brief description of one set of programs will illustrate the types of facilities which are available.

The AUTOMAT methods generator is available commercially as part of a broader range of programs for computer-aided work study.[4] Using the AUTOMAT programs the work study practitioner may input certain information relating to the work method, the layout of the workplace, and the tools and equipment employed, from which the program determines the most appropriate work method and provides a detailed workplace layout with tool positions, etc. (The program will also produce a standard time for this method for subsequent use in the development of work standards; see Chapter 8.) The program uses the MTM notation for this purpose, so details of the work method must be input using the MTM notation, and the output is normally in the form of a type of SIMO chart (see above).

The system is quite flexible, so the work study practitioner can specify the work method in a variety of ways, and in different levels of detail, ranging from an outline operation description to a more detailed analysis of the method. Similarly, the workplace layout input can be in as much detail as is considered appropriate. The computer automatically generates a detailed workplace layout with positions of parts, tools, equipment, etc., and generates and prints an MTM description of an appropriate work method together with the standard times for that method. The program uses a set of heuristic procedures to

---

[4] Schofield, N. A. (1980) Computer aided work study using AUTOMAT and COMPUTE—practical tools for the industrial engineer, *International Journal of Production Research*, **18** (2), pp. 153–168. (Available as part of 'TIMELINK' system from Compeda, now part of Prime CAD/CAM Ltd.)

generate good work methods from the input information. If the initial input description of a method is in relatively little detail, i.e. if it is an outline description, then the computer program is capable of generating a detailed statement of an appropriate work method. The work method developed by the program takes into account the need to seek motion economies, etc. While developing the work method from the input data the program keeps and accumulates information to describe the operator's movements, idle time, distance travelled, number of body motions, etc. These measures can then be used to highlight bad methods of working, or as criteria for evaluating alternative methods. These measures of the 'efficiency' of the method can also be printed out together with the SIMO chart type description of a work method.

The type of program described above provides an opportunity not only for automatic development of work methods but also for rapid comparison of alternative work methods. For example, by varying the input slightly different methods will be developed and these can be compared against the criteria mentioned above, e.g. percentage idle time of each hand, distance travelled of each hand, percentage time spent in body movements, number of body movements, number of difficult motions. Other computer programs which are commercially available also provide such a facility. For example, the 4M DATA[5] computerized work measurement system (see also Chapter 8) also provides 'simulation capability'. This permits the work study engineer to try out several methods interactively with the computer before selecting the one to be used and requesting the computer program to develop a detailed statement of work standards etc. for that method.

Methods description

Less ambitious than methods development programs are those which seek only to provide detailed methods descriptions. These (e.g. the MOST computer system; see Chapter 8) require as input a description of a work method in at least outline and coded form. Then, using stored information from which detailed element descriptions can be obtained, and using one of the PMTS notations, the computer prints out a description in, for example, SIMO chart format of the job (usually with element and operation times; see Chapter 8). In this type of application the computer is taking over the detailed, often time-consuming task of preparing printed work-method descriptions in a usable format, often also drawing upon filed data for standard or commonly used elements or sequences of elements.

Data storage and retrieval

Most of the computerized work study programs provide a facility to store information on work elements, sequences of work elements and complete work methods together with information on tools, equipment, layouts and time standards. Such data will be of particular relevance in the development of work standards for jobs, and this will be discussed in the following chapter. Additionally, in developing and specifying work methods for new jobs, it may be possible to 'build up' a method simply by fitting together

---

[5] The 4M DATA MOD II computerized work measurement system, MTM Association for Standards and Research, 16-01 Broadway, Fairlawn, New Jersey 07410 USA.

appropriate sequences, etc., from the data file. With this type of facility it is possible to reduce considerably the time required to develop and specify the new work method. The method study analyst need only identify the major parts of the total job, and the computer program can then construct detailed methodology using the filed data.

CHECKLIST FOR CHAPTER 7

Work study
  The nature of work study
  History of work study
    F. W. Taylor
    F. and L. Gilbreth
    C. Bedeaux
  Applications of work study
  Structure and purposes of work study
    Definitions
    Aims of work study
    Which jobs to study
Method study
  Definition
  Seven steps of method study—purpose of
  each step—existing jobs—new jobs
  1. Select job to study
  2. Record work method
    Type of record
      Diary
      Flow diagrams
        Flow diagrams
        String diagrams
        Travel chart
      Multiple activity charts
      Process charts
        Symbols
        Types
        Outline
        Flow process

        worker
        material
        worker and material
        equipment
      Two-handed
      SIMO chart
      Memomotion
      Cyclegraphic
        cyclegraph
        chronocyclegraph
    Recording procedure
      Direct visual
      Recollection/memory
      Video and cine
      Electronic
  3. Examine the method
  4. Develop improved method
    Process improvement formulae
    Principles of motion economy
      Body
      Workplace
      Tools and equipment
  5. Define the new method
  6 and 7. Install and maintain method
    Training
    Maintenance
Computers in method study
  Method development and analysis
  Methods description
  Data storage and retrieval

FURTHER READING

Barnes, R. M. (1969) *Motion and Time Study*, 6th edition. New York: Wiley. This is still one of the best books on work study, though slightly confusingly arranged.

BS 3138, *Glossary to Terms in Work Study*, British Standards Institute, London, 1969.

Nadler, G. (1967) *Work Systems Design: The 'Ideals' Concept*. Homewood, Illinois: Irwin. A description of the ideals concept (ideal design of effective and logical systems), i.e. the design of the work system which will be the most effective in achieving a necessary function.

Seabourne, R. G. (1971) *Introduction to Work Study. 2, Statistics*. Harlow: Longman. An introductory book, also covering statistics and incentive payment systems.

Semprevivo, P. C. (1982) *Systems Analysis*, 2nd ed. Henley: Science Research Associates. This reference and the following one will be of interest to readers who also wish to consider systems analysis and management services—both topics related to the material covered in this chapter.

Walley, B. H. (1973) *Management Services Handbook*. Beekman.

QUESTIONS

7.1 Describe, with examples, the method study techniques you would use to investigate the work of:
  (a)   a team of six workers in a hotel reception/cashier area;
  (b)   a single worker on a short-cycle repetitive clerical task.

7.2 The Gobust Co. packs 'nick-nacks'. They are imported and weighed out in lots of $\frac{1}{2}$ kg. There are 12 'nick-nacks' to the kg, on average. The 'nick-nacks' must be inserted in a jar, to which a portion of 'nick-nack' juice is added. The jar is then sealed with a twist cap.
  (a)   Analyse the job. Develop a good sequence of work elements.
  (b)   Sketch the process flow and layout.
  (c)   Use an operation chart to detail the work involved.

7.3 The electric plug shown in Question 3.2 is to be assembled manually in large quantities. Develop a method of assembling the components of the plug and sketch the workplace layout. Use a two-handed process chart to indicate your method. You may approximate the element times.

7.4 Develop a method for manually assembling the pipe clip shown in Figure 7.4. Sketch the workplace layout and approximate the element times.

7.5 Draw up a micromotion analysis of the two-handed operation shown in Figure 7.6, using a SIMO chart and Therbligs.

7.6 What are the six important steps involved in performing a method study? Describe very briefly the principal techniques available for the execution of the second of these steps, and describe also the logical sequence or 'formula' which constitutes step 4.

7.7 Discuss the problems in human relations which are likely to occur during a method study exercise and indicate how they might be minimized. In your answer show how the problems differ at various stages of the investigation.

CHAPTER 8

Work Measurement and Work Standards

NOTATION USED IN THIS CHAPTER

BM	Basic minute
L	Required limits of accuracy
MOST	Maynard operation sequence technique
MTA	Motion time analysis
MTM	Methods time measurement
N	Actual number of observations
N^1	Required number of observations for given confidence level and accuracy
p	Percentage of total time occupied by activity under consideration
PMTS	Predetermined motion time system
SM	Standard minute
TMU	Time measurement unit (0.0006 min.)
x	Observed element time

Work measurement is defined in British Standard 3138 as the 'application of techniques designed to establish the time for a qualified worker to carry out a specified job at a defined level of performance', and time study as 'a work measurement technique for recording the times and rates of working for the elements of a specified job carried out under specified conditions, and for analysing the data so as to obtain the time necessary for carrying out the job at a defined level of performance'. Time study is considered, then, as that part of work measurement concerned with the direct timing of job elements by means of a suitable device such as a stopwatch. This is not the only method of obtaining times for jobs, as we shall see later. In fact, there are two classes of work measurement: direct time study and indirect time study, which does not rely on the use of the stopwatch. (see also Figure 7.1.)

USES OF WORK STANDARDS

Some of the uses of work time estimates and work standards are outlined in Figure 8.1. Times are necessary for the comparison of work methods, for operations scheduling and for capacity planning. The proper co-ordination of operations depends on the availability of accurate time estimates.

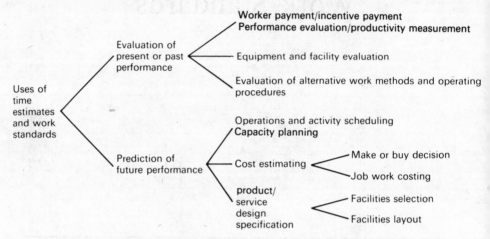

Figure 8.1 *Uses of work time estimates and standards.*

The allocation of facilities to a single worker and the even distribution of work among members of a team cannot be accomplished without estimates of the duration of all operations. The output of flow process systems depends, to a large extent, on the output of the workers with the longest work cycle; consequently the balanced allocation of work is essential.

Standard times for jobs, once established, may be used to set labour standards for payment purposes, to determine the operating effectiveness of equipment, workers, groups of workers, departments or factories, and to determine standard costs of operations for pricing or estimating purposes. (Payment systems are discussed in Chapter 10.)

MEASUREMENT OF WHAT?

Work study is concerned primarily with manual work. To a lesser extent it is concerned with work performed by machines, but hardly ever directly with mental work.

There is normally little difficulty in measuring machine work, since machine times are usually a function of machine speeds, etc. However, even where human manual work is highly rationalized and repetitive, there is a need for most workers to exercise some mental ability. As far as work study and work management are concerned, mental work is often too difficult to measure directly.[1] Part of the process of establishing standard times for a

---

[1] There have been some attempts, however, to develop work measurement procedures for use in the study of mental work, e.g. Vansanten, H. G. (1973) 'Mento-Factor', *Work Study*, January, pp. 36–43.

job involves the adoption of allowances, i.e. provision of additional time to compensate for atmospheric conditions, contingencies, etc. Mental effort is dealt with in precisely the same way, i.e.

1. Physical human work is measured.
2. Machine work is calculated.
3. Mental human work is allowed for.

WORK MEASUREMENT PROCEDURES

There are two categories of work measurement procedures (see Figure 7.1). Direct time study is the traditional stopwatch procedure and accounts for the majority of the exercises conducted. Indirect methods are on occasion either desirable or necessary. In the case of a new job it is impossible to conduct direct studies and, where jobs are to be undertaken for a comparatively short period of time, there may not be enough time to conduct direct work measurement. With the exception of analytical estimating, the indirect methods are of more recent origin. They have many advantages in terms of consistency and accuracy, and possibly additional developments may increase their future scope and value.

Table 8.1 summarizes the conventional procedures for work measurement, which are discussed in more detail below.

DIRECT WORK MEASUREMENT

Time study

As with method study, we can break down time study procedure into a series of simple, logical and important steps, as follows.

Obtain all necessary information

Our objective in conducting a work measurement exercise is to determine the time required for a job carried out under specified conditions. It is necessary, therefore, to have a record of these conditions in case the exercise is referred to or used at a later date. There is usually provision for recording information about the worker, machine, material, layout, output, method, quality standard etc., on one of the forms used during the study or, alternatively, it may be sufficient to refer to the appropriate method study for this information.

Table 8.1 *Procedures for work management* (From Wild, R. (1980) *Management and Production*, 2nd edition. Harmondsworth: Penguin. Reproduced with permission.)

	Technique	Definition (BS 3138)	Steps involved	Accuracy detail	Applications
Direct work measurement	1. Time study	'A work measurement technique for recording the times and rates of working for the elements of a specified job carried out under specified conditions, and for analysing the data so as to obtain the time necessary for carrying out the job at a defined level of performance	1. Get all information concerning job to be measured 2. Divide job into *elements* 3. Time and rate the elements 4. Determine number of cycles to time 5. Determine allowances 6. Calculate standard time for job	Amount of detail is determined by step 2 and accuracy is determined largely by the process of *rating* (step 3), which is largest subjective area of time study	Widely used, particularly for direct work. May be used as a preliminary to generating synthetic data

	2. Activity sampling	A technique in which a large number of instantaneous observations are made over a period of time of a group of machines, processes or workers. Each observation records what is happening at that instant and the percentage of observations recorded for a particular activity or delay is a measure of the percentage of time during which that activity or delay occurs	1. Get all details of job(s) to be measured
			2. Divide job into activities
			3. Conduct pilot study to:
			  (a) determine number of observations
			  (b) check method
			4. Conduct study; make readings
			5. Calculate proportion of time for each activity
				Gives information about proportion of time spent on each activity only	Intermittent work. Long cycle times. As a preliminary investigation

Indirect work measurement				
1. Synthetic timing	A work measurement technique for building up the time for a job at a defined level of performance by totalling element times obtained previously from time studies on other jobs containing the elements concerned, or from synthetic data	1. Get all details of job to be measured 2. Divide job into elements 3. Select times from synthetic data 4. Determine allowances 5. Calculate standard time for job	Usually as much detail as time study, since data have usually been obtained from prior time studies. Accuracy depends on amount of data available and care in application usually consistent	Where adequate data have been gathered usually provides a sufficiently accurate and rapid method of determining times, often without recourse to stopwatch, and prior to starting job
2. Pre-determined motion time systems	A work measurement technique whereby times established for basic human motions (classified according to the nature of the motion and the conditions under which it is made) are used to build up the time for a job at a defined level of performance	1. Get all details of the job to be measured 2. Determine amount of detail required 3. Construct time for job 4. Determine allowances 5. Calculate standard time for job	Systems are available to provide various levels of detail. Consistency is ensured, and accuracy with many systems is greater than that of time study	Where consistency and accuracy are important. Detailed systems are time consuming to apply. Later systems forfeit detail for speed of application. Suitable for use on indirect workers and for intermittent work
3. Analytical estimating	A work measurement technique, being a development of estimating, whereby the time required to carry out elements of a job at a defined level of performance is estimated from knowledge and practical experience of the elements concerned	1. Get all information concerning job to be measured 2. Divide job into elements 3. (a) Apply synthetic data where available (b) Estimate or time element durations 4. Determine allowances 5. Calculate standard time for job	Uses synthetic data supplemented by either time studies or estimates. Slightly less accurate and consistent than synthesis	Where insufficient synthetic data are available. Rapid method, suitable for intermittent work. e.g. maintenance

Divide the job into elements

This is necessary for the following reasons:

(a)   to provide a better understanding of the nature of the job;
(b)   to break a time study exercise up into manageably sized 'pieces';
(c)   to permit a more accurate study;
(d)   to distinguish different types of work;
(e)   to enable 'machine' elements, i.e. machine-paced work, to be isolated from 'worker' elements;
(f)   to enable detailed job descriptions to be produced;
(g)   to enable time standards to be checked or modified;
(h)   to enable times for certain common or important elements to be extracted and compared.

Jobs may consist of constant or variable elements, manual or machine elements, repetitive, occasional, or even 'foreign' elements. Constant elements are of identical specification and have the same duration whenever performed, unlike variable elements, the times of which vary according to characteristics such as weight, size, distance, etc. Machine elements are often constant while worker elements are often variable. Occasional elements do not occur in every cycle but nevertheless are an essential part of the job, whereas foreign elements are unnecessary.

The ease with which the study is conducted, as well as the data obtained, is very much dependent on the definition of the job elements; fortunately, there are some general and well-tried rules which can be used at this stage.

1.   The elements selected will be timed separately and repeatedly; consequently it is essential that clearly defined beginning and ending points should be available to identify the element.
2.   Elements should be as short as possible yet not too short to be conveniently timed.
3.   Elements should be as unified as possible. Whenever possible, elements consisting of a logical sequence of basic motions should be used.
4.   Worker and machine elements should be separated.
5.   Regular and irregular elements should be separated.
6.   Elements involving heavy or fatiguing work should be separated out.
7.   Finally, constant elements should be separated from variable elements.

Timing elements

A variety of mechanical and electronic devices are available to assist in the timing of work elements. Traditionally, analogue stopwatches were used for timing elements. Work study stopwatches are calibrated in seconds, milliminutes, centiminutes or centi-hours, the latter three being the more common and the more useful. There are two alternative methods of using stopwatches, i.e. 'continuous' and 'flyback' timing, the choice being dependent on the circumstances and personal preference. In continuous timing the watch runs throughout the study, times are read off, and element durations are obtained by subtraction. No time is lost in stopping the watch and every element must be recorded. Flyback timing records the duration of each element separately. The watch is zeroed after every element and element times are known immediately; consequently it is easy to spot errors and irregularities. A more sophisticated system of flyback timing using two analogue watches mounted together on a special board is also available. A mechanism operates to stop one watch and start the other at the end of each work element. The advantage of this method, sometimes known as accumulative timing, is that ease and accuracy of reading a stopped watch is combined with the principal advantage of continuous timing, namely that a minimum of time is wasted during an element timing.

Digital stopwatches can be used in exactly the same manner as indicated above. In using both analogue and digital watches the watches are usually mounted on an observation board to which are clipped record sheets on which the observer writes the element, reserve time, ratings, etc.

More sophisticated electronic equipment is now available and in widespread use in element timing. A variety of types of 'event recorder' are available which combine ease of use with accuracy and versatility. Electronic data capture terminals are also used, particularly where summary statistics and calculations are to be performed locally on the data, or where data are to be input directly to a computer for subsequent analysis. Such terminals are in effect alpha/numeric keyboard devices with some internal storage and a small LCD display. Such devices can be programmed to 'prompt' the observer with element descriptions in code form so that times can be recorded and then stored within the device. Summary calculations can be performed, and in some cases by interfacing the device directly with a typewriter a list of element times can be printed out for editing and for checking for missing observations, etc. In most cases such devices provide for interfacing with the computer so that the stored information can be 'down loaded' to the computer for subsequent analysis.

There are also available a variety of 'proprietary' devices to provide specific facilities. Electronic 'time study boards' are available with keys marked with work study terminology for recording information on a tape cassette carried in a shoulder pack by the observer. Other boards are available with 'built-in' electronic clocks and one or more displays. These are in effect sophisticated versions of the traditional clip board with paper and the analogue clock recording devices described above.

We shall look in more detail at electronic data capture terminals later in this chapter.

Some methods of timing elements involve filming. A cine or, more usually, video film can be made of the operation for subsequent analysis 'off the job'. In some cases the filmed record can incorporate a clock so that detailed timings can be obtained, or the film can be run at a known and constant speed so that a frame by frame or 'foot by foot' analysis can be undertaken.

The number of cycles to be timed

We must take enough readings to be reasonably confident of an accurate result. Direct time study is a sampling process, and the accuracy of the sample as a measure of the elements themselves is determined by the variability of the elements and the size of the sample. The number of observations to be taken depends on:

(a) the variation in the times of the element;
(b) the degree of accuracy required;
(c) the confidence level required.

A 95 per cent confidence level and an accuracy of ± 5 per cent or ± 10 per cent are usually adopted. This means that the chances are at least 95 out of 100 that the mean or average we obtain from the observations will be in error by ± 5 per cent or ± 10 per cent of the true element time.

Before the number of observations necessary to fulfil this requirement can be calculated, we must establish the variability of the element time by conducting a brief 'pilot' study. We can then use one of the following formulae to calculate the required number of observations.

95 per cent confidence $\pm$ 5 per cent accuracy:

$$N^1 = \left(\frac{40 \sqrt{N \Sigma x^2 - (\Sigma x)^2}}{\Sigma x} \right)^2$$

95 per cent confidence $\pm$ 10 per cent accuracy:

$$N^1 = \left(\frac{20 \sqrt{N \Sigma x^2 - (\Sigma x)^2}}{\Sigma x} \right)^2$$

where N^1 = required number of observations for given confidence and accuracy
N = actual number of observations taken in pilot study
x = each observed element time from the pilot study

Rating the worker

So far we have been concerned only with the observed or actual times required by a worker to perform elements of work, but the object of work measurement and time study is to determine not how long it *did* take to perform a job or elements of a job, but how long it *should* take. It is necessary, therefore, to compare the actual rate of working of the worker with a standard rate of working so that the observed times can be converted to basic times, i.e. the time required to carry out an element of work at standard performance. In fact every observation we make must be rated and the appropriate rating factor recorded on the record chart before the observed time is recorded.

Performance rating is the comparison of an actual rate of working against a defined concept of a standard rate of working. The standard rate corresponds to 'the average rate at which qualified workers will naturally work at a job, provided they know and adhere to the specified method, and provided they are motivated to apply themselves to their work' (BS 3138). On the British Standard Performance Scale (which we shall use throughout this chapter) standard rating is equal to 100, i.e. a rating of 50 is equal to half the standard rate of working. In the USA the '60/80 scale', where standard performance is 80, is used.

Although standard rate is defined above, it is really only a concept. In practice the standard rate of working is a function of the situation, e.g. the physical conditions, the type of labour, company policy, and may differ greatly between companies. Consequently, the company must train the time study analyst to recognize what the company or industry regards as standard performance.

Several systems of rating have been developed. *Effort rating*[2] is concerned primarily with work speed, the operator being rated according to the speed of his or her movement, adjustments being made to the rating according to the perceived difficulty of the job being done. *Objective rating* is a similar method depending on the consideration of two factors: speed and difficulty. The operator is rated first according to the speed of his or her movement, irrespective of the nature of the job. After this speed rating an adjustment is made depending on the nature of the job being performed, particularly:

---

[2] Presgrave, R. (1945) *The Dynamics of Time Study*. New York: McGraw-Hill.

(a) how much of the body is used;
(b) the use of footpedals;
(c) the need for bimanualness;
(d) eye–hand coordination;
(e) the handling requirements;
(f) the weight of objects handled.

Tables of adjustment factors are available for various categories of each of these six factors.[3]

The Westinghouse Company devised a system in about 1927 in which four characteristics were considered: the skill used, the effort required, the conditions prevailing and the consistency required. A numerical scale is attached to each of these characteristics (Table 8.2). Unlike the two systems mentioned above, the Westinghouse system is used to rate a job rather than the separate elements of the job. For this reason it is sometimes referred to as a *levelling system* rather than a rating system. A separate rating for each element is made for each area and the sum of the four figures represents the final rating factor for each element, e.g.

$$\text{Observed (actual) element time} = 0.45 \text{ minutes}$$

$$
\begin{aligned}
\text{Element rating} \quad &= +0.06 \text{ (skill)} \\
&\quad +0.12 \text{ (effort)} \\
&\quad +0.00 \text{ (conditions)} \\
&\quad +0.01 \text{ (consistency)} \\
\hline
&\quad +0.19
\end{aligned}
$$

$$
\begin{aligned}
\text{Basic time for element} \quad &= 0.45 \times (1.00 + 0.19) \\
&= 0.54 \text{ minutes}
\end{aligned}
$$

Whichever one of these or other methods of rating or levelling is used the basic time corresponds to the observed time after rating, i.e.

$$\text{basic time for element or job} = \text{observed time} \times \frac{\text{rating}}{100}$$

Table 8.2 *Factors and point values in the Westinghouse system of performance rating or levelling*

Skill			Effort			Conditions			Consistency		
+0.15	A1	Superskill	+0.13	A1	Excessive	+0.06	A	Ideal	+0.04	A	Perfect
+0.13	A2		+0.12	A2		+0.04	B	Excellent	+0.03	B	Excellent
+0.11	B1	Excellent	+0.10	B1	Excellent	+0.02	C	Good	+0.01	C	Good
+0.08	B2		+0.08	B2		0.00	D	Average	0.00	D	Average
+0.06	C1	Good	+0.05	C1	Good	−0.03	E	Fair	−0.02	E	Fair
+0.03	C2		+0.02	C2		−0.07	F	Poor	−0.04	F	Poor
0.00	D	Average	0.00	D	Average						
−0.05	E1	Fair	−0.04	E1	Fair						
−0.10	E2		−0.08	E2							
−0.16	F1	Poor	−0.12	F1	Poor						
−0.22	F2		−0.17	F2							

[3] Mundel, M. E. (1960) *Motion and Time Study.* Englewood Cliffs, NJ: Prentice-Hall.

Allowances

We have not yet obtained the standard time for the elements of the job, since it may be necessary now to provide allowances to compensate for fatigue, personal needs, contingencies, etc. The basic time does not contain any allowances and is merely the time required by the worker to perform the task at a standard rate without any interruptions or delays. Allowances are normally given as a percentage of the basic element times and usually include:

1. Relaxation allowances:
    (a) fatigue allowances to give the workers time to recover from the effort (physiological and psychological) required by the job;
    (b) personal needs—to visit toilets, washrooms, etc.
2. Contingency allowances given to compensate for the time required by the workers to perform all necessary additional and periodic activities which were not included in the basic time because of infrequent or irregular occurrence and the difficulty of establishing the times, e.g. reading drawings, cleaning machinery.
3. Tool and machinery allowance to compensate the worker for the time necessary for adjusting and sharpening tools, setting up equipment, and so on.
4. Reject allowance, necessary where a proportion of defective items must necessarily be produced.
5. Interference allowance to compensate for time unavoidably lost because of the stoppage of two or more machines, attended by one worker, at the same time.
6. Excess work allowance to compensate for the extra work necessary because of unforeseen or temporary changes in the standard conditions.

Total allowances are often of the order of 15 to 20 per cent, so inaccuracies are of some consequence. Nevertheless, practice is again very much a function of the situation. Allowances intolerable in one company may be perfectly acceptable elsewhere; consequently the time study analyst should be trained in this area as carefully as in performance rating.

Calculate standard time

The standard time for an element or a job is calculated as follows:

$$\text{Standard time} = \left(\text{observed time} \times \frac{\text{rating}}{100} \right) \times \text{per cent total allowance}$$

For example, where the worker is observed to be working at greater than the standard rate the three element times may bear a relationship to one another, as shown in Figure 8.2.

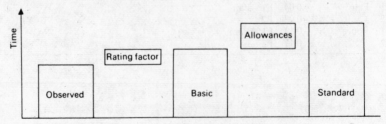

Figure 8.2 *Breakdown of the standard minute.*

The *standard minute* is the unit of measurement of work, consisting partly of work and partly of relaxation. It represents the output in one minute if the work is performed at the standard rate. By means of work measurement we can express the work content of jobs in terms of single units—standard minutes (SMs)—irrespective of the differences between the jobs themselves.

Note that an SM is a measure of *work* and not a measure of time. It is connected with time only in that one SM of work will take one minute of time at 100 performance. SMs can therefore be used in calculating wages and performance. For example, performance can be measured by:

$$\frac{\text{Output of work in SMs}}{\text{Total labour time in minutes}}$$

Activity sampling

The work measurement techniques we have described so far are appropriate where we are concerned with short-cycle repetitive work. If, however, it is necessary to establish work standards in situations where long, irregular-cycle work is conducted, or where many different jobs are performed, these techniques may be quite inappropriate.

It may be necessary to study the activities of several workers on several machines in order to establish the proportion of time each worker spends on various activities, or to determine the utilization of resources, space, etc., and in such cases some form of sampling procedure is invaluable.

Memomotion photography, discussed in the previous chapter, was a sampling technique by which, in particular circumstances, we are able to obtain enough information about jobs or activities without conducting a continuous study. In memomotion study the sampling interval was constant, but in certain cases we may wish to sample at irregular intervals in order to avoid any chance of our observations regularly coinciding with some particular feature of the activity being studied.

The accuracy of our sample as a measure of the actual activity is clearly dependent on the number of observations we take. If we are willing to take many observations, our confidence in the result can be high, but this will have been obtained only at higher cost.

Again, we must decide what confidence level and accuracy we require before we can decide how many observations to take. Furthermore, a pilot study must be conducted to establish the frequency of occurrence of the activity being studied; then for a confidence level of 95 per cent the formula to determine the number of observations required is:

$$N^1 = \frac{4p(100 - p)}{L^2}$$

Where N^1 = number of observations needed

p = percentage of total time occupied by the activity with which we are concerned, as obtained from a pilot study.

L = required limits of accuracy (expressed as a percentage)

Activity sampling is normally used to determine the percentage of the total time that a person or machine spends on certain activities. In the simplest case, the requisite number of random observations is taken to determine the percentage of total time spent by either a worker or a machine in working or not working.

Rated activity sampling

Occasionally it is practical to sample activities at regular rather than random intervals because of the random nature of the activities concerned. In such circumstances it is possible to use an extension of activity sampling known as *rated activity sampling* or *rated systematic sampling*.

EXAMPLE: A PHOTOCOPIER

Observation number (one-minute intervals)	Machine running	Machine not running
1	1	
2	1	
3	1	
4		1
5	1	
6	1	
7		1
8	1	
9	1	
10	1	
Total	8	2

A photocopier is either working or not working. A series of observations is made at regular one-minute intervals to determine the proportion of the total time devoted to each of these activities. The table gives the results of the survey; each of the marks in the table has resulted from an observation.

If the production of items from this machine during the period observed was 25, and if we assume standard performance, then the *basic minutes (BM)*[4] for each product is given as follows:

$$BM/product = \frac{8}{25} = 0.32$$

EXAMPLE: A PACKING JOB

A woman is performing a packing job which has an irregular cycle and consists of a maximum of three elements of work. Observations are made at regular intervals of 0.1 minute; the number of items produced during the period of the study is determined and the operator is rated at each observation. Determine the *basic minutes* for each element and for each item produced.

The table shows the results of the sampling. The figures in the columns indicate not only which element was being performed on each observation, but also the performance rating for that element at that time.

The output during this two-minute study was ten items.

---

[4] i.e. after rating but before the addition of allowances

Observation number (0.1 minute intervals)	Element 1	Element 2	Element 3	Idle
1	100			
2		100		
3	95			
4			110	
5	95			
6				100
7		100		
8	95			
9	100			
10			105	
11		100		
12				100
13		100		
14	95			
15		100		
16	110			
17		110		
18			95	
19				100
20	100			
Total ('00)	7.9	6.1	3.1	3.0

The basic minutes for each element per product can be calculated using the following formula:

$$BM/element = \frac{\text{sum of all ratings}}{100} \times \frac{\text{observation interval}}{\text{output}}$$

i.e. For element 1:
$$BM = 7.9 \times 0.1/10$$
$$= 0.079$$

For element 2:
$$BM = 6.1 \times 0.1/10$$
$$= 0.061$$

For element 3:
$$BM = 3.1 \times 0.1/10$$
$$= 0.031$$

The total basic minutes for each item is of course the sum of the above figures, i.e. 0.171.

Indirect work measurement

Synthetic timing (elemental, standard or basic data)

Work measurement data are often classified and stored with this possible use in mind, and the process of reconstruction is usually referred to as synthesizing. As time studies are completed the 'elemental' data are coded and stored. Periodically these data are examined to determine whether there is any consistency between times for similar elements. When enough consistent data have been gathered the information can be condensed as tables, graphs or equations for easy future application. If elemental times are being collected for this purpose the definitions of work elements should be more precise than would normally be required. Furthermore, because of the slow accumulation of data suitable for synthesizing, it is often preferable to plan the entire work measurement activity with the object of obtaining accurate data.

The generation of data for machine elements normally involves comparatively little trouble, since such times are often either constant or the functions of known variables. Similarly, constant 'worker' elements provide little difficulty, since an equal time will be required whenever the job or element is performed.

It is more difficult to deal with variable elements. First, we must examine the variations in time which occur in our accumulated data to establish whether the variation is a result of a difference in the nature of the element itself, or whether it results from the action of one or more variables. If the variations are particularly large there may be fundamental differences in the nature of the elements, in which case the data cannot be assembled together. The remaining variation can usually be attributed to variables such as distance, size and weight, and graphs or tables can then be constructed.

Synthetic data are reliable and consistent, since normally they have resulted from many studies over a period of time. They can be used to establish time standards for short-run work on which there would be insufficient time to conduct a direct time study, and to construct time standards for jobs not yet begun.

A practical advantage is that there is no need for the use of a stopwatch, but it can be expensive and time consuming to develop synthetic data. It is normal to synthesize basic times to which allowances must be added. The need to rate the job under consideration is avoided and, since the synthetic data will probably have been derived from numerous studies, the consequence of inaccuracies in the original studies is reduced.

Predetermined motion time systems (PMTS)

In BS 3138 PMTS is defined as 'a work measurement technique whereby times established for basic human motions (classified according to the nature of the motion and the conditions under which it is made) are used to build up the time for a job at a defined level of performance'. A PMT system therefore consists of a list of all motions that a worker can use in doing a task, together with time values for these motions at a specified level of performance and in specified circumstances.

MTM-1

Methods time measurement (MTM) was developed by Maynard, Stegemerton and Schwab during the latter part of the Second World War, and was first published in book form in 1946.[5]

The first MTM system (MTM−1) provided times for basic motions, the argument being that, because such motions approximated to the 'lowest common denominators' of all

---

[5] Maynard, H. B., Stegemerton, G. T. and Schwab, J. L. (1946) *Methods-time Measurement*, London: McGraw-Hill. 1946.

work, it was possible, theoretically at least, to construct time standards for all jobs from a set of tabular data. In addition to this assumption, that all work can be divided into basic units, i.e. given a qualitative description, a further assumption was made, i.e. that for each of these qualitative units a universal time value can be obtained. It was assumed, for example, that the time required for a particular elemental motion is not influenced unduly by preceding or succeeding motions.

To establish the time of each motion under various conditions was a tremendous job, and was usually accomplished by analysing motion films. The problem of rating still remained, but at least all times were derived from ratings by small groups of observers working under carefully controlled conditions.

Many of the better PMT systems are extremely comprehensive and attempt to take into account as many variables as possible. Nevertheless, factors such as the influence of the sequence of units, the overall complexity of the task, the repetitiveness of the sequence of units, the direction of movement, etc. must necessarily be omitted from even the better systems.

MTM−1 quickly became the most widely used PMT system, largely because unlike the others of that time, it was non-proprietary and was backed up by a widespread association which provided both momentum to the system and training for practitioners.

MTM−1 classifies all hand motions into basic units as follows:

Reach (R) the basic element employed when the predominant purpose is to move the hand to a destination or general location

Move (M) the basic element employed when the predominant purpose is to transport an object to a destination

Turn (T) a movement which rotates the hand, wrist and forearm

Apply pressure (AP) the element employed whenever pressure is applied

Grasp (G) a hand or fingers element employed when an object is required for further operation

Position (P) the basic element employed to align, orient or engage one object with another, when motions used are minor and do not justify classification as other basic elements

Release (RL) the basic element employed to relinquish control of an object by the fingers or hand

Disengage (D) the basic element employed to break contact between objects

Eye travel and eye
focus (*ET, EF*)
Body, leg and
foot motions

The times for various sub-groups of each of these units, and under various conditions, are shown in Figure 8.3. In addition Table 8.3 shows how the MTM−1 notation is constructed, and Figure 8.4 indicates the ease or difficulty with which simultaneous motions are achieved.

The time units used in MTM are 'time measurement units' where:

$$1 \text{ TMU} = 0.0006 \text{ min.}$$

It should be noted that because MTM−1 was developed in America, TMU values do not necessarily correspond to 100 on the BS rating scale. There has been a good deal of controversy over the relationship of the ratings included in the TMU values and the BS

TABLE I—REACH—R

Distance Moved Inches	Time TMU A	B	C or D	E	Hand In Motion A	B	CASE AND DESCRIPTION
¾ or less	2.0	2.0	2.0	2.0	1.5	1.6	A Reach to object in fixed location, or to object in other hand or on which other hand rests.
1	2.5	2.5	3.6	2.4	2.3	2.3	
2	4.0	4.0	6.9	3.8	3.5	2.7	
3	5.3	6.3	7.3	5.3	4.5	3.6	
4	6.1	6.4	8.4	6.8	4.9	4.3	B Reach to single object in location which may vary slightly from cycle to cycle.
5	6.5	7.8	9.4	7.4	6.3	5.0	
6	7.0	8.6	10.1	8.0	5.7	5.7	
7	7.4	9.3	10.8	8.7	6.1	6.5	
8	7.9	10.1	11.5	9.3	6.5	7.2	C Reach to object jumbled with other objects in a group so that search and select occur.
9	8.3	10.8	12.2	9.9	6.9	7.9	
10	8.7	11.5	12.9	10.5	7.3	8.6	
12	9.6	12.9	14.2	11.8	8.1	10.1	
14	10.5	14.4*	15.6	13.0	8.9	11.5	D Reach to a very small object or where accurate grasp is required.
16	11.4	15.8	17.0	14.2	9.7	12.9	
18	12.3	17.2	18.4	15.5	10.5	14.4	
20	13.1	18.6	19.8	16.7	11.3	15.8	
22	14.0	20.1	21.2	18.0	12.1	17.3	
24	14.9	21.5	22.5	19.2	12.9	18.8	E Reach to indefinite location to get hand in position for body balance or next motion or out of way.
26	15.8	22.9	23.9	20.4	13.7	20.2	
28	16.7	24.4	25.3	21.7	14.5	21.7	
30	17.5	25.8	26.7	22.9	15.3	23.2	

TABLE II—MOVE—M

Distance Moved Inches	Time TMU A	B	C	Hand In Motion B	Wt (lb.) Up to	Fact-or	Con-stant TMU	CASE AND DESCRIPTION
¾ or less	2.0	2.0	2.0	1.7	2.5	1.00	0	
1	2.6	2.9	3.4	2.3				
2	3.6	4.6	5.2	2.9	7.5	1.06	2.2	A Move object to other hand or against stop.
3	4.9	5.7	6.7	3.6				
4	6.1	6.9	8.0	4.3	12.5	1.11	3.9	
5	7.3	8.0	9.2	5.0				
6	8.1	8.9	10.3	6.7	17.5	1.17	5.6	
7	8.9	9.7	11.1	6.5				
8	9.7	10.6	11.8	7.2	22.5	1.22	7.4	
9	10.5	11.5	12.7	7.9				
10	11.3	12.2	13.5	8.6				B Move object to approximate or indefinite location.
12	12.9	13.4	15.2	10.0	27.5	1.28	9.1	
14	14.4	14.6	16.9	11.4				
16	16.0	15.8	18.7	12.8	32.5	1.33	10.8	
18	17.6	17.0	20.4	14.2				
20	19.2	18.2	22.1	15.6	37.5	1.39	12.5	
22	20.8	19.4	23.8	17.0				
24	22.4	20.6	25.5	18.4	42.5	1.44	14.3	C Move object to exact location.
26	24.0	21.8	27.3	19.8				
28	25.5	23.1	29.0	21.2	47.5	1.50	16.0	
30	27.1	24.3	30.7	22.7				

TABLE III—TURN AND APPLY PRESSURE—T AND AP

Weight		Time TMU for Degrees Turned										
		30°	45°	60°	75°	90°	105°	120°	135°	150°	165°	180°
Small	0 to 2 Pounds	2.8	3.5	4.1	4.8	5.4	6.1	6.8	7.4	8.1	8.7	9.4
Medium	2.1 to 10 Pounds	4.4	5.5	6.5	7.5	8.5	9.6	10.6	11.6	12.7	13.7	14.8
Large	10.1 to 35 Pounds	8.4	10.5	12.3	14.4	16.2	18.3	20.4	22.2	24.3	26.1	28.2

APPLY PRESSURE CASE 1 16.2 TMU.   APPLY PRESSURE CASE 2 10.6 TMU.

TABLE IV—GRASP—G

Case	Time TMU	DESCRIPTION
1A	2.0	Pick Up Grasp—Small, medium or large object by itself, easily grasped.
1B	3.8	Very small object or object lying close against a flat surface.
1C1	7.3	Interference with grasp on bottom and one side of nearly cylindrical object. Diameter larger than ½".
1C2	8.7	Interference with grasp on bottom and one side of nearly cylindrical object. Diameter ¼ to ½".
1C3	10.8	Interference with grasp on bottom and one side of nearly cylindrical object. Diameter less than ¼".
2	5.6	Regrasp.
3	5.6	Transfer Grasp.
4A	7.3	Object jumbled with other objects so search and select occur. Larger than 1" × 1" × 1".
4B	9.1	Object jumbled with other objects so search and select occur. ¼" × ¼" × ⅛" to 1" × 1" × 1".
4C	12.9	Object jumbled with other objects so search and select occur. Smaller than ¼" × ¼" × ⅛".
6	0	Contact, sliding or hook grasp.

TABLE V—POSITION—P

CLASS OF FIT		Symmetry	Easy To Handle	Difficult To Handle
1—Loose	No pressure required	S	5.6	11.2
		SS	9.1	14.7
		NS	10.4	16.0
2—Close	Light pressure required	S	16.2	21.6
		SS	19.7	25.3
		NS	21.0	26.6
3—Exact	Heavy pressure required	S	43.0	48.6
		SS	46.5	52.1
		NS	47.8	53.4

* Distance moved to engage—1" or less.

TABLE VI—RELEASE—RL

Case	Time TMU	DESCRIPTION
1	2.0	Normal release performed by opening fingers as independent motion.
2	0	Contact Release.

TABLE VII—DISENGAGE—D

CLASS OF FIT	Easy to Handle	Difficult to Handle
1 Loose Very slight effort, blends with subsequent move.	4.0	5.7
2 Close Normal effort, slight recoil.	7.5	11.8
3 Tight Considerable effort, hand recoils markedly.	22.9	34.7

TABLE VIII—EYE TRAVEL TIME AND EYE FOCUS—ET AND EF

Eye Travel Time = $15.2 \times \dfrac{T}{D}$ TMU, with a maximum value of 20 TMU.

where T = the distance between, points from and to which the eye travels.
D = the perpendicular distance from the eye to the line of travel T.

Eye Focus Time = 7.3 TMU.

TABLE IX—BODY, LEG AND FOOT MOTIONS

DESCRIPTION	SYMBOL	DISTANCE	TIME TMU
Foot Motion—Hinged at Ankle.	FM	Up to 4"	8.6
With heavy pressure.	FMP		19.1
Leg or Foreleg Motion.	LM—	Up to 6"	7.1
		Each add'l. inch	1.2
Sidestep—Case 1—Complete when leading leg contacts floor.	SS-C1	Less than 12"	Use REACH or MOVE Time
		12"	17.0
		Each add'l. inch	.6
Case 2—Lagging leg must contact floor before next motion can be made.	SS-C2	12"	34.1
		Each add'l. inch	1.1
Bend, Stoop, or Kneel on One Knee.	B, S, KOK		29.0
Arise.	AB, AS, AKOK		31.9
Kneel on Floor—Both Knees.	KBK		60.4
Arise.	AKBK		76.7
Sit.	SIT		34.7
Stand from Sitting Position.	STD		43.4
Turn Body 45 to 90 degrees—			
Case 1—Complete when leading leg contacts floor.	TBC1		18.6
Case 2—Lagging leg must contact floor before next motion can be made.	TBC2		37.2
Walk.	W-FT	Per Foot	5.3
Walk.	W-P	Per Pace	15.0
Walk.	W-PO	Per Pace	17.0

Figure 8.3 *MTM-1 application data in TMU.*

Table 8.3 *Examples of MTM–1 notation*

Motion	Code	Meaning and TMU value
Reach	R7A	Reach, path of movement 17.5 cm, class A. Hand not in motion at beginning or end (7.4 TMU)
Move	M6A	Move, 15 cm, class A, object weighs less than 1.1 kg (8.9 TMU)
Turn	T90M	Turn, 90° object weighing 0.95 to 4.5 kg (8.5 TMU)
Grasp	G1C1	Grasp, case 1C1 (7.3 TMU)
Position	P2NSE	Position, close fit, non-symmetrical part. Easy to handle. (21.0 TMU)
Release	RL1	Release, case 1 (2.0 TMU)
Disengage	D1D	Disengage, loose fit, difficult to handle (5.7 TMU)
Eye travel	ET10/12	Eye travel, between points 25 cm apart, line of travel 30 cm from eye (12.7 TMU)

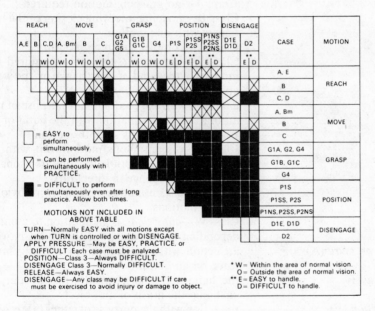

Figure 8.4 *Simultaneous motions. (Figures 8.3 and 8.4 reproduced with the permission of the MTM Association of UK.)*

scale, but recently it has been suggested that for all practical purposes job times derived using MTM values should be accepted as equivalent to a BSI rating of 83.[6]

[6] Burman, P. M. et al. (1969) MTM and the BSI rating scale, *Work Study and Management Services*, **13**, p. 97.

MTM–2

The advantages of a PMTS are much the same as the advantages of synthetic standards, but the main disadvantage of the use of such systems is the considerable amount of time normally needed to construct element and job times from such detailed information. This was perhaps the main reason why PMT systems were slow to be accepted in many companies, particularly in the United Kingdom, and as a result certain 'second generation' systems were developed which relied on the use of elements rather than basic motions. MTM–2 is such a system. It was developed in Europe with the purpose of fulfilling several objectives, one of which was that the data should be easily and rapidly handled in practice.

MTM–2 was synthesized from MTM–1 data and consists of nine motions – Get; Put; Apply pressure; Regrasp; Eye action; Crank; Step; Foot motion; Bend and arise. Only Get and Put have variable categories, so the MTM–2 data card has only 39 time standards. As with MTM–1, the motions and their various sub-categories are closely defined and precise rules govern their use.

Get (G)	a motion with the predominant purpose of reaching with the hand or fingers to an object, grasping the object, and subsequently releasing it
	Class A—no grasping motion required
	Class B—grasping involving closing of the hand or fingers with one motion
	Class C—complex grasping motion
	Class W—*get weight*, the action required for the muscles of the hand or arm to take up the weight of an object
Put (P)	a motion with the predominant purpose of moving an object to a destination with the hand or fingers
	Class A—continuous smooth motion
	Class B—discontinuous motion, but without obvious correcting motion (i.e. unintentional stop, hesitation or change in direction)
	Class C—discontinuous motion with obvious correcting motions
	Class W—*put weight*, is an addition to a put action depending on the weight of the object moved
Apply pressure (A)	an action with the purpose of exerting muscular force on an object
Regrasp (R)	the hand action performed with the purpose of changing the grasp of an object
Eye action (E)	the action with the purpose of either (a) recognizing a readily distinguishable characteristic of an object, or (b) shifting vision to a new viewing area
Crank (C)	a motion with the purpose of moving an object in a circular path more than $180°$ with hand or fingers
Step (S)	either (a) a leg motion with the purpose of moving the body or (b) a leg motion longer than 30 centimetres
Foot motion (F)	a short foot or leg motion the purpose of which is *not* to move the body
Bend and arise (B)	bend, stoop or kneel on one knee and subsequently arise

The time standard, in TM units, for each of the motions is easily obtained from the MTM–2 data card (Figure 8.5). The values for the seven motions without variable categories are given at the bottom of the card, while the remaining figures on the card relate to Get and Put. The time standard for both of these is determined by the category of the motion and the distance involved. The left-hand column gives distance in centimetres. The time standards for GW and PW are shown on the card; in the case of the former, a time value of 1 TMU per kilogram applies, and in the case of the latter 1 TMU per 5 kilograms, i.e. the TMU associated with 'Getting' an object of effective net weight 10 kg (GW 10) is 10 TMU, whereas the time standard for PW 10 is 2 TMU.

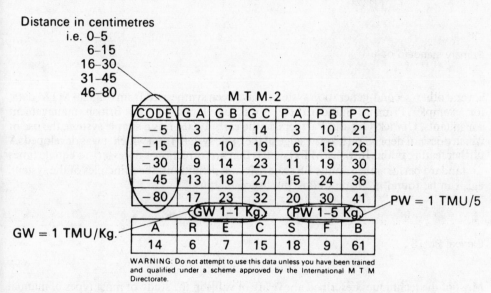

Figure 8.5 *The MTM–2 data card. Reproduced with the permission of the MTM Association of UK.*

Other MTM-derived PMTS

MTM–3

MTM–3 is a development of MTM–2. Introduced in 1970, it is more quickly applied and intended primarily for small-batch work where there is considerable variation in work method from cycle to cycle.

4M DATA

There are many other MTM-based PMTS. The 4M DATA system (O'Neil and Moore (1980)), developed specifically for use in a computerized PMTS, combines the basic MTM–1 motions into only two categories: GET and PLACE.

MOST

The MOST (Maynard Operations Sequence Technique) (Zandin (1980)) was derived from MTM–1 with the objective of simplifying and accelerating application without loss of accuracy. MOST identifies eight key activities which occur in three fixed sequences. Index numbers ascribed to the variables for each activity reflect the relative simplicity or complexity of the sequence or move. Thus the 'compression' of a single activity into a short formula is achieved, enabling MOST to be used (it is claimed) up to 40 times faster than MTM–1 and up to 15 times faster than MTM–2.

Primary standard data

Several other 'second-generation systems' have been synthesized from original MTM data; for example, Primary Standard Data was developed by the British management consultants, Urwick-Orr and Partners, in the early 1960s. It is a simple system, the use of which does not depend on a knowledge of the basic system from which it was developed. A further feature of this British PMT system is that no correction is necessary to equate times to standard performance on the BS scale. Motion definitions, the principles of the system, etc., can be found in Neale's book published in 1967.[7]

Clerical PMTS

Most of the techniques described above are of value in the study of most types of manual work. However, a MTM-derived PMTS has been developed specifically for use in work study for clerical jobs. MTM–C is a two-level standard data system. Synthesized from MTM–1 motion data, MTM–C covers a wide range of filing, typing, key entry, and general clerical tasks. The activities covered include:

1. *Get/place*
2. *Open/close*
3. *Fasten/unfasten*
4. *Organize/file*
5. *Read/write*
6. *Typing*
7. *Handling*
8. *Walking/body motions*
9. *Office machines*

Level 1 of MTM–C, the more detailed, provides three distance ranges for elements involving reach and move. Level 2 provides these elements in the intermediate distance range.

---

[7] Neale, F. J. (1967) *Primary Standard Data*. London: McGraw-Hill.

Analytical estimating

Analytical estimating is described as 'a work measurement technique, whereby the time required to carry out elements of a job at a defined level of performance is established from knowledge and practical experience of the elements concerned' (BS 3138).

Analytical estimating is intended to replace a procedure known as *rate fixing*, which was occasionally used to establish time standards for non-repetitive work such as maintenance. In such circumstances there are often insufficient synthetic data available to allow time standards to be established, and consequently standards must be constructed using whatever data are available, plus estimates of the basic times for the remaining elements. Clearly a requirement in analytical estimating is that the estimator is completely familiar with, and perferably skilled and experienced in, the work concerned.

The procedure used is much the same as before, in that jobs are first divided into appropriate elements, synthetic data being used for as many of those elements as possible while basic times are estimated for the remainder. Rather than applying allowances to individual elements, relaxation and contingency allowances are applied as overall or blanket figures for the whole job.

COMPUTERS IN WORK STUDY *(see also pp. 181–183)*

Table 8.4 outlines some of the computer programs and computer systems currently available to the work study practitioner. Study of this list indicates that computer programs and computer systems might be of value to the work study practitioner in the following areas:

(a) preparation of detailed work methods description;
(b) methods development and analysis (and workplace layout);
(c) storage and retrieval of data on work methods and times;
(d) development of workplace layout;
(e) analysis of direct time study data;
(f) determination of time standards;
(g) computerized PMTS.

Of the above, (a), (b) and (c) relate specifically to method study and were discussed in Chapter 7, while (e) (f) and (g) relate specifically to work measurement and are discussed below. The remaining area (c) relates to both method study and work measurement.

In the remainder of this chapter we shall look first at computer applications in work measurement before concluding with a review of the impact of computers in the broad field of work study.

Computers in work measurement

At the simplest level, computer programs have been written to analyse direct time study data. For example (referring to Table 8.4) the program described by Aston is a simple program which takes observed times for elements with ratings, and information on the frequency of the elements per cycle, etc., and provides a listing with observed data, cumulative element times, average times and average ratings for elements. Such applications are simple 'number-crunching' uses of a computer to take over some of the more tedious aspects of work measurement. At a slightly more sophisticated level, programs such as that described by Anderson and Hosni (see Table 8.4) attach element times to elements by reference to PMTS tables. Thus if the elements are identified by appropriate code (in the case of the Anderson and Hosni programs by the work factor PMTS code) reference can be made to the table of element times and these can then be attached to the elements and standard times for the job, etc., can be calculated. This application is in fact one step removed from that of a fully computerized PMTS system. In such a system element and job times will be calculated, for a given job description, by reference to PMTS tables. In addition, by reference to filed data, the computer is able to print out a fully detailed statement of the job method using full element description, PMTS code, etc., and also perhaps by checking against certain rules or heuristics is able to ensure that the method does not violate any of the rules and procedures for effective work methods, e.g. by checking that sequences of elements do not incorporate any difficult motion sequences. In addition such a program might determine various indices as measures of the effectiveness of the method, e.g. the number of difficult motions used. The 'MOST' computer system provides such facilities (see Table 8.4).

Using computers in work measurement, indeed in the whole field of work study, it will often be appropriate to employ some form of 'data capture'. Some such equipment is described in Table 8.5. In its simplest form such data-capture equipment simply replaces

Table 8.4   *Some computer programs and systems for work study*

Name	Source	Facilities	PMTS employed	Computer/ Language
ADAM	MTM Association	*Work method description* and *time standard development* Methods outline, using MTM or other work element descriptions, input via keyboard. Work methods description and labour standards computed and output. *Data storage and retrieval* available with editing facilities for maintenance of standards, etc. ADAM–C uses MTM–C clerical standard data system (both levels). ADAM–V uses MTM–V data for production work. ADAM–2 uses MTM–2 data.	MTM	48K Micro or Mini/Pascal
AUTOMAT	Schofield (1980) *and* Prime CAD/CAM	*Work method development and analysis* and *time standards development* Information on work-place and equipment, and on work method (MTM notation) is input. Program develops and outputs detailed layout and appropriate work method (in MTM–2) with standard time. MTM rules and heuristics for good work methods used by program. Measures of efficiency of method are calculated and output for methods comparison evaluation. *Data storage and retrieval.* Batch or interactive processing available.	MTM	Mini or Mainframe (or Bureau)/ FORTRAN IV

Name	Source	Facilities	PMTS employed	Computer/ Language
COMPUTE	Schofield (1980) *and* Prime CAD/CAM	*Time standards syntheses* The computer holds data on machines, equipment, etc., together with time standards from previous studies. Formulae, etc., are used by the program to enable the work study engineer to obtain a time study for an element or operation previously studied or one which differs in a defined way from such a job, e.g. different allowances, sizes, materials, etc.	—	Mini or Mainframe or Bureau/ FORTRAN IV
CSD	Brisley and Dossett (no details)	*Computerized use of companies' synthetic data* for methods description and time standard development	—	?/?
4M DATA	O'Neal and Moore (1980) *and* MTM Association	*Methods development and analysis* Methods description, using 4M DATA (derivative of MTM−1) notation input to computer via keyboards, cards, etc.). Computer applies MTM 'rules' to develop efficient work method. Outputs include SIMO charts, operation analysis and standard report, MTM−1 analysis and methods improvement indices. Provides *data storage and retrieval* facilities and 'interfacing' with other programs for scheduling, line balancing etc. (4M–MODII A for batch processing on computer. (4 M–MODII B for on-line processing.)	4M/MTM 1, 2 and 3	IBM, Honeywell, and Data General or Time Sharing/COBOL
MOST Computer System	Zandin (1980) (see Chapter 9) *and* H.P. Maynard & Co. Inc. *and* Maynard & Barry Ltd	*Methods description* and *time standard development* and *Workplace layout development* Outline workplace and methods descriptions entered (using MOST terminology) via keyboard. Computer defines workplace layout, specifies work method in detail, calculates standard times, and provides printouts. *Data storage and retrieval* with editing, etc. Interfacing possible with machining data, and line balancing programs.	MOST	DEC PDP Mini/ Fortran
TS20 Time Study System	Duncanson (1981) *and* Optech Automation Ltd	*Collection and analysis of direct time study data.* Direct time study data collected via electronic data recorded on cassette (and with automatic timing). Cassette then read by micro-computer to produce input listing for error check and editing, then various listings with full element descriptions, times, etc.	—	Micro/?
UNIVATION	Brisley and Dossett (1980) (no details)	*Computerized PMTS* for methods description and time standard development	?	?/?

Table 8.4 (*contd.*)

Name	Source	Facilities	PMTS employed	Computer/ Language
WOCOM	Brisley and Dossett (1980) (no details)	*Computerized PMTS* for methods description and time standard development	?	?/?
—	Anderson and Hosni (1981)	*Determines time standard* for a job, using work factor PMTS notation and element times. Operation description is input, then elements and times are listed in output with total operation time (program listing provided)	Basic Work Factor	Tandy Micro/Basic
—	Aston (1982)	*Analysis of direct time study data.* Observed (direct time study) times. Ratings are input for each observation for each element with frequencies per cycle, directly via computer keyboard. Output comprises study reference, element listing with observed data, cumulative element times, average times and ratings	—	PET/Micro Basic

Table 8.5 *Some electronic data-capture equipment for use in work study*

Name	Description	Computer Interfacing: Computer/ Language	Source
MicroTIME System	General-purpose, hand-held alpha/numeric portable device (Microfin) is used for data collection and transmission (direct or remote) to a computer. Device is programmed to record event under observation, the time taken (in min/100 or seconds) together with performance rating. At end of the study the device is connected to a micro-computer and data are transferred to 'floppy disc' file for subsequent processing to provide sequential element lists for checking/editing, element details, study summary, etc.	Apple/?	Microfin Systems Ltd
DATAMYTE	General-purpose, hand-held alpha/numeric portable terminal for data collection and transmission (direct or remote) to and from a computer. Built-in clock for automatic timing of elements. Prompting of observations and remote editing. Up to 64k storage. Facility to list data direct from terminal. Computer programs available in BASIC for time study analyses (data check average time, extreme times element list, time summaries, etc.) and work sampling (determine number of observations and time schedule, summary of unrated and rated times).	8k micro/Basic	Electro General Corporation
OS Event Recorder	A hand-held alpha/numeric programmable event recorder and computer, with facilities for local data analysis, editing of data and output of summary statistics, for use in time study and work sampling	Facility to input programs from cassette to set up machine for different jobs	Observational Systems Inc.

Name	Description	Computer Interfacing: Computer/ Language	Source
Optech Time Study Board	A data-capture device to permit data recording on a cassette for subsequent input to a computer. The keys are labelled in a work study format. Elapsed time for elements are recording automatically on a cassette tape which runs at a constant speed. The cassette data are input directly to a micro-computer	Micro/?	Optech Automation Ltd

the traditional analogue stopwatch and time study record sheets. At a more sophisticated level, data-capture equipment is available to enable observers to time elements automatically (for example using a built-in clock or cassette recorder running at a known speed), to store element descriptions and times for a particular job and then input that data either directly or remotely to a computer for subsequent editing and analysis, or to perform some local analysis on the data, e.g. checking for missing times, determining job times, etc. It can be seen from Table 8.5 that most such equipment is now able to interface with a computer and in effect therefore operates as a remote terminal for that computer, but provides for storage of data on the terminal during the period in which the observer is measuring or describing the job.

Increasingly, in using computer systems, data-capture terminals, etc., the objective is to deploy the facilities for the benefit of both method study and work measurement. Although at present computer systems perhaps provide greater benefits in work measurement than in method study, there is now a trend towards the development of more comprehensive applications.

Comprehensive work study

A comprehensive computerized work study system will provide facilities in the seven categories listed earlier and will therefore be of relevance and value to the work study practitioner in all aspects of his or her work. Such comprehensive systems will involve not only the use of computers (with printers, disc files, etc.) but also electronic equipment for gathering and inputting data of the type listed in Table 8.5. None of the systems described in Table 8.4 provides a fully comprehensive computer-based work study system but their further development will rapidly lead to such a system becoming available. Consideration of a hypothetical system will give some indication of the scope for the use of computers in work study. The scope of a hypothetical 'comprehensive' computer-based work study system is illustrated by Figure 8.6 (which in turn is derived from Figure 7.1, which was used to outline the structure of work study). The facilities provided by a comprehensive computer-based work study system are described in this diagram. The configuration required to support such a system might resemble that shown in Figure 8.7.

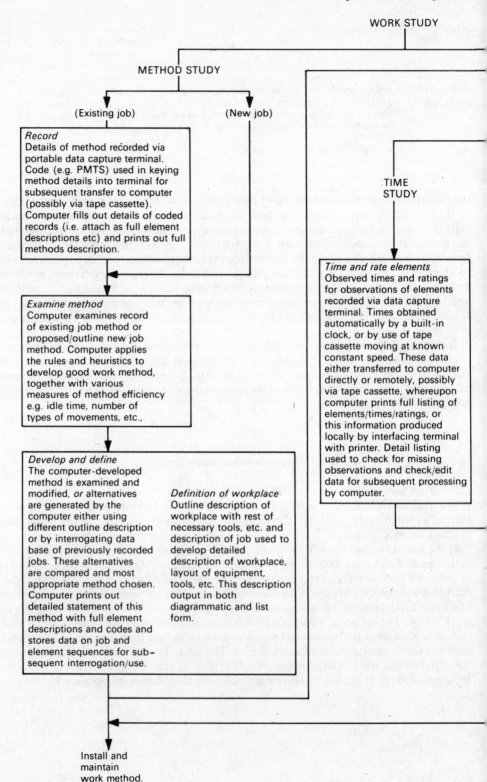

WORK STUDY

METHOD STUDY

(Existing job)   (New job)

TIME STUDY

Record
Details of method recorded via portable data capture terminal. Code (e.g. PMTS) used in keying method details into terminal for subsequent transfer to computer (possibly via tape cassette). Computer fills out details of coded records (i.e. attach as full element descriptions etc) and prints out full methods description.

Examine method
Computer examines record of existing job method or proposed/outline new job method. Computer applies the rules and heuristics to develop good work method, together with various measures of method efficiency e.g. idle time, number of types of movements, etc.,

Time and rate elements
Observed times and ratings for observations of elements recorded via data capture terminal. Times obtained automatically by a built-in clock, or by use of tape cassette moving at known constant speed. These data either transferred to computer directly or remotely, possibly via tape cassette, whereupon computer prints full listing of elements/times/ratings, or this information produced locally by interfacing terminal with printer. Detail listing used to check for missing observations and check/edit data for subsequent processing by computer.

Develop and define
The computer-developed method is examined and modified, *or* alternatives are generated by the computer either using different outline description or by interrogating data base of previously recorded jobs. These alternatives are compared and most appropriate method chosen. Computer prints out detailed statement of this method with full element descriptions and codes and stores data on job and element sequences for sub-sequent interrogation/use.

Definition of workplace
Outline description of workplace with rest of necessary tools, etc. and description of job used to develop detailed description of workplace, layout of equipment, tools, etc. This description output in both diagrammatic and list form.

Install and maintain work method.

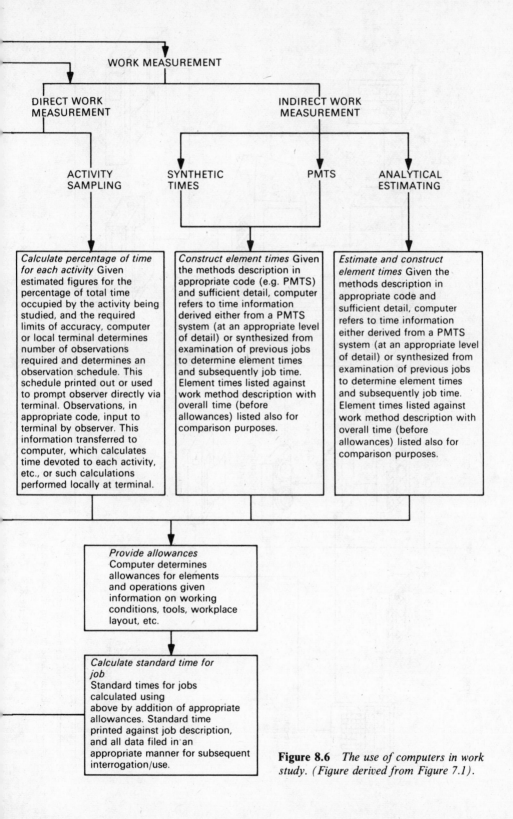

Figure 8.6 *The use of computers in work study. (Figure derived from Figure 7.1).*

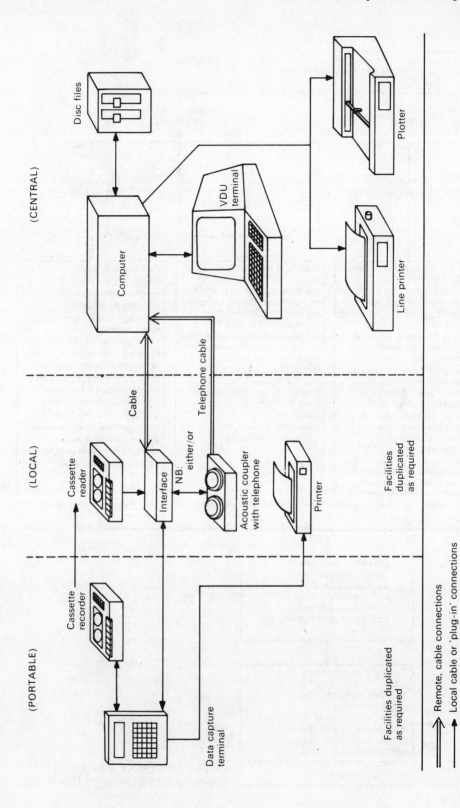

Figure 8.7 Possible configuration of a computer system's hardware for work study applications.

CHECKLIST FOR CHAPTER 8

Definition of work measurement (BS 3138)
Use of work standards
    Evaluation of present and past performance
    Prediction of future performance
Measurement of what?
    Manual work
    Machine work
    Mental work
Work measurement procedures
Direct work measurement
    Time study
        Obtain all necessary information
        Divide job into elements
        Time elements
            Number of cycles to be timed
        Rate the worker
        Allowances
        Calculate standard time
    Activity sampling
        Rated activity sampling
Indirect work measurement
    Synthetic timing

PMTS
    History of PMTS
    Work factor
    MTM–1
    MTM–2
    Other MTM-based systems
        MTM–3
        4M data
        MOST
        Primary standard data
        Clerical PMTS
            MTM–C
    Analytical estimating
Computers in Work Study
    Seven areas of application
    Computers in work measurement
        Analysis of time study data
        Computerized PMTS
        Data capture
    Comprehensive computer-based work study
        Facilities of a hypothetical system
        Configuration of a system

FURTHER READING

Dudley, N. A. (1968) *Work Measurement—Some Research Studies*. London: Macmillan. This book will be of interest to readers anxious to pursue the subject in greater depth, since it contains descriptions of some of the more important British research studies in work measurement.

Karger, D. W. and Bayha, F. H. (1955) *Engineered Work Measurement*, 2nd edition, New York: Industrial Press. Deals with MTM.

Maynard, H. B. Stegemerton, G. T. and Schwab, J. L. (1946) *Methods-time Measurement*. London: McGraw-Hill. This was the first detailed presentation of MTM.

Seabourne, R. G. (1971) *Introduction to Work Study and Statistics*. Harlow: Longman.

Computers (and electronic equipment) in work study

Anderson, J. and Hosni, Y. A. (1981) Time standards by microcomputers, *Industrial Engineering*, September, pp. 18–21.

Aston, E. (1982) Micro computers—a work measurement application, *Management Services*, March, pp. 12–19.

Brisley, C. L. and Dossett, R. J. (1980) Computer use and non-direct labour measurement will transform profession in the next decade, *Industrial Engineering*, August, p. 34–42.

Duncanson, G. (1981) Electronic time study really arrives, *Management Services*, February, pp. 6–8.

Electro General Corporation
14960 Industrial Road
Minnetouka
MN 55343, USA

Maynard & Barry Ltd
Berkeley Square House
Berkeley Square
London W1X 5PB, UK

H.P. Maynard & Co. Inc.
Pittsburgh
Pennsylvania, USA

Microfin Systems Ltd
Winslade House
Egham Hill
Egham
Surrey TW20 OAZ, UK

MTM Associations for Standards and Research
16-01 Broadway
Fair Lawn
NJ 07410, USA

Observational Systems Inc.
1103 Grand Avenue
Seattle
Washington 98122, USA

O'Neal, M. H. and Moore, C. (1980) Multi-plant computer systems for standards provides tool for overall manufacturing control, *Industrial Engineering*, August, pp. 54–80.

Optech Automation Ltd
Units 12/13
Loomer Road Industrial Estate
Newcastle under Lyme
Staffs, UK
Prime CAD/CAM, Stevenage, UK
Schofield, N. A. (1980) Computer-aided work study using AUTOMAT and COMPUTE—practical tools for the Industrial Engineer, *International Journal of Production Research*, **18** (2), pp. 153–168.
Zandin, K. B. (1980) *MOST Work Measurement Systems*. New York: Dekker

Observation number (N)	Time for element (in 1/100 min.)
1	40
2	45
3	43
4	42
5	45
6	47
7	40
8	48
9	47
10	42
11	40
12	39
13	42
14	41
15	43
16	44
17	46
18	43
19	42
20	42
21	44
22	43
23	40
24	42
25	45

QUESTIONS

8.1 The figures below are the observed times obtained by stopwatch during 25 observations of a single element of a manual task. Have sufficient observations of this element been made to provide an accuracy of ± 5 per cent with a confidence interval of 95 per cent?

8.2 The Westinghouse method of rating (see Table 8.2) was used to rate the performance of the element for which the observed times given in the previous question were also obtained. The rating is to be made on a basis of the following:

Skill	C1
Effort	B2
Conditions	E
Consistency	D

Calculate the standard time for the element if a personal allowance of 5 per cent is given.

8.3 Using the data given on the sheet shown below and the following information, calculate the output of a worker at standard performance for an eight-hour shift.

8.4 The following task relates to a series of four time studies which were taken of a worker assembling an electric plug which had two identical terminal pins.

Study	Worker				Times	Date		Sheet			
	Male				1/10 min.			1			
Element number	Rating	Observed time	Ineffective time	Basic time	Element number	Rating	Observed time	Ineffective time	Basic time		
1	110	0.45			1	105	0.45				
2	100	0.70			2	110	0.70				
3	110	0.35			3	115	0.40				
1	105	0.50			1	100	0.45				
2	110	0.65			2	100	0.80				
3	105	0.40			3	90	0.50				
1	100	0.45			1	95	0.52				
2	100	0.72			2	100	0.75				
3	100	0.42			3	110	0.45				
					1	100	0.45				
—			3.80		2	100	0.75				
					3	100	0.40				
1	100	0.47			1	110	0.52				
2	90	0.85			2	100	0.75				
3	110	0.50			3	100	0.38				
1	100	0.45									
2	100	0.75									
3	110	0.48			Adjust jig every 25 cycles						

Allowances: Fatigue 5 per cent   Personal 10 per cent   Delay 2 per cent

Description of operation

The worker removes a completed plug from a jig and sets it aside; he takes a base for a new plug and fits this in the jig. He then takes two terminal pins and inserts these through the base, and a lid is placed on top of the base. By exerting pressure on the lid a mechanical screwing device, situated under the jig automatically fastens the base and the lid together. The cycle then starts again.

After every 1000 plugs assembled, the screwdriver blade in the mechanical screwing device has to be resharpened.

Four studies were made of this operation and the results tabulated

Study number		1	2	3	4
	Repetitive elements				
A	Remove complete plug and fit new base in jig (BM)	1.61	3.31	2.55	1.72
	Number of occurrences	20	40	30	20
B	Insert one terminal pin through base (BM)	2.11	4.06	3.31	2.05
	Number of occurrences	40	80	60	40
C	Locate lid on base and fix with mechanical device (BM)	1.96	3.92	3.05	2.04
	Number of occurrences	20	40	30	20

      Occasional elements

D   Remove, sharpen and refit screw-
      driver blade (BM)   7.60   —   —   7.30
      Number of occurrences   1   —   —   1

      Contingencies

E   (BM)   1.3   —   0.9   —
      Number of occurrences   2   —   1   —

Note: (a) BM in each case is the total basic minutes (i.e. the observed time adjusted for rating) spent on that element during the study.

        (b) A relaxation allowance of 10 per cent is appropriate for all the elements except the occasional element. For this element a relaxation allowance of 15 per cent should be given.

Determine the standard time for assembling one plug.

8.5   Assume that after the application of appropriate work simplification techniques you have taken a direct time study and, after subtraction, you get the following results (time in minutes):

Cycle number	Element number				
	1	2	3	4	5
1	0.15	0.62	0.33	0.51	0.23
2	0.14	0.58	0.20	0.50	0.26
3	0.13	0.59	0.36	0.55	0.24
4	0.18	0.61	0.37	0.49	0.25
5	0.22	0.60	0.34	0.45	0.27

(a) Elements 2 and 4 are machine paced.

(b) You have a decision rule which states that any reading which varies by more than 25 per cent from the average of all readings for an element will be considered 'abnormal'.

(c) The operator is rated at 120 per cent.

(d) Allowances have been set at (for an eight-hour shift):

           personal time   30 minutes
           unavoidable delay   36 minutes
           fatigue   5 per cent

(e) The operator, who is paid on a straight time rate, receives 50p per hour.

(f) Material costs are 3p per piece.

(g) Overhead costs are calculated at 80 per cent of the sum of direct labour and material costs.

How many pieces per shift should each operator produce and what is the production cost per piece? Discuss the appropriateness of these estimates for planning purposes.

8.6   The principal benefit in using predetermined motion time systems to develop work standards is the avoidance of performance rating, and hence the avoidance of undue dispute over the resultant standards. Discuss.

8.7   Discuss the function of performance rating in the determination of work standards. Compare stopwatch study and work sampling in the determination of work standards. You have obtained the following work sample from a study during a 40-hour work week:

           idle time   20 per cent
           performance rating   135 per cent
           total parts produced   280

The allowance for this particular type of work is 10 per cent. Determine the standard time per part.

8.8   Activity sampling has been used as a convenient means of studying the activities of an operator tending a photocopier in an office.

The following figures have been calculated from the results of such a survey, in which the sampling interval was a constant five minutes and in which the total non-stop duration of the survey was three hours.

Percentage of total time operator idle	30 %
Percentage of total time operator adjusting machine	40 %
Percentage of total time operator cleaning workplace	10 %
Percentage of total time stacking printed sheets	20 %

What is the percentage accuracy of each of these figures at a 95 per cent confidence interval?

8.9   'Inherent worker variability invalidates conventional time study.' Discuss.

8.10 The table below gives details of the data obtained during a rated activity sampling or rated systematic sampling exercise. The observations were made at 0.4-minute regular intervals, and the figures in the columns are the performance ratings (on the BS scale) for each of the elements during particular observations. (Notice that each element does not necessarily occur during each work cycle.)

If a total allowance of 15 per cent of the basic time is to be provided, what is the standard time in SM for the assembly of one product?

Observation number	Assembly element Numbers				
	1	2	3	4	Idle
1	100				
2		100			
3	105				
4		95			
5					100
6			100		
7			95		
8	90				
9		105			
10	95				
11			90		
12					105
13	100				
14					100
15		110			
16			105		
17	110				
18				105	
19	95				
20		90			

Number of assemblies produced during this eight-minute exercise = 12.

8.11 The technique of rated activity sampling is used to study the activities of three workers employed on an assembly line. The first two workers on the line have two elements to perform on each item, whereas the third worker has one element of work for each item.

At the beginning of the study the line is empty. Sufficient parts to enable the assembly of ten items are then provided, and observations are taken at 0.1-minute intervals as follows:

Time	Observed worker
0.1	A
0.2	B
0.3	C
0.1	A
0.2	B
0.3	C
etc.	etc.

These observations result in the ratings shown in the table below.
What are the basic times for each of the five work elements and for each of the three workers?

Observation number			Worker A			Worker B			Worker C	
A	B	C	El 1	El 2	Idle	El 3	El 4	Idle	El 5	Idle
1	2	3	80					100		100
4	5	6		110		90				100
7	8	9		100				100	75	
10	11	12		90			80		85	
13	14	15			100			100	90	
16	17	18	110					100		100
19	20	21		100		100				100
22	23	24			100	100			100	
25	26	27		75			85		110	
28	29	30	120			110			100	
31	32	33			100	85			120	
34	35	36			100			100		100

8.12 What are the basic objectives of work measurement? Describe briefly the main techniques and give in detail the situations suitable for one particular technique. Measured work standards are frequently used as a basis for operations scheduling and control. Comment briefly on the required accuracy of the work standards.

8.13 You are to determine the standard time for a manual job which has not previously been studied, and for which there is no detailed work method record. A computer-based work study system has been made available to you for the first time. You have a 'Microfin'-type device and a micro-computer in your office equipped with a VDU, line printer and 'floppy' disc storage. You are led to believe that all the necessary computer programs are available. How would you expect to collect information on the job to be studied, and use the computer? What output would you want to obtain from the computer?

CHAPTER 9

Human Factors
in Work System Design

NOTATION USED IN THIS CHAPTER

a	Work hours for first unit or task repetition
b	Exponent representing rate of improvement through learning
x	Number of completed units or task repetitions
$\overline{y}$	Cumulative work hours

In this chapter we shall concentrate on working conditions and the worker. The topics covered here are complementary to those covered in Chapters 7 and 8. To a large extent this chapter introduces the 'behavioural' dimension into our consideration of the design of work and work systems.

This chapter is divided into two parts as follows:

1. *Working conditions*. In this part we shall look at the design of the workplace and ergonomics. We shall also consider health and safety considerations.
2. *The worker*. Here we shall look at the design of jobs in the work organization from the worker's viewpoint and also consider aspects of worker variability and learning.

THE WORKING CONDITIONS

Ergonomics

In this section we shall be concerned with people at work, and particularly with the design of workplaces and equipment with people in mind.

220

The period between the two world wars saw the beginning of the large-scale study of working conditions and their influence on the worker's behaviour. Many psychologists were concerned during this period with the causes of fatigue, and in the United Kingdom bodies such as the Industrial Fatigue Research Board (later the Industrial Health Research Board) were established. In the USA the famous Hawthorne studies conducted by Elton Mayo at the Hawthorne plant of the Western Electric Company at Chicago began with a study of the working environment, lighting levels, etc. The Second World War stimulated this type of research work, but by this time the emphasis had, of necessity, changed. Complex military equipment placed new demands on workers and operators, who were required to exercise considerable dexterity and concentration in using radar and other equipment.

It was during this period that the term 'ergonomics' was coined in Britain, while in America the phrases 'human engineering' and 'human factors engineering' were in use to describe basically the same activities.

The worker–machine system

Despite increasing mechanization of work in industry and business, people are still associated with, and are essential to, most operating systems. Certainly the worker's role is changing, the worker being relieved of many routine and/or hazardous tasks. This trend will continue, but there will always be a need for some people, and the emphasis will therefore move to the design and management of worker–machine systems. We shall consider the nature and effects of mechanization and automation in the next chapter. Here we shall look briefly at the nature of worker–machine systems as a preliminary to further consideration of ergonomics. (We should stress that, throughout, our use of 'machine' implies equipment of all types.)

Consider the situation in which worker and machine are interdependent, in which neither can work effectively or continually without the other. When a worker uses a machine, a loop or closed system results. The worker will receive certain information from the machine, either from dials, displays, etc., designed for that purpose, or by observation of the machine itself. He or she will process this information and make decisions on what action, if any, to take and may then manipulate controls or attend to the machine in some other way so as to affect its behaviour in the desired manner. This worker–machine system is depicted diagrammatically in Figure 9.1.

The efficiency with which the worker functions depends on environmental factors, on his or her own characteristics, such as age, motivation, training and experience, and on the efficiency with which the machine provides the information feedback and accepts control measures.

If we accept, for our present purposes, that workers and their characteristics are largely fixed, this leaves us with only three aspects of the worker–machine system to discuss:

(a) design of information displays;
(b) design of controls;
(c) environmental factors.

Design of information displays

The most common means of displaying or communicating information is visual. We can identify two categories of visual display: analogue and digital. Analogue methods, such as

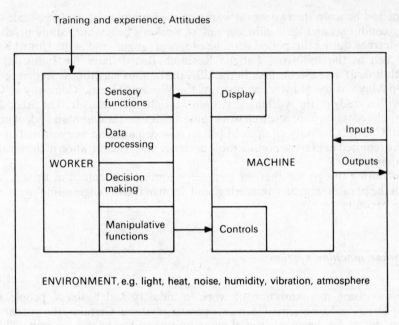

Figure 9.1 *Simplified worker–machine system.*

the circular graduated scale, are in common use, but this is mainly due to expediency rather than functional merit. The use of digital displays is a more recent phenomenon.

We can further classify visual display as follows:

1. Displays used without controls:
   (a) for quantitative measurement, e.g. clocks, voltmeters; the purpose of these is to determine whether the correct value exists, or whether corrective action is necessary;
   (b) for check reading, i.e. to determine the proximity of a characteristic to a desired value, and not for obtaining a precise measurement;
   (c) for comparison, e.g. to compare the readings on two dials;
   (d) for warning; although warning systems often include audible devices, lights are also frequently used.
2. Displays used with controls:
   (a) for controlling, i.e. to extract information and measure the effect of corrective action;
   (b) for setting, i.e. to use a control and display to ensure that a correct value is obtained, for example setting the running speed of an engine after starting up;
   (c) for tracking, i.e. to use a control continuously to correct movement or to compensate for external factors, for example keeping two indicators synchronized, or on target, by means of a control.

Many of the handbooks on ergonomics and human engineering present standards and design data for visual displays. They are not identical in their recommendations, but the following list contains most of the important points relating to the design of dials, etc.

1. Instruments should enable the worker to read information as accurately as necessary, but not more so.
2. The scale used should be both simple and logical, using the minimum number of suitable divisions.

3. The scale should provide information in an immediately usable form, and no mental conversions should be necessary.
4. Scales that must be read quantitatively should be designed so that workers need not interpolate between marks.
5. Vertical figures should be used on stationary dials and radial figures used on rotating dials.
6. Scales should not be obscured by the pointer.

Also in the visual category are written or printed information, radar, and VDUs. Visual methods of communication involving permanent copies, such as line output from computers, are particularly valuable where the message must be retained for future reference, where there is no urgency in the transmission of the information, and where long or complex messages are involved.

Instruments such as gauges and dials are of value where many sets of information are to be transmitted, and where the worker's job permits him or her to receive such information when it arrives.

Aural information 'displays', such as telephones, buzzers, bells and speech, are more appropriate where speed of transmission is important, where messages are short and uncomplicated, and where a record of the message need not be retained. Often aural communication is essential in industry, where visual channels are overloaded or where the environment does not permit visual communication. However, within the context of the worker–machine, aural communication is infrequent, except where workers are able to determine the state of equipment from the sound of operation.

Design of controls

The types of controls commonly used and their suitability for various tasks are shown in Table 9.1. The first and most important step is to select the type of control best suited to the requirements. This will involve answering the following questions:

1. What is the control for?
2. What is required, e.g. in terms of precision, force, speed, number of settings?
3. What information must be displayed by the control, i.e. must the control be identified from the others, must it be picked out in the dark, and should the worker be able to tell how the control is set?
4. How do environmental conditions affect or limit the use of the control?

Finally, having selected the most appropriate types of controls to use, they should be logically arranged, clearly marked and easily accessible. They should suit the capabilities of the operator and should be positioned to distribute the loads evenly among them. Functionally similar controls may be combined, as for example in the combined sidelights, headlights and flasher switch on many cars; also, as far as possible, controls should 'match' the changes they produce in the machine or the system (e.g. clockwise rotation to 'increase' something, etc.). There should be consistency in the direction of movement of controls and they should be close to, and identifiable with, their associated displays.

Table 9.1 *Suitability of various controls for different purposes* (Reproduced from 'Ergonomics for Industry No. 7', Ministry of Technology, 1965, by permission of the Controller, HMSO.)

Type of control	Speed	Accuracy	Force	Range	Loads
Cranks					
small	Good	Poor	Unsuitable	Good	Up to 40 in/lb
large	Poor	Unsuitable	Good	Good	Over 40 in/lb
Handwheels	Poor	Good	Fair/Poor	Fair	Up to 150 in/lb
Knobs	Unsuitable	Fair	Unsuitable	Fair	Up to 15 in/lb
Levers					
horizontal	Good	Poor	Poor	Poor	Up to 25 lb[a]
vertical (to–from body)	Good	Fair	{ Short Poor { Long Good	Poor	Up to 30 lb[a]
vertical (across body)	Fair	Fair	Fair	Unsuitable	{ One hand up to 20 lb[a] { Two hands up to 30 lb[a]
joysticks	Good	Fair	Poor	Poor	5–20 lb
Pedals	Good	Poor	Good	Unsuitable	(30–200 lb; depends on leg flexion and body support (Ankle only up to 20 lb)
Push buttons	Good	Unsuitable	Unsuitable	Unsuitable	2 lb
Rotary selector switch	Good	Good	Unsuitable	Unsuitable	Up to 10 in/lb
Joystick selector switch	Good	Good	Poor	Unsuitable	Up to 30 lb

[a] When operated by a standing operator depends on body weight.

Environmental factors

The provision of good workplace lighting, heating, ventilation, etc., is often a statutory requirement, and is necessary, though insufficient, to motivate workers and provide job satisfaction.

Lighting. Good lighting is not achieved merely by adding extra lights, since the type of lighting system adopted will depend on the type of work being performed, the size of objects, the accuracy, speed and duration of the work, etc. An adequate lighting system should provide:

(a) sufficient brightness;
(b) uniform illumination;
(c) a contrast between brightness of job and of background;
(d) no direct or reflected glare.

Although a considerable amount of research has been conducted to establish optimum levels of illumination for various jobs, there is little agreement on the subject, and American recommendations in particular differ from British in suggesting higher levels of illumination.

Lighting should be arranged to avoid 'flicker' and to provide an acceptable amount of shadow. Notice that freedom from shadow is not always desirable, since in certain circumstances, e.g. inspection, shadows can be used to improve the visibility of details by accentuating or 'modelling' surface details.

Noise. We can make the obvious distinction between continuous and intermittent noise, both of which are to some extent inevitable in industry; both can have detrimental effects on behaviour and may even cause physical damage to the worker.

Noise levels and the effect on workers can be reduced by controlling noise at its source, by putting barriers between the worker and the source of noise, by providing protective devices for the workers, or by modifying work processes to reduce workers' exposure to noise. Prolonged exposure to continuous noise levels in excess of 90 dB (decibels) is likely to result in hearing loss; 40 dB is an acceptable maximum level for comfort.

Sudden noises greatly in excess of the background noise level can and do produce a reaction, shock, or startling effect which could have disastrous consequences for workers employed on or close to machinery. Regular intermittent noise is a common feature in industry where, for example, automatic machines such as presses are involved, but there is a danger of underestimating its effect by assuming an eventual adjustment by the worker to the situation.

Temperature and ventilation. Figure 9.2 shows that the type of work and its duration determines the individual's tolerance to heat, and Table 9.2 indicates the relationship between space requirements and ventilation.

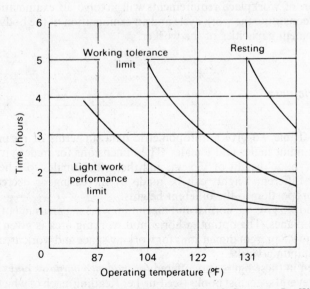

Figure 9.2 *Tolerance to heat. From Woodson, W. E. and Conover, D. W. (1964) Human Engineering Guide for Equipment Designers. Berkeley: University of California Press.*

Table 9.2 *Relationship between space requirements and ventilation.* (From Fogel, L. J. 1963 *Biotechnology: Concepts and Applications.* New Jersey: Prentice-Hall. Reproduced with permission.)

Net volume of space (cubic feet) Fresh air supply (cubic feet per minute)	Volume of space required per person (cubic feet)
1000	500
600	450
400	400
200	300
100	200
60	150
35	100
22	65

Workplace design

The design of workplaces and equipment was mentioned in Chapter 7, and all the comments made there are relevant here.

In many jobs the worker has to remain sitting or standing for long periods of time while performing a given series of tasks. Rarely is the detailed design of the product or its components influenced by the ergonomic requirements of the workers responsible for making it, except of course in such cases as the need for access during assembly. Commonly, however, other aspects of workplace design are influenced by ergonomic considerations. Inadequate design of workplaces will inhibit the ability of the worker to perform his or her tasks and may result in injuries, strain or fatigue, or a reduction in quality or output.

Determination of workplace requirements will involve an examination of the work elements which constitute the work cycle and an examination of the body measurements, reach and movement capacities of the worker.

Anthropometric data

Figure 9.3 and Table 9.3 give anthropometric data, in terms of mean dimensions in centimetres, for adult males and females. The dimensions for males given in Table 9.3 correspond to a 'nude' height of 175 cm, and those for females to a height of 163 cm. Corrections for different heights can be made by increasing or decreasing the given dimensions in proportion to the different heights.

Figures 9.4 and 9.5 give the normal and maximum working areas in both the horizontal and the vertical planes. The optimum horizontal working area is given in Figure 9.6.

Figures 9.7 and 9.8 present dimensions for working space and work area height for both sedentary and standing work.

The data given in these figures are offered *for guidance purposes only*. They have been extracted from several specialist books (see Further Reading) each of which provides more detailed information should this be required.

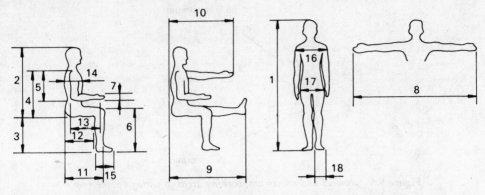

Figure 9.3 *Anthropometric data. (For dimensions see Table 9.3.)*

Table 9.3 *Anthropometric data (mean dimensions, adult males and adult females).* See Figure 9.3.

Measurement	Adult male (mean dimension, cm)	Adult female (mean dimension, cm)
1	175	162
2	90	85
3	48.5	45.5
4	58	55.5
5	36	34
6	55	51
7	9	8.5
8	178	162
9	107	101.5
10	87	79
11	59.5	56
12	47.5	46.5
13	47	43
14	22.8	–
15	27.5	24.5
16	44.5	39.5
17	33	34.5
18	9	8.8

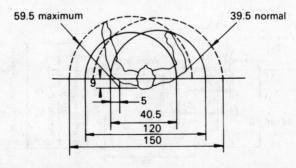

Figure 9.4 *Normal and maximum working areas in horizontal plane (cm).*

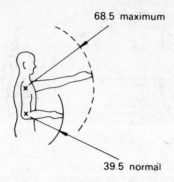

Figure 9.5 *Normal and maximum working areas in vertical plane (cm).*

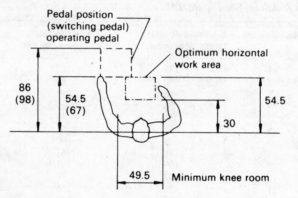

Figure 9.6 *Optimum working area, pedal positions and knee room (cm).*

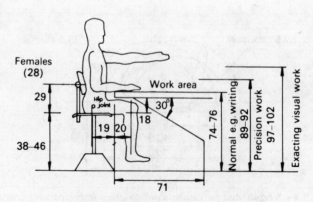

Figure 9.7 *Space for seated work (cm).*

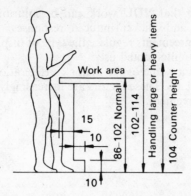

Figure 9.8 *Space for standing work (cm).*

VDU (visual display unit) work[1]

A substantial proportion of workers in offices and factories work with VDUs. In the typical situation the worker works with a VDU and keyboard connected to a computer. Such working situations are commonplace in all types of office work, in retailing, banking and insurance, and in many aspects of factory work, as well as in computer installations. Similar situations exist in connection with the use of microfilm readers, VDU readout terminals (without input keyboards), etc. The VDU, with or without input keyboard, as a self-contained unit or linked to a remote computer, is increasingly becoming a dominant feature in people's working environments.

The impact of VDUs on work will continue to increase, and already we see the evolution of 'Homo termino-videns' (terminal-viewing man) at work. Such is the importance of the VDU that the design of VDU-dominated working environments merits special reference in this chapter.

Trade unions and workers' representatives, employers and legislators have come to be particularly concerned about the effects of VDUs on workers. There is evidence of VDU work giving rise to physical discomforts, especially relating to visual fatigue, headaches, back and shoulder ache, etc. Clearly adequate ergonomic design of a VDU-dominated workplace is essential. Much of the previous discussion is also relevant in this context, but here there are additional factors which in some countries have given rise to legislation or publication of guidelines governing VDU work. For example in 1978 the Swedish Welfare Council issued directives which included the requirement for an ambient lighting level lower than that normally found in office premises, the provision of anti-glare arrangements, the requirement for movable/adjustable display screens, the avoidance of windows in the 'background' to VDUs, the provision of an appropriate level of workplace illumination, recommendations in respect of operators who wear spectacles, and the provision of rest periods.

These and other similar regulations specify the minimum workplace design requirements, beyond which specific provisions will be required for particular situations. For

---

[1] This section deals with a topic on which there is considerable current research. New findings and recommendations are published frequently; the information in this section summarizes the situation as at 1982 and is based largely on the 'European Foundation' research programme conclusions (see 'Further Reading' at the end of the chapter).

example, there is evidence that VDU work can be injurious to health through, for example, X-ray emission and 'flicker'-induced responses. In some cases local employer/union or industry agreements regulate the type of display which can be used and the maximum periods of uninterrupted use.

The sections below outline some of the major considerations in the design of VDU-dominated work environments. These factors are increasingly likely to be the subject of legislation or collective agreement.

Visual conditions

A major problem in designing VDU workplaces is the distribution of luminescences (light emissions) at the workplace. A compromise must be found between the low luminescence required of the display screen and the high luminescence required for reading the keyboard and printed documents.

Symbols on the VDU are produced by an electron beam which excites an emission of light in the phosphor coating of the screen. There is a choice of different phosphors, and this influences not only luminous intensity but also colour, flicker, and the life of the screen. The legibility of symbols on the screen depends on the contrast, and it has been suggested that a contrast of 10:1 is near optimum, while the maximum and minimum values are 15:1 and 2.5:1 respectively. Depending on the level of illumination in the room the symbol luminescence of 90 cd/m² is near optimum, with maximum and minimum values of 160 and 20 respectively. Symbol colour is not considered to be of critical importance; however, 'flicker' is a major factor. A 'critical flicker frequency' is that at which the individual can just detect a flicker in a light source. This varies from person to person but is normally in the range 20 to 60 Hz. It is dependent also on the flicker area, the shape of the light source, its illumination, location in the visual field, etc. The closer the worker to the screen and the higher the luminescence, the higher the critical flicker frequency. The surface of VDUs, being convex and glossy, can reflect surrounding features, and this can reduce symbol contrast and increase strain. Such reflections can be muted by surface treatment or the use of filters.

The cabinet surrounding the VDU tube should have a higher reflection factor than the screen itself to provide a smooth transition to the normally brighter surroundings. The luminescence of keyboards should not differ substantially from that of screens, which in most situations will necessitate the use of a dark-coloured keyboard. Concave keys can result in reflections.

Normally the level of illumination required for reading a manuscript will be higher than that required for other aspects of VDU work. However, substantial contrast with the level of illumination at the workplace is undesirable, so in most cases 'manuscript illumination' will be lower than provided for normal office work; hence legibility must be good. Printed character size, character colour and paper colour will affect legibility.

Ambient lighting conditions in working environments where VDUs exist will often be influenced by the needs of other workers on different types of work. In such cases VDUs must be positioned and oriented to prevent glare and to minimize the contrast between screen, keyboard and manuscript illumination, and levels of background illumination. It has been suggested that the area surrounding the VDU workplace should have a horizontal illumination of 300 lx and a background luminescence of 20 to 40 cd/m².

Heat and noise

The power delivered to the VDU and associated equipment is partly converted to heat and can result in a higher temperature than is desirable unless adequate local ventilation is provided. The largest contributor to local heat production will be the control unit for the VDU; the heat output of such units, typically in the range 75 to 100 W, must be considered in determining the thermal balance for working environments. Convection effects which might produce draughts and humidity requirements must also be considered.

Several sources of noise are associated with the operation of a VDU: mechanical ventilation of a VDU can add considerably to the local noise level, and keyboard noise and the noise caused by printers can be substantial. A recommended noise level below 55 dB(A) has been recommended, while VDU tasks requiring high levels of mental concentration might be adversely affected by background noise levels greater than 45 dB(A).

Ergonomic considerations

The checklists below deal specifically with a VDU working environment comprising VDU screen, keyboard, manuscript or printed material (being read) and operator.

Terminal desk

1. Adjustable desk height is desirable. A height indicator to facilitate adjustment by different workers is beneficial.
2. The desk top should be large enough to allow for all items used by the operator and for readjustment/repositioning of those items.
3. The desk top should consist of one piece with no gaps, joints, etc.
4. The desk top should have a non-reflecting surface and a pleasant (not a cold) feel.

Keyboard

1. The thickness/height of the keyboard should not exceed 20 mm including the second row of keys and it should be as narrow as possible.
2. Keyboards with a height greater than 30 mm should be sunk into the desk (although this reduces the possibility of relocation, etc.).
3. It should be easy to push or turn the keyboard.
4. The keyboard should stand firmly.
5. The keyboard should not be attached to the screen unit.
6. The slope of the keyboard should be as small as possible.
7. The keyboard should not have more keys than are needed for the work in question.
8. It will often be better to change from one keyboard to another to accommodate different types of work rather than have a comprehensive, over-large keyboard to accommodate all requirements.

Keys

1. The force required to press a key should be 0.25 to 1.5 N.
2. The distance of travel in key depression should be 3 to 4.8 mm.
3. The length of a square key should be 12 to 15 mm.
4. The distance from centre to centre of adjacent keys should be 18 to 20 mm.
5. The function keys should be larger than, and perhaps a different colour from, other keys.
6. The symbols should be engraved in the key surface or printed below a non-reflecting transparent cap.
7. The keys should be concave but only enough to match the convexity of fingers and not so much as to cause undue reflection.
8. Guide keys should be marked with a small raised dot for easier location in touch typing.

Screen unit

1. It should be possible to adjust the height of the screen unit and to tilt or turn it without tools.
2. It should be possible to push the screen unit backwards and forwards on the desk. Distance markers will facilitate readjustment.
3. The screen unit should stand firmly and not be too heavy to move.

Manuscript

1. A manuscript stand should be stable and adjustable in height and sideways. It should also tilt.
2. The best position for the manuscript is at the same distance from the eyes as the screen, and as close to the screen as possible. Abrupt changes in luminescence and reflection must be avoided.

Work schedules

Views on the definition of fair rest periods for VDU workers are numerous and varied. An early report published in Austria recommended that a break of at least one hour should follow not more than one hour's work at a VDU, but more recently collective agreements in industry have envisaged rather shorter breaks after rather longer periods, e.g. 15 minutes minimum after two hours' work at a VDU. Clearly the 'relaxation' allowance provided (see Chapter 8) in VDU work will be significant in most situations. This is an area in which legislation and collective agreements will undoubtedly have considerable impact.

Health and safety

Our discussion of working conditions and job design leads us to consider issues relating to health and safety at work—important aspects for operations managers who in many cases are legally responsible for the health and safety of their subordinates. For example in the UK, with the enforcement of Health and Safety at Work Act 1974, much of the legal responsibility for the health and safety of workers is placed on management. Employees are of course required to carry responsibility for the safety of themselves and their colleagues through both the observance of safety practices and the adoption of those working methods in which they have been instructed. The employer or manager is required to provide an overall working environment, including adequate training of the operator, so that it is safe and healthy for employees to undertake their jobs. In effect, therefore, the safety of workers becomes the individual responsibility of managers responsible for departments as well as the responsibility of the employing organization as a whole. In such circumstances individual managers become legally responsible and therefore liable to criminal prosecution for failure to observe the requirements of the Act.

In considering health and safety we are concerned in effect with the prevention of accidents or ill health. Such subjects should of course be considered in a preventive rather than a remedial sense, since it is in the interests of all parties to prevent the occurrence of illness or accidents, but in order to indicate the magnitude of the problem it will be appropriate to remind ourselves of the effects of accidents and the extent to which accidents have occurred in industry and commerce in the past.

Industrial accidents

Currently in the UK and in most other industrialized countries the number of work days lost through industrial injury exceeds those lost through industrial disputes, strikes and grievance activity. In the UK at the present time the relationship is of the order of two to one. Approximately 300 000 accidents are reported in factories annually in the UK, approximately 1 per cent of which are fatal. It should be noted, however, that in general a large proportion of the accidents which occur in industry and business are never reported and therefore do not feature in local or national statistics. Statistics concerning accidents are therefore a poor indicator of the magnitude of the problem, since for such purposes an accident is considered to be something which 'causes disablement for more than three days' and is therefore legally notifiable. Thus a large number of accidents are not reported and, furthermore, a large number of the accidents which do cause disablement for more than three days are reported under other headings, e.g. sickness, absence, etc.

In general, at least in factories, the major source of accidents is concerned with the handling of goods, e.g. lifting, placing, movement, etc., at the workplace and between workplaces. Falls, and accidents caused by machinery, are the next most important source of accidents. Most severe accidents occur as a result of individuals becoming 'involved' with machinery, while accidents occurring during the handling of goods comprise a major proportion of those accidents causing lesser or shorter periods of disablement. Fires and explosions are also a major source of accidents. Table 9.4 gives some indication of the causes and severity of accidents in industry.

Among the economic implications to the employer deriving from the occurrence of an accident are the following:

Table 9.4   *UK industrial accidents: cause and severity*

Primary cause	Severe (including fatalities) (%)	Resulting in absence from work of > 28 days (%)	Resulting in absence from work of < 28 days (%)	Percentage of total for all causes
Machinery	33	22	45	17
Transport	25	28	47	7
Hand tools	17	22	61	6
Falls of persons	22	30	48	16
Striking against an object	12	28	60	9
Handling goods	11	28	61	28
Struck by falling object	21	29	50	7
Others	14	24	62	10
			Total	100

(Based on reports of UK Chief Inspector of Factories, *c.* 1980)

(a)   working time lost by the employee;

(b)   time lost by other employees who choose to or must of necessity stop work at the time of or following the accident;

(c)   time lost by supervision, management and technical staff following the accident;

(d)   proportion of the cost of employing first aid, medical staff, etc.;

(e)   cost of disruption to the operation;

(f)   cost of any damage to the equipment or any cost associated with the subsequent modification of the equipment;

(g)   cost of any compensation payments or fines resulting from legal action;

(h)   costs associated with increased insurance premiums;

(i)   reduced output from the injured employee on return to work;

(j)   cost of reduced morale, increased absenteeism, increased labour turnover among employees.

This is, of course, only one side of the equation, since the injured person, his or her dependants, colleagues, etc. must also 'pay' some cost as a result of the occurrence of an accident. Certainly it would be socially, morally and probably legally unacceptable to consider accidents only in terms of direct and indirect cost to the employers.

Preventive action

The prevention of illness and accidents requires efforts on the part of employees and management, the latter including those responsible for the design of the operating system and its staffing. Some of the steps which might be taken to reduce the frequency and severity of accidents are as follows:[2]

---

[2]   Gedye, R. (1979) *Works Management and Productivity.* London: Heinemann.

(a) developing a safety consciousness among staff and workers and encouraging departmental pride in a good safety record;
(b) developing effective consultative participation between management, workers and unions so that safety and health rules can be accepted and followed;
(c) giving adequate instruction in safety rules and measures as part of the training of new and transferred workers, or where working methods or speeds of operation are changed;
(d) materials handling, a major cause of accidents, to be minimized and designed as far as possible for safe working and operation;
(e) ensuring a satisfactory standard from the safety angle for both basic plant and auxiliary fittings such as guards and other devices;
(f) good maintenance—apart from making sound job repairs, temporary expedients to keep production going should not prejudice safety.

Fire prevention and control represent a further area for preventive action. The main causes of fire in industry and commerce tend to be associated with electrical appliances and installations. Smoking is a major source of fires in business premises. The Fire Protection Association (of the UK) suggest the following guidelines for fire prevention and control:

1. Management should accept that fire prevention policies and practices must be established and reviewed regularly.
2. Management should be aware of the possible effects and consequences of fires in terms of loss of buildings, plant and output, damage to records, effects on customers and workers, etc.
3. Fire risks should be identified, particularly as regards sources of ignition, presence of combustible materials, and the means by which fires can spread.
4. The responsibility for fire prevention should be established.
5. A fire officer should be appointed.
6. A fire prevention drill should be established and practised.

As for other sources of illness and accidents, there are detailed guidelines for fire prevention and checklists for use in assessing the adequacy of existing procedures and in designing new procedures.

THE WORKER

Job design and work organization

No longer is the design of work and jobs simply the application of method study and work measurement. There is a need to give considerable thought to the behavioural aspects of work and job design, and this is the focus of this section.

In order to put the subject in perspective, and in order to understand fully current theory and practice, it will be beneficial first to examine briefly its history.

The theories of job design

Since the work of Taylor and Gilbreth and the birth of the scientific management movement, many theories of work and job design (we can use the two terms synonymously for the time being) have been advanced, a great deal of research work has been conducted and a great deal learned. Both Taylor and Gilbreth were intent on finding the best method of working. Taylor's two fundamental objectives were to:

(a)   select the best person for the job;
(b)   instruct him or her in the best method of doing the job.

In 1911 Taylor said, 'Those who have anything to do with Scientific Management realize, however, that there is a best way in doing everything, and that the best way can always be formulated into certain rules'.[3] Similarly, Gilbreth was anxious to discover the best way to work, although, unlike Taylor, he sought this through the elimination of wasteful and inefficient motions. Both Taylor and Gilbreth, despite their differing emphases, considered the worker as being like any other production facility, as something that could be 'set up' to work continuously and efficiently in a predetermined manner. The scientific management movement brought an engineering approach to the study and design of work.

This approach was to be modified first by industrial psychologists. Until about 1935 their focus was on the causes and consequences of boredom and fatigue. Britain took a lead in this work through bodies such as the Industrial Fatigue Research Board. An ergonomic approach to work and job design then evolved in which the emphasis was on the influences of working conditions (heat, light, rest pauses, etc.) on worker behaviour. The limitations of this approach became apparent in about 1925, when the first of several experiments was conducted at the Bank Wiring Department of the Hawthorne works of the Western Electric Company in Chicago.[4]

The human relations theory

To come to terms with these new-found complexities there evolved an approach later known as the human relations theory, which emphasized the social needs of the worker. The human relations theorists investigated factories as social systems rather than as collections of workers and their jobs. In searching for optimum methods of job design these theorists placed emphasis on the workers' social and affiliation needs. However, people are no more exclusively social animals than they are financial animals; consequently in some respects the human relations theory was as abstract as earlier theories, since it was concerned primarily with only one dimension—the social—which was considered to be of overriding importance. For this reason the human resources approach began to emerge.

---

[3]   From a paper presented at the first conference on scientific management at the Amos Tuck School, Dartmouth College, USA, October 1911.
[4]   Roethlisberger, F. J. and Dickson, W. J. (1939) *Management and the Worker*. Harvard: Harvard University Press. (The Hawthorne experiments were begun on the then classical lines that the objective was to investigate the influence of physical working conditions on working behaviour, with particular reference to fatigue and output. The first experiment concerned the influence of lighting on worker output. Two groups of workers were observed: one a control group and the other a test group. Lighting levels were adjusted for the test group, but, irrespective of what changes were made, the output for both groups increased. Similar results were obtained in the experiment begun in 1927, in which the influence of work hours, particularly rest periods, was examined. Irrespective of the changes made in the hours and the frequency and duration of rest periods, output showed an encouraging upward trend. The conclusion drawn from these experiments was that the worker was not an isolated machine whose performance was influenced only by the type of work he or she was asked to do and the conditions in which he or she was asked to do it. The early concepts of work were now seen as oversimplified.)

The human resources theory

McGregor presents two theories relating to the worker and his or her job. First, theory X, the assumptions of which are as follows:

1. The average worker dislikes work and prefers to avoid it.
2. Workers must be coerced and controlled in order to work for organizational objectives.
3. The average worker prefers to be directed, to avoid responsibility; he or she has little ambition and seeks security foremost.

In contrast to this theory McGregor suggests a theory Y, the basis of which is as follows:

1. The capacity for physical and mental effort is a natural ability of the average worker.
2. External control is not the only means of motivating workers, since the average worker will exercise self-direction and self-control in the service of objectives to which he or she is committed.
3. Commitment to objectives is a function of the rewards associated with their achievement.
4. The average worker learns under proper conditions not only to accept, but also to seek, responsibility.
5. The capacity to exercise a relatively high degree of imagination, ingenuity and creativity is widely, not narrowly distributed among the population.
6. Under the conditions typical of modern industry the intellectual potentials of the average worker are only partially utilized.

This concept of the worker, with its implications for job design, while appealing, initially did not influence job design practice significantly until the emergence of a further approach: the job enlargement and enrichment philosophy (job redesign).

The job enlargement and enrichment philosophy (job redesign)

Throughout the period up to the 1970s, despite these various theories, there was a continuing trend towards the increasing rationalization of work. The principles of work study developed and first applied by Taylor and Gilbreth were adopted widely and largely unquestioningly, but increasingly the further rationalization of work is being condemned. It is argued that such work is incapable of fulfilling the basic work needs, i.e. the needs for achievement, recognition and so on, and that as a consequence job satisfaction is minimal.

Over the past ten years, therefore, a philosophy has evolved which advocates the design or redesign of jobs so that workers can use their skills and abilities more, determine their own work pace, make decisions about work methods, quality, etc. The emphasis here is on worker self-motivation[5] and job satisfaction *alongside* operational efficiency and productivity. We shall refer mainly to job redesign, since much of the information we shall draw upon comes from situations in which jobs have been redesigned, i.e. changed. However, our discussion, in particular the identification of objectives in the redesign of jobs, applies also to the design of new jobs.

---

[5] A full understanding of the concepts and theories of job enrichment requires an understanding of aspects of behavioural science, in particular topics relating to motivation theory. For further details readers may wish to consult books such as Lawler, E. E. (1973) *Motivation in Work Organisations*. Monterey: Brooks-Cole.

The nature of job redesign and work organization

The job redesign 'experiments' which have been undertaken in effect have involved one or both of two basic approaches, i.e. the *enlargement* of work content through the addition of one or more related tasks, and job *enrichment*, involving the increase in the motivational content of jobs through, for example, the addition of different types of tasks or the provision of increased worker involvement and participation. Both approaches are concerned with the content of jobs. A quite different approach involves the way in which jobs are organized. The provision of job rotation, i.e. workers moving between jobs in either a self-organized or a scheduled manner, and the provision of some opportunities for workers to organize their own jobs are examples of this approach. We shall describe this approach as work organization. This two-part categorization is summarized in Figure 9.9. The distinction between job enlargement and enrichment permits examination of the degree to which the changes employed are likely to increase the motivational content of jobs. It is argued that the opportunity for the satisfaction of higher-order needs is provided through job enrichment but not through the simple enlargement or extension of the existing content of jobs. The difference between job redesign and work organizational changes helps highlight the fact that, although the objective of many changes is the

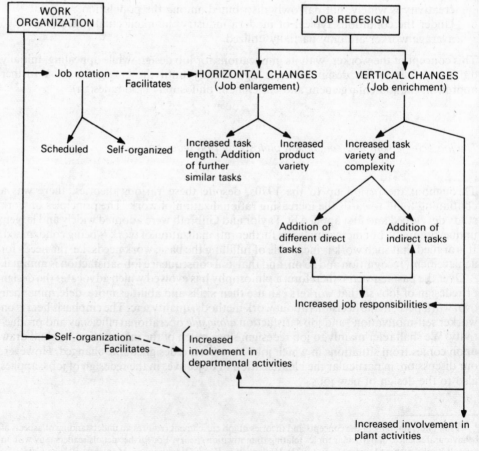

Figure 9.9

modification of the tasks undertaken by workers, such changes are often dependent on, or perhaps brought about only by, appropriate organizational change. Thus job rotation, an organizational change, may provide for job enlargement, and some degree of worker self-organization may give rise to, or be a necessary prerequisite for, certain types of job enrichment.

A procedure for job redesign and work organization

Our primary objective here is to attempt to develop a succinct yet comprehensive model or checklist which can be used in the redesign of jobs and in work organizations. In particular we must look in more detail at the mechanics of redesign and organizational changes (i.e. the means) and at the objectives (i.e. the ends) of such change in order to provide a common practical framework.

Table 9.5 identifies most of the desirable job characteristics which have been advocated by authors, i.e. those characteristics which are considered to give rise to job satisfaction and worker motivation.[6] These are further considered below.

Work content and method

Examination of the nature of the 14 job characteristics listed in Table 9.5 reveals a three-level structure, i.e.

1. Tasks:
    new and more difficult tasks to be added;
    inclusion of some auxiliary and preparatory tasks.
    The characteristics listed also provide some examples of the above, i.e.
    inspect own work;
    repair defects;
    set up machines;
    responsibility for cleanliness of work area;
    responsibility for maintenance.
2. Task relationships:
    'closure'—perform complete module of work;
    obvious relationship between tasks.
3. Work attributes:
    perceivable contribution to product utility;
    increased task variety;
    use of workers' valued skills and abilities;
    meaningful and worthwhile job.

These three levels might be seen to have cause and effect relationships, i.e. it might be advocated that tasks (1) should be structured so that the tasks done bear a holistic relationship (2) in order to provide certain work attributes (3).

---

6   Wild, R. and Birchall, D. W. (1973) Means and ends in job restructuring, *Personnel Review,* Autumn, pp. 18–24.

Table 9.5 *Desirable characteristics of jobs (for job satisfaction and motivation)*

Job/Work
1. Work content
   A   'Closure', i.e. complete module of work
   B   Obvious relationship between tasks
   C   New and more difficult tasks added
   D   Increased variety of tasks
   E   Make use of workers' valued skills and abilities
   F   Include some auxiliary and preparatory tasks
   G   Individual inspects own work
   H   Assembler repairs defective items
   I   Operator sets up machines
   J   Operator responsible for cleanliness of work area
   K   Operator responsible for maintenance
   L   Perceived contribution to product's utility
   M   Work content such that job is meaningful and worth while
2. Work method
   A   No machine pacing

Organization
3. Work organization
   A   Give worker some choice of method
   B   Worker discretion
   C   Operator plans own work
   D   Operator organizes own work
   E   Self-regulation
   F   Worker responsible for controlling own work
   G   Operator sets own performance goals
   H   Subgoals to measure accomplishment
   I   Individual accountable for own work
   J   Job responsibilities (generally)
   K   Worker autonomy
   L   Operator involved in solving problems
   M   Workers participate in design and improvement of own job
   N   Workers involved in decision-making concerning work
   O   Workers receive performance feedback at regular intervals
4. Job opportunity
   A   More than minimum required training provided
   B   Worker able to learn new things about process
   C   Promotion prospects for worker
   D   Specific or specialized tasks enable worker to develop expertise
   E   Increased challenge for worker
5. Social conditions/relations
   A   Conversation either easy or impossible
   B   Facilitates workers' movement about factory

Work organization

Examination of the work-organization characteristics listed in Table 9.5 reveals a possible two-level structure: work organization and work attributes.

1. Work organization:
   worker has some choice of work method;
   worker plans/organizes own work;
   worker controls own work/self-regulation;
   workers set performance goals;
   regular performance feedback;

      worker participates in job design/improvement;
      worker involved in work problem-solving.
2. Work attributes:
      worker discretion/decision-making;
      worker accountability/responsibility;
      worker autonomy.

Group 1 above may be seen to give rise to the attributes of 2 and, further, some work-method characteristics may be seen as prerequisites for certain organizational characteristics.

Job opportunity

Of the five cited characteristics, four relate to personal development while one relates to job advancement. Worker involvement in the organization (involvement, identity, feelings of importance) and self-actualization (growth and advancement, self-development and pride) are given as consequences of opportunities for worker development, but no specific effects are associated with opportunities for promotion. It could be argued that personal development, e.g. increase in skills, abilities and accomplishment, will give rise to openings in employment and hence promotion opportunities, although it is not clear whether authors advocating development characteristics had this consequence in mind.

Social conditions

Both characteristics in this section relate to ease of social interaction. We would suggest that a job should facilitate social interaction in the interests of job satisfaction, although it is recognized that complete lack of verbal contact may be preferable to contact with difficulty.

Examination of the tentative structures developed above suggests a breakdown of the original job characteristics or 'means' category into two sections: first, work and job attributes, and second, those characteristics (tasks, task relationships, work methods and organization) which in some combination provide for the existence of such attributes. From this interpretation it appears that it is largely the provision and manipulation of these latter characteristics which give rise to the existence of work and jobs with attributes capable of causing worker responses. While the processes of job restructuring and work organization do not necessarily follow such a neat path, this three-part process does provide a useful reference framework. The model is summarized in Figure 9.10, in which certain additions have been made as a result of the findings cited earlier in this chapter. This model does not necessarily provide a complete checklist, nor does the information reviewed above yield only to this interpretation. However, the structure is of value in that it helps to distinguish between those aspects of jobs which might be manipulated and those job features which changes might affect but which cannot be directly treated. The job attributes identified here might, in many circumstances, provide more appropriate objectives for job changes than many of those usually identified in the literature, since these attributes are more easily associated with the 'enabling' job characteristics.

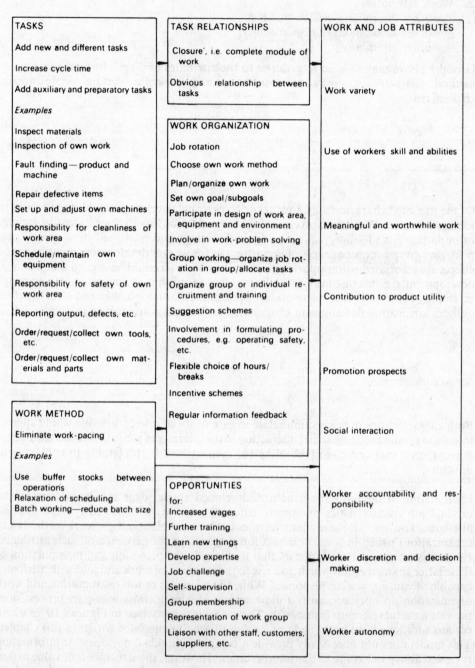

Figure 9.10 *Model relating the characteristics and attitudes of work and jobs. From Wild, R. (1975) Work Organization. New York: Wiley.*

Job redesign: the present situation

In discussing work study in Chapters 7 and 8 we showed that its objective was the determination of the most efficient work method, while the objective of work measurement was the determination of a standard time for such a method. Quite apart from the fact that work study tends to lead to specialization and work rationalization, these objectives have been criticized. For example, how appropriate or reasonable is it to expect a worker to execute any task, large or small, in precisely the same way and in precisely the same time on each repetition? Is it not reasonable to expect the worker's pace to vary, and to expect him or her to vary the work method in order to achieve more variety? Indeed it can be said that the whole concept of work study, in that it seeks to impose a rigidity of method and duration, is ill-conceived and inappropriate. Such an argument, however, again assumes the homogeneity of the workforce, as did the job redesign philosophy. It is undoubtedly true that some workers would prefer to avoid work pacing, method imposition and highly rationalized work, but, equally, others will willingly tolerate and even prefer such circumstances.

There is no doubt that the activities of the industrial engineer or work study practitioner are of prime importance in determining job satisfaction, since despite the importance of such aspects of the job as social relations, supervision and environmental conditions, the nature of the work is a determinant of job satisfaction.

The influence of the industrial engineer, the work study practitioner, and hence the operations manager on job satisfaction is very clear. However, one thing that is immediately apparent from our discussion is the futility of generalization. A frequent mistake has been the belief that the relationship between the worker, the work and the job is a simple one, a belief which has often led to the formulation of oversimplified and abstract theories of job design.

Job satisfaction can be regarded as a function of the extent to which job needs are fulfilled. Workers, however, exhibit different needs with different emphases. For some people the need for achievement is particularly important, and for them an interesting, challenging job is essential. For others the achievement need is less important than the financial or social needs.

Clearly, highly rationalized work is not universally detrimental, but equally, in the present situation, job enlargement could often be beneficial.

Ideally one would wish to design a job appropriate to the requirements of the individual, but even if this were possible it is unreasonable to expect that it would be practical. If we regard the objective of job design as being the design of jobs appropriate to the requirements of the individual, so as to maximize job satisfaction and productivity, then alternatively we can consider the problem as being one of labour selection and placement. In the former case jobs are designed appropriate to the requirements of an available labour force, whereas in the latter case labour is selected and placed into available jobs. Ostensibly, the former is the responsibility of the industrial engineer and the latter the responsibility of the personnel manager, but since neither job design nor labour selection and placement can be performed independently of knowledge of the other, the complete division of responsibilities is perhaps no longer appropriate.

In the short term, neither job design nor labour selection and placement can be fully effective because sufficient knowledge is not yet available. Further research must be conducted to determine the relationships between job design, situational variables and individual characteristics and their influence on job satisfaction and behaviour before adequate procedures and principles can be evolved. In the short term, therefore, the responsibility of the industrial engineer must extend to an awareness of this problem, since without sympathy from management and the professions involved the present situation cannot be improved. In practical terms the responsibility of the industrial engineer must at present be to ensure that a variety of jobs are available within any firm, so that job dissatisfaction, once identified, can be remedied by means of internal transfers of workers to jobs more appropriate to their requirements.

EXAMPLE: WORK REORGANIZATION IN CONTRACT CLEANING

Organization:	Texas Instruments, USA
Jobs:	Factory and office cleaners
Original arrangement:	Contract workers do all cleaning
Problem:	Poor standard of work of contract cleaners
New arrangement:	Groups of cleaners established (employed by company)
	Groups given specific areas of responsibility
	Groups responsible for organizing their own work in each area
	Groups plan and control own work schedules
	Groups given training in work simplification
Results:	Cleanliness improved
	71 personnel used in place of 120
	Turnover of staff substantially reduced
	Saving $103 000 p.a.

EXAMPLE: JOB ENRICHMENT IN A TELEPHONE EXCHANGE

Changes are to be made to two existing telephone operator jobs: directory assistance and toll, in an exchange situated in a medium-sized town. Currently directory assistance involves looking up telephone numbers at the request of customers. Operators are required to use a very precise phraseology with customers, they are not allowed to leave their positions without their supervisor's permission, and they are not permitted to swop jobs on their own initiative. The operators cannot make decisions about whether or not to serve a customer who has a large number of requests.

The redesign of the jobs was undertaken by both specialist staff and line management. Operators had the changes explained to them. The specific changes were as follows: (a) operators were given more freedom concerning phraseology used with customers, emphasis being placed on helpfulness and efficiency; (b) operators were no longer required to state their number at the beginning of conversations; (c) operators could move from directory assistance to toll operations at their own discretion if the workload appeared unequal; (d) operators themselves could decide whether to deal with a large number of requests and call customers later; (e) greater freedom of movement was permitted; (f) operators were allowed to take and report their own counts of the calls they had handled. As a result of the changes, training was reduced from five days to less than two days, but little change was reported in levels of job satisfaction.

EXAMPLE: JOB ENLARGEMENT IN ASSEMBLY WORK

The previous method of assembly of the several types of typewriters involved the use of two parallel, non-mechanical type flow lines staffed by both male and female workers. Each line was divided into five main sections and staffed by approximately 65 workers working at a cycle time of three minutes. The sections at the beginning of the line had the more complex tasks, those towards the end being concerned with more simple assembly tasks prior to quality checks and rectification work. Each section had a supervisor. The payment system employed consisted of a base rate plus an individual bonus which accounted for as much as 25 per cent of the total earnings.

Following the redesign the cycle time of the new operations is now 20 minutes and the layout of the line has been rearranged to facilitate greater interpersonal contact. The groups are given responsibility for checking quality and fault rectification. The piecework scheme has been replaced by a monthly time rate. Social areas have been provided adjacent to each of the lines, and workers arrange their own breaks among themselves, with the freedom to rearrange work methods if they so desire. Improvements include a 35 per cent increase in output, a cheaper cost for the desired product quality, less floor space required, better worker/management relations and an increase in production flexibility.

Worker variability and learning effects

An implicit assumption in work measurement is that of worker consistency. Certainly in establishing work times through direct measurement it is normal to average several readings or observations. To some extent this overcomes the problems of worker variability, and of course minimizes the effects of inaccuracies of measurement. However, the objective nevertheless is to obtain a single time estimate or measure. This single figure is then frequently used without recognition of the fact that, in practice, work times will vary around it, and that at best it represents only the mean work time. In virtually all circumstances human manual work times will vary and some account must be taken of this characteristic. For example, where work is undertaken in a series of sequential operations, unless some allowance is made for work time variability at each stage, substantial idle time and/or work congestion will result. Such worker variability will be considered in more detail in Chapter 15 in the discussion of flow system design.

Learning

The concept of learning is complex, so much so that there is as yet little agreement about the true nature of the processes involved. We cannot examine this complex subject here and it will be sufficient for our present purposes to consider learning as the process by which an individual (e.g. manager, worker) acquires skill and proficiency at a task which, in turn, has the effect of permitting increased productivity in his or her performance of that task. Here we shall be concerned only with worker task learning, the speed at which a task can be executed, the extent to which the learning can increase this speed, and the influence of various factors on the learning phenomenon. We shall consider the nature and use of the *learning curve* (sometimes called the *improvement curve* or the *progress function*). The learning curve of the type shown in Figure 9.11 reflects three factors:

1. The time required to complete a task or unit of work will reduce with repeated performance of that task.
2. The rate of reduction will decrease over time.
3. This reduction in time will follow a general pattern.

The learning curve shown in Figure 9.11 represents a 75 per cent rate of improvement. The curve shows a performance improvement resulting from learning equivalent to a constant rate of improvement of 75 per cent, i.e. the first performance of the task requires one hour

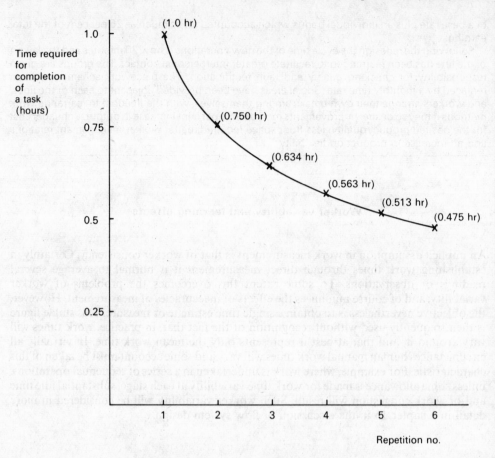

Figure 9.11   *75 per cent learning curve.*

and thereafter every doubling of the number of performances or number of repetitions shows a 75 per cent improvement. Thus the second performance requires 1×0.75, i.e. 0.75 hours, the fourth performance requires 0.75×0.75, i.e. 0.56 hours, etc. This performance improvement, shown on arithmetic scales as in Figure 9.11, shows a characteristic asymptotic pattern. Alternatively such curves can be plotted on logarithmic paper as straight lines. The same 75 per cent learning curve is shown with others on log scales in Figure 9.12. This type of plot serves to demonstrate one of the most important aspects of the learning effect, i.e. its *predictability*.

$$\bar{y} = ax^b$$

where $\bar{y}$ = accumulative work hours for any quantity, x, of units produced by x repetitions of the task.

a = work hours for first unit, i.e. for first performance of the task
x = number of completed units, i.e. number of repetitions of the task
b = exponent representing the rate of improvement (i.e. the percentage learning rate divided by 100)

Thus the work hours required for a total of ten repetitions of a task where the first performance takes one hour and where a 75 per cent learning effect exists = $1 \times 10^{0.75} = 5.59$ hours.

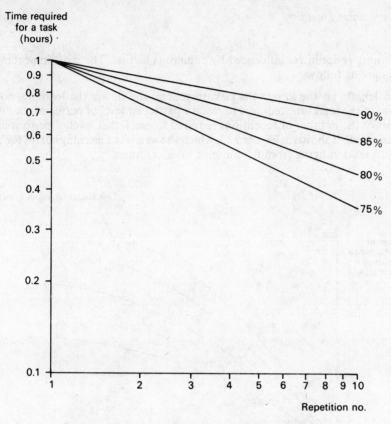

Figure 9.12 *Learning curves (75–90 per cent).*

The following examples illustrate further types of learning curve calculations in which the coefficients in Table 9.6 are used.

EXAMPLES OF LEARNING CURVE CALCULATIONS

1. A worker is to repeat a job 20 times. It is estimated that the first time the job is done it will take 1.5 hours. It is estimated that an 80 per cent learning effect will exist. How long will it take to finish all 20 jobs?
   Answer. For 20 units at 80 per cent learning, total time $= 1.5 (10.484) = 15.73$ hours
2. It is known that the average time for a job over a 'run' of 15 identical jobs is three hours. What is the time required for the first and the last jobs if the learning rate is 75 per cent?
   Answer. Total time for 15 units (for an initial time of 1 hour $= 7.319$

   Average time for 15 units (for an initial time of 1 hour) $= \dfrac{7.319}{15} = 0.4879$ hours

   Hence:

   Time for first unit $\dfrac{3}{0.4879} = 6.149$ hours

   Time for last unit $0.325 (6.149) = 1.998$ hours

Factors influencing learning

Task learning is doubtless influenced by numerous factors. The most important for our purposes are as follows:

1. Task length, i.e. the longer the task, in general the slower the learning, not only in terms of the total time required to reach a particular level of performance, but also in terms of the number of repetitions required to reach that level of performance. This relationship is shown in Figure 9.13, which shows a set of learning curves for different-length tasks ranging from 0.5 minutes to 3.5 minutes.

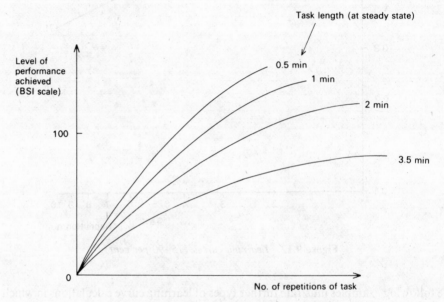

Figure 9.13 *Effect of task length on learning.*

2. Task complexity.
3. The capability or skill of the worker and his or her familiarity with the type of work to be learned.
4. Task similarity, i.e. the extent to which the task being learned is similar to that undertaken previously by the worker.
5. Worker motivation and personal characteristics.
6. External influences, e.g. physical conditions, etc.

In certain circumstances, particularly where work has begun on a particular task, it will be possible to estimate the learning percentage and thus to predict, using the formula above, the time required to complete a task or the performance level at some future date. Thus it will be possible to predict the relatively steady state performance, i.e. the work standard for a particular task. In other circumstances, especially where work has not begun on a particular task, it will be necessary to estimate the learning percentage in order to predict the 'relatively steady state' work standard. Prediction might be undertaken either by comparing the task to be completed with similar work undertaken in similar circumstances or by analysing the nature of the task by comparison with other tasks.

Table 9.6 *Learning curve coefficients*

Unit number	70% Unit time	70% Total time	75% Unit time	75% Total time	80% Unit time	80% Total time	85% Unit time	85% Total time	90% Unit time	90% Total time
1	1.000	1.000	1.000	1.000	1.000	1.000	1.000	1.000	1.000	1.000
2	.700	1.700	.750	1.750	.800	1.800	.850	1.850	.900	1.900
3	.568	2.268	.634	2.384	.702	2.502	.773	2.623	.846	2.746
4	.490	2.758	.562	2.946	.640	3.142	.723	3.345	.810	3.556
5	.437	3.195	.513	3.459	.596	3.738	.686	4.031	.783	4.339
6	.398	3.593	.475	3.934	.562	4.299	.657	4.688	.762	5.101
7	.367	3.960	.446	4.380	.534	4.834	.634	5.322	.744	5.845
8	.343	4.303	.422	4.802	.512	5.346	.614	5.936	.729	6.574
9	.323	4.626	.402	5.204	.493	5.839	.597	6.533	.716	7.290
10	.306	4.932	.385	5.589	.477	6.315	.583	7.116	.705	7.994
11	.291	5.223	.370	5.958	.462	6.777	.570	7.686	.695	8.689
12	.278	5.501	.357	6.315	.449	7.227	.558	8.244	.685	9.374
13	.267	5.769	.345	6.660	.438	7.665	.548	8.792	.677	10.052
14	.257	6.026	.334	6.994	.428	8.092	.539	9.331	.670	10.721
15	.248	6.274	.325	7.319	.418	8.511	.530	9.861	.663	11.384
16	.240	6.514	.316	7.635	.410	8.920	.522	10.383	.656	12.040
17	.233	6.747	.309	7.944	.402	9.322	.515	10.898	.650	12.690
18	.226	6.973	.301	8.245	.394	9.716	.508	11.405	.644	13.334
19	.220	7.192	.295	8.540	.338	10.104	.501	11.907	.639	13.974
20	.214	7.407	.288	8.828	.381	10.485	.495	12.402	.634	14.608
21	.209	7.615	.283	9.111	.375	10.860	.490	12.892	.630	15.237
22	.204	7.819	.277	9.388	.370	11.230	.484	13.376	.625	15.862
23	.199	8.018	.272	9.660	.364	11.594	.479	13.856	.621	16.483
24	.195	8.213	.267	9.928	.359	11.954	.475	14.331	.617	17.100
25	.191	8.404	.263	10.191	.355	12.309	.470	14.801	.613	17.713
26	.187	8.591	.259	10.449	.350	12.659	.466	15.267	.609	18.323
27	.183	8.774	.255	10.704	.346	13.005	.462	15.728	.606	18.929
28	.180	8.954	.251	10.955	.342	13.347	.458	16.186	.603	19.531
29	.177	9.131	.247	11.202	.338	13.685	.454	16.640	.599	20.131
30	.174	9.305	.244	11.446	.335	14.020	.450	17.091	.596	20.727
31	.171	9.476	.240	11.686	.331	14.351	.447	17.538	.593	21.320
32	.168	9.644	.237	11.924	.328	14.679	.444	17.981	.590	21.911
33	.165	9.809	.234	12.158	.324	15.003	.441	18.422	.588	22.498
34	.163	9.972	.231	12.389	.321	15.324	.437	18.859	.585	23.084
35	.160	10.133	.229	12.618	.318	15.643	.434	19.294	.583	23.666
36	.158	10.291	.226	12.844	.315	15.958	.432	19.725	.580	24.246
37	.156	10.447	.223	13.067	.313	16.271	.429	20.154	.578	24.824
38	.154	10.601	.221	13.288	.310	16.581	.426	20.580	.575	25.399
39	.152	10.753	.219	13.507	.307	16.888	.424	21.004	.573	25.972
40	.150	10.902	.216	13.723	.305	17.193	.421	21.425	.571	26.543
41	.148	11.050	.214	13.937	.303	17.496	.419	21.844	.569	27.111
42	.146	11.196	.212	14.149	.300	17.796	.416	22.260	.567	27.678
43	.144	11.341	.210	14.359	.298	18.094	.414	22.674	.565	28.243
44	.143	11.484	.208	14.567	.296	18.390	.412	23.086	.563	28.805
45	.141	11.625	.206	14.773	.294	18.684	.410	23.496	.561	29.366
46	.139	11.764	.204	14.977	.292	18.975	.408	23.903	.559	29.925
47	.138	11.902	.202	15.180	.290	19.265	.405	24.309	.557	30.482
48	.136	12.038	.201	15.380	.288	19.552	.403	24.712	.555	31.037

Table 9.6 *(contd.)*

Unit number	70%		75%		80%		85%		90%	
	Unit time	Total time	Unit time	Total time	Unit time	Total time	Unit time	Total time	Unit time	Total time
49	.135	12.173	.199	15.579	.286	19.838	.402	25.113	.553	31.590
50	.134	12.307	.197	15.776	.284	20.122	.400	25.513	.552	32.142
51	.132	12.439	.196	15.972	.282	20.404	.398	25.911	.550	32.692
52	.131	12.570	.194	16.166	.280	20.684	.396	26.307	.548	33.241
53	.130	12.700	.192	16.358	.279	20.963	.394	26.701	.547	33.787
54	.128	12.828	.191	16.549	.277	21.239	.392	27.094	.545	34.333
55	.127	12.955	.190	16.739	.275	21.515	.391	27.484	.544	34.877
56	.126	13.081	.188	16.927	.274	21.788	.389	27.873	.542	35.419
57	.125	13.206	.187	17.144	.272	22.060	.388	28.261	.541	35.960
58	.124	13.330	.185	17.299	.271	22.331	.386	28.647	.539	36.499
59	.123	13.453	.184	17.483	.269	22.600	.384	29.031	.538	37.037
60	.122	13.574	.183	17.666	.268	22.868	.383	29.414	.537	37.574

Because of this learning phenomenon it will be unrealistic to assume that a constant time is required for the completion of particular tasks, i.e. that a particular work standard will always apply. Thus in direct time study it will be necessary to take some account of the level of learning accomplishment of the worker in order to 'correct' the work standard based on the observed time. Thus if the worker being observed during direct time study is inexperienced, it must be assumed that a more experienced worker will be able to perform the task in a shorter time. However, if a work standard is being determined for a new job, the learning effect must be allowed. Similarly, in establishing work standards for jobs some account must be taken of the 'life' of such jobs. If a worker is to perform a job for some considerable length of time then it is reasonable to assume that he or she will achieve a level of performance equivalent to the relatively steady state level. If, however, the task is to be performed for a relatively short time it might be assumed that learning will still be taking place when the last cycle is completed. In applying indirect work measurement, e.g. PMTS, an allowance must also be made for the learning effect. In general, PMTS times will provide work standards for fully trained, skilled and accomplished workers, i.e. steady state learned performances. Some allowances must be made in such times to provide for the learning effect during the start-up period.

Learning effects

It follows from the above that consideration of learning effects, as shown by learning curves, will be of relevance wherever it is necessary to establish a time for a worker to perform a task, and wherever such times are to be used. For example, learning curves, as a means of determining the amount of time required for tasks and/or the amount of capacity available for undertaking work, are of relevance in applications such as the following:

1. In capacity planning. It is suggested in Chapter 11 that capacity will increase over time as increasing familiarity with the task increases labour efficiency.
2. Pricing products and services. If the labour cost component for a product or service is to be costed in terms of the labour hours required to execute the task then the cost will decrease over time. Thus a long 'run' involving greater repetition should result in reduced cost, therefore perhaps reducing price.

3. Scheduling. If the time required for a task is reduced because of the effects of learning, this fact should be taken into account in scheduling repetitive operations. It is possible that, initially at least, increasing repetition of a task will lead to greater efficiency not only in terms of the time required to complete the task but also in the achievement of quality standards, i.e. greater standards of accuracy, etc. This form of learning effect may need to be taken into account in the planning and implementation of quality control procedures. (Notice, however, that equally it might be argued that excessive repetition might lead to a form of 'over-familiarity' and lack of attention, which might result in reduced quality.)

CHECKLIST FOR CHAPTER 9

Working conditions
  Ergonomics and workplace design
    The worker machine system
      Design of information displays
        with controls
        without controls
      Design of controls
        suitability of controls
      Environmental factors
        Lighting
        Noise
        Temperature and ventilation
      Workplace design
        Anthropometric data
          Working areas and space
  VDU work
    Visual factor
    Temperature and noise
    Ergonomic factors
    Work patterns
  Health and safety
    Industrial accidents
      Economic implications
    Preventive action

      Six steps
    Fire prevention
      Six steps
  The worker
    Job design and work organization
    Theories of job design
      Human relations theory
      Human resources theory
      Job enlargement and enrichment
    Nature of job redesign and work organization
      Job enlargement
      Job enrichment
    A procedure for job redesign and work organization
      Desirable job characteristics
    Examples
      Job redesign: the present situation
  Worker variability and learning effects
    Learning
      The learning curve
      Learning curve coefficients
      Learning curve calculations
      Factors influencing learning

FURTHER READING

Corlett, E. N. and Richardson, J. (1981) *Stress, Work Design and Productivity*. Chichester: Wiley. Ergonomics and human factors engineering with case examples, etc.

Dainoff, M. J. (1979) *Occupational Stress Factors in Secretarial/Clerical Workers*. Washington DC: US Department of Health.

Davis, L. E. and Taylor, J. C. (ed.) (1972) *Design of Jobs*. Harmondsworth: Penguin. A book of readings.

European Foundation for the Improvement of Living and Working Conditions (1981) *The Working Environment and VDUs*. Shankill: Euro Foundation.

Hirschmann, W. B. (1964) Profit from the learning curve, *Harvard Business Review*, February, p. 118.

Mackay, C. (1983) People and VDUs, *Archimedes*, February, pp. 28–30. A good review of the topic.

Meister, D. (1971) *Human Factors and Theory of Practice*. New York: Wiley. A comprehensive treatment of ergonomics.

Osborne, D. (1982) *Ergonomics at work*. Chichester: Wiley. Practical ergonomics.

Powell, P. I., Hale, M. Martin, J. and Simon, M. (1971) 2000 *Accidents*. London: National Institute of Industrial Psychology. Booklets describing current health and safety requirements are available from HMSO, London.

Wild, R. (1975)*Work Organization*. New York: Wiley. A comprehensive treatment of job design and work organization with particular reference to mass production work. Chapter 4 also deals with mechanization and automation.

QUESTIONS

9.1 State, discuss and compare the principal requirements of displays used for the following purposes:
   (a)   indicating road speed of car to driver;
   (b)   indicating domestic oven temperature required (i.e. set) and actual temperatures;
   (c)   indicating time of day in an airport departure lounge.

9.2 State, discuss and compare the principal requirements of controls used for the following purposes:
   (a)   setting temperature required for a domestic oven;
   (b)   emergency off' control for metal-cutting lathe;
   (c)   controls for a hi-fi stereo radio receiver.

9.3 Outline and justify the ambient conditions required for the following working environments:
   (a)   an engineering drawing office;
   (b)   an electronic instrument assembly workshop;
   (c)   a hospital operating room

9.4 How might anthropometric data be used in the design of the following items:
   (a)   an adult's cycle;
   (b)   a typist's chair;
   (c)   the driver's seat and controls of a car?

9.5 Discuss and compare the nature of the manual jobs likely to be associated with a moving-belt, fixed-item assembly line for small products (see Chapter 15) and a toolroom grinding machine.

9.6 How might the following jobs be enriched:
   (a)   copy typist;
   (b)   bank teller;
   (c)   domestic appliance service repair worker?
indicate any assumptions made about the jobs and their circumstances.

9.7 (a)   An 80 per cent learning effect is known to exist in a situation in which the first performance of a manual task takes 100 hours; what is the average performance time for the task after 32 task repetitions?
   (b)   How many hours are required for the eighth performance of the task?
   (c)   How many repetitions of the task are required before a target performance level of 41 hours is achieved?

9.8 What factors might be expected to influence the learning, i.e. the rate of performance improvement, of a worker operating a new piece of office machinery? How might the standard performance for such a task be determined for operations scheduling purposes, and what factors would influence the procedure employed?

CHAPTER 10

Organizational Factors in Work System Design

NOTATION USED IN THIS CHAPTER

E	Earnings for a given period
H	Hours worked
N	Number of pieces/units
P	Piece rate
R	Base pay rate
S	Standard hours allowed for job ($= s \times N$)
s	Standard hours allowed for each piece/unit
X	Performance level at which incentive participation begins
Y	Extent of gearing of an incentive payment system
VA	Value added
PBR	Payment by results

This chapter completes our examination of the four sets of factors or considerations which are of principal relevance in the design of work systems. Our focus in this chapter is an 'organizational' one. We shall look at the type of organization structure which must exist in order to support particular types of job design and work organization. We shall also consider the process of change, in particular technological change within the organization, and finally the design and operation of the reward or incentive system for work undertaken within the organization. These topics complement those discussed in Chapters 7, 8 and 9, and should be considered alongside them.

ORGANIZATION DESIGN AND THE OPERATIONS MANAGER

In Chapter 9 we looked at job design, but we cannot consider this in isolation, since the design of satisfactory jobs is contingent upon other factors and conditions. For example,

253

the establishment of a semi-autonomous group working within an organization will depend for its success and indeed viability on the existence of an appropriate organization structure, i.e. one which permits the delegation of authority and responsibility down the organization and therefore facilitates decentralized decision-making. Equally, the existence of this type of organization will tend to encourage such forms of job design and work organization and may tend to militate against the existence of a highly structured work situation.

These topics were also considered in Chapter 3. It will be recalled that certain types of organizational structure were found to be associated with certain types of work technology, where 'work technology' was defined in terms of the types of tasks, their relationships and the nature of work flows.

From our discussion in Chapter 3 it should be noted in the context of job and work design that for the existence of jobs and work organizations which provide enriched jobs with autonomy and discretion for the individual and for work groups, certain organizational features must exist, such features reflecting a relatively unstructured and decentralized organization. Thus, in seeking to introduce job enrichment, autonomous group working, etc., some consideration must be given to the organization structure, since a high degree of structuring and centralizing can only militate against, complicate, and perhaps prevent such developments.

TECHNOLOGICAL CHANGE AND WORK

We have noted in Chapter 9 that because of continuing mechanization and automation of operations, workers' roles are changing. It is appropriate now, having also discussed organization design and technology, to look more closely at the nature and effects of mechanization and automation.

The nature of mechanization and automation

Bright, attempting to overcome some of the problems of definition, suggests that, in general usage, automation suggests something significantly more automated than that which existed previously; hence 'automation' in one industry may contrast both in level of development and in characteristics with automation elsewhere. Other authors have taken the view that the elimination of direct manual involvement in *control* is the principal feature of automation. Mechanization may be viewed as an aspect of automation, the latter also being seen as a function of the integration of operations and the use of control systems which are largely independent of manual involvement. It is reasonable, therefore, to view both mechanization and automation as trends rather than states, both being associated with the replacement of human activities by the activities of inanimate objects. Mechanization is therefore an aspect of, or component part of, automation; it is concerned with activities, while automation of such activities implies the use of control procedures which are also largely independent of human involvement. The two terms will be used in this manner throughout the remainder of this chapter, i.e. automation will be taken to subsume mechanization.

We can identify four basic components of operations in order to aid examination of the nature and effects of automation:

(a)   power technology—sources of energy used;
(b)   processing technology—tools and techniques used in operations performed on materials;
(c)   materials handling technology—transfer of materials and items between processes;
(d)   control—regulation of quality and quantity of output and throughput.

It has been suggested that the substitution of inanimate for human work, i.e. the process of automation, usually occurs in the order: first, processes; second, handling; and third, control. Thus a hierarchy of levels of automation such as that shown in Table 10.1 might be envisaged. In each case level 1 is fully manual work, while levels 2, 3 and 4 are the intermediate steps to the achievement of level 5, where fully automatic work is obtained.

Table 10.1   *Dimensions of automation*

Automation of process (i.e. assembly, measurement, etc.)

Level 1.   Use of hand and handtool
      2.   Use of powered handtool
      3.   Use of machine—hand controlled
      4.   Use of machine—automatic cycle—hand activated
      5.   Use of machine—automatic

Automation of handling (i.e. transport, load/unload, location, storage)

Level 1.   Use of hand and handtool
      2.   Use of powered handtool
      3.   Use of machine—hand controlled
      4.   Use of machine—automatic cycle—hand activated
      5.   Use of machine—automatic

Automation of control (i.e. (a) activation, (b) monitoring, (c) regulation and (d) rectification and maintenance of processes and handling)

Level 1.   Manual (a), (b), (c) and (d)
      2.   Product activated or timed with manual (b), (c) and (d)
      3.   Automatic (a), (b); manual (c), (d)
      4.   Automatic (a), (b), (c); manual (d)
      5.   Fully automatic

The effects of automation

The effects of increasing mechanization and the trend towards process automation of the skills and behaviour of workers, supervisory patterns, etc., have been studied extensively. Such research has relied on comparative studies of operating systems commonly held to represent different degrees of mechanization or automation, as well as on studies conducted within one industry.

Studies of the effect of automation have typically involved examination of work undertaken in process industries. Automation in such situations tended to give rise to wide basic changes in the content and structure of jobs, working conditions, career patterns, security, pay and the prestige of the work performed. With increasing automation jobs tend to become more demanding, varied, interesting and challenging for many workers, although in some cases such changes may be of a temporary nature—a result of a 'start-up' situation. Technical know-how tends to become more important and workers may expect increased job content resulting from automation, together with increased demands on skills, knowledge and training. In general, greater job complexity and responsibility, and therefore greater intrinsic rewards, are associated with work in automated systems, but often at the expense of increased worker inactivity.

A further consideration is that of social interaction. Often the greater distance between workers in automated systems results in reduced social interaction. However, as full automation is approached, the central grouping of controls gives rise to grouping of workers. Up to a certain level, therefore, automation increases the ratio of working space to people and therefore inhibits social relationships. The relationship of operators and their supervisors is also considered to be affected by automation, the general view being one of increased contact and improved worker/supervisor relations. An increased separation of workers from both operations and their outputs is often found. Increased training needs are often associated with the wider responsibilities of automated jobs, while emphasis on vigilance and monitoring duties, the importance of minimizing process disruption, the consequences of breakdowns, and the comparative inactivity of workers are considered to lead occasionally to increased stress.

The above comments relate mainly to situations approaching full automation, i.e. those in which there is automation of control. The effects of lower levels of automation have received less attention; however, we can conclude tentatively that such developments tend to give rise to:

(a) the increasing isolation of workers and hence a reduction in social interaction;
(b) a reduction in the amount of physical effort required, largely due to reduced handling requirements;
(c) a loss of worker control of work pace and worker independence from the machine cycle;
(d) improved working conditions and increased safety;
(e) increased use of shift working.

The degree to which workers' jobs are affected is one area in which many authors have been at pains to distinguish between the effects of mechanization and automation. For example, it has been suggested that the principal effect of mechanization is to restrict workers' actions, while automation takes over these actions: workers who are 'in-line' with the operating system may have work tasks which have the repetitiveness and tensions of similar, non-mechanized work. It would seem that in many cases mechanization affects jobs adversely by increasing the division of labour, rendering certain skills obsolete, removing control of the work pace and increasing the 'distance' between worker and product. It is generally accepted that both in mechanization beyond a certain stage and in automation, the emphasis on inspection, monitoring and control tasks increases while the amount of direct work activity decreases. High levels of mechanization appear to necessitate the use of greater skills, wider knowledge and the performance of supervisory duties, and thus the effects may differ little from those of automation. However, to achieve this situation the various stages of partial mechanization, characterized by the retention of some manual work in either processing or handling, appear to necessitate a somewhat different role for the worker.

Although the manner and characteristics of the development of automation are affected by the factors identified in the previous section, researchers appear to be in general agreement that, at higher levels of automation, work becomes more varied and demands greater use of skills and knowledge, offset to some degree by physical inactivity coupled with the need for vigilance, which could give rise to a stressful situation. Equally, it is clear that what has generally been referred to as mechanization, because of continued dependence on manual intervention in control, offers few of these job characteristics.

PAYMENTS AND INCENTIVES

A detailed treatment of payments and incentive systems is beyond the scope of this book. However, since we have discussed work measurement (one application of which is in the design of pay systems) it will be appropriate in this chapter to provide a brief review of the principles of payment and incentive systems. Further, since motivation is important in job design (Chapter 9), we shall consider one possible motivator, i.e. financial reward. This section therefore provides a summary of the context, purposes and objectives of payment system design followed by a slightly more detailed treatment of two topics which are both of some relevance to operations managers: job evaluation and the design and operation of incentive payment systems. The focus throughout will be on payments and incentive payment systems as they relate to and/or are influenced by operations managers. It should be noted, however, that a detailed treatment of this subject would entail some consideration of industrial relations and social, organizational and legal factors. Readers who wish to pursue the subject in greater depth are referred to the 'further reading' list at the end of the chapter.

Nature of remuneration

Here we are concerned with the remuneration of work in an employment context. All such work will be associated with some form of remuneration, the major element of which will be financial. We shall focus on financial rewards, particularly wages. In fact we might identify four classes of financial remuneration as follows:

(a) wages, i.e. payment received by employees on a periodic basis, e.g. weekly or monthly;
(b) bonuses, e.g. lump sum awards, often provided on an annual basis;
(c) benefits, e.g. insurance benefits, pensions, allowances, non-monetary rewards such as the use of company cars, etc.;
(d) long-term rewards, i.e. lump sum rewards over a long period of time, typically five years and/or on termination of contract or on completion of contract employment period.

Our focus here will be on wages and wage-related factors, in particular the establishment of wage payment systems and structures, and on forms of incentive wage payment.

The significance of wages

Although it would be an oversimplification to claim that people worked solely for financial reward, it is undoubtedly true that adequate wages and acceptable wage systems are a matter of considerable importance to most working people. We must distinguish between those factors which encourage an individual to work and those factors influencing satisfaction at work. Financial reward is undoubtedly a major factor in the former, although beyond a certain level and in certain circumstances job satisfaction may be influenced largely by factors other than wage levels and the wage system. Certainly in many countries in recent years there has been a growing interest in non-wage aspects of remuneration, and increasing importance is now attached to such factors. However, without adequate wages and without the use of an acceptable and equitable wage payment system such interest would decline. Adequate wage levels and an acceptable wage payment system may therefore be seen as a foundation or 'platform' upon which other aspects of remuneration might be built and without which other aspects might not exist.

Needless to say, payment of wages represents a major cost source in many organizations. Not only do companies compete with one another as regards wage levels, but also their competition in the marketplace, being affected by price, is indirectly affected by wages as one factor affecting price and margins. The value added during operations, e.g. the value added to materials, is influenced by wage levels, and the ability to recruit and retain labour (and the attitudes and therefore to some extent the behaviour of labour) is also influenced by wage levels and the nature of payment systems. In these respects, therefore, the design and administration of wage payment systems are of relevance to the operations manager.

Wage payment systems and structures

The objectives of any payment system are numerous and might include the following (see Bowey (1975) in Further Reading):

(a) to enable the employee to earn a good and reasonable salary or wage;
(b) to pay equitable sums to different individuals, avoiding anomalies;
(c) to be understandable and acceptable to the employees and their seniors;
(d) to reward and encourage high-quality work;
(e) to encourage employees to accept transfers between jobs;
(f) to encourage employees to accept changes in methods of working;
(g) to discourage waste of materials or equipment;
(h) to encourage employees to use their initiative and discretion;
(i) to encourage employees to develop better methods of working;
(j) to reward and encourage high levels of output;
(k) to discourage and lead to a decrease in overtime working.

In general, the design of a wage payment system to meet some or all of the above objectives will require some consideration of (a) pay structure and (b) pay systems.

The development of an adequate pay structure will require some consideration of the pay to be provided and the differentials between various jobs, i.e. the establishment of the 'relative worth' of different jobs in different circumstances. In most cases it will be necessary to establish some scale or grading of jobs based on some objective assessment and to relate jobs measured on this scale to pay rates or levels in the manner shown in Figure 10.1. The establishment of such a scale will often provide some form of career or job structure for employees.

Various schemes are available under the general heading '*job evaluation*' for the establishment of such structures; however, it should be remembered that in many cases the establishment of pay levels or pay bands for particular jobs will be a matter of negotiation between employees (often represented by trade unions) and employers. In many cases, of course, there will be national agreements between employers or employers' associations and trade unions. Such agreements will often stipulate pay bands or minimum pay levels for particular jobs and conditions of service, etc.; in supplementing such national agreements there may be certain local negotiating and bargaining machinery to establish pay and wage structures at local or company level. In periods of pay restraint and Government intervention in wage and pay bargaining, companies are rarely entirely free to

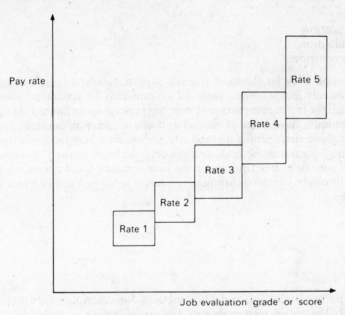

Figure 10.1 *A pay/job structure.*

establish, change or manipulate pay structures. However, given such complicating factors it will be necessary in most cases to develop and employ some consistent method of job evaluation if differentials are to be recognized and wage drift is to be avoided.

The design of the wage payment system will require the consideration of questions such as: 'To what extent will the wage be paid through some form of incentive payment system? How might such an incentive payment system operate? How will standards of performance be established and what control system will be introduced to monitor payment levels, earnings, etc?'. In many cases some form of incentive payment system will be employed, although, as we have noted, in recent years there has been a move towards the introduction of non-financial incentives.

The following sections consider in outline both job evaluation and incentive systems.

Job evaluation

'Job evaluation' is a term used to cover a number of separate and distinct methods of systematically measuring the relative worth of jobs, using yardsticks which are derived from the content of the jobs. A job evaluation scheme will enable new jobs to be placed in a proper relationship with existing jobs by the use of easily explained and acceptable facts and principles. Thus the principal purpose of job evaluation is to rank jobs as a basis for a pay structure. It aims, therefore, to compare all jobs under review using common criteria, to define the relationship of one job to another. It is essentially concerned with establishing relationships and not with absolutes. In comparing jobs it is the job content which is considered, and job evaluation is used primarily for establishing basic pay levels or wage bands.

There are four main methods of job evaluation:

1. Job ranking.
2. Job classification.
3. Points evaluation.
4. Factor comparison.

Points evaluation is by far the most popular system, followed by job classification, job ranking and finally factor comparison. All systems may be applied to jobs at different levels, although the factor comparison system has perhaps more limitations in this respect.

Other techniques have been developed and are in use. For example, the job profile method,[1] the guide chart profile method (the well-known Hay job evaluation method),[2] the time span of discretion method[3] and the decision band method[4] are among those in fairly general use. Brief descriptions of the four schemes listed above are given below. Further details can be obtained through the sources listed in 'Further Reading' at the end of this chapter.

Job ranking

This is perhaps the simplest job evaluation method. Job descriptions are prepared for each job to identify the duties, responsibilities and qualifications necessary for the job. Such descriptions may be developed jointly by management and unions, and should certainly be agreed by both parties. In some cases 'key' jobs are chosen which adequately cover the whole range of jobs and these are compared with one another in order to produce a ranking of jobs. Where few jobs exist it will be possible to develop a ranking for the entire list at the outset. Given this ranking of jobs on the basis of difficulty, importance to the firm, etc., job grades are established through an examination of the relative importance or merit of adjacent jobs on the scale. Thus grade boundaries may be established between jobs in the ranking which are agreed to have substantially different importance or difficulty ratings. Pay levels or ranges are then attached to each job grade. A somewhat more sophisticated approach involves the use of paired comparisons. Again, where many jobs exist, key jobs will be chosen and each pair of jobs compared with one another by a panel of judges. This process will enable a ranking to be established and thereafter the above procedure is followed.

The job ranking method is simple and straightforward. It is relatively cheap to install and is flexible. It does, however, suffer the disadvantage of relying heavily on judgement and having a relatively minor objective or quantitative content. In the use of this job ranking system there is a tendency to rank jobs to reflect current pay systems. Furthermore, the resultant ranking of jobs reflects only their rank order importance and does not provide for the quantitative assessment of differences between jobs.

---

[1] Butterworth, J. 'The job profile method', Chapter 5 in Bowey (1975) (see Further Reading at the end of this chapter).
[2] Younger, W. F. 'The guide chart profile method', Chapter 15 in Bowey (1975) (see Further Reading at the end of this chapter).
[3] Jaques, E. (1961) Time span of discretion method, *Equitable Payment*. London: Heinemann.
[4] Patterson, T. I. (1966) Decision band method, *Management Theory*. London: Business Publications.

Job classification

Using this procedure a number of job grades are first determined and then the existing jobs are allocated to these predetermined grades. Each grade will normally have recognizable characteristics, taking into account features such as the skill required in jobs, and their responsibilities. Each grade may be represented by a 'benchmark' job, which, taking into account the majority of factors, is most representative of the job grade. The job descriptions are then prepared for each of the existing jobs or each of the jobs to be allocated to the job structure. These jobs are then allocated to the existing grades through a process of comparison with the job grade descriptions or with the predetermined 'benchmark' jobs. Thus the procedure is much the same as in job ranking, except that jobs are allocated against an existing or required job structure. In both cases whole jobs may be treated and in both systems jobs may be evaluated on a variety of factors as agreed or as considered important within the particular circumstances. Skill and responsibilities are usually considered, and job difficulty and job-holder qualifications are also usually of some importance.

Points evaluation

This, one of the most popular job evaluation schemes, was developed in 1924 in America by M. R. Lott. Unlike the above systems, it relies on the identification and comparison of job factors rather than the whole job. Factors, e.g. skill, effort, responsibility and working conditions, are selected which are common to all or most of the jobs within the organization. These *compensatable* factors are defined and a weighting is allocated to each to indicate its relative importance to the organization. Thus for a total points weighting of 200, skill may be allocated 50 points, effort 50 points, responsibility 60 points and job conditions 40 points. Each of these factors is then broken down into sub-factors which are again defined and weighted, the sum of the weighting for each sub-factor being equal to the points weighting given to the main factor. Table 10.2 lists eleven sub-factors as identified in the NEMA (National Electrical Manufacturers Association of the USA) version of the points evaluation scheme. In some cases sub-factors are further broken down and again points allocated to each. Job descriptions are then prepared for each job to be evaluated and jobs are evaluated against the factors or sub-factors, points being allocated to each job for each sub-factor. The total points score for each job then represents the total evaluation or 'merit' of the job. Jobs are then ranked according to the total points score, job grades are established and pay scales or ranges agreed for each job grade as in the above scheme.

Unlike the above systems, the points evaluation system provides a semi-objective means of job evaluation. Because of the detail which might be introduced through the identification and definition of sub-factors, the scheme might be employed consistently and agreement may be achieved relatively easily. The use of this scheme provides not only a means of establishing job rankings and a job structure but also a way of quantitatively identifying differentials between jobs and grades.

Factor comparison

This method is an extension of points evaluation and uses five factors:

Table 10.2 *Job evaluation by points rating*

Factors	Possible points rating
Skill	*(50)*
1. Education	10
2. Experience	30
3. Initiative/ingenuity	10
Effort	*(50)*
4. Physical	30
5. Mental/visual	20
Responsibility	*(60)*
6. Equipment or process	15
7. Material or product	15
8. Safety of others	15
9. Work of others	15
Job conditions	*(40)*
10. Working conditions	25
11. Unavoidable hazards	15
	(200) 200

1. Mental effort required in the job.
2. Skills required for the job.
3. Physical effort required for the job.
4. Responsibility of the job.
5. Job conditions.

A number of key jobs are selected and then a panel of 'experts' determines the proportion of the total wage paid for each constituent factor. Each factor is given a monetary value for the key jobs. This allows a scale to be established for each factor and other jobs can then be compared with them, factor by factor, to yield a ranking of all jobs. Since the initial exercise is carried out in terms of monetary values, interpolation will yield wage rates for all jobs. This method is more complex and difficult both to describe and implement because it uses, in one process, job evaluation and the allocation of monetary values.

'Payment by results' incentive schemes (PBR)

Individual incentives

Although the use of incentive payment systems is not a necessary corollary of a work measurement exercise, it is a fact that the installation or use of an incentive payment scheme is one of the usual reasons for work measurement.

It is also a fact that there is a great deal of confused thinking about the merits, design and use of methods of incentive payments. Consequently, while we shall not comment directly on the merits of such schemes, it will be worth while to describe some of the more popular schemes so that their basic principles are understood. We shall deal first with some traditional PBR schemes.

100 per cent participation or one for one schemes

This is one of the simplest and most widely used incentive payment systems. Under this system, increases in performance above a certain level lead to directly proportional increases in wages. In its simplest form, incentive payment is provided for throughput or output above 100 performance, there being a guaranteed payment of the base rate for performances at 100 or less (see Figure 10.2). In other words, earnings are calculated on a time basis as follows:

$$E = RH + R(S - H)$$

where E = earnings for a given period
R = base pay rate
H = hours worked
S = standard hours allowed for job
= standard hours for each piece[5] (s) × number of pieces (N)

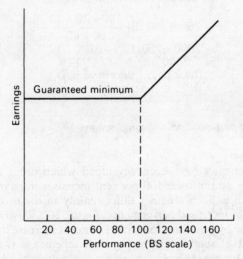

Figure 10.2 *100 per cent participation incentive payment scheme beginning at 100 performance.*

EXAMPLE

Base pay rate	= 250 pence/hour
Hours worked	= 8
Standard minutes (SM)/piece	= 20
Output	= 30 pieces

$$E = 250(8) + 250\left[\left(\frac{20}{60} \times 30\right) - 8\right]$$

$$= 2000 + 250(10 - 8)$$

$$= \quad 2000 \quad + \quad 500$$
$$\text{(base pay)} \quad \text{(incentive pay)}$$

$$= 2500 \text{ p (total pay)}$$

---

[5] Each item or unit processed or produced.

Often 100 per cent participation or 'one for one' schemes begin at a level less than 100 performance, i.e. incentive payment is offered to workers who exceed a performance of perhaps 75 or 80. As with the previous scheme, it is usual to guarantee minimum base rate earnings. In this case earnings are calculated as follows:

$$E = RH + R\left(\frac{100S}{X} - H\right)$$

where X = the performance at which participation begins, e.g. 75 or 80

EXAMPLE

Base pay rate	= 250 pence/hour
Hours worked	= 8
SM/piece	= 20
Output	= 30 pieces

Participation from 80 performance

$$E = 250(8) + 250\left(\frac{100 \times 20 \times 30}{60 \times 80} - 8\right)$$
$$= 2000 + 250(12.5 - 8)$$
$$= \quad 2000 \quad + \quad 1125$$
$$\text{(base pay)} \quad \text{(incentive pay)}$$
$$= 3125 \text{ p (total pay)}$$

Less than 100 per cent participation or geared schemes

A large number of schemes have been developed which differ from those described previously in that they do not offer 100 per cent increases in payment for 100 per cent increases in performance. Such schemes differ mainly in the extent to which workers participate as a result of increased performance. Figure 10.3 illustrates a 50/50 scheme in which earnings increase by $\frac{1}{2}$ per cent for every 1 per cent increase in performance beyond 100. The main benefit of such incentive payment schemes is that they provide some measure of safeguard for management in circumstances where allowed times may have been inaccurately estimated. An additional safeguard can, of course, be provided by applying an upper limit to incentive earnings.

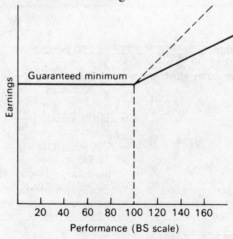

Figure 10.3 *50/50 geared incentive scheme.*

The formula for calculating earnings for geared schemes without an upper earnings limit, and starting at a performance level of 100, is as follows:

$$E = RH + YR(S - H)$$

where Y = the extent of the gearing, e.g. 0.5 for a 50/50 plan

---

EXAMPLE

$$
\begin{aligned}
\text{Base pay rate} &= 250 \text{ pence/hour} \\
\text{Hours worked} &= 8 \\
\text{SM/piece} &= 20 \\
\text{Output} &= 30 \text{ pieces} \\
\text{Gearing} &= 50/50
\end{aligned}
$$

$$E = 250(8) + 0.5(250)\left(\frac{20 \times 30}{60} - 8\right)$$

$$= 2000 + 125(10 - 8)$$

$$= 2000(\text{base pay}) + 250(\text{incentive pay})$$

$$= 2250 \text{ p (total pay)}$$

As before, participation may begin at a level below 100, in which case earnings are calculated by the following formula:

$$E = RH + YR\left(\frac{100S}{X} - H\right)$$

Piece-work

This is one of the oldest methods of incentive payment, under which workers are paid a fixed amount for each piece processed. In fact the piece-work system is very similar to the 100 per cent participation or one for one system previously described, the principal difference being that in piece-work the standard is described in terms of money and not time. As with the previous systems, it is usual to operate the incentive payment system in conjunction with a guaranteed minimum payment level.

The piece-rate (P) is defined as follows:

$$P = Rs$$

consequently earnings (E) over a period of time are calculated by means of the following simple equations:

$$E = RsN \text{ (where performance is above 100)}$$

$$E = RH \text{ (where performance is below 100)}$$

EXAMPLE

$$
\begin{aligned}
\text{Base pay rate} &= 250 \text{ pence/hour} \\
\text{Hours worked} &= 8 \\
\text{SM/piece} &= 20 \\
\text{Output} &= 30
\end{aligned}
$$

Piece-rate $= Rs$

$$= 250 \times \frac{20}{60}$$

$$\text{Performance} = \frac{\text{standard hours produced}}{\text{hours worked}} \times 100$$

$$= \frac{\frac{20}{60} \times 30}{8} \times 100$$

$$= 125$$

$$\therefore \text{Earnings } (E) = RsN$$

$$= 250 \times \frac{20}{60} \times 30$$

$$= 2500 \text{ p}$$

It should be noted that certain practical complexities must be accommodated during the operation of any incentive payment method. For example, a certain amount of waiting time will be incurred throughout most working periods and, in addition, unmeasured work may be undertaken. It is usual to pay both of these at base rate or at day-work rate and, consequently, care must be taken to include them in the wage calculations.

EXAMPLE

Base pay rate	= 250 pence/hour
Total hours worked	= $9\frac{1}{2}$
Hours worked on unmeasured work	= $\frac{1}{2}$
Waiting hours	= 1
SM/piece for measured work	= 20
Output of measured work	= 30 pieces

Using a 100 per cent participation system above a 100 performance.

$$E = 250(9\tfrac{1}{2}) + 250 \left[\left(\frac{20}{60} \times 30 \right) - (9\tfrac{1}{2} - 1\tfrac{1}{2}) \right]$$

$$= 2375 + 500 \text{ (incentive pay)}$$

$$= 2875 \text{ p (total pay)}$$

Measured day work

The use of the measured day work system avoids some of the problems normally encountered in the design and administration of the type of incentive wage systems described above. It avoids the need for continual measurement of performance and adjustment of wage levels based on such performance, yet it provides a form of incentive wage system. Measured day work offers a fixed rate of pay for a defined standard of performance. Work measurement is used to establish standard times for various jobs and to negotiate the pay rate for such jobs at different levels of performance. Workers are then guaranteed a regular weekly wage if they are able consistently to achieve a given level of performance. Having demonstrated the ability to maintain a level of performance over a minimum period, they are paid an appropriate wage. Subsequent failure to achieve this level of performance results first in some form of discipline or review by management, and subsequently in a reduction to a lower wage level. Measured day work therefore incorporates elements of normal incentive pay with some other benefits of a straight time rate system, in that wage levels do not fluctuate as much as in incentive pay, yet an incentive element remains.

EXAMPLE: COMPUTER DATA INPUT

A bank operates a measured day work scheme for computer terminal operators in a particular department. Four pay rates exist: £50, £55, £60 and £65 a week. Based on clerical work measurement there are four performances standards: ≤ 80, 80–100, 100–120 and ⩾ 120 BSI. New employees are paid at £50 a week during a four-week training period. Thereafter their performance is measured weekly. If they are able to perform at ⩾ 80 BSI for four consecutive weeks they are upgraded to £55 a week. If thereafter, at any time for four consecutive weeks, they can perform at ⩾ 100 BSI they are then upgraded to £60 a week, etc. Subsequent failure to achieve the appropriate performance level leads after two consecutive weeks to a formal review which can be followed, after a further two consecutive weeks of performance less than target, by a reduction of the weekly wage to the next lowest category. Certain wage premiums (e.g. for length of service, skill level, etc.) are paid to some workers on top of the weekly wage, whatever the level.

Premium payment scheme

The approach here is similar to that of measured day work, but the time scale is often extended so that performance reviews take place at long intervals; hence stability is high.

Multi-factor incentives

Increasingly, incentive payment schemes are based on multiple performance or achievement criteria. In particular such schemes take into account factors other than the output-related or throughput-related criteria used in the schemes described above. At the simplest level, multi-factor schemes will also provide for the reward of quality, attendance and timekeeping achievements. At this level they can readily be applied to individuals, but in general multi-factor schemes are more appropriate for group incentive payment (see below). In these cases, factors such as output (or throughput) quality, resource utilization and customer service criteria can be accommodated. With this approach a high base rate is supplemented by an 'incentive' earning usually calculated on a 'points' basis, points being awarded for a level of achievement on each factor. Factors may carry different weightings to reflect their relative importance in the particular situation, and the total incentive earning may be obtained by adding the weighted points achievements for each factor and converting the total to a money equivalent, to be added to the base pay.

Such schemes offer the following benefits:

1. The incentive has a broad base and can be designed more readily to reflect the organization's needs.

2. Overall performance/achievement is rewarded, and the risk of high achievement on one factor being achieved at the expense of another is reduced.
3. The setting and weighting of factors offer opportunities for the participation of all groups involved.
4. Flexibility can be built into the scheme by allowing for changes in factors weighting.

Group incentive schemes

The schemes described above are *primarily* applied to individuals. Derivatives of these schemes, in particular measured day work, premium payments and multi-factor schemes, may be applied to small groups of people employed in related tasks in a particular area, but in general other types of schemes, with a distinctive philosophy, are used to provide incentive pay to groups of workers. Many such schemes exist, ranging from the schemes developed for a particular application, e.g. the Scanlon plan, to those based on general principles, which are relevant in a variety of organizations. Such group incentive schemes might be applied to small groups of workers engaged together on a task and working interdependently, to departments, and in some cases to entire organizations. In general the larger the group involved in such incentive pay the greater the problem of designing a scheme which has perceived *relevance* and *immediacy*. In other words, the larger the group and the more 'remote' the criteria for determining the amount of incentive pay, the greater the likelihood that individuals will see the factors which influence their incentive pay as being beyond their direct influence, and the greater the risk that the time lag in providing the incentive pay will limit the development of individuals' motivation. These, therefore, are the principal motivational obstacles of such schemes, but on the other hand such schemes do emphasize the sharing of achievements and productivity gains, and with that the need for team working, and perhaps the development of some greater identification with organizational goals, etc.

Group incentive payment schemes will, in general, emphasize participation in productivity improvement. Such schemes may be based on productivity improvements as measured by reduced labour costs, or increased value added, or other criteria, including many of those outlined in our discussion of performance measurement in Chapter 21. An alternative approach allows the beneficiaries of such schemes to participate in their design through the establishment of some form of representative committee whose task will be to identify objectives associated with productivity/performance improvement and thus specify the criteria for group incentive reward. Such approaches require considerable employee/management discussion and 'negotiation' during the design process, but have been common replacements for individual, and in particular piece-work, systems in the manufacturing industries, and are especially appropriate in industries where output cannot be measured easily. Thus such schemes are popular in retailing, transport, etc.

Some approaches to group incentive payment are outlined below.

Profit-sharing schemes

An index or formula can be negotiated to relate incentive payments to profits (usually pre-tax), normally above a base level. Generally profits are shared between the company and its employees, e.g. a 60:40 share.

Employees' bonus for period = 0.4 (profit earned less base line profit)

The major disadvantage of such schemes, apart from problems of 'immediacy' (see above), is that profits can be affected by factors which are beyond employees' control.

Sales value schemes

Such schemes are similar to the above except that increases of sales value over a base line are distributed between employees and the organization. Again there can be the problem of 'immediacy', and of course sales revenue will be influenced by pricing policy decisions, as well as by factors influenced by employees. Such schemes, however, are a popular means of incentive payment in supply organizations, where sales targets are often established and used as a base from which to calculate PBR for sales personnel, etc.

Added value (AV) schemes

The use of the AV concept permits changes in performance, particularly labour productivity, to be expressed in terms of value.

AV can be defined as 'the value added to input materials', i.e. the difference between the value of output (e.g. sales) and the costs of the materials used in creating those sales. From this added value must be paid all the other costs incurred in the operation, e.g. wages, administrative costs, capital charges. Hence (see Figure 21.1):

$$AV = \text{Sales revenue } less \text{ Total external purchases}$$
$$AV \text{ productivity} = \frac{\text{Added value}}{\text{Labour costs} + \text{Capital charges}}$$
$$= \frac{\text{Added value}}{\text{Internal expense}}$$

The major benefits of using the AV productivity measure as an indication of the overall performance of a unit and a basis for incentive payment include:

1. It clearly demonstrates that increases in wages must be met from increases in the value of outputs, not simply from sales or turnover (which might result from non-profitable activity).
2. Value can be increased in numerous ways, e.g. rationalization of activities (eliminating low-value work), increased capital expenditure, improved resource utilization, modified pricing; thus the AV productivity criterion emphasizes overall effort, not simply output and worker-controlled factors.
3. The comparison of the performance of different units or organizations is easier, since AV (unlike profit measure) is not influenced by depreciation, etc.
4. The measurement of AV productivity requires consideration of the whole organization's activities and therefore demands meaningful participation and negotiation within the organization.

One method of calculating AV-based incentive bonus is described in the example below.

EXAMPLE: AV BONUS SCHEME

Step 1   Agree a value added/employee cost ratio, e.g. average of annual for past five years:

		£
Net sales revenue		10 000 000 p.a.
Total external purchases		3 000 000 p.a.
VA		7 000 000 p.a.

which is represented by:

	£
Labour costs	5 000 000
Capital charges	1 000 000
Profits	1 000 000
	7 000 000

Hence:

$$\frac{\text{Value added}}{\text{Employee cost}} = \frac{7\,000\,000}{5\,000\,000}$$

$$= 1.4$$

Step 2   Agree basis for sharing of VA/employee cost improvement, e.g. 50 per cent to company, 50 per cent to employees (subject to 50 per cent payment to reserve for use in periods where no improvement is obtained).

Step 3   Calculate periodic results, e.g. monthly.

		£
Net sales revenue for period	=	1 000 000
Total external purchases for period	=	400 000
VA for period		600 000
which includes labour costs		£400 000

Hence:

$$\frac{\text{VA for period}}{\text{Employee cost}} = \frac{600\,000}{400\,000}$$

$$= 1.5$$

Step 4   Determine bonus payment.

Agreed employee labour cost for given VA

$$= \frac{600\,000}{1.4}$$

	£
	429 000
Allocation to the company	214 500
Available as bonus	214 500
Less payment to reserve	107 250
∴ Available for bonus payment this period	107 250

CHECKLIST FOR CHAPTER 10

The 'organizational focus' in work system design
Organizational design and the operations manager
   Organization structure and job design
Technological change and work
   The nature of mechanization
   The nature of automation
   The 'process' or stages of automation
   The dimensions of automation
   The effects of automation on jobs and work
Payments and incentives
The nature of remuneration
   Wages
   Bonuses
   Benefits
   Long-term rewards
The significance of wages
Wage payment systems and structures
   The objectives of a payment system
   Pay/job structures

Job evaluation
   Job ranking
   Job classification
   Points evaluation
   Factor comparison
Incentive wage systems
   Individual schemes
   100 per cent or 'one for one' systems
   Less than 100 per cent or 'geared' systems
   Piece-work
   Measured day work
   Premium payment schemes
   Multi-factor schemes
Group schemes
   Problems of 'immediacy' and 'relevance'
   Profit-sharing schemes
   Sales value schemes
   Added value schemes

FURTHER READING

Bowey, A. (ed.) (1975) *Handbook of Salary and Wage Systems.* Epping: Gower.

Fein, M. (1979) Lets return to MDW for incentives, *Industrial Engineering*, January, pp. 34–37.

Husband, T. M., (1976) *Work Analysis and Pay Structure.* New York: McGraw-Hill. The structure and organization of rewards, job analysis, job evaluation and pay systems.

Industrial Engineering, **14** (11) (1982) Incentive systems—another look. Four articles on pp. 52–80.

Lupton, T. and Bowey, A (1982) *Wages and Salaries.* Aldershot: Gower. A comprehensive and modern study of the design and implementation of wage and salary systems.

QUESTIONS

10.1 Refer to Question 8.3. The worker on that job produces 2600 pieces during an eight-hour working shift. He is working on a 10 per cent participation incentive scheme, in which the basic rate is £3 per hour and in which incentive payment is given for outputs in excess of 75. What are the worker's total gross earnings for the shift?

10.2 Show how any two of the job evaluation schemes described in this chapter would be used to evaluate:
   (a) the job of a supermarket check-out desk operator;
   (b) the job of a draughtsman or draughtswoman;
   (c) your job.

10.3 A worker is capable of giving a regular 125 performance over a working week of 40 hours. If she is employed on testing work and if the standard hour (SH) per item tested is 0.75, what would the gross total pay per week be on a base rate of 270 pence per hour under the following systems of payment:
   (a) 100 per cent participation with incentive payment for performances over 100;
   (b) 100 per cent participation with incentive payment for performances over 75;
   (c) 50/50 scheme with incentive payment for performances over 100;
   (d) 50/50 scheme with incentive payment for performances over 75?
   What piece-rate must be paid to the worker if her gross total weekly earnings under a

piece-work system are to equal the largest gross total weekly earnings provided by one of the above incentive schemes?

10.4 In order to monitor the performance of an organization, and as a basis for a value added PBR scheme, calculate some value added ratios for each of the following, using whichever of the given data are relevant. Explain your ratios and comment on the results.

Case	A	B	C
Number of employees	216	202	195
	£	£	£
Net sales (including changes in stocks)	2 562 100	2 884 600	3 600 500
Cost of materials	1 000 000	1 000 500	1 000 750
Wages and salaries	800 500	750 750	1 100 000
Profit	250 000	175 000	300 000
Fixed assets	3 000 000	2 000 100	1 500 000
Current assets	1 500 000	500 000	575 000

10.5 What are the principal benefits, disadvantages and applications of a value added incentive payment scheme?

PART 5

CAPACITY MANAGEMENT

In this chapter we deal in some detail with what is perhaps the most difficult, and certainly the most important, problem and decision area for operations management. Unless the capacity of the operating system is managed effectively, the operations manager is unlikely to achieve his or her twin objectives. Good decision-making and effectiveness in other areas are unlikely to compensate for or conceal poor capacity management.

This is one of the 'principal' problem areas of operations management as defined in Chapter 1. The strategies which might be adopted for the management of capacity can be: (a) limited by feasibility constraints (associated mainly with the structure of the operating system); (b) influenced by desirability factors (deriving from the objectives of the organization and operations managers); and (c) influenced by the operations manager's own preferences.

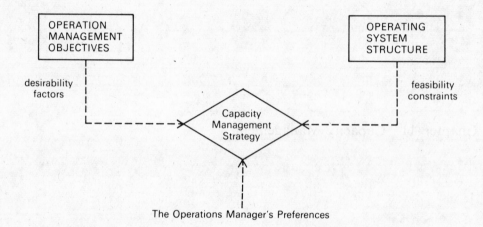

CHAPTER 11

Capacity Management

NOTATION USED IN THIS CHAPTER

C_I	Cost of storage/unit/period
C_O	Cost of overtime production/unit/period
C_R	Cost of regular production/unit/period
I_i	Inventory level at end of period i
L	Average number of units in system
L_q	Average number of units in queue
O_i	Maximum overtime production in period i
p	Throughput rate
P_n	Probability of n units in system (i.e. queue+one being serviced)
R_i	Maximum regular time production in period i
S_i	Sales for period i
W	Average time units spend in system
W_q	Average time units spend in queue
λ	Average arrival rate (units/period of time)
μ	Average service rate (units/period of time)
ρ	λ/μ

Although in this chapter we shall be considering capacity management, it will be appropriate first to consider the broader operations planning and control context within which the management of capacity takes place.

OPERATIONS PLANNING AND CONTROL *(see also Chapter 12)*

In this book it is our intention to treat operations planning and operations control separately. We shall regard operations planning as a *pre*-operating activity, i.e. the

275

determination of the facilities needed to provide the required goods or services and the construction of a schedule by means of which this will be achieved. Operations control we consider to be essentially a *during*—operating activity involving the implementation of operations planning decisions. Our definition of the two functions is, therefore, as follows:

> *Operations planning is concerned with the determination, acquisition and arrangement of all facilities necessary for the future operations.*

> *Operations control is concerned with the implementation of a predetermined operations plan or policy and the control of all aspects of operations according to such a plan or policy.*

Notice, however, that operations planning and control are very closely linked and entirely interdependent. Decisions during planning will determine the problems, and often the nature, of control, and experiences during control will influence future planning.

In Chapter 1 we identified planning and scheduling problems as being 'characteristic' of operating systems. In other words, we considered these to be distinguishing problem areas, the nature of the problems encountered being influenced by the nature of the operating system, in particular the structure of the system and vice versa. For this reason we must consider the nature of planning problems in different types of operating systems, the strategies available for operations planning, and the appropriateness of each of these in different situations.

In this chapter we shall consider only capacity management. Activity scheduling will be introduced in the next chapter, and inventory management will be dealt with in Chapter 17. Both activity scheduling and inventory management decisions may be considered to be subsidiary to capacity management. A particular approach to, or strategy for, the management of capacity will often be implemented largely through scheduling and inventory decisions.

THE NATURE OF CAPACITY MANAGEMENT

The effective management of capacity is perhaps the most important responsibility of operations management. It is the planning responsibility of operations managers. All other operations planning takes place within the framework set by capacity decisions.

Capacity management is concerned with the matching of the capacity of the operating system and the demand placed on that system.

A system has capacity if it has at least some of *each* of the types of resources which are needed to perform its function. For example, a taxi service has capacity to transport a person if it has a vacant cab, a driver, fuel, etc., and a manufacturing system has capacity to produce if it has manufacturing equipment, raw materials, labour, etc. Some of *each* of the necessary resources must exist if capacity is to exist. However, in measuring capacity we shall often refer only to the principal, or most costly, or most greatly used, or most commonly used resource in the operating system. Table 11.1 identifies some of the resources which might be used to describe or measure the capacity of different types of systems.

One approach to the capacity management problem is to try to plan the capacity required and then manipulate that capacity so that it matches the changing demands placed on it. If insufficient capacity is provided it will be possible to meet only some of the demand, and so some customers must wait or go elsewhere. If too much capacity is provided there will be some under-utilization of resources. Another approach is to try to

Table 11.1 *The capacity of operating systems: measures of capacity*

Operating system	Resources which may be used in measuring the capacity of the system
Manufacture	
Electricity generation	Megawatt capacity
Steel manufacture	Number of mills or blast-furnaces
Craft manufacture	Labour force
Transport	
Airline	Number of seats
Taxi service	Number of cabs
Telecommunications	Number of lines
Service	
Hospital	Number of beds
Library	Number of books/journals
Restaurant	Number of tables
Supply	
Warehouse	Volume
Retail shop	Shelf area
Petrol station	Number of pumps

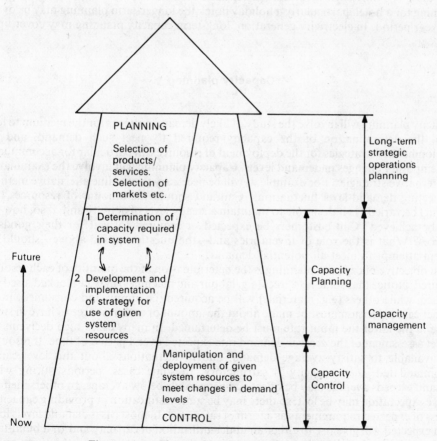

Figure 11.1 *The timescale of capacity management.*

manipulate demand to match available capacity. Demand might be increased through advertising, increased promotion, lower prices, etc., and this might help avoid under-utilization of available capacity. However, if there is insufficient capacity available, demand may be allowed, or even encouraged, to fall.

In most cases an organization will seek to match capacity and demand by a combination of these two approaches. However, operations managers will be concerned mainly with the former, and in most cases they will see their task as that of trying to ensure that a forecast or given demand can be satisfied. From the operations manager's viewpoint, one of the major problems is uncertainty of demand. The existence of a stable and known demand would simplify the problems of capacity management considerably, and changing demand can be accommodated relatively easily providing changes can be predicted accurately. However, the expectation of changing demand levels without the possibility of accurate prediction gives rise to extremely complex capacity problems. We should perhaps note that this uncertainty of demand level may be caused by:

(a) uncertainty about the number of orders to be received; and/or
(b) uncertainty about the amount of resources required for the satisfaction of customer orders.

The management of capacity involves both planning and control. In total it is a medium- to long-term problem area. Figure 11.1 locates the two elements along such a timescale. The planning aspect is a longer-term, 'future' activity while control is a more medium-term task. The timescales involved will depend on the situation. For example, in capacity planning for a hotel, particularly a holiday hotel, the longer-term planning may be over a one-year period. In electricity generation, long-term capacity planning may cover up to ten years.

Capacity planning

Capacity planning will involve the study of likely demand patterns for the medium to long term, the determination of the capacity required to meet such demand, and the development of strategies for the deployment of resources, in particular for accommodating temporary changes in demand levels. Capacity planning will involve the examination of alternative strategies. For example, it will be necessary to examine alternative methods of meeting demand-level fluctuations. Can and should the amount of resources (e.g. labour) be varied? Is it desirable to maintain a steady level of activity and, if so, how can this be achieved? Can customers be expected or required to wait for their goods or services? What is the role of inventories and—the question posed above—should the system attempt to meet all potential demand?

An objective of capacity planning is the determination of the quantity of each resource required. Notice that some resources (e.g. labour and machines) may be stocked, used and re-used, while others (e.g. materials) will be acquired, i.e. input, and consumed. In the former case a decision must be made about the amount of each resource to have in stock, while in the latter the input rate must be determined. In many cases such decisions will reflect assessment of the *average* demand rate expected over a period of time. If resources are available to satisfy average demand, and if fluctuations about this level can be accommodated, then capacity is satisfactory. In some cases, periods during which demand exceeds average may be offset against periods below average. In others, demand above expectation may be lost, so there may be some justification in providing capacity in excess of expected requirements as a form of safeguard. In most cases demand levels lower than expected will give rise to either an under-utilization of capacity and/or a build-up of resources beyond expectations. Failure to satisfy either resource productivity and/or customer service criteria can therefore result from inaccurate assessment of average demand levels and hence the provision of too little or too much capacity, or failure to provide for adequate adjustment to fluctuations about these levels through either underestimation of the extent of demand fluctuations or insufficient capacity flexibility. For example, in any system where resources are stocked, an overestimate of demand will lead to an underutilization of resources, while an underestimate of demand may, sooner or later, affect customer service—sooner in the case of systems without output stocks and later where output stocks exist. In anticipation of demand, an overestimate of demand will lead to increasing stock. Temporary under- or over-capacity resulting from inability to adapt to demand-level fluctuations may give rise to precisely the same effects.

Although it is convenient to consider capacity planning as occurring in two stages—determination of average levels and planning for meeting variations about this level—these two aspects are clearly interdependent. The capacity provided may be influenced by the manner in which adjustments may be made. Constraints on adjustment, particularly limitations on ability to accommodate short-term excess demand, may necessitate provision of 'excess' capacity.

Capacity control

This is the shorter-term aspect of capacity management. It involves the manipulation and deployment of system resources and is achieved mainly through inventory management and activity scheduling. The nature of these two activities is therefore influenced by capacity planning decisions. This chapter deals with capacity planning. Topics relating to capacity control will be dealt with in subsequent chapters.

The nature of capacity management, and its relationships with other management decision areas, are shown diagrammatically in Figure 11.2. Examples of capacity planning in different types of operating systems are given in Table 11.2. The next section considers in more detail the two major decision areas of capacity planning. These are interrelated areas, since decisions about the capacity required will be influenced by the choice of strategy for the use of capacity and vice versa.

CAPACITY PLANNING

The capacity required

The objective of this aspect of capacity planning will be the determination of the general or overall level of capacity required for the medium-term to long-term future period. This will be achieved through either measurement or estimation of the demand to be placed on the system. Estimation or forecasting of future demand will normally be necessary where the operating system operates in anticipation of demand, but where the system responds only to known customer orders demand can be measured, so estimation is unnecessary and the capacity planning problem is considerably simplified.

When forecasting future demand for capacity planning purposes, fluctuations will be expected but to some extent ignored. For example, where there is no trend in expected demand, a capacity equal to average expected demand might be provided (i.e. capacity X

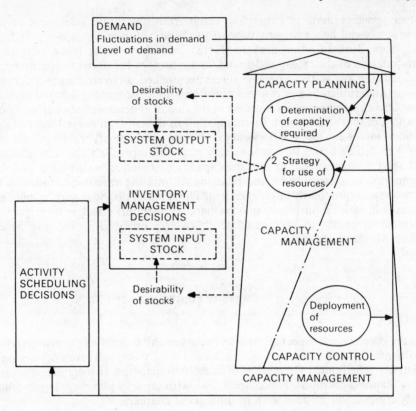

Figure 11.2 *The relationships between capacity management and scheduling and inventory decisions.*

Table 11.2 *Examples of capacity planning problems*

Examples of operating systems	Type of capacity planning problem
Manufacture Builder (of 'one-off' houses to customer order)	Houses are built as, when, how and where required by particular customers. Resources must be obtained for each job but, since each house is different, it will not be possible to predict exactly how many resources are needed. The builder must complete the houses on time and therefore must provide excess resources or be able to subcontract.
Supply Wholesaler	The wholesale business supplies retailers in an area with goods. They need to provide a good service, but don't want to hold too much stock. They will try to forecast demand, in particular to identify seasonal variations. They will then have to decide how much of each item to stock, and what to do if stocks are insufficient at any time.
Transport Furniture removal	The furniture remover will want to give a good service, and in particular will not want customers to wait too long. However, it is known that demand will fluctuate. The business doesn't want to have too many spare, unused vans, drivers, etc., so will hope to have enough resources to deal with most demand most of the time.
Service Fire service	A fire service cannot keep its customers waiting; nor can demand be forecast accurately. It will probably be necessary to have enough capacity (e.g. vehicles, staff, etc.) to deal with most situations, but also to arrange for other facilities to be 'on call', e.g. from other towns.

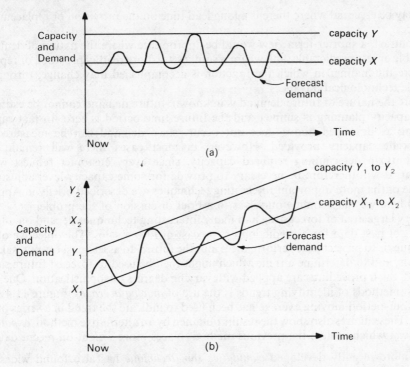

Figure 11.3 *Demand or capacity forecasts.*

in Figure 11.3(a)). If, however, a strategy of providing some excess capacity is employed, a higher level may be provided (e.g. capacity *Y* in Figure 11.3(a)). Where demand is expected to increase or fall, e.g. Figure 11.3(b), correspondingly increasing or reducing capacity may be provided, again taking into account the strategy adopted for the use of system resources. It is for this reason that the determination of the overall or general medium-term to long-term capacity for the system requires consideration of the strategy for meeting demand fluctuations. Precisely the same considerations apply when demand can be measured, since in most cases there will be fluctuations in the level of demand.

Demand forecasting *(see also Appendix II)*

In many situations the first step in capacity planning will be demand forecasting, the objective of which is to estimate the future demand which is to be placed on the operating system. Often the responsibility of forecasting will not rest with the operations manager. However, he or she must know something of how the forecasts are obtained, and that is our purpose in this section.[1]

The length of the forecast period will depend largely on the nature of system resources and the nature of the market. Capacity plans may involve periods in excess of five years where there is sufficient stability or predictability of the nature of demand. A long-term

---

[1] Forecasting techniques are discussed in detail in Appendix II.

view may be essential where there is a long lead time on the provision or replacement of resources.

In contrast, a shorter-term view would be appropriate where the nature of demand is less stable or less predictable, and where resources are more readily provided or replaced, or where the manner in which the function is accomplished may change, through for example technological advances.

Where the nature of future demand is unknown, future demand cannot be estimated. Here capacity planning is simpler and the future time period is zero. In fact capacity planning as described above does not occur, since demand can be measured and appropriate capacity provided. However, in most cases there will remain some uncertainty in determining required capacity, since every customer request will be different. It will therefore be necessary to provide for some capacity-level adjustment.

Some of the more important forecasting techniques are described briefly in Appendix II, and here we shall confine ourselves to a brief discussion of the problem.

A very large area of forecasting and many forecasting techniques depend on a formal analysis of past data for a prediction or forecast of future sales. The objective of such techniques is to project past performances into the future, to assess past output, sales and demands, and to determine a trend which might then be used to forecast future sales or demand. Such procedures are applied with varying degrees of sophistication. One of the simplest methods of identifying trends is the use of *moving averages*. Figure 11.4 shows how a four-period moving average has been used to indicate the trend in a series of sales figures. These figures also show the results obtained by an alternative method, *exponential smoothing*, which, unlike the previous method, places more weight on recent data.

The more recently developed *cumulative sum technique* has also found widespread application in short-term forecasting, and is particularly valuable for examining data with the object of detecting significant changes in mean or average values.

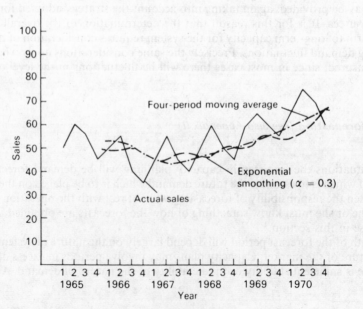

Figure 11.4   *Sales trends plotted by four-period moving average, and exponential smoothing methods.*

Another approach to forecasting involves the use of *economic indicators* or *associative predictions*. Many companies have found that there is a close relationship between the sale of their goods or services and certain of the indices of economic conditions produced by the government or by trade associations. Where such relationships exist a change in the index or indices might usefully be regarded as an indication of a likely change in demand. The objective, therefore, is to find one or more indices whose fluctuations are *afterwards* reflected in changes in demand. (Without this time lag, the association is useless.) For example, the sales of cars might be regarded as a useful prediction of the subsequent sale of accessories, and the building of houses as a prediction or an index for the sale of furnishings. To develop forecasting techniques based on associative predictions can be a rather lengthy business which usually involves an extensive examination of the statistical relationship of past sales data and various likely indices. The closeness of the statistical association of variables can be measured by calculation of a *correlation coefficient*. Once indices bearing a close correlation with historical data have been found, this relationship can be used for forecasting. The relationship is expressed mathematically by means of a *regression equation*.

Each of these techniques and terms will be discussed more fully in Appendix II.

Some factors affecting demand

In forecasting demand for goods or services it is appropriate to recognize that in many cases demand is a function of time. The classic life-cycle curve shown in Figure 11.5 illustrates one such relationship. This curve will normally apply in the case of goods or services consumed directly by the public (e.g. domestic appliances, sport and leisure facilities). The timescale will depend on the nature of the product or service. While there is a tendency to assume continued growth for goods and services such as raw materials, basic services and transport, (e.g. steel, fuel, medical care, rail and air transport), a similar life-cycle relationship may in fact exist, although the timescale may be considerable. Demand for energy, particularly electricity, has recently begun to decline after a considerable period of growth. The use of canal and rail transport also shows this relationship. Various mathematical formulae exist for the description of such curves. Exponential functions are often employed to describe the incubation and growth periods.

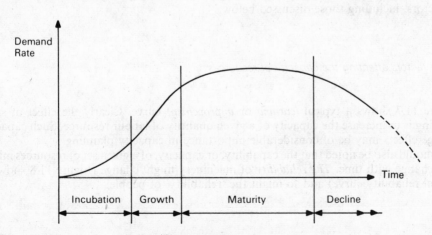

Figure 11.5 *A life-cycle curve.*

Various policies might be employed for the provision of capacity to satisfy such demand. At one extreme, sufficient capacity to meet all expected demand might be provided from the outset, with attendant benefits of economies of scale in ordering, acquisition, training, etc. Alternatively, capacity might be matched to demand by incremental change over time, with benefits in utilization, etc. Systems providing several outputs from common resources might, despite the life-cycle characteristics, expect relatively steady total demand. Figure 11.6 illustrates this.

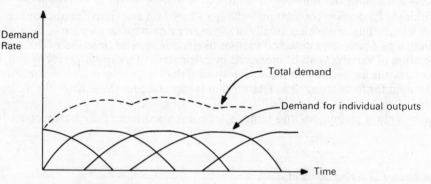

Figure 11.6   *Combination of individual demand curves.*

Determining the capacity required

Given a forecast or a measure of demand for a future period, the next step in capacity planning is to decide what overall or general level of capacity to provide for that period, about which some small variations may be possible in order to accommodate known or expected fluctuations in demand.

Before proceeding further we must recognize that a given quantity of resources does not necessarily provide a fixed level of capacity. For example, in one situation a labour force of ten people may provide a greater capacity than in another. The absence of a fixed relationship between a quantity of physical resources and capacity is a result of a variety of factors, including those discussed below.

Some factors affecting the capacity of resources

Figure 11.7 shows a typical *learning* or *improvement* curve. Clearly the effect of such learning is to increase the capacity of a given quantity of labour resource. Such capacity change effects may be of considerable importance in capacity planning.

It should also be noted that the capability, or capacity, of a given set of resources might also change with time. *The reliability* of machinery might change (Figure 11.8 shows a typical reliability curve) and so might the 'reliability' of people.

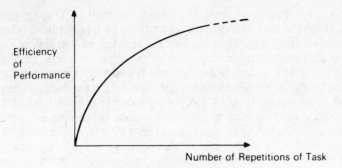

Figure 11.7 *A learning curve.*

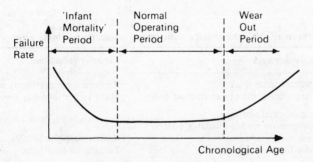

Figure 11.8 *A reliability curve.*

Strategies for the use of capacity

Faced with fluctuating and uncertain demand levels there are two basic capacity planning strategies which might be employed: (a) providing for efficient adjustment or variation of system capacity; and (b) eliminating or reducing the need for adjustments in system capacity.

Strategy 1: Provide for efficient adjustment or variation of system capacity

In most situations it will be both possible and desirable to adopt this strategy. Usually system capacity can be changed within certain limits, perhaps not instantaneously but certainly with little delay. Temporarily more useful capacity might be created by providing more resources and/or providing for their more efficient or intense utilization. Temporary reductions in capacity might be achieved through the transfer of resources to other functions or of course the temporary reduction in the resources on hand or the input rate of resources consumed.

In *supply* systems, e.g. supermarkets, such a strategy is employed as the principal means of accommodating inevitably fluctuating demand levels. Consider the supermarket check-out system. In periods of low demand some of the resources, i.e. the staff, can be transferred to other functions such as re-stocking shelves. During periods of high demand, staff resources may be increased temporarily by transfer from other functions to provide 'double-staffing', e.g. operation of cash register, and wrapping and loading, in turn providing for more intensive utilization of the other resources, i.e. the cash register and the counter. Similarly in certain *manufacture* systems capacity released during periods of low demand might be employed on rectification or service work, while peak demand periods might be accommodated by temporary increase in resource levels through, for example, overtime working and more intensive use of equipment, perhaps through deferral of maintenance work. In some cases capacity might effectively be increased by subcontracting work. To some extent this strategy might be appropriate in the management of *transport* and *service* systems. In both cases maintenance and service work might be scheduled for periods of low demand, and flexible work shift patterns might be employed, overtime working introduced, etc.

Table 11.3 lists some of the means available for the adjustment of system capacity.

Table 11.3   *Means available for capacity adjustment (capacity planning strategy 1)*

Resources	Capacity increases	Capacity reductions
All	Subcontract some work	Retrieve some previously subcontracted work
	Buy rather than make (manufacture only)	Make rather than buy (manufacture only)
Consumed	Reduce material content	
Material	Substitute more readily available materials	
	Increase supply schedules	Reduce supply schedules
	Transfer from other jobs	Transfer to other jobs
Fixed	Scheduling of activities, i.e. speed and load increases	
Machines	Scheduling of maintenance, i.e. defer, hire or transfer from other functions	Scheduling of maintenance, i.e. advance Subcontract or transfer to other functions
Labour	Hours worked, i.e. overtime rearrangement of hours, shifts, holidays	Hours worked, i.e. short time rearrangement of hours, shifts, holidays
	Workforce size, i.e. staffing levels temporary labour transfer from other areas	Workforce size, i.e. layoffs, transfer to other areas

Strategy 2: Eliminate or reduce the need for adjustments in system capacity

In some cases it may be impossible, undesirable or time-consuming to provide for temporary adjustment in system capacity. In general it will be difficult to provide for temporary capacity adjustments in systems which employ large quantities of a large variety of resources without incurring considerable expense and/or delay. Complex process plants which normally work around the clock present little scope for capacity adjustments to meet temporary demand increases, while reductions in demand will often give rise to underutilization of major resources. Similarly, in systems which use highly specialized resources such as skilled labour, it may be desirable to avoid the need for temporary capacity adjustments.

In such situations a strategy of minimizing the need for system capacity adjustments will be more appealing. The adoption of such a strategy might involve the provision of excess capacity and therefore the acceptance of perhaps considerable underutilization of resources, in order to increase the probability of being able to meet high or even maximum demand. Such an approach might be desirable where there is little possibility of providing temporary increases in capacity, and where customer service is of paramount importance. Examples of such situations might include an emergency ambulance service, power station or hospital emergency ward. The provision of some excess capacity, yet insufficient to meet maximum demand, necessitates the acceptance that during periods of peak demand either customers will be lost or they must wait or queue until demand levels fall. In practice such an approach is frequently adopted, for in many cases very considerable excess resources must be provided to ensure that peak demand can be satisfied.

In systems where output stocks can exist, the provision of inventories of goods is a conventional strategy for the smoothing of demand. Such inventories not only insulate the function from fluctuations in demand levels and thus facilitate the use of relatively stable resource levels and high utilization, but also enable customers to be provided with goods with little delay. Many systems operate in this fashion, e.g. the production of domestic appliances, vehicles, building materials, etc. The manufacture of Christmas cards, fireworks and goods subject to seasonal demand fluctuations is often undertaken on this basis, especially where resources cannot readily be used for other purposes. A similar situation exists where customer waiting or queuing is feasible. In such cases, despite a fluctuating demand rate, the rate at which customers are dealt with, i.e. the system capacity, might remain fairly stable. Bus and rail services are frequently intended to operate in this manner. Similar situations might exist at times of peak demand in both manufacture and supply, e.g. the bespoke tailor and the retail shop.

This strategy for capacity management is summarized in Table 11.4, from which it will be seen that there are four basic approaches which might be adopted individually or in combination, i.e.

(a) Maintain 'excess' capacity (and reduced resource productivity).
(b) (i) Accept loss of customers.
     Require customer queuing or waiting (reduced customer service).
     (ii) Provide output stocks.

Table 11.4 *Approaches for eliminating or reducing the need for adjustments in system capacity (capacity planning strategy 2)*

Approach		Relevance	
		Accommodation of temporary demand increases	Accommodation of temporary demand reductions
(a)	Maintain 'excess' capacity	Yes	Not directly relevant
(b) (i)	Accept loss of customers	Yes—in effect some demand ignored	Not directly relevant
	Customer queuing or waiting	Yes—queue increases	Yes—queue reduces
(ii)	Output stocks	Yes—stocks reduce	Yes—stocks increase

Notice that only part of 2(b)(i) and 2(b)(ii) permit the accommodation of temporary demand reduction without the risk of reductions in capacity utilization. Notice also that the provision of excess capacity alone is rarely a sufficient basis for accommodating demand fluctuations. In most cases it will be necessary to take some action aimed at reducing or smoothing the *effect* of fluctuations on the function, i.e. approaches 2(b)(i) and (b)(ii) above.

Factors influencing capacity planning

Operating system structure and function (feasibility factors)

In many cases organizations would prefer to have demand level fluctuations eliminated or reduced. To some extent they may be able to smooth demand by offering inducements or by requiring customers to wait. Failing or following these efforts to reduce the effects of demand level fluctuations, operating systems will seek to accommodate fluctuations by adjusting capacity. However, the opportunities (or indeed the need) to adopt these strategies for capacity planning will be influenced or limited by the structure of the system. We shall consider only those structures in which resource stocks are maintained, since capacity planning as outlined above is needed only where resources are acquired in anticipation of requirements. In these cases capacity planning will aim to deal with uncertainty about the number of orders to be received and perhaps also uncertainty about the resources needed to satisfy the orders received. The feasibility of each strategy for each of the four structures is outlined in Figure 11.9 and discussed below.

Operating systems which provide for output stocks permit accommodation of fluctuations in demand level through the use of physical stocks, which not only protect the function against unexpected changes in demand level but also permit a relatively stable level of function activity and thus high capacity utilization. The stock levels employed will often reflect the variability of demand and the 'service level' to be provided, i.e. the acceptable level of probability of stock-out situations with the consequent risk of loss of trade or customer waiting. Systems which are unable to operate with output stocks will in most cases have relatively fixed capacity, hence during temporary high-demand periods they will either require customer waiting or suffer loss of trade. Since some excess capacity will normally be provided, capacity utilization will often be low, especially when demand is highly variable.

Transport and service systems do not permit function in anticipation of demand, so either a relatively fixed capacity will be under-utilized despite efforts to maximize the ability of the system to adjust, or customer queuing will be required. The queue size will depend on relative levels and variabilities of demand and function capacity, and in some cases, through the use of scheduling (e.g. appointment) systems, customer queuing can be planned.

The relative values of strategy 1 (provide for efficient adjustment of system capacity) and strategy 2 (eliminate or reduce the need for adjustment in system capacity) are influenced by operating system structure feasibility. However, other factors will influence the choice of strategy. If, for example, there is a limit to the size of output stocks, then although strategy 2(b) is feasible it may not be possible to rely on it for meeting demand level changes. In most situations it will be desirable to consider providing effective capacity adjustment to meet demand-level change, but in most cases effective capacity management will also depend on a preventive strategy, either through the absorption of fluctuation through stock or through customer queuing and waiting. Systems which permit function in anticipation of demand will normally use output stock to protect against demand-level fluctuations. Hence the management of the finished goods inventory is of crucial importance. Other systems will normally rely on customer queuing and, where possible, will seek to schedule customer arrivals.

STRATEGY / STRUCTURE	1. PROVIDE FOR EFFICIENT ADJUSTMENT OF SYSTEM CAPACITY	2. ELIMINATE OR REDUCE NEED FOR ADJUSTMENT OF SYSTEM CAPACITY			
		a. Maintain excess capacity	b. Reduce or smooth effect of demand level fluctuations		(ii) Use stock to absorb demand fluctuations
			(i) Fix upper capacity limit with effect of		
			Loss of trade	Customer queuing/waiting ••	
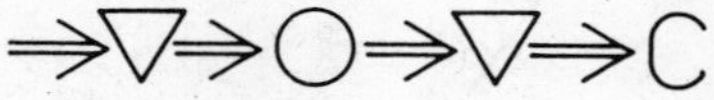 ⇉▽⇉○⇉▽⇉C	Feasible and often desirable to supplement strategy 2b(i)	Feasible, but not necessary	Feasible, but not normally necessary	Waiting feasible but not normally necessary	Feasible, and normally adopted
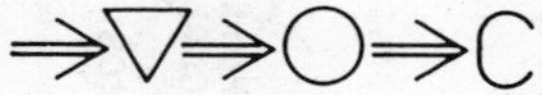 ⇉▽⇉○⇉C	Feasible and often desirable to supplement strategy 2b(ii)	Feasible, and may be necessary in conjunction with or instead of 2b1	Feasible and normally adopted	Waiting feasible and normally adopted	Not feasible
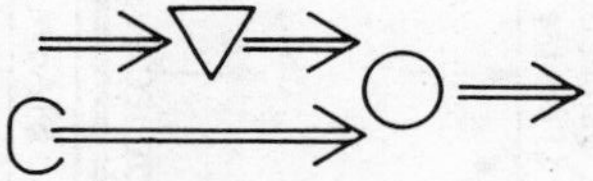 (diagram)	Feasible and desirable in conjunction with 2a	Feasible and normally adopted	Might be feasible depending on nature of function	Not feasible	Not feasible
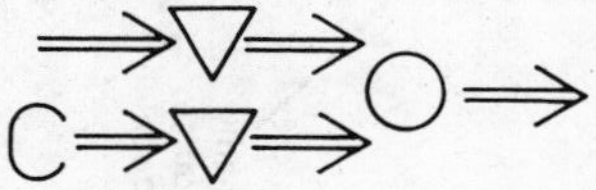 (diagram)	Feasible and often desirable to supplement strategy 2b(i)	Feasible, but not necessary	Feasible and might be adopted	Queuing feasible and normally adopted	Not feasible

• Customer push
•• Customer pull

Figure 11.9 *Capacity planning strategies for systems with resource stocks. From Wild, R. (1977) Concepts for Operations Management. New York: Wiley.*

Operations management objectives (desirability factors)

In Chapter 1 we identified the 'twin' objectives of operations management as providing customer service and achieving resource utilization. The emphasis given to these objectives will vary, and this relative emphasis will influence the approach employed in capacity planning. For example, the need to provide high customer service even at the expense of resource utilization will encourage the provision of excess capacity and/or output stocks. The influence of objectives on capacity planning is illustrated in the following cases, while Figure 11.10 provides a 'decision tree' type of approach to the

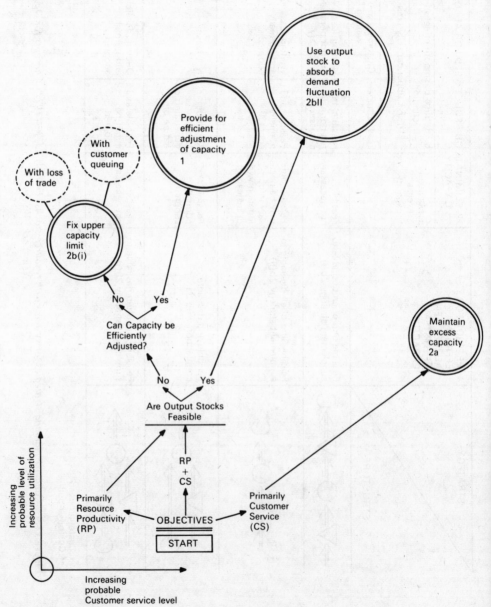

Figure 11.10 *'Decision tree' type approach to the selection of capacity management strategies. Derived from an original by B. Melville, University of Waikato, New Zealand.*

selection of capacity management strategies and suggests the relationship of these strategies to the two basic operations management objectives.

EXAMPLE CASES

The types of approach which may be used in capacity planning in three contrasting cases are summarized in Table 11.5 and outlined below.

Builder (of 'one-off' houses to customer order)

Here we shall consider the special 'one-off' house builder who neither has a permanent labour force nor owns much equipment. In effect, on receipt of an order from a customer the builder acquires all the resources necessary for the satisfaction of the order. In this case the capacity management problem is relatively simple. The determination of capacity needs is a straight-forward problem, since no capacity (i.e. no resources) is provided prior to receipt of the customer's order. There is therefore no need to attempt to forecast demand. Demand is in effect measured and sufficient capacity is then provided to meet that demand, i.e. to satisfy that order. Theoretically at least, the development of a strategy for the utilization of resources is straightforward, since there is never the need to provide for efficient adjustment of capacity or the need to eliminate or reduce the need for such adjustment. In practice, however, since in such situations all orders will be different, it may be difficult to determine exactly how much of each resource is required. For example, the quantity of each type of building material can only be estimated and the amount of labour required will depend on a variety of factors. In practice, therefore, there will be a need to *either* ensure that further capacity can be provided if enough is not obtained initially *and/or* to eliminate or reduce the need for adjustment in system capacity by the provision of excess capacity. Hence the capacity planning strategy adopted will often consist of:

(a)   provision for efficient adjustment of system capacity through, for example, subcontracting, transferring material, labour and machinery from other jobs, increasing hours worked and/or labour force; and/or
(b)   eliminating or reducing the need for adjustment in system capacity by providing excess capacity.

Customer service will be one principal objective in determining and managing capacity in such systems. Apart from price, which in part will be influenced by the resource utilization expected, delivery or completion time will be the main variable affecting the probability of receiving orders. The customer service objective will therefore be manifest in attempts to minimize building time. In addition the building operations manager will of course seek to ensure that resource productivity is high, so that costs can be kept down, and will therefore seek to satisfy a partly competing objective by ensuring that equipment, labour and materials are all sufficiently highly utilized. Therefore strategy 2b(i) above may be favoured when requirements are being planned.

Fire service

In this case we can consider the normal system structure to provide input resource stocks but no input queue of customers, since it will usually be the intention of the fire service to ensure that appliances, etc., are 'standing by' for calls. There will, of course, be situations, such as major disasters, in which all available resources are committed and hence new customers must wait,

Table 11.5 *The nature of capacity: examples.*

Example	Operating system structure	Capacity planning		Principal objectives
		Determination of capacity required	Capacity planning strategy (see Tables 11.3 and 11.4)	
Builder (of 'one-off' houses)		Demand is measured. Capacity is provided to meet each demand.	1 and/or 2(b)(i) i.e. Provide for capacity adjustment and/or some excess capacity	Maximum customer service (in particular through minimizing completion time) + Maximum utilization of (consumed) resource
Fire service		Expected demand is forecast. Capacity is provided to meet maximum or near maximum demand.	2(a) with some possibility of 1. i.e. Eliminate or reduce need for adjustment in system by providing excess capacity with further possibility of providing some capacity adjustment	No customer queuing + High resource productivity
Furniture removal		Expected demand is forecast. Capacity is provided to meet average or 'sufficient' demand.	2(b)(i) (with customer queuing and possibly loss of trade), with possibility of 1. i.e. Eliminate or reduce need for adjustment in system capacity by smoothing effect of demand level fluctuations through fixing upper capacity limit and accepting loss of trade with the further possibility of providing some capacity adjustment.	Minimum customer queuing and/or loss of trade + High resource productivity

but here we shall consider the capacity management problem for the normal, i.e. the intended, situation.

Expected demand will be forecast and enough capacity will doubtless be provided to meet substantially more than average demand. In effect, therefore, capacity planning strategy 2, i.e. eliminate or reduce need for adjustment in system capacity' through the 'provision of excess capacity', is adopted. Undoubtedly the emphasis will be on this approach.

However, there may also be some possibility of providing for some degree of capacity adjustment (i.e. strategy 1) through, for example, subcontracting work (to neighbouring fire services), transferring resources from other jobs (e.g. maintenance, practices, etc.) and temporary yet rapid increases in the labour force or hours worked (use of standby labour, etc.).

The principal objective in capacity planning will be the maintenance of the system structure, i.e. to ensure that no customer queuing occurs, coupled of course with reasonably high capacity utilization. In practice the customer service criterion will often be satisfactorily attained at the cost of poor resource productivity.

Furniture removal

This differs from the above example in offering a far wider range of alternative approaches to capacity management. Here input resources will be stocked and will be utilized on jobs drawn from an available queue.

Again expected demand will be forecast and on this basis a certain capacity will be provided. Unlike the fire service, there will be no necessity to meet high demand and in practice capacity will be provided which is sufficient to meet near average demand or 'sufficient' demand— 'sufficient' being defined by management as that proportion of available demand which management choose to seek to satisfy. Having established a normal capacity in this way, the operations manager must choose whether, and if so how, to provide for efficient capacity adjustment (strategy 1) and/or whether, and if so how, to eliminate or reduce the need for such adjustments (strategy 2). Both strategies are feasible and might be implemented as follows:

(a) provision for efficient adjustment of system capacity, through for example subcontracting work, transfer of resources from other jobs, rescheduling activities, temporary changes in staffing or hours;

(b) eliminating or reducing the need for adjustment in system capacity through
  (i) providing excess capacity (although this is normally neither necessary nor adopted);
  (ii) reducing or smoothing the effect of demand level charges by fixing an upper capacity limit and normally requiring customers to queue, and in some cases accepting some loss of trade.

The principal objective in capacity planning here will be the provision of an acceptable level of customer service by minimizing average waiting time or queue length and thus minimizing the loss of customers, coupled with providing for high resource productivity, i.e. utilization of resources.

CAPACITY PLANNING PROCEDURES

In this section we shall describe some of the procedures which may be used in capacity planning. Before going into detail two general points will be made.

Aggregation

The term *aggregate planning* is often employed in the capacity context. The implication is that such planning is concerned with *total* demand, i.e. all demands collected together. This is of relevance in operating systems where different goods or services are provided, and in such cases capacity planning will seek to estimate or measure all demands and express the total in such a way as to enable enough of all resources (or total capacity) to be provided. Demand for all outputs must therefore be expressed in common capacity-related units such as the number of resources or resource hours required (see for example, Table 11.1). An operating system may, for example, provide three types of service, or service three types of customer. The estimated demand for each source expressed in, for example, hours per unit time (e.g. week) required for each type of resource must be identified and totalled. Given this aggregate demand, an overall capacity plan can be developed to cope with all demands.

Economic operating levels *(see also Chapter 4)*

Figure 11.11 shows the relationship between the unit cost of processing and the throughput rate for a hypothetical situation. It will be evident from the figure that the economic throughput rate is p^1 since this is the rate at which the unit cost is least. The use of a higher throughput rate involves higher unit costs, as does a lower throughput rate. Such a situation will often exist, especially where an operating system has been designed specifically to process items or customers at a particular rate. For example, in a flow processing system involving a series of interdependent facilities, the entire system must be designed to provide a particular output or throughput rate. If the output rate is reduced then costs will increase because of facility idle time, etc., and if the output rate is increased then subcontracting, overtime work, duplicate facilities, etc., will be required, all of which will contribute to the unit output costs.

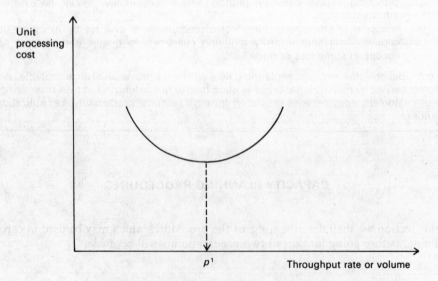

Figure 11.11   *Unit cost/volume relationship.*

If, in an operating system comprising a set of resources which provide the relationship shown in Figure 11.11, it is now considered appropriate to increase the level of resources in order to provide for a greater throughput rate, then it may be possible to shift the entire curve as shown in Figure 11.12. This implies that the facilities have been rearranged or set up in a different manner so that the intended rate is now p^2. Again, departures from this throughput rate p^2 can incur increased unit costs.

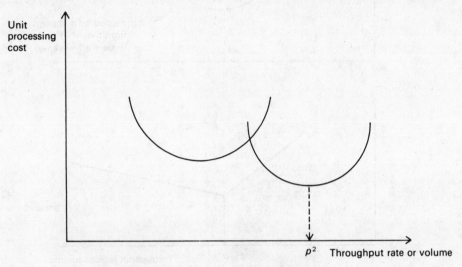

Figure 11.12 *Unit cost/volume relationships.*

This concept of an 'economic operating level' is relevant in many situations and is of value in capacity planning since, where curves such as those shown in Figures 11.11 and 11.12 are available or can be approximated, the cost of changing capacity through the adoption of capacity planning strategy 1 can be established for different magnitudes of change.

Notice that in some situations the cost/throughput rate relationship is not a 'smooth' one. For example, in some situations a throughput rate can be increased only incrementally, so relationships similar to those shown in Figure 11.13 may apply. However, whatever the nature of the relationship, providing it is known or can be approximated, the economic level of operations can be found and the cost of capacity changes above or below a particular level can be obtained.

In the remainder of this chapter we shall look at capacity (or aggregate) planning procedures. We shall consider only a few of the many procedures which are available, the intention being to illustrate the types of approach which might be employed rather than to provide a comprehensive 'tool-kit'.

Most of the available procedures are relevant only in particular situations and deal only with particular types of capacity planning problems. In introducing each of the procedures below we shall first try to indicate where the approach might be employed and for what particular purpose.

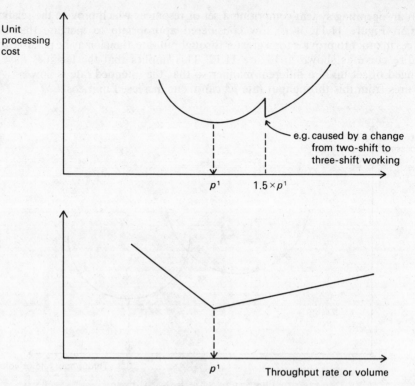

Figure 11.13   *Unit cost/volume relationships (discontinuous).*

Cumulative graphs (a procedure for comparing alternative capacity plans for a period, particularly where there is a need to balance the costs of changing capacity against cost of insufficient or extra capacity, e.g. comparison or combination of strategies 1 and 2).

The capacity provided to satisfy estimated or measured demand will, as shown above, be influenced by the strategy employed for meeting demand fluctuations. The use of cumulative graphs is a method of examining alternatives.

Table 11.6 gives the estimated monthly demand for a one-year period. The figures are plotted cumulatively in Figure 11.14, which also shows three possible cumulative capacity curves. Curve 1 corresponds to a capacity of 37.5 resource hours per day—the minimum required to ensure that capacity is always equal to or in excess of expected demand for this period. The adoption of a strategy of providing sufficient excess capacity to eliminate the need for capacity adjustment (strategy 2(a)) would lead to the provision of such capacity. The provision of approximately 30 resource hours per day (curve 2) might result from the adoption of a different strategy for the use of resources (strategy 2(b)(i)). Such an arrangement would mean either increasing output stock or reducing customer waiting time during the period up to day 50 and after day 160, when capacity exceeds demand. Day 50 to day 160 would see:

(a)   stock diminishing or depleted; and/or
(b)   increased customer waiting time; and/or
(c)   loss of trade

since capacity would be lower than expected demand.

Both curves 1 and 2 require no capacity adjustment during this period. The adoption of an approach relying wholly on or involving the strategy of providing for efficient adjustment in capacity (strategy 1) might give rise to the provision of capacity in the manner of curve 3, in which one capacity adjustment is made (at day 75) and which provides for the satisfaction of all forecast demand without the use of output stocks, customer queuing or loss of trade, yet with better capacity utilization than curve 1.

It will be possible to cost these three (and other) alternative strategies if the cost of changing capacity and the costs of having insufficient capacity (e.g. cost of lost customers) and extra capacity (e.g. cost of stock) are known.

Note: In practice the use of cumulative graphs in capacity planning must take into account the lead time normally required between the use of capacity or resources and the satisfaction of customers. For example, the expected customer demand in April equivalent to 900 resource hours (Table 11.6) would necessitate the provision of appropriate capacity at an earlier period. Hence the capacity curves in Figure 11.14 should in fact be displaced forward by the amount of this lead time. Similarly, the use of such curves must take into account the situation which exists at the start of the planning period. For example, if an output stock exists at day 0 then any cumulative capacity curve must start above point 0 on the y axis.

Table 11.6 *Estimated monthly demand*

Month	Working days	Cumulative days	Estimated demand (in resource hours)	Cumulative estimated demand
Jan.	20	20	500	500
Feb.	18	38	650	1150
Mar.	22	60	750	1900
Apr.	18	78	900	2800
May	21	99	700	3500
June	20	119	500	4000
July	20	139	300	4300
Aug.	10	149	300	4600
Sept.	20	169	450	5050
Oct.	21	190	500	5550
Nov.	20	210	550	6100
Dec.	18	228	300	6400

The reaction rate[2] (a procedure for determining by how much and how often to adjust capacity to meet changes in demand—particularly relevant where both capacity strategies 1 and 2 are to be employed).

The 'reaction rate' of adjustment of capacity determines how much capacity adjustment is made to meet a forecast fluctuation in demand. Capacity adjustment by the full amount of demand variation gives a 100 per cent reaction rate, hence fluctuations in demand are transmitted directly to the function. This might lead to severe problems and costs in acquiring or disposing of resources, e.g. personnel. Reaction rates can take any value from 0 to 100 per cent. Low reaction rates lead to stable operation but higher inventories, and higher reaction rates would lead to the reverse conditions. Short review periods between decisions lead to small capacity fluctuations and smaller inventories for a given reaction rate.

The selection of a reaction rate and review period depends on the balance of inventory

---

[2] Buffa, E. S. (1973) *Modern Production Management*, 4th edition. Chichester: Wiley.

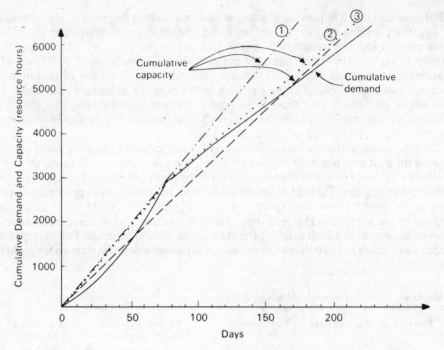

Figure 11.14 *Cumulative demand and capacity curves.*

carrying costs in relation to the costs of capacity change. The mathematical analysis of the reaction rate approach indicates the optimum combination for a given application. If much of the fluctuation in demand derives from random causes there is little need to react quickly. Lower reaction rates and short review periods will cause small adjustments fairly often. In general, high reaction rates and long review periods tend to overcontrol. The optimal amount of control minimizes the sum of the two types of cost, rather than minimizing one at the expense of the other. (*Note*: The reaction rate procedure adopts a similar approach to that used in the exponential smoothing method of forecasting. See Appendix II.)

Linear programming (see also Appendix 1) (the 'transportation' approach described here provides a means of allocating available capacity and inventories against a forward demand in such a way as to balance these costs and smooth the level of operations—relevant only where strategy 2 (b)(ii) is employed, possible alongside other strategies).

Various linear programming methods have been used in this context. Here we shall concentrate on the use of the transportation algorithm. The transportation method of linear programming provides a means of minimizing a combination of capacity and inventory costs. Various alternative means of providing capacity are recognized, typically normal working, overtime working and subcontracting. The use of the method requires that demands for each of several periods are satisfied from inventory and/or from the use of normal plus, if necessary, additional capacity in such a manner that total costs are minimized. The approach has one major disadvantage in that it is static, i.e. it is a method for formulating policy for a given period assuming no changes in circumstances, etc., during that period. Repeated recalculations for a forward period will overcome this to some extent, but there is a danger of suboptimization.

For the sake of easy illustration let us consider a manufacturing situation in which planning is necessary for only four sales and production periods ($n = 4$). The sales demand during each of these periods is represented by S, i.e. S_1, S_2, S_3 and S_4 and this demand may be met from one of the following:

(a) stock;
(b) 'regular' production during the normal shifts;
(c) overtime production.

The costs associated with each of these are:

(a) storage—C_I—cost of storage per unit per period;
(b) regular production—C_R—cost of production per unit per period;
(c) overtime production—C_O—cost of production per unit per period.

We might further assume that items produced during one period are not available to the customer until the following period; consequently some initial stock must be available to satisfy demand for sales period 1. We can now represent the unit costs as a transportation matrix as shown in Table 11.7.

Table 11.7 *Matrix of costs associated with production, stock and demand during four periods*

Production period		Sales period				Final stock	Total capacity
		1	2	3	4		
0	Opening stock	0	C_I	$2C_I$	$3C_I$	$4C_I$	I_0
1	Regular production	—	C_R	$C_R + C_I$	$C_R + 2C_I$	$C_R + 3C_I$	R_1
	Overtime production	—	C_O	$C_O + C_I$	$C_O + 2C_I$	$C_O + 3C_I$	O_1
2	Regular production	—	—	C_R	$C_R + C_I$	$C_R + 2C_I$	R_2
	Overtime production	—	—	C_O	$C_O + C_I$	$C_O + 2C_I$	O_2
3	Regular production	—	—	—	C_R	$C_R + C_I$	R_3
	Overtime production	—	—	—	C_O	$C_O + C_I$	O_3
Total demand during period		S_1	S_2	S_3	S_4		

Notation I_i = stock level at end of ith period
R_i = max. no. of units that can be produced on regular time during ith period
O_i = max. no. of units that can be produced on overtime during ith period

Notice that certain cells contain dashes, since these represent impossible routes. (The production from one period cannot be used to satisfy demand for an earlier period. In order to ensure that these cells do not feature as part of the solution it is conventional to allocate extremely high cost values to them.) To indicate how this table has been constructed, consider period 2. Sales during this period may be satisfied from stock which has incurred cost associated with storage for one period, i.e. C_I, or from production which was undertaken during the previous period at cost C_R for regular production and C_O for overtime production. The case shown in Table 11.7 deals only with one product; however, this method can easily be extended to cover production planning for two or more products merely by constructing two or more columns for each of the sales periods and for final stock.

Furthermore, it is not necessary that the costs of production, C_R and C_O, or the costs of storage, C_I, should be the same for each period or each product.

EXAMPLE

Two very similar products, A and B, are to be manufactured. The total demand for each for three future periods is:

Period 1	A = 100	B = 50
Period 2	A = 70	B = 105
Period 3	A = 50	B = 125

It is estimated that the stock of products at the beginning of period 1 will be:

$$A = 150$$
$$B = 75$$

The cost of stockholding per product per period, C_I, is £2. The costs of production are as follows:

For production during period 1:
    Product A $C_R = £1$ per product
                               $C_O = £2$ per product
    Product B $C_R = £1$ per product
                               $C_O = £2$ per product

For production during period 2:
    Product A $C_R = £2$ per product
                               $C_O = £3$ per product
    Product B $C_R = £2$ per product
                               $C_O = £3$ per product

The production capacity per period is as follows.

Period 1	regular production =	125 units (of either type)
	overtime production =	50 units (of either type)
Period 2	regular production =	125 units (of either type)
	overtime production =	50 units (of either type)

What is the optimal production plan and what is the cost associated with satisfying the above demands?

The cost matrix is shown in Table 11.8. Using the transportation methods of linear programming described in Appendix I, the solution shown in Table 11.9 can easily be obtained. The cost associated with this production plan is as follows:

$$
\begin{aligned}
&100(0) + 50(0) + 70(2) + 5(2) \\
&+ 100(1) + 25(3) \\
&+ \ \ 25(4) + 25(4) \\
&+ 100(2) + 25(4) \\
&+ \ \ 50(5) \qquad\qquad = £1075
\end{aligned}
$$

Table 11.8 *Costs associated with a three-period production plan for three products*

PRODUCTION PERIOD		Sales period 1 Product A	B	Sales period 2 Product A	B	Sales period 3 Product A	B	Final stock Product A	B	Total capacity (both products)
0	Opening stock	0	0	2	2	4	4	6	6	225
1	Regular production			1	1	3	3	5	5	125
1	Overtime production			2	2	4	4	6	6	50
2	Regular production					2	2	4	4	125
2	Overtime production					3	3	5	5	50
	Total demand during period	100	50	70	105	50	125	75		(575)

Table 11.9 *Three-period production plan for two products*

PRODUCTION PERIOD		Sales period 1 Product A_0	B_0	Sales period 2 Product A_2	B_2	Sales period 3 Product A_4	B_4	Final stock Product $A+B_6$	Total capacity (both products)
0	Opening stock $_0$	100	50	70_2	5_2	$_4$	$_4$	6	225
1	Regular production–1			100_1	25_1	$_3$	$_3$	$_5$	125
1	Overtime production $_0$			$_2$	$_2$	25_4	25_4	$_6$	50
2	Regular production–2					$_2 100_2$		25_4	125
2	Overtime production–1					$_3$	$_3$	50_5	50
	Total demand	100	50	70	105	50	125	75	

Notice that in this solution a proportion of both regular and overtime production during production period 2 is delivered to stock. This is necessary because production capacity during this period is in excess of demand. If, however, the total production capacity in any period need not be used then our solution would have involved the production of 100 of product A during regular production in period 2. This would result in a saving of 25(4) + 50(5), i.e. £350 during this period, but of course no opening stock would be available for the next period.

Linear decision rule[3] (a procedure for smoothing operations taking into account labour costs, workforce change cost, inventory costs, etc., in order to determine the best capacity plan for future periods—relevant where strategies 1 and 2(b)(ii) are employed).

The objective of this sophisticated mathematical approach is the derivation of a series of linear equations (or decision rules) for use in specifying the output rate and capacity required to meet forecast demand and minimize total costs. The costs of carrying inventory and payroll costs (including overtime) and the cost of changing the size of the labour force are considered. The procedure, like linear programming, produces an optimal result, but must be tailored to fit each application, i.e. to take into account particular cost structures, etc.

Heuristic methods[4] (largely concerned with workforce or capacity smoothing, such procedures may be of relevance where there is a need to balance costs of capacity change with costs of inventories, i.e. strategies 1 and 2(b) (ii)).

A 'heuristic' method provides a good, but not necessarily the best, solution. In reality most operations management decisions are heuristic or, more colloquially, 'rules of thumb'.

The *management coefficients* model uses a simplified version of the workforce production level decision rules incorporated in the linear decision rule method. Coefficients for these rules are determined by regression analysis on historical performance, i.e. managers' actual past behaviour. The equation is then used to indicate the future decision as with the linear decision rules.

An alternative approach involves a *search* of feasible solutions to establish the coefficients for the linear decision rule method. The coefficients are established to minimize total cost and the two equations are then used for planning purposes. Two approaches have been developed. The parametric production planning model deals with inventory, workforce changes, overtime costs and customer queuing. The search decision rule is of a similar nature.

Queuing theory methods (such approaches may be of relevance in determining the capacity required in service and transport systems and/or in deciding levels of utilization of capacity and customer service levels).

Transport and service systems depend on an input provided by the beneficiary of the service and 'processing' cannot take place until that is available. Because of this time dependence, capacity planning is constrained and such systems cannot usually achieve the same levels of resource productivity as manufacture or supply systems. However, some such systems improve utilization by scheduling inputs, i.e. by controlling them (e.g. appointment systems for GPs, dentists, etc., and certain types of transport system). In

[3] Holt, C. C., Modigliani, F., Muth, J. and Simon, H. (1960) *Planning Production Inventories and Workforce*, Englewood Cliffs, NJ: Prentice-Hall.
[4] For example see Bowman E. H. (1963) Consistency and optimality in management decision making, *Management Science*, **9**(2) and Taubert, W. H. (1965) Search decision rule for aggregate scheduling problems, *Management Science*, **14**(6).

other situations (e.g. roads, hospitals, shops), since there is little control of input arrival rate, adequate capacity must be provided to meet peak demand without excessive 'customer' waiting time (strategy 2(a) and (b)). Outside peak demand periods, low utilization must be tolerated unless alternative services may be provided. Queuing theory may be used in capacity planning in such situations.

Although input 'arrivals' may follow specific patterns, the overall pattern in many cases is random. This gives rise to queuing situations. The methods used to describe and analyse queuing situations depend on the form of the system, in particular:

(a) number of servicing units;
(b) configuration of servicing units, i.e. whether in parallel or in series;
(c) queue discipline;
(d) distribution of arrival times;
(e) distribution of service times.

The simplest case is shown in Figure 11.15.

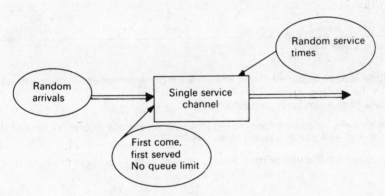

Figure 11.15 *Simple queuing situation.*

Let:

P_n = probability of n units in system (i.e. queue + one being serviced)
L = average number of units in system
L_q = average number of units in queue
W = average time units spend in system
W_q = average time units spend in queue

where:

λ = average arrival rate (units/period of time)
μ = average service rate (units/period of time)
ρ = utilization parameter = $\dfrac{\lambda}{\mu}$

$\mu > \lambda$

If there are λ arrivals/h and the system has a capacity of μ/h, the system will be busy $\dfrac{\lambda}{\mu}$ proportion of time and idle $\left(1 - \dfrac{\lambda}{\mu}\right)$ proportion of time. Thus:

$$P_0 \text{ (probability of no units in system)}$$

$$= 1 - \frac{\lambda}{\mu}$$

It can also be shown that:

$$L = \frac{\lambda}{\mu - \lambda}$$

$$L_q = \frac{\lambda^2}{\mu(\mu - \lambda)} \qquad \text{NB: } L_q \text{ does not equal. } L - 1 \text{ since for some of the time the service channel is empty; the average number being served} \neq 1.$$

$$W = \frac{1}{\mu - \lambda}$$

and $W_q = \dfrac{\lambda}{\mu(\mu - \lambda)}$

EXAMPLE

A new hospital is to be designed. If one ambulance is provided, what will be its utilization, and what will be the average waiting time for the ambulance?
    Taking data from a similar community:

1. Emergency calls for ambulances are random with an average of one per hour (half due to accidents and half due to various illnesses).

2. Time required for ambulance round trip is random with an average of $\frac{1}{2}$ hour (i.e. two per hour).

Hence $\lambda = 1$
         $\mu = 2$

$$W_q = \frac{1}{\mu(\mu - \lambda)} \quad = \frac{1}{2} \text{ hour}$$

$$P_0 = 1 - \frac{\lambda}{\mu} \quad = \frac{1}{2}$$

$$L_q = \frac{\lambda^2}{\mu(\mu - \lambda)} \quad = 0.5$$

i.e. for one ambulance, average waiting time $= \frac{1}{2}$ hour, but the ambulance is busy only half of the time.

CHECKLIST FOR CHAPTER 11

Operations planning and control   Nature of capacity management
  Operations planning: definition   Capacity management: definition
  Operations control: definition   Nature of capacity

FURTHER READING

Eilon, S. (1973) The production smoothing problem, *Production Engineer*, **52**, pp. 123–129.

Fisk, J. C. and Seagle J. P. (1978) The integration of aggregate planning with resource requirements planning, *Production and Inventory Management*, 3rd quarter, pp. 81–89. (Part reprinted as Chapter 16 in Wild, R. (ed.) (1981) *Management and Production Readings*. Harmondsworth: Penguin.)

Morris, W. T. (1967) *The Capacity Decision system*. Homewood, Illinois: Irwin. Focuses mainly on the investment decisions and budgeting.

Wild, R (1980) *Operations Management—A Policy Framework*. Oxford: Pergamon. Chapter 7 discusses capacity management in the context of business policy.

Zimmerman, H. J.and Sovereign M. G. (1974) *Quantitative Methods for Production Management*. Englewood Cliffs, NJ: Prentice-Hall. Chapter 6 deals with aggregate planning. It gives and illustrates the use of several quantitative approaches including linear programming.

QUESTIONS

11.1 A small company is engaged in the manufacture of automatic gigglecocks for three principal customers, Smith, Brown and Jones. These three customers are in the habit of placing their orders for a four-week period three weeks in advance; a set of orders has just been received by the company and are shown below.

Customer	Quantity to be delivered during week number			
	26	27	28	29
Smith	10	14	20	15
Brown	14	20	25	17
Jones	7	9	10	7
Total	31	43	55	39

Given the following information, determine the optimal production plan and the cost associated with the satisfaction of these orders for automatic gigglecocks according to such a plan.

Stockholding cost per gigglecock per week $= £1$
Production cost per gigglecock $= £10$ during normal shift work
                                                   $= £15$ during night-shift work
'Free' stock of gigglecocks at end of week 25 $= 35$
Production capacity each week $= 35$ gigglecocks per normal shift
                                                   $= 15$ gigglecocks per night shift

No stock is required at the end of week 29.

11.2 What are the two basic capacity planning strategies? Describe with examples the use of each and their use together.

11.3 Table 1 below shows the number of each of two products, A and B, which have recently been ordered from company X for delivery to customers during the four months May to August.

Each of the two products consists of two sub-assemblies (I and II or II and III) as shown in Table 2. Table 2 also gives the work hours of production required for each sub-assembly.

The company works a three-shift system. The production capacity in work hours per shift is shown in Table 3.

The company is in the habit of planning production for several months ahead, each additional customer order being included in the production plan when it is received. The production plan prior to the receipt of the recent orders is shown in terms of work hours of production capacity required in Table 4.

Table 5 shows the unit production costs for each sub-assembly for each shift, while Table 6 gives the unit storage cost per sub-assembly per month.

Assume: (a) that the details of the existing production plan cannot be altered; (b) that sub-assemblies manufactured during one month enable the products of which they are a part to be delivered to customers no later than the last day of the same month; (c) that there will be no sub-assemblies in stock at the end of April.

Formulate this planning problem as a linear programming problem; arrange the data in a manner which permits a linear programming algorithm to be used, but do not solve the problem Comment on any important characteristic of the solution which is evident from the initial formulation

Table 1 *Demand from new orders*

Product	May	June	July	August
A	20	40	25	40
B	30	25	50	32

Table 2 *Sub-assemblies/product, and work hours/sub-assembly*

Product	Number of sub-assemblies per product		
	I	II	III
A	1	1	—
B		1	1
Work hours production	5	7	5

Table 3 *Production   capacity   (work hours)/month*

	March to July inc.	August
Shift 1	400	400
Shift 2	400	300
Shift 3	400	300

Table 4 *Work hours committed to previous orders*

	March	April	May	June	July	August
Shift 1	300	250	250	200	150	100
Shift 2	300	200	200	100	100	50
Shift 3	300	200	200	50	100	50

Table 5 *Unit production cost (£)/sub-assembly*

	Sub-assembly					
	I		II		III	
Shift 1	5	6	6	7	4	5
Shift 2	7	8	8	9	6	7
Shift 3	7	8	8	9	6	7
	March–July	August	March–July	August	March–July	August

Table 6 *Unit storage cost /month*

Sub-assembly	£/month
I	0.5
II	0.6
III	0.5

11.4 Identify and discuss the relevance of the various approaches available for the adjustment of capacity. Indicate what factors or considerations might encourage or prevent the use of each.

11.5 A company has decided to set up a computer bureau. It will provide a computing service for local organizations and will offer not only the hardware but also a programming service. What type of capacity planning problems might be encountered in designing the bureau (i.e. deciding the types and quantities of resources to be provided)?

PART 6

OPERATIONS SCHEDULING

INTRODUCTION TO PART 6

Here we deal with the scheduling (or planning or timing) of the conversion activities of the operating system. We try first to identify the different types of scheduling problems which can be encountered in different types of operating systems, and then consider some techniques for their solution. The techniques and the types of problems which are of particular importance are dealt with in depth in Chapters 13, 14 and 15.

The scheduling of the activities within the operating system is another principal problem area of operations management, as defined in Chapter 1. As with capacity management (see Introduction to Part 5), the strategies employed in activity scheduling will again be influenced by:

(a) *feasibility constraints (influenced mainly by the operating system structure);*
(b) *desirability factors (influenced mainly by the organization's and operations manager's objectives);*
(c) *the operations manager's own preferences.*

The nature of the activity scheduling problem will be influenced by the operating system structure, but equally, activity scheduling decisions can change the operating system structure. Further, the objectives being pursued by the operations manager, in particular the relative importance of resource utilization and customer service, will influence the selection of an activity scheduling strategy but, given some freedom of choice, the operations manager may prefer to employ an approach which insulates the operating system from external uncertainties, e.g. demand changes.

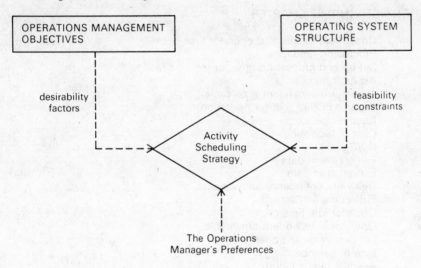

CHAPTER 12

Activity Scheduling

NOTATION USED IN THIS CHAPTER

a	Concurrent facility and operator time/cycle
a_i	Processing time for i
A_i	Set-up and processing time for job i on facility A
A_n	Ashcroft number
b	Operator independent time/cycle
c	Expected delay cost for operation
C_o	Cost of operator/h
C_m	Cost of facility/h
E	C_o/C_m
EF	Earliest finish date
ES	Earliest start date
f_i	Delay or contingency allowance
FCFS	First come first served
i_o	Operator idle time/cycle
i_m	Operator independent time/cycle
LIO	Longest imminent operation
LOB	Line of balance
L_q	Average queue length
m	Number of facilities ($j = 1 \ldots m$)
MRP	Materials requirements planning
n	Number of jobs ($i = 1 \ldots n$)
n	Number of facilities assigned
n^1	Ideal number of facilities for one worker
N	Number of remaining operations
ρ	λ/μ
Q_i	Order quantity for item i
S	Job slack
SIO	Shortest imminent operation
t	Processing time (in COVERT)
t	Facility independent activity time/cycle
t_0	Scheduled completion date

t_1	Present date
T	Total throughput time
x_i	Time at which i must begin
Y_n	Cost/unit of processing with n facilities
λ	Mean arrival rate
μ	Mean service rate
Δpq	Interval between end of p and start of q

Activity scheduling is one of the principal and 'characteristic' problem areas of operations management. The type of activity scheduling problem which might be encountered may be different in different types of operating systems. This is the *feasibility* constraint described in Chapter 1. Additionally, the operations manager's approach to scheduling will be influenced by *desirability* associated with the need to pursue certain objectives and by the operation manager's own *preferences*.

This chapter considers the nature of the scheduling problem in operations management. It identifies different types of activity scheduling situations so that we might then identify which problem-solving techniques are relevant in each situation. The last part of the chapter introduces some activity scheduling techniques, while subsequent chapters in this part of the book deal in more detail with other scheduling techniques and procedures for use in other situations.

NATURE OF THE ACTIVITY SCHEDULING PROBLEM

Activity scheduling is concerned with the activities which take place *within* the operating system. An activity schedule will show the times (or dates) at which all of these activities are to be undertaken. The fixing of such times determines the manner in which items will flow through the operating system. The activity scheduling problem (sometimes called activity planning) is concerned with the fixing of these times in advance. The manner in which the problem is tackled will depend largely on the situation in which activity scheduling is undertaken. For example, if an operating system is working in anticipation of demand, the scheduling problems will differ from those in an operating system which is working specifically to satisfy individual customers' 'due date' requirements. Other factors will influence the nature of the activity scheduling problem and therefore the techniques which might be appropriate for the solution of that problem. In order better to understand the nature of the activity scheduling problem we shall first consider two factors:

(a) whether scheduling is to be 'internally' or 'externally' oriented;
(b) whether demand is 'dependent' or 'independent'.

Factors influencing the activity scheduling problem

Here we shall consider 'feasibility' and 'desirability' factors influencing the nature of the activity scheduling problem strategies.

Internally and externally oriented scheduling

Activity scheduling is concerned with the timing of activities, but these times must be fixed in relation to some other requirements. Consider as an example a situation in which products are manufactured against a specific customer order. Each customer order specifies exactly what is to be produced and when it is required—the 'due date'. Here the internal activities which create end products (e.g. the manufacture of components and sub-assemblies) must all be scheduled so that each end product is available on the required 'due' or delivery date. A similar situation can exist in non-manufacturing organizations. Here those activities which are necessary to satisfy a particular service or transport requirement must be performed in time to satisfy a particular customer's request. In all such cases the customer has a *direct* influence on the timing of activities within the operating system, so activity scheduling can be seen to be *externally* oriented in that the timing of all activities are fixed to satisfy *particular* external customer timing requirements.

In contrast, consider a situation in which items are manufactured for stock in anticipation of future customer orders. Here there need be no *direct* influence from a particular customer on the internal activity schedule. Customers are satisfied from stock and the need to replenish this stock gives rise to the need to schedule activities within the operating system. A similar situation can exist in service and transport systems, where a system is 'buffered' from its customers by an input queue. In these circumstances the activity scheduling can be mainly *internally oriented*, and in such cases there can be more freedom in activity scheduling, so schedules can be fixed more easily to maximize resource utilization, etc.

Thus the nature of the activity scheduling problem can in part be defined by the *orientation* of scheduling.

Externally oriented scheduling strategy

Externally oriented scheduling strategy is scheduling of activities within an operating system specifically to satisfy particular customer timing requirements. This will normally involve due date considerations. One approach to externally oriented scheduling is shown in Figure 12.1, which illustrates the due date scheduling procedure in Gantt chart form. Three particular cases are considered:

(a) An operating system in which there is a 'function from stock, direct to customer order' (see Chapter 1). Here the customer due date is fixed and activity scheduling involves subtracting from this date the duration of the function which must be undertaken to satisfy the customer's requirements. This reverse scheduling gives rise to a start date for the function.

(b) An operating system in which there is a 'function from source, direct to customer'. Here a similar situation exists but in this case it is necessary, by reverse scheduling, to establish a start date for the function, and then the order date for the acquisition of resources for that function.

(c) An operating system in which there is a 'function from stock and from customer'. In this situation the customer's due date is the date on which the customer *arrives* into the system. This in fact is the start date for the function, the end date of which is found by adding the function duration to the start date.

This is a simple scheduling technique. Others are also available for tackling the externally oriented scheduling problem, and these will be described in this and subsequent chapters.

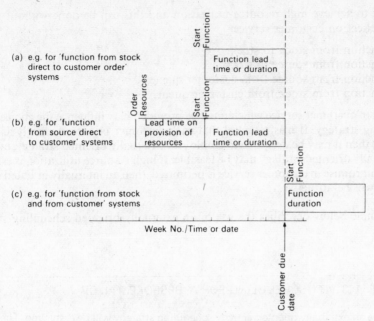

Figure 12.1 *Due date activity scheduling.*

Internally oriented scheduling strategy

With this approach the activities within the operating system are scheduled without direct reference to individual customers' due date requirements. Such a situation can exist where there are stocks or queues between the activities and the customer. In these circumstances there is a greater opportunity to schedule activities to provide for efficient flow, high resource utilization, economic batching, etc., within the operating system. The emphasis therefore may be on the maximization of resource utilization, with relatively little direct concern for *individual* customers' due date requirements. Several techniques may be appropriate for tackling the internally oriented activity scheduling problem. For example, the use of *dispatching* procedures will often be relevant. This approach involves deciding which of several available jobs to do next on a particular facility. Other techniques will be described later in this chapter and in subsequent chapters.

From the above it will be seen that an internally oriented strategy will *not* normally be *feasible*, hence an externally oriented (i.e. due date) strategy will normally be employed for the following operating system structures, since in these cases an internal orientation will not normally be feasible, and will be undesirable:

(c) Function from stock to customer order.
(d) Function from source to customer order.
(e) Function from stock, direct from customer.

An internally oriented activity scheduling strategy is *feasible* for all other operating system structures. Further, such an approach will often be employed, since it will normally be desirable to achieve high resource utilization and this can be done without substantial adverse effect on customer service:

(a) Function from stock to stock.
(b) Function from source to stock.
(c) Function from source from customer queue.
(d) Function from stock from customer queue.

The level of customer service which must be provided may influence the choice of activity scheduling strategy. If it is essential that each customer be served exactly as and when required, then it may be *desirable* to employ an externally oriented strategy, even though an internally oriented strategy may be feasible. If high resource utilization is essential and some compromise in customer service is permitted, then an internally oriented scheduling strategy will be attractive.

The example below describes the use of an externally oriented scheduling strategy.

EXAMPLE: ACTIVITY SCHEDULING FOR A 'BESPOKE' TAILOR

In this case an externally oriented activity scheduling strategy will be employed. The customers will influence the entire system directly, excluding input resource stocks. Customer orders, together with their required, quoted and/or agreed delivery dates, will be fed directly into the activity scheduling function along with necessary information on the work content, method of manufacture and resource requirements. A reverse scheduling procedure will normally be applied, all separate operations being scheduled to commence so that, given available capacity limits, the garment will be completed on or before the required due date. For simple garments this reverse scheduling procedure might involve one operation only (i.e. 'manufacture garment'), the normal throughput time for manufacture of such a garment being known with some accuracy. For more complicated garments, especially those requiring several different operations using different resources, the reverse scheduling procedure may recognize several separate operations, each with known or estimated throughput time and each scheduled to be performed sequentially or, in some cases, concurrently (e.g. concurrent manufacture of the pieces of a suit).

Materials will be withdrawn from input resource inventories according to the specified manufacturing schedule. Inventories of consumable items will therefore be depleted; this in turn will lead to the placing of replenishment orders.

The principal objective of activity scheduling in this case will be the provision of high due date performance, that is, the provision of a high proportion of goods on or before due date or the minimization of lateness, for example average lateness of jobs or the percentage of late jobs. A simultaneous objective will be the achievement of adequate resource utilization.

Dependant and independent demand

Another way of describing the activity scheduling situation is to consider the relationship between demand for the outputs of the operating system (i.e. the products or services) and the need to perform the various activities which take place within the operating system. Consider as an example the manufacture of a complex product consisting of several components, parts, sub-assemblies, etc.

If in this case we know the parts and components which are required to produce a particular end product, and if we know the demand for that product, then we can, for a particular period of time, calculate exactly what activities must be performed within the system to satisfy that demand. Thus there is a completely *dependent* relationship between demand, which is known, and the activities required within the operating system. A similar situation can exist in the non-manufacturing organization where the satisfaction of a particular customer requirement, e.g. a service or transport, requires the performance of particular activities within the system and where demand for that service is known and hence the particular activities which must be performed can be calculated and known with certainty.

Thus we can describe a *dependent activity demand situation* as one in which a knowledge of customer demand in terms of both *what* is required and *when* it is required permits us to calculate what activities must be performed within the operating system in a particular period of time. Notice that in most cases we shall be concerned with a particular scheduling period, i.e. the need to schedule particular activities to be performed within a particular period, e.g. a month. This will often correspond to the planning period, or the period for which demand is forecast.

It will be appreciated that, in many respects, the scheduling of activities in a dependent activity demand situation is relatively straightforward, since there are few uncertainties. All that is required is that a known amount of work is scheduled to take place so that known customer requirements are satisfied by particular times or dates. In addition to this objective it will, of course, be appropriate to try to schedule these activities to take place, within these constraints, in such a manner that resource utilization is maximized.

In contrast, an *independent activity demand situation* can be said to exist where it is impossible to calculate exactly what activities are required within the operating system in a particular period of time. Such a situation can exist *either* where there is not enough knowledge about demand, i.e. customers' orders are not known in advance or there is a good deal of uncertainty about future customer orders, *or* where there is no clear relationship between the nature of the product, service, transport, etc., required by the customer and the nature of the activities which must be performed by the operating system to satisfy that customer requirement. In an independent activity demand situation, therefore, the activity scheduling problem is more complex since there are more uncertainties. In this type of situation it will often be necessary to estimate or forecast in some way the amount of activities required to satisfy some future, as yet unknown, demand, and then to schedule those activities to take place so that the end products are available at what is expected to be the right time, or so that the service or transport is available when customers arrive.

TYPES OF ACTIVITY SCHEDULING PROBLEM

The distinction between the internal and external orientation of scheduling, and that between dependent and independent activity demand, are relevant in identifying different types of activity scheduling situations. These two factors are *interrelated* and normally those responsible for the scheduling of activities will find themselves dealing with a situation in which there is either dependent activity demand and externally oriented scheduling or, in total contrast, independent activity demand and internally oriented activity scheduling. These are the two normal and distinctive activity scheduling situations but a third situation is possible, as outlined in Table 12.1. These three situations are described in more detail below.

Table 12.1 *Activity scheduling situations*

	Externally oriented activity scheduling	Internally oriented activity scheduling
Dependent activity demand	① *Situation* Customer demand known in terms of what is required, quantities and due dates. Hence the activities required to satisfy this demand can be calculated. *Activity scheduling problems* Determine when known activities must be done to satisfy given customer due dates while also satisfying internal requirements. *Appropriate techniques* MRP (Chapter 12). 'Reverse' network analysis (i.e. with scheduled project completion dates) (Chapter 13). Line of balance (Chapter 14). Reverse scheduling (Chapter 12) for production and supply. Forward scheduling (Chapter 12) for service and transport.	③ *Situation* Customer demand known in terms of what is required, quantities and due dates, but due dates not taken into account *or* demand stated only in terms of what is required and the quantities (i.e. no due date requirement). The activities which are needed can be calculated. *Activity scheduling problems* Determine when known activities must be done to satisfy internal requirements. *Appropriate techniques* Forward network analysis (i.e. without scheduled project completion dates (Chapter 12). Sequencing (Chapter 12). Batch scheduling (Chapter 14). Dispatching (Chapter 12). Assignment (Chapter 12). Forward scheduling for production and supply (Chapter 12). Flow scheduling (Chapter 15). Timetabling (Chapter 12).
Independent activity demand	④ Does not normally exist	② *Situation* Activities to be completed in a given time period must be *estimated*. *Activity scheduling problems* Determine when activities must be done to satisfy the estimated overall requirements for the period while satisfying internal requirements. *Appropriate techniques* Forward network analysis (i.e. without scheduled project completion dates) (Chapter 12). Sequencing (Chapter 12). Dispatching (Chapter 12). Assignment (Chapter 12). Forward scheduling for production and supply (Chapter 12). Batch scheduling (Chapter 14). Flow scheduling (Chapter 15). Timetabling (Chapter 12).

Externally oriented activity scheduling with dependent activity demand

The nature of the customers' demand on the system is known, whether for products, services or transport. The customers have been identified and their requirements determined in terms of both the nature of the things required and the time when those things are required. There is a known relationship between the nature of products or services provided by the organization and the types of activities which must be performed within the organization so that these outputs are available. Thus given the knowledge of demand and given this relationship, the activities required by the operating system and the dates by which these activities must be completed can be calculated. Here the activity scheduling problem is that of determining when to do given activities such as to satisfy given customer due date requirements, while also satisfying certain internal requirements, e.g. capacity requirements.

Appropriate scheduling techniques for this type of activity scheduling situation will include:

1. Materials requirements planning (see this chapter).
2. Network analysis using scheduled project completion dates (see Chapter 13).
3. Line of balance (see Chapter 14).
4. Reverse or forward scheduling (see this chapter).

Internally oriented activity scheduling with independent activity demand

Here we have little information about customer demand. It is not possible to calculate actual activity requirements, so the nature and quantity of the activities which must be performed within the operating system will be obtained by direct forecasting of activity requirements. The activity scheduling problem in this situation therefore involves the timing of an estimated activity requirement in order to satisfy a period's estimated needs while also satisfying internal, e.g. capacity, requirements. In this situation there are no known customers and no definite due dates.

Appropriate techniques for use in this type of situation might include:

1. Network analysis without the use of schedule end dates (see Chapter 13).
2. Sequencing (see this chapter).
3. Dispatching (see this chapter).
4. Assignment (see this chapter).
5. Forward scheduling (see this chapter).
6. Batch scheduling (see Chapter 14).
7. Flow scheduling (see Chapter 15).
8. Timetabling (see this chapter).

Internally oriented activity scheduling with dependent activity demand

This situation will not occur often. However, it is possible to envisage such an approach where, even though knowledge of customer demand permits the calculation of the activities required within the system in terms of quantity, nature and due dates, it is nevertheless intended that scheduling of these activities is undertaken primarily to satisfy internal requirements. The situation therefore differs from (1) in Table 12.1 in that the scheduling problem is not specifically concerned with due date requirements. It differs from (2) in Table 12.1 in that the activities which are to be performed during a particular period of time are known with certainty rather than being a result of the estimates.

Such a situation might occur where it is necessary to manufacture goods against specific customer orders without a due date requirement, or where items are to be supplied to particular customers without any due date/dates being imposed by such customers. In transport or service industries such a situation may exist where it is necessary to deal with particular customers and their requirements over a period of time, but where the timing of this provision is not imposed by customers.

The scheduling techniques which might be appropriate in this situation are similar to those described in (2) in Table 12.1.

Externally oriented scheduling with independent activity demand

It is difficult to envisage such a situation existing, since the two requirements are mutually contradictory.

NATURE OF OPERATIONS, AND ACTIVITY SCHEDULING TECHNIQUES

The discussion above has identified which types of scheduling techniques might be appropriate in different activity scheduling situations. A third factor will influence which type of technique is employed in a particular situation: this factor is concerned with the nature of the process involved within the operating system. Let us take as an example a system in which the operating system provides services to satisfy different customer requirements. No two customers ever come to the system with precisely the same requirements, so the operating system must respond to quite different customer needs. This is a form of 'one-off' situation. A similar situation can exist in the manufacturing industry where items are to be manufactured against specific customer orders and where such orders are never repeated. In the manufacturing context this will be referred to as project production.

In contrast, there are manufacturing systems which produce one type of item only to satisfy the needs of a particular set of customers; this might be a form of repetitive production. A similar situation can exist in service or transport industries where an operating system exists solely to provide one particular service or transport for customers who require or are prepared to accept that service or transport. There are also intermediate situations in which jobbing or batch processes are employed.

The type of scheduling technique used in a particular situation will depend on the factors outlined in Figure 12.2, and in addition on whether the activities are to be scheduled in a project, jobbing, batch or repetitive manner. This distinction is rather simplistic, since there are areas of overlap between the four categories; however, it is sufficient for our present purposes. Table 12.2 lists the activity scheduling techniques previously introduced in Table 12.1. Each technique is described briefly and some indication is given of whether the technique will be appropriate for project and/or jobbing and/or batch and/or repetitive processes.

Reference to Tables 12.1 and 12.2 will indicate which scheduling technique might be appropriate for a given situation.

MATERIALS REQUIREMENTS PLANNING (MRP)
(see also Chapter 17)

The principal applications of MRP are in manufacture, particularly batch manufacture. In this context it has some similarities with the line of balance technique (see Chapter 14). There are also similarities with group technology (see Chapter 14) and the reverse scheduling method (see this chapter). MRP is, however, in principle, of relevance in other situations, both in manufacture and in service operations. Where an MRP approach is appropriate it will often provide the framework within which all scheduling and also inventory decisions are made (see Chapter 17).

Table 12.2 *Activity scheduling techniques for project, jobbing, batch and flow systems*

	Scheduling technique	Brief description	Project	Jobbing	Batch	Flow	See Chapter:
A	Materials requirements planning (MRP)	A technique by which known customer demand requirements are 'exploded' to produce 'gross' parts, components or activity requirements. These 'gross' requirements are compared with available inventories to produce 'net' requirements which are then scheduled within available capacity limitations. MRP is for scheduling and also for inventory management and capacity management.	?	?	√		12
B	Reverse scheduling (Gantt charts)	A technique by which the durations of particular activities are subtracted from a required completion date, i.e. the schedules for all the activities required for the satisfaction of some particular customer requirement are determined by scheduling in reverse from the required due date.	√	√	√		12
C	Forward scheduling (Gantt charts)	The opposite of reverse scheduling, where the scheduled times for a particular set of activities are determined by forward scheduling from a given date in order ultimately to obtain a date for completion of a particular set of activities or project.	√	√	√		12
D	Sequencing	The determination of the best order for processing a known set of jobs through a given set of facilities in order to, for example, minimize total throughput time, minimize queuing, minimize facility idle time, etc.		√	?		12
E	Dispatching	A technique by which it is possible to identify which of an available set of jobs to process next on an available facility in order to minimize, over a period of time, throughput times, lateness, etc.		√	?		12
F	Assignment	A technique by which it is possible to assign or allocate an available set of jobs against an available set of resources (where each job may be undertaken on more than one resource), in order to minimize throughput time, maximize resource utilization, etc.	?	√	?		12

Table 12.2 (*contd.*)

Scheduling technique	Brief description	Project	Jobbing	Batch	Flow	See Chapter:
G Timetabling	Techniques resulting in the development of a schedule, timetable or rota indicating when certain facilities or resources will be available to those wishing to use them.				✓	12
H Network analysis (or critical path analysis)	A technique by which the various interrelated and interdependent activities required in the completion of a complex project can be scheduled, with any slack or free time being identified. The technique can be used in scheduling activities from a start date (forward NA) or by working backwards from a required completion data (backward NA).	✓	?	?		13
I Batch scheduling	A technique involving the determination of optimum batch sizes and a schedule for the completion of such batches on a set of facilities. The batch sizes are determined by comparing set-up (or change) costs with holding or inventory costs. The schedule is determined by reference to these batch sizes. The technique is concerned with both scheduling and inventory management.			✓	?	14
J Line of balance (LOB)	A technique which permits the calculation of the quantities of the particular activities or parts and components which must have been completed by a particular intermediate date, in order that some final delivery schedule might be satisfied. It is therefore a scheduling and a control technique.			✓		14
K Flow scheduling	A technique for establishing appropriate facilities for the processing of items and customers where each item or customer passes through the same facilities in the same order. The technique is concerned primarily with meeting certain output requirements in terms of cycle time and balancing the use of the resources within the system.			?	✓	15

The principles of MRP

Materials requirements planning is concerned primarily with the scheduling of activities and the management of inventories. It is particularly useful where there is a need to produce components, items or sub-assemblies which themselves are later used in the production of a final product or, in non-manufacturing organizations, where the provision of a transport or service for a customer necessitates the use or provision of certain sub-systems. For example it may be used when a customer orders a motor vehicle from a manufacturing organization, which must first manufacture or obtain various components which are then used in the final assembly of that vehicle for that customer. Similarly, in treating a patient in a hospital, e.g. for a major operation, the hospital must, in order to satisfy this service requirement, provide accommodation for the patient, diagnostic tests, anaesthetics and post-care facilities as well as surgical facilities so that the patient's total requirements are satisfied. In these two cases the product or service requested by the customer can be seen to be the 'final' output of the system, which derives from certain lower-level provisions. These lower-level provisions are considered to be *dependent* on the customer's final requirement. Given a measure or forecast of the total number of customers requiring the final provision of the system, the demand at lower levels can be obtained. The materials requirement planning technique is used for precisely this purpose, i.e. to break down or explode the final customer requirements into their component parts and then, taking into account available capacity, existing inventories, etc., to schedule the provisions of these component parts so that the customer's final requirement is satisfied on schedule. The materials requirement planning procedure therefore takes as one of its inputs the measured or forecast demand for the system's outputs. It breaks down this demand into its component parts, compares this requirement against existing inventories, and seeks to schedule the parts required against available capacity. The MRP procedure produces a schedule for all component parts, if necessary through to purchasing requirements, and where appropriate shows expected shortages due to capacity limitations. The basic procedure is illustrated in Figure 12.2. The procedure will be undertaken on a repetitive basis, the 'explosion' and scheduling procedure being repeated at regular intervals perhaps corresponding to the intervals at which demand forecasting is undertaken or as and when required as a result of changes in known demand. The use of this procedure involves considerable data processing, even for relatively simple outputs. The popularity of the MRP technique and its extensive use have resulted largely from the availability of cheap computing power within organizations.

The use of MRP

The manner in which MRP operates will be described by reference to a manufacturing situation. The principal *inputs* to the MRP process are as follows:

1. The *bill of requirements*. This, in effect, identifies the component parts of a final output product. (The terms 'bill of materials' or 'product structure record' might be employed.) At each 'level' the different components, materials or sub-assemblies are shown, thus the bill of requirements shows not only the total number of sub-parts but also the manner in which these parts eventually come together to constitute the final product. The lead time between levels is also shown. The arrangement is shown diagrammatically in Figure 12.3. There are several different methods of structuring the bill of requirements data. The most appropriate

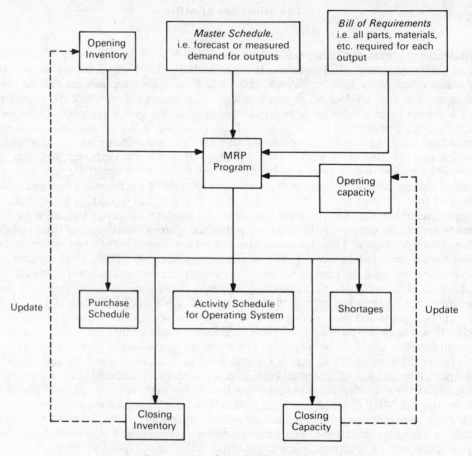

Figure 12.2 *Basic MRP procedure.*

structure will depend on the nature of the application and on computing requirements, e.g. file structures. In general, however, the final product level will be referred
to as level zero. Below this, at level 1, are the principal sub-assemblies, etc., which
together make up the final product. At level 2 are the components, etc., of the
principal sub-assemblies, and so on through as many levels as appropriate to reach
the level of raw materials or bought-in items. Each item is assigned to one level only,
and each item at each level has a unique coding. The different levels and/or branches
may correspond to different design or manufacturing responsibilities. For example,
in organizing the components of a motor vehicle in this format, level 1 may comprise
major sub-assemblies such as engines, bodies, frames, etc., such that below that level
the various component parts in effect correspond to particular areas of manufacturing responsibility. Where complex end products may be made in several different
possible configurations from a large number of parts or sub-assemblies which may be
assembled in different ways, it is common to use a 'modular' bill of requirements
structure. Using this approach, even though there may be a very large range of end
products differing in detail from one another, it will not be necessary to have a large
number of different, unique bill of requirements structures, but will be enough to
specify those modules from a composite bill of requirements structure which together
constitute the required end product.

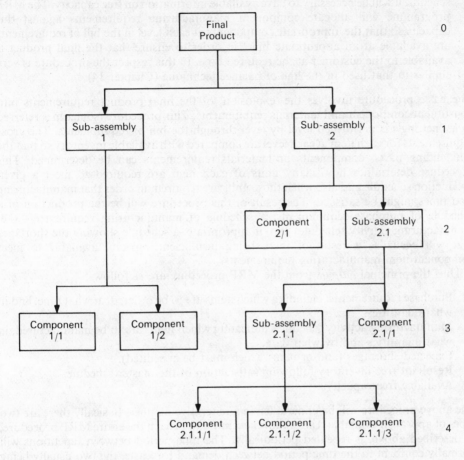

Figure 12.3 *Bill of requirements structure (five levels).*

2. The *master production schedule* is based on known or forecast demand for a specified future period, e.g. the forecasting period. The schedule shows how much of each end item is wanted and when the items are wanted. It is in effect the delivery or the 'due date' schedule for each product expressed in terms of both quantity and timing. The period over which this demand is expressed will depend on the type of product concerned and the capacity planning procedures used by the organization. In general, however, the time period should allow enough time for the acquisition of all materials, the manufacture of all componens, parts and sub-assemblies, and the assembly of the final product.

3. *Opening inventory*. This record will show the available inventories of all materials, components, sub-assemblies, etc., required for the manufacture of the end product. In general the file will show both total and free (i.e. unallocated) inventory. The latter is more important in the context of MRP, since the objective is to compare component or parts requirements against available stock (i.e. excluding those items already committed to the manufacture of other products), in order to determine purchase and manufacture requirements for items for a particular delivery schedule.

4. *Opening capacity*. If the MRP procedure is to be used to provide a production schedule it will be necessary to have available information on free capacity. The MRP programme will allocate component manufacturing requirements against this capacity so that the appropriate components at each level in the bill of requirements are available at an appropriate time, in order to ensure that the final product is available to the customer at the required time. In this respect the procedure is very similar to that used in the line of balance technique (Chapter 14).

The basic procedure involves the 'explosion' of the final product requirements into constituent component and materials requirements. This procedure (sometimes referred to as 'netting') is performed level by level through the bill of requirements. The gross requirements for each item at each level are compared with available inventory so that the outstanding parts, components or materials requirements can be determined. This procedure determines how many units of each item are required to meet a given production schedule and also when those units are required, in order that manufacturing lead times might be satisfied. The result of this procedure will be the production of a schedule of purchase requirements, a schedule of manufacturing requirements (i.e. manufacturing activity schedule) and, if appropriate, a schedule showing the shortages that will occur as a result of there being insufficient capacity available to meet component/item manufacturing requirements.

Thus the principal *outputs* from the MRP procedure are as follows:

1. Purchase requirements: including which items are to be ordered, at what time, and in what quantities.
2. Manufacturing activity schedules indicating which items are to be manufactured, in what quantities and by what date.
3. Expected shortages (and/or items which must be expedited).
4. Resultant free inventory following satisfaction of the master schedule.
5. Available free capacity.

The above procedure will be undertaken in a reiterative manner. Basically there are two types of approach available. Using the *regenerative* approach the entire MRP procedure, as described above, is repeated periodically. The time period between repetitions will normally conform to the time period between demand forecasts, the two usually being undertaken on a regular basis, e.g. once a month. The approach using the regenerative system is in effect to undertake an entirely new MRP calculation on each occasion, i.e. to undertake each set of calculations as if there had been no previous MRP study. In such cases the inventory inputs to the system will assume that all current stocks are free and that none of the available capacity is committed. Thus each MRP repetition takes into account all known demand for the schedule period, and from the demand, bill of requirements, inventory and capacity data, calculates a new schedule. Such an approach may be appropriate where the output schedule changes to a relatively small extent. In such circumstances the amount of computation may not be too great and the differences between the schedules produced for successive calculations may not be substantial. An additional advantage of the regenerative approach is that data errors are not repeated or compounded.

Where there is considerable change in the output schedule, or where forecasts are subject to large margins of error, or where the bill of requirements details change, e.g. as a result of design changes, it may be more appropriate to adopt a *net change* approach to materials requirements planning. Using this procedure only the alterations to the master schedule and/or the other input data are taken into account as and when necessary. These changes are considered and their effects on purchase and manufacturing schedules, inventories, capacity factors, etc., are considered. While the regenerative approach might be useful in a relatively stable situation, in a volatile situation the net change approach might be more appropriate. The net change system requires more processing and will not normally be used when the volumes are high.

Other factors in the use of MRP

Batch sizes

The operation of an MRP procedure as described above results in the purchase and/or manufacture of items in the quantities required and when required. But this takes no account of the need to purchase and manufacture economic batch sizes (see Chapters 14 and 16) which balance ordering or set-up costs against the holding costs. If these economies are to be obtained the MRP procedure must accommodate an economic batching procedure. One method of achieving this is to issue an order, whether a purchase or a manufacturing order, for a fixed (i.e. most economic) quantity of an item whenever there is a requirement for that item. Items surplus to requirements are then placed in stock, and when at a later date an item is required again, stock is depleted or a further economic batch quanity is manufactured. In fact the need for inventories of items over a period of time results mainly from the need to manufacture items in economic batches unless there are safety stock considerations at these levels.

Table 12.3 *Use of economic batches and safety stocks in MRP (for one component)*

	Period				
	1	2	3	4	etc.
Quantity required at end of period	45	40	20	10	
Free stock at beginning of period[a]	65	20	30	60	50
Quantity to be made during period[b]	0	50	50	0	

[a] Safety stock to be held = 20
[b] Economic batch quantity = 50

Safety stock

Where an MRP procedure is used against forecast end-product demand there is a risk that the forecast may be inaccurate and therefore that on occasions more end products are required than had been anticipated for a given period. To protect against such a situation it would be necessary to hold some safety stocks. Where customer requirements are concerned exclusively with end products rather than also being expressed in terms of components of parts (e.g. for spares or replacement purposes) such safety stock is best held at the higher levels within the bill of requirements structure, e.g. at final sub-assembly or final product assembly levels. In these circumstances the MRP procedure itself tends to protect against shortage of lower-level items by producing them in time to meet the final master production schedule. Hence safety stock is normally held only at lower levels where customer demand can be expressed in terms of component parts as well as finished products.

Table 12.3 gives an example of component-level batch and safety stock calculations.

MRP and capacity, inventory and scheduling decisions

In the above the relationship between the MRP procedure and capacity planning is clear. MRP, where used, can be seen as the next logical step after that of capacity planning as described in Chapter 11. As most capacity planning is undertaken in aggregate terms, and as activity scheduling requires the development of detailed schedules for particular items or particular processes, the MRP procedure can be seen as a logical intermediate step. Where MRP is used the activity schedule will be an outcome of MRP, and likewise where an MRP procedure is adopted, inventory management will be an integral part of it except for the need, separately, to accommodate batch requirements, etc. Clearly also, the use of MRP has considerable implications in purchasing (see Chapter 17).

REVERSE SCHEDULING

External due date considerations will directly influence activity scheduling in certain structures. The approach adopted in scheduling activities in such cases will often involve a form of reverse scheduling of the Gantt chart type illustrated in Figure 12.1(a) and (b).

A major problem with such reverse or 'due date' scheduling is in estimating the total time to be allowed for each operation, in particular the time to be allowed for waiting or queuing at facilities.

Some queuing of jobs (whether items or customers) before facilities is often desirable since, where processing times on facilities are uncertain, high utilization is achieved only by the provision of such queues.

Operation times are often available, but queuing times are rarely known initially. The only realistic way in which queuing allowances can be obtained is by experience. Experienced planners will schedule operations, making allowances which they know from past performances to be correct. Such allowances may vary from 50 per cent to 2000 per cent of operation times and can be obtained empirically or by analysis of the progress of previous jobs. It is normally sufficient to obtain and use allowances for groups of similar facilities or for particular departments, since delays depend not so much on the nature of the job, as on the amount of work passing through the departments and the nature of the facilities.

Operations schedules of this type are usually depicted on Gantt or bar charts. The advantage of this type of presentation is that the load on any facility or any department is clear at a glance, and available or spare capacity is easily identified. The major disadvantage is that the dependencies between operations are not shown and, consequently, any readjustment of such schedules necessitates reference back to operation planning documents. Notice that, in scheduling the processing of items, total throughput time can be minimized by the batching of similar items to save set-up time, inspection time, etc.

FORWARD SCHEDULING

For a manufacturing or supply organization a forward scheduling procedure will in fact be the opposite of that illustrated in Figure 12.1(a) and (b). This approach will be particularly relevant where scheduling is undertaken on an internally oriented basis and the objective is to determine the dates or times for subsequent activities, given the times for an earlier activity, e.g. a starting time.

In the case of supply or transport organizations the forward scheduling procedure will be as illustrated in Figure 12.1(c). Here the objective will be to schedule forward from a given start date, where that start date will often be the customer due date, e.g. the date at which the customer arrives into the system. In these circumstances, therefore, forward scheduling will be an appropriate method for dealing with externally oriented scheduling activities.

SEQUENCING

Sequencing procedures seek to determine the best order for processing a set of jobs through a set of facilities.

Two types of problems can be identified. First, the static case, in which all jobs to be processed are known and are available, and in which no additional jobs arrive in the queue during the exercise. Second, the dynamic case, which allows for the continuous arrival of jobs in the queue. Associated with these two cases are certain objectives. In the static case the problem is merely to order a given queue of jobs through a given number of facilities, each job passing through the facilities in the required order and spending the necessary amount of time at each. The objective in such a case is usually to minimize the total time required to process all jobs: the throughput time. In the dynamic case the objective might be to minimize facility idle time, to minimize work in progress or to achieve the required completion or delivery dates for each job.

Sequencing: two facilities and n jobs (static case)

This example considers the situation where n jobs are to be processed on each of two facilities (A and B) with the same order (A, B) and no passing.

Let A_i = set-up time + processing time for job i on facility A ($A_i > 0$; $i = 1 \ldots n$)
  B_i = the same for facility B
Objective: to minimize T (total throughput time) for all n jobs

Solution procedure:

1. List information as shown in Table 12.4.

Table 12.4.

i	A_i	B_i
1	A_1	B_1
2	A_2	B_2
3	A_3	B_3
↓	↓	↓
n	A_n	B_n

2. Select shortest time (or remaining time).
3. If this is A_i put that job first (or nearest first).
4. If this is B_i put that job last (or nearest last).
5. Delete this job from the table.
6. Return to 1.

EXAMPLE

A two-facility, six-job sequencing problem and its solution using this procedure are shown in Table 12.5 and Figure 12.4.

Table 12.5

i	A_i	B_i	Order
1	5	1 ——————————→	6th
2	4 ———————————	5 ——————————→	3rd
3	6	5 ——————————→	5th
4	7	6	4th
5	2 ———————————	6 ——————————→	1st
6	3 ———————————	4 ——————————→	2nd

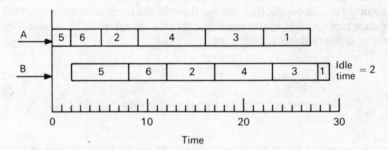

Figure 12.4 *Program to minimize T (T = 29).*

Sequencing: special case of $m=3$ (A, B, C) (static)

This considers the situation where n jobs are to be processed on each of three facilities (A, B and C) with the same order (A, B, C) and no passing.

Let A_i = set-up time + processing time for job i on facility A ($A_i > 0$; $i = 1 \ldots n$)
    B_i = the same for facility B
    C_i = the same for facility C

Either one or both of the following requirements must be satisfied:

1. min. $A_i \geqslant$ max. B_i
2. min. $C_i \geqslant$ max. B_i

Objective: to minimize T (total throughput time) for all n jobs

EXAMPLE

The example shown in Table 12.6 satisfies requirement 2 above (min. C_i = max. B_i).

Table 12.6

i	A_i	B_i	C_i
1	6	5	5
2	8	3	7
3	4	2	8
4	3	2	11
5	5	5	9

Solution procedure:

1. Calculate $(A_i + B_i)$ and $(B_i + C_i)$.
2. Proceed as before (Table 12.5) using two 'imaginary' facilities whose processing times are $(A_i + B_i)$ and $(B_i + C_i)$.

Table 12.7

i	$A_i + B_i$	$B_i + C_i$	Order
1	11	10 ⟶	5th
2	11	10	4th
3	6 ⟶	10 ⟶	2nd
4	5 ⟶	13 ⟶	1st
5	10 ⟶	14 ⟶	3rd

Solution: 4, 3, 5, 2, 1 or 4, 3, 5, 1, 2. $T = 45$.

Sequencing: two jobs ($n = 2$) and m facilities (static)

A graphical solution procedure can be used for the problem where two jobs are to be processed on each of m facilities but in different orders.

EXAMPLE

Consider the example shown in Table 12.8 where there are five facilities, A, B, C, D and E. The solution is shown in Figure 12.5. The graph shows job 1 plotted on the x axis and job 2 plotted on the *y* axis. Ordinates (0, 0) represent the time at which the programme begins and ordinates (13, 12) the time the programme finishes. Because each facility can process only one job at a time the shaded rectangular areas represent unfeasible areas. The problem is, therefore, to travel

Table 12.8

Job (*i*)	1		2	
	Order	Time (hours)	Order	Time (hours)
First operation	A_1	4	A_2	2
Second operation	B_1	3	D_2	2
Third operation	C_1	1	C_2	4
Fourth operation	D_1	3	B_2	2
Fifth operation	E_1	2	E_2	2

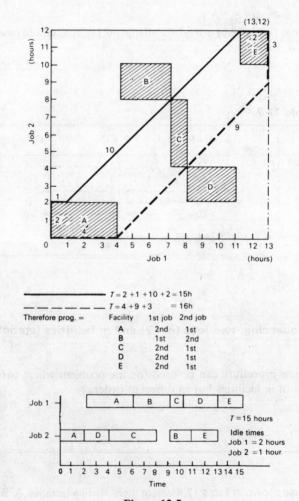

———————— $T = 2 + 1 + 10 + 2 = 15h$

— — — — — $T = 4 + 9 + 3 \quad = 16h$

Therefore prog. =

Facility	1st job	2nd job
A	2nd	1st
B	1st	2nd
C	2nd	1st
D	2nd	1st
E	2nd	1st

$T = 15$ hours

Idle times
Job 1 = 2 hours
Job 2 = 1 hour.

Figure 12.5

from (0, 0) to (13, 12) by the shortest route (to minimize T) using only vertical (processing job 2) or horizontal (processing job 1) or 45° lines (processing jobs 1 and 2). The graph shows two possible solutions. The minimum throughput time (T) is 15 hours.

Sequencing by linear programming (static)

With a little ingenuity the sequencing of jobs on facilities can be represented by a series of linear equations or inequalities, e.g.

let x_i = time at which operation i must begin
and a_i = processing time for operation i

Then, since each facility can process only one job at a time, one job must precede the other by an interval equal to or greater than its processing time.

Either $x_2 - x_1 \geqslant a_1$ (job 1 precedes job 2) or
$x_1 - x_2 \geqslant a_2$ (job 2 precedes job 1)

Additional requirements can be represented in a similar manner, e.g.

1. Order requirements

$x_l + a_l \leqslant x_m$ (operation l precedes operation m)
$x_m + a_m \leqslant x_n$ (operation m precedes operation n)

2. Delay requirements

$x_p + a_p + \Delta_{pq} = x_q$ (There must be a given interval Δ_{pq} between the end of operation p and the start of operation q.)

Linear programming is a method of solving a set of such simultaneous linear equations or inequalities. The use of this technique in the treatment of sequencing problems was undoubtedly an important development in the field of operational research, since it was the first major step towards a more general technique capable of providing an optimal solution to a wide range of problems. However, even with the aid of powerful computers, the extensive computations necessary obviate its use in any but simple problems.

DISPATCHING

Many of the techniques described above offer optimum solutions to sequencing problems, but a question that should be asked is whether or not optimum solutions are necessary or even desirable. Clearly, if a solution to a problem can be obtained only after excessive computation or through over-simplification then there is little to recommend it.

Furthermore, all of the foregoing methods have dealt only with the static rather than the dynamic problem. When the dynamic situation arises there is no practical and general method of ensuring an optimum solution. If this fact is accepted, then it is reasonable to consider such problems in simpler 'dispatching' terms, i.e. considering the immediate priority of jobs on one facility, rather than attempting explicitly to consider several facilities at once. The efficiency with which dispatching is performed determines to a large extent the overall operations efficiency, since it can affect such crucial things as operations time, work-in-progress, facility loading, etc.

The principal method of job dispatching is by means of *priority rules*. The use of priority rule dispatching is an attempt to formalize the decisions of the experienced 'human' dispatcher. Most of the simple priority rules that have been suggested are listed below.

1. *Job slack (S)*. This is the amount of contingency or free time, over and above the expected processing time, available before the job is completed at a predetermined date, i.e.

$$S = t_0 - t_1 - \Sigma a_i$$

where t_0 = future date (e.g. week number)
t_1 = present date (e.g. week number)
Σa_i = sum of remaining processing times (e.g. weeks)

Where delays are associated with each operation, e.g. delays caused by interfacility transport, this rule is less suitable, hence the following rule may be used.

2. *Job slack per operation*, i.e. S/N, where N = number of remaining operations. Therefore where S is the same for two or more jobs, the job having the most remaining operations is processed first.

3. *Job slack ratio*, or the ratio of the total remaining time to the remaining slack time, i.e.

$$\frac{S}{t_0 - t_1}$$

In all the above cases, where the priority index is negative the job cannot be completed by the required date.

4. *Shortest imminent operation* (SIO), i.e. process first the job with the shortest processing time.

5. *Longest imminent operation* (LIO). This is the converse of (4).

6. *Scheduled start date*. This is perhaps the most frequently used rule. The date on which operations must be started so that a job will meet a required completion date is calculated, usually by employing reverse scheduling from the completion date, e.g.

$$x_i = t_0 - \Sigma a_i$$
$$\text{or} \quad x_i = t_0 - \Sigma(a_i + f_i)$$

where x_i = scheduled start date for an operation
f_i = delay or contingency allowance

Usually some other rule is also used, e.g. first come, first served, to decide priorities between jobs with equal x_i values.

7. *Earliest due date*, i.e. process first the job with the earliest due or completion date.

8. *Subsequent processing times*. Process first the job that has the longest remaining process times, i.e. Σa_i or $\Sigma(a_i + f_i)$.

9. *Value*. To reduce work-in-progress inventory cost, process first the job which has the highest value.

10. *Minimum total float*. This rule is the one usually adopted when scheduling by network techniques. (see Chapter 13.)

11. *Subsequent operation*. Look ahead to see where the job will go after this operation has been completed and process first the job which goes to a 'critical' queue, that is a facility with a small queue of available work, thus minimizing the possibility of facility idle time.

12. *First come, first served* (FCFS).

13. *Random* (e.g. in order of job number).

Rules 12 and 13 are random since, unlike the others, neither depends directly on job characteristics such as length of operation, value, etc.

Priority rules can be classified further, as follows:

1. *Local rules* depend solely on data relating to jobs in the queue at any particular facility.
2. *General rules* depend on data relating to jobs in the queue at any particular facility and/or data for jobs in queues at *other* facilities.

Local rules, because of the smaller amount of information used, are easier and cheaper to calculate than general (sometimes called *global*) rules. All the above rules with the exception of rule 11 are local rules.

One further classification of rules is as follows:

1. *Static rules* are those in which the priority index for a job does not change with the passage of time, during waiting in any one queue.
2. *Dynamic rules* are those in which the priority index is a function of the present time.

Rules 4, 5, 6, 7, 8, 9, 10, 11, 12 and 13 above are all static, whereas the remainder are dynamic.

A great deal of research work has been conducted in an attempt to determine the merit of priority rule dispatching, and in particular to evaluate the relative merit of the numerous rules that have been suggested. This research work has normally taken the form of simulation studies. In general, researchers have used computers to simulate jobbing shop conditions, and have often relied on many simplifying assumptions such as the following.

1. The operation times (including set-up times) for all jobs are known and are independent of the order in which jobs are processed on facilities.
2. Operations, once started, must be completed.
3. No facility may process more than one job at a time.
4. Transport time of jobs between facilities can be neglected.
5. Each job must be processed on facilities in a predetermined order.
6. Facilities do not break down.
7. Facilities and labour resources are available in known quantities.
8. The splitting of job batches is not permitted.

Several criteria for assessing the results of the simulations have been used, the following measures of dispatching performance being adopted by many researchers.

1. *Due date criteria*, i.e. assessing the performance of priority rule dispatching by whether or not jobs satisfy specified 'due' or completion dates.
   (a) *Mean of the completion distribution.* The completion distribution shows the relative frequency with which jobs are completed early, on time, and late. The mean of the distribution represents the average dispatching efficiency. Early completion is assumed to offset late completion.
   (b) *The variance of the completion distribution.* The variance is a measure of the dispersion of values or the spread of a distribution; hence the variance of the completion distribution is a measure of the consistency of dispatching results.
   (c) *Mean lateness.* If we consider that only the *late* completion of a job is detrimental, then the mean lateness is a measure of dispatching efficiency.
   (d) *The number of jobs late.*

2. Criteria related to *throughput*, or *waiting time* and the *congestion* of jobs, e.g.
   (a) mean throughput time;
   (b) throughput time variance;
   (c) mean number of jobs in process;
   (d) variance of number of jobs in process.

As a result of the enormous amount of research that has been conducted in this area, many researchers have suggested and tested variations or extensions of many of the simple priority rules listed above. For example, at least five variations of the 'shortest imminent operation' rule have been developed and tested, in attempts to overcome the main disadvantage of this rule, namely the long waiting times incurred by jobs with long processing times. These SIO derivatives include:

1. *Truncated SIO rule.* An upper limit is placed on waiting time, so jobs which have waited for longer than a given time take precedence.
2. *Two-class SIO rule.* Operations are considered to be either short or long. A further rule such as FCFS is used to select jobs from each class.
3. *SIO with FCFS.* The simple SIO rule is used along with the FCFS rule, the purpose of which is to reduce the backlog of jobs with long operation times.
4. *SIO rule with imperfect prediction* of operation times.
5. *Two-class truncated SIO rule.* The job with the shortest operation within a critical class of jobs is selected, or if this class is empty the SIO is taken.

More complex rules have been developed,[1] including two 'sequential' rules, the simplest of which is as follows:

$$\text{Priority index} = \frac{(t_i - x_i) - f_i}{N \pm K}$$

where
t_i = present date
x_i = scheduled start date for operation
f_i = flow or contingency allowance
K = empirically derived constant
N = number of remaining operations

This priority index is a comparison of the flow allowance (f_i) with the deviation from the planned start date ($t_i - x_i$). When $(t_i - x_i) - f_i$ is a positive value then all the flow allowance has been consumed by the late start, therefore the first jobs to be processed are those with high priority indices.

There has been some attempt to simplify priority rules by the addition of *heuristic decision rules.* Gere tested eight such heuristic rules, but concluded that only three of these offered significant improvements over the results obtained by the priority rules. These three heuristics were:

1. *Alternative operation.* The simple priority rule is used, but before processing the job with the highest priority according to this rule (say job 1), check to see whether or not by so doing any of the remaining jobs becomes even more critical. If so, give highest priority to this job (say job 2). Check again to see if this makes any of the remaining jobs more critical. If none of the others is more critical, process job 2; otherwise process job 1.
2. *Look ahead.* Before processing the next job (say job 1) according to the priority rule, look ahead to see whether a more critical job (say job 2) is due to arrive at the machine before job 1 is finished. If so, leave the machine vacant and await that job.
3. *Insert.* (To be used in conjunction with 'look ahead'.) Rather than leave a machine idle through the 'look ahead' heuristic, process the longest of the available jobs that can be completed before job 2 arrives.

An important priority rule has been developed by Carroll which has been given the mnemonic COVERT, standing for c over $t \left(\dfrac{c}{t} \right)$ where c = the expected delay cost of an operation and t = processing time for an operation. The purpose of this rule, which has been tested with encouraging results, is to give a high priority to jobs with a high ratio of expected lateness to operation time.

Various combinations of priority rules have been suggested and tested, perhaps the best

[1] Rowe, A. J. (1960) Towards a theory of scheduling, *Journal of Industrial Engineering,* **11,** March.

known being: *scheduled start date* + *total float*. Such a rule is invariably used as a means of selecting jobs to be processed when network analysis has been used during production planning. For example if we refer to the network analysis computer printout shown in Figures 13.37 and 13.38 we see that jobs are listed in order of 'planned start date' (first) and 'total float'. These documents list, for the benefit of shop-floor personnel, jobs in the order in which they are to be done; in other words, jobs are listed according to the priority index *planned* (or *scheduled*) *start date* + *total float*.

In conclusion, perhaps the most effective rule according to present research is the SIO rule, and more particularly, the various extensions of this rule. Massive simulation studies have shown that of all 'local' rules, those based on the SIO rule are perhaps the most effective, certainly when considered against criteria such as minimizing the number of jobs in the shop, the mean of the 'completion distribution' and the throughput time. The SIO rule appears to be particularly effective in reducing throughput time, the truncated SIO and the two-class SIO rules being perhaps the most effective derivatives, having the additional advantage of reducing throughput time variance and lateness.

The 'first come, first served' priority rule has been shown to be particularly beneficial in reducing average lateness, whereas the 'scheduled start date and total float' rule has been proved effective where jobs are of the network type.

A matrix method

Wright[2] has developed a matrix method for computing job/facility schedules. The method is best described by means of an example.

EXAMPLE

Consider a four-job ($n = 4$), four-facility ($m = 4$) problem. The four jobs arrive in the order A, B, C, D and are each to be processed on each of the four facilities in the order 1, 2, 3, 4. Processing times (in minutes) are shown in Table 12.9.

Table 12.9 *Processing times for jobs (in minutes)*

Job (i)	Facility (j)			
	1	2	3	4
A	6	4	9	2
B	7	3	7	4
C	8	6	9	4
D	5	3	6	7

A schedule is to be determined using the first come first served dispatching rule. The merit of the schedule is to be assessed by reference to:

(a) the total throughput time for all jobs;
(b) the average job throughput time;
(c) the average job queue time;
(d) facility utilization;
(e) the average job tardiness or lateness against a 25-minute target completion time.

Using the procedures below, the matrix shown in Figure 12.6 can be set up.

---

[2] Wright, G. (1978) City University Business School, London, private communication, September.

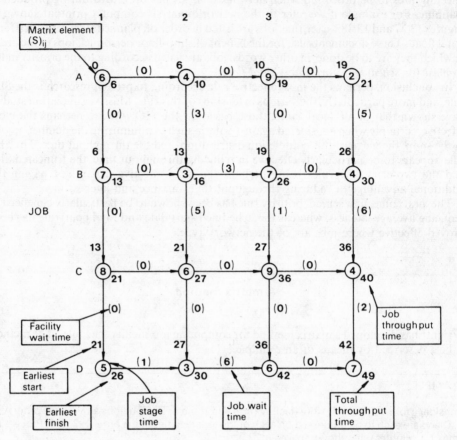

Figure 12.6 *Matrix calculations for the problem from Table 12.9 (FCFS).*

1. Assign first processing stage of first job to matrix element $(S)_{1,1}$.
2. Calculate earliest start (ES) and earliest finish (EF) times for this job for this stage.
3. Assign first processing stage of second job to matrix element $(S)_{2,1}$.
4. Calculate ES and EF times.
5. Repeat steps 1 to 4 for $(S)_{3,1}$ and $(S)_{4,1}$.
6. Repeat steps 1 to 5 for all jobs for second processing stage, i.e. matrix elements $(S)_{1,2}$ to $(S)_{4,2}$ using the rules:

$$\left.\begin{array}{l} ES(S)_{ij} = EF(S)_{i-1,j} \\ \qquad \text{or} \\ EF(S)_{i,j-1} \end{array}\right\} \text{whichever is the greater}$$

$$EF(S)_{ij} = ES(S)_{ij} + \text{processing time of job } (i) \text{ on facility } (j)$$

7. Repeat steps 1 to 5 for all jobs for third and fourth processing stages.

The other figures given in Figure 12.6 are calculated as follows:

$$\text{Facility wait time} = ES(S)_{ij} - EF(S)_{i-1,j}$$
$$\text{Job (stage) wait time} = ES(S)_{ij} - EF(S)_{i,j-1}$$

For this example, taking figures from Figure 12.6:

1. Total throughput time = 49 minutes.

2. Average job throughput time = $(21 + 30 + 40 + 49) \div 4 = 35$ minutes.
3. Average job wait time (including time waiting for jobs to be started) =
    $[(6 + 13 + 21) + (3 + 6 + 1)] \div 4 = 12.5$ minutes
        waiting to   internal
        be started   waiting time
4. A measure of facility utilization can be obtained by expressing the total processing time for a facility as a percentage of total time for which a facility is 'tied up', i.e. the time from the commencement of the first job to the completion of the last job, i.e.

    for facility 1. $26 \div 26 = 1.0$
    2. $16 \div 24 = 0.66$
    3. $31 \div 32 = 0.96$
    4. $17 \div 30 = 0.56$

5. Average job tardiness against target:

    for job A = $21 - 25 = 4$
          B = $30 - 25 = 5$
          C = $40 - 25 = 15$
          D = $49 - 25 = 24$
    Average $40 \div 4$
                       $= 10$ minutes

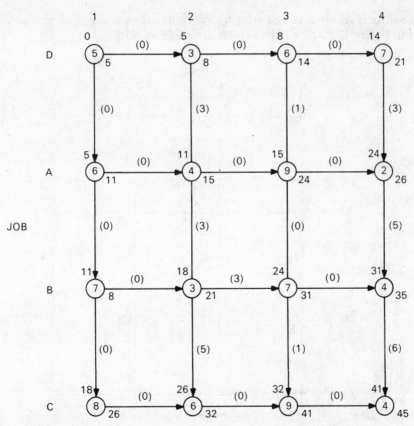

Figure 12.7 *Matrix calculations for the problem from Table 12.9 (SIO).*

Now, using a shortest operation time rule based on the shortest first operation, jobs in the above example would be processed through facilities in the order D, A, B, C, giving the matrix shown in Figure 12.7.

The example above required *ordered sequential processing*, i.e. all jobs are processed on all facilities and in the same sequence. This matrix method can also be used to deal with *broken ordered sequential processing* in the manner described below.

For broken ordered sequential processing some processing stages for specified jobs may not exist, but the general job flow sequence is the same. For example, for the arrangement shown in Table 12.10 jobs A and C are not processed on facility 3 and job B is not processed on facility 2, otherwise jobs are processed on facility in the order A, B, C, D.

Table 12.10 *Processing times for jobs (in minutes)*

Job (*i*)	Facility (*j*)			
	1	2	3	4
A	6	3	—	5
B	4	—	2	8
C	5	4	—	9
D	7	2	3	6

The matrix is set up as before using 'ghost' or dummy job stages of zero duration as shown in Figure 12.8 and all calculations are made as before.

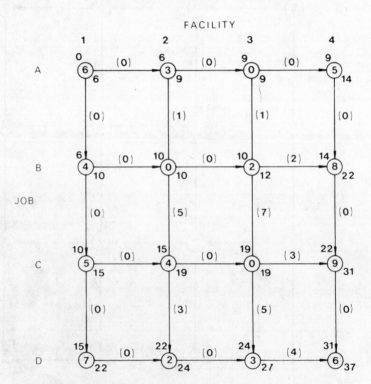

Figure 12.8 *Matrix calculations for the problem from Table 12.10.*

ASSIGNMENT *(see also Appendix I)*

Often, when attempting to decide how orders are to be scheduled onto available facilities, one is faced with various alternative solutions. For example, many different facilities may be capable of performing the operations required on one customer or item. Operations management must then decide which jobs are to be scheduled onto which facilities in order to achieve some objective, such as minimum cost or minimum throughput time. We shall look at two methods of tackling this problem.

The index method

This simple, rapid, but approximate method of facility/job assignment is best described by means of an example.

EXAMPLE: A COMPUTER BUREAU

A computer bureau must process five orders in a period of time. Each order in effect comprises several very similar jobs, and each can be run on any one of three computer facilities A, B and C. Table 12.11 gives the operation time for each job on each of the available facilities.

Table 12.11 *Operation time per job, on each facility*

Order no. (*i*)	No. of jobs in order (Q_i)	x_{ij} Operation time per job on facility *j* (min.)		
		A	B	C
1	30	5.0	4.0	2.5
2	25	1.5	2.5	4.0
3	45	2.0	4.0	4.5
4	15	3.0	2.5	3.5
5	10	4.0	3.5	2.0

The available capacity for these facilities for the period in question is:

$$A = 100 \text{ minutes}$$
$$B = \ 80 \text{ minutes}$$
$$C = 150 \text{ minutes}$$

The index number for a facility is a measure of the time disadvantage of using that facility for processing, and is obtained by using this formula:

$$I_j = \frac{x_{ij} - (x_i \text{ minimum})}{(x_i \text{ minimum})}$$

where: I_j = index number for facility

x_{ij} = operation time for job *i* on facility *j*

x_i min. = minimum operation time for job *i*

For order 1:

$$I_A = \frac{5.0 - 2.5}{2.5} = 1.0$$

$$I_B = \frac{1.0 - 2.5}{2.5} = 0.6$$

$$I_C = \frac{2.5 - 2.5}{2.5} = 0$$

Table 12.12 shows the index numbers for all facilities and orders. Using Table 12.12 and remembering that the index number is a measure of the time disadvantage of using that facility, we can now allocate orders to facilities. The best facility for order 1 is C ($I_C = 0$); the processing time for that order (75 minutes) is less than the available capacity. We can, therefore, schedule the processing of this order on this facility. Facility A is the best facility for order 2, but also the best for order 3. Both cannot be accommodated because of limitations on available capacity, so we must consider the possibility of allocating one of the orders to another facility. The next best facility for order 2 is facility B ($I_B = 0.67$) and for order 3 the next best facility is also facility B ($I_B = 1$). Because the time disadvantage on B is less for order 2, allocate order 2 to B and 3 to A. The best facility for order 4 is B but there is now insufficient capacity available on this facility. The alternatives now are to reallocate order 2 to another facility or to allocate order 4 elsewhere. In the circumstances it is better to allocate order 4 to facility C. Finally, order 5 can be allocated to its best facility, C.

Table 12.12

Order no.	No. of jobs in order	Facility A		Facility B		Facility C	
		Index no.	Processing time for order (min)	Index no.	Processing time for order (min)	Index no.	Processing time for order (min)
1	30	1.0	150	0.6	120	0	75
2	25	0	37.5	0.67	62.5	1.67	100
3	45	0	90	1.0	180	1.25	202.5
4	15	0.2	45	0	37.5	0.4	52.5
5	10	1.0	40	0.75	35	0	20
Capacity (% utilization)			100 (90)		80 (78)		150 (98)

The disadvantages of this method are readily apparent. First, with problems involving more orders and facilities than the one used here, the allocation and reallocation of orders might be very tedious. Second, we have not considered the possibility of splitting an order.

Linear programming method

The problem of assigning jobs to available facilities discussed above can also be solved by linear programming. The objectives and the constraints can be formulated as a set of linear inequalities which might then be solved using, say, the Simplex method described in Appendix I. Let us assume, for the sake of simplicity, that the operating costs of the facility are not dependent on the type of job assigned to them and that, unlike previously, individual orders may be assigned to more than one facility. Consider our previous three-facility, five-order problem (Table 12.13).

Table 12.13

Order no. (i)	No. of jobs in order (Q_i)	Throughput per minute per facility (jobs)		
		A	B	C
1	30	0.20	0.25	0.40
2	25	0.67	0.40	0.25
3	45	0.50	0.25	0.22
4	15	0.33	0.40	0.29
5	10	0.25	0.29	0.50
Capacity available (m)		100	80	150
Operating cost ($\pounds$/m) C_j		1.0	0.75	0.85

We can represent the assignment of items to facilities by using the following notation:

$$Q_{i,j} \text{ where } i = \text{order no.}$$
$$j = \text{facilities}$$

i.e. $Q_{1,A}$ = Quantity of order 1 assigned to facility A

$Q_{1,B}$ = Quantity of order 1 assigned to facility B

Our objective is to obtain the least cost assignment of jobs to facilities; we must therefore minimize the following objective function:

$$\text{Total cost} = C = 1.0 \left(\frac{Q_{1,A}}{0.20} + \frac{Q_{2,A}}{0.67} + \frac{Q_{3,A}}{0.50} + \frac{Q_{4,A}}{0.33} + \frac{Q_{5,A}}{0.25} \right)$$

$$+ 0.75 \left(\frac{Q_{1,B}}{0.25} + \frac{Q_{2,B}}{0.40} + \frac{Q_{3,B}}{0.25} + \frac{Q_{4,B}}{0.40} + \frac{Q_{5,B}}{0.29} \right)$$

$$+ 0.85 \left(\frac{Q_{1,C}}{0.40} + \frac{Q_{2,C}}{0.25} + \frac{Q_{3,C}}{0.22} + \frac{Q_{4,C}}{0.29} + \frac{Q_{5,C}}{0.50} \right)$$

Since the number of jobs allocated to facilities must not exceed the quantity in the order, the following constraints must be observed:

$$Q_{1,A} + Q_{1,B} + Q_{1,C} = 30$$
$$Q_{2,A} + Q_{2,B} + Q_{2,C} = 25$$
$$Q_{3,A} + Q_{3,B} + Q_{3,C} = 45$$
$$Q_{4,A} + Q_{4,B} + Q_{4,C} = 15$$
$$Q_{5,A} + Q_{5,B} + Q_{5,C} = 10$$

Also:

$$Q_{i,j} \left(\begin{array}{l} i = 1, 2, 3, 4, 5 \\ j = A, B, C \end{array} \right) \geq 0$$

These inequalities may be solved simultaneously and the objective function minimized by using the Simplex method of linear programming. The situation in which facility operating cost is dependent on the type of job being processed may be formulated in the same manner.

Machine interference

When more than one facility is assigned to a single operator a phenomenon known as machine interference may occur. For example, if one operator attends three machines, when one stops (either at the end of its operating cycle or for any other reason, e.g. breakdown) then the operator will attend to it. If, however, while the operator is attending to it one of the other machines stops, then, since he or she is unable to attend to both, a certain amount of machine idle time must result. This is known as machine interference.

The assignment of two or more facilities to one operator is a common feature in many industries, and, of course, the nature of the work being done on such facilities will determine the amount of attention required from the operator. This, in turn, will determine the optimum number of facilities to assign to the operator. This worker—facility assignment, since it determines the system capacity, is of considerable importance during operations planning.

The mathematical treatment of multi-facility assignments has been attempted by many authors, but the problem is a particularly complex one, especially when the operators have duties other than simply attending to the facility and when the characteristics of the facilities differ. In this section we will confine ourselves to a simple deterministic case in which facilities, all of which are the same, behave in some predictable manner.

We can identify three types of activity:

1. *Independent activities* performed by either facility or operator without the need for the services or attention of the other.
   (a) Facility-independent activity time per cycle $= t$.
   (b) Operator-independent time per cycle $= b$.
2. *Concurrent activities* which must be performed by operator and facility together $= a$.
3. *Idle time*, when either operator or facility is waiting for the other.
   (a) Operator idle time per cycle $= i_o$.
   (b) Facility idle time per cycle $= i_m$.

For example, if an operator attended only one facility the situation in Figure 12.9 might result.

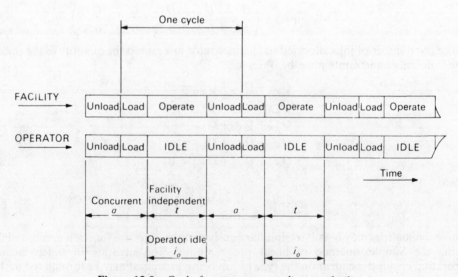

Figure 12.9 *Cycle for operator attending one facility.*

Unless the operator is able to perform other duties during the period in which the facility operates independently, a great deal of operator idle time must result. In such a case the operator might reasonably be asked to attend to more than one of these facilities. (In the example in Figure 12.9 he or she could attend to at least two facilities.)

The ideal number of facilities to allocate to one operator (n^1) can be calculated using this formula:

$$n^1 = \frac{a+t}{a+b}$$

Unless we are particularly fortunate, n^1 will not be a whole number, but as it is usually possible to assign only whole facilities to operators we must decide whether to allocate the next whole number smaller than n^1 and hence incur operator idle time, or the next whole number larger than n^1 and incur facility idle time, i.e.

$$(n) < n^1 < (n+1)$$

This decision, of course, will depend on the relative cost of operator and facility idle time. If

$$C_o = \text{Cost of operator/h}$$
$$C_m = \text{Cost of facility/h}$$

and

$$E = \frac{C_o}{C_m}$$

then the best multi-facility assignment can be found by using the formula:

$$\frac{Y_n}{Y_{(n+1)}} = \frac{E+n}{E+n+1} \times \frac{n^1}{n}$$

Y_n is the cost per unit of processing with an assignment of n facilities, and $Y_{(n+1)}$ likewise for an assignment of $n+1$ machines.

If $Y_n/Y_{(n+1)}$ is greater than 1, then $n+1$ facilities should be used, and if $Y_n/Y_{(n+1)}$ is less than 1, then n facilities should be used.

When the facility-independent time (t) and the concurrent activity time (a) per cycle are constant, then we can calculate, as above, the assignment arrangement to avoid interference; but when either or both of those times vary the problem is considerably more difficult.

One of the best-known treatments of this complex, queuing-type situation was presented by Ashcroft over thirty years ago. He made the following assumptions:

1. The probability of a facility requiring service by the operator is independent of the time it has been running hitherto.
2. All service times (a) are constant.
3. No priority system of servicing operates.
4. All facilities have similar operational characteristics.

Such assumptions are seldom completely justified in practice, but often the situation does not differ too much and, in such cases, the Ashcroft treatment has been found to provide good results. Using a statistical queuing theory approach, Ashcroft derived a table of numbers which gives the average number of facility running hours per clock hour. The Ashcroft number, therefore, is a measure of the expected output from facilities when these are all assigned to one operator. Consequently they are of value during operation planning for determining the facility output in multi-facility assignments.

Table 12.14 gives Ashcroft numbers for one to ten facilities and for ratios of concurrent (service) time (a) to facility-independent running time (t) from 0.01 to 1.00.

Table 12.14 *Ashcroft numbers* (From O'Connor, T. F. (1952) *Productivity and Probability.* Manchester: Emmott & Co. Ltd. Reproduced with permission.)

p	$n=1$	$n=2$	$n=3$	$n=4$	$n=5$	$n=6$	$n=7$	$n=8$	$n=9$	$n=10$
0.00	1.00	2.00	3.00	4.00	5.00	6.00	7.00	8.00	9.00	10.00
0.01	0.99	1.98	2.97	3.96	4.95	5.94	6.93	7.92	8.91	9.90
0.02	0.98	1.96	2.94	3.92	4.90	5.88	6.85	7.83	8.81	9.78
0.03	0.97	1.94	2.91	3.88	4.84	5.81	6.77	7.74	8.70	9.66
0.04	0.96	1.92	2.88	3.84	4.79	5.74	6.69	7.64	8.58	9.52
0.05	0.95	1.90	2.85	3.79	4.74	5.67	6.61	7.53	8.45	9.37
0.06	0.94	1.88	2.82	3.75	4.68	5.60	6.51	7.42	8.31	9.19
0.07	0.93	1.86	2.79	3.71	4.62	5.52	6.42	7.29	8.15	8.99
0.08	0.93	1.85	2.76	3.67	4.56	5.44	6.31	7.16	7.89	8.76
0.09	0.92	1.83	2.73	3.62	4.50	5.36	6.20	7.01	7.78	8.50
0.10	0.91	1.81	2.70	3.58	4.44	5.28	6.08	6.85	7.57	8.21
0.11	0.90	1.79	2.67	3.53	4.38	5.19	5.96	6.68	7.33	7.89
0.12	0.89	1.77	2.64	3.49	4.31	5.10	5.83	6.50	7.08	7.55
0.13	0.88	1.76	2.61	3.44	4.24	5.00	5.69	6.31	6.81	7.19
0.14	0.88	1.74	2.58	3.40	4.18	4.90	5.55	6.10	6.53	6.83
0.15	0.87	1.72	2.55	3.35	4.11	4.80	5.40	5.90	6.25	6.48
0.16	0.86	1.71	2.52	3.31	4.04	4.70	5.25	5.68	5.97	6.14
0.17	0.85	1.69	2.50	3.26	3.97	4.59	5.10	5.47	5.70	5.82
0.18	0.85	1.67	2.48	3.22	3.90	4.48	4.94	5.26	5.44	5.52
0.19	0.84	1.66	2.44	3.17	3.83	4.37	4.79	5.05	5.19	5.24
0.20	0.83	1.64	2.41	3.12	3.75	4.26	4.63	4.85	4.95	4.99
0.21	0.83	1.62	2.38	3.08	3.68	4.15	4.48	4.66	4.73	4.75
0.22	0.82	1.61	2.35	3.03	3.61	4.04	4.33	4.47	4.53	4.54
0.23	0.81	1.59	2.33	2.98	3.53	3.94	4.18	4.30	4.34	4.34
0.24	0.81	1.58	2.30	2.94	3.46	3.83	4.04	4.13	4.16	4.16
0.25	0.80	1.56	2.27	2.89	3.39	3.72	3.90	3.98	4.00	4.00
0.26	0.79	1.55	2.24	2.85	3.31	3.62	3.77	3.83	3.84	3.84
0.27	0.79	1.53	2.22	2.80	3.24	3.52	3.65	3.69	3.70	3.70
0.28	0.78	1.52	2.19	2.75	3.17	3.42	3.53	3.56	3.57	3.57
0.29	0.77	1.51	2.16	2.71	3.10	3.33	3.42	3.44	3.45	3.45
0.30	0.77	1.49	2.14	2.67	3.03	3.23	3.31	3.33	3.33	3.33
0.31	0.76	1.48	2.11	2.62	2.97	3.14	3.21	3.22	3.22	3.22
0.32	0.76	1.46	2.09	2.58	2.90	3.06	3.11	3.12	3.12	3.12
0.33	0.75	1.45	2.06	2.53	2.84	2.98	3.02	3.03	3.03	3.03
0.34	0.75	1.44	2.03	2.49	2.77	2.90	2.93	2.94	2.94	2.94
0.35	0.74	1.42	2.01	2.45	2.71	2.82	2.85	2.86	2.86	2.86
0.40	0.71	1.36	1.89	2.25	2.43	2.49	2.50	2.50	2.50	2.50
0.45	0.69	1.30	1.78	2.07	2.19	2.22	2.22	2.22	2.22	2.22
0.50	0.67	1.24	1.67	1.90	1.98	2.00	2.00	2.00	2.00	2.00
0.55	0.64	1.19	1.57	1.76	1.81	1.82				
0.60	0.62	1.14	1.48	1.63	1.66	1.67				
0.65	0.61	1.10	1.40	1.51	1.54	1.54				
0.70	0.59	1.05	1.32	1.41	1.43	1.43				
0.75	0.57	1.01	1.25	1.32	1.33	1.33				
0.80	0.55	0.97	1.19	1.24	1.25	1.25				
0.85	0.54	0.94	1.13	1.17	1.17	1.18				
0.90	0.53	0.91	1.07	1.11	1.11	1.11				
0.95	0.51	0.87	1.02	1.05	1.05	1.05				
1.00	0.50	0.84	0.98	1.00	1.00	1.00				

EXAMPLE: A LAUNDRY

An operator must attend to several washing machines. Determine the efficiency in terms of average running hours/clock hour for different operator/machine assignments if service time/(unload and load machine)/complete cycle (i.e. a) = 5 minutes and unattended machine running time/cycle (i.e. b) = 10 minutes

$$p = \frac{a}{t} = 0.5$$

No. of washing machines (n)	Ashcroft no. A_n	Efficiency (%) $\frac{A_n}{n} \times 100$
1	0.67	67
2	1.24	62
3	1.67	56
4	1.90	48
5	1.98	40

In fact to determine the best assignment, operator and facility costs must be taken into account. The cost per clock hour is the cost of one operator per hour, plus n times the cost of a facility per hour:

$$Y = C_o + nC_m$$

The best assignment is that which minimizes the ratio:

$$\frac{Y}{A_n C_o}$$

which can also be expressed as:

$$\frac{1 + (nC_m/C_o)}{A_n}$$

EXAMPLE: A 'SUPER' LAUNDRY

Find the best machine assignment.
In this case:

$$p = 0.1$$
$$C_o = \pounds 2$$
$$C_m = \pounds 6$$

Hence:

No. of machines operator (n)	A_n	$\frac{1 + nC_m/C_o}{A_n}$	
1	0.91	4.40	
2	1.81	3.87	
3	2.70	3.71	
4	3.58	3.63	
5	4.44	3.61	
6	5.28	3.60	← best assignment = 6 machines/operator
7	6.08	3.62	
8	6.85	3.65	

EXAMPLE: ANOTHER 'SUPER' LAUNDRY

Find the best machine assignment.
  In this case:

$$\rho = 0.25$$

$$\frac{C_m}{C_o} = 2.0$$

n	A_n	$\dfrac{1 + (nC_m/C_o)}{A_n}$	
1	0.80	3.75	
2	1.56	3.21	
3	2.27	3.08	◄——————— best assignment = 3 machines operator
4	2.89	3.11	
5	3.39	3.24	
6	3.72	3.50	

TIMETABLING

The timetabling of activities is of particular relevance in respect of repetitive functions. Bus, train and air services usually operate to a timetable. Similarly, the activities of certain service systems, e.g. cinemas, are timetabled. These are customer push systems, so customers have to take advantage of the function at predetermined times. The function is not performed at other times, so customers arriving at the wrong time must wait, and of course, if there are no customers at the time selected for the performance of the function, or if not enough customers are available to utilize fully the facilities provided, there will be under-utilization of capacity. In many situations timetables are necessary, since common resources are deployed to provide a variety or series of functions. In many transport systems, for example, vehicles travel a set route providing movement for individuals between points along that route. In certain service systems, for example hospitals, common resources such as specialists provide a service in a variety of departments, or for a variety of types of customers, in a given period of time. Certain out-patient clinics operate in this fashion. In all such cases a timetable will normally be developed and made available to customers. Much the same situations may apply in 'customer pull' systems, where functions occur at given times. It follows that in all such cases the nature of demand must be predictable since, in effect, function is undertaken in anticipation of demand. In fact, in such cases, the absence of (sufficient) customers at the time selected for the performance of the function may give rise to the creation of output stock. Alternatively, output may be lost or wasted. The timetabling of such activities is an exercise in internally oriented scheduling, since no direct account is taken of individual customers' demands. The development of timetables will take into account the time required for, or the duration of, activities, and in many cases (e.g. transport systems) the required or preferred order or sequence.

Few quantitative techniques are relevant in the development of such timetables. 'Routeing', flow planning and vehicle scheduling procedures are of relevance in timetabling transport systems. In some cases the problem will resemble that of sequencing outlined above, while in others it may be convenient to use Gantt charts and simulation procedures in both the development and the evaluation of timetables.

CRITERIA FOR SCHEDULING

In most situations it will not usually be feasible, and in some cases not desirable, to attempt to develop optimum activity schedules. Because of the dynamics of situations and the unpredictability of demand, a degree of control is essential. The relative importance attached to scheduling or control will depend to some extent on the type of situation and particularly the type of system structure existing. In general, scheduling will be more complex in 'function to order' situations where scheduling decisions will be required to absorb external (i.e. demand) fluctuations directly. Furthermore, in such situations the degree of function repetition may be less, therefore the need for control may be greater. In contrast, in 'function to stock' situations, scheduling will be somewhat easier, therefore the need for control somewhat less. In 'demand push' situations, where stocks exist between function and customer, scheduling will tend to be easier and the need for control less. Demand levels may also influence the relative complexity and importance of scheduling and control activities. In general, high demand levels will be associated with function repetition and the provision of special-purpose resources together with product or service specialization. In contrast, relatively low demand levels may be associated with relatively low function repetition, high product or service variety and the use of general-purpose resources, hence scheduling may be complex and there will be a relatively greater dependence on control. In situations where demand predictability, i.e. the nature of demand, permits the provision, i.e. stocking, of resources and where demand levels are high, the provision of special-purpose equipment may give rise to an emphasis on the provision of balance, the avoidance of interference and consideration of learning or improvement effects. In such situations much of the internally oriented scheduling will be 'built into' the system. In contrast, in situations where demand predictability is low and where demand levels are also low, accurate scheduling will be impossible, hence low equipment utilization, high work-in-progress and or customer queuing will be evident. In these situations the use of local dispatching rules, resource smoothing, allocation of jobs, etc., together with an emphasis on control, will be evident.

Criteria or measures of effective activity scheduling and control might include the following:

(a) the level of finished goods or work-in-progress (for systems with output stocks);
(b) percentage resource utilization (all systems);
(c) percentage of orders delivered on or before due date (for function to order systems only);
(d) percentage stock-outs/shortages (for systems with output stocks only);
(e) number of customers (all systems);
(f) down time/set-ups, etc. (all systems);
(g) customer queuing times (for systems in which customers wait or queue).

In virtually all cases there will be a need to avoid sub-optimization, that is, it will be easy in most cases to satisfy each of the above criteria individually. However, the objective of operations management, and therefore an objective of activity scheduling, is to obtain a satisfactory balance between customer service criteria and resource utilization criteria.

CHECKLIST FOR CHAPTER 12

Nature of the activity scheduling problem
Internally/externally oriented scheduling
   strategies

Dependent/independent demand
External orientation/dependent demand
   Nature of scheduling problems

Appropriate techniques	Reverse scheduling
Internal orientation/independent demand	Forward scheduling
Nature of scheduling problem	Sequencing
Appropriate techniques	2 facilities/n jobs
Internal orientation/dependent demand	3 facilities/n jobs
Nature of scheduling problem	m facilities/2 jobs
Appropriate techniques	Dispatching
Nature of operations, and activity scheduling	Priority rules
techniques	Local/general
Project	Static/dynamic
Jobbing	Criteria
Batch	Effectiveness of dispatching rules
Process	Matrix method
Activity scheduling techniques and their	Assignment
applications	Index method
Materials requirements planning (MRP)	Linear programming
Procedure	Machine interference
Inputs	Timetabling
Regenerative/net change	Criteria for scheduling

FURTHER READING

Colley, J. L., Lande, R. R. D. and Fair, R. R. (1977) *Production Operations Planning and Control*. San Francisco: Holden-Day. A massive (850 pages) book, the principal merit of which is its case studies (28 in all) covering various topics including those covered in Chapters 11 to 16.

Eilon, S. (1979) Production scheduling. In Haley, K. B. (Ed.) *OR '78*. pp. 237–264. North Holland Publishing Co. A review of scheduling problems and methods for their solution.

Freeland, J. R. and Colley, J. L. (1982) A simple heuristic method for lot sizing in a time-phased reorder system, *Production and Inventory Management*, First Quarter, pp. 15–22. Deals with the determination of batch sizes in an MRP situation.

Lock, D. (1971) *Industrial Scheduling Techniques*. Epping: Gower. A 'catalogue' of techniques including network methods.

Niland, P. (1976) *Production Planning, Scheduling and Inventory Control*. London: Macmillan. Deals largely with scheduling decisions in manufacture, including forecasting and inventory control.

Orlicky, J. (1974) *Materials Requirements Planning*. Maidenhead: McGraw-Hill.

Schroeder, R. G. et al. (1981) A study of MRP benefits and costs, *Journal of Operations Management*, **2** (1) pp. 1–9.

Van Hees, R. N. and Monhemius, W. (1972) *An Introduction to Production and Inventory Control*. London: Macmillan. This and the following book provide perhaps the most detailed treatment of the subject, largely from a manufacturing viewpoint.

Van Hees, R. N. and Monhemius, W. (1973) *Production and Inventory Control Theory and Practice*. London: Macmillan.

QUESTIONS

12.1   Five patients, 1, 2, 3, 4 and 5, must be examined on each of three hospital diagnostic tests, A, B and C, in that order. Process times are given below. Use Johnson's rule to determine the best sequence for the five patients and use a Gantt chart to show an optimum schedule.

Table of process times (hours)

	Patients				
	1	2	3	4	5
Test A	5	4	9	7	6
Test B	3	2	4	3	1
Test C	8	3	7	5	2

12.2 Distinguish between the sequencing and the dispatching problems. How important is the sequencing problem in activity scheduling and how useful in practice are the various algorithms which can be used to provide optimal solutions to such problems?

12.3 Solve the following sequencing problems, the objective in each case being to minimize the throughput time of all customers.

(a) Two facilities: A, B.
Seven customers: 1, 2, 3, 4, 5, 6, 7.
Each customer to be processed on each facility in order A–B.
No overtaking of customers.

Table of process times (hours)

	Facility	
Customer	A	B
1	8	5
2	6	7
3	3	10
4	7	8
5	6	4
6	5	10
7	7	7

(b) Two facilities: X, Y.
Six customers: 1, 2, 3, 4, 5, 6.
Customers to be processed on each facility in order XY.
No overtaking of customers.
Customer 4 process on facility Y only.
Customer 1 process on facility X only.

Table of process times (hours)

	Facility	
Customer	X	Y
1	5	–
2	7	6
3	5	9
4	–	8
5	7	4
6	9	3

(c) Three facilities: X, Y, Z.
Four customers: 1, 2, 3, 4.
Each customer to be processed on each facility in order X–Y–Z.
No overtaking of customers.

Table of process times (hours)

Customer	Facility		
	X	Y	Z
1	4	3	3
2	2	4	2
3	4	4	4
4	6	2	4

12.4   Two cars (1, 2) must be serviced on all of five garage facilities (A, B, C, D, E). The servicing times and the order of the operations for each car are given below. Draw a bar chart showing the minimum throughput time programme for the servicing of the two cars.

Operation number	Car 1		Car 2	
	Facility	Time (hours)	Facility	Time (hours)
1	A	4	A	5
2	D	3	C	7
3	E	5	D	4
4	B	6	B	3
5	C	4	E	5

12.5   Ten jobs are waiting to be run on a computer.
(a)   Given the information below, arrange these jobs in priority order (the one with highest processing or dispatching priority first) according to the following priority rules:
   1. job slack;
   2. job slack per operation;
   3. job slack ratio;
   4. shortest imminent operation;
   5. longest imminent operation;
   6. scheduled start date;
   7. earliest due date;
   8. subsequent processing time;
   9. first come, first served.

Job	Scheduled completion date (week no.)	Sum of remaining processing times (weeks)	Number of remaining operations	Duration of operations on this machine	Arrival order at this machine
1	17	4	2	1	1
2	15	6	3	2	10
3	17	3	4	1	2
4	16	5	1	3	4
5	19	7	2	0.5	9
6	21	4	5	2	3
7	17	2	4	0.5	5
8	22	8	3	3.5	8
9	20	6	2	2	6
10	25	10	1	2	7

NB: The present date is week no. 12.

    (b) Use the 'first come, first served' (FCFS) priority rule to resolve 'ties' given by the above rules.

12.6   Describe some of the activity scheduling problems which may occur and the techniques available for their solution, in the following situations:
    (a) an emergency ward in a hospital;
    (b) a furniture removal company;
    (c) a take-away food shop (e.g. a hamburger shop).

12.7   Holdtight Company Ltd have just received orders from four customers for quantities of different 'expanderbolts'. Each order is to be manufactured over the same very short period of time, during which three machines are available for the manufacture of the bolts.

    The table below shows the manufacturing time in hours/bolt for each of the three machines and the total available hours' capacity on each for the period in question.

    Assuming that each order is to be manufactured on one machine only, how should orders be allocated to machines?

Order no.	Number of expanderbolts	Manufacturing time (hours/bolt)		
		M/c A	*M/c* B	*M/c* C
1	50	4	5	3
2	75	3	2	4
3	25	5	4	3
4	80	2	5	4
Total capacity (hours)		175	275	175

12.8   Five orders are received by a company, each order being for a quantity of one type of agricultural bucket. Each type of bucket can be made on any of the five machines which happen to have available production capacity. The table below gives details of the numbers of buckets in each order, the manufacturing time (in hours/bucket) for each machine, and the total hours of production capacity available on each machine.

    Using the index method described in this chapter, determine the optimum allocation of orders to machines, assuming (a) that orders cannot be split between several machines, and (b) that individual orders can be manufactured on a maximum of two machines.

Order no.	No. of products	Machine A	B	C	D	E
1	30	2.0	2.5	3.0	4.0	3.5
2	25	3.0	3.0	3.5	4.0	2.5
3	40	4.0	5.0	2.0	3.0	2.5
4	25	3.5	2.0	3.5	2.5	3.0
5	30	4.0	2.0	2.5	3.0	4.0
Total hours available		175	150	130	120	120

12.9 If the hourly operating costs of each of the three machines described in Question 12.7 are as follows:

Machine	Operating cost/hour (£)
A	2.0
B	3.0
C	2.5

express the allocation problem given in Question 12.7 as a set of equations or inequalities suitable for solution using the Simplex method of linear programming.

12.10 Demand forecasting is an essential prerequisite of capacity planning for certain types of operating systems. Which systems and why?

12.11 Products A and B can be produced at factories I and II. The production time required per product unit is one hour for A and two hours for B—the same at both factories.
   The demand for A and B, the time available at each factory, and production costs and inventory holding costs per product unit are given for the forthcoming two months in the tables below.

Product	Demand (product units)	
	May	June
A	100	110
B	150	190

	Time available (hours)		Cost per product unit (£)	
	May	June	Product A	Product B
Factory I				
Normal time	200	200	3.0	6.2
Overtime	40	10	3.6	6.8
Factory II				
Normal time	250	200	3.1	6.4
Overtime	60	40	3.9	7.2

Inventory holding costs
(£ per product unit per month)

Factory I	0.6
Factory II	0.4

Determine an optimum production plan that will meet demand at minimum cost. What is the total cost of this optimum programme?

12.12 A worker is required to attend to one or more semi-automatic office machines. The cycle of operations for each machine is as follows:

Worker loads/unloads machine: 5 minutes
Machine operates without requiring attention of worker: 12 minutes
Repeat

During this cycle the worker must stack up the items which he has unloaded from the machine. This takes him 2 minutes.
What is the ideal number of such identical machines to allocate to one worker, given the following additional information?
Total cost associated with each machine = £50/h
Total cost associated with each worker = £5/h

12.13 A telephonist is required to deal with (i.e. answer and then monitor) incoming calls only on four telephone lines. Each call for each line takes an average of three minutes of the operator's time, and after each call each line is silent for an average of ten minutes. (During this period the operator is not required to perform any work.) The total hourly cost associated with each line, which is independent of the proportion of time the line is idle, is five times the total hourly cost associated with the telephonist.
(a) What is the efficiency of each line in terms of the percentage of total time devoted to operation?
(b) How many should be allocated to a telephonist?
(c) What assumptions have you made in arriving at your answer?

12.14 Describe a matrix method of job shop scheduling for the n job, m machine case. Evaluate the following set of jobs on the machines as shown using the following scheduling decision rules:

(a) first come, first served;
(b) shortest total operation time;
(c) shortest first operation.

Show how the results vary by using the above rules in respect of:

(i) throughput rate;
(ii) machine idle time;
(iii) job waiting time;
(iv) average job lateness against a target of 20 hours from time zero.
Job Times:

Job	Machine			
	1	2	3	Total
A	10	15	8	33
B	4	9	12	25
C	12	15	10	37
D	8	10	12	30

Jobs are processed in the order machine 1, 2, 3.
What is the principal disadvantage of the SOT rule and how can this be overcome?

12.15 Explain why and how the type of procedure used in MRP might be of relevance in activity scheduling in the following situations:
(a) a major hotel which, nightly, provides large formal dinners for different companies, business societies, clubs, etc.;
(b) an advertising agency which prepares TV advertisements for a large range of different types of customers.

CHAPTER 13

Network Scheduling

NOTATION USED IN THIS CHAPTER

a	Optimistic estimate of activity duration
b	Pessimistic estimate of activity duration
σ	Standard deviation ⎱ of duration distribution
σ^2	Variance ⎰
CPM	Critical path method
d	Activity duration
EF	Earliest finish date
ES	Earliest start date
GERT	Generalized evaluation review technique
LF	Latest finish date
LS	Latest start date
m	Most likely duration of activity
PERT	Programme evaluation review technique
s	Schedule date
t	Expected time or mean duration
TF	Total float
x	Standardized value

This chapter will deal exclusively and in detail with the use of network techniques in activity scheduling and planning. The topic was introduced in Chapter 12, where it was noted that this approach provides a means of establishing schedules for sequentially interdependent activities. It is useful for internally or externally oriented scheduling. The technique is of wide relevance, is used extensively in the scheduling of complex projects, and merits consideration in detail. Our description throughout will refer to projects, the planning of projects, etc., and it should be noted that such projects might relate to manufacture, supply, service or transport (see also Chapter 12).

The rudimentary steps in operations planning by network analysis are as follows:

1. Construct an arrow or network diagram to represent the project to be undertaken, indicating the sequence and interdependence of all necessary jobs in the project.
2. Determine how long each of the jobs will last and insert those times on the network.
3. Perform network calculations to determine the overall duration of the project and the criticalness of the various jobs.
4. If the project completion date is later than required, consider modifying either the network and or the individual job durations so that the project may be completed within the required time.

This is the extent of the planning phase of simple network analysis; there are, however, subsequent steps concerned with the control of the operation and these will be dealt with later. Furthermore, this simple description of the procedure has omitted all considerations of costs and resources, and these will be dealt with later in this chapter.

THE CONSTRUCTION OF NETWORK DIAGRAMS

Any project may be represented by means of an arrow diagram in which the arrangement of arrows indicates the sequence of individual jobs and their dependence on other jobs. Arrow diagrams consist of two basic elements: *activities* and *events*.

An activity is a time-consuming task and is represented by an arrow or line. An event is considered as instantaneous, i.e. a point in time. An event may represent the completion or the commencement of an activity and is represented by a circle. A sequence of events is referred to as a path.

Unlike bar charts, the scale to which activities are drawn has no significance. The length of an activity arrow on a network diagram is unrelated to the duration of that activity. It is normal to number events as in Figure 13.1 so that paths within the network can easily be described but, other than for identification, event numbers have no significance. Also for convenience we shall identify each activity with a letter and/or description.

The network diagram is constructed by assembling all activities in a logical order. For example, the networks shown in Figures 13.2 and 13.3 relate to a decorating job.

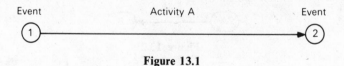

Figure 13.1

Throughout the *main text* in this chapter we shall employ one particular approach in the construction of networks, i.e. the *activity on arrow* method. This is the most widely used method. In some situations, however, the alternative approach—*activity on node*—may be preferred; this approach is used throughout this chapter in the footnotes. Those wishing to adopt this approach should first read the Appendix to this chapter.

Activity on node diagrams
An activity is a time-consuming task and is represented here by ⊂⊃ . Arrows are used to join activities, to show the precedence relationships of activities. Thus the activities in the network are represented by the *nodes* of the network (not the arrows).

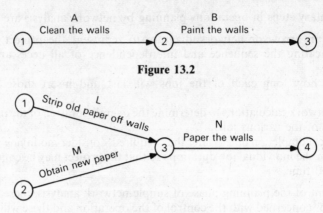

Figure 13.2

Figure 13.3

No activity may begin until all the activities leading to it are completed. In Figure 13.2 only after the walls have been cleaned can they be painted. In Figure 13.3 starting to paper the walls is dependent not only on the old paper having been removed but also on the new paper being available.

Activities occurring on the same path are *sequential* and are directly dependent on each other. *Parallel* activities on different paths are independent of one another (Figure 13.4).

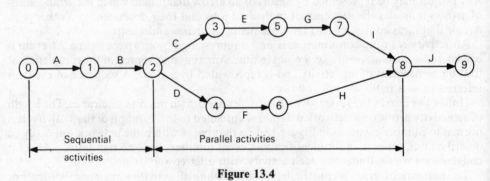

Figure 13.4

Activity on node diagrams

Figure 13.2

Figure 13.3

Figure 13.4

The convention in drawing networks is to allow time to flow from left to right and to number events in this direction so that events on the left of the diagram have smaller numbers than, and occur before, events on the right of the diagram.

It is not usually possible to use network diagrams in which 'loops' or 'dangles' occur; a loop such as that in Figure 13.5 may be a perfectly legitimate sequence of operations where, for example, a certain amount of reprocessing of materials or rectification takes place but, because of the calculations which must later be performed on the diagram, it cannot be accepted in network analysis.

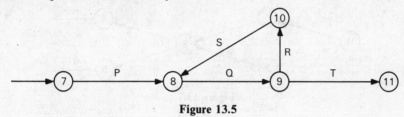

Figure 13.5

Although there are certain computer programs which will accept multiple-finish and multiple-start events on networks, it is not normally possible to leave events 'dangling' as in Figure 13.6.

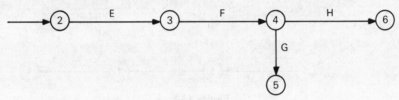

Figure 13.6

Dummy activities

The activities discussed above represent some time-consuming operation or job to be performed during the project. Dummy activities consume no time; they are of zero

---

Activity on node diagrams

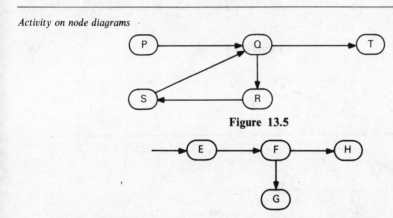

Figure 13.5

Figure 13.6 *The problem of 'dangles' does not occur with activity on node diagrams.*

Dummy activities.
There is no need to use dummy activities in activity on node diagrams.

duration and are used solely for convenience in network construction. Dummy activities, represented by dotted lines, may be necessary on the following occasions:

1. To provide the correct logic in the diagram. In Figure 13.7 the completion of activities C and D is necessary before either E or F may begin. If in practice, only activity E depends on the completion of both activities C and D, and activity F depends on D alone, to represent this logic a dummy activity is required (Figure 13.8).

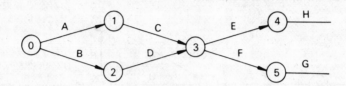

Figure 13.7

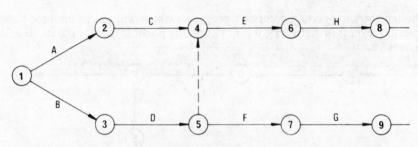

Figure 13.8

2. To avoid having more than one activity with the same beginning and end event (Figure 13.9). It is not usually possible to represent activities in this manner since activities B and C would be described from their event numbers as 3–4, so a dummy activity is necessary (Figure 13.10).

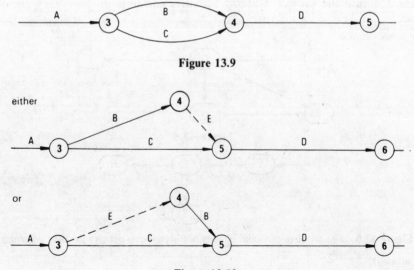

Figure 13.9

Figure 13.10

3. For convenience in drawing. The two networks in Figure 13.11 are equivalent, but the use of dummy activities facilitates representation. This is often necessary in complex networks.

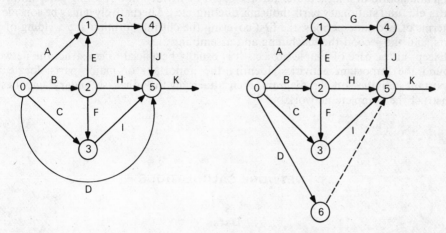

Figure 13.11

It may be necessary to use dummy activities when initially constructing networks to avoid complicated and untidy diagrams. Nevertheless, since the amount of subsequent analysis is dependent on the number of activities in a diagram, redundant dummies should be eliminated in order to save calculation time.

In drawing large networks for projects with many activities we have often found it to be easier to begin from the end of the project and work backwards. It is often helpful to

Activity on node diagrams

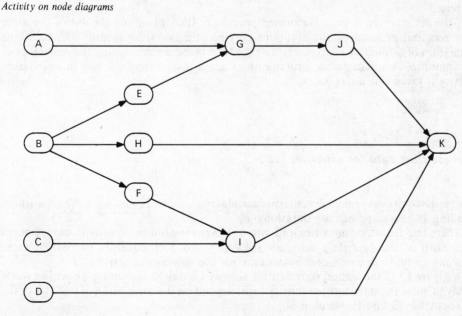

Figure 13.11

consider large projects in separate parts, i.e. certain sections of the project or, if more appropriate, certain periods during the project, and then to piece together several smaller networks rather than try to construct the complete network from scratch. For example, the manufacture of a large water turbine could be divided into rotating parts (impeller, shafts, etc.) and stationary parts (housing, ducting, etc.). Alternatively it may be considered in terms of two time periods, the first covering the cutting, forming and welding of the parts, and the second the machining and assembling.

Except in the case of simple projects it is usually beneficial to construct the network around the important activities. Identify the important or major parts, locate the important activities on the diagram, then attach all the other, secondary activities to construct the complete network.

NETWORK CALCULATIONS

Dates

The objective of initial network calculations is to determine the overall duration of the project so that either a delivery date can be given to the customer or we can consider what alterations are necessary for the project to be completed on or before a date to which we are already committed.

To perform the network calculations two things are required: first an *activity network* representing the project, and second the durations of all the activities in that network. Network analysis is only a tool: its value depends entirely on the way in which it is used and the information on which it is based. Consequently, the collection of activity durations from records, or the estimation of durations, is an important part of the exercise.

If the activities have been performed previously then, assuming the use of the same resources and procedures, the durations may be obtained from records. On occasions some form of estimation is necessary. For the time being we shall ignore the possibility of using multiple estimates of activity durations and consider only the case in which each activity is given one duration.

Earliest start date for activities (ES)

The earliest start date for each activity is calculated from the *beginning* of the network by totalling all preceding activity durations (d).

Where two (or more) activities lead into one event the following activity cannot begin until both of the preceding activities are completed. Consequently the last of these activities to finish determines the start date for the subsequent activity.

In Figure 13.12 the earliest start date for activity I is day 17 (assuming the project starts at day 0), since the start date for activity I will depend on the completion of the later of the two activities G and H, which is H.

Therefore, when calculating *ES* dates, work from the *beginning* of the network and use the *largest* numbers at junctions.

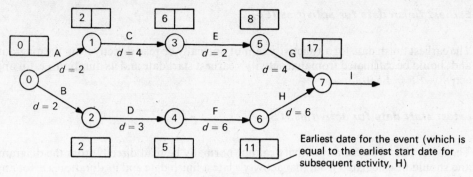

Figure 13.12

Latest finish date for activities (LF)

This is calculated from the *end* of the project by successively subtracting activity durations (*d*) from the project finish date.

Where two (or more) activities stem from one event the earliest of the dates will determine the latest finish date for previous activities.

In Figure 13.13 the latest finish date for activity A is day 3, since activity B must start on day 3 if the project is not to be delayed.

Therefore, when calculating *LF* dates begin from the *end* of the network and use the *smallest* numbers at junctions.

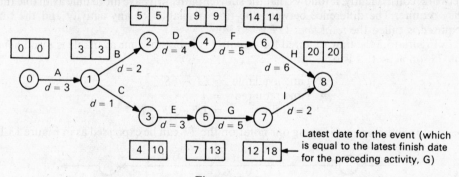

Figure 13.13

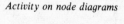

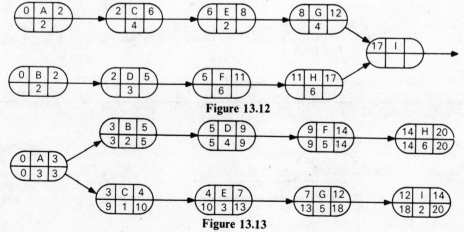

Figure 13.12

Figure 13.13

Earliest finish date for activities (EF)

The earliest finish date for any activity cannot normally be read directly from the diagram, and should be calculated from that activity's earliest start date and its duration, i.e. for any activity: $EF = ES + d$.

Latest start date for activities (LS)

The latest start date for any activity cannot normally be read directly from the diagram, and should be calculated from that activity's latest finish date and its duration, i.e. for any activity: $LS = LF - d$.

Float

In the previous example the earliest completion date for the project, i.e. the date of event 8, is determined by the *EF* dates for activities H and I. Activity I could finish on day 14 (the *EF* date for activity I is $ES + d = 12 + 2$), but activity H cannot finish until day 20 and it is this activity which determines the finish date for the project. In fact, it is path ABDFH which determines the project's earliest finish date rather than path ACEGI.

The earliest finish date for any project is determined by the longest path through the network; consequently, it follows that the shorter paths will have more time available than they require. The difference between the time available for any activity and the time required is called the *total float (TF)*.

In Figure 13.3 the time required for activity I is 2, but the time available is 8 and hence the *TF* on activity I is 6.

$$\text{Time available} = LF - ES$$
$$\text{Time required} = d$$
$$\text{Total float} = LF - ES - d$$

i.e. for any activity (say G), using our notation the *TF* can be expressed as in Figure 13.14.

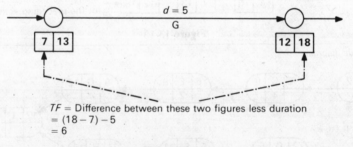

TF = Difference between these two figures less duration
= (18 − 7) − 5
= 6

Figure 13.14

Activity on node diagrams

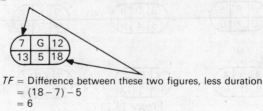

TF = Difference between these two figures, less duration
= (18 − 7) − 5
= 6

Total float is a characteristic of a path and not a characteristic of a single activity. For example, in Figure 13.13 the total float on activities A, C, E, G and I is 6. If the total float is used up at any time by delays or lateness in one of the activities then it is no longer available to any of the other activities on that path.

The critical path

The *critical path* is the longest path through the network and is, therefore, the path with minimum total float (zero *TF* in the above example). Any delay in the activities on the critical path will delay the completion of the project, whereas delay in activities not on the critical path will initially use up some of the total float on that path and not affect the project completion date.

Slack and other types of float

This is perhaps an appropriate point at which to mention two additional items. The term 'slack' is sometimes used with reference to network analysis. It is often taken as equivalent to float but, strictly speaking, whereas float relates to activities, slack relates to events. So far we have mentioned only total float, but two further types of float exist, i.e. *free float* and *independent float*. In this chapter we shall be concerned only with total float but, for the sake of completeness, free float is the difference between the time required for an activity and the time available for that activity if both preceding and succeeding activities occur either as early or as late as possible (free float early and free float late respectively). Independent float is the difference between the time required for an activity and the time available for that activity without affecting any other activities; i.e. it is the spare time available when the preceding activity occurs as late as possible and the succeeding activity as early as possible.

These four principal types of float are compared below.

1. *Total float*. The maximum free time available for an activity if preceding and succeeding activities are as far apart as possible:

    Total float for an activity
    = Latest start date of succeeding event – Earliest finishing date of preceding event – Activity duration

    Unlike 2 and 3 below, total float will be identical for activities which are in series. Total float is shared for such activities.

2. (a) *Free float/early*. The amount of free time available for an activity when every activity occurs at the earliest possible point in time:

    Free float/early for an activity
    = Earliest start date of succeeding event – Earliest start date of preceding event – Activity duration

    Free float is not a shared float in the sense that the calculation does not cause the same float to be shown on different activities.

    (b) *Free float/late*. This is the amount of free time available to an activity when every activity occurs at the latest possible point in time.

    Free float/late for an activity
    = Latest start date for succeeding event – Latest start date for preceding event – Activity duration

3. *Independent float.* The amount of free time available to an activity without displacing any other activity, i.e. the maximum amount of free time available to an activity if the preceding and succeeding activities are as near together as possible.

> Independent float on an activity
> = Earliest start date of suceeding event − Latest start date of preceding event
> − Activity duration

EXAMPLE 13.1

The following table lists all the activities which together constitute a small project. The table also shows the necessary immediate predecessors for each activity and the activity durations.

1. Construct an activity network to represent the project.
2. Determine the earliest finish date for the entire project, assuming the project begins at day 0.

Activity	Immediate predecessors	Activity duration (days)
A	—	2
B	A	3
C	A	4
D	A	5
E	B	6
F	CD	3
G	D	4
H	B	7
I	EFG	2
J	G	3

Answer:

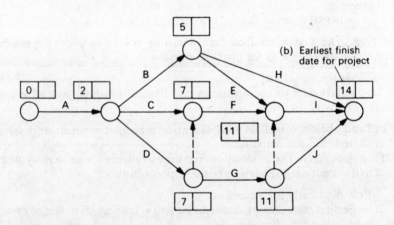

(b) Earliest finish date for project

EXAMPLE 13.2

For the project described in Example 13.1 determine:

(a)   the total float on each activity;
(b)   the critical path;

(c)   the latest start date for activity B;
(d)   the earliest finish date for activity F;
(e)   the effect on the project duration if activity I were to take three days;
(f)   the effect on the project duration if activity F were to take six days.

Answer:

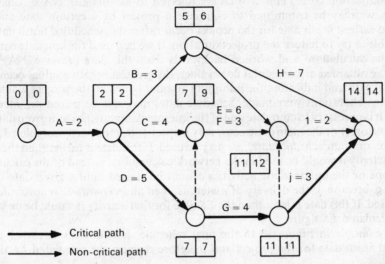

(a) *Activity* A B C D E F G H I J
     TF   0 1 3 0 1 2 0 2 1 0

(b) Critical path = A D G J

(c) Latest start date for B $= LF -$ duration
                              $= 6 - 3$
                              $=$ day 3

(d) Earliest finish date for F $= ES +$ duration
                                 $= 7 + 3$
                                 $=$ day 10

(e) No effect, but since increase in duration is equal to the total float on the activity, this activity would become critical.

(f) Project would be delayed by one day since only two days *TF* are available on the activity.

Activity on node diagrams

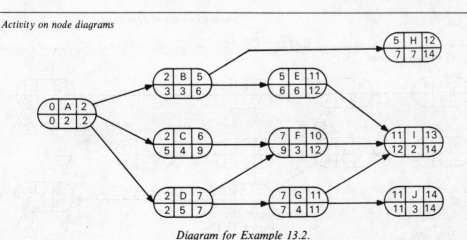

Diagram for Example 13.2.

Schedule dates

At the beginning of this section we indicated that one approach in network calculations is to calculate the earliest completion date for the project and if necessary compare this with the desired completion date. (This is what we referred to as 'forward' NA in Chapter 12.) However, we may be committed to complete a project by a certain date and, if the calculated earliest finish date for the project occurs after this scheduled finish date, it will be desirable to try to reduce the project duration. If we had used the schedule completion date in the calculations and worked backwards from this date ('reverse' NA) then we would have obtained negative total float values, the greatest negative values occurring on the critical path and indicating the minimum amount by which the project would be late unless some alterations were made. Schedule dates may also be placed on intermediate events. If it is necessary to complete one of the intermediate activities by a given date, e.g. so that the customer or the main contractor may inspect or test the partly completed product, then an *intermediate schedule date/late* may be used. If this date is earlier than the *LF* date for that activity it would be used in the network calculations instead of the calculated *LF* date. If one of the intermediate activities cannot be started until a given date for some reason, e.g. because of the delivery of materials, then an *intermediate schedule date/early* may be used. If this date is later than the *ES* date for that activity it would be used instead of the calculated *ES* figure.

In the example in Figure 13.15 the final schedule date, day 20, is earlier than the calculated finish date for the project and therefore replaces the calculated *LF* date. The

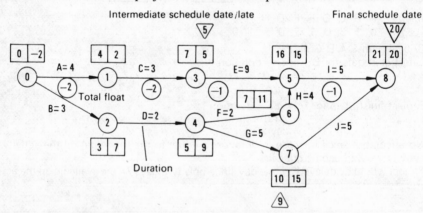

Figure 13.15

Activity on node diagrams

Figure 13.15

same applies to the intermediate schedule date/late for the completion of activity C. The intermediate schedule date/early for the start of activity J has no effect, since this date is earlier than the calculated *ES* date for that activity.

Using schedule dates it is possible to obtain not only negative values of total float but also different values along the critical path. In the example in Figure 13.15 the *TF* on activities A and C is -2, and on E and I it is -1, but all four activities form a critical path.

The matrix method

The two figures which are written at each event on the network are sometimes called *event dates*. The first figure, which we have obtained by considering the earliest finish date for the activities, is referred to as the earliest event date or time, while the second one is referred to as the latest event date or time.

To facilitate network calculations the *matrix* method is sometimes preferred. Any network diagram can be represented as a matrix; for example, the matrix shown in Figure 13.16 represents the network diagram in Figure 13.17. The event numbers are listed across the top of the matrix and also down the left-hand side. The figures in the cells are the durations of the activities connecting pairs of events. For example, event 1 is connected to event 2 by an activity of duration 4, i.e. event 1 is the initial event for activity A, and 2 is the ending event for that activity. Similarly, event 2 is connected to event 3 by an activity of duration zero, i.e. a dummy. Because the network shown in Figure 13.17 has events numbered sequentially, all the entries in the matrix are above the diagonal. However, this situation will not always occur; for example, if the direction of the arrow for activity E had been reversed, then an entry would have occurred below the diagonal in the matrix.

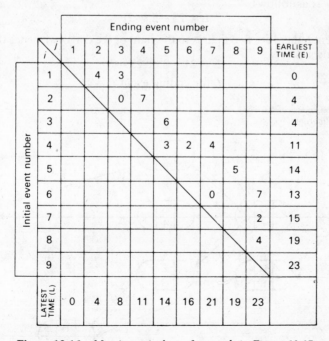

i \ j	1	2	3	4	5	6	7	8	9	EARLIEST TIME (E)
1		4	3							0
2			0	7						4
3					6					4
4					3	2	4			11
5								5		14
6							0	7		13
7									2	15
8									4	19
9										23
LATEST TIME (L)	0	4	8	11	14	16	21	19	23	

Figure 13.16 *Matrix equivalent of network in Figure 13.17.*

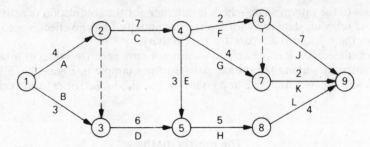

Figure 13.17 *Network diagram from matrix in Figure 13.16.*

The earliest times (E) for each of the events are calculated as follows. The earliest time (zero) for initial event 1 is entered opposite 1 in the column on the right of the matrix. Now referring to initial event 2, move along the second row of the matrix until the diagonal is reached. Read the figure(s) from above the diagonal in this column (i.e. 4) add them to the E values for their rows (i.e. 0) and enter the largest answer as E for initial event 2. Similarly, for initial event 3 move along the third row to the diagonal, read the figures from above the diagonal in this column (3 and 0), add them to the E values for their rows (0 and 4) and enter the largest answer as E for initial event 3 (i.e. 4).

For initial event 4 there is only one figure above the diagonal (7); add this to the E values for that row (4) and enter the answer (11) as the earliest time for initial event 4.

The latest times are calculated in the reverse manner. First the latest time for the last event is entered. In this case the last event is 9 and the latest time is the same as the earliest time; hence 23 is entered under ending event 9 in the L row. Now move to ending event 8; move up the column to the diagonal, read the figure(s) to the right of the diagonal in this row (i.e. 4), subtract them from the L values for those columns (23) and enter the smallest answer as the latest time for ending event 8. Similarly, the calculation of the latest time for ending event 7 is as follows:

$$L = 23 - 2 = 21$$

For ending event 6 there are two figures to the right of the diagonal, hence the calculation of L is as follows:

$$L = 21 - 0 \text{ or } 23 - 7$$

$$\therefore \quad L \text{ for ending event 6 is 16}$$

Activity on node diagrams

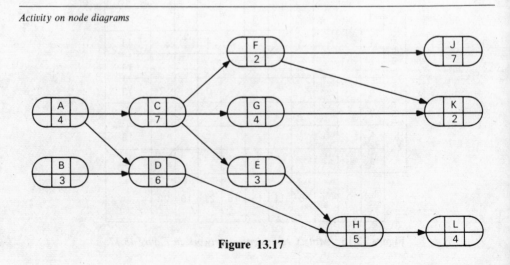

Figure 13.17

The matrix method of calculating dates gives precisely the same result as the method used previously. It is perhaps preferable in that it is a simple, routine procedure, but of course, unlike the previous method, it gives no indication of the reasons for, or the logic of, the calculations. For this reason it is preferable first to master the original method. In this example calculations by either method reveal that the critical path for the network is 1 2 4 5 8 9.

MULTIPLE TIME ESTIMATES (PERT)

We have previously assumed that a single time can be given for the duration of every activity. There are many occasions, however, when the duration of activities is not certain or when some amount of variation from the average duration is expected. For example, in maintenance work unexpected snags may occur to increase the activity duration, or failures may be found to be less serious than had been expected and the activity duration is thus reduced. In construction work jobs may be delayed because of unfavourable weather, etc.

In such cases it is desirable to be able to use a time distribution rather than a single time for activity durations, to represent the uncertainty that exists.

In network analysis uncertainty in durations can be accommodated and the following notation is usually used:

m = the most likely duration of the activity
a = the optimistic estimate of the activity duration
b = the pessimistic estimate of the activity duration

These three estimates can be used to describe the distribution for the activity duration. It is assumed that the times are distributed as a 'beta' distribution (Figure 13.18).

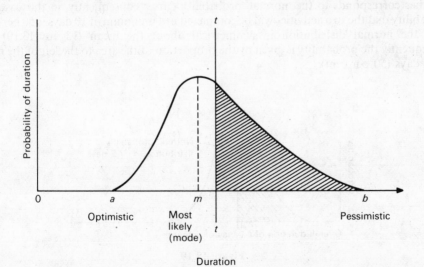

Figure 13.18

where t = the expected time—the mean of the distribution
          σ = the standard deviation (which is a measure of the spread
                of the distribution)
          $\simeq$ the range between the extreme values divided by 6

$$\equiv \frac{b-a}{6}$$

If certain assumptions are made about the distribution, the mean (t) and the variance (σ^2) can be expressed as follows:

$$\text{Mean (the expected time) } t = \frac{a+b+4m}{6}$$

$$\text{Variance} \qquad\qquad \sigma^2 = \frac{(b-a)^2}{36}$$

(For the derivation of these formulae see the Appendix to Battersby, A. (1970) *Network Analysis for Planning and Scheduling*, 3rd edition. London: Macmillan.)

Probability of achieving scheduled dates

Suppose we have two sequential activities, A and B, for which the durations are:

$$a_A = 0.5 \text{ days} \qquad a_B = 4 \text{ days}$$
$$b_A = 3.5 \text{ days} \qquad b_B = 12 \text{ days}$$
$$m_A = 2 \text{ days} \qquad m_B = 8 \text{ days}$$

Using these formulae, for activity A the expected duration t_A is 2 days and the variance $\sigma^2 = 0.25$ days, and for activity B the expected duration t_B is 8 days and variance $\sigma^2_B = 1.75$ days. Assuming activity durations to be independent, the expected duration for the pair of activities is 10 days and, since the variances may be added together, the variance for the pair is 2 days. It is usually assumed that the distribution for the duration of a series of activities corresponds to the 'normal' probability curve; consequently, in this case, the probability that the two activities will be completed in a minimum of 10 days is 50 per cent, since the normal distribution is symmetrical about the mean (Figure 13.19) and consequently the probability is given by the proportion of the area to the left of the mean of 10 days (50 per cent).

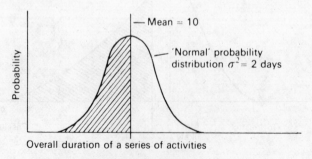

Figure 13.19

Suppose we have three activities which represent the critical path in a network, as in Figure 13.20. If we assume that these durations are independent, i.e. that the duration of activity A does not affect that of B, and so on, and that the normal distribution applies for the project duration, then we can calculate the probability that the project will be completed on or before the required schedule date.

$$\text{Expected project duration } (t) = 2 + 8 + 5 = 15$$
$$\sigma^2 = 3$$

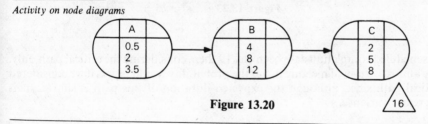

Figure 13.20

In the distribution shown in Figure 13.21 the probability of meeting the schedule date is represented by that portion of the area under the curve to the left of the 16-day ordinate. This area can be obtained from normal distribution tables if the diagram is first converted to a standardized scale.[1] In this case the probability of completing the project by day 16 is

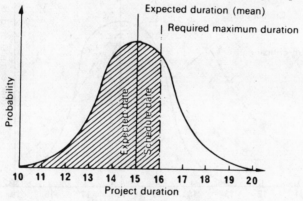

Figure 13.21

Activity on node diagrams

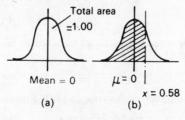

Figure 13.20

---

[1] The standardized scale is used solely for convenience. The standardized normal distribution has a total area of 1.00, a mean value of 0, and variance σ^2 of 1 (Figure 13.22a):

Total area
=1.00

Mean = 0
$\mu = 0$
$x = 0.58$
(a)   (b)

Figure 13.22

continued over

0.72, since the area to the left of the 16-day ordinate is 72 per cent of the total area.

The assumptions underlying the use of probabilities in this way in network analysis are, to say the least, of doubtful validity. The assumptions that the distribution for each activity duration corresponds to a 'beta' distribution and that the distribution of the duration of a sequence of activities can be regarded as 'normal' are not based on thorough research and should be regarded only as empirical rules which, over a period of time, have been found to work. Furthermore, in calculating the probability on project end dates only the critical path is used, but where the duration of each activity in the network is uncertain any path through the network has a certain probability of being critical and we should perhaps examine more than one path.

Suppose that in a network in which most of the activities' durations are uncertain the critical path has an expected duration of 16 days and a standard deviation of 1 day. In the same network there is a path of expected duration 15 days with a standard deviation of 3 days. According to the usual practice we ought to consider only the critical path in calculating our probabilities, but to do so in this case would mislead us, since there is a possibility that it will be the second path which will determine the project duration (Figure 13.23).

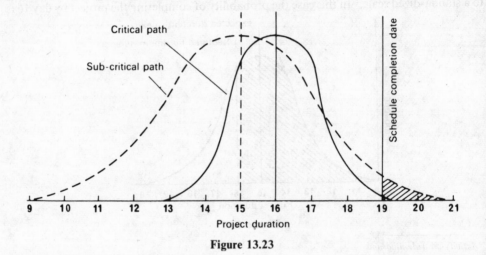

Figure 13.23

Had our scheduled completion date been day 19 then, considering the critical path only, we would be almost certain of meeting it, but the probability would be less if we considered the sub-critical path since, although the expected duration of this path is shorter, it is subject to greater variance.

---

footnote continued

where s = schedule date

t = expected date

σ = standard deviation

x = standardized value for the ordinate required, i.e. the schedule date

$$x = \frac{s-t}{\sigma} = \frac{16-15}{\sqrt{3}} = 0.58$$

When this value is located in normal distribution tables (Figure 13.22b), the area to the left of this value is found to be 72 per cent.

EXAMPLE 13.3

The three time estimates (optimistic, likely, pessimistic) for the duration of the individual activities which form a small project are shown on the network diagram below.

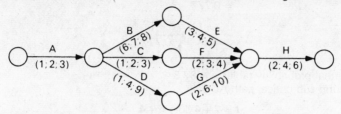

(a) Calculate the expected project duration.
(b) Determine the probability of finishing the project by day 18 or earlier.

Answer:

(a)

Activity	t days	σ^2
A	2	4/36
B	7	4/36
C	2	4/36
D	4⅓	64/36
E	4	4/36
F	3	4/36
G	6	64/36
H	4	16/36

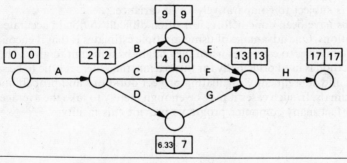

Activity on node diagrams

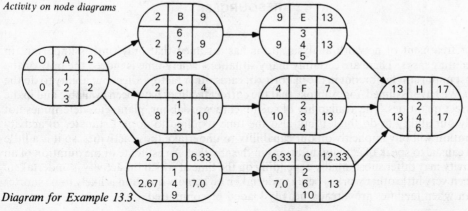

Diagram for Example 13.3.

Expected project duration = 17 days.
(b)   Considering critical path ABEH:

$$t = 17$$
$$\sigma^2 = 4/36 + 4/36 + 4/36 + 16/36$$
$$= 0.777$$

$$x = \frac{s-t}{\sigma} = \frac{18-17}{\sqrt{0.777}}$$

$$x = 1.14$$

From normal probability tables $x = 87.3\%$
Considering sub-critical path ADGH:

$$t = 2 + 4.33 + 6 + 4$$
$$= 16.33$$
$$\sigma^2 = 4/36 + 64/36 + 64/36 + 16/36$$
$$= 4.1$$

$$x = \frac{s-t}{\sigma} = \frac{18-16.33}{\sqrt{4.1}}$$

$$x = 0.825$$

From normal probability tables $x = 79.6\%$

In using three activity duration estimates to calculate the probabilities of completing projects or parts of projects on or before given scheduled completion dates, it is important to consider sub-critical paths. This is particularly important when the length of such a path approaches the length of the critical path, and also where the duration of the activities on such a path is subject to comparatively large variance.

Unless jobs have been done before, it is often difficult to obtain accurate estimates of activity durations. One advantage of using multiple estimates is that it encourages people to commit themselves to estimates when they might be reluctant to give a single estimate. But if this method is used principally for this reason, then there is little to be said for using these figures and subsequently calculating project durations and probabilities to several places of decimals. In such cases it may be enough merely to take the average of the three estimates; in fact many computer programs provide this facility.

RESOURCES

Our treatment of network analysis so far has assumed that only time is important in executing tasks. There are certainly many situations where time is indeed the only or the most important factor, but in the majority of cases other factors affect our ability to do the job. We have assumed, for example, that the correct facilities have been available and in the correct quantities. The availability of such facilities as labour, plant, etc., determines not only our ability to do the job but also the time required to do it. Estimates of activity duration will rely implicitly on our capability to undertake those activities, so it is a little unrealistic to speak of activity durations in the abstract. An estimate of the duration of an activity may differ substantially depending on the time at which the activity is undertaken. When very little other work is being undertaken an activity duration is likely to be shorter than when facilities are already heavily loaded or committed.

Each estimate of durations is based on the assumed use of a certain amount of resources, and consequently, when the project duration is calculated initially, we may also calculate the forward resource utilization, e.g. Figure 13.24.

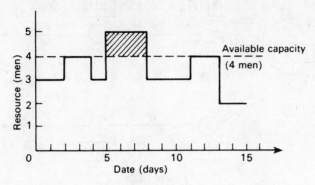

Figure 13.24

In this example an overload occurs from day 5 to day 8; consequently, unless we arrange to either subcontract this work or obtain additional resources, we cannot expect to meet our project completion date. The only remaining alternative is to reschedule some of the jobs which constitute this overload. We can, for example, delay three work-days of work from this period until days 8 to 11 and avoid overloading the resources.

Consider the part of a network shown in Figure 13.25. To be completed in four days, activity C requires six workers and four machines; activity D requires eight workers and five machines for three days. The total resources available are eight workers and six machines, therefore activities C and D cannot occur together. The solution is to:

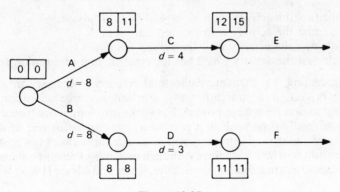

Figure 13.25

1. Subcontract one of the activities.
2. Obtain additional resources.
3. Reschedule one or both of the activities.

Solutions (1) and (2) are particularly suitable where large overloads would occur and where this can be predicted well in advance. Often rescheduling is undertaken, and certainly where the overload is small and has occurred unexpectedly this is perhaps the only solution. The question is how can we reschedule the project to avoid overloading the resources and yet incur a minimum delay in completion? Activity D is on the critical path (it has a total float of 0) and the total float of activity C is three days, so activity D should be undertaken before C and this results in no additional project delay (Figure 13.26).

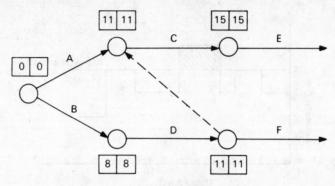

Figure 13.26

This is, in effect, a *resource levelling* procedure (see also Chapter 11) concerned with the allocation of resources to activities in order to level or smooth the resource requirement for a project for which an initial network has been constructed and activity dates calculated. This levelling approach is used where it is not possible, because of resource limitations, to perform all activities according to the original dates. In other words it is a method for modifying either the initial network logic (as in Figure 13.26) and/or the activity dates to take resource limitations into account. The example above used the 'priority rule': total float to reschedule activities. This is the normal approach and is the basis of many computer-based resource allocation/levelling procedures for network planning (see later in this chapter). Using such an approach a straightforward procedure such as that described in Figure 13.27 can be employed. Notice, however, that other priority rules are available, some of which are listed below:

1. Reschedule first the activity with least total float (as above).
2. Reschedule first the activity with shortest duration.
3. Reschedule first the activity with the earliest ES date.
4. Reschedule first the activity which has the smallest sum of duration and total float.

Resource aggregation, i.e. calculating the total resources necessary in any period to complete the project, is a straightforward job, but resource allocation can involve extensive computation for a large project. Networks involving more than a few hundred activities are normally processed on a computer, but the use of one of the numerous computer/network analysis programs is still economic for networks of fewer activities if resource allocation is to be undertaken. Although methods of resource allocation suitable for manual processing are available (see Shaffer, Ritter and Meyer (1965), Weist and Levy

---

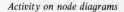

Activity on node diagrams

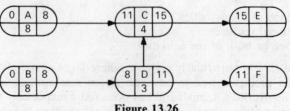

Figure 13.26

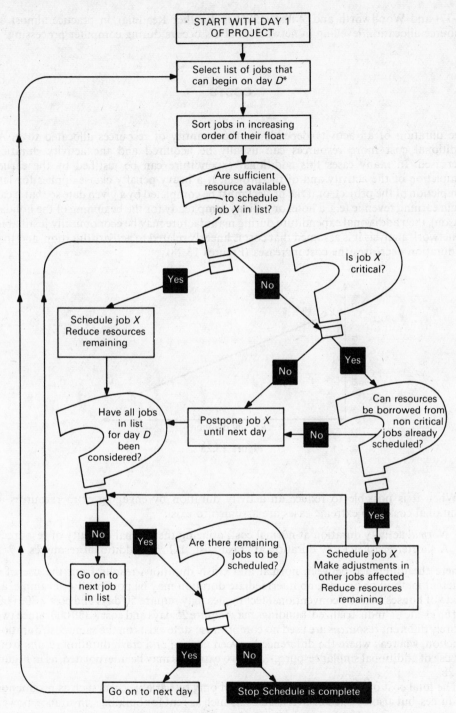

Figure 13.27 *Heuristic program for resource allocation. From Wiest, J. D. (1966) Heuristic programs for decision making, Harvard Business Review, 44(5), pp. 129–143. Reproduced with permission.*

(1977) and Woodworth and Willie (1975) in Further Reading), in practice almost all resource allocation/levelling in network analysis occurs during computer processing.

COSTS

The duration of an activity depends on the quantity of resources allocated to it. At additional cost more resources can usually be acquired and the activity duration decreased. In many cases this additional expenditure can be justified by the earlier completion of the activity and of the project. If a heavy penalty clause applies for late completion of the project, or if the project must be completed by a given date so that it can begin earning revenue (e.g. a hotel or holiday camp ready for the beginning of the holiday season), then additional expenditure during manufacture may be economically justifiable. In network analysis it is assumed that cost is linearly related to activity duration, and that as duration decreases the cost increases (Figures 13.28).

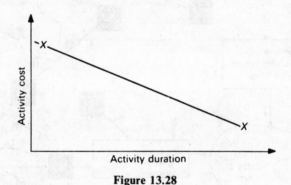

Figure 13.28

When it is possible to reduce an activity duration by engaging extra resources at additional cost, two extreme cases are assumed to exist:

1. *Normal* activity duration at normal cost, utilizing the normal quantity of resources.
2. A shorter *crash* activity duration at crash cost, utilizing additional resources.

Where the difference between normal and crash durations results from the use of a different method or process, no intermediate duration may be possible. For example, an estate of houses built by conventional techniques may require 50 days and cost £200 000, but an estate of 'industrialized' buildings may require 25 days and cost £330 000. Since two entirely different resources are used no compromise state exists on the same cost/duration function, whereas where the difference between normal and crash duration results from the use of additional similar resources, the two extremes may be interpolated, as in Figure 13.28.

The total cost of a project is determined not only by variable costs such as production resources, but also by fixed or overhead costs such as rent for buildings, insurance, power, administration, etc. Consequently the project duration involving minimum total cost is not necessarily the duration with minimum cost of resources.

The network diagram for a small construction project, activity cost data and network dates is shown in Figure 13.29(a). Only the activities on the critical path affect the project duration, therefore reduction in project duration must be sought on the critical path and

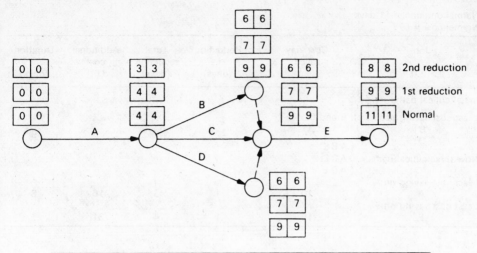

Figure 13.29(a) *Network diagram and comparison between cost of normal and crash activities.*

Activity	Normal		Crash	
	Duration (days)	Cost (£)	Duration (days)	Cost (£)
A	4	30	3	40
B	5	12	2	18
C	3	10	2	20
D	5	10	3	12
E	2	15	1	30
	Total 77			

N.B. Indirect fixed cost—£5/day

from those activities offering time savings at least cost. Initially there are two critical paths—ABE and ADE—and the least cost time saving is two days from both activities B and D. After activities B and D have been reduced from five to three days all three paths are critical and, since no further reduction is possible on activity D, savings must be obtained from activities A and E. Activity A can be reduced by one day at a cost of £10, then activity E by one day at a cost of £15. This procedure for reducing the project duration is given in the table in Figure 13.29(b), which also shows the construction of the total cost/project duration curve. The least cost project duration is nine days.

Before terminating our discussion of costs we must draw attention to a rather interesting 'twist' or variation of the procedure followed in the preceding example. Again we shall consider a simple example in order to explain the variation. Consider the simple project represented by Figure 13.30. Let us calculate the total cost associated with the completion of this project in first one and then two days less than the normal duration.

The normal duration of the project is 32 days at a normal cost of £1620. Under those conditions the critical path is 0 1 4 3 5 6 (see Figure 13.30 and Table 13.1). To reduce this duration by one day, one of the jobs on the critical path must be reduced by one day. The cheapest reduction is available on job 1–4 (£15), consequently a project duration of 31 days is achieved at a cost of £1635.

There are now three critical paths (0 1 4 3 5 6, 0 2 4 3 5 6 and 0 1 3 5 6), consequently a reduction of the project duration by a further day is achieved by reducing each of these paths by one day. Job 1–4 cannot be reduced any further, hence the cheapest direct method

Normal duration = 11 days
Normal cost = £77

Job	Cost/day saved	Reduction (days)	Total reduction (days)	Additional cost (£)	Duration (days)
Initial critical paths = $\begin{cases} ABE \\ ADE \end{cases}$					
Least cost saving occurs on B and D					
$\left.\begin{matrix} B \\ D \end{matrix}\right\}$	2 + 1	2	2	6	9
Now three critical paths = $\begin{cases} ABE \\ ACE \\ ADE \end{cases}$					
Least cost saving on A					
A	10	1	3	16	8
Least cost saving on E					
E	15	1	4	31	7

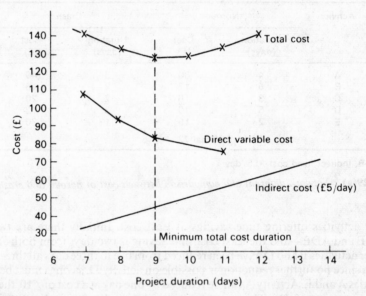

Figure 13.29(b)   *Activity variable cost/duration relationships for Figure 13.29(a).*

of reducing the project duration from 31 to 30 days is reducing by one day the duration of job 1–3 (thereby reducing critical path 0 1 3 5 6) and the duration of job 4–3 (thereby reducing the duration of *both* paths 0 1 4 3 5 6 and 0 2 4 3 5 6). Thus the additional cost incurred is £40 and the total cost for a project duration of 30 days is £1675. Notice that although three critical paths were involved, job 4–3 was common to two of those and it was necessary only to alter the duration of two jobs.

Job 0–1 is also common to two critical paths and we could therefore have reduced the duration of this job and that of either job 0–2 or 2–4 to reduce the duration of the project, but such a solution would have been more expensive than that outlined previously. One further means of reducing the duration of the project would have been to reduce the duration of jobs 0–1 and 4–3. This again would have been a more expensive solution than the original. Notice, however, that both jobs 0–1 and 4–3 are common to two paths. Reduction of job 0–1 would reduce both path 0 1 3 5 6 and path 0 1 4 3 5 6, while

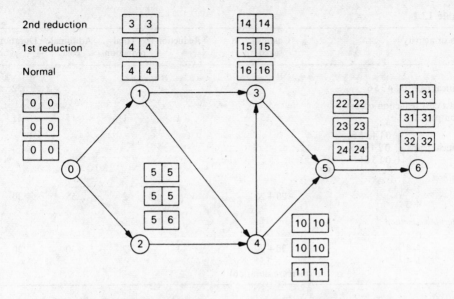

Activity	Normal		Crash	
	Duration (days)	Cost (£)	Duration (days)	Cost (£)
0–1	4	200	3	230
0–2	5	180	4	200
1–3	11	200	9	240
1–4	7	150	6	165
2–4	5	150	4	170
4–3	5	170	4	190
3–5	8	170	7	265
4–5	8	200	8	200
5–6	8	200	8	200
		Total 1620		

N.B. Indirect fixed cost considered to be zero.

Figure 13.30

reduction of job 4–3 would reduce path 0 1 4 3 5 6 and path 0 2 4 3 5 6. The reduction of both of these jobs by one day would reduce path 0 1 4 3 5 6 by two days, hence an alternative method of obtaining a project duration is to reduce, by one day, jobs 0–1 and 4–3, and to *increase* by one day job 1–4. In fact this alternative is cheaper than the previous one, the cost of the reduction being 30 + 20 − 15, i.e. £35 compared with the £40 cost of the previous method.

This interesting twist occurs only infrequently; nevertheless it is worth while keeping a lookout for this type of solution when the analysis involves more than one critical path: when two or more reducible activities are common to these paths which themselves contain previously reduced activities.

Table 13.1

Job or activity	Cost/day saved	Reduction	Total reduction	Aditional cost	Duration
Critical path 0 1 4 3 5 6					32
Least cost reduction occurs on path 1–4	15	1	1	15	31
Critical paths $\begin{cases} 0\,1\,4\,3\,5\,6 \\ 0\,2\,4\,3\,5\,6 \\ 0\,1\,3\,5\,6 \end{cases}$					
Method 1					
$\left.\begin{array}{l} 1{-}3 \\ 4{-}3 \end{array}\right\}$	$20+20$	1	2	55	30
Alternative method					
$\left.\begin{array}{l} 0{-}1 \\ 4{-}3 \\ 1{-}4 \end{array}\right\}$	$30+20$ -15 (increase duration)	1	2	50	30

COMPUTER-BASED NETWORK PLANNING

Operations planning using network analysis is normally undertaken with the assistance of a computer. The following example concerns a manufacturing project. The example is based on a program developed by ICL, but numerous other mainframe, mini- and micro-computer-based programs are available.

When more than 200 or 300 activities are involved the use of a computer is advisable, particularly if regular updating of the network is envisaged for operations control purposes or if resource allocation is necessary. The important stages during network analysis based production planning are:

1. Construct the network.
2. Estimate the duration of each activity and the resources required.
3. Define any necessary schedule dates.
4. Define the maximum amount of resources available and the working hours available.
5. Perform network calculations.
6. Compare schedule dates and calculated dates.
7. Modify network and/or activity durations if necessary.
8. Recalculate network.
9. Repeat 6, 7 and 8 as necessary.
10. Issue operations plan to all necessary departments.

The input for the network analysis program will normally inlude the following:

1. List of activities, described by the beginning and ending event number.
2. The duration(s) for each activity.
3. Schedule dates on intermediate and/or finish events.
4. The description of each activity. This is not necessary for the program but forms part of the output so that the information is meaningful and activities can easily be recognized.

5. The *responsibility code* for each activity, i.e. whether it is performed in the drawing office, foundry, and so on, so that, if desired, the output can be broken down into separate lists showing the production plan for each department or area.
6. Description of the work week and the holidays, etc., so that the work will not be scheduled during holidays and so that activity durations in hours or days can be used to calculate project durations in weeks or months.
7. The resource levels normally available, i.e. normal work and machine hours per week.
8. Additional resources available due to overtime, etc.
9. Maximum activity delay which, if necessary, can be tolerated because of the rescheduling of activities to conform to resource availability.
10. Computer run parameters, e.g. customer's name, name of project.
11. Output parameters to determine the type of output required, etc.

Figure 13.31 shows part of the input for a small project: building a motor yacht. Single time estimates are being used and no resources are defined. The beginning and the scheduled end dates are given, as are the departments responsible for each activity. The network for the project is shown in Figure 13.32. Most programs provide for output in several different forms suitable, for example, for the customer, production planning department, production control, etc., and some of the input will consist of instructions to specify the type and format of output required. It is usual in the output to have the definitions (event numbers, descriptions, etc.) on the left-hand side of the page and the results on the right of the page. Each line of output represents one activity, and each activity is identified by its event numbers and, for convenience, by its description.

PROJECT   MOTOR YACHT 39   RUN NO
DATE . . . . PAGE . . . . .OF

TRAN CODE	BEGIN EVENT	END EVENT	DURATION/ DATE	OPTIONAL FIELDS. (MAX 16 SPACES/ 3 FIELDS)			DESCRIPTION
AB		1	05 APR 65		MY39		
AA	1	2	30	office			Draw plans
AA	2	9	60	office			Order and await engine
AA	9	10	20	yard			Prepare engine
AA	10	11	10	yard			Install engine
AA	11	12	30	yard			Construct deck & clean off
AA	12	13	40	yard			Paint & varnish
AA	13	14	20	yard			Final fit-out
AA	2	3	40	office			Order and await timber
AA	3	11	40	yard			Cut timber for deck
AA	2	4	60	office			Order and await joinery fittings
AA	4	8	30	yard			Assemble joinery units & fittings
AA	8	11	20	yard			Install joinery
AA	2	5	20	yard			Make hull templates
AA	5	6	40	yard			Cut hull timber
AA	6	7	40	yard			Construct hull
AA	7	12	10	yard			Clean off hull
AA	2	12	40	office			Order and await paint & varnish
AA	3	4	30	yard			Make joinery units
AA	3	5	0				Dummy
AA	7	8	0				Dummy
AA	7	10	0		↓		Dummy
AF		14	08 OCT 65		MY39		
							→
							→

* PLEASE MARK OFF COLUMNS REQUIRED WITH DOUBLE LINE SEPARATORS

Figure 13.31 *Part of input for small project: building a motor yacht.*

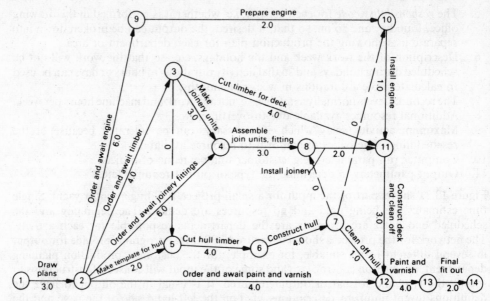

Figure 13.32 *Network for building a motor yacht.*

In this example the output from the first run is shown in Figure 13.33, which gives the results in the format specified by the output parameters. The activities are listed in order of increasing total float. The least total float is −1.8 weeks and the critical path is 1 2 3 5 6 7 8 11 12 13 14. The project cannot be completed by the scheduled end date and consequently either activity durations and/or the network itself must be modified.

FLOATSHIP + CO. LTD

BEGIN EVENT	ENDING EVENT	DEPT.	PROJECT	DESCRIPTION	ACT DUR	EARL FINISH	LATEST FINISH	TOTAL FLOAT
*1	2	OFFICE	MYO39	DRAW PLANS	3 0	28APR65	13APR	−1.8
2	3	OFFICE	MYO39	ORDER AND AWAIT TIMBER	4 0	26MAY65	13MAY	−1.8
3	5		MYO39	D	0	26MAY65	13MAY	−1.8
5	6	YARD	MYO39	CUT TIMBER FOR HULL	4 0	24JUN65	11JUN	−1.8
6	7	YARD	MYO39	CONSTRUCT HULL	4 0	22JUL65	09JUL	−1.8
7	8		MYO39	D	0	22JUL65	09JUL	−1.8
8	11	YARD	MYO39	INSTALL FITTINGS + JOINERY	2 0	05AUG65	23JUL	−1.8
11	12	YARD	MYO39	CONSTRUCT DECK + CLEAN OFF	3 0	26AUG65	13AUG	−1.8
12	13	YARD	MYO39	PAINT + VARNISH	4 0	07OCT65	24SEP	−1.8
13	14*	YARD	MYO39	FINAL FIT OUT	2 0	21OCT65	08OCT	−1.8
7	10		MYO39	D	0	22JUL65	16JUL	−0.8
10	11	YARD	MYO39	INSTALL ENGINE	1 0	29JUL65	23JUL	−0.8
2	5	YARD	MYO39	MAKE TEMPLATE FOR HULL	2 0	12MAY65	13MAY	0.2
3	4	YARD	MYO39	MAKE JOINERY UNITS	3 0	17JUN65	18JUN	0.2
4	8	YARD	MYO39	ASSEMBLE JOINERY UNITS + FITTINGS	3 0	08JUL65	09JUL	0.2
2	4	OFFICE	MYO39	ORDER AND AWAIT JOINERY FITTINGS	6 0	10JUN65	18JUN	1 2
					1.0	29JUL65	13AUG	−2 2
7	12	YARD	MYO39	CLEAN OFF HULL	6 0	10JUN65	02JUL	3 2
2	9	OFFICE	MYO39	ORDER AND AWAIT ENGINE	2 0	24JUN65	16JUL	3 2
9	10	YARD	MYO39	PREPARE ENGINE	4 0	24JUN65	23JUL	4 2
3	11	YARD	MYO39	CUT TIMBER FOR DECK				
2	12	OFFICE	MYO39	ORDER AND AWAIT PAINT + VARNISH	4 0	26MAY65	13AUG	11.2

CONSTRUCTION OF A MOTOR YACHT
RUN NUMBER 1
REPORT DATE 08MAR65

ACTIVITY PERT

ORDER: TOTAL FLOAT
BY SEQUENCE ORDER

PAGE 1

Figure 13.33 *Output from first run on construction of the motor yacht.*

The second network shows the modified arrangement and duration of activities designed to reduce the project duration by at least 1.8 weeks and meet the scheduled finish date of 8 October (Figure 13.34).

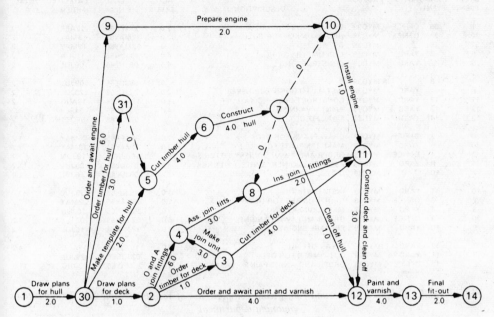

Figure 13.34 *Network for building the motor yacht, revised to meet scheduled date.*

The output from the second run is shown in the sequences from Figure 13.35 to Figure 13.41. Figure 13.35 is a complete list of results suitable for use by the planning department. The activities are listed in order of increasing total float, hence the most critical activities appear at the top of the page. There is now a positive total float of 0.2 weeks, the critical path being through event numbers 1 30 31 5 6 7 8 11 12 13 14. Dummies are still included in this output, but since they are of little practical value they can be, and are, omitted from the other outputs.

Figure 13.36 contains precisely the same information as the previous output, but in this case the activities are ordered by the earliest finish date. This type of output would be of value to the customer, who could use it to evaluate the progress of the project. If the project is running according to plan, the activities above the current date in the earliest finish date column should have been completed.

Figures 13.37 and 13.38 are departmental printouts with the activities listed in order of planned start (earliest start) dates. All the activities for that department are listed and this document, therefore, is the operations plan for the department. Notice that no finish dates are included but a blank column is provided in which the actual finish date may be entered. This information can be fed back to the operations control department and used for updating the network. The use of a *planned start* date rather than an *earliest start* date has obvious psychological advantages!

Figures 13.39 and 13.40 are the bar chart equivalents of the previous two figures, showing earliest start and finish dates. (Latest dates—either start or finish—have been excluded from all outputs intended for use on the shop floor, lest they should provide encouragement for delays.)

Finally, Figure 13.41, unlike all the previous outputs, is concerned with events and not

CONSTRUCTION OF A MOTOR YACHT
          RUN NUMBER 2
          REPORT DATE 15MAR65

FLOATSHIP · CO LTD
ACTIVITY PERT

ORDER TOTAL FLOAT
       BY SEQUENCE ORDER

PAGE 1

BEGIN EVENT	ENDING EVENT	DEPT	PROJECT	DESCRIPTION	ACT DUR	EARL FINISH	LATEST FINISH	TOTAL FLOAT
1*	30	OFFICE	MYO39	DRAW PLANS FOR HULL	2.0	21APR65	22APR	.2
30	31	OFFICE	MYO39	ORDER TIMBER FOR HULL	3.0	12MAY65	13MAY	.2
31	5		MYO39	D	.0	12MAY65	13MAY	.2
5	6	YARD	MYO39	CUT TIMBER FOR HULL	4.0	10JUN65	11JUN	.2
6	7	YARD	MYO39	CONSTRUCT HULL	4.0	08JUL65	09JUL	.2
7	8		MYO39	D	.0	08JUL65	09JUL	.2
8	11	YARD	MYO39	INSTALL FITTINGS · JOINERY	2.0	22JUL65	23JUL	.2
11	12	YARD	MYO39	CONSTRUCT DECK · CLEAN OFF	3.0	12AUG65	13AUG	.2
12	13	YARD	MYO39	PAINT + VARNISH	4.0	23SEP65	24SEP	.2
13	14*	YARD	MYO39	FINAL FIT OUT	2.0	07OCT65	08OCT	.2
30	2	OFFICE	MYO39	DRAW PLANS FOR DECK	1.0	28APR65	06MAY	1.2
30	5	YARD	MYO39	MAKE TEMPLATE FOR HULL	2.0	05MAY65	13MAY	1.2
2	4	OFFICE	MYO39	ORDER AND AWAIT JOINERY FITTINGS	6.0	10JUN65	18JUN	1.2
4	8	YARD	MYO39	ASSEMBLE JOINERY UNITS · FITTINGS	3.0	01JUL65	09JUL	1.2
7	10		MYO39	D	.0	08JUL65	16JUL	1.2
10	11	YARD	MYO39	INSTALL ENGINE	1.0	15JUL65	23JUL	1.2
2	3	OFFICE	MYO39	ORDER TIMBER FOR DECK	1.0	05MAY65	27MAY	3.2
3	4	YARD	MYO39	MAKE JOINERY UNITS	3.0	26MAY65	18JUN	3.2
30	9	OFFICE	MYO39	ORDER AND AWAIT ENGINE	6.0	02JUN65	02JUL	4.2
9	10	YARD	MYO39	PREPARE ENGINE	2.0	17JUN65	16JUL	4.2
7	12	YARD	MYO39	CLEAN OFF HULL	1.0	15JUL65	13AUG	4.2
3	11	YARD	MYO39	CUT TIMBER FOR DECK	4.0	02JUN65	23JUL	7.2
2	12	OFFICE	MYO39	ORDER AND AWAIT PAINT · VARNISH	4.0	26MAY65	13AUG	11.2

Figure 13.35 *Output from second run, giving complete list of results suitable for the operations planning department.*

CONSTRUCTION OF A MOTOR YACHT
          RUN NUMBER 2
          REPORT DATE 15MAR65

FLOATSHIP + CO LTD
ACTIVITY PERT

ORDER EARLIEST FINISH
       BY TOTAL FLOAT

PAGE 1

DEPT	PROJECT	DESCRIPTION	ACT DUR	EARL FINISH	LATEST FINISH	TOTAL FLOAT
OFFICE	MYO39	DRAW PLANS FOR HULL	2.0	21APR65	22APR	.2
OFFICE	MYO39	DRAW PLANS FOR DECK	1.0	28APR65	06MAY	1.2
YARD	MYO39	MAKE TEMPLATE FOR HULL	2.0	05MAY65	13MAY	1.2
OFFICE	MYO39	ORDER TIMBER FOR DECK	1.0	05MAY65	27MAY	3.0
OFFICE	MYO39	ORDER TIMBER FOR HULL	3.0	12MAY65	13MAY	.2
YARD	MYO39	MAKE JOINERY UNITS	3.0	26MAY65	18JUN	3.2
OFFICE	MYO39	ORDER AND AWAIT PAINT + VARNISH	4.0	26MAY65	13AUG	11.2
OFFICE	MYO39	ORDER AND AWAIT ENGINE	6.0	02JUN65	02JUL	4.2
YARD	MYO39	CUT TIMBER FOR DECK	4.0	02JUN65	23JUL	7.2
YARD	MYO39	CUT TIMBER FOR HULL	4.0	10JUN65	11JUN	.2
OFFICE	MYO39	ORDER AND AWAIT JOINERY FITTINGS	6.0	10JUN65	18JUN	1.2
YARD	MYO39	PREPARE ENGINE	2.0	17JUN65	16JUL	4.2
YARD	MYO39	ASSEMBLE JOINERY UNITS + FITTINGS	3.0	01JUL65	09JUL	1.2
YARD	MYO39	CONSTRUCT HULL	4.0	08JUL65	09JUL	.2
YARD	MYO39	INSTALL ENGINE	1.0	15JUL65	23JUL	1.2
YARD	MYO39	CLEAN OFF HULL	1.0	15JUL65	13AUG	4.2
YARD	MYO39	INSTALL FITTINGS + JOINERY	2.0	22JUL65	23JUL	.2
YARD	MYO39	CONSTRUCT DECK + CLEAN OFF	3.0	12AUG65	13AUG	.2
YARD	MYO39	PAINT + VARNISH	4.0	23SEP65	24SEP	.2
YARD	MYO39	FINAL FIT OUT	2.0	07OCT65	08OCT	.2

Figure 13.36 *Output from second run with activities ordered by earliest finish date.*

FLOATSHIP + CO LTD

CONSTRUCTION OF A MOTOR YACHT			ACTIVITY PERT			ORDER: DEPT		PAGE 1
RUN NUMBER: 2						BY PLANNED START		
REPORT DATE: 15MAR65						BY TOTAL FLOAT		

DEPT	PROJECT	DESCRIPTION	ACT DUR	PLANNED START	PLANNED FINISH	ACTUAL FINISH	REMARKS
YARD	MYO39	MAKE TEMPLATE FOR HULL	2.0	21APR65	05MAY		
YARD	MYO39	MAKE JOINERY UNITS	3.0	05MAY65	26MAY		
YARD	MYO39	CUT TIMBER FOR DECK	4.0	05MAY65	02JUN		
YARD	MYO39	CUT TIMBER FOR HULL	4.0	12MAY65	10JUN		
YARD	MYO39	PREPARE ENGINE	2.0	02JUN65	17JUN		
YARD	MYO39	CONSTRUCT HULL	4.0	10JUN65	08JUL		
YARD	MYO39	ASSEMBLE JOINERY UNITS + FITTINGS	3.0	10JUN65	01JUL		
YARD	MYO39	INSTALL FITTINGS + JOINERY	2.0	08JUL65	22JUL		
YARD	MYO39	INSTALL ENGINE	1.0	08JUL65	15JUL		
YARD	MYO39	CLEAN OFF HULL	1.0	08JUL65	15JUL		
YARD	MYO39	CONSTRUCT DECK +CLEAN OFF	3.0	22JUL65	12AUG		
YARD	MYO39	PAINT + VARNISH	4.0	12AUG65	23SEP		
YARD	MYO39	FINAL FIT OUT	2.0	23SEP65	07OCT		

Figure 13.37 *Departmental printout with activities listed in order of planned start dates.*

FLOATSHIP + CO LTD

CONSTRUCTION OF A MOTOR YACHT			ACTIVITY PERT			ORDER: DEPT		PAGE 1
RUN NUMBER: 2						BY PLANNED START		
REPORT DATE: 15MAR65						BY TOTAL FLOAT		

DEPT	PROJECT	DESCRIPTION	ACT DUR	PLANNED START	PLANNED FINISH	ACTUAL FINISH	REMARKS
OFFICE	MYO39	DRAW PLANS FOR HULL	2.0	05APR65	21APR		
OFFICE	MYO39	ORDER TIMBER FOR HULL	3.0	21APR65	12MAY		
OFFICE	MYO39	DRAW PLANS FOR DECK	1.0	21APR65	28APR		
OFFICE	MYO39	ORDER AND AWAIT ENGINE	6.0	21APR65	02JUN		
OFFICE	MYO39	ORDER AND AWAIT JOINERY FITTINGS	6.0	28APR65	10JUN		
OFFICE	MYO39	ORDER TIMBER FOR DECK	1.0	28APR65	05MAY		
OFFICE	MYO39	ORDER AND AWAIT PAINT + VARNISH	4.0	28APR65	26MAY		

Figure 13.38 *Departmental printout with activities listed in order of planned start dates.*

FLOATSHIP + CO LTD

CONSTRUCTION OF A MOTOR YACHT			ACTIVITY PERT			ORDER: DEPT		PAGE 1
RUN NUMBER: 2						BY PLANNED START		
REPORT DATE 15MAR65						BY TOTAL FLOAT		

DEPT	PROJECT	DESCRIPTION	05APR 1	21APR 1	05MAY 1	19MAY 1	02JUN 1	17JUN 1
YARD	MYO39	MAKE TEMPLATE FOR HULL		XXXXXXXXXX				
YARD	MYO39	MAKE JOINERY UNITS			XXXXXXXXXXXXXX			
YARD	MYO39	CUT TIMBER FOR DECK			XXXXXXXXXXXXXXXXXXX			
YARD	MYO39	CUT TIMBER FOR HULL				XXXXXXXXXXXXXXXXXXX		
YARD	MYO39	PREPARE ENGINE						XXXXXXXXXX
YARD	MYO39	CONSTRUCT HULL						XXXXXXXXXXXXXXX
YARD	MYO39	ASSEMBLE JOINERY UNITS + FITTINGS						XXXXXXXXXXXXXXX
YARD	MYO39	INSTALL FITTINGS - JOINERY						
YARD	MYO39	INSTALL ENGINE						
YARD	MYO39	CLEAN OFF HULL						
YARD	MYO39	CONSTRUCT DECK + CLEAN OFF						
YARD	MYO39	PAINT - VARNISH						
YARD	MYO39	FINAL FIT OUT						

Figure 13.39 *Bar chart equivalent of Figure 13.37 showing earliest start and finish dates.*

```
                                              FLOATSHIP + CO LTD
    CONSTRUCTION OF A MOTOR YACHT                ACTIVITY PERT                  ORDER: DEPT                    PAGE 1
              RUN NUMBER   2                                                             BY PLANNED START
              REPORT DATE  15MAR65                                                       BY TOTAL FLOAT

    DEPT    PROJECT                        05APR      21APR     05MAY     19MAY     02JUN     17JUN
                              DESCRIPTION    1          1         1         1         1         1

    OFFICE  MYO39  DRAW PLANS FOR HULL      XXXXXXXXXX
    OFFICE  MYO39  ORDER TIMBER FOR HULL              XXXXXXXXXXXXXXXX
    OFFICE  MYO39  DRAW PLANS FOR DECK                XXXXX
    OFFICE  MYO39  ORDER AND AWAIT ENGINE             XXXXXXXXXXXXXXXXXXXXXXXXXXXXXXX
    OFFICE  MYO39  ORDER AND AWAIT JOINERY FITTINGS        XXXXXXXXXXXXXXXXXXXXXXXXXXXXXX

    OFFICE  MYO39  ORDER TIMBER FOR DECK                   XXXXX
    OFFICE  MYO39  ORDER AND AWAIT PAINT · VARNISH         XXXXXXXXXXXXXXXXXXX
```

Figure 13.40   *Bar chart equivalent of Figure 13.38 showing earliest start and finish dates.*

```
                                              FLOATSHIP + CO LTD
    CONSTRUCTION OF A MOTOR YACHT                 EVENT PERT                   ORDER: PLANNED DATE           PAGE 1
              RUN NUMBER:  2                                                            BY SLACK
              REPORT DATE: 15MAR65

                        EVENT       REP                                  PLANNED     SLACK
                       NUMBER       CODE        DESCRIPTION               DATE

                         30         MD    PLANS FOR HULL COMPLETED        21APR        .2
                          2         MD    PLANS FOR DECK COMPLETED        28APR       1.2
                          7         MD    HULL CONSTRUCTED                08JUL        .2
                         11         MD    INSTALLATIONS COMPLETED         22JUL        .2
                         12         MD    DECK LAID                       12AUG        .2

                         14*        MD    READY FOR SEA TRIALS            07OCT        .2
```

Figure 13.41   *Output showing key events in order of planned start dates. (Figures 13.31 to 13.41 reproduced with the permission of International Computers Ltd.)*

activities. In the input, certain key events were specified corresponding to major landmarks in the project. This output lists the key events in order of their planned (earliest) start dates. The slack on each event is given. This type of output is designed for the project manager or company executive, who, although concerned with the overall progress of the project, is normally unconcerned with the details.

Resources: aggregation and allocation

Resource aggregation is a comparatively simple procedure and the output consists of either lists or histograms showing the total requirements per resource per period. There are occasions where such information might be of value. When the computer program does not provide for resource allocation or levelling an aggregation of resources will indicate which periods and which resources are overloaded. It is then possible either to manually reschedule the activities using these resources during the overload periods to obtain extra resources, or to subcontract some of the work.

Unless the factory is working considerably under capacity, some form of resource allocation is normally necessary, and a procedure often adopted in computer-based network analysis is as follows:

1. Aggregate resources.
2. Identify periods of overload.

3. Reschedule activities during these periods as follows:
   (a) delay activities in order of decreasing total float by a period up to the allowed maximum delay;
   (b) if overload still occurs use additional resources available;
   (c) if overload still occurs allow overload to stand.

This is far from perfect procedure. No attempt has been made to overcome resource overloads by moving activities forward, nor is any attempt made to compare the cost of extra resources with either the cost of project delay or the cost of subcontracting work. The difficulty of dealing with resource allocation in a routine manner is illustrated by the fact that only recently has resource allocation become a feature of network analysis computer programs. Allocation is often a time-consuming routine by computer standards and, although it is no doubt possible to devise more exhaustive routines, it is doubtful whether the extra cost in computing time is worth the marginal extra benefits. The procedure outlined above has been available for several years and is regarded by many users as sufficiently accurate and exhaustive for all practical purposes.

Multi-project operations planning

Network analysis was originally developed for use on large single projects of the type mentioned at the beginning of this chapter, and this still remains the most important application of the technique. Recently, however, greater use has been made of network planning procedures in the simultaneous manufacture of several items. This type of application is best dealt with on a computer, and contemporary network analysis programs, which have provision for up to 15 000 activities, are easily capable of dealing with several quite large projects.

Perhaps the main thing to avoid is compromise. Network analysis is such an effective planning procedure that, unless all the projects in any particular situation are planned in this way, there is a very real danger that those to which network analysis is applied will progress at the expense of the remainder. One of the important advantages of this procedure is that it highlights critical activities and encourages those responsible to make a real effort not only to meet the required finish dates but also to 'get off the critical path'. Under this sort of influence there is little incentive to worry unduly about other projects which do not appear in the limelight.

To use network analysis on several projects the following additional information is required:

1. The activities in each network must be separately identifiable, either by using different event numbers or by the use of a prefix letter to identify the project.
2. In addition to responsibility codes to identify which department is responsible for the activities, a further code must be used to identify the project so that the output for each project and each department can be collected together if necessary.

One of the difficulties in using this method for multi-project planning is to define the relative importance of each project. For example, if three projects are running concurrently and at any time one department is responsible for processing an item from each and each item has the same total float and start date, which is the most important? To some extent this problem can be overcome by deciding on the order of priority of the projects and communicating this to all concerned; alternatively, schedule dates may be used to indicate priorities. Nevertheless, this assumes first that priorities remain constant and that decisions about activities will necessarily be resolved in relation to the priority of the overall projects, whereas there may be occasions when it is preferable to do jobs from less important projects first (when, for example, the set-up cost of a machine is substantially less if two or more jobs are done in this order rather than in order of project priority).

THE USE OF GANTT (BAR) CHARTS

It will often be useful to represent the activities of a project diagrammatically against a timescale. The normal network diagram has no timescale, but it is possible to use a form of Gantt or bar chart, as shown in the previous example (Figures 13.39 and 13.40). The use of Gantt charts to represent activities, their start dates, etc., will be appropriate when using network techniques to develop schedules which must then be communicated to others and/or displayed for easy reference. Gantt charts are easily read and can be used to show the progress of work on activities or projects. They can easily be updated and changed, and various proprietary 'kits' are available for the construction of such charts, with colour coding for different types of resources, etc. However, the main problems with this approach are that: (a) it is difficult to show the interdependence of activities; and (b) it is difficult to show all the dates for each activity, which are determined from the network calculations. The first problem can be overcome with ingenuity. The second problem is normally overcome by showing only earliest start and finish dates (in the manner employed in Figures 13.39 and 13.40).

Figure 13.42 is a Gantt chart representation of the project previously described in network form in Example 13.2. This chart also shows the resource requirements for the activities. Figure 13.43 shows how this type of representation can be used to develop a resource aggregation for this project.

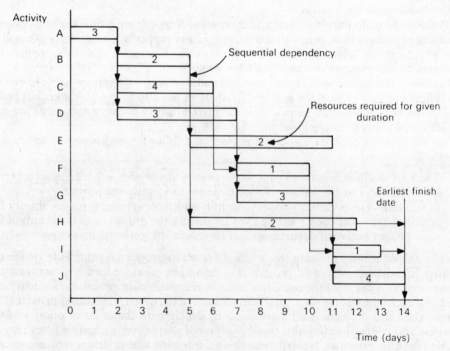

Figure 13.42 *Gantt chart representation of project described in Example 13.2.*

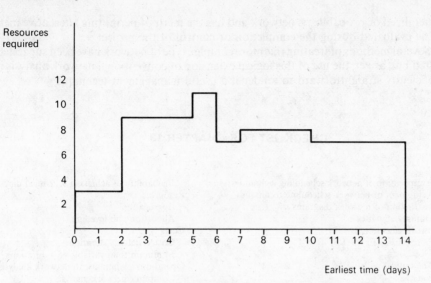

Figure 13.43 *Resource aggregation for Figure 13.42.*

GERT NETWORKS

In the past, network analysis has been criticized because of the difficulty of altering the network construction in the light of experience or circumstance during the actual performance of jobs. In other words, it has been suggested that there is inadequate connection between the planning stage, during which the network is constructed, and the usage stage, during which the network and the activity start and finish dates are used to schedule and control the overall project.

In some cases, particularly when concerned with new or novel projects never before undertaken, the initial network drawn up during the project planning stages proves either impractical or disadvantageous in use. In many cases, for example because of a delay in certain parts of the project or because of unforeseen snags and circumstances, it becomes necessary to modify part of the network in order to undertake part of the project in a different manner from that initially envisaged. Often during the planning stage alternative methods of undertaking the project are evident, but because such alternatives cannot be included in conventional network analysis, one of these alternatives is chosen in the hope that in practice this will prove to be the best method.

In order to ensure that projects are completed in the optimum manner, it would be necessary for:

(a)   all alternative methods of completing the project, i.e. different job durations and technological orderings, to be included in the network;
(b)   the effects and the merits of alternative methods to be considered at the planning stage and throughout the usage or control stage of the project.

In this chapter we are concerned primarily with operations planning using network analysis; nevertheless, it is pertinent to point out that, in order to overcome the discontinuity between planning and control, attempts have been made to devise methods of constructing and using networks which show the several possible ways of completing the project rather than only one method. This type of network can be described as a generalized or probabilistic network and has the merit of permitting alternative methods to be evaluated during the completion or control of the project.[2]

Several methods of treating this more complex type of network have been suggested and tested but, as yet, the use of this logical extension of conventional network analysis is not sufficiently straightforward to render it a useful management technique.

CHECKLIST FOR CHAPTER 13

The application of network scheduling techniques	Probability of achieving scheduled dates
Development of network scheduling techniques	Resources
Construction of network diagrams	Aggregation
Dummy activities	Allocation and levelling
Network calculations	Costs
Dates (EF, LF, ES, LS)	Cost v. activity duration
Float	Minimum total variable cost durations
The critical path	Operations planning with network analysis
Slack	Computer network analysis
Free and independent float	Resource aggregation and allocation
Schedule dates	Multi-project operations planning
Event dates	Gantt (or bar) chart representations
Matrix method of calculation	'GERT' networks
Multiple time estimates (PERT)	Activity on node (precedence) diagrams

FURTHER READING

Battersby, A. (1978) *Network Analysis for Planning and Scheduling Studies in Management*, 3rd edition, London: Macmillan. Possibly the best British book on network methods.

Lockyer, K. G. (1970) *An Introduction to Critical Path Analysis*, 3rd edition. London: Pitman. Provides a simple introduction to the subject.

Shaffer, L. R., Ritter, J. B. and Meyer, W. L. (1965) *The Critical Path Method*. Maidenhead: McGraw-Hill.

Weist, J. D. and Levy, F. K. (1977) *A Management Guide to PERT/CPM*, 2nd edition. Englewood Cliffs, NJ: Prentice-Hall. A well-established American book which also presents several 'heuristic' rules for resource allocation. This topic is also covered in Shaffer, Ritter and Meyer (1965) and Woodworth and Willie (1975).

Woodgate, H. S. (1977) *Planning by Network*, 3rd edition. London: Business Books. A simple introduction to the subject.

Woodworth B. M. and Willie, C. J. (1975) A heuristic algorithm for resource levelling in multi-project, multi-resource scheduling. *Decision Sciences*, **6** (3).

---

[2] Crowston, W. and Thompson, G. L. (1967) Decision CPM: a method for simultaneous planning, scheduling, and control of prospects. *Operations Research*, **15** (3), pp. 407–426.
Elmaghraby, S. E. (1966) On generalized activity networks, *Journal of Industrial Engineering*, **XVII** (11).
Pritsker, A. A. B. (1968) GERT networks, *Production Engineer*, **47** (10), pp. 499–506.

QUESTIONS

13.1   Construct a network diagram for the following activities:

Activity	A	B	C	D	E	F	G	H	J	K	L	M	N	O
Necessary preceding activities	—	—	A	AB	C	C	D	D	E	EF	GH	H	JK	LM

13.2   Redraw the following network diagram so that the logic is retained and dummy activities are used correctly.

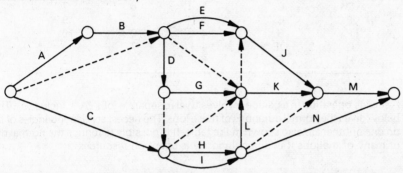

Figure Q13.2

13.3   Draw an activity network for the following activities. Assuming that the project starts at day 0, calculate the earliest start and latest finish dates for all activities, and the project earliest completion date. Calculate also the total float on all activities and identify the critical path.

Activity	A	B	C	D	E	F	G	H	I
Immediate predecessors	—	—	A	AB	BC	CD	CD	EF	EGF
Activity duration (days)	3	5	6	2	4	7	3	4	5

13.4   In the following network, assuming that the project starts at day 0, what is the probability that the project will be completed by day 26?

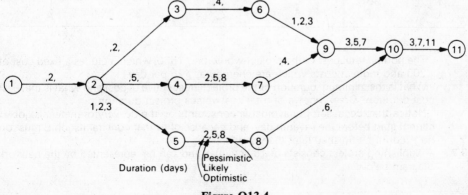

Figure Q13.4

13.5   The following table describes the various activities of a small project. What is the probability that the project will be completed in $22\frac{1}{2}$ days or less?

Activity	Immediate predecessor(s)	Estimates of activity duration (days)		
		Optimistic	Likely	Pessimistic
A	—	2	4	6
B	A	1	5	9
C	A	—	9	—
D	C	5	6	7
E	B	5	7	9
F	B	4	10	16
G	DE	—	7	—
H	F	6	9	12

13.6   A service operation in a garage involves twelve separate jobs (A–L inclusive). The table below gives the normal durations of these jobs. The necessary dependencies of the jobs on one another are also shown in the table. It is possible to reduce the normal duration of many of the jobs if additional money is spent on resources.

Job	Predecessors	Normal duration (days)	Number of days by which job may be reduced	Cost of shortening job duration (£/day)	Increments by which job might be reduced (days)
A	—	4	3	50	1
B	—	8	0	—	—
C	—	3	1	100	1
D	A	6	3	50	2
E	C	5	2	80	1
F	D	8	3	100	$\frac{1}{2}$
G	D	2	1	75	1
H	E	6	2	75	1
I	E	2	1	60	1
J	F	1	0	—	—
K	GBH	6	3	50	1
L	I	5	2	35	2

The normal total cost of the project would be £1500, which includes a fixed cost of £200 and indirect costs which are charged at £25 per day.

What is the minimum duration of the project irrespective of cost and what is the least cost duration? Draw a curve of total cost versus project duration.

Notice that, because of unavoidable constraints on the delivery of materials, job H cannot start before the seventh day, and because of further constraints job B must on no account be finished later than day 14.

13.7   A publishing project consists of 15 activities and can be represented by the network diagram below.

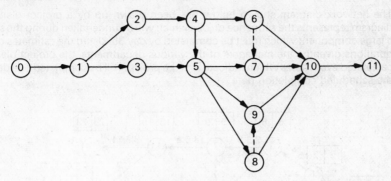

Figure Q13.7

The duration of each of the activities is as follows:

Activity		Duration (days)
Begin event	End event	
0	1	10
1	2	5
1	3	6
2	4	3
3	5	4
4	5	3
4	6	8
5	7	4
5	8	5
5	9	9
6	7	Dummy
6	10	7
7	10	2
8	10	3
9	8	Dummy
9	10	6
10	11	9

(a) If the project is to start at, say, day 0 and is to end as soon as possible, calculate the total float (TF) on each activity and identify the critical path.

(b) Activity 3–5 is 'copy edit the manuscript'.
Activity 6–10 is 'check book cover design'.
The project is begun on day 0 but the publishers discover that the manuscript will not be delivered from the author until week 18, and that the artwork for the book cover will not come from the artist until week 24.
(i) What effect do these deliveries have on the earliest completion date of the project?
(ii) What is the new critical path?

13.8 If certain multiple time estimates are used for the duration of individual jobs in a project, probabilities may be calculated for the completion of the project or part of the project by certain schedule dates.
What are the basic assumptions necessary for such calculations, and how justified are such assumptions in practice?
Under what circumstances is this procedure likely to be beneficial, and in what circumstances are the results likely to be either inaccurate or unrealistic?
Wherever possible, construct numerical examples to illustrate your answer.

13.9 The network diagram shown below has been drawn up by a project planner. The diagram represents the sequence of jobs which will be undertaken during the service of a large component which must be completed by day 35. Using the estimates of the job durations given by the managers of the various departments, the project planner has calculated event dates which indicate that the project will be completed one day before the scheduled completion date.

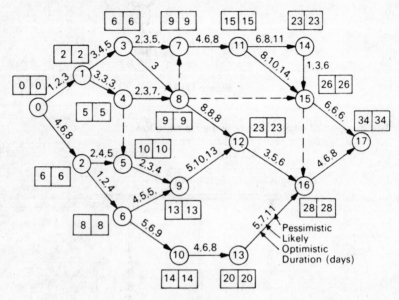

Figure Q13.9

The information given on the diagram has been submitted to you, the project executive, for approval prior to being distributed to the various departments. What are your reactions and why?

13.10 The following table gives the durations of the individual jobs in a complex project and shows the sequential relationship between the jobs. The activities are not listed in order of occurrence and the letters refer to events. It is possible to reduce the durations of some of the jobs to the extent shown in column (4) at an incremental cost per week saved as shown in column (5).

The target time for completing the project is 23 weeks, and the benefits of completion before the target date are estimated at £160 per week saved.

Find the most economical duration for the whole project and the corresponding durations for individual jobs.

(1) Job designation	(2) Prior job(s)	(3) Duration of job (weeks)	(4) Number of weeks by which job can be shortened	(5) Cost of shortening job by 1 week (£)
P–L	—	5	2	120
P–D	—	10	0	—
P–M	—	9	2	80
L–Z	P–L	7	2	100
Z–D	L–Z	0	0	—
Z–Y	L–Z	5	3	50

(1) Job designation	(2) Prior job(s)	(3) Duration of job (weeks)	(4) Number of weeks by which job can be shortened	(5) Cost of shortening job by 1 week (£)
D–Y	L–D P–D M–D Z–D	6	3	80/week for first week, thereafter 100/week
Y–R	Z–Y D–Y	3	1	170
M–R	P–M	10	2	30
M–D	P–M	2	0	—
L–D	P–L	4	3	100

13.11 From the information given below construct a network diagram.
(a) Neglecting resource considerations, what is the earliest finish date for the project?
(b) Assuming that each activity begins as early as possible, construct a graph showing the amount of resources used during each period.
(c) The maximum number of resources available is 19 workers. Again, assuming that activities are begun as soon as possible, redraw the network so that the resources used at any time do not exceed 19 workers and so that a minimum project delay is incurred.
(d) What project delay is incurred through this adherence to the resource limit?

Activity	Immediate predecessor	Duration (days)	Number of workers used
A	—	8	4
B	—	7	8
C	A	6	5
D	B	8	4
E	B	4	8
F	B	8	6
G	CD	5	5
H	E	6	4
I	F	6	5
J	GHI	10	6

NB: Because of the nature of the work, jobs cannot be interrupted and must be finished once begun.

13.12 Unit Construction Ltd is a small company engaged in the manufacture of high-class furniture. About once a year a new product is added to the already extensive range. In the past some difficulty has been experienced in co-ordinating the various activities involved in introducing the new product, so this year it has been decided to draw up an activity network for the entire job. The managing director of the company has described the entire design and 'launching' process as follows, and this information is to be used in constructing the activity network:

Basic designs are prepared by our furniture design department, following which detailed drawings are produced and several prototypes made. The prototypes are tested in the laboratories, after which it is usually necessary to make minor design modifications.

Preliminary market research is normally begun after the detailed drawings have been produced, but of course full-scale market research cannot be started until after the prototypes have been made. Incidentally, customer reactions uncovered during the full-scale market research are normally included in the final design along with modifications resulting from prototype laboratory testing. The main purpose of full-scale market research is to establish (1) the likely demand for the product—information which is required before we can begin to tool-up for production or lay out the factory for manufacture, and (2) the nature of press adverts and TV commercials (we always do both).

Final design details are required before these two types of advertisement can be designed. Following the preparations of the TV film and the press copy, both sets of advertisements are approved by myself, then released. Copies of the press adverts are sent to the showroom for point-of-sale advertising.

Once a final design has been established, the prototypes are modified and sent to our showroom where displays are established. When these displays are established and copies of the press adverts have been received, the showroom manager designs the final display. The display material is made by the showroom artists and should, of course, be ready in time for the delivery of the products to the showroom.

13.13 The diagram given below shows the sequence and interdependence of the eleven activities (A–K) which together are necessary in the launch of a new product. Each of the circles represents an activity and the arrows show the interdependence of these activities. This type of diagram is known variously as an *activity on node, precedence,* or *circle and link* diagram and is sometimes adopted in preference to the more usual *activity on arrow* diagram when using network analysis.

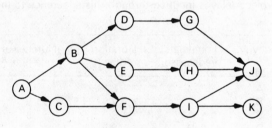

Figure Q13.13

Activity	Duration (days)	Workers required
A	2	4
B	4	3
C	3	6
D	5	5
E	6	7
F	3	4
G	4	6
H	7	8
I	6	3
J	8	7
K	4	10

The durations (in days) of each of the activities are given in the table. Also given are the numbers of workers required to complete each activity in the given time.

(a) Either using the type of diagram given or redrawing the diagram in the conventional form, calculate the earliest completion date for the project, identify the critical path and calculate the total float on each activity. (Assume that the project is begun at day 0.)

(b) Assuming (i) that each activity is begun as soon as possible, and (ii) that each activity once begun cannot be interrupted, draw a table to indicate the labour requirements for each day during the project.

(c) What are the advantages of the *activity on node* type of network construction over the more conventional method?

13.14 This morning the following information collected by the previous company network analyst on the installation of new operations facilities was presented to you. Make a full analysis and propose a work schedule for the project. Report on what actions may be necessary to ensure that the facilities are ready for the September/October production peak this year.

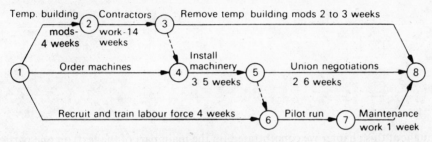

Figure Q13.14

The machines were ordered on 1 January, with a six months delivery promise. The plant manager requires a one-week or two-week pilot production run, extending to at least three weeks if building modification work is in progress. The engineering department is to produce sub-nets for the temporary building modification and their removal, and machine installation. Approximate durations which assume that these three jobs do not overlap are given, together with other durations on the skeleton network.

13.15 Construct an activity on node network from the following data, and then draw a Gantt chart equivalent to the network, using earliest dates. Show any float which exists on activities on the Gantt chart.

Activity	Predecessors	Duration (hours)
A	—	7
B	A	4
C	A	5
D	B, E	3
E	C	8
F	C	9
G	F	2
H	C, D	6

APPENDIX TO CHAPTER 13

'Activity on Node' Diagrams

Throughout this chapter we concentrated (in the main part of the text) on one particular method of constructing network diagrams, the method in which activities or jobs are represented by arrows. i.e. the *arrow diagram* or *activity on arrow* method. An alternative approach represents activities or jobs by circles or nodes, and is known variously as the *activity on node*, *precedence*, or *circle and link* method. For example, the two arrow diagrams shown in Figure 13.44 can be redrawn as the activity on node diagrams shown in Figure 13.45.

The advantages of this type of network construction, which nevertheless is not generally adopted (except in flow process design—see Chapter 15), are:

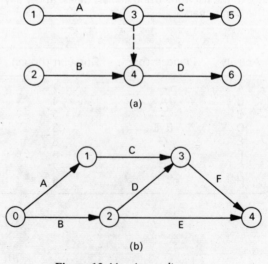

(a)

(b)

Figure 13.44 *Arrow diagrams.*

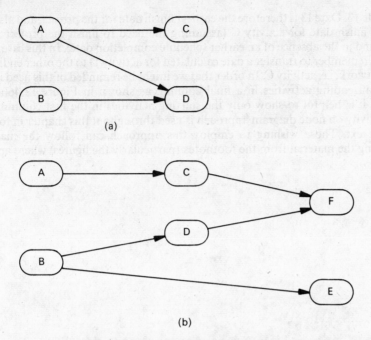

(a)

(b)

Figure 13.45 *Activity on node diagrams.*

1. The diagrams are simpler both to construct and to interpret, mainly because it is unnecessary to use dummies.
2. The diagrams are easy to modify.
3. Description of activities by a single number rather than a pair of numbers is possible.

Network calculations are performed in much the same manner as described in the main part of the text. For example, consider the simple network shown in Figure 13.45(a). Given the duration of each of the activities, the earliest and latest start and finish dates can be calculated (see Figure 13.46).

Notice that with activity on node networks there is often no single point on the network to represent the start or the finish point. For example, in Figure 13.46 the project is complete when C and D are finished. C can be finished by date 9, but D cannot be finished

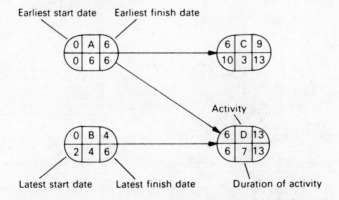

Figure 13.46 *Network calculations for activity on node diagrams.*

before date 13. Date 13 is therefore the earliest finish date for the project, and also becomes the latest finish date for activity C (assuming the need to finish the project as soon as possible and in the absence of an earlier schedule completion date). In this case, therefore, we had to remember to transfer a date calculated for activity D to the other ending activity for the network, i.e. activity C. In order that we might be reminded of this need it is helpful to show all ending activities in a final column, as shown in Figure 13.46(a) and (b). Similarly, it is helpful to show only the starting activities in the first column.

The activity on node diagram approach is used throughout this chapter in footnotes to the main text. Those wishing to employ this approach can follow the main text by substituting the material from the footnotes (particularly the figures) where appropriate.

CHAPTER 14

Scheduling for Batch Processing

B	Buffer stock
c	Allowable increase (proportion) of C over $C*$
C	Total cost of set-up and holding
C_1	Stock-holding cost/item/unit of time
C_2	Shortage cost/item/unit of time
C_{1i}	Stock-holding cost/item i/unit of time
C_s	Set-up or preparation cost/batch
C_{si}	Set-up cost/batch item i
$C*$	Minimum total cost
GT	Group technology
LOB	Line of balance
N	Number of complete processing cycles
q	Processing rate
q^1	Actual batch size/$Q*$
q_i	Processing rate for item i
Q	Batch size
$Q*$	Optimum batch size
Q_i	Batch size for item i
Q_i*	Optimum batch size for item i
r	Consumption rate
r_i	Consumption rate for item i
t	Processing cycle time
$t*$	Optimum processing cycle time
T_p	Processing period for a batch

In the previous chapter we discussed planning in relation to project operations. In the next chapter scheduling for repetitive operations will be discussed. Both types of systems are comparatively easy to describe since, in both cases, reference can be made to their *pure* forms, i.e. the processing of unit quantities of different types of items or customers, and the

405

continual processing of a single type of item or customer respectively. Since batch processing exists between these two extremes it is more difficult to envisage and describe. It is unlike flow processing, since the operating system must deal with a variety of types of items or customers and the processing rate is not normally equal to the demand rate; and it is unlike project systems since a greater variety of types of items or customers must be dealt with.

BATCH PROCESSING SITUATIONS

Although batch processing tends to be associated with batch manufacture, it will exist in other types of operating systems. A batch flow system might exist in supply, in that the function might seek to transfer items from input stock to customers in batches rather than in unit quantities. For example, where the cost of supply, i.e. transfer from input stock to customer, is high there may be some benefit in dealing with several customers at one time given the possibility of accumulating 'customers' for particular types of item. Equally, in supply systems which operate without input stocks, i.e. in which items are acquired for particular customers, there may be benefits in operating on a batch processing system. The acquisition and sale of shares, some commodities, etc., is undertaken in this way. In service systems customers may be processed in batches. For example, certain entertainment services operate in this way in that the service is provided when a given number or minimum number of customers are available. Such a situation might exist in systems in which resources are stocked, as in certain entertainment facilities or in situations which must acquire resources to satisfy customer needs. Likewise certain transport systems might operate on a batch processing arrangement. Transport, for example, might be available only when a certain number of customers have presented themselves. Thus a function might be triggered by the growth of the queue of customers to or beyond a certain minimum limit.

Thus batch processing systems may exist in all four functions and for most system structures. A common characteristic is the need to identify appropriate batch sizes at which the function is triggered. Equally there is usually a need to utilize the resources within the system for the processing of the different types of item or customer; indeed, it is because the available resources normally provide capacity in excess of that required for a particular type of item or customer that batch working is employed; thus, between the times at which particular items are processed, facilities may be used for processing different items or customers. In manufacture, batch processing might be employed in systems which have output stocks, i.e. batches of items are produced in anticipation of demand. Also the batch processing method might be employed in the manufacture of items to order, providing, of course, orders are received for sufficiently similar items. (See 'Group Technology in Manufacture' later in this chapter.)

For transport and service systems it is likely that batch processing can be employed only where customer input queues exist, since it is unlikely that batches of customers will present themselves to the organization but rather that they will be allowed to accumulate over time. In all cases, of course, the use of batch processing at the expense of customer waiting or queuing time is feasible only in certain market situations, while the use of batch processing to provide a stock of items in anticipation of demand will be appropriate in circumstances where customer waiting or queuing is to be minimized.

Much of what will be discussed in this chapter will relate to and overlap with that introduced in Chapter 17 on inventory management. Many of the problems of planning for batch processing are similar to those involved in inventory management, and in general, detailed treatments, particularly of more sophisticated aspects, will be covered in Chapter 17.

BATCH PROCESSING DECISIONS

In general the planning of batch processing requires the solution of three problems:

(a) batch sequencing, i.e. the determination of the order in which batches of different items (or customers) will be processed;
(b) the determination of batch sizes, i.e. the quantity of each type of item (or customer) to be processed at one time;
(c) batch scheduling, i.e. the timing of the processing of batches of items (or customers).

Table 14.1 gives examples of batch processing in manufacture, supply, transport and service systems. The common features of all such batch processing situations are: (a) the processing of different types of items (or customers) on a common set of facilities; and (b) a processing rate for each type of item (or customer) which is greater than the demand or usage rate. The table also indicates where each of the three basic batch processing decisions will be required. Notice that in all cases the batch size decision will be needed.

Table 14.1 *Examples of batch processing*

Operating system function	Examples of batch processing situation	1. Determine sequence of batches	2. Determine batch sizes	3. Determine schedule for batches
A Manufacture and B Supply	I Make (or supply) several items, each in predetermined quantities for output stocks, to satisfy future customers' demands	Yes	Yes	Yes
	II Make (or supply) several items, each in predetermined quantities, for known customers, but only when enough customers have been obtained (i.e. without output stocks)	Probably	Yes	Probably
C Transport and D Service	I Transport (or service) customers in predetermined quantities, each batch drawn from a larger number of customers in a queue	Probably	Yes	Probably
	II As I, but taking an entire queue when it reaches the predetermined quantity	No	Yes	No

Figure 14.1 illustrates the manner in which batch processing systems can operate. Consider first Figure 14.1(a)(1), which shows changes in an output stock over a period of time. At time 0 the processing of a batch begins and items are delivered continually into the output stock. Simultaneously items are consumed from that output stock, but since the processing rate is greater than the consumption rate the stock builds up to a level X. At time 1 processing finishes, the batch having been completed. During period 1–2 consumption only occurs, so the stock is depleted to time 2, at which point the processing of a further batch must begin. This type of situation might exist in manufacture where items are made in predetermined quantities for output stock. Referring to Table 14.1, this type of situation might describe examples AI and AII and the less common examples BI and BII.

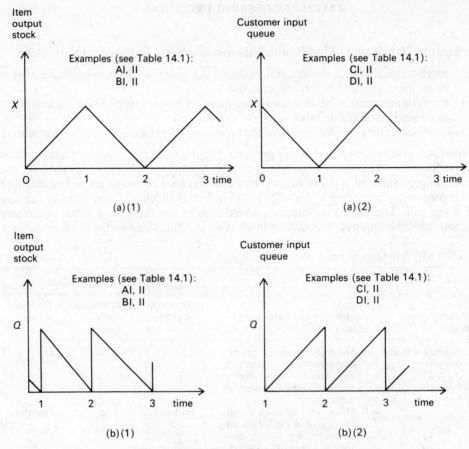

Figure 14.1 *Types of batch processing.*

Referring now to Figure 14.1(b)(1), here at time 1 a complete batch of items is delivered into stock, and then from time 1 to time 2 only consumption takes place and thus stock is depleted to a level at time 2 at which a further batch must be delivered. Unlike the situation in Figure 14.1(a)(1), processing takes place instantaneously. This is less likely to exist in practice, but could describe a situation (Table 14.1) similar to examples AI, AII, BI and BII where the batch of items is processed instantaneously, or where no items are released from the process until the entire batch is completed.

Both the above cases apply to situations in which items are processed for an *output stock*. In transport and service customers exist on the input side of the function. Here input stocks of customers may build up, and then be depleted as batches are processed through the system. If we take, for example, Figure 14.1(a)(2), in the period 0–1 the input stock, i.e. the waiting queue of customers, falls, since during this period customers or items are being taken from the queue to be processed at a greater rate than that at which they arrive. From 1 to 2 the processing stops and the input queue of customers builds up. Such a situation might exist in examples CI, CII, DI and DII (Table 14.1), where items or customers are taken from stock continually during the processing of a given quantity or batch of items. Where items are taken from the input queue in a complete batch for processing, the situation shown in Figure 14.1(b)(2) will exist. Here during period 1–2 the queue will build up, since no processing is taking place. Instantaneously at time 2 an entire batch of customers is taken from the queue for processing, thus the queue falls by that batch quantity, only to build up again during period 2–3.

Clearly, in each of the situations shown in Figure 14.1, there will be some need to determine the *size of the batch* to be processed. The size of the batch will influence the average stock level. Thus, for example, in Fig. 14.1(b) the maximum stock level shown is in fact equal to the batch quantity. Thus for larger batch sizes the average stock level will increase, and be equal to the batch processing size divided by two. In Figure 14.1(a) the maximum stock quantity is less than the batch processing size, since consumption takes place simultaneously with processing. Nevertheless, an increase in batch size will increase the stock level. Thus the principal penalty of processing larger batches is the need to hold larger stocks and thus incur larger stock-holding costs, whether these be the costs of output stocks or the costs of customer input queues. However, in processing larger batches, for a given demand fewer batches must be processed over a given period of time. Since the processing of one batch will incur certain set-up costs, the use of larger batches will incur lower set-up costs over a period of time. In other words, the problem of determining the batch size is that of determining the best balance to strike in the cost of stock-holding and the cost of set-up.

In a typical batch processing situation several different types of items or customers are to be processed on one set of facilities. In these circumstances a batch set-up cost may be influenced not only by the type of item which is to be processed, but by the type of item which the facility was previously set up to process. Thus the set-up cost may be a function of batch sequence. In these circumstances it will be appropriate to try to determine the sequence which minimizes the total cost of set-up over a period of time. Where this situation exists, the batch sequence must be determined *before* determining batch sizes, since not until the batch sequence is determined can the cost of set-up be found, and the cost of set-up is required in order to determine the batch size (see above).

Also, in most cases, it will be necessary to determine the timing for the processing of batches of different items, i.e. the time at which each batch process is to begin. This problem is also related to that of batch size determination, since with a larger batch size, for a given demand, fewer batches must be produced, thus the intervals between processing will be greater. Conversely, for a smaller batch size, with a given demand, the intervals between the processing of batches will be smaller.

We shall deal with these three interrelated problems in the following sections. We shall deal first with the problem of batch sequencing before considering the determination of batch sizes and the batch scheduling problem. Throughout we shall concentrate on the types of situations shown in Figure 14.1(a)(1) and 14.1(b)(1). These are the more common batch processing situations; however, the formulae which we shall develop will also be relevant to the types of situations shown in Figure 14.1(a)(2) and 14.1(b)(2).

BATCH SEQUENCING *(see also Chapter 15)*

It is possible that the cost of setting up, i.e. preparing, a set of facilities for the processing of a particular batch of items or customers will depend not only on the type of items or customers to be processed in that batch, but also on the type which was previously processed on the same facilities. Thus, for example, if, among other items, two very similar types of items (A and B) are to be processed in batches on a set of facilities, the cost of changing the set-up of facilities from that which is appropriate for processing item A to that which is appropriate for processing item B may be relatively low compared with the cost of changing the set-up from that appropriate for processing either of these types of items to that appropriate for processing quite a different type of item. Here the set-up cost is a function of the sequence of items, and it is appropriate to try to determine the appropriate sequence in order to minimize total set-up costs. Thus if four types of items, A, B, C and D, are to be processed in batches on a common set of facilities, and the set-up cost for each batch is influenced by the type of item which was previously processed on the facilities, and where that cost is known, an optimum sequence for these four items can be determined to minimize total set-up cost for the processing of a batch of each of the four types of items. The assumption here, of course, is that each batch must be processed the same number of times, i.e. that a repetitive sequence involving one batch of each item can be established. This is the normal situation, and a solution can often be found using the assignment method of linear programming, which is described in Appendix I. (The problem is identical to that of determining the optimum sequence for batches of items to be processed on a mixed-model repetitive/flow processing system. This is described in Chapter 15.)

Processing 'families' of items

A situation might exist in which several different types of item each require a similar, but not identical, set-up, while other items which must be processed on the facility require a different type of set-up. In this situation those items which require the same type of set-up may be seen as a 'family' of similar items. It will be sensible when setting up the facilities to process a batch of any one of the items in the family to take advantage of that set-up and process a batch of all the other items within the family, especially where the cost of the set-up is relatively high.

For example, in the situation shown in Table 14.2, the set-up costs incurred between the processing of items B, C and D are small whereas the cost of setting up the process between either A or E and any of the family B, C and D is relatively high. In this case, therefore, there will be some merit in processing the 'family' of items B, C and D in succession, possibly in the order C, B, D, with the other two items produced at another time, possibly in the order A, E. In fact the sequencing problem shown in Table 14.2 is an example of the type of situation which *cannot* be solved using the assignment method referred to above; this is because of the configuration of the cost within the matrix. In such cases, particularly where a 'family' of items exist, an alternative approach will be required.

One approach to the solution of the 'family' sequencing problem is as follows:

1. Identify the items within a 'family'.
2. Determine the 'processing cycle' for these items (i.e. the time interval between the successive processings of the family) together with the batch quantity for each item.
3. Determine the optimum sequence for the remaining items and process these items as required between families.

Table 14.2

Preceding item	Succeeding item				
	A	B	C	D	E
A	0	100	90	110	60
B	105	0	10	5	60
C	95	20	0	25	70
D	100	15	10	0	80
E	70	75	80	75	0

The procedure for determining the optimum processing cycle for a set of items is given later in this chapter.

(Notice that the 'family' processing problem has some similarities with the approach discussed in the section on group technology later in this chapter.)

DETERMINATION OF BATCH SIZES *(see also Chapter 17)*

The normal approach here is to seek to determine batch sizes which in some way minimize total cost. Certainly other approaches exist, e.g. maximization of profits, but the cost minimization approach is the most important, and is the only approach which will be dealt with in this chapter.

Batch quantities which are too large will result in high stock levels and cause a large amount of capital to be tied up in stock which might otherwise be invested elsewhere. Additionally, unduly high stock levels with incur other costs, such as the cost of stock-keeping, insurance and depreciation. On the other hand, batch quantities which are too small will result in the need for a large number of batches to be processed for a given period of time and thus incur large set-up costs.

Perhaps the most important point to note is that in practice batch sizes are rarely constant. It will often be appropriate to 'split' batches during processing and/or to use a batch size which differs from the theoretical optimum. Our discussion of batch sizes should be taken in this context and the formulae which are developed should be used with discretion rather than rigidly.

Figure 14.2 shows the relationship of these costs to batch size. Clearly the problem is to determine the batch size which minimizes total variable costs. Our aim is to determine the economic batch size Q^* associated with minimum total variable cost C^*.

We shall deal first with *deterministic* situations in which demand, etc., is considered to be known and to be constant. We shall deal with three such situations, as shown in Figure 14.3.

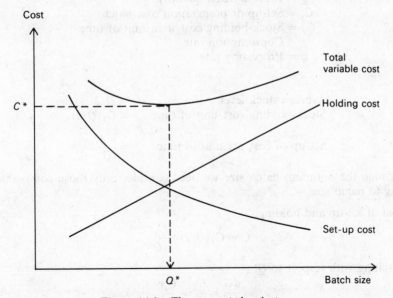

Figure 14.2 *The economic batch size.*

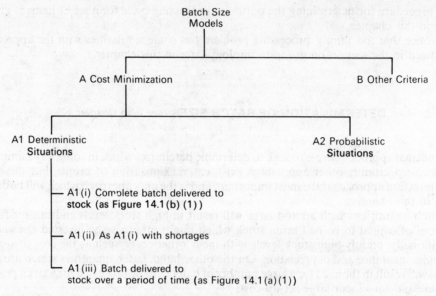

Figure 14.3 *Batch size models.*

A1: Deterministic situations

A1(i): Complete batch delivered to stock, as Figure 14.1(b)(i)

Our notation is as follows:

Q = Process batch quantity
C_s = Set-up or preparation cost/batch
C_1 = Stock-holding cost/item/unit of time
r = Consumption rate
q = Processing rate

Then:

Average stock level $= Q/2$
Stock-holding cost/unit of time $= C_1(Q/2)$

Set-up of cost per unit of time $= \dfrac{C_s r}{Q}$

To determine the optimum batch size we need consider only those costs which vary according to batch size.

Total cost of set-up and holding:

$$C = C_1(Q/2) + \frac{C_s r}{Q} \tag{1}$$

Differentiating with respect to Q:

$$\frac{\mathrm{d}C}{\mathrm{d}Q} = \frac{C_1}{2} - \frac{C_s r}{Q^2}$$

Equating this to zero to obtain the minimum cost gives:

$$\text{Minimum cost batch size} = Q^* = \sqrt{\frac{2C_s r}{C_1}} \tag{2}$$

Substituting (2) into (1) gives the total cost per unit of time associated with this processing policy, i.e.

$$C^* = \sqrt{2rC_s C_1} \tag{3}$$

Notice also the optimum processing cycle time for this item:

$$t^* = \frac{Q^*}{r}$$

EXAMPLE: WATERTIGHT LTD

Watertight Ltd are the manufacturers of a range of plastic overshoes. The complete range consists of 14 different types (i.e. sizes and styles). Type BB (Big and Black) is sold in the largest quantities, demand being reasonably stable at 4500 pairs per month.

All overshoes are manufactured in batches, the production process being such that the entire batch is completed at the same time.

(a) Given the following information, use the formulae above to determine the economic batch production quantity:

> Machine set-up cost per production batch = £150
> Stock-holding cost per pair   = £3.75 per annum

(b) The present production policy is to manufacture BB overshoes in batch sizes of 3000 pairs at regular intervals. How does the actual production cycle time compare with the optimum production cycle time?

(a)

$$r = 4500 \text{ per month}$$

$$C_s = £150$$

$$C_1 = 3.75 \times \frac{1}{12} = £0.313 \text{ per month}$$

$$\therefore Q^* = \sqrt{\frac{2C_s r}{C_1}} = \sqrt{\frac{2 \times 150 \times 4500}{0.313}}$$

$$= 2077 \text{ pairs}$$

(b)

$$t^* = \frac{Q^*}{r} = \frac{2077}{4500}$$

$$= 0.46 \text{ months}$$

$$\text{Actual } Q = 3000 \text{ pairs}$$

$$\therefore \text{ Actual } t = \frac{Q}{r} = \frac{3000}{4500}$$

$$= 0.67 \text{ months (46 per cent longer interval than optimum policy)}$$

A1(ii): As A1(i) with shortages

One might extend the simple model above to include the possibility of stock shortages or 'stock-outs'. This introduces an additional cost factor, the cost of shortages, C_2. The model, which still assumes known and constant demand, is depicted in Figure 14.4. The areas below the horizontal axis, i.e. periods t_2, represent demand which would have been satisfied had adequate stock been available. The cost of such shortage in terms of loss of profit, etc., must be introduced into the formula, since it will influence the choice of batch size.

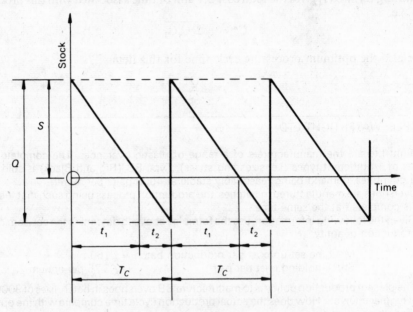

Figure 14.4 *A stock/batch processing model allowing shortages.*

Using the previous notation, plus C_2 = shortage cost/item/unit of time:

$$\text{Stock-holding cost per unit of time} = \frac{S}{2}\left(\frac{t_1}{t_1+t_2}\right)C_1$$

$$= \frac{C_1 S}{2}\left(\frac{S}{Q}\right)$$

$$= \frac{C_1 S^2}{2Q}$$

$$\text{Shortage cost per unit of time} = C_2 \frac{(Q-S)}{2}\left(\frac{t_2}{t_1+t_2}\right)$$

$$= \frac{C_2(Q-S)^2}{2Q}$$

$$\text{Set-up cost per unit of time} = \frac{C_s r}{Q}$$

Total set-up, holding, shortage cost/unit time:

$$C = \frac{C_1 S^2}{2Q} + \frac{C_2(Q-S)^2}{2Q} + \frac{C_s r}{Q} \qquad (1)$$

Differentiating with respect to S:

$$\frac{\partial C}{\partial S} = \frac{SC_1}{Q} - \frac{(Q-S)C_2}{Q}$$

$$= 0 \text{ for maximum or minimum}$$

$$\therefore S^* = \frac{QC_2}{C_1 + C_2} \tag{2}$$

Differentiating with respect to Q:

$$\frac{\partial C}{\partial Q} = \frac{-S^2 C_1}{Q^2} + \left[\frac{4Q(Q-S) - 2(Q-S)^2}{4Q^2}\right] C_2 - \frac{C_s r}{Q^2}$$

$$= 0 \text{ for maximum or minimum}$$

$$Q^* = \sqrt{\frac{2rC_s}{C_1}} \sqrt{\frac{C_1 + C_2}{C_2}} \tag{3}$$

Substituting (3) into (1)

$$C^* = \sqrt{2rC_1 C_s} \sqrt{\frac{C_2}{C_1 + C_2}} \tag{4}$$

EXAMPLE: A SHOE WHOLESALER

$$r = 9500 \text{ per month}$$
$$C_1 = \text{£}5 \text{ per item per annum}$$
$$C_s = \text{£}1250$$
$$C_2 = \text{£}2 \text{ per item per month}$$

(a) Compare the optimum delivery quantities for:
   (i) a policy in which stock-outs are permitted;
   (ii) a policy in which stock-outs must not occur.

(b) What is the maximum set-up cost per batch which can be accepted under policy (ii) if the total cost per month associated with this policy is not to exceed the total cost per month of policy (i)? (Assume all other data above to apply except C_s for policy (ii).)

(a) (i)

$$Q^* = \sqrt{\frac{2C_s r}{C_1}} \sqrt{\frac{C_1 + C_2}{C_2}}$$

$$= \sqrt{\frac{2 \times 1250 \times 9500}{5/12}} \sqrt{\frac{5/12 + 2}{2}}$$

$$= 7550 \times 1.1$$

$$= 8305$$

(ii)

$$Q^* = \sqrt{\frac{2C_s r}{C_1}}$$

$$= 7550$$

(b) (i)

$$C^* = \sqrt{2rC_1 C_s} \sqrt{\frac{C_2}{C_1 + C_2}}$$

$$= \sqrt{\frac{2 \times 9500 \times 5 \times 1250}{12}} \sqrt{\frac{2}{5/12 + 2}}$$

$$= 3146 \times 0.910$$

$$= \text{£}2863 \text{ per month}$$

(ii)
$$£2863 = \sqrt{2rC_sC_1}$$
$$C_s = \frac{2863^2}{2rC_1}$$
$$= \frac{2863^2 \times 12}{2 \times 9500 \times 5}$$

Maximum $C_s = £1035$

A1(iii): Batch delivered to stock over a period of time, as Figure 14.1(a)(ii)

Now instead of considering the total processing batch to be delivered into stock at the same time, we shall consider a situation in which the items which constitute the batch are delivered into stock continuously throughout the process period. (See Figure 14.5.)

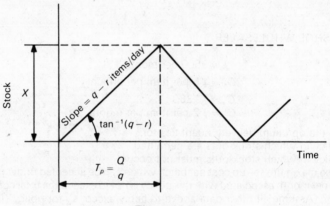

Figure 14.5

We can again calculate optimum batch quantities, etc., as follows (adopting the notation used above):

$$\text{Maximum stock level} = X$$
$$= \frac{Q}{q}(q-r)$$
$$\text{Average inventory} = \frac{Q}{2}[1-(r/q)]$$
$$\therefore \text{Stock-holding cost per unit time} = C_1\left[\frac{Q}{2}(1-(r/q))\right]$$

Total cost of set-up and holding per unit of time:

$$C = \frac{C_1 Q}{2}[1-(r/q)] + \frac{C_s r}{Q} \tag{1}$$

Differentiating with respect to Q:

$$\frac{dC}{dQ} = \frac{-C_s r}{Q^2} + \frac{C_1}{2}[1 - (r/q)]$$

Equating this to zero gives the maximum or minimum point of the function. Hence:

$$\text{Minimum cost batch size} = Q^* = \sqrt{\frac{2C_s r}{C_1[1 - (r/q)]}} \tag{2}$$

The total cost per unit of time associated with this processing policy is given by substituting equation (2) into equation (1):

$$C^* = \sqrt{2rC_s C_1}\sqrt{1 - (r/q)} \tag{3}$$

EXAMPLE: EXPRESS DRINKS COMPANY (1)

A product is sold at a constant rate of 600 per day, the processing rate for the item being 2000 per day. It is known that set-up costs are £10 per batch and that stock-holding costs, including notional loss of interest on capital, are £0.5 per item per year. What is the minimum cost processing batch quantity?

$$C_S = £10$$
$$q = 2000$$
$$r = 600$$

Assuming that there are 250 working days per year:

$$C_1 = \frac{0.5}{250} = £0.002 \text{ per item per day}$$

$$Q^* = \sqrt{\frac{2 \times 10 \times 600}{0.002[1 - (6/20)]}}$$

$$Q^* = 2928$$

A2: Probabilistic situations—dealing with uncertainty

The preceding discussion assumed an entirely deterministic situation, i.e. the assumption was made that all the relevant information for the determination of batch sizes was known with certainty. It was assumed, for example, that the demand rate was known and that it would not change from that known quantity. It was assumed that the production or processing rate was known and was not subject to any variation. Clearly this highly simplified situation may not exist in practice. We must be able to deal with situations in which demand rate varies, production rate varies, and costs are uncertain. These sources of uncertainty are discussed below, their implications are identified, and ways in which they might be accommodated for the planning of batch production are considered.

Uncertainties in costs

The procedures described above seek to determine the economic batch size by balancing the cost of set-up and the cost of stock-holding. If either of these costs is unknown or cannot be estimated accurately enough then these procedures cannot be employed. In determining the formula for economic batch size, etc., it was assumed that the set-up cost, i.e. the cost of preparing for the processing of a particular batch of items, was independent of the batch size. It was further assumed that the stock-holding cost could be expressed as cost per item per unit of time, irrespective of inventory level. In practice both these assumptions may be invalid. It is possible, however, through modifications of the above procedures, to determine the economic batch size where a set-up cost is not constant and where the stock-holding cost is a function of stock quantity. One of these approaches is discussed in Chapter 17.

Rarely will C_s and C_1 be known with certainty. In most cases they must be estimated. Since the objective of the economic batch size procedure is to determine the batch size which corresponds to the minimum total variable cost it will be of interest to identify to what extent the total variable cost is sensitive to changes in batch sizes, etc. This is considered later in the section entitled 'The Production (or Processing) Range'.

Uncertainties in usage or consumption rate (only)

Consider the situation in which only the usage rate is uncertain and the effect that this single source of uncertainty might have on the stock position as shown by diagrams such as those in Figure 14.1

For example, in Figure 14.1(a)(1), the processing of a batch is finished at time 1 and the processing of the next batch is not due to commence until time 2. If the demand between times 1 and 2 is greater than expected then stock will fall to zero before time 2 and a stock-out situation will exist. A similar situation might exist in the type of batch processing shown in Figure 14.1(b)(1). A complete batch is delivered to stock at time 1 and the next batch is due to be delivered at time 2. If demand between times 1 and 2 is greater than expected then again a stock-out situation can exist. The equivalent situations can exist for customer input queue situations, as shown in Figures 14.1(a)(2) and 14.1(b)(2).

One way of protecting against the risk of stock-outs resulting from higher than expected demand is through the use of a buffer stock. Figure 14.6 shows the use of a buffer stock in

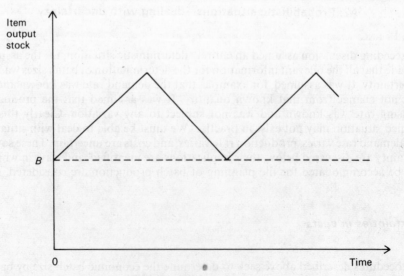

Figure 14.6 *The use of buffer stocks (in the type of batch processing shown in Figure 14.1(a)(1).*

the type of batch processing situation shown in Figure 14.1(a)(1). The buffer stock quantity B is a measure of the degree of protection provided against increases in demand. A large buffer stock reduces the risk of a stock-out situation but of course increases the stock-holding cost, while a lower buffer stock quantity B provides less protection against stock-outs but incurs less stock-holding cost. Whatever the buffer quantity B, the economic batch size can be determined in the same manner as described above and will be unaffected by the value B. However, the use of a buffer stock together with the economic batch size approach which employs a formula assuming constant demand should be employed with caution (see below).

For the batch processing system shown in Figure 14.6:

Total cost of set-up and stock-holding/unit of time, C

$$= C_1 B + \frac{C_1 Q}{2}\left[1 - \left(\frac{r}{q}\right)\right] + \frac{C_s r}{Q} \tag{1}$$

Differentiating with reference to Q:

$$\frac{dC}{dQ} = \frac{-C_s r}{Q^2} + \frac{C_1}{2}\left[1 - \left(\frac{r}{q}\right)\right]$$

hence

$$Q^* = \sqrt{\frac{2C_s r}{C_1\left[1 - \left(\frac{r}{q}\right)\right]}} \tag{2}$$

(as before). But, substituting (2) into (1) gives:

$$C^* = \sqrt{2rC_s C_1}\sqrt{1 - \left(\frac{r}{q}\right)} + C_1 B$$

Similarly, a buffer stock can be used to protect against fluctuations in demand or usage in the type of batch processing in which complete batches of items are delivered to stock (Figure 14.1(b)(1), and again if the economic order quantity is determined using the previous approach, it is not influenced by B but, of course, the minimum total variable cost associated with this batch size is increased by the cost of the buffer quantity multiplied by the holding cost ($C_1 B$).

Where a buffer stock is used the buffer quantity will be determined by reference to two factors:

(a) the extent of the variation in demand or usage, possibly expressed as a standard deviation about a mean demand;
(b) the degree of protection required in stock-outs, possibly expressed as the maximum probability or risk of stock-out which can be tolerated.

It may be possible, however, to protect against uncertain demand without having to use a buffer stock. For example, if arrangements can be made for stock to be replenished immediately the stock level falls to zero then no buffer stock is required even though the rate at which stock is depleted is unknown. Quite often it will not be possible to arrange for stock to be replenished, or for stock replenishment to begin, at a given time. For example, there may be a delay (or lead time) between the making of a decision to replenish stock and the time at which the first items or the complete batch are received into stock. If that lead time is known for certain then it may be possible to accommodate uncertainties in demand without the use of buffer stocks, but more often the lead time will be uncertain. In these circumstances we must protect against uncertain demand and lead time. In this, the normal situation, the problem is that of accommodating *uncertain lead time usage*. Again a buffer stock approach will be appropriate, and this approach is discussed in detail in Chapter 17.

We have seen that buffer stocks can be used to protect against usage variations and variations in lead time without the need to modify the batch quantity. Remember, however, that the determination of batch quantity assumes a known usage rate. If the variation in usage about a mean rate is not great, and there is no overall trend towards increasing or reducing usage, it is still possible, without introducing substantial errors, to determine the batch size as discussed above for the deterministic situation and to use in conjunction with that approach a buffer stock strategy to protect against demand/lead time uncertainties. This will be the normal approach in the management of batch processing where the need to begin the processing of a batch is 'triggered' *at a particular inventory level*. In other words, where the scheduling, i.e. the timing, of the processing of batches is determined by the inventory level, this approach will be appropriate. In these situations therefore there will be no fixed or regular interval between the processing of batches. (This type of situation is directly analogous to the re-order level (or perpetual) inventory control system described in Chapter 17).

There is an alternative approach to the scheduling of batch processing which relies on the processing of batches of items or customers at predetermined or *fixed intervals of time*. Such an approach will often be necessary where the processing of several different items or customers on common facilities uses most of the capacity of those facilities. In these circumstances it will be necessary to plan ahead in order to ensure that the requisite number of each item is processed over a period of time without the penalties of under-utilization of capacity at certain times, and insufficient capacity and hence the need to subcontract at other times. (Such an approach is directly analogous to the re-order interval (or periodic) method of inventory control described in Chapter 17.) For this type of system a somewhat different approach will be required to accommodate demand uncertainties since, in the circumstances, it may not be possible to determine a fixed optimum batch quantity for each item being processed. This situation is discussed in detail in Chapter 16.

Processing rate uncertainties

One type of batch processing involves the processing and consumption of items simultaneously over a period of time (Figure 14.1(a)(1) and (2)). In determining the economic batch size for this situation it was assumed not only that usage was constant, but also that the processing rate was known and constant. Such a 'simple' situation may not exist in practice because, as we have seen, usage may be uncertain, but also because the processing rate may be affected by the breakdown of equipment, wastage rates, or the need for reprocessing. In general the level of uncertainty associated with the processing rate will be less than that associated with usage. However, it can be an additional source of uncertainty. Hence there can be a risk that a stock-out situation might occur or be aggravated because less than the expected quantity of items were delivered to stock. Equally, a variation in processing rate may offset a variation in usage rate.

A similar situation may exist in batch processing situations in which complete batches of items are delivered into stock. In these cases there may be some uncertainties in the delivered quantity; thus, for example, stock may be replenished to a lower level than had been expected, and therefore a stock-out situation can occur or be made worse.

Both these situations can again be accommodated along with or in the absence of uncertainties in usage by using a buffer stock type of approach as outlined above.

The production (or processing) range

Because of the frequent difficulty of accurately establishing costs such as C_1 and C_s it is fortunate that the total cost curve (see Figure 14.2) is fairly flat at the point of minimum cost, since this means that the total variable cost is not very sensitive to deviations from optimal batch size. It is possible, therefore, to adopt a batch size which differs slightly from the optimal without incurring substantially increased costs. This feature of the total cost curve gives rise to the 'production range' concept. Batch quantities within this range are considered as acceptable. In Figure 14.7 the production range is between Q_1 and Q_2, corresponding to a maximum increase in cost from the minimum C^* to C.

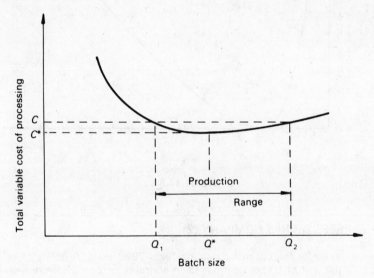

Figure 14.7 *Economic batch size.*

Eilon[1] has developed a procedure for the determination of an acceptable processing range which is dependent on knowing the allowable increase in the total variable costs of production, c. Thus:

$$c = \frac{\text{Actual variable costs per unit}}{\text{Minimum variable costs per unit}}$$

and let:

$$q^1 = \frac{\text{Actual batch size}}{\text{Minimum cost batch size}}$$

It can be shown that:

$$q^1 = c \pm \sqrt{c^2 - 1} \qquad (1)$$

and thus the two limits of 'production' range are:

$$Q_1 = Q^*(c - \sqrt{c^2 - 1}) = Q^* q_1^1$$
$$Q_2 = Q^*(c + \sqrt{c^2 - 1}) = Q^* q_2^1$$

[1] Eilon, S. (1969) *Elements of Production Planning and Control*. London: Collier-Macmillan.

The values of q_1^1 and q_2^1 can be found by using formula (1) or from the curve given in Figure 14.8, and the production range can then be calculated.

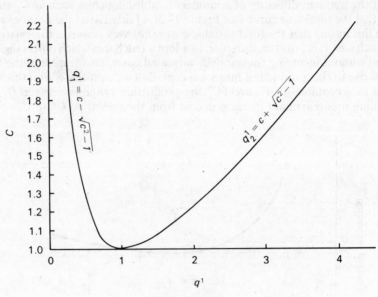

Figure 14.8

EXAMPLE: EXPRESS DRINKS COMPANY (2)

In our previous example the optimal batch size was 2928 units. A policy of an allowable increase in cost per unit of 10 per cent has been adopted, i.e. $c = 1.1$. From Figure 14.8:

$$q_1^1 = 0.64$$
$$q_2^1 = 1.56$$
$$Q_1 = Q^* q_1^1 = 2928(0.64) = 1874$$
$$Q_2 = Q^* q_2^1 = 2928(1.56) = 4568$$

SCHEDULING FOR BATCH PROCESSING *(see also Chapter 12)*

Having now decided the batch size for each item which is to be processed on a common set of facilities, and the sequence or order in which those items will be processed, we must consider the timing of the processing of these batches.

Given the processing batch size Q and the consumption rate r, the processing cycle time t can be determined as follows:

$$t = \frac{Q}{r}$$

Thus for a batch size of 100 items with a production rate of 400 items/month the processing cycle time will be 1/4 month (i.e. approximately one week). Therefore a batch of size 100 must be manufactured each week.

In fact, as shown previously, the processing cycle time for the optimum batch quantity Q^* can be determined directly and can be shown, for the three situations which were dealt with in this chapter, to be as follows, where $t^* = $ optimum.

Processing cycle time (i.e. interval between starting the processing of successive batches of one type of item)

A1(i) $\quad t^* = \sqrt{\dfrac{2C_s}{rC_1}}$

A1(ii) $\quad t^* = \sqrt{\dfrac{2C_s}{rC_1}}\sqrt{\dfrac{C_1 + C_2}{C_2}}$

$\left.\begin{array}{l}\\ \\ \\ \\ \\ \end{array}\right\}$ assuming deterministic situation (e.g. see Figure 14.3)

A1(iii) $\quad t^* = \sqrt{\dfrac{2C_s}{rC_1\left[1 - \left(\dfrac{r}{q}\right)\right]}}$

The schedule for the processing of batches of items can be determined in the above fashion, but this approach takes each item separately. No consideration is given to the fact that because of limited capacity on a set of facilities, there may, for example, not be enough time available to process each item in the optimum batch quantity at the optimum production cycle. Where there is considerable excess capacity such an approach may be appropriate, but where capacity is limited a somewhat different approach will be necessary, since in these situations the multi-batch schedule problem occurs.

As an illustration of the batch scheduling problem consider a situation in which only two items (A and B) are to be processed successively on the same equipment. The economic (minimum cost) batch quantity for each item has been calculated by use of one of the previous formulae and the processing schedule is shown in Figure 14.9. In this case there is no idle time on the equipment and the optimum and individually calculated processing policies for the two batches do not clash, so we must think ourselves particularly lucky. Quite easily we could have found ourselves in a far from ideal situation in which, for example, the sum of the processing times for the batches of items was either greater or less than the time available. Alternatively a situation might have resulted in which processing of successive batches of one item was constrained to take place at greater than the desired interval and consequently stocks of that item would fall to a level below the desirable safety

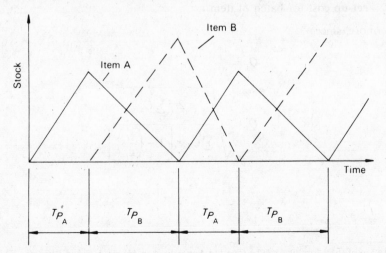

Figure 14.9 *Successive processing of batches of A and B on the same equipment: ideal situation.*

or buffer stock level. Any of these situations is quite likely to arise if, in a multi-item situation, we attempt to calculate batch sizes and processing cycles for items individually and without reference to their effect on one another.

Very often the order or sequence in which the different items are to be processed will be determined either by the process itself or by the setting-up or preparation requirements for each item. For example, in a paint-manufacturing process it is desirable to manufacture lighter colours first and darker colours later. In the manufacture of engineering components, the order in which batches of items are manufactured is often determined by the change-over costs of jigs and tools. In such cases the only problems to be solved are the desirable length of the complete manufacturing cycle (i.e. the time required to manufacture one batch of all the products) and the frequency of the cycles.

The problem is to find the most economical cycle, i.e. that which minimizes set-up and holding or inventory costs. As before, the set-up costs increase and the holding costs decrease as the number of cycles increases.

It is clear from the foregoing discussion that to obtain a satisfactory solution the cycle time for all items must be set simultaneously. Furthermore, the processing and consumption rates for each item in the sequence must be expressed in common units. The unit normally used is 'hours of processing'; hence consumption is expressed as 'hours of processing used per unit of time'. Of course, using this convention the process rate for all items will be the same.

When a number of items are to be processed successively, and when processing is of the type shown in Figure 14.9, the total number of complete cycles per unit time, N, is given by the following formula:[2]

$$N = \sqrt{\frac{\sum_i C_{1i} r_i \left[1 - \left(\frac{r_i}{q_i} \right) \right]}{2 \sum_i C_{Si}}}$$

where N = number of complete processing cycles per unit time, each consisting of the processing of a batch item

r_i = consumption rate for item i

q_i = production rate for item i

C_{1i} = holding cost/unit of time for item i

C_{Si} = set-up cost for batch of item i

Furthermore, since:

$$Q_i = \frac{r_i}{N}$$

$$Q_i = \sqrt{\frac{2 r_i^2 \sum_i C_{S_i}}{\sum_i C_{1i} r_i \left[1 - \left(\frac{r_i}{q_i} \right) \right]}}$$

---

[2] The derivation of these formulae can be found in Appendix A in Magee, J. F. and Boodman, D. M. (1967) *Production Planning and Inventory Control.* London: McGraw-Hill.

EXAMPLE

Four items, A, B, C and D, are to be processed successively in batches on the same facility. The consumption and process rates, batch set-up and item holding costs for each product are shown in Table 14.3. To use the formula, the processing and consumption rates for all items must be expressed in common units. The unit used will be 'days of processing per year'. If there are 250 working days per year, then the new consumption rates can be calculated; e.g. for item A, with a processing rate of 250/day, 40 days' processing are needed per year to satisfy an annual consumption of 10 000.

Table 14.3

Item	Consumption per year	Processing rate per day	Holding cost per item per year ($£$)	Set-up cost of batch ($£$)
A	10 000	250	0.005	10
B	5 000	100	0.005	5
C	8 000	200	0.010	8
D	12 000	300	0.008	6

Notice also that the holding cost must also be related to 'days of processing', e.g. for item A, C_1 is $250 \times 0.005 = 1.25$, i.e. the holding cost for a day's processing of item A per year. The process rate for each item is the same, since, in each case, it requires one day to process one unit of each (i.e. one day's processing). The rescaled figures are shown in Table 14.4.

Table 14.4

Item	r_i	q_i	C_1	C_s
A	40	250	1.25	10
B	50	250	0.50	5
C	40	250	2.00	8
D	40	250	2.40	6

The consumption rate (r_A) for item A is 40 in the new units because days at 250 per day are necessary to process 10 000. Similarly:

$$r_B = \frac{5000}{100} = 50, \text{ etc.}$$

Referring now to the formula for N:

Table 14.5

Item	$\dfrac{r_i}{q_i}$	$1 - \dfrac{r_i}{q_i}$	$C_1 r_i$	$C_1 r_i\left[1 - \left(\dfrac{r_i}{q_i}\right)\right]$	C_{Si}
A	0.16	0.84	50	42	10
B	0.20	0.80	25	20	5
C	0.16	0.84	80	67.2	8
D	0.16	0.84	96	80.6	6
				$\sum C_1 r_i\left[1 - \left(\dfrac{r_i}{q_i}\right)\right]$	$\sum C_{Si}$
				$= 209.8$	$= 29$

Hence:

$$N = \sqrt{\frac{209.8}{2 \times 29}}$$

$$N = 1.9 \text{ cycles/year}$$

Consequently, for minimum cost, 1.9 complete runs per year should be made. Each complete cycle will consist of four batches as follows:

$$Q_A = \frac{r_A}{N} = \frac{10\,000}{1.9} = 5250 \text{ items}$$

$$Q_B = \frac{r_B}{N} = \frac{5000}{1.9} = 2630 \text{ items}$$

$$Q_C = \frac{r_C}{N} = \frac{8000}{1.9} = 4220 \text{ items}$$

$$Q_D = \frac{r_D}{N} = \frac{12\,000}{1.9} = 6300 \text{ items}$$

and each complete run lasting:

$$t_A = \frac{5250}{250} = 21.0 \text{ days}$$

$$t_B = \frac{2630}{100} = 26.3 \text{ days}$$

$$t_C = \frac{4220}{200} = 21.1 \text{ days}$$

$$t_D = \frac{6300}{300} = 21.0 \text{ days}$$

89.4 days

Since the process rate for each product is such that total annual consumption or demand can be satisfied by substantially less than one year's processing, unless consumption is increased or additional items are manufactured, equipment will spend some time idle each year.

THE LINE OF BALANCE TECHNIQUE

Our previous discussion has taken for granted the fact that batch processing proceeds in a series of steps. For example, we have assumed that in a process consisting of several operations, 1, 2, 3, etc., the entire batch is completed on operation 1 before being passed to operation 2, and so on. This type of situation is desirable to some extent, since it provides easier operations control. On the other hand, there are disadvantages in this iterative type of procedure. For example, the throughput time for any batch will be high, the work-in-progress will be high and, consequently, a large amount of storage space will be required. Ideally, therefore, we must look for a procedure in which batches of items might be divided, i.e. processing begun on subsequent operations before the complete batch has been processed on previous operations, and yet a procedure which enables adequate control of operations to be exercised. Such a situation might be desirable in manufacture, supply or service systems in certain conditions.

When batches are kept complete during processing and when an activity schedule for each batch on each operation is available, it is an easy matter to determine whether processing is proceeding according to plan. If the dividing of batches is allowed then the situation is more complex and it is often quite difficult both to establish an activity schedule and to determine whether progress is satisfactory or not. It is difficult, for example, to determine whether, at a given time, sufficient items have completed sufficient operations.

For example, consider the completion schedule shown in Table 14.6. Twelve finished items must be completed at the end of week 1, another fourteen at the end of week 2, and so on. It is clear from this that, at the end of the fifth week, forty items should have completed the final operation. What is not clear, however, is how many items should have passed through the previous operations at this date so as to ensure completion of the required quantity of items in later weeks.

Table 14.6 *Job completion requirements*

Week no.	Delivery of finished items required	Cumulative completions required
0	0	0
1	12	12
2	14	26
3	8	34
4	6	40
5	10	50
6	12	62
7	14	76
8	16	92
9	18	110
10	22	132

The 'line of balance' technique was developed to deal with precisely this type of situation. It originated at the US Goodyear Company in the early 1940s, was developed during the 1950s at the request of the US Department of Defence, and has been used largely by the US Army and Navy.

The line of balance technique is an example of 'management by exception' since it deals only with the important or crucial (exceptional) operations in a job, establishes a schedule or plan for them and attracts attention to those which do not conform to this schedule (those about which something must be done if the progress of the entire job is not to be jeopardized). It is particularly useful where large batches of fairly complex items requiring many operations are to be delivered or completed over a period of time.

The technique can be regarded as a slightly more sophisticated form of the Gantt chart, the objective being to study the progress of jobs at regular intervals, to compare progress on each operation with the progress necessary to satisfy the eventual delivery requirements, and to identify those operations in which progress is unsatisfactory.

We can best describe the technique by means of a simple example. Two pieces of information are required, first the completion requirements and second an operation programme, i.e. the sequence and duration of the various operations. Four stages are involved in the use of the technique:

(a) the completion schedule;
(b) the operation programme;
(c) the programme progress chart;
(d) analysis of progress.

The completion schedule

Construction of the completion schedule is the first step. The cumulative complete requirements must be calculated and presented either as a table (Table 14.5) or, and this is more useful later, as a graph (Figure 14.10), which may also be used to record deliveries in the manner shown.

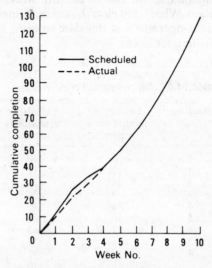

Figure 14.10   *Cumulative completions.*

The operation programme

The operation programme depicts the 'lead time' of the various operations, i.e. the length of time prior to the completion of the final operation by which intermediate operations must be completed.

In a simple job it is possible to show such information for *all* operations in the job, but in more complex jobs we concern ourselves only with those operations which are important or critical to the progress of the job and the satisfaction of the schedule.

The operation programme is best depicted as a chart, with the final delivery date as zero. Figure 14.11 is such an operation programme. The final completion date (completion of operation 15) is zero and the timescale runs from right to left. This programme shows that items B and C must be combined (operation 14) two days before completion. Item C, prior to this combination, undergoes two conversion operations; the second must be finished five days before final completion, and the first two days before that. Purchase of the material for item C must be completed ten days before final combination. The item with longest lead time, 17 days, is B.

These two pieces of information—completion schedule and operation programme—are prerequisites for use of the line of balance technique. They need to be constructed only once for any job, unlike the following documents, which must be constructed each time the schedule and progress are examined.

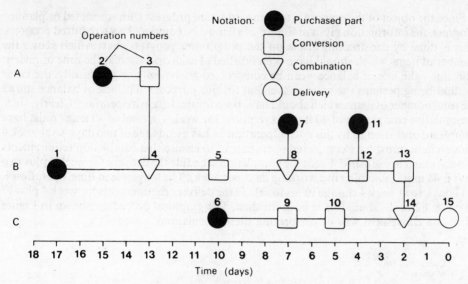

Figure 14.11 *Operation programme.*

The programme progress chart

This chart shows the number of items which have been finished at each of the critical or important operations at a given date. Suppose, for example, the review date is week 4, by which, according to the completion schedule, 40 items should have been completed, i.e. 40 items should have passed operation 15 of the operation programme. The number of items that have completed this and each of the other operations can be obtained simply by checking inventory levels. The results can then be depicted by means of a histogram. Figure 14.12 shows the programme performance at week 4.

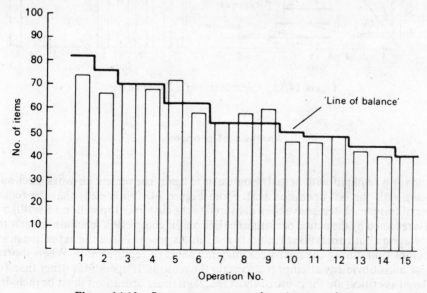

Figure 14.12 *Programme progress chart (as at week 4).*

Since the object of the exercise is to compare actual progress with scheduled or planned progress, the information given in Figure 14.12 must be compared with required progress. This is done by constructing a line on the programme progress chart which shows the number of items which should have been finished at each operation at the time of review. This line—the line of balance—can be constructed analytically or graphically, the latter method being perhaps the more convenient for our purposes. The line of balance shows the total number of items which should have been finished at each operation. Clearly, since a cumulative completion of 40 items is required for week 4, a total of 40 items must have completed operation 15 by this date. Operation 14 has a lead time of two days, so at week 4 enough items must have completed operation 15 to ensure that completion requirements two days later are satisfied. From the completion schedule the delivery for week 4 plus two days is 44 units (assuming five working days per week). The longest lead time, operation 1, is 17 days, so at week 4 enough items to satisfy the delivery requirements for week 4 plus 17 days, i.e. 82 units, should have been finished. The graphical procedure shown in Figure 14.13 is a convenient way of performing these calculations.

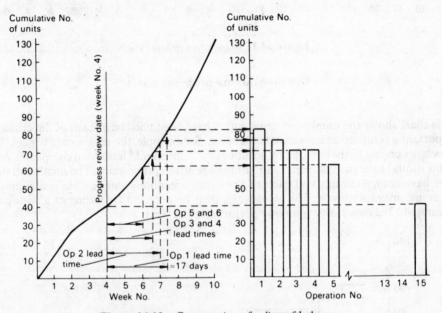

Figure 14.13   *Construction of a line of balance.*

Analysis of progress

In comparing required with actual progress it is again convenient to work backwards, beginning with the last operation (15). From Figure 14.12 it is clear that the required number of completed items have been delivered to the customer (operation 15 = 40), a fact which is reflected by the actual performance line on the completion schedule. Clearly there is a shortage on both operations 13 and 14 and, unless processing can be expedited in some way, completion during the next week may fall short of requirements. When shortages occur we must obviously attempt to ascertain the reasons. If operations other than those considered as critical are the cause of shortages then those operations must be included in subsequent versions of the progress and line of balance chart. As an aid to control, colour codes might be used for the 'bars' on the progress chart to depict responsibility; alternatively, additional charts might be constructed containing progress information on operations in various processing areas. Figure 14.14 shows three additional programme progress charts, each containing one type of operation. From these it is clear that performance on the purchasing operations may well jeopardize future deliveries. We must therefore attempt to ensure that items, particularly on operations 1 and 2, are purchased more quickly, or failing this we should alter the lead time on these operations. Charts such as these might be issued to and used by departmental managers or production controllers.

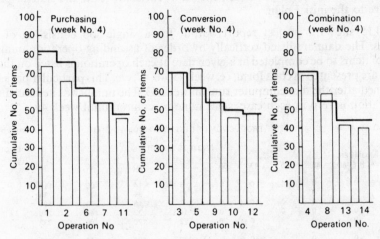

Figure 14.14 *Additional programme progress charts.*

The line of balance is a simple and useful planning and control technique, its main advantage being, like network analysis, that it formalizes and enforces a planning discipline which in itself is useful. It is a simple but powerful procedure which relies on several assumptions. For example, we have assumed that the lead times shown in Figure 14.11 are constant, and that the type and sequence of operations are independent of production quantities. Such assumptions are very often justified in practice and consequently the technique as it has been presented here is of direct value.[3]

LOB computer procedure

Several computer programs have been written[4] and use of these, particularly where many operations are involved and progress reviews are frequent, simplifies the application of line of balance. One typical program is described below.

---

[3] It is possible to use a modified version of the line of balance technique in situations where lead times are variable. See Turban, E. (1968) The line of balance—a management by exception tool, *Journal of Industrial Engineering*, September, pp. 440–448.

[4] Levitt, H. P. (1968) Computerized line of balance technique, *Journal of Industrial Engineering*, February, pp. 61–66.

Hosni, Y. A. and Guediri, F. (1981) Line of balance (LOB) using a microcomputer, *Industrial Engineering*, August, pp. 22–24.

Data, i.e. 'milestone' number (a 'milestone' for the purpose of this program is equivalent to an 'operation' as used in the description in this chapter), lead time, quantity required, etc., are input to the computer. Output is in line-printed form. There are three types of output:

1. Project reports—an output which shows, in tabular form, the target quantities for each operation.
2. Progress reports—an output which shows, in tabular form, the state of processing relative to the initial plan.
3. Progress charts—an output which shows, in bar chart form, the state of processing relative to the initial plan.

Figure 14.15 shows a project report output for a single job consisting of only 14 operations. The data are listed vertically by order of ascending operation number. The quantity of items to be completed at a given date at each operation is listed on the output. The dates are presented in code form, i.e. week 45, 46, 47, etc. This particular project report was obtained after the first computer run, on week 43. The number of items completed at each operation is zero in each case, since none is required until week 46.

PROJECT NO. XB/41 A   PRODUCTION OF DESKS/AO MODIFIED C/41   PROJECT REPORT

LINE OF BALANCE   DATE 07 07

PROJECT TARGETS   CODED DATE 43

MILESTONE NUMBER	NUMBER ACHIEVED	45	46	47	50	55	60	80	90
OA32	0	0	0	0	0	5	14	65	117
OB16	0	0	0	0	0	42	96	420	738
OB32	0	0	0	0	0	7	16	70	121
OB41	0	0	0	0	0	14	32	140	246
OC08	0	0	0	0	36	72	120	400	632
OC21	0	0	0	0	0	72	132	510	840
OC24	0	0	0	0	54	108	180	600	948
OC27	0	0	0	0	0	72	132	510	840
OC32	0	0	0	0	9	18	30	100	158
OC40	0	0	0	0	0	72	132	510	840
OC90	0	0	0	0	18	36	60	200	316
OCA6	0	0	0	0	0	144	264	1020	1680
OD22	0	0	40	56	96	176	280	896	1352
ODA9	0	0	20	28	48	86	140	448	676

SEQUENCED BY ASC MILESTONE NUMBER   PAGE 1/1

Figure 14.15   *Line of balance project report.*

PROJECT NO XB/41/A   PRODUCTION OF DESKS/AO MODIFIED C/41   PROJECT REPORT

LINE OF BALANCE   DATE 26/07

PROJECT TARGETS   CODED DATE 88

MILESTONE NUMBER	NUMBER ACHIEVED	55	70	85	88	91	94	97	·100
OA32	103	5	37	90	106	123	140	158	175
OB16	700	42	240	570	672	774	876	978	1050
OB32	95	7	40	95	112	129	146	163	175
OB41	243	14	80	190	224	258	292	326	350
OC08	629	72	220	516	584	652	700	700	700
OC21	763	72	282	672	774	876	978	1050	1050
OC24	655	108	330	774	876	978	050	1050	1050
OC27	701	72	282	672	774	876	978	1050	1050
OC32	100	18	55	129	146	163	175	175	175
OC40	1001	72	282	672	774	876	978	1050	1050
OC90	226	36	110	258	292	326	350	350	350
OCA6	1700	144	564	1344	1548	1752	1956	2100	2100
OD22	1352	176	480	1120	1264	1400	1400	1400	1400
ODA9	651	88	240	560	632	700	700	700	700

SEQUENCED BY ASC MILESTONE NUMBER   PAGE 1/1

Figure 14.16   *Line of balance project report.*

PROJECT NO. XB/41/A   PRODUCTION OF DESKS/AO MODIFIED C/41   PROGRESS REPORT

PROJECT NO. XB/41/A   PRODUCTION OF DESKS/AO MODIFIED C/41   PROGRESS REPORT
LINE OF BALANCE   DATE 27/07
PROJECT TARGETS   CODED DATE 88

MILESTONE NUMBER	NUMBER PER ITEM	LEAD TIME	NUMBER ACHIEVED	TARGET	CRITICALITY ABSOLUTE	RELATIVE
OD22	8	9	1352	1264	88	11
ODA9	4	9	651	632	19	5
OCO8	4	7	629	584	45	11
OC24	6	7	655	876	−221	−37
OC90	2	7	226	292	−66	−33
OC32	1	7	100	146	−46	−46
OC27	6	4	701	774	−73	−12
OC21	6	4	763	774	−11	−2
OC40	6	4	1001	774	227	38
OCA6	12	4	1700	1548	152	13
OB16	6	1	700	672	28	5
OB32	1	1	95	112	−17	−17
OB41	2	1	243	224	19	10
OA32	1	0	93	106	−13	−13

SEQUENCED BY DSC. LEAD TIME   PAGE: 1

Figure 14.17   *Line of balance project report.*

Figure 14.16 is a project report for the same job for week 88. Again the output shows the target requirement for each operation for several future dates. Figure 14.17 is the progress report produced during the same computer run; the output shows the progress at each operation by comparing the number of items completed with the target requirements. The final two columns give a measure of the criticality of the situation. 'Absolute criticality' is a measure of over-production at an operation, whereas 'relative criticality' is a measure of the over-production in terms of the final operation. For example, for operation OD22 the target for week 88 is 1264, whereas 1352 have been completed; hence the 'absolute criticality' is $1352 - 1264 = 88$. The 'relative criticality' is 88 divided by the number of items required for the final operation, i.e. 88/8, which is 11. It is therefore a measure of over-completion in terms of finished items rather than individual components.

Under-completion is emphasized, of course, by negative criticality values, as in the case of OC24, where a severe under-achievement has resulted for week 88.

This progress information may also be presented in terms of a bar chart (Figure 14.18). Here targets are represented by 1s and achievements by Xs. For further information, target quantities for the next report date may also be shown by extending the 1s with the symbol z.

GROUP TECHNOLOGY IN MANUFACTURE

In Chapter 3 we discussed methods of component or workpiece coding and classification and indicated that one of the principal benefits of an effective classification system was the possibility of group technology or family manufacturing. Although group technology has little directly in common with the topics previously discussed in this chapter and is of particular relevance in *manufacture*, it is appropriate to consider it here since, by definition, it is concerned with the processing of components in combined batches in order to obtain the benefits normally associated with large batch processing and absent from unit or small batch processing.

The principal precondition for large-scale (large batch and mass) processing is a stable and high demand for items. The principal benefits of this type of processing are high

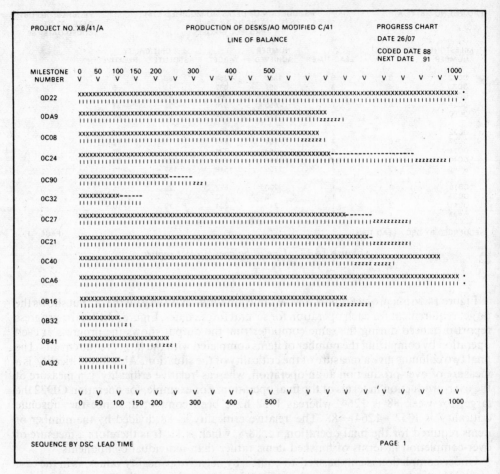

Figure 14.18   *Line of balance progress chart. (Figures 14.15 to 14.18 reproduced with permission, Line of Balance Users' Guide, International Computers Ltd.)*

machine utilization, few machine set-ups and low work-in-progress. Group technology is an attempt to obtain these benefits in situations where the necessary precondition does not exist and it attempts to do this by concentrating on components rather than products.

In conventional batch processing work, batch sizes and operations sequences are determined from the information available to the appropriate manager. Such information normally derives directly from the sales order or works order documents; consequently batch sizes are usually related directly to customer order sizes. The net result of this type of situation is that similar parts are often passed through widely differing sequences of operations and usually constitute different processing batches. This situation leads directly to low efficiency because of frequent machine set-ups and high work-in-progress.

Adopting a group technology method, the following stages are achieved:

1. The parts of each of the items processed are examined and placed into logical classes or families and the operations sequence for each class of parts is determined and specified.
2. Groups of facilities suitable for the processing of these classes of parts are specified using the operations planning details and forecasted demand for the items and hence the components.

3. The sequencing of each class of parts for each group of facilities.

For purposes of implementing group technology, two types of family or group and three methods of processing can be identified. The two types of family are:

1. *Type A*, consisting of parts which are similar in shape and which have all or the majority of processing operations in common.
2. *Type B*, consisting of apparently dissimilar parts which are related by having one or more processing operations in common.

The three methods of processing using group technology are therefore as follows:

1. *Method* 1—processing of a type-A family on a group of different conventional machines.
2. *Method* 2—processing of a type-A and/or type-B family on one or more similar and conventional machines.
3. *Method* 3—processing of a type-B family on a group of different machines.

In conventional terms the processing of a large quantity of type-A parts by method 1 corresponds to flow processing, which is of course an efficient method since it maximizes machine utilization. It is the object of group technology, by identifying common features in parts, to extend this type of application and to obtain increased efficiency in processing by adopting one of the three methods described above.

Formation of parts families

Clearly an important decision influencing both the nature and the success of group technology is the classification of parts. Some of the approaches which might be employed are discussed below.

On occasions the selection of the parts for inclusion in a family may be relatively simple so the use of one of the more rigorous techniques will be unnecessary. Such a situation may occur when the item range is fairly static, when there are large numbers of parts with similar shapes, and when several obviously exclusive categories of parts exist.

Classification (see the Appendix to Chapter 3) in this context refers to the assignment of parts into predefined groups or classes, while *coding* is the allocation of identities to these groups. The type and amount of information contained in the code depend on the potential uses of the system. A designer may wish to retrieve designs to obtain relevant information and to utilize existing parts in new items, while retrieval is also necessary in connection with costing, planning, variety reduction, etc. For this reason the design of a classification and coding system is normally a compromise that attempts to satisfy as many potential demands as possible.

The demands made on the system require not only that it should establish what types of parts are being processed, but also that it should facilitate the arrangement of parts into groups suitable for manufacture by the group method. The size of some groups formed will be such that their process is not economically feasible, but by merging such groups together their group processes may become economic.

Various classification systems have been developed, and some details were given in the Appendix to Chapter 3.

A different type of approach relies on the classification of operation or process routes for parts to identify families which use the same group of facilities, or which can be readily re-routed to do so. In production flow analysis a progressive form of analysis is used, consisting of three basic steps as follows:

1. *Factory-flow analysis.* The objective of this is to identify the best division of facilities into departments. The operations routeings for all parts (obtained from route cards) are coded to indicate the department visited by each item and then sorted by this code to create groups of parts with the same interdepartmental routeings.
2. *Group analysis.* The route cards for all parts processed in each department are analysed to identify the best division into groups. This is achieved by sorting cards into packs containing items with the same operation routeing, these packs then being combined to form viable facility/operation groupings.
3. *Line analysis.* The objective here is to obtain the best sequence of facilities in groups through study of the flow patterns within these groups. This is the layout problem in group technology, which will be discussed more fully in the next section.

Facilities grouping

The facilities necessary to perform all operations on the parts family, and the expected load on each piece of equipment, can be listed for each family identified. It may be necessary at this stage to eliminate certain parts from families or to add others to avoid low or uneven machine utilization. Rarely, however, will it prove possible to achieve full utilization of all machines in a group, and some flexibility of labour is probably required—a characteristic which distinguishes group technology from classic flow processing.

Several techniques suitable for assisting in the determination of the arrangement of facilities in a group technology system have been developed. Singleton[5] outlined a simple method for determining a layout sequence for a number of operations or machines through which a variety of parts are processed, each part having a particular route through the operations. This method involves converting the process or operation sequence for each part to a common length scale of 100 units, the spacing of operations on this scale being equal to $100/N$, where N is the number of operations for that part. Histograms are plotted for each operation showing its placing on the percentile scale for each part, the occurrences being weighted by the processing quantity for each part. These distributions are then ranked in order of their means to give a suitable sequence of operations, i.e. the operation with the lowest mean is placed first on the line and the one with the highest mean is placed last. Backtracking or bypassing of operations by parts is indicated by the overlapping of the distributions, while distributions with a large spread or range might suggest that alternative operations routeings for parts be examined to improve part flow.

Travel or cross charts are of some value in developing layouts (see Chapter 6). Such a chart can show the nature of inter-operation movements for all parts for a given period of time. The row totals on the chart show the extent of movement from an operation, and the column totals show movement to an operation. Each cell of the chart shows the relative frequency of movement between two operations; an ideal movement pattern suitable for use on a flow line is indicated when all the entries in the matrix appear in the cells immediately above the diagonal. Such travel charts can be used to help develop a sequence of operations. For example, operations with a low 'to/from' ratio (i.e. row-total/column-total ratio)[6] receive parts from relatively few sources but distribute work to a large number of destinations. Hence, if in-sequence movement is to be maximized and backtracking is to

---

[5] Singleton, W. T. (1962) Optimum sequencing of operations for batch production, *Work Study and Industrial Engineering*, **3**, pp. 100–110.

[6] Hollier, R. H. (1963) The layout of multi-product lines, *International Journal of Production Research*, **2**, (1) pp. 47–57.

be minimized, such operations should be placed at the beginning of the sequence of operations. Conversely, operations with a high 'to/from' ratio should be placed towards the end of the sequence, since they receive work from a large number of sources but distribute to comparatively few destinations. This heuristic approach is simple and attractive, and clearly has considerable practical merit.

Sequencing

The determination of the sequence in which batches of parts are loaded onto a group technology cell or 'line' will be influenced by the desire to reduce setting cost and minimize throughput time. The problem is entirely congruent with the multi-model line batch sequencing problem and can be approached in the same way (see Chapter 15). If component batching is not adopted, individual components will be launched into the cell in much the same manner as in mixed-model line production. However, in this case, launch discipline and model sequence are unlikely to be important because of the far greater throughput time and component idle time.

CHECKLIST FOR CHAPTER 14

Batch processing situations
Batch processing decisions
Examples of batch processing situations and problems
Types of batch processing
  Processing to output stock
  Processing from input queues
Batch sequencing
  Processing families of items
Determination of batch sizes
  The economic batch size
  A1: Deterministic situations
    (i) Complete batch from/to stock
    (ii) As (i) with shortages
    (iii) Batch from/to stock over period of time
  A2: Probabilistic situations
    Uncertainties in costs

Uncertainties in usage or consumption rates
  Buffer stocks
  Processing rate uncertainties
  The production (processing) range
Scheduling for batch processing
  Optimum processing cycles
  Scheduling for multiple items
Line of balance
  The completion schedule
  The operation programme
  The programme progress chart
  Analysis of progress
  Computer procedure
Group technology in manufacture
  Formation of families
  Facilities grouping
  Sequencing

FURTHER READING

For books on techniques, particularly analytical techniques related to batch sizes, schedules, etc., see 'Further Reading' in Chapter 17.

Burbidge, J. L. (1975) *The Introduction of Group Technology*. London: Heinemann. The techniques of group technology.

Fox, B. (1982) OPT, *Inventories and Production Magazine*, November–December. Outlines a comprehensive approach to batch scheduling in manufacture.

Lumsden, N. P. (1972) *Line of Balance Method*. Oxford: Pergamon. A clear and concise treatment of the subject. Possibly the best book on line of balance.

QUESTIONS

14.1   What circumstances necessitate the use of batch processing in manufacture, supply, transport and service systems? What are the principal characteristics of this method of processing and what are the principal managerial problems involved?

14.2   (a) Calculate:
   (i)   the optimum processing batch quantity;
   (ii) the processing cycle time, given the following information

Set-up cost per batch	$= £17$
Stock-hoding cost per item per month	$= £0.05$
Buffer stock required	$= 25$ items
Demand rate per year	$= 12\,000$ (stable)
Process rate per month	$= 1500$
Processing cost per item	$= £25$

The process is such that all items in a batch are completed at the same time.

   (b) Because of deterioration in the processing facilities, the processing rate per month drops from 1500 to 900. How does this change affect the economic batch quantity?

14.3   Experimental Brewers Ltd are the sole manufacturers of 'Instant Beer'. Because of the market potential for this new style of beverage an entirely new manufacturing facility has been established, the capacity of which is 5000 litres (equivalent) per day. At the moment demand for 'Instant Beer' is stable at 3000 litres (equivalent) per day. The product is manufactured intermittently, set-up costs for the facility being £250 and storage costs per day per 10 000 litres (equivalent) being £100.

The company is prepared to tolerate the occasional stock-out, which it estimates to cost £500 per 10 000 litres (equivalent) per day.

In what batch quantities should 'Instant Beer' be manufactured?

14.4   Pizza is made at a rate of 240 pieces per hour by an automatic cooking machine. The pizza is sold (cold) through a shop on the same premises at a rate of 100 per hour (virtually constant). The cost of setting up the machine for production of the pizza is £15. (The same machine is also used to produce other items.) The cost of stocking cold pizza is £1 per 1000 per hour.

What is the optimum batch production quantity and how frequently should such batches ideally be produced (neglecting limitations caused by the need to produce other items)?

14.5   Refer to the situation faced by Experimental Brewers Ltd (Question 14.3). The company decides to adopt a policy of allowing a variation in production batch quantities equivalent to a variation of plus or minus 8 per cent of the cost associated with the economic batch quantities.

What is the 'production range' in such circumstances?

14.6   A hospital uses a certain medication at a rate of 200 units per day. The medication is prepared in the hospital's own laboratories in batches. The set-up cost is £100. The processing cost is £5 per unit, and the refrigerated storage is £0.1 per unit per day.

If the management is prepared to tolerate an increase of up to 1 per cent in the minimum total cost per unit, what flexibility does this give in the choice of batch quantities and what is the total cost per unit of the cheapest solution if, for chemical reasons, processed batches are restricted to multiples of 50 units?

14.7   Assuming processing of equal batch sizes at regular intervals and given the following, calculate the processing cycle time:

   (a) $C_s = £150$
   $C_1 = 50$ p per item per annum
   $r = 5000$ per month

   (b) $C_s = £150$
   $C_1 = 50$ p per item per annum
   $r = 5000$ per month
   $C_2 = £1$ per item per month

(c) $C_s = £150$
$C_1 = 50\,$p per item per annum
$r = 5000$ per month
$q = 50\,000$ per month

14.8 Discuss the advantages, disadvantages and limitations of the line of balance planning and control technique.

Compare and contrast it with any other planning and control technique, such as network analysis, with which you are familiar.

14.9 Ornamental Doorknobs Ltd assemble four types of door knocker—Elizabethan, Victorian, Georgian and Modern—in batches on the same equipment. The following table gives the annual demand, the assembly rate and the inventory cost per item per annum for each type of knob. A change in the equipment set-up is necessary whenever there is a change in the type being assembled. This set-up cost is £10 irrespective of the type of change. Assume a working year of 250 days.

Calculate the processing batch sizes for each type of knocker and how many complete runs of all four types should be made per year.

Knocker	Demand (per year)	Assembly rate (per day)	Inventory cost (per item p.a.)
Elizabethan	7 000	150	0.008
Victorian	10 000	250	0.006
Georgian	15 000	300	0.005
Modern	5 000	100	0.007

14.10 The delivery schedule of items and the operations programme for the making of these items are given below.

Week no.	Delivery required	Cumulative delivery
0	0	0
1	12	12
2	15	27
3	12	39
4	20	59
5	5	64
6	10	74
7	15	89
8	10	99
9	27	126
10	15	141
11	20	161
12	17	178

Cumulative delivery requirements:

Construct the line of balance for weeks 3, 6 and 10. Indicate how you would use the line of balance to analyse progress in the several different departments involved in the making of the items.

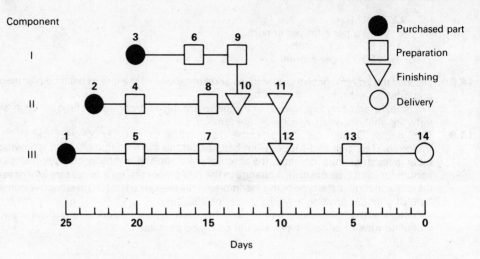

Figure Q14.10 *Operations programme for each item.*

14.11 What is group technology and what benefits are likely to be obtained by introducing group technology, if appropriate, into a company?

Whatsteps would be followed during an investigation to determine whether group technology is appropriate in a given manufacturing situation?

Describe briefly the principal methods of component classification, designed for use in group technology.

CHAPTER 15

The Design and Scheduling of Flow Processing Systems

NOTATION USED IN THIS CHAPTER

C	Cycle time
C_i	Cycle time for unit i
C_j	Cycle time for model j
C_n	Cycle time for $n\,(n = 1 \ldots i)$
COMSOAL	Computer method for sequencing operations for assembly lines
$\bar{c}$	Average work station time
K	Constant
L_1	Unit inventory cost/unit time
L_2	Idle facilities cost/unit time
N	Number of items to be produced
N_j	Total number of model j required
n	Number of work stations
n_{min}	Minimum number of work stations
PW	Positional weight
RPW	Ranked positional weight
T	Production time period
T_F	Feed interval
T_T	Tolerance time
t	Element time
$\bar{t}$	Mean work time for element
X	Optimum buffer capacity
x_i	Time of launching unit i
Z	Cumulative work station time
γ	Regular item launch interval
α	Time interval between successive stations starting work on any one unit
σ	Standard deviation of normally distributed work times

In this chapter we shall concentrate on the design and scheduling of flow processing systems, which because of their importance deserve individual attention. Fundamentally, most types of operating systems provide a form of flow processing, i.e. customers, materials or products arrive into the system and proceed through several departments or facilities before emerging from the end of the system. For example, each of the following could be considered as a form of flow processing:

(a) passage of paperwork through an office;
(b) passage of patients through a hospital;
(c) passage of data through a computer;
(d) passage of children through classes and schools in an educational system;
(e) passage of a car down a vehicle assembly line.

The manner and nature of 'flow' in these cases differ. In some cases items or customers will flow through a system by different *routes*, i.e. visiting different departments or facilities (e.g. (a) and (b) above). In some cases the *flow rate* will be low and/or the *throughput time* high (e.g. (b) and (d) above). In some cases the consistency of routes, the flow routes, and the desire to minimize throughput times will justify a 'product'-type arrangement of facilities, e.g. as a 'line' (as in (e) above), but in others a functional/process layout will be appropriate.

In this chapter we shall take as our principal focus the manufacturing flow processing system, in particular the 'flow line' (e.g. (e) above). This will provide us with a clear case or application, and through it we shall be able to identify most of the important characteristics and problems of flow processing systems. These will also apply to similar systems in other types of organizations. Familiarity with the design of flow lines may help us to identify flow systems in other situations where similar problems exist and where the procedures described in this chapter are of some relevance.

MASS PRODUCTION

Flow lines are a principal feature of mass production systems. Although the details may differ, the concept remains the same: the items are manufactured or assembled as they pass through a series of work stations. Raw materials or components are fed in at the beginning of, and at certain points along, the line, and goods are delivered from the end of the line. In the assembly of motor vehicles the body unit is delivered to the first work station on the line and the workers at subsequent stations add the engine, transmission, suspension, trim and so on, until the vehicle is completed.

The mass production of complex discrete items such as cars using the flow principle is one of the most important achievements in manufacturing technology and one of the most important aspects of mass production. However, the general term 'mass production' embraces two technologies (Figure 15.1), the development of the simpler *quantity*

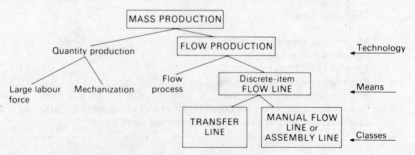

Figure 15.1 *Mass production systems. From Wild, R. (1972) Mass Production Management. New York: Wiley. Reproduced with permission.*

production having preceded the development of *flow production*. We use the term 'quantity production' here to describe the manufacture, in large quantities, of relatively simple items using single facilities. In such cases there is no flow through facilities. Mass production and flow production are therefore not necessarily the same, since mass production gives rise to flow production only when necessitated by the nature of the product, i.e. where it is sufficiently complex to require the use of several facilities or production 'stages'.

Flow production consists of two basic subsections: flow processes, designed for the manufacture of large quantities of bulk, fluid or semi-fluid products, and flow lines, which use the same principle of efficient material and product flow in the manufacture of large quantities of complex, discrete items.

Flow lines which are engaged, essentially, in product assembly are often referred to as manual flow lines or assembly lines, while those which use automatic material transfer between the automatic machining 'stations' are normally referred to as transfer lines.

We have identified two classes of production flow line, and can now identify various subdivisions of these classes (Table 15.1). Both classes of flow line can be used for the manufacture of one or more products. The production of one product or model on either class of line can be accomplished without the need to alter the 'set-up' of the line, i.e. without the need to change tools or work allocations, etc. The production of more than one product, however, gives rise to more complex situations. In such cases two alternative strategies are available:

1. The production of the two or more products in separate batches. This we shall refer to as the multi-model situation, and it necessitates the rearrangement of the flow line between batches.
2. The production of the two or more products simultaneously on the line. This we shall call the mixed-model situation, which gives rise to rather complex design problems and will be discussed in some detail later.

Table 15.1   *Classes and varieties of flow line (From Wild, R. (1972) Mass Production Management. New York: Wiley. Reproduced with permission.)*

Flow line description		Number of products	Product changes	Flow of items	Setting of equipment and allocation of work
Class	Variety				
Transfer line	Single model	1	None	Regular	No changes required
	Multi-model	>1	Batch changes	Regular batches	Changes of equipment setting and/or work allocation required on change of batch
Manual flow line or assembly line	Single model	1	None	Irregular[a]	No changes required
	Multi-model	>1	Batch changes	Irregular[a]	Changes of equipment setting and/or work allocation required on batch change
	Mixed model	>1	Continual[c]	Irregular	Changes of equipment setting and/or work allocation normally required[b]

[a] Because of variable work-station times—characteristic of manual flow lines.
[b] Alternatively, as in 'group technology', tools and equipment might be permanently allocated a specific group of components.
[c] At any time the line contains a mixture of product types.

Whichever strategy is adopted, if more than one model or product is to be manufactured on the line, these products must have similar work contents. The greater the similarity, the easier it will be to provide either multi-model or mixed-model production. More flexibility is normally available on assembly lines; consequently in certain circumstances it may be possible to design such lines for either multi-model or mixed-model operation. For example, many car assembly lines work on the mixed-model principle, different 'builds' of the same vehicle, and occasionally different types of vehicle, being produced simultaneously on the line. The use of reprogrammable or flexible tools, such as industrial robots, facilitates this flexibility. In contrast, transfer lines are far less flexible. They are normally confined to single-model, or occasionally large-batch multi-model, operation.

There is only one fundamental prerequisite for mass production, and that is mass demand. Since flow-line production is one means of mass production, its use also depends on mass demand. The term 'mass demand' must be qualified; in particular, we must consider not only the level of demand, but also the continuity. In practice, flow-line production will be justified for certain products when demand is both high and reasonably continuous. Nevertheless, in certain circumstances it may be justifiable to establish a flow line to produce items to satisfy one very large order (i.e. to accommodate high-level, but not continuous, demand). In practice such situations are likely to be rare, and some degree of demand continuity will normally be a prerequisite of flow-line production. The nature of the product will determine the means of mass production to be used; consequently, a further prerequisite of each of the means of mass production is the availability of a suitable product.

THE DESIGN OF 'SIMPLE' FLOW LINES

We must begin by considering the nature and design of 'simple' flow lines. The reason for the use of the term 'simple' will become apparent later in the chapter, and here it is sufficient to recognize that certain simplifying assumptions will be made.

A production flow line consists, essentially, of a series of work stations, these stations consisting either of (in a transfer line) one or more machines or of (in a manual flow line) one or more workers, probably equipped with some tools.

The total work content of the product or item, i.e. the total time required to complete the item, is divided among these stations so that, as the item travels down the line, it becomes incrementally more complete at each station.

One objective in designing flow lines is to attempt to allocate equal amounts of work to each station, i.e. to divide the total work content of the job as evenly as possible between the stations. This is known as *line balancing*. Without such balance, a certain amount of inefficiency or loss must inevitably occur, since some stations will have more work to perform than others. All stations will normally be required to process the same number of items within a given period of time.

The time required to complete the work allocated to each station is known as the *service time*. The time available at each station for the performance of the work is known as the *cycle time*—the cycle time normally being longer than the service time. The cycle time at a station is the time interval between the completion or the starting of work on successive items, and therefore includes both productive and non-productive work as well as any idle time. Non-productive work in both manual flow lines and transfer lines will include the transfer of the product between stations, and in the former will also include a certain amount of handling, movement, etc. (Figure 15.2).

$$\text{Cycle time} = \text{service time} + (\text{idle time or loss})$$
$$= \frac{\text{productive}}{\text{work time}} + \frac{\text{non-productive}}{\text{work time}} + (\text{idle time or loss})$$

The total work content of the job consists of the total productive work plus the total non-productive work.

$$\text{Total work content} = (\text{total productive work}) + (\text{total non-productive work})$$

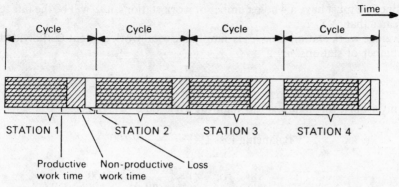

Figure 15.2

The manner in which work can be allocated to stations on the line is influenced by certain constraints. Each job will consist of certain work elements, and normally the order in which some of these elements of work can be performed will be influenced by technological or *precedence* constraints. For example, it is necessary to drill a hole before it can be tapped. Such precedence constraints will limit the flow-line designer's ability to achieve balance in allocating work (i.e. work elements) to stations.

The allocation of elements to stations will also be limited by *zoning* constraints. Such constraints will necessitate or preclude the grouping of certain work elements at certain stations. For example, it may be essential that two work elements are not allocated to the same station if they might in some way interfere with one another, e.g. the grouping at one station of a delicate assembly and a heavy forging operation. Such a constraint is known as a negative zoning constraint, in contrast to a positive zoning constraint, which necessitates the grouping of two or more work elements at one station, as might be the case when the maximum utilization of a single expensive piece of equipment is to be achieved. Because of such constraints perfect line balance is rarely achieved in practice, and a certain amount of *balancing delay* or *balancing loss* is normally inevitable. Balance delay is the difference between the total time available for completion of the job and the total time required. For example, at any one station the balance delay is the difference between the cycle time and the service time. The percentage balancing loss for any station is given by the difference between the cycle time and the service time, expressed as a percentage of the cycle time. Similarly, the balancing loss for a complete line is given by the difference of the total time available (e.g. the sum of the cycle times) and the total time required (i.e. the sum of the service times), expressed as a percentage of the total time available.

Line balancing

The cycle time can be calculated, at least theoretically, from the required output. For example, if N items are to be produced in T minutes, then the cycle time (C) should be:

$$C = \frac{T}{N}$$

Furthermore, given these two figures and knowing either the total work content or each of the element times (t), the minimum number of work stations ($n_{min.}$) can be calculated.

$$n_{min.} = \frac{N\Sigma t}{T}$$

In fact, since we must have a whole number of work stations, $n_{min.}$ will be the integer equal to or greater than $N\Sigma_t/T$.

The average work station time ($\bar{c}$) is simply the total work content (Σt) divided by the actual number of stations, n.

$$\bar{c} = \frac{\Sigma t}{n}$$

Almost invariably, this figure is less than the cycle time (C). Hence:

$$\text{Balancing loss } (\%) = \frac{C - \bar{c}}{C} \times 100$$

$$\text{or } (\%) = \frac{n(C) - \Sigma t}{n(C)} \times 100$$

In practice, when designing assembly lines we cannot normally achieve the perfect balance shown in Figure 15.3. A situation such as the one shown in Figure 15.4(a) will result if we are lucky, but often it will be as shown in Figure 15.4(b), in which neither the work station times are balanced nor is the maximum work station time equal to the desired cycle time.

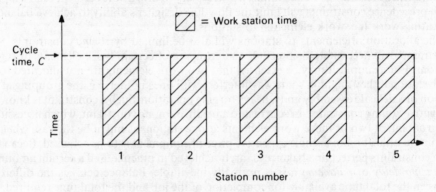

Figure 15.3 *Perfectly balanced five-station assembly line.*

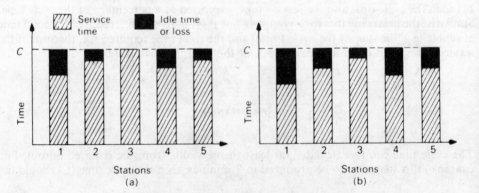

Figure 15.4 *Five-station assembly line balances.*

Although we have spoken of and depicted idle time resulting from imperfect line balance, in practice periods of idleness caused by the difference between cycle times and work station times rarely exist because a worker will normally be inclined to perform his or her work operations in the time available. In fact, a Parkinson's law type of situation will exist in which the work will expand to fill the available time. Nevertheless, the consequences are precisely the same because an under-utilization of labour will result.

It has been estimated that the balancing loss occurring in industry today is between 5 and 20 per cent.

The objective of assembly line balancing is that, given a desired cycle time or output rate, the minimum rational work elements and their standard times, and other constraints, one should attempt to assign work elements to work stations in order to:

(a) minimize idle time or balancing loss;
(b) minimize the number of work stations;
(c) distribute balancing loss evenly between stations;
(d) avoid violating any constraints.

Methods of simple assembly line balancing

The first analytical treatment of the assembly line balancing problem was developed by Bryton in 1954, while Salveson published a linear programming solution in 1955,[1] as did Bowman in 1962.[2] Similar rigorous procedures have been suggested by Mitchell,[3] Hoffman[4] and Klien[5] but they all suffer from the same disadvantage: they are impractical for large and realistic problems. Because of the nature of the problem and the inadequacy of these treatments, several authors and several organizations have developed heuristic methods of assembly line balancing, those suggested by Helgerson and Birnie,[6] Tonge,[7] Kilbridge and Wester[8] and Arcus[9] being perhaps the best known and the most suitable (they are described below). Many of the heuristic treatments bear some resemblance to intuitive procedures and some are little more than formal statements of such procedures, a situation which may be taken as an endorsement of the basic suitability of some traditional practice.

The Kilbridge and Wester method

This simple heuristic method of assembly line balancing is best described by means of an example.

Assembly of a simple component requires the performance of 21 work elements which are governed by certain precedence constraints, as shown in Figure 15.5. This precedence

[1] Salveson, M. E. (1955) The assembly line balancing problem, *Transactions of the American Society of Mechanical Engineering*, **77**, August, p. 939.
[2] Bowman, E. H. (1962) *Operational Research*, **8** (3), p. 385.
[3] Mitchell, J. A. Report No. 6–94801–1–R3, Westinghouse Research Laboratories.
[4] Hoffman, T. R. (1957) *Management Science*, **9** (4), p. 551.
[5] Klien, M. (1962) *Operational Research*, **11** (2), p. 274.
[6] Helgerson, N. B. and Birnie, D. P. (1961) Assembly line balancing using the ranked positional weight technique, *Journal of Industrial Engineering*, **XII** (6), p. 394.
[7] Tonge, F. (1960) Summary of heuristic line balancing procedure, *Management Science*, **7** (1), p. 21.
[8] Kilbridge, K. and Wester, L. (1961) A heuristic method of assembly line balancing, *Journal of Industrial Engineering*, **VXII** (4), p. 292.
[9] Arcus, A. L. (1966) COMSOAL – a computer method of sequencing operations for assembly lines, *International Journal of Production Research*, **4** (4).

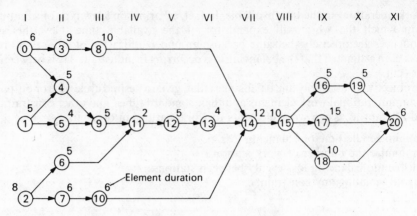

Figure 15.5 *Precedence diagram of work elements.*

diagram shows circles representing work elements placed as far to the left as possible, with all the arrows joining circles sloping to the right. The figures above the diagram are column numbers. Elements appearing in column I can be started immediately, those in column II can be begun only after one or more in column I have been completed, and so on.

The data shown on this diagram can now be represented in tabular form as shown in Table 15.2. Column (c) of this table describes the lateral transferability of elements among columns; for example, element 6 can be performed in column III as well as in column II without violating precedence constraints. Element 8 can also be performed in any of the columns IV to VI, as can element 10. Element 3 can also be performed in any of the columns III to V provided element 8 is also transferred, as can element 7.

Suppose it is our objective to balance the assembly line for a cycle time of 36. In this case we would proceed as follows:

1. Is there a duration in column (f) of the table equal to the cycle time of 36? *No.*
2. Select the largest duration in column (f) less than 36, i.e. 19 *for column I.*
3. Subtract 19 from 36 = 17.
4. Do any of the elements in column (II), either individually or collectively, have a duration of 17? *No, the nearest is 16 for elements 4, 6 and 7, which will give a work station time of 35 for station 1.*
5. Select the smallest duration from column (f) which is larger than 36, i.e. 48 *for columns I and II.*
6. Can one or more of the elements in columns I and II be transferred beyond column II so as to reduce the duration as near as possible to 36? *No, but element 3 (with 8) plus 6 can be transferred to give a work station time of 34.*
7. Select the next largest duration from column (f), i.e. 69 *for columns I, II and III.*
8. Can one or more of the elements in columns I, II and III be transferred beyond column III so as to reduce the duration to 36? *No, the nearest are elements 3, 7, 8 and 10, which would give a duration of 38, which is too large.*
9. Will an improved allocation of elements for this station be obtained by considering a large duration from column (f)? *No.*
10. Adopt the best allocation found previously, *i.e. step 4, which gave a work station time of 35.*
11. Rewrite the table to show this allocation and calculate new cumulative figures for column (f) (Table 15.3).
12. Is there a duration in column (f) of the new table equal to 36? *Yes, for columns III and IV.*

Table 15.2 *Tabular presentation of data in Figure* 15.4

Column no. in precedence diagram (a)	Element no. (b)	Transferability of element (c)	Element duration (d)	Duration for column (e)	Cumulative duration (f)
I	0 1 2		6 5 8	19	19
II	3 4 5 6 7	III–V (with 8) III III–V (with 10)	9 5 4 5 6	29	48
III	8 9 10	IV–VI IV–VI	10 5 6	21	69
IV	11		2	2	71
V	12		5	5	76
VI	13		4	4	80
VII	14		12	12	92
VIII	15		10	10	102
IX	16 17 18	 X X	5 15 10	30	132
X	19		5	5	137
XI	20		6	6	143

13.   Allocate the elements in these columns to the second work station and redraw the table showing new figures for column (f) (Table 15.4).
14.   Is there a duration in column (f) of the new table equal to the cycle time of 36? *No.*
15.   Select the largest duration in column (f) which is less than 36, *i.e.* 31 *for columns V, VI, VII and VIII.*
16.   Subtract 31 from 36 = 5.
17.   Does one or more of the elements in the next column (IX) equal 5? *Yes, element* 16.
18.   Allocate the columns concerned and that element to the work station and redraw the table (Table 15.5).
19.   Is there a duration in column (f) of the new table equal to 36? *Yes, for columns IX, X and XI.*
20.   Allocate the element in these columns to the work station.

All 21 elements have now been assigned to four work stations in the manner shown in Figure 15.6, the balancing loss involved being:

$$\frac{n(C) - \Sigma t}{n(C)} \times 100$$

$$= \frac{4(36) - 143}{4(36)} \times 100$$

$$= 0.7 \text{ per cent}$$

Table 15.3

Column no. in precedence diagram (a)	Element no. (b)	Transferability of element (c)	Element duration (d)	Duration of column (e)	Cumulative duration (f)
I	0		6		
	1		5		
	2		8		
II	4		5		
	6		5		
	7		6		(35)
III	3	III–V (with 8)	9		
	5		4		
	9		5		
	10	IV–VI	6	24	24
IV	8	V–VI	10		
	11		2	12	36
V	12		5	5	41
VI	13		4	4	45
VII	14		12	12	57
VIII	15		10	10	67
IX	16		5		
	17	X	15		
	18	X	10	30	97
X	19		5	5	102
XI	20		6	6	108

(Station 1 spans columns I–II, cumulative (35).)

Table 15.4

Column no. in precedence diagram (a)	Element no. (b)	Transferability of element (c)	Element duration (d)	Duration of column (e)	Cumulative duration (f)
	0				
	1				
	2				
	4				
	6				
	7			35	(35)
III	3		9		
	5		4		
	9		5		
	8		10		
	10		6		
IV	11		2	36	(36)
V	12		5	5	5

(Station 1 spans the first block, (35); Station 2 spans column III–IV block, (36).)

Column no. in precedence diagram (a)	Element no. (b)	Transferability of element (c)	Element duration (d)	Duration of column (e)	Cumulative duration (f)
VI	13		4	4	9
VII	14		12	12	21
VIII	15		10	10	31
IX	16 17 18	 X X	5 15 10	30	61
X	19		5	5	66
XI	20		6	6	72

Table 15.5

Column no. in precedence diagram (a)	Element no. (b)	Transferability of element (c)	Element duration (d)	Duration of column (e)	Cumulative duration (f)	
	0 1 2 4 6 7		 35	(35)		Station 1
	3 5 9 8 10 11		 36	(36)		Station 2
V VI VII VIII IX	12 13 14 15 16		5 4 12 10 5	36	(36)	Station 3
IX	17 18		15 10	25	25	
X	19		5	5	30	
XI	20		6	6	36	

As can readily be seen from the example, this heuristic method is rapid, easy and often quite efficient. The allocation of elements is basically determined by precedence relationships, lateral transferability of elements being used to aid allocation when necessary. The originators of this method offer the following comments to aid in the application of the method.

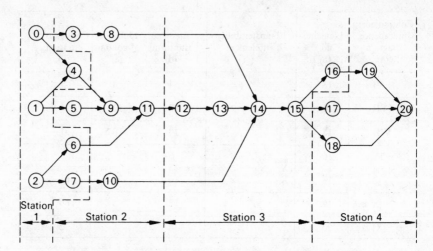

Figure 15.6   *Allocation of 21 elements to four work stations.*

1. Permutability within columns is used to facilitate the selection of elements (tasks) of the length desired for optimum packing of the work stations. Lateral transferability helps to deploy the work elements (tasks) along the stations of the assembly line so they can be used where they best serve the packing solution.
2. Generally the solutions are not unique. Elements (tasks) assigned to a station which belong, after the assignment is made, in one column of the precedence diagram can generally be permuted within the column. This allows the line supervisor some leeway to alter the sequence of work elements (tasks) without disturbing optimum balance.
3. Long-time elements (tasks) are best disposed of first, if possible. Thus, if there is a choice between the assignment of an element of duration, say, 20 and the assignment of two elements of duration, say 10 each, assign the larger element first. Small elements are saved for ease of manipulation at the end of the line. The situation is analogous to that of a paymaster dispensing the week's earnings in cash. He will count out the largest bills first. Thus, if the amount to be paid a worker is $77, the paymaster will give three $20 bills first, then one $10 bill, one $5 bill and two $1 bills in that order.
4. When moving elements laterally, the move is best made only as far to the right as is necessary to allow a sufficient choice of elements for the work station being considered.

In view of point 3 above, the *ranked positional weight* (*RPW*) method of assembly line balancing, described next, might be considered a logical extension of the present method, since in the RPW method a heuristic procedure is used which allocates elements to stations according to both their position in the precedence diagram and their duration.

Ranked positional weights

The ranked positional weight procedure (developed by Helgerson and Birnie) is a rapid, but approximate, method which has been shown to provide acceptably good solutions quicker than many of the alternative methods. It is capable of dealing with both precedence and zoning constraints. The procedure is best illustrated by considering a simple example.

Assembly of a very simple component involves 11 minimum rational work elements. There are constraints on the order in which these elements are to be undertaken, but there are no zoning constraints. Figure 15.7 is a precedence diagram in which the circles depict work elements. Element 2 must follow elements 0 and 1 and must precede element 5, etc. The standard element times (hours) are also shown in Figure 15.7. In Figure 15.8 this same information is listed: in the first column the element number is given, and in the second its standard time. The middle of the table shows the element precedences; for example, element 0 is immediately followed by element 2, which in turn is followed by 5, which is followed by 6 and 7, and so on. A single mark indicates the element which follows immediately and crosses indicate elements which follow because of their relationship with other elements. The final column of the table gives the *positional weight* (*PW*) for each element. This is calculated by summing the element's own standard time and the standard time for all following elements. Thus, in the case of element 0:

$$\begin{aligned} PW = \text{element} \quad 0 &= 0.32 \\ + \text{element} \quad 2 &= 0.20 \\ + \text{element} \quad 5 &= 0.23 \\ + \text{element} \quad 6 &= 0.20 \\ + \text{element} \quad 7 &= 0.05 \\ + \text{element} \quad 8 &= 0.32 \\ + \text{element} \quad 9 &= 0.10 \\ + \text{element} \ 10 &= 0.30 = 1.72 \end{aligned}$$

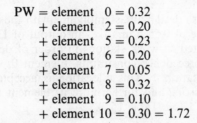

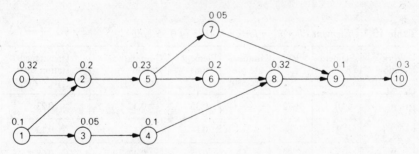

Figure 15.7   *Element precedence diagram.*

Element number	Element time (hours)	0	1	2	3	4	5	6	7	8	9	10	Positional weight
0	0.32			I			+	+	+	+	+	+	1.72
1	0.1			I	I	+	+	+	+	+	+	+	1.65
2	0.2						I	+	+	+	+	+	1.40
3	0.05					I				+	+	+	0.87
4	0.1									I	+	+	0.82
5	0.23							I	I	+	+	+	1.20
6	0.2									I	+	+	0.92
7	0.05										I	+	0.45
8	0.32										I	.+	0.72
9	0.1											I	0.40
10	0.3												0.30

Figure 15.8   *Precedence and positional weights table.*

The positional weight is therefore a measure of the size of an element and its position in the sequence of elements.

In Table 15.6 the elements, their times and the immediate predecessors are given in order of decreasing positional weights.

Table 15.6   *Elements in order of positional weights*

Element no.	0	1	2	5	6	3	4	8	7	9	10	Total
Element time	0.32	0.1	0.2	0.23	0.2	0.05	0.1	0.32	0.05	0.1	0.3	1.97
PW	1.72	1.65	1.4	1.2	0.92	0.87	0.82	0.72	0.45	0.40	0.30	
Predecessors (Immediate)	–	–	0,1	2	5	1	3	4,6	5	7,8	9	

We are required to design an assembly line with the minimum number of stations to provide a cycle time of 0.55 hours (i.e. an output of 1.82 per hour). Using Table 15.6, elements are allocated to work stations in order of decreasing positional weights and without violating precedence constraints. Element 0, with the highest PW of 1.72, is allocated first to station 1. This allocation is acceptable because element 0 has no immediate predecessors, and furthermore its element time is less than the spare time available in station 1 (see Table 15.7).

Table 15.7   *Element allocation for cycle time of 0.55 hours*

Work station	Element	PW	Immediate predecessor	Element time	Cumulative station time (Z)	Unassigned station time ($C - Z$)
	0	1.72	—	0.32	0.32	0.23
1	1	1.65	—	0.1	0.42	0.13
	3	0.87	1	0.05	0.47	0.08
	2	1.4	0,1	0.2	0.2	0.35
2	5	1.2	2	0.23	0.43	0.12
	4	0.82	3	0.1	0.53	0.02
3	6	0.92	5	0.2	0.2	0.35
	8	0.72	4,6	0.32	0.52	0.03
	7	0.45	5	0.05	0.05	0.50
4	9	0.4	7,8	0.1	0.15	0.40
	10	0.3	9	0.3	0.45	0.10

$C = 0.55$

Balancing loss $= \dfrac{4(0.55) - 1.97}{4(0.55)} \times 100 - 10.4\%$

Element 1 is the next to be allocated since it has the next highest PW. It is acceptable in station 1 since no precedence constraints are violated and there is sufficient unassigned cycle time left to accommodate it.

The next highest PW belongs to element 2, but this cannot be assigned to station 1, even though its immediate predecessors have been assigned, because the unassigned station time remaining (0.13) is less than the element time (0.2).

Element 5 cannot be allocated because it must follow element 2; nor is there enough time available.

Element 6 cannot be allocated to station 2 for the same reasons.

Element 3 can be allocated to station 1 since its immediate predecessor is already allocated and there is enough time available.

Of the remaining elements only 7 is short enough for accommodation in station 1, but it cannot be allocated here because it must follow element 5.

The same procedure is now repeated for the remaining stations.

Four work stations are required for this assembly line, and the initial allocation gives a balancing loss of 10.4 per cent. Notice that there is unassigned time at each station, the largest work station time of 0.53 hours occurring at station 2. In fact we now have a situation similar to the one depicted in Figure 15.4(b).

For the specified output required (1.82 per hour) there is no better solution than the one given above, but, if other considerations permit, the cycle time could be reduced to 0.53 hours with a corresponding increase in output to 1.89 per hour and a reduction of balancing loss to 7 per cent. A reduction of the cycle time to less than 0.53 hours would necessitate the use of five work stations.

There is really little point in retaining a cycle time of 0.55 hours in this case, since to do so is merely to introduce inefficiency into the system for the sake of obtaining a given output. Here, as in many cases of assembly line balancing, it is desirable to modify output in order to minimize balancing loss. In this case, therefore, the assembly line balancing procedure would be first to seek a balance for a given cycle time C, and then to minimize the cycle time for the same number of work stations. A flow diagram for such a procedure using the ranked positional weight (RPW) technique is shown in Figure 15.9.

COMSOAL

An interesting method of assembly line balancing called COMSOAL (computer method of sequencing operations for assembly lines) was developed around 1965 by Arcus. COMSOAL uses a computer to sample data and simulate possible assembly line balances. The simulation follows the following comparatively simple basic procedure:

1. Consider the job in terms of a precedence diagram of minimum rational work elements of the type shown in Figure 15.7. Construct a list (List A) showing, in one column, all work elements and, in an adjacent column, the total number of elements which *immediately precede* them in the precedence diagram. (Such a list based on Figure 15.7 is shown in Table 15.8.)
2. Construct a list (List B) showing all elements which have *no* immediate predecessors (i.e. elements with a zero in the second column of List A (Table 15.9).
3. Select at random one element from List B, say element 0.
4. Eliminate the selected element from List B and move all elements below the selected element up one position.
5. Eliminate the selected element from the precedence diagram and update List A.
6. Add to List B those elements which immediately follow the selected element and now have no immediate predecessors.

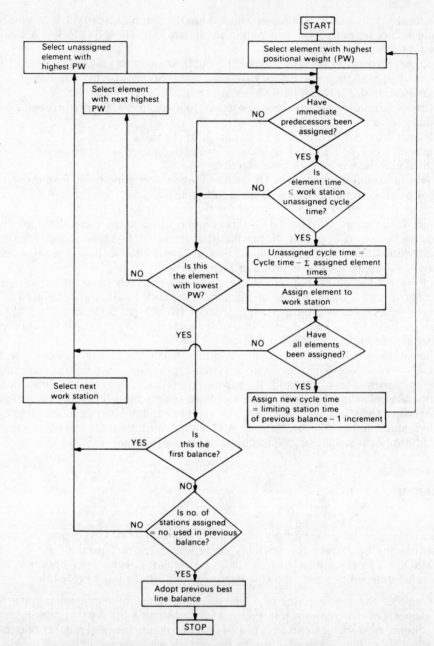

Figure 15.9   *Assembly line balancing (RPW method) (line first balanced for a given time C and then minimum cycle time obtained for the same number of stations).*

This simple procedure is then repeated until a sequence containing all elements has been constructed. The elements (in this order) are then assigned to station 1, 2, 3, etc., the cycle time at each station being diminished until no further elements can be accommodated, at which stage the next element is assigned to the next station. The number of stations used in the balance is counted, and compared with the previous best balance. If there is an improvement the new balance is stored in the computer and the previous best discarded;

thus by generating a fairly large set of possible solutions a good assembly line balance can be obtained.

Arcus improved this basic procedure by extracting from List B a further list, C, consisting of those elements whose times did not exceed the time available at the station under consideration, and then selecting elements randomly from this new list. A further improvement was achieved by using a biased or weighted sampling procedure to select elements from List C, in place of purely random selection. Arcus also incorporated a procedure by which a solution could be aborted before completion if the total station idle time of the incomplete solution exceeded that of the previous best solution.

Table 15.8 *List 'A'—COMSOAL*

Element No.	No of immediate predecessors
0	0
1	0
2	2
3	1
4	1
5	1
6	1
7	1
8	2
9	2
10	1

Table 15.9 *List 'B'—COMSOAL*

Elements without immediate predecessors
0
1

Multi-model and mixed-model line design

The use of flow-line techniques certainly leads to highly efficient production when product variety is small or non-existent, but any increase in the variety of the product not only leads to more complex design and management problems but also results inevitably in reduced operating efficiency. Increasing consumer discretion and increasing competition from other manufacturers restrict a company's ability to rationalize production, and consequently, for example, few if any motor vehicle assembly lines are now devoted to the continuous production of single uniform products, and a similar situation exists in many other industries. Multi-model or mixed-model lines must therefore be used and hence designed.

1. *Multi-model line*
    Again assuming a simple line design problem, this approach requires the following major decisions to be made:
    (a) How will the line be 'balanced'?
    (b) What will be the production batch sizes of the models?
    (c) In what order will the batches be manufactured? (The batch sequencing problem.)

2. *Mixed-model line*

   Here the major decisions are:
   (a) How will the line be balanced?
   (b) In what order will the models be launched into the line? (The model sequencing problem.)

Multi-model lines

The several models processed in batches on a multi-model line may either be different products or different versions of the same product, but in either case the different models or products will have similar, though not identical, manufacturing requirements, since otherwise there would be little justification in manufacturing them on the same basic assembly line.

Steyn[10] has shown that, in designing multi-model lines, it is necessary to take into account not only work content but also the processing costs and the model demand situation. The determination of the batch sizes to be processed for each model type is dependent on demand conditions and processing costs (i.e. set-up and holding costs) in precisely the same manner and for the same reasons as outlined in our discussion of batch processing in Chapter 14. Similarly, the cycle times to be employed on multi-model lines are dependent on the work content of models and the demand for each model. It follows that if the line is to be balanced, and the separate batches of items are to be scheduled against a specific cycle time or output rate, these problems cannot be tackled until production costs, market conditions, etc., have been taken into account. Steyn has developed a methodology for designing multi-model lines within this broader context. Our approach below recognizes these broader considerations but takes each line design problem individually.

In practice, in running a multi-model line, the line is set up for one model, then adjustments are made to the line prior to the manufacture of a batch of the second model, and so on. We can therefore consider the line design problem as being a succession of separate assembly-line design problems, hence decisions (a) and (b) above may be considered in the manner outlined previously. Decision (b), batch sizes, was dealt with in detail in Chapter 14, so we shall be concerned here only with decision (c), the batch sequencing problem.

The optimum manufacturing sequence for the batches of different models is clearly influenced by the cost of setting up the assembly line. The total cost of setting up the line comprises the cost of tool and machine change-overs, tool and machine resetting, machine and labour idle time, etc., and is clearly influenced by the nature of the preceding and succeeding models. The problem, therefore, is to determine the sequence order of the model batches to minimize the total setting-up cost over a given period of time. It is highly unlikely that line set-up costs will be constant, but, of course, if this were the case the sequence order of model batches would be immaterial.

One attractive and simple technique which will *often* give a solution to the batch sequencing problem is the assignment method of linear programming.[11] The matrix shown in Figure 15.10 shows the setting-up cost associated with pairs of models, i.e. the figures in the matrix are the costs of changing the assembly line from a set-up suitable for production of the 'preceding' model to one suitable for production of the 'succeeding'

---

[10] Steyn, P. G. (1977) Scheduling multi-model production lines *Business Management*, **8** (1). (Steyn deals specifically with paced lines but his point is also relevant in this context.)
[11] See Appendix 1.

Cost	Succeeding model			
Preceding model		A	B	C	D
	A	0	100	150	80
	B	50	0	100	75
	C	80	40	0	110
	D	115	100	60	0

Figure 15.10 *Setting-up cost associated with pairs of models.*

model. The zeros appear in the diagonal of this matrix, because these batch sequences involve no changes in the line set-up; however, since our objective is to determine the least cost of changes, we must ensure that the diagonal elements do not feature in the solution by attaching very high cost values to them (in this case a cost of 1000).

The solution to this assignment problem, which is shown in Figure 15.11 and can be derived easily by inspection, indicates that for minimum setting-up cost, model D must follow model A, model A must follow model B, B must follow C and C must follow D. In other words, starting with model A, the model batch sequence would be as follows:

$$A–D–C–B–A–D–C–\text{and so on}^{12}$$

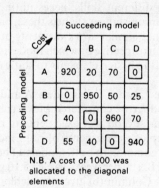

N.B. A cost of 1000 was
allocated to the diagonal
elements

Figure 15.11 *Least cost solution to the assignment problem in Figure 15.10.*

Mixed-model lines

The advantage of this type of production is that, unlike multi-model lines, a steady flow of models is produced in order to meet customer requirements, theoretically without the need for large stocks of finished goods. The major disadvantages arise from the differing work contents of the models, resulting in the uneven flow of work and consequent station idle time and/or congestion of semi-finished products.

---

[12] It is possible to extend this technique to cover the situation in which the initial state of the line is important, e.g. in which the initial state of the line is a result of the production of a model now discontinued. See Young, H. H. (1967) Optimising models for production lines, *Journal of Industrial Engineering*, **XVIII** (1), pp. 70–78.

This type of assembly line undoubtedly presents the most complex design and operating problems; indeed some of these problems are so complex that adequate analytical techniques have not yet been developed.

A certain amount of research has been undertaken, but a great deal more has yet to be learned before fully satisfactory management techniques are developed. We can therefore only attempt to summarize the issue involved and describe briefly some of the solutions that have been suggested. We shall deal mainly with the line balancing and the model sequencing problems, the latter being the more complex. Some computer programs have been developed by companies to deal with their own particular balancing and sequencing problems, but none of these is available for general use.

Line balancing for mixed-model assembly lines might be considered merely as several single-model balancing problems, i.e. each model could be considered separately and the total work content divided as equally as possible between the work stations. Consider a case where a line is built for the assembly of two similar models of a product, A and B. The work elements of model A are allocated to the work stations so that during the periods in which A is being assembled, balancing loss is minimized. Similarly, the work elements of B are allocated to work stations in order to minimize balancing loss during the assembly of model B. Such a procedure is often adopted and is fairly satisfactory when the models to be produced are of a similar nature, i.e. when the production of each model involves similar work elements to be undertaken in a similar order or when the production of all models merely involves the repetition of similar work elements. When such circumstances apply, the workers at each station will be required to do the same type of work irrespective of which model is being produced. If, on the other hand, basically dissimilar models are to be produced then independent line balancing for each will often result in dissimilar work elements, e.g. work involving different skills, necessitating different training, etc., being allocated to each station. In circumstances such as these, balancing should be undertaken in such a way as to ensure that similar work elements are allocated to the same work stations or groups of stations, irrespective of which model is being produced. A method by which this might be achieved is to assign elements to stations on a total time rather than a cycle time basis.

Consider the case mentioned above. Two models, A and B, are to be assembled on the same line. Model A is the product we considered previously (Figure 15.7) and model B is dissimilar but nevertheless has several work elements in common with model A.

The precedence relationship of the elements of both models is shown in Figure 15.12 (elements 1, 3, 4, 7, 8 and 9 are common to both models). The production requirements are: model A, 200 per week; model B, 100 per week. Table 15.10 gives all the details that we shall require for balancing the line. Column (b) gives the element duration. Column (e) shows the number of times the work element must be performed during the week to satisfy the output requirements of both models. The total time required for each work element per week is given in column (f) (total time/week = b × e).

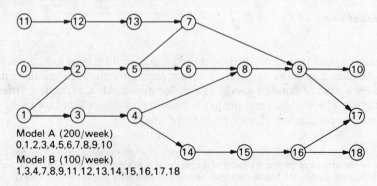

Figure 15.12 *Precedence diagram for elements of two models (A and B).*

Table 15.10 *Data for two-model line balancing problem*

(a) Element no.	(b) Element duration (hr)	(c) No. of	(d) times elements	(e) must be	(f) Total time/wk (hr)	(g) Positional weight (using total
		A	B	Total/wk	$\Sigma = 569$	times)
0	0.32	200	0	200	64	411
1	0.1	200	100	300	30	463
2	0.2	200	0	200	40	347
3	0.05	200	100	300	15	292
4	0.1	200	100	300	30	277
5	0.23	200	0	200	46	307
6	0.2	200	0	200	40	246
7	0.05	200	100	300	15	125
8	0.32	200	100	300	96	206
9	0.1	200	100	300	30	110
10	0.3	200	0	200	60	60
11	0.1	0	100	100	10	167
12	0.15	0	100	100	15	157
13	0.17	0	100	100	17	142
14	0.08	0	100	100	8	61
15	0.07	0	100	100	7	53
16	0.13	0	100	100	13	46
17	0.2	0	100	100	20	20
18	0.13	0	100	100	13	13

The line balance is obtained using the ranked positional weights technique, but instead of calculating positional weights by summing element times, they are found by summing total times. All that now remains is to allocate elements to work stations. The available time per station per week is considered to be 40 hours (five eight-hour days) and the element allocation is shown in Table 15.11. Balancing loss is 5.1 per cent but it has been necessary to combine several work stations because the total time for four elements (0, 5, 8 and 10) is greater than the available 40 hours.

These figures indicate that, in respect of one week's production, we have achieved quite a respectable line balance: a 5.1 per cent balancing loss is very good. Notice, however, that such a method of line balancing is justified *only* when production is truly *mixed*-model. Had there been a tendency to send models through the line in batches rather than individually, a quite unsatisfactory situation would have resulted. If a batch of model A is being assembled, stations 1, 8, 9, 10, 11, 13, 14 and 15 will be under-utilized and incur a great deal of balancing loss, and while the batch of model B is being assembled stations 2, 3, 4, 5, 6, 7, 13 and 14 will be under-utilized. Only if model A and model B are produced concurrently on the line, and particularly if the line has been designed to include buffer stocks between stations, will a satisfactory situation result from the allocation shown in Table 15.11. In other words, this method of 'combined' line balancing for a shift's or a week's production of all models is beneficial where:

(a) models are to be produced concurrently on the line, and not in batches;
(b) dissimilar work elements are involved and it is desirable to ensure that work of a similar nature is allocated to separate stations or groups of stations.

The efficient design and operation of mixed-model assembly lines depends on the solution of two problems: first, the line balancing problem just discussed, and second, the model sequencing problem. The latter problem, for which there is yet no satisfactory general solution, is concerned both with the time interval between the 'launching' or starting of models onto the line, and also with the *order* in which models are launched onto and flow along the line. The objective of such sequencing is to provide for the best utilization of the

Table 15.11 *Two-model assembly line balance*

Station no.	Element no.	Total time per week for element (hr)	Time remaining from 40–hour week (hr)
1	1	30	10
	11	10	0
2, 3	0	64	16
	3	15	1
4	2	40	0
5, 6	5	46	34
	4	30	4
7	6	40	0
8, 9, 10	8	96	24
	12	15	9
	14	8	1
11	13	17	23
	7	15	8
	15	7	1
12	9	30	10
13, 14	10	60	20
	16	13	7
15	17	20	20
	18	13	7

assembly line, high utilization being associated with minimum station idle time and minimum congestion of work along the line (item waiting).

Two systems of launching are used: *variable rate* and *fixed rate*. In variable-rate launching the time interval between the starting of successive models down the line is equal to the station cycle time of the leading model. For example, if three models, C, D and E, whose station cycle times are 4, 2 and 1 minutes respectively, are to be assembled on a line, a variable-rate launching system such as that shown in Figure 15.13 might be used.

It is quite clear from this figure that the time interval between successive stations starting work on any one model (α) is equal to the longest model cycle time, and consequently, when models with shorter cycle times are being assembled, a considerable amount of item waiting time results. Notice also that this same idle time results even when none of the models with the longer cycle time is present on the line. (After the 19th minute there are no model Cs on the line, yet the time interval is still four minutes.)

There is little that can be done by way of model sequencing to minimize this item waiting time, since, assuming that for each model the cycle time remains constant, and is equal at each station, the amount of item waiting time will always be determined by the difference in model cycle times. A reduction in item waiting time would be obtained by launching models with shorter cycle times first, but unless complete batching of models were possible, i.e. assembly of all model Es, then all model Ds and finally model Cs, the improvement would last only until it was necessary to launch one model C (see Figure 15.14)

An important practical disadvantage of variable-rate launching occurs where there is a need for related activities to be synchronized with the assembly line, e.g. the supply of materials at points along the line or the joining of two or more assembly lines (such as the merging of power train and body assembly lines in car manufacture). In such a case these related activities must be carefully planned and controlled to synchronize with the variable launching on the assembly line. In such circumstances a system of fixed-rate launching

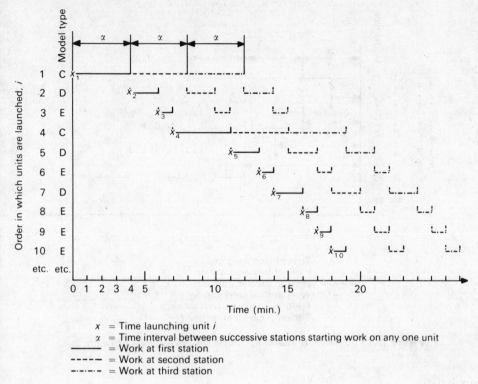

Figure 15.13 *Variable-rate launching of three models onto a three-station assembly line.*

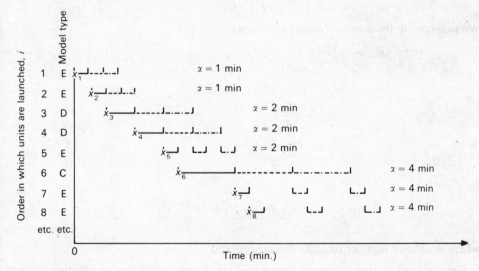

Figure 15.14 *Increase in item waiting time after launch of model C with longer cycle time.*

may be preferable, in which units are launched or started on the line at regular intervals (γ).

It is clear from Figure 15.15 that the fixed launching interval must not be greater than the time of the first unit or model launched, otherwise station idle time will result.

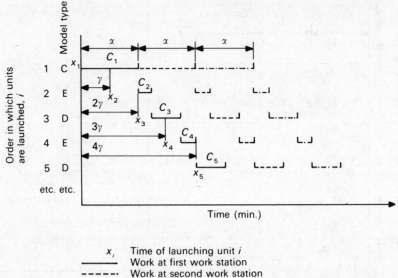

x_i   Time of launching unit *i*
――――   Work at first work station
------   Work at second work station
-·-·-··   Work at third work station
γ   Fixed launching interval for units
C_i   Station cycle times for unit *i*

Figure 15.15 *Fixed-rate launching system for three-station assembly line.*

Similarly:

$$\gamma \leqslant C_1$$

$$2\gamma \leqslant C_1 + C_2$$
$$3\gamma \leqslant C_1 + C_2 + C_3$$
$$4\gamma \leqslant C_1 + C_2 + C_3 + C_4$$

We can rewrite these requirements as follows:

$$\gamma \leqslant C_1$$

$$\gamma \leqslant \frac{C_1 + C_2}{2}$$

$$\gamma \leqslant \frac{C_1 + C_2 + C_3}{3}$$

$$\gamma \leqslant \frac{C_1 + C_2 + C_3 + C_4}{4}$$

$$\vdots$$

$$\gamma \leqslant \frac{C_1 + C_2 + C_3 + C_4 + \ldots + C_m}{m}$$

where m = total number of units to be produced.

Each of the requirements must be satisfied simultaneously if station idle time is to be avoided.

From Figure 15.15 it can also be seen that α, the time interval between successive stations starting work on any one unit, must ideally be equal to the longest station cycle time:

$$\alpha_{\text{optimum}} = \text{Max. } C$$

and it can be shown that the optimum value for γ is equal to the average of the station cycle times for all units:

$$\gamma_{\text{optimum}} = \frac{\Sigma N_j C_j}{\Sigma N_j}$$

where N_j = total number of model j required
C_j = cycle time for model j.

In order to avoid both operator idle time and the congestion of work on the line, the following double inequality must be satisfied each time a unit is launched onto the line:[13]

$$0 \leqslant \left(\sum_{h=1}^{i} C_h \right) - i\gamma \leqslant \alpha - \gamma$$

where C_h = cycle time.

It is usually impossible, unless both models and station times are very carefully chosen, to avoid both station idle time and work congestion, but, by careful ordering of the models, both of these inefficiencies can be minimized. To select the correct order a decision must be made every time a unit is launched onto the line, i.e. every step i. For example, in order to avoid station idle time and minimize work congestion, models should be launched onto the line so that for every launching or step i, the following function is minimized:

$$\left(\sum_{h=1}^{i} C_h \right) - i\gamma$$

EXAMPLE

Three models, A, B and C, of a particular product are assembled concurrently on an assembly line.

The quantities required over a given period and the model cycle times are as follows:

Model j	No. of units required N	Model cycle time C_j
A	60	0.5
B	110	0.6
C	55	0.8

Calculate the fixed interval at which units must be launched onto the line, and show how the sequence of models might be determined in order to avoid station idle time.

$$\gamma = \frac{\Sigma N_j C_j}{\Sigma N} = \frac{30 + 66 + 44}{60 + 110 + 55}$$

$$= 0.62$$

Units must be launched onto the line in such a way that multiples of the launching interval $(i\gamma)$ are less than, but as nearly equal as possible to, the sum of the model cycle times.

$$\left(\sum_{h=1}^{i} C_h \right)$$

Such a method of launching is illustrated in Table 15.12.

---

[13] For the derivation of this and the other formulae in this section see Wester, L. and Kilbridge, M. (1964) The assembly line model – mix sequencing problem, *Proceedings of 3rd International Conference on Operations Research* 1963, Dunod, Paris.

Table 15.12 *Fixed-interval launching of units onto an assembly line*

Unit i	$i\gamma$	Model	Model cycle time C_i	$\sum_{h=1}^{i} C_h$	$\left(\sum_{h=1}^{i} C_h\right) - i\gamma$
1	0.62	C	0.8	0.8	0.18
2	1.24	A	0.5	1.3	0.06
3	1.86	B	0.6	1.9	0.04
4	2.48	B	0.6	2.5	0.02
5	3.10	B	0.6	3.1	0.00
6	3.72	C	0.8	3.9	0.18
7	4.34	A	0.5	4.4	0.06
8	4.96	B	0.6	5.0	0.04
9	5.58	B	0.6	5.6	0.02
10	6.20	B	0.6	6.2	0.00
11	6.82	C	0.8	7.0	0.18
12	7.44	A	0.5	7.5	0.06
13	8.06	B	0.6	8.1	0.04
14	8.68	B	0.6	8.7	0.02
15	9.30	B	0.6	9.3	0.00
16	9.92	C	0.8	10.1	0.18
17	10.54	A	0.5	10.6	0.06
18	11.16	B	0.6	11.2	0.04
19	11.78	B	0.6	11.8	0.02
20	12.40	B	0.6	12.4	0.00
21	13.02	C	0.8	13.2	0.18
22	13.64	A	0.5	13.7	0.07
. . .	. . .	. . .	. . .	. . .	. . .
etc.	etc.	etc.	etc.	etc.	etc.

Notice that in this example the optimum sequence of models results from the repeated launching of models in the order:

$$C\text{–}A\text{–}B\text{–}B\text{–}B$$

but notice also that the continual launching of units in this order would not lead to the assembly of the required number of each model in the given time period (too many of model B and too few of models A and C would be completed). Consequently, in practice it would be necessary to depart from this optimal procedure to some extent in order to satisfy manufacturing requirements. Had the figure in the final column ($\Sigma C_h - i\gamma$) been greater than $\alpha - \gamma$ (0.18) at any time, this would have indicated that the operator would have been forced out of his or her work station in order to complete the work on the particular unit, or alternatively that the unit would continue to the next station incomplete.

The only other published treatment of the mixed-model assembly line sequencing problem is by Thomopolous. He deals with the fixed-rate launching system but develops a more comprehensive treatment of the subject than that presented briefly here. He attempts, by means of a simulation procedure (which, in cases involving many models and/or units, would be very long), to determine the ordering of models to minimize total cost of station idle time and work congestion. In many respects both these treatments are inadequate and a great deal of progress must be made before practical, comprehensive and efficient methods of mixed-model assembly line design are available.

THE DESIGN OF 'COMPLEX' FLOW LINES

Human aspects of assembly line design *(see also Chapter 9)*

The major assumption in our discussion of simple flow-line design was that elements of work require a given constant time, the standard element time. In the chapters on work study the validity of the assumption that there was a single best method of doing a job and consequently a single time for the job was criticized. But even assuming this to be the case, or assuming that for some other reason a worker continually adopts the specified work method, it still does not follow that the time required will be constant. There may be occasions when faulty materials or parts are received and consequently more time is required to assemble them. Workers may drop or fumble with the parts or the tools, or their attention may be distracted. They may talk to their neighbours or think about something else, and all these things may affect the time required to complete the operation.

This phenomenon of variability is the fundamental difference between assembly lines involving human operators and those depending exclusively on machines, i.e. transfer lines. It is not invalid to assume that machines at stations on transfer lines require a constant time for elements of work, but it certainly is quite unrealistic to make the same assumption about human beings. The procedures described above are adequate by themselves for the design of transfer lines, but insufficient for the design of assembly lines involving human workers.

After a considerable amount of research it has been found that unpaced work time distributions (the time taken by workers to perform elements of work or operations) are usually unimodal and positively skewed, i.e. the distributions have a single peak, and a long 'tail' to the right of the peak. The distribution shown in Figure 15.16 is that of work times for a packing task.

Clearly, if we were to design assembly lines in which workers were allowed a fixed standard time, neither more nor less, in which to complete an operation, we might find that on some occasions the worker would easily complete the task within this time, while on other occasions he or she would be prevented from doing so. This type of situation is referred to as *rigid pacing*. There is no 'freedom' for workers, since they are confined to perform each and every operation in a given time.

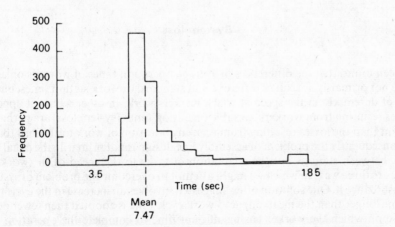

Figure 15.16 *Work time distribution for an unpaced task. From Conrad, R. and Hille, D. A. (1955) Comparison of paced and unpaced performance at a pacing task, Occupational Psychology, 24(15). Reproduced with permission.*

Consider the time distribution for the unpaced task shown in Figure 15.17. This is the distribution which would result in the absence of any pacing influence or imposed work time. If an assembly line is designed in which there is rigid pacing and in which the worker is allowed the mean time to complete the task, then on some occasions he or she may be unable to complete the task, and the product would pass on down the line partially completed, later to be rejected. On the remaining occasions the worker would have more time available than required, and while idle time may not necessarily result, there would certainly be an under-utilization of the worker.

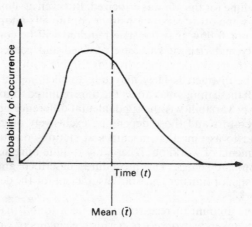

Figure 15.17 *Unpaced work time distribution.*

This phenomenon is referred to as *system loss* and often occurs where workers on assembly lines are subject to some form of pacing. In practice, rigid pacing rarely occurs (except on transfer lines) but some degree of pacing, involving a tolerance about a given time, often occurs. For example, in motor-vehicle assembly, pacing is not rigid since the workers can ride along or follow the line while completing their jobs.

System loss

It has been found that the differences in average operation times of workers on assembly lines are not primarily a result of differences in standard or work station times, but largely a result of differences in the speed at which workers work. In other words, it appears that the losses resulting from workers' variable operation times (system loss) are perhaps more important than the losses resulting from uneven allocation of work to stations (balancing loss). Consequently the problem of assembly line design is not primarily the equal division of work between stations but the adaptation of tasks to the speed of the workers.

There are three ways in which we might attempt to overcome the problem of system loss, or at least reduce it. One solution often suggested involves an increase in the cycle time. If a cycle time longer than the mean unpaced work cycle time is adopted then fewer occasions will arise on which the worker has insufficient time to complete the operation. This is, however, quite unsatisfactory, and is not really a solution at all, since there are now more occasions on which the worker could complete the operation in less than the time available. There may be some marginal benefit in increasing the cycle time if the cost of faulty or incomplete items is particularly high, but in general such a 'solution' does not reduce total system loss. Nevertheless, there is often a temptation to increase cycle time. For example, if 10 per cent of the output from an assembly line is defective because of uncompleted operations, a corresponding increase in cycle time will perhaps reduce the defective output level, but only at the cost of lower utilization of labour.

A second and superior solution is to eliminate or reduce the cause of the problem, i.e. the pacing effect. There are two ways in which we can attempt to do this, both involve making the items available to the worker for a longer period of time. Take, for example, an assembly line consisting of workers sitting at a bench above which jobs travel by means of a conveyor belt with suspended baskets. The worker must take the job off the belt, perform the operation and replace it on the belt, which carries it to the next station. Jobs spaced at 5 m intervals on a belt moving at 5 m/min will produce an output of 60 products/hour. The same output will result from a spacing of 10 m and a belt speed of 10 m/min, or a spacing of 2.5 m and a belt speed of 2.5 m/min. But each of these different arrangements has different consequences for the seated worker, who can reach only a certain distance either side of the work station. If the worker can reach 2.5 m either way, then in the first case each job will be within reach and available for one minute only, in the second case for half a minute, and in the last case two minutes. Clearly the greater the time the job is available to the worker the lower is the pacing effect, and system loss is reduced.

On assembly lines where jobs pass directly from one worker to the next, every worker, except the one at the first station on the line, is dependent on the previous worker. Under such conditions the work must be strictly paced in order to avoid excessive labour idle time. If, for example, because of faulty material or a mistake in assembly, a worker at one station takes longer than the cycle time to complete the operation, then the worker at the next station on the line will have to wait for work (unless coincidentally he or she also has exceeded the cycle time for his or her operation). This coupling or interdependence of stations necessitates pacing, but if the stations could be decoupled in some way the pacing effect, and also system loss, could be reduced.

Buffer stocks *(see also Chapter 17)*

The way in which this is done is to introduce buffer stocks of several jobs between stations, so that temporary hold-ups or delays at stations do not immediately result in idle time at subsequent stations. There are certain disadvantages in using buffer stocks on assembly lines. Work-in-progress stock and hence tied-up capital will be increased, and additional space will be required. In fact, in many cases, because of the size of the items, it may be quite unrealistic to consider using buffer stocks. (Introducing inter-station buffer stocks onto a motor vehicle final assembly line would not be a suggestion that the company accountant or the works manager would receive too enthusiastically.) However, in many situations buffer stocks are an important feature of assembly line operation.

Figure 15.18, showing the performance of perfectly balanced assembly lines of various lengths, indicates that the use of buffer stocks of only one item has a significant effect on system loss and, furthermore, that system loss increases as the number of stations increases.

It is possible using statistical queuing theory to calculate the effect of inter-station buffer stocks on assembly line efficiency. In order to be able to use the conventional formulae, one must assume that work time distributions conform to the negative exponential distribution. Furthermore, using this approach it is difficult to treat lines of more than two stations. Despite these assumptions the results of such calculations merit examination. If

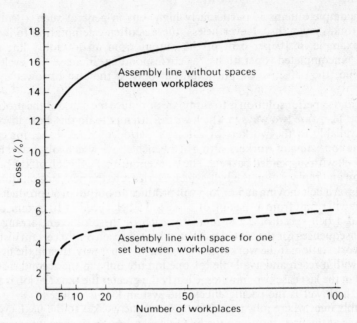

Figure 15.18 *System losses related to length and layout of assembly line. From Van Beek, H. G. (1964) The influence of assembly line organisation on output, quality and morale, Occupational Psychology, 38, pp. 161–172. Reproduced with permission.*

we assume that an infinite stock is available for the first station[14] and that no stock is allowed between the stations, then the utilization of the line is only 67 per cent, whereas the introduction of buffer stocks between the stations increases utilization as follows:[15]

Buffer stock	Utilization (%)
2	75
3	80
4	83
8	90

A certain amount of research work has been undertaken in an attempt to determine the optimum inter-station buffer stock capacity (i.e. the maximum amount of buffer stock to allow between stations) under more practical conditions. This research has again depended on assumptions about the nature of work time distribution and also on the assumption of a 'steady state', i.e. that the assembly line has been operating for a sufficient time to allow a steady or stable condition to arise at each station. Of all the conventional statistical probability distributions it is perhaps most realistic to assume that the work time conforms to the normal distribution. Young,[16] using a model previously developed

[14] This is not such an unreasonable assumption, since it implies only that there are sufficient stocks of raw materials or components to maintain the line continually.

[15] Hunt, G. C. (1956) Sequential arrays of waiting lines, *Operations Research*, **4**, p. 675.

[16] Young, H. H. (1967) Optimization models for production lines, *Journal of Industrial Engineering*, **XVIII**(1), pp. 70–78.

by Barten,[17] assuming steady state conditions and the normal work time distribution, has developed a formula for the optimum buffer stock capacity, as follows:

$$X = \frac{K L_2 \sigma^{0.61}}{L_1}$$

where X = optimum buffer capacity at stages in a balanced production line
L_2 = idle facilities cost per unit time
L_1 = unit inventory cost per unit time
σ = standard deviation of the normally distributed work times
K = a constant which depends on the number of stations, e.g.
K = 0.39 for four stages
0.43 for six stages
0.47 for eight stages

Young used a computer to simulate assembly lines (in which no machine maintenance time was required) to test the above formula. He found that the buffer capacities calculated by the formula were very close to the simulated optimum buffer capacities.

More recently, computer simulation has been used by Anderson and Moodie[18] to determine optimum buffer stock capacity. Theirs was a somewhat involved piece of research which cannot be described in detail here, but their simulation and analysis '. . . showed that both the numbers of stages and the in-process inventory buffer capacity have a significant effect on the average delay of the production line and the average in-process inventory'.

Complex line balancing

Our previous description of assembly line balancing concerned the relatively simple situation in which only precedence and zoning constraints were considered and in which standard, fixed work cycle times were assumed to apply. Already we have discovered one additional complexity, that work cycle times usually vary, and we should therefore re-examine assembly line balancing in the light of this situation. In practice the previous assumption is usually implicit in assembly line balancing, an approach which, although theoretically incorrect, can perhaps be justified in the case where buffer stocks are included to absorb the effect of work cycle time variations. Indeed there is very little alternative to this practice, since as yet there is no completely acceptable, widely adopted method of balancing assembly lines for probabilistic work cycle times. There are some published papers which deal specifically with the problem, but none are concerned primarily with obtaining line balances.[19, 20] Perhaps the most attractive method of dealing with this complexity was developed by Arcus, who extended his COMSOAL method (described previously) to deal with the assembly line balancing problem in its more complex form. As well as probabilistic work cycle times, the COMSOAL method is claimed to be able to

[17] Barten, K. A. (1962) A queueing simulator for determining optimum inventory levels in a sequential process, *Journal of Industrial Engineering*, **XIII**(4).
[18] Anderson, D. R. and Moodie, C. L. (1969) Optimal buffer storage capacity in production lines, *International Journal of Production Research*, **7**(3), pp. 233–240.
[19] Moodie, C. L. and Young, H. H. (1965) A heuristic method of assembly line balancing for assumptions of constant or variable work element times, *Journal of Industrial Engineering*, **XVI**(1).
[20] Mansoor, E. M. and Ben-Tuvia, S. (1966) Optimizing balanced assembly lines, *Journal of Industrial Engineering*, **XVII**(3).

balance lines subject to numerous other complexities, such as work elements larger than the cycle time, zoning constraints, work elements requiring more than one operator, etc. Because of this flexibility, the COMSOAL method is undoubtedly an attractive technique, but even so it has not been widely adopted in practice, industry preferring, it seems, to use simpler, more subjective procedures rather than the computationally complex but more comprehensive methods such as COMSOAL and others.

Types of manual flow lines

When discussing the simple lines above it was unnecessary to distinguish between different methods of line operation since, in the simple case, there is really only one logical operating method, i.e. all stations have the same fixed cycle time, and work flow along the line is regular, since the transfer or movement of items between all stations takes place at the same time. In practice not only is the manner in which manual flow lines operate somewhat more complex than that described above, because of the characteristic work element and service-time variability, but there are also many possible methods of operation. In concluding our brief discussion of 'complex' (i.e. real) flow lines we shall consider alternative operating methods.

We can first identify two basic types of manual flow line:

1. *Non-mechanical lines*, consisting of lines which do not use a moving belt or conveyor for the transfer of work along the line or between stations. Such lines, although probably making use of power and hand tools, are essentially, manually operated.
2. *Moving-belt lines*, consisting of all those types of lines which use a continually moving belt or conveyor for the transfer of items along the line and/or between stations.

Moving-belt lines can be broken down into two further categories:

(a) Items are removable from the belt
(b) Items are fixed to the belt.

And the second of these two categories can be further divided to give a total of five types of line. The five types are described briefly below and their characteristics are summarized in Table 15.13.

Non-mechanical lines

If all the stations on the flow lines are able to retain items until they have been completed and are able to pass items to the next station on completion, there is a variable-cycle-time situation in which, because there is no maximum limit, incomplete items should not be produced. Furthermore, if such a method of operation were used, there should be no under-utilization of stations or idle time, since the cycle time would always be equal to the service time. In practice, it is not normally possible to operate a line in this manner because of the interdependence of stations. While it is possible to avoid the production of incomplete items, idle time cannot be avoided, and will occur for two reasons:

(a) because, on occasions, stations will be starved of work, i.e. once an item has been passed to the next station, a delay will follow before another item becomes available from the previous station;

Table 15.13　Types of manual flow lines and their characteristics (From Wild, R. (1972) *Mass Production Management*. New York: Wiley.)

	Non-mechanical lines	Moving-belt lines			
		Items removed from line	Items fixed to line		
			Station overlap possible	No station overlap possible	
				More than one item available to station ($T_F < T_T$)	Only one item available to station ($T_F \geq T_T$)
Cycle time	Variable	Variable	Variable	Variable	Fixed (determined by station length and feed rate)
Work flow	Irregular	Irregular	Regular	Regular	Regular
Buffer stocks	Would reduce idle time	Would reduce number of incomplete items and idle time	Physical stocks not possible	Physical stocks not possible	Physical stocks not possible
Feed rate (interval = T_F)	None, except perhaps for first station	Fixed for first station only	Fixed	Fixed	Fixed
Limits on maximum service time	None	None	Determined by station length, feed rate and previous station	Determined by station length and feed rate	Maximum service time = cycle time
Tolerance time (T_T)	Does not apply	Yes	Yes	Yes	Yes
Mechanical pacing	None	With margin	With margin	With margin	With margin
Incomplete items	None	Possible	Possible	Possible	Possible
Station idle time { through blocking	Possible	Not possible	Not possible	Not possible	Possible because of fixed cycle time (can be considered as either 'blocking or starving')
through starving	Possible	Possible	Possible	Possible	

(b)   because, on occasions, a worker will be prevented from passing a completed item to the next station because that station is still engaged on its work on the previous item, i.e. the station which has completed its work is blocked by the subsequent station.

In practice, if stations operating in this manner are not decoupled by the provision of space for buffer stocks of items between stations, idle time caused by both starving and blocking will be considerable. Thus, in practice, it is normal for this type of line to incorporate buffer stocks. A buffer stock can be defined, therefore, as 'items located between stations to reduce the probability of station starving or blocking'.

This method of line operation involves no work pacing, since there is no maximum cycle time or, theoretically, a limit to the minimum cycle time.

Since the cycle time on this type of line is variable, the flow of work along the line is irregular. Because this type of line does not depend on the use of a moving belt or conveyor, a fixed feed rate does not exist, except perhaps at the first station.

Moving-belt lines

Items removed from line

There are several types of operating line in which item movement is by means of moving belts. Perhaps the most complex type of line is the one in which workers at stations remove an item from the line to perform their work, placing it back on the line on completion of the work before picking up the next item. If we consider any one station on such a line, we can identify the following possibilities:

1.   Idle time or station under-utilization may occur if, on completion of one item, the subsequent item is not available to the operator, i.e. idle time may occur because of starvation at the station. The possibility of blocking does not arise because of the continuous movement of the belt and because:
2.   Items may pass a station without being worked on at the station. If a worker finds it necessary to spend considerably more time than usual working on a particular item, it is possible that, during this time, the moving line may carry the next item past the station. Thus, on this type of line, the production of incomplete items is a possibility.

On such lines there is likely to be a fixed feed rate for the first station, since items will probably be fed to the moving line at regular intervals. However, for subsequent stations the fixed rate is likely to be irregular and dependent on the service time of preceding stations. Work flow, therefore, is irregular, and line output is determined by the average feed rate or the fixed feed rate of the first station. The cycle time on these lines is variable, and since there is (theoretically, at least) no maximum cycle time, there is no work pacing, at least not in a mechanical sense. (Notice, however, that on both this and the previous type of line there may be a psychological pacing factor, since excess time spent on one item will result in either the accumulation of large buffer stocks or the production of incomplete items.)

Buffer stocks may be introduced into these lines if workers at stations remove items from the line rather than letting them pass by while completing work on a previous item. Even so, station blocking will not occur, since, when such buffer stocks reach the maximum level, provided the stock is off the line, it will always be possible for the previous station to place items on the line.

On such lines the tolerance time is an important concept. The tolerance time is the time period during which an item is available to be taken from the line, and therefore it is determined by the belt speed and the length of the station through which it passes.

Items fixed to line

Station overlap possible. Very often, on a flow line in which a moving belt is used, the items on which work is to be performed are, in effect, fixed to the line. By this we mean that they are attached to the line or, because of their weight or other characteristics, cannot be removed from the line. The latter situation exists in motor-vehicle assembly lines. In this type of line the work must be performed at each station while the item is in motion. This requires workers at stations to either reach up and down the line or to move with the line to complete their work. In such cases, depending on the physical nature of the line, it is possible for some overlapping of stations to occur, the extent of the possible overlap being determined by the spacing, reach or permitted movement of workers.

On lines of this type the work flow is regular and the cycle time is variable.

Since there will be a limit to either the reach or the permitted movement of workers in either direction, the cycle time is subject to a maximum limit, and thus the work is paced with margin. The maximum cycle time available for an item at a station will be determined by the time at which it is completed by the previous station, the line speed, and the maximum permitted reach or movement of the station down the line. It will be possible for incomplete items to pass from stations because of the limit on cycle times. Idle time may also occur because of work starvation at stations, but blocking is not normally possible, and neither is it possible to introduce physical stocks of items (i.e. buffer stocks) onto such lines. Notice that the term 'tolerance time' is useful in describing this type of line.

No station overlap possible. On occasion, the class of line described above is used without the facility for station overlap, although this is perhaps less usual than the previous case. Depending on the spacing of the items on the belt and the length of work stations, two alternatives are available:

(a)   lines on which more than one item is available to the station;
(b)   lines on which only one item is available to each station.

Alternative (a) is the more usual case, and we shall examine this first. The characteristics of such lines are very similar to fixed item/station overlap lines in that:

(a)   the cycle time is variable with a maximum determined by the length of the station and the line speed and item spacing; thus
(b)   work is paced with margin;
(c)   work flow, as in all lines with fixed items, is regular; and
(d)   the feed rate is fixed;
(e)   the production of incomplete items is possible because of the limit of the maximum cycle time; and
(f)   idle time is possible because of starving, but blocking is not possible;
(g)   the use of physical buffer stocks of items is not possible.

This type of line is not, perhaps, in widespread use, although often individual stations on other types of line have to operate in this mode. The best example of this is the case of a spray booth on a flow line. This is a 'closed' station, and overlap with the stations on either side of it is normally impossible.

The fundamental difference between this type of line and the type described previously concerns the influence of preceding stations. Since the preceding station cannot encroach on the subsequent station, the cycle time is limited only by station length and feed rate, and is independent of the service time or completion time of the previous station.

Alternative (b), in which only one item is available to non-overlapping stations, is a more abstract case, and here we are departing from our principle of defining basic types of line according to their practical use. The reason for the inclusion of this type will become clear shortly. In this type of line the cycle time is fixed and is determined by the station length and the feed rate (line speed and item spacing). As before, work flow is regular and the feed rate fixed. Again, it is possible for incomplete items to be produced because of the limited cycle time, and, furthermore, it is possible for station idle time or under-utilization to occur, but in this case the cause of idle time differs from that described previously. Here idle time or under-utilization can and will occur because, irrespective of the time required for work at a station (the service time), the item remains at the station for a fixed time (the cycle time). The obligation for a worker at a station to take a fixed time for each item and the resultant idle time which may occur can be likened to either starving or blocking, but, strictly speaking, it is quite a different phenomenon. On such lines pacing is with margin, and again it is, strictly speaking, different from the pacing experienced by workers on the other types of line because the maximum service time available for any station is the same for each cycle.

This type of moving-belt flow line is rarely found in practice. However, its operating characteristics are identical to those of a type of line which does not incorporate the moving-belt principle.

Rather than add a further category to our classification to accommodate this type of line, it is more convenient to describe it in terms of our existing class. In practice, therefore, fixed-cycle-time lines of this type often take the form described below.

Visual or audible signals are often used to enforce this method of line operation, i.e. to prompt the passage of items between stations. For example, in suitably arranged lines in which all workers are facing in one direction, a 'traffic-light' type arrangement at the head of the line is sometimes used. These lights flash or change colour at cycle time intervals, at which times workers are required to pass the item on which they have been working to the next station. Alternatively an audible signal such as a bell or buzzer may be used if more convenient, workers being required to pass their work down the line on hearing the signal. In lines operating in this manner all stations have the same maximum time in which to complete their work, i.e. the cycle time, which is determined by the line output requirement. This is the maximum time available, but the work could be completed in less than this cycle time. Thus pacing with margin applies, the time available ranging in theory from zero time to the cycle time. Because items remain at each station for the cycle time, irrespective of the work station time for the particular item, the work flow on this type of line is regular, idle time may occur and incomplete items may be produced.

COMPUTERS IN FLOW PROCESSING DESIGN

Much of the work in designing flow processing systems requires simple but repetitive calculations. The balancing of lines, particularly the balancing of mixed and multi-model lines, the determination of batch sizes, the sequencing of models, etc., are all relatively straightforward analytical procedures. In many cases these line design problems will be tackled infrequently, especially in the case of single-model flow processing systems. In designing these flow processing systems it is important that adequate solutions be found, since the introduction of inefficiencies will be costly. In other circumstances, in particular in the design of mixed-model and multi-model flow lines, line design decisions will be made more often, perhaps at the changeover from one model to the next, changeover of shifts, etc. Again it is important that adequate solutions be found to the line design problems, and also that these solutions should be found relatively quickly and at minimum cost. All these requirements point to the advantages of using computer-based line design methods. Many computer programs are available for line balancing, for simulating different types of line operation, etc. The information shown in Table 15.14 is no more than an indication of the types of programs which are available, and thus an indication of the way in which computers are now used extensively in the design of flow processing systems.

Table 15.14 *Computer programs for flow line design*

Program name	Source/origin	Description
BAL-ANCE	Harris, R. D. and Maggard, M. J. (1972) *Computer Models in Operations Management.* London: Harper and Row.	Line balancing program written in Fortran IV. Program offers the user a choice of five different heuristic rules to balance lines. User must also choose whether to balance for a desired number of stations or against a desired cycle time. Heuristics are: 1. Assign to station feasible element with largest work element time. 2. Assign to station feasible element with smallest work element time. 3. Assign to station first available feasible work element. 4. Assign to station the feasible work element with the next highest element number. 5. Assign feasible element selected randomly.
(No name)	American Institute of Industrial Engineers, 25 Technology Park, Atlanta, Norcross, Georgia, 30092 USA	Program for line balancing. Program applies a COMSOAL approach to solve the line balancing problem iteratively. The program attempts to minimize the number of work stations and the time assigned to the work station with the maximum service time. For micro-computers, e.g. TRS 80 and Apple II.
LINBAL	Nicholson, T. A. J. and Pullen, R. D. (1974) *Computers in Production Management Decisions.* London: Pitman.	Line balancing program. Interactive program to help designer to evaluate alternative line arrangements. All elements are pre-assigned to stations and input together with details on staffing of stations. Program then calculates station times and balance loss and prints out station element allocations. Designer can then manipulate design by: moving elements between stations; moving elements off the line; assigning new times to elements; cancelling elements not needed; inserting new elements; inserting new stations; changing staffing at stations.
(No name)	Fiske, T. S. (1981) *Industrial Engineering*, August, pp. 58–62.	Program considers learning effects and length of run to determine tightness of line balance. Written in BASIC for a micro-computer (TRS 80).
(No name)	Whitehouse, G. E. and Washburn, D. (1980) Solve simple assembly line balance problems, *Industrial Engineering*, 12(9), pp. 22–24.	Solves simple line balancing problems. Takes precedence and element times, and balances line against a maximum cycle time. No zoning constraints. Written in BASIC for a micro-computer (TRS 80).
CALB GALS CABS CAML etc.	Advanced manufacturing methods program, Illinois Institute of Technology, Research Institute, Chicago, USA	Comprehensive set of programs for use in various aspects of flow line design, e.g. CALB—line balancing GALS—flow line operation simulation CABS—batch scheduling CAML—machine loading

CHECKLIST FOR CHAPTER 15

Types of flow processing system
Mass production
  Mass production systems
  Classes and varieties of flow line
    Single-model lines
    Multi-model lines
    Mixed-model lines
Design of 'simple' flow lines
  Line balance
    Cycle time
    Service time
    Production and non-productive work
    Precedence
  Line balancing
    Objectives
    Methods
      Kilbridge and Wester
      Ranked positional weights
      COMSOAL
  Multi-model lines
    Nature
    Line balancing
    Batch sizes
    Batch sequencing
  Mixed-model lines
    Line balancing

Launching
  Variable rate
  Fixed rate
  Model sequencing
Design of 'complex' flow lines
  Human aspects
  Work time distributions
  Pacing
    Rigid
    With margin
  System losses
  System loss problems
    Solutions
      Cycle time choice
      Buffer stocks
  Complex line balancing
  Types of manual flow line
    Non-mechanical lines
    Moving belt lines
      Removable items
      Fixed items
        Station overlap
        No station overlap
Use of computers in flow process design
  Line balancing programs

FURTHER READING

Buxey, G. M., Slack, N. D. C. and Wild, R. (1973) Production flow systems design—A review, *AIIE Transactions*, **5**(1), pp. 37–48. A survey and summary of flow line design procedures.

Chase, R. B. (1975) Strategic considerations in assembly line selection, *Californian Management Review*, **18**(1), pp. 17–23.

Dar-el, E. M. and Rubinovitch, Y. (1979) MUST—A multiple solutions technique for balancing single model assembly lines, *Management Science*, **25**(11), pp. 1105–1124.

Mastor, A. A. (1970) An experimental investigation and comparative evaluation of production line balancing techniques, *Management Science (Theory)*, **16**(11), pp. 728–784. A detailed comparative study of line balancing procedures.

Wild, R. (1972) *Mass Production Management*. New York: Wiley. A comprehensive treatment of discrete item mass production flow systems. The only book currently available on the subject.

QUESTIONS

15.1 A multi-station flow line is to process a minimum of 6000 completed items per 40-hour working shift. Each item requires 25 elements of work together constituting a total work content of 11 minutes.

    What is the minimum number of work stations for this line and what will the cycle time (C) ideally be?

15.2 What will the balancing loss be of the line, the requirements of which are given above?

15.3   The diagram shown below indicates the necessary precedence requirements of 12 work elements which together constitute the total work content of a simple service task.

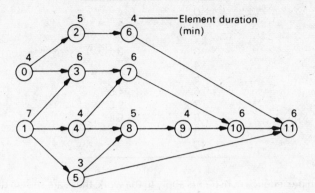

Figure Q15.3

Using the line balancing technique devised by Kilbridge and Wester, design a line (i.e. assign work elements to the required number of work stations) to produce as near as possible to, and no less than, three items per hour.

What is the balancing loss for the line that you have designed?

15.4   Use the Kilbridge and Wester line balancing technique to balance a simple line, with the minimum number of work stations, to process a minimum of 60 items per hour. The processing of each item consists of 21 work elements, some of which must be performed in a given order as shown by the precedence diagram below.

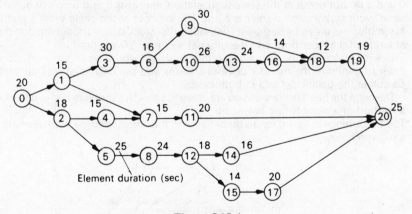

Figure Q15.4

15.5   The work involved in assembling a small component can be described in terms of 11 minimum rational work elements whose element times are as follows:

Element	Time (min.)
0	4
1	3
2	3
3	3
4	7
5	5
6	4.5
7	9.5
8	5
9	7
10	7

Certain precedence constraints apply to the work; these are shown diagrammatically below.

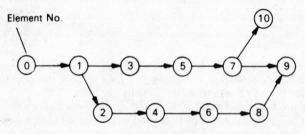

Figure Q15.5

Furthermore, because of the nature of the work it is necessary to ensure that elements 0 and 3 *do not* occur at the same work station, elements 3 and 5 *do not* occur at the same work station, and elements 8 and 10 *do* occur at the same work station. Two assembly lines are to be designed (without buffer stocks), one producing components at a rate of 4.61 per hour and the other at a rate of 5.0 per hour.

Use the ranked positional weight method to assign work elements to work stations in order to minimize the number of work stations and the balancing loss on each line. Calculate the balancing loss in both cases.

Describe the heuristic device you are using to solve this problem and justify its use as a method of assembly line balancing.

15.6 The precedence diagram for an operation and the corresponding work element times are given below.

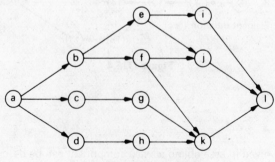

Figure Q15.6

Work element	Time (min.)	Work element	Time (min.)
a	0.20	g	0.30
b	0.65	h	0.45
c	0.40	i	0.65
d	0.10	j	0.40
e	0.30	k	0.35
f	0.15	l	0.25

If there are three operators available for this work determine the maximum output that can be achieved by the line.

15.7 What is 'system loss', how is it caused, and how can it be reduced?

15.8 Analytical line balancing procedures are sufficient for the successful design of 'transfer lines' but are they adequate themselves for the design of mass production systems in which human operators are involved in executing the work?

What are the 'human' problems associated with the design and operation of mass production systems such as flow lines?

15.9 Determine the optimal' inter-station buffer stock capacities for a flow line consisting of six stations. Assume that the station work times are distributed normally with (a) a variance of 1.6 and (b) a variance of 3.2. The unit inventory cost per hour is £0.005 and the unit cost of the facilities per hour is £0.007.

Which formula have you used in calculating the optimal buffer capacity, and on what other assumptions does this treatment of the problem depend?

15.10 Describe briefly the following:
(a) a multi-model assembly line;
(b) a mixed-model assembly line;
(c) simple assembly line balancing;
(d) complex assembly line balancing;
(e) batch sequencing on assembly lines;
(f) model sequencing on assembly lines.

15.11 The matrix below shows the costs incurred through changing an assembly line from a set-up suitable for the production of one type of item to a set-up suitable for the production of a different type of item.

During each shift, each of the five types of item must be produced once. A batch of item type A must be produced first. In what order must the batches of the five items be produced-if the cost of setting up the line is to be minimized?

What is the total line set-up cost per shift?

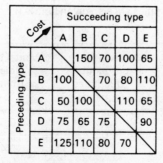

Figure Q15.11

15.12 Two models (A and B) of a simple product are to be produced on a short 'manual' assembly line. Because of the nature of the demand for these items, it is preferable to design the assembly line for mixed production of the two models rather than for separate production in batches.

The line output for the two types, per eight-hour shift, must be:

$$A = 500 \text{ products}$$
$$B = 250 \text{ products}$$

The diagrams below show the precedence relationships of the work elements which constitute both models. Certain of the elements are common to both models, and the remainder are peculiar to each. (Common elements have the same numbers in both diagrams.)

Design an assembly line with the minimum number of stations and allocate work elements to stations.

What is the average balancing loss of your line over a period of one shift?

Model A

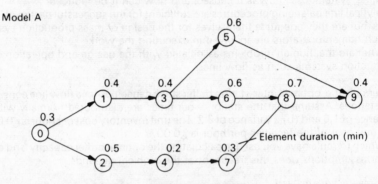

Figure Q15.12(a)

Model B

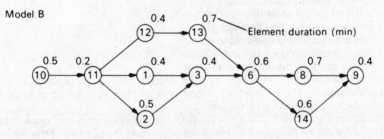

Figure Q15.12(b)

15.13 Four models of a product are to be produced on a 'mixed-model' line. The relative proportions of each of the models to be produced over any given period are given below. The model cycle times are also given below (i.e. the cycle times for each model at each station).

Model	Relative production (quantities required)	Model cycle times (min.)
A	0.2	0.6
B	0.3	0.3
C	0.3	0.4
D	0.2	0.7

The models must be launched onto the line at fixed intervals. Determine the sequence in which models must be launched onto the line to minimize congestion on the line
    Comment on this model sequence.

15.14 The minimization of balancing loss should be a secondary objective during the design of assembly lines, particularly mixed-model assembly lines.' Discuss.

15.15 The diagrams below indicate the precedence relationships for the work elements of two jobs. Certain of the elements are common to both jobs (i.e. elements 1, 2, 3, 4, 6), while the remainder are peculiar to one job. At the moment product A is made on assembly line A and product B is made on assembly line B. The allocation of work elements to stations, and the line outputs, are also shown below.

Product A

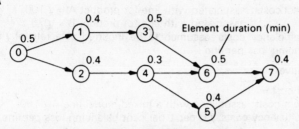

Figure Q15.15(a)

Output required = 60 per hour (i.e. cycle time = 1 min.)

Station	Elements	Work station time (min.)
1	0, 2	0.9
2	1, 4	0.7
3	3, 5	0.9
4	6, 7	0.9

Product B

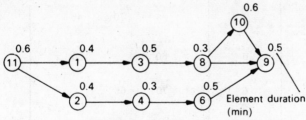

Figure Q15.15(b)

Output required = 50 per hour (i.e. cycle time = 1.2 min.).

Station	Elements	Work station time (min.)
1	11, 1	1.0
2	2, 3	0.9
3	4, 6,8	1.1
4	10, 9	1.1

The company manufacturing these two products is anxious to evaluate the merits of three possible methods of manufacture:

1.   The manufacture of both A and B together on a mixed-model assembly line.
2.   The manfacture of A and B separately in batches on an existing larger assembly line which would also be expected to manufacture batches of another product, C.
3.   The present arrangement.

The evaluation of the three methods of manufacture is to be accomplished by comparing the total costs of each alternative, as follows:
   Present situation

   Total cost =
   Indirect costs: associated with line for product A = £100
                    : associated with line for product B = £75
   + Inefficiency costs: assumed to be incurred at a rate of £5 per 1 per cent balancing loss per line

Alternative 1

   Total cost =
   Indirect costs: associated with a mixed-model line = £150
   + Inefficiency costs: £5 per 1 per cent balancing loss per line.

Alternative 2

   Total cost =
   Indirect costs: addition to indirect costs for existing product C line = £50
   + Inefficiency costs: associated with balancing loss and calculated to be £50.
   + Change-over costs, incurred when the set-up of the multi-model line is changed between production of batches of two different products. The matrix below details such costs (assume the production of one batch of each model only and three line set-ups).

Preceding product \ Succeeding product	A	B	C
A	—	70	45
B	60	—	80
C	70	65	—

Figure Q15.15(c)

   Which is the most economic method of producing products A and B in the quantities specified?

PART 7

MATERIALS MANAGEMENT

INTRODUCTION TO PART 7

Here we deal with the management of items, products and customers throughout the operating system, from inputs to outputs. We first identify different approaches to this task of materials management, and then consider those topics which are of particular and direct relevance to the operations manager.

Again, especially when dealing with inventory management in Chapter 17, we shall consider 'principal' or 'characteristic' operations management problem areas, i.e. problems which are influenced by the operating system structure and where the approaches employed are influenced by the operations objectives.

CHAPTER 16

Materials Administration, Purchasing and Distribution

NOTATION USED IN THIS CHAPTER

B	Buffer or safety stock
B_1	Buffer stock for location 1
B_n	Total buffer stock for n locations
MRP	Materials requirement planning
n	Number of stock locations at a given level in a customer channel
PDM	Physical distribution management

Materials administration has been defined[1] as the methods and principles by which we endeavour to plan, organize, co-ordinate, control and review the flow of materials throughout an organization. It involves, therefore, some form of overall control of materials throughout an organization, and offers a distinctive and increasingly popular approach to materials management. In the absence of a materials administration approach within an organization the management (i.e. the planning, organizing, co-ordinating, controlling and reviewing) of materials, materials stocks, materials flows, parts stocks, materials in progress and, where appropriate, the flow of customers will be the responsibility of several departments or individuals. This is the more decentralized approach and has been the traditional approach in most businesses to date.

Figure 16.1 shows the relationships and overlap between responsibilities for materials management for two different types of operating systems. It will be seen that the entire materials administration responsibility can be subdivided into three main areas:

(a) *purchasing or procurement,* i.e. responsibility for obtaining and managing incoming materials through to input stocks;

---

[1] Ericsson, D. (1974) *Materials Administration* (Translation). Maidenhead: McGraw-Hill.

Example 1

Manufacturing, from stock, to stock, to customer

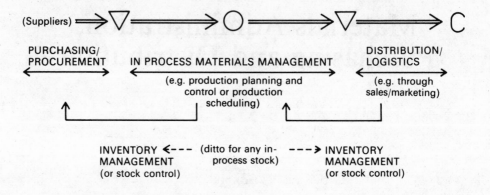

PURCHASING/
PROCUREMENT

IN PROCESS MATERIALS MANAGEMENT

(e.g. production planning and
control or production
scheduling)

DISTRIBUTION/
LOGISTICS

(e.g. through
sales/marketing)

INVENTORY ◄--- (ditto for any in- ---► INVENTORY
MANAGEMENT   process stock)   MANAGEMENT
(or stock control)   (or stock control)

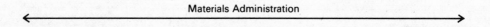

Materials Administration

Example 2

Service, from stock, from customer queue

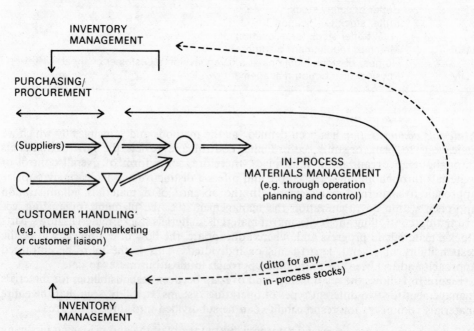

INVENTORY
MANAGEMENT

PURCHASING/
PROCUREMENT

(Suppliers)

IN-PROCESS
MATERIALS MANAGEMENT
(e.g. through operation
planning and control)

C

CUSTOMER 'HANDLING'
(e.g. through sales/marketing
or customer liaison)

(ditto for any
in-process stocks)

INVENTORY
MANAGEMENT

Figure 16.1 *Materials management responsibilities in two types of operating systems.*

(b) *in-process materials management*, i.e. the management of materials, items and, where appropriate, customers through the transformation process (see also Chapters 12–15);

(c) (i) in the case of manufacture supply systems, *distribution/logistics* for the transfer of items, products, etc., to the customer from the system, where appropriate from output stock;

(ii) in the case of transport and service systems, *customer handling*, i.e. the management of customers joining the operating system through, where appropriate, to the input queue situation.

Within these areas of responsibility there will exist physical stock situations. In Example 1 in Figure 16.1 there are two stocks: (a) incoming materials, components, parts, products, etc.; and (b) outputs. Similarly, in Example 2 there is an input stock of items from suppliers and also an input queue of customers. In many cases in practice, such stocks are the responsibility of an inventory control or inventory management function. The inventory management function links together the three areas of responsibility identified above, and will be responsible either to an overall materials administration function or to one of those three areas (see also Chapter 17).

CENTRALIZED v. DECENTRALIZED MATERIALS MANAGEMENT

The benefits of a centralized or overall approach to materials management, e.g. through the use of the materials administration concept, might be seen to include:

1. Avoidance of problems of divided responsibility.
2. Avoidance of possible conflicting objectives and priorities.
3. Avoidance of duplication of effort.
4. Ease of communications throughout the organization.
5. Ease of, and better representation of, the materials management function at board/policy level.
6. Better career/developmental opportunities.
7. Economies of scale.

The benefits of a decentralized approach to materials management, i.e. through the use of different departments or functions operating essentially individually but with appropriate communication and perhaps overall control from board level, might be seen to include:

1. Greater opportunity for functional specialization.
2. Greater flexibility.
3. Greater opportunity for materials managers to act as integral parts of geographically dispersed organizations (rather than being seen as separate head office/personnel staff).

The type of approach employed for materials management within an organization will depend largely on the relevance of the above advantages and the circumstances in which the organization is to work. For example it might be argued from organizational theory (see Chapter 3) that a centralized (materials administration), approach might be more appropriate in 'static' situations subject to few uncertainties. In such situations the organization will face fewer changes in markets, demand, customer behaviour, supplier behaviour, technological change, etc., and thus it may be possible to implement and stick to relevant rules, procedures, etc., for materials management throughout the organization. Where there is a greater degree of uncertainty, for example because of demand changes, product changes, changes in the nature of the service and technological changes, particularly where these affect different parts of the organization in different ways, then there may be some merit in a decentralized approach which facilitates rapid response to their changing circumstances from different parts of the organization. Two brief case examples of centralized and decentralized approaches to materials management follow.

EXAMPLE 1: CENTRALIZED MATERIALS ADMINISTRATION IN A NATIONAL RETAIL STATIONERY ORGANIZATION

This organization has several hundred retail shops throughout the country. Each shop sells stationery, records, some toys and some confectionery, but mainly magazines and popular books. It maintains a central national materials administration directorate operating from the corporate headquarters. The materials administration director and his staff are responsible for the acquisition of all products sold through the retail branches, their delivery to the three warehouses, their stocking in the warehouses, subsequent distribution to shops, retail stock at shops, point-of-sale display and local promotion of items. All the retail shops offer the same stock lines and all shops must obtain all their supplies from the company's warehouses. A catalogue is available offering a limited part of this range on mail order to customers. Such orders are satisfied directly from one of the warehouses through a mail-order distribution function which is also the responsibility of the materials administration director.

   The materials administration director has regional staff who liaise with retail branches in various areas. These staff operate from the warehouse locations. Their responsibility is primarily to advise local retail shop managers of merchandising policy, new lines which are to be introduced, local and point-of-sale promotion requirements, etc. The company maintains a centralized computer-based system for materials records. Point-of-sale returns are made directly from check-out machines to retail branch stock records and from there to warehouse records on a weekly basis. Deliveries are made to retail shops on a weekly basis.

EXAMPLE 2: DECENTRALIZED MATERIALS MANAGEMENT IN A COLLEGE BOOKSHOP COMPANY

This organization runs about twenty bookshops on college and university campuses. It gives considerable autonomy to bookshop managers, in particular in respect of the books which they choose to stock and any point-of-sale advertising, promotion displays, etc. The quantities of items stocked in bookshops are also the responsibility of individual bookshop managers. However, the bookshop managers are required to order books through a company purchasing system; the system is run from the company headquarters, but deliveries are made from publishers directly to individual bookshops. Unsold books can be returned either to the publishers, depending on the conditions of their supply, or to a company 'clearing' inventory which either holds the items in stock against future occasional orders from individual bookshops or redistributes them to other shops where the demand might be greater. The smaller retail outlets are run, in some cases single handed, by a local manager, possibly with a part-time assistant. He or she is responsible for receiving books into stock, displaying them, selling them and making his or her financial returns to the company. In the larger shops the retail manager will have staff responsible for ordering and stock-holding, for sales and for finance.

In this book our description of materials management is a decentralized one. The remainder of this chapter deals with purchasing and distribution, while in Chapter 17 we concentrate on inventory management, i.e. the management of input and output, and process inventories. Together these two chapters will cover most of the materials management tasks for most types of organization.

PURCHASING AND SUPPLY

Although rarely their sole responsibility, the purchasing or procurement function clearly concerns operations managers. Operations managers are responsible for providing goods or services of the right specification and quality, at the right time, in the right quantity and at the right price, and purchasing or procurement managers are, in the same terms, responsible for purchasing materials and items of the right specification and quality, at the right time, in the right quantity, from the right source and at the right price. Theirs, in other words, is the responsibility of obtaining those items required by the operating system. They are concerned with the input to the operating system, i.e. the flow of physical resources to the operating system.

The objectives of purchasing

The objectives of purchasing have been identified (see Baily and Farmer (1977) in 'Further Reading') as follows:

1. (a) To supply the organization with a steady flow of materials and services to meet its needs.
   (b) To ensure continuity of supply by maintaining effective relationships with existing sources and by developing other sources of supply either as alternatives or to meet emerging or planned needs.
2. To obtain efficiently, by any ethical means, the best value for every unit of expenditure.
3. To manage inventory so as to give the best possible service at lowest cost.
4. To maintain sound co-operative relationships with other departments, providing information and advice as necessary to ensure the effective operation of the organization as a whole.
5. To develop staff, policies, procedures and organization to ensure the achievement of the foregoing objectives.

Reference to the management of inventories above raises the question of the relationship of purchasing as a process to inventory management as discussed in Chapter 17. Purchasing will, in some cases, become concerned with the provision of goods to input inventories, i.e. in those system structures in which inventories exist, the purchasing function, whether a part of the operations management area of responsibility or not, will be concerned with the link between customers and input inventories. In some cases this responsibility for supplying items and materials to input inventory will be matched with some responsibility for the maintenance of such inventories. In other situations inventory replenishment needs will be identified, thus giving rise to purchase requirements executed by the purchasing function. Again it is unimportant to argue about the responsibility for such input inventories. We shall deal with inventory management in Chaper 17. The topics covered there are of relevance in purchasing, as indeed the topics covered here are relevant to inventory management.

Deriving from the above objectives, we might identify the following as being the principal benefits to be gained from the effective management of the purchasing process:

(a) lower prices for materials and items used;
(b) faster inventory turnover;
(c) continuity of supply;
(d) reduced replenishment lead times;

(e)   reduced transport cost;
(f)   reduced materials obsolescence;
(g)   improved vendor relationships;
(h)   better control of quality;
(i)   effective administration and minimization of organizational effort;
(j)   maintenance of adequate records and provision of information for the operations managers.

Clearly the purchase of items and materials has relevance in all types of operating system, since in all such systems there will be some dependence on the use of physical items. While the principles and objectives of purchasing might also be applied in the acquisition of labour, capital, etc., the purchasing process is concerned primarily with obtaining physical items for use in, and conversion through, the operating system. Most operating systems need such items. Hospitals, for example, need a regular reliable supply of consumable items such as medicines and sterile equipment and transport operations are dependent on an adequate supply of consumable materials such as fuel and tyres. Supply organizations naturally are dependent on an adequate, reliable and efficient supply of those items which are to be passed to customers, while manufacturing organizations are entirely dependent on the supply of consumable and non-consumable materials and items.

The organization of purchasing

A major issue in this context is the degree to which purchasing as a function should be centralized. In recent years there has been a trend towards the establishment of centralized purchasing functions. This trend has been particularly noticeable in health services and in local and central government supply, as well as in manufacturing. The principal benefits thought to be associated with central purchasing are summarized below:

(a)   The possibility of standardizing specifications and establishing common needs, as regards quantity, quality, specification, etc.;
(b)   the possibility of more economic purchase through, for example, larger batch quantities;
(c)   the reduction in administrative cost through the purchase of larger quantities on few occasions, possibly from fewer sources;
(d)   the possibility of purchase staff specialization and thus increased knowledge of sources and supplies;
(e)   the possibility of the use of more effective, detailed and accurate purchase information and records;
(f)   the possibility of more detailed accurate and rapid budgetary and financial control procedures;

The principal advantages derive from the possibility of increased purchase volumes, from standardization, and from specialization. Disadvantages of centralized purchasing, however, might include:

(a)   difficulties of communication within the organization, deriving perhaps from geographical separation;
(b)   slow response to new or unusual supply needs from the organization;
(c)   possible increased dependence on a smaller number of suppliers resulting from increased volume and from standardization.

Thus the merits of centralized purchasing will depend on the possible financial savings through volume and variety considerations as against the possibility of reduced response times and flexibility.

Sourcing and suppliers

An important function of purchasing is the identification of suitable sources of supply. The systematic investigation and comparison of sources, the evaluation and monitoring of performance of supply sources and the development of appropriate procedures with suppliers are therefore of importance. Vendor rating is discussed briefly below and in more detail in Chapter 19. Although market research will not be discussed in detail here, it will be appreciated that supplier market research is of importance in obtaining adequate supply sources for the organization.

Figure 16.2 outlines the procedure normally involved in selecting suppliers. The model suggests that the buyer, on receipt of a request to purchase, first checks whether the

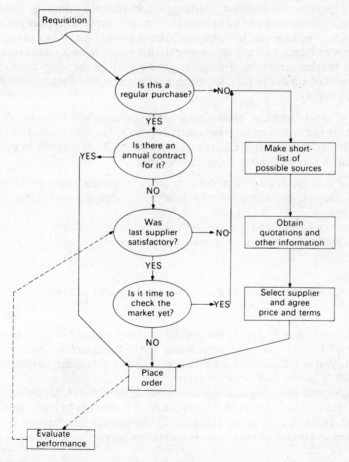

Figure 16.2 *Outline of procedures for selecting suppliers. The broken line indicates steps taken after the order has been placed. From Baily, P. J. H. (1970) Design of Purchasing Systems and Records. Epping: Gower Press. Reproduced with permission.*

organization is currently committed to the particular supplier for the supply of such items and, if not, whether an existing source might satisfy the requirement. Repeat ordering with an existing source would be normal unless for some reasons necessitating a review of such an arrangement. Such reasons might include recent price increases, recent extensions in supplier supply lead time, failing to meet specifications, decline in vendor rate perform- ance, etc. Buyer source loyalty is a well-documented phenomenon, and clearly offers benefits in terms of reduced administrative difficulty, improved vendor/buyer understand- ing and relationship. In fact, benefits accrue both to supplier and to vendor. Vendors tend also to give preference to existing customers.[2]

Often an investigation of possible sources for the supply of new items and materials will reveal several alternatives, hence the question of single or multiple sourcing often arises. Factors to be considered in this respect include the following:

1. Effect on price, i.e. single sourcing of increased quantities may reduce purchase price. Alternatively, in certain circumstances, multiple sourcing may in fact reduce price as a result of supplier competition for orders.
2. Effect on supply security, i.e. while organization of supply will be simpler with a single source, the organization will be dependent and thus at great risk as a result of any disruptions through, for example, strikes, etc.
3. Effect on supplier motivation. Although the security resulting from regularly supplying large quantities to an organization might increase supplier motivation, and thus increase willingness to improve specifications, etc., undoubtedly in some circumstances increased motivation might also result from a competitive situation.
4. Effect on market structure of single sourcing may in the long term result in the development of a monopolistic situation with the eventual elimination of alternative sources of supply.

The process of identifying and determining supply sources will often involve obtaining competitive bids and analysing such bids and proposals. The latter will often involve price and delivery comparisons, but in most cases more detailed analysis will be necessary. The following factors may be among those considered:

(a) price and cost factors, i.e. cost, delivery costs, insurance costs, price breaks etc.;
(b) delivery factors, including delivery lead times, delivery quantities and delivery frequencies;
(c) specifications factors and quality control/assurance practices;
(d) legal factors, e.g. warranty, in terms of condition etc.

Considerations in purchasing policy and procedures

Special considerations will apply in the purchasing of commodities in which speculation, the purchase of 'futures' and price forecasting are of considerable importance.

This specialist area will not be dealt with here. Further details can be obtained from the 'Further Reading' at the end of the chapter.

Value analysis and value engineering have been dealt with in Chapter 3 and, while the make or buy decision has already been introduced, it is relevant to refer again to the issue in this context. Table 16.1 provides a checklist for the make or buy decision. Such decisions can be complex and therefore past, present and future market conditions will normally be analysed.

---

[2] See, for example, Farmer, D. H. and MacMillan, K. (1976) The benefits of reducing opportunism in buyer–supplier relationships, *Journal of Purchasing and Materials Management*, Winter.

Table 16.1 *A make or buy checklist* (From Baily, P. and Farmer, D. H. (1977) *Purchasing Principles and Techniques*. London: Pitman. Reproduced with permission.)

If currently purchased from an outside source	If currently being manufactured within the company
(1) Does capacity exist within own company?	(1) Is there a matter of secrecy to be considered?
(2) If so, is such capacity likely to be available for the planning period involved?	(2) If the item is withdrawn from production, would redundancies result?
(3) Is the necessary raw material available now at economic rates?	(3) If 'yes', what action would need to be taken by management regarding these redundancies?
(4) Will that material continue to be available at economic rates for the planning period?	(4) If tooling is involved, what is its condition? Can it be used by the prospective source?
(5) If tooling is involved: (a) what is the cost? (b) what is the expected life? (c) what is the delivery?	(5) Will the machinery involved on current manufacture be fully utilized for alternative work if the part is withdrawn?
(6) Are we satisfied that the current suppliers are the most economic source?	(6) Is there a possibility of development work being done on the part? If so, can this be done satisfactorily in conjunction with an outside supplier?
(7) Is there a patent involved and thus the possibility of royalties to be paid?	(7) Will the quantities involved interest an outside supplier?
(8) Is VAT chargeable (e.g. printing)?	(8) Do we know the true cost of alternative supply against manufacture (e.g. transport and handling costs)—present and forward?
(9) Are the current suppliers doing development work towards an improved version of the item?	(9) Is the item part of an integral production route involving several stages of manufacture? If so, can outside manufacture be satisfactorily co-ordinated with production schedules and machine loading in our shops?
(10) Have the current suppliers had difficulty with quality, quantity or time factors, and have their costs escalated as a result, thus affecting their selling price?	(10) What is the forward market position for the item concerned for the relevant planning period?
(11) If their quality has been affected: (a) has the suppliers' quality system been vetted? (b) what has been the extent of quality failures? (c) is our production department confident that the specified quality can be economically maintained in internal production? (d) are we over-specifying?	(11) Are all drawings current?
(12) If their other costs are escalating: (a) what are the reasons? (b) are we confident that we will not be affected in the same way?	(12) Is there any advantage in our supplying raw materials/components if a decision to buy is made?
(13) If the item is currently being imported, what is the cost breakdown? If duty is payable, what rates are applied? What duty, if any, will be payable on the relevant raw materials/components if they are imported?	(13) Can we indicate to the potential supplier the remaining life of the product?
	(14) Can the potential supplier suggest ideas for taking cost out of the product?

Documentation procedures for purchasing will not be considered here; however, it should be noted that, because of the often considerable amount of money involved in purchase and purchase decisions, adequate records must be maintained, and because of the often complex situations which exist, computer-based records and control procedures are often desirable. Figure 16.3 shows in outline a computer-based system used by one aircraft-manufacturing organization. The system was designed to provide a bank of reliable and readily available information for interrogation using terminals. It aims to increase the amount of time the buyer is able to spend in negotiating with suppliers and to reduce the amount of time spent in maintaining information on supply. The system also provides benefits in offering interface with company production and financial systems.

It covers all purchases including bought-out equipment, standard parts, raw materials, subcontract work, repairs, services, commercial equipment and stationery. It assists in the following functions:

(a) accumulation of the requirement to buy;
(b) printing of purchase orders;
(c) recording the progression of the purchase order;

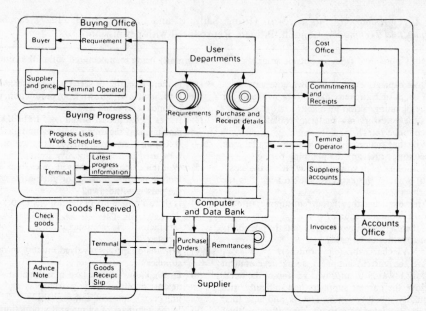

Figure 16.3 *A computer-based purchase record system. From Baily, P. and Farmer, D. F. (1977) Purchasing Principles and Techniques. London: Pitman. Reproduced with permission.*

(d)   receipts;
(e)   inspection;
(f)   accumulation of the purchase history;
(g)   supply analysis.

Materials requirements planning *(see also Chapter 12)*

Although developed primarily for use in batch manufacturing situations, materials requirements planning has potential in other manufacturing and non-manufacturing situations. The procedure is discussed in detail in Chapter 12 and will only be summarized here.

The principles involved in MRP differ little from those employed for the purchase of materials and parts in many organizations in recent years. Justification for the discussion of these procedures as a separate topic derives largely from the fact that the recent application of computers in this area has made possible the use of a purchasing procedure of a scale not hitherto generally feasible.

In batch manufacture, particularly in situations where items are assembled in batches, certain components may be required in large quantities at infrequent intervals, i.e. to suit the batch assembly schedule. In many such situations, therefore, there will be little benefit in maintaining stocks of all parts and items at all times, since at most times these stocks will not be drawn upon. Thus if a procedure can be developed by which those items required for assembly are available at the times required and stocks of these items are not maintained, or are maintained at a far lower level, at other times, an efficient purchasing/stock-holding policy may result. Given this situation the high cost of maintaining unnecessary stock is avoided while items will still be available when required. Materials requirements planning provides such a procedure. It is based on the use of a 'bill of materials' file and a production or assembly schedule. The bill of materials file provides information on all parts and materials required for all finished products and the production schedule provides information on the production or assembly schedule for all finished products.

Co-ordination of this information together with a knowledge of supply lead times permits the procurement of parts as and when required by the production/assembly schedule. MRP, which has some similarities with reverse or due date scheduling and network analysis (see Chapter 13), aims to keep inventories low in order to facilitate purchasing, to ensure a supply of parts and materials when needed and to highlight exceptions and priorities. It is an effective means to an adequate link between the purchasing or procurement and the manufacturing function.

In non-manufacturing situations the materials requirements planning procedure may be of relevance, particularly when the system requires the acquisition of inputs specific to particular operations, jobs or outputs, i.e. when a batch processing procedure is employed. In, for example, certain supply operations where items are acquired against particular customer orders, a materials requirements procedure may be of value in that it might provide an effective means of planning, controlling and monitoring the purchase of large quantities of a large range of items in order to satisfy the requirements of a large number of customers each of whom has particular delivery or due date requirements.

PHYSICAL DISTRIBUTION AND CUSTOMER CHANNELS

Figure 16.1 locates the responsibility of distribution within materials management. In goods output systems (i.e. manufacturing and supply) the responsibility of distribution is that of getting goods *to* the customer. A similar responsibility exists in 'customer input' type systems (i.e. service and transport), where the responsibility is to get customers, whether they be people or things, into the system. In the simplest situation these responsibilities involve the organization in direct relationships with the ultimate or end customers, possibly through inventories, and the input of customers, possibly through customer queues. In more complex cases there will be intermediate stages.

In this section we shall deal with the management of both types of 'channel'. The term 'customer channels' will be used to remind us that we are concerned with flows from or to customers. We shall consider the terms 'distribution' or 'physical distribution' to apply to the management of physical flows through both types of customer channels.

Physical distribution management (PDM)

PDM, concerned with the dynamics of distribution and with customer channel behaviour, may be defined in our context as the process by which appropriate quantities of items or customers are passed through the distribution channel to or from customers. This definition suggests that, given certain channels, the task of PDM is to make them work. However, it begs the question of 'influence' or 'control'. An enterprise may have a one-stage customer channel as shown in Figure 16.1, i.e. dealing directly with its own ultimate customers, perhaps through a stock or customer queue over which it has some direct control. The manner in which it operates, i.e. its stock-holding, the service level provided to customers and its coverage of the market, can therefore be determined entirely by itself. If, however, more stages exist, e.g. there are intermediaries between the organization and its end customer, then each party may have some influence over such decisions. Figure 16.4 shows, diagrammatically, different types of customer channels, and gives examples for: A, service and transport organizations; and B, manufacture and supply organizations. The figure shows the channels as perceived by the organization. Notice that each stage in the channel might be viewed as a single input/output stage in the way shown in Figure 16.1, but here the emphasis is on multiple-stage channels.

Ideally an enterprise would like to influence all stages in the distribution channel between itself and the final customer, and this is easily achieved for organizations with one-stage customer channels. The extent of the influence or the 'reach' of the enterprise along the customer channel will affect its PDM decision. An enterprise which controls its entire distribution channel to or from the final customer will make decisions affecting all stages in that channel, whereas an enterprise with less influence may make decisions affecting only a part of of the channel.

PDM decisions

The principal interrelated decision areas in PDM are as follows:

(a) the choice, design and implementation of a channel of distribution;
(b) the 'level of service' to be provided to customers;
(c) inventory decisions.

These are outlined in the following section, which can provide only an introduction to this subject.[3] Notice that for single-stage channels the PDM decisions are principally (b) and (c) above, and in such cases the problem can be seen largely as one of inventory management. We shall be dealing with inventory management in this context in Chapter 17, so here we shall concentrate on the more complex PDM case of multi-stage channels where the approach required is somewhat different because of both (a) above and the more complex situations in (b) and (c).

Channel decisions

We can identify four important questions to be asked in deciding on 'customer channels':

(a) the question of *level*—the number of levels or stages which should exist in the channel;
(b) the question of *type*—which type or types of intermediary should be employed once the level has been decided;
(c) the question of *intensity*—how many of each type of intermediary are to be used;
(d) the question of *control*—what degree of control should the organization seek to exercise, and where appropriate what degree of control should it accept from others.

---

[3] For further details see Kotler, P. (1976) *Marketing Management*, Englewood Cliffs, N J: 3rd edition. Prentice-Hall, or books on PDM, e.g. Bowersox, D. J. (1974) *Logistical Management*. London: Macmillan.

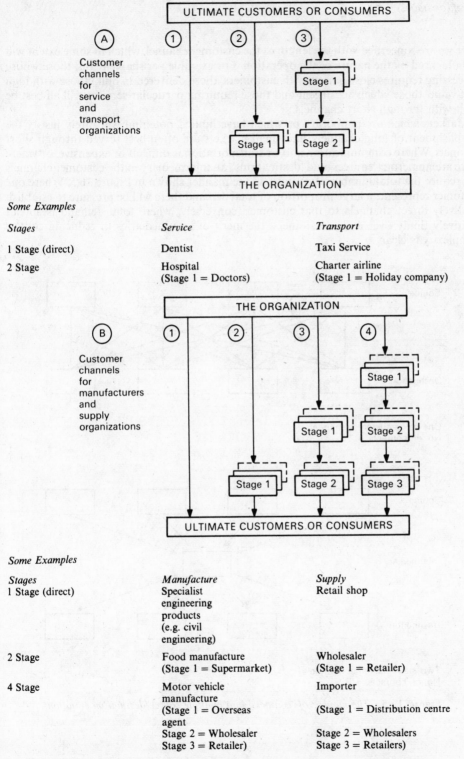

Figure 16.4 *Types of customer channel for an organization, and examples.*

Level (or stages)

Here we are concerned with the length of the customer channel, which to some extent will be influenced by the nature of the operation. For example perishable items, those whose processing requires close liaison with customers, those delivered in bulk, those with high unit value, those which are urgent and those requiring particular services will all best be dealt with through short channels.

Markets which are temporary or which have limited potential will rarely justify the establishment of long channels, and small markets are often best served through short channels. Where communication and/or transportation is difficult or expensive, or where there are numerous 'sources' and 'destinations', an intermediary in the customer channels can reduce the total number of contacts in the manner shown in Figure 16.5. Where one customer represents a large proportion of total demand there will be pressure to establish relatively direct channels to that customer; conversely, where total demand is spread relatively thinly over many customers, the merit of intermediaries in reducing contact complexity is clear.

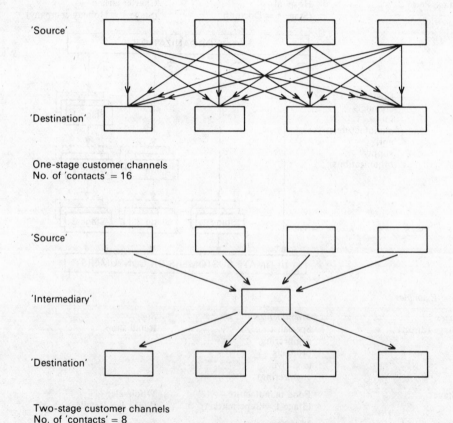

Figure 16.5 *The number of 'contacts' in a multiple source/destination situation.*

Type

Which types of intermediary are most suited to particular channels? The nature of the 'end' market of customers should influence the choice of 'type' rather than vice versa. Items, transports or services must be available to 'end' customers where they expect to find them. It will therefore be difficult to break with tradition unless service to the end customer is clearly improved, although there are obvious examples of successful innovation, e.g. in new forms of retailing and in direct selling.

Intensity and control

At one extreme there is the possibility of limited distribution through an exclusive channel, and a move from this situation will involve an organization in dealing with a greater number and range of intermediaries. This, however, may be justified where greater market coverage or 'presence' is required yet where the organization does not aspire to maintain close control over all intermediaries. The increased 'coverage' of the market might justify the use of more intensive distribution through multiple intermediaries at each stage with increased PDM costs. However, the use of a greater number of 'contact' points with the market will influence the stock levels required in order to provide a given level of service (see below).

Service level decisions *(see also Chapter 17)*

The level of service provided to end customers might be expressed in terms of:

(a) percentage of customer orders satisfied in a given period of time;
(b) average delivery or waiting time before a customer order is satisfied;
(c) percentage of customer orders which are satisfied after a quoted delivery or waiting time;
(d) percentage of total demand satisfied in a given period.

The type of measure employed in setting objectives for, and then in monitoring, customer service will depend on the type of organization, and in particular the type of product or service which is being provided. For example, (a) above will be relevant in a 'manufacture to stock' situation where the customer is normally to be satisfied from stock. Measure (b) above will be relevant where goods or service are provided against a specific order, i.e. where customers will normally expect to wait to be served, or where capacity is insufficient to create output stocks of goods or avoid input queues of customers, even though the nature of customer needs is known in advance.

Whatever the measure of customer service, it will generally be the case that the provision of higher levels of service will incur greater costs to the organization. The type of relationship shown in Figure 16.6 will often apply.

Clearly there is a cost penalty in providing high customer service, so the justification for aiming for high service must be demonstrable. The obvious reason is the need to conform to what customers expect, i.e. what competitors provide; indeed this will be essential unless some compensatory satisfaction is provided, e.g. through lower price. Equally, inability to compete in the market through price or specification will necessitate the provision of better service through better delivery, short waiting times, etc. (see Chapter 1).

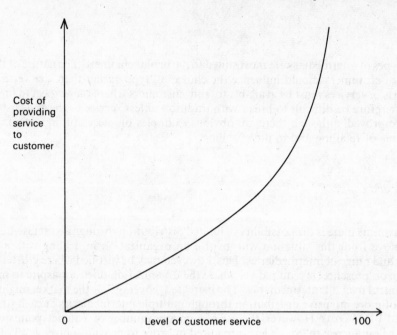

Figure 16.6 *The relationship of customer service and cost.*

Where inventories of items exist, clearly service-level decisions can influence inventory decisions in terms of not only the levels of inventory to be provided, but also their location throughout the customer channel. We must now therefore clarify the PDM factors influencing inventory decisions.

Inventory decisions *(see also Chapter 17)*

Chapter 17 will deal in detail with inventory management decisions. The emphasis there will be on the management of 'single-stage' inventories (e.g. the management of each stock in an operating system, i.e. each triangle in systems such as those in Figure 16.1). Here we must consider inventories *throughout* customer channels. For example in a three-stage distribution channel there may be three levels of inventory of the same type of items, with several different stock-holdings at each level.

Among other purposes, inventories provide service to the next stage in the channel. For example, an input stock of raw materials in a hospital helps to ensure that the medical activities of the hospital are not held up. An output stock in a manufacturing company helps to ensure that those directly served by that organization are able to get what they want when they want it. In other words, for each stock there is an immediate customer and a purpose of the stock is to provide service to that customer. We shall see in Chapter 17 that where demands on stock are uncertain, as is often the case, or when the time required to replenish stocks is uncertain, it is necessary to provide some buffer or safety stock to ensure that most customers get what they want most of the time, i.e. that 'stock out' situations are normally avoided. Two related PDM questions, themselves related to the service-level question, therefore are: what stock levels to provide and where to provide them.

The determination of safety (or buffer) stock levels to provide given levels of service will be dealt with in detail for the 'single-stage' problem in Chapter 17. These single-stage methods can be modified to deal with stocks in multi-stage systems. Here we shall consider only the basic principles to be remembered in making inventory decisions in multi-stage systems.

The number of stock locations at a given stage

If one stock location is established from which demand throughout a given market is to be satisfied, then a safety stock must be provided in addition to a base stock. The base stock is that amount of inventory necessary to satisfy average demand during a given period of time, while the safety stock is that extra amount provided to protect against uncertainties. The way in which this safety stock can be determined is explained in Chapter 17. If we establish several stock locations *each* for a given sector of the market, e.g. a region, then base stock and safety stock must be provided at each. The sum of the base stocks for each stock location will be the same as the original single base stock, but the sum of the safety stocks at each location to provide the original level of service will exceed the safety stock required for the single location.

The general relationship between the sum of the safety stocks required for n stock-holdings and that required for a single holding can be shown to be as follows:[4]

$$B_n = \frac{B_1(n)}{\sqrt{n}}$$

where B_n = total safety or buffer stock for n locations
B_1 = safety or buffer stock for 1 location
n = number of locations

The general nature of the relationship is shown in Figure 16.7.

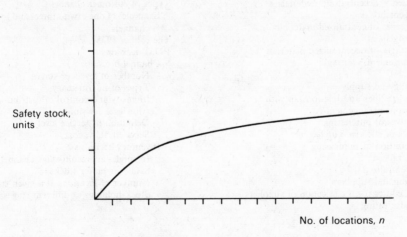

Figure 16.7 *Safety stock v. number of stock locations at a given stage or level.*

[4] Smykay, E. W. (1973) *Physical Distribution Management*, 3rd edition. London: Macmillan.

Stock-holdings at different levels

In considering safety stock provision it should be noted that less total safety stock will be needed to provide a given level of end customer service if that stock is provided at a 'higher' level in the customer channel, providing of course that when required it can quickly be deployed to the end customer. For example, in a customer channel which has a wholesale and several retail stocks, safety stock provided at the wholesale level can protect against uncertain demand at all retail outlets, but since high demand at one can be offset by low demand at another, the safety stock-holding at the warehouse level will be less than the total safety stock required by all retailers if each is required to operate entirely separately in its own market sector.

The existence of stocks at 'higher' levels in the customer channel should not simply permit the duplication of stocks held at 'lower' levels, but should complement lower-level stocks. For example, low-usage and/or high-cost items should be stocked at higher levels to reduce cost, while high-usage/low-cost items should be concentrated in lower-level stocks since this permits high customer service at low cost.

CHECKLIST FOR CHAPTER 16

Materials administration
  Definition
Materials management responsibilities
  Purchasing/procurement
  In process materials management
    (cf. Operations planning and control)
  Distribution (logistics)
    (cf. Marketing and sales)
  Inventory management
Centralized v. decentralized materials
  management
  Advantages of centralized materials
    management
  Advantages of decentralized materials
    management
  Examples
Purchasing and supply
  Responsibilities and relationship with
  operations management
  Objectives of purchasing
  Benefits of effective purchasing
  Organization of purchasing
    Centralized
    Decentralized
  Sourcing and suppliers
    Procedures for the selection of suppliers
    Vendor rating

Single or multiple sourcing: factors to be
  considered
Purchasing policy and procedures
  Make or buy policy
  Documentation and computer procedure
  Materials requirements planning
Physical distribution and customer channels
  The role of distribution in materials
    management
  Types of customer channel
    Examples of one-, two-, three- and four-stage
      channels
  The role of PDM
  PDM decisions
    Channel decisions
      Number of levels or stages
      Types of intermediary
      Intensity and control of distribution
    Service level decisions
      Definition of service level
      Service level v. cost
    Inventory decisions
      In single- and multi-stage channels
      Safety or buffer stocks
      Number of locations at a given stage
      Stock-holdings at different stages

FURTHER READING

Ammer, D. S. (1980) *Materials Management*, 4th edition. Homewood, Illinois: Irwin. A comprehensive treatment of the entire subject.

Baily, P. and Farmer, D. H. (1977) *Purchasing Principles and Techniques*, 3rd edition. London: Pitman. A well established, detailed and comprehensive text on purchasing, covering the purchasing function as relevant to most types of business organization.

Baily, P. and Farmer, D. (1982) *Materials Management Handbook*. Aldershot: Gower.

Coombs, R. H. (1971) *Handbook of International Purchasing*. Cahner Books.

Meitz, A. A. and Castleman, B. B. (1975) How to cope with supply shortages, *Harvard Business Review*, January/February, pp. 91–96.

Miller, J. G. and Sprague, L. G. (1975) Behind the growth in materials requirements planning, *Harvard Business Review*, September/October, pp. 83–91.

QUESTIONS

16.1 Discuss the merits of centralized purchasing procedure for a series of small retail domestic hardware stores.

16.2 What factors might influence the make or buy decision for a manufacturing organization, and how might similar considerations operate in a transport or service organization?

16.3 'Materials requirements planning is little more than the extension of reverse scheduling from operations to the purchasing function.' Discuss.

16.4 Give examples of one-stage and two-stage customer channels for :
   (a) a manufacturing organization;
   (b) a supply organization;
   (c) a transport organization;
   (d) a service organization.
   Explain why such channels are employed in these cases.

16.5 Select *one* of the following organizations and outline and explain the types of decision likely to be required in PDM in that organization (i.e. in the planning, management and control of flows through the customer channels):
   (a) a book publisher dealing with college books;
   (b) a micro-computer manufacturer.

CHAPTER 17

Inventory Management

NOTATION USED IN THIS CHAPTER

B	Buffer or safety stock
σ	Standard deviation of demand
C	Total cost of ordering and holding
C_1	Holding cost/item/unit time
C_2	Shortage or stock-out cost/item/unit time
C_{11}	Fixed portion of C_1
C_{12}	Variable portion of C_1
C_{1A}	Variable holding cost/unit time, for one increment of storage
C_{1i}	Holding cost/item of item i/unit time
C_s	Ordering cost/order
$C*$	Minimum total cost
MRP	Materials requirements planning
N	Number of items ($i = 1 \ldots N$)
$P(U)$	Probability of usage U
p	Cost/unit
p_i	Price for order quantity q_i $\Big\}$ for discount price
q_i	Order quantity
Q	Order quantity
Q_i	Order quantity for item i
q	Delivery or production rate
$Q*$	Optimum order quantity
R	Re-order level
r	Usage or demand rate
r_i	Usage or demand rate for item i
S	Stock level after replenishment
t	Order cycle
t_i	Order cycle for item i
$t*$	Optimum order cycle
U	Lead time usage
$\bar{U}$	Mean lead time usage

We discussed the management of inventories in the context of physical distribution management in Chapter 16. There we concentrated on multi-stage systems and attempts to manage inventories throughout such systems. For example, we recognized that in many goods distribution systems inventories might exist at three stages in the channel of distribution, i.e. at the manufacturer, wholesaler and retailer levels. We noted that the management of multi-stage inventory systems was in some ways a different problem from that of managing single-stage inventories, i.e. single stock-holdings. Here we shall concentrate on the management of single-stage inventories. All of what will be discussed will be relevant in the context of PDM, since not only in some cases will it be appropriate to manage each stock-holding as a separate entity, but also in many cases each stock-holding will be the property or responsibility of a different organization, and thus there will be little opportunity for co-ordinated control of inventories at different levels.

THE NATURE AND PURPOSES OF SINGLE-STAGE INVENTORIES
(see also Chapter 1 and Chapter 11)

Stocks will exist in operating systems if they are feasible, and if they serve some useful purpose. For example, it will be feasible to employ system output stocks in manufacturing or supply systems if the nature of future customer demand is known, i.e. if we know what future customers will want (see Chapter 1). In this case, therefore, such stocks will exist if they also serve some useful purpose, e.g. if they effectively protect the operating system from fluctuations in demand.

Similar considerations apply to all the stocks which might exist before, within and after any operating system. If they are feasible, they will be used if they are useful, and the latter will often depend on the capacity management strategy which is being employed (see Chapter 11).

For our purposes we can consider stocks to comprise either *consumed* or *non-consumed* items. Consumed items (e.g. materials or products) are utilized by the operating system or taken by the customer and must therefore be replaced. Non-consumed items (e.g. capital equipment and labour) are used repeatedly by the system and need repair and maintenance. In this chapter we deal only with consumed items, and therefore with three types of inventory:

(a) *system output inventory* (in manufacturing and supply systems) e.g. of goods produced or provided by the operating system;
(b) *system input resource inventory* (in manufacturing, supply, transport or service systems), e.g. of materials which will be consumed by the operating system;
(c) *customer input queues* (in transport or service systems) i.e. in effect, the input stocks of customers that will be processed through the system. (They are a resource which is input to the operating system, since the system cannot operate without them.)

Notice that 'work-in-progress' inventory, i.e. partially processed items or customers, is really the output stock of one part of the operating system and the input to the next. It is therefore contained within categories (a) and (b) above.

Inventory management is concerned essentially with the use and control of the inventories associated with operating systems. The need for inventory management is influenced by capacity management decisions, since the existence of inventories will, in part, be determined by the capacity management strategies which are to be employed. If inventories exist, they should serve some useful purpose, and therefore must be carefully managed. These 'purposes' might include:

1. *For output stocks* (in manufacture and possibly supply systems):
    (a) to provide good service to customers;
    (b) to protect the function from uncertainties in demand, e.g. permitting stable level of operating of function despite fluctuating demand;
    (c) to permit manufacture or supply of items in economic batches.
2. *For input resource stocks* (in manufacture, supply, transport and service systems):
    (a) to permit favourable purchase/provision arrangements (e.g. price discounts and economic quantities);
    (b) to protect the function from uncertainties in supply, e.g. permitting stable/undisrupted operation despite fluctuating/interrupted supplies.
3. *For customer input queues* (in transport and service systems): to protect functions from uncertainties in demand, e.g. permitting stable level of operating of functions despite fluctuating demand.

From a capacity viewpoint, output inventories provide a form of damper, insulating the function from fluctuations in demand level. The management of output inventories is concerned with regulation of the flow of items, and the management of input stocks of consumed items is much the same type of flow control problem. Output stocks exist to accommodate short-term differences between demand and system output rates. Similarly, input stocks of consumed items exist to accommodate short-term differences between the supply and consumption rates. The extent to which the level and composition of stocks vary is therefore a measure of their usefulness: lack of variation might suggest that stock is not needed.

INVENTORIES OF CONSUMED ITEMS

System output inventory

Certain operating system structures provide for output stocks. Customer demand is satisfied from such stocks, which in turn are replenished from the function. The information flows in the opposite direction to the physical flow; hence, in the case of intermittent stock replenishment, customer orders will be received at output inventory, depletion of which will give rise to the dispatch of replenishment orders to the function.

Stocks may be replenished *intermittently* or *continuously*, although in some cases the distinction is more evident in the type of inventory management decisions that are required than in the physical flow into stock.

For our purposes we can consider the nature of customer demand to be given; however, a knowledge or estimate of the nature of demand, in particular the demand level and fluctuations, will influence inventory management. The stock levels maintained and/or the amount of buffer (or safety) stock provided will reflect expected demand levels and fluctuation.

The complexity of the inventory management problem and the likely effectiveness of inventory management depend on the variability or unpredictability of stock input and output levels and also on the opportunities for, and the extent of, control. Thus in certain systems inventory management is likely to be more effective than in others simply because there is the opportunity for the exercise of closer control.

The classic stock control problem is that of establishing an inventory policy based on some *control over stock inputs* to satisfy unpredictable demand or output. Given a forecast output or usage rate per unit time and the variability of that output rate, the following inventory parameters might be established:

1. For intermittent stock replenishment:
   (a) either re-order level *or* interval; and
   (b) order quantities.
2. For continuous replenishment:
   (a) input rate; and
   (b) average stock level required.

System input resource inventory

Certain systems require input stocks. The problem of managing the stocks of input resources closely resembles that of system output inventory management. If the function is considered as the customer for input resource stocks then, as with output stocks, demand is satisfied from stock, which in turn is replenished from supply. The activity scheduling function will be responsible for the manner in which input stocks are depleted. Either consumable resources will be scheduled intermittently through the function or a regular throughput rate will have been fixed. In either case we can again consider the nature of demand on stocks to be given; however, a knowledge or estimate of the nature of demand, in particular demand level and fluctuations, will again influence input inventory management. As with output stocks, the amount of buffer (or safety) stock provided will reflect expected demand levels and fluctuation as well as the predictability and degree of control available over *inputs to stock*.

Again the following parameters might be established:

1. For intermittent stock replenishment:
   (a) either re-order level *or* interval; and
   (b) order quantities.
2. For continuous replenishment:
   (a) input rate; and
   (b) average stock level required.

Customer input queues

Two operating system structures require input queues (or stocks) of customers (see Chapter 1). In such systems, customers, or items provided by them, are consumed resources. We have argued that in transport and service systems the customers themselves, or something provided by them, are an input which differs from other consumed resources only in being beyond the direct control of system management. In other words there is little or no control over the input or arrival of such resources, i.e. their input is unpredictable. Since there is no opportunity for control over inputs, the inventory is in effect managed through *control over the output*.

Given an estimate of the input rate and the variability of that rate, the following inventory parameters might be established.

1. For intermittent depletion:
   (a) output intervals *or* the stock levels at which output is to occur; and
   (b) output quantities.

2. For continuous depletion:
   (a) output rate; and
   (b) average stock level required.

INVENTORY MANAGEMENT DECISIONS

The decisions required in inventory management, from above, are summarized in Table 17.1. Table 17.2 indicates where the two types of inventory control might be encountered.

Table 17.1 *Inventory management decisions (consumed items)*

Nature of flow	Location of flow control	
	On stock inputs	On stock outputs
Intermittent	Determine stock replenishment level *or* interval Determine input quantity	Determine stock levels *or* intervals at which output is to take place Determine output quantity
Continuous	Determine average (or safety) stock levels required Determine stock replenishment (input) rate	Determine average stock levels required Determine stock output rate

Table 17.2 *Control of inventories* v. *operating system structures*

Type of control		Application	
Model	Description	System structures (see Chapter 1)	Inventory
 Control	Control of stock input	Functions from stock to stock Function from stock to stock Function from stock to customer Function from stock from customer Function from stock from customer queue	Output Input Input Input Input
 Control	Control of stock output	Function from source from customer queue Function from source from customer queue	Customer input Customer input

The following example indicates the manner in which inventories are controlled in a particular situation. Some of the decisions required in this situation (Table 17.1) and the type of control situation which exists (Table 17.2) are seen to be influenced by the structure of the operating system, while the objectives to be achieved clearly influence the operations manager's decisions.

EXAMPLE: A HOSPITAL ACCIDENT WARD

Inventories will exist on the input side of the function only and will consist of cnsumed and non-consumed resources. There will be no stocks of finished goods or, ideally, stocks or queues of customers. Taking first the consumed item input stocks, management will seek to control such inventory through control of input flow, such flow being either intermittent or continuous. In the case of intermittent flow, management will seek to establish either a replenishment level or a replenishment interval, and replenishment batch sizes. In the case of the control of continuous or almost continuous input flow, management will seek to establish a safety or average stock level sufficient to accommodate unexpectedly high demand. Consumed item input stocks in hospital accident wards might comprise medications, bandages, disposable items, intermediate materials, direct materials, etc. In contrast, non-consumed items will of course be all physical facilities, equipment, buildings, etc., together with labour, i.e. medical, nursing and administrative staff. Here replacement is almost certainly likely to be on an intermittent basis, the task again being to determine the timing of replacement, such replacement being either replacement of resources lost or the renewal of exhausted resources. The objective in the management of such input resource inventories in the hospital accident ward will be concerned principally with the provision of adequate customer service. Here customer service will be considered satisfactory only inasmuch as the system structure is maintained, i.e. only inasmuch as customer queuing is avoided. A deterioration in customer service reflected in the queuing of customers will of course reflect a change in system structure. In the latter case somewhat different inventory management problems will occur.

COSTS IN INVENTORY MANAGEMENT

Two sets of costs are of immediate relevance in inventory decision-making: inventory costs and customer service costs.

Inventory costs

Items held in stock incur costs. *Holding costs* comprise the costs of storage facilities, provision of services to such facilities, insurance on stocks, costs of loss, breakage, deterioration, obsolescence, and the opportunity cost or notional loss of interest on the capital tied up. In general, an increase in the quantity of stocks held will be reflected in an increase in holding costs, although the relationships may not be linear. For example, costs of increasing stock-holdings may be in the form of a step function, since increased space is required when stocks reach certain levels. The cost of capital, insurance, etc., may also be discontinuous through the effect of price breaks or quantity discounts. Stock-holdings of a certain level may permit replenishment in quantities sufficient to attract quantity discounts. Other things being equal, higher costs of holding will result in lower stock quantities and vice versa. Certain stock-change costs apply particularly in intermittent flow systems, e.g. in input control systems change costs will consist of the cost of *ordering* replenishment and in some cases the cost of delivery of replenishment items and the cost of receipt, inspection, placing in stock, etc. In output control systems change costs will consist of the cost of ordering or initiating depletion and the cost of dispatch, etc.

Customer service costs

Customer service considerations influence inventory decisions in operating systems in which output stocks exist. Here customer service might be measured in terms of the number of occasions over a given period on which customer orders cannot immediately be satisfied from stock, i.e. the number of 'stock-outs'. Equally, the *probability* of such stock-outs might also provide a measure of customer service. In such a situation customers are in effect being starved by the system. In transport and service systems, customer service may be measured by the occurrence or duration of queuing. Where queuing is required, customer service may be measured by the average time spent in the queue or the number of items in the queue. Where queuing is not normally required, customer service may be measured by the probability that queuing will occur. In such situations customers are in effect being 'blocked' by the system. This customer service, whether in input or output control systems, has inventory cost implications, e.g. costs of shortage, loss of trade.

WHICH ITEMS TO CONTROL

Many companies subject all items, purchased or produced, irrespective of their value, usage or quantity, to the same type of stock control procedure. Such a policy can be a waste of time and effort.

Although high usage rate does not necessarily mean high stock levels, fast-moving items, i.e. those for which the usage rate is high, and expensive items are likely to incur greater stock costs than slow-moving, inexpensive items. Consequently it should be our primary aim in the management of inventories to control the 'fast-moving/expensive' items, since by doing so greater potential savings are possible than by concentrating effort on inexpensive items.

One of the ubiquitous phenomena of business is described by the so-called Pareto or ABC curve (see Figure 17.1). In relation to inventory control the curve demonstrates the 'law' that a small proportion of the stocked items account for a large proportion of inventory cost or value. Their relationship is often referred to as the 80/20 'law', i.e. up to 80 per cent of the firm's total inventory cost or value is accounted for by about 20 per cent of items. This relationship encourages us to categorize inventory items into three classes, A, B and C. Category A would be those relatively few types of items which account for a relatively large proportion of total inventory cost or value, category B would be the slightly larger number of items which account for a smaller percentage of total cost, and category C would be that large proportion of items which account for a very small proportion of total cost.

Category A items should be closely controlled by an inventory management system and category B items should be subject to less control, whereas for category C items a simple control procedure is probably sufficient.

The following example shows how an ABC curve can be constructed and items appropriate for category A, B and C treatment identified.

EXAMPLE: A CLOTHING WHOLESALER

The table below shows the bought-in price and annual sales of the set of different types of garments which are held in stock by a wholesaler. Construct an ABC chart for these items and suggest which items should be treated as classes A, B and C.

Item type	Purchase price (£)	Annual sales (items per year)
a	8	1250
b	18	450
c	30	75
d	25	10
e	3	280
f	4	80
g	18	45
h	7	250
i	12	150
j	26	30

Solution

Step 1: Calculate annual value

Item type	*Annual value* (£)
a	10 000
b	8 100
c	2 250
d	250
e	840
f	320
g	810
h	1 750
i	1 800
j	780

Total number of item types stocked   10

Total annual value   £26 900

Step 2: Order items by descending annual value and calculate cumulate percentage of total annual value.

Item type	*Annual value* (£)	*Cumulative percentage of £26 900*
a	10 000	37
b	8 100	67
c	2 250	76
i	1 800	82.5
h	1 750	89
e	840	92
g	810	95
j	780	98
f	320	99
d	250	100

Step 3: Draw ABC chart (see Figure 17.1).

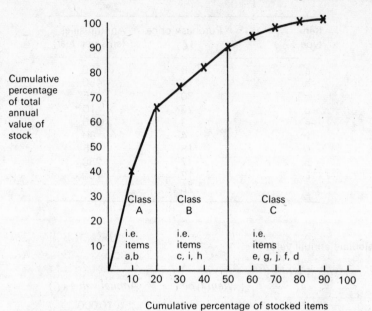

Figure 17.1 *ABC chart (example).*

INVENTORY MANAGEMENT SYSTEMS

We can now look more closely at the types of problems posed by the adoption of the inventory management strategies outlined in Table 17.1. We shall focus on the more usual case of intermittent flow/input control.

Intermittent flow/input control

Most published treatments of inventory management deal with input control of intermittent flow systems, that is, they deal with the management of inventory through manipulation of supply with the objective of satisfying a given output need or criterion. There are two basic approaches that might be adopted (see Table 17.1):

(a)   fixed input level;
(b)   fixed input interval.

The two aproaches are compared in Figure 17.2. Fixed input level control relies on the replenishment of stock by a given input quantity, actuated at a given inventory level. In other words, inventory will fall to a re-order level, when replenishment is initiated or takes place. This approach is sometimes known as the 'maximum–minimum' or 'two-bin' system.

  The fixed input interval approach relies on the replenishment of inventory at fixed intervals of time. The replenishment quantity in such situations is often determined such as to replenish inventory to a given maximum level. Replenishment of stock in input

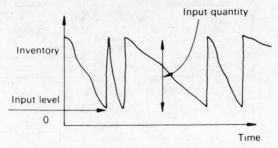

A   Fixed input level and quantity

Input quantity

Inventory

Input level

0

Time

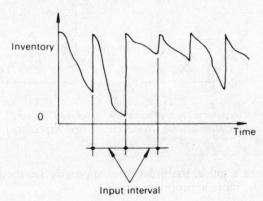

B   Fixed input interval

Inventory

0

Time

Input interval

Figure 17.2   *Input control inventory: types of control.*

control/intermittent flow systems might take place instantaneously or over a period of time. The stock level traces on Figure 17.2 rely on instantaneous replenishment, i.e. replenishment of stock by a whole quantity at one time. Figure 17.3 compares (A) intermittent input/instantaneous with (B) intermittent input/with usage. The latter relies on replenishment of stock intermittently yet over a period of time during which usage or output continues to occur.

The input level approach to inventory control is in effect a form of *perpetual* inventory management. Stock is replenished when it falls to a particular level, so it will be necessary to maintain some 'perpetual' monitoring of the inventory in order to ensure that action is taken when the appropriate stock level is reached. The input interval system is in effect a *periodic* inventory control system. There will be no need to check stock level except at the times when the replenishment order is to be placed. The type of system which is employed will depend largely on the circumstances. In some situations it will be very difficult, or expensive, to maintain a perpetual check on inventory levels in order to be able to operate the order level approach. However, where the number of transactions, i.e. the number of times the stock is depleted, is low compared with the annual usage, or where the unit cost of items is high, it may be more appropriate to use the perpetual inventory control system.

Table 17.3 compares the two systems. In many cases the cost of running a perpetual inventory control system (order level approach) will be greater than that of running a periodic inventory control system (order interval approach). However, the cost of carrying inventory may be less with the perpetual inventory control system than with the periodic system, especially where the periodic control system involves the replenishment of stock

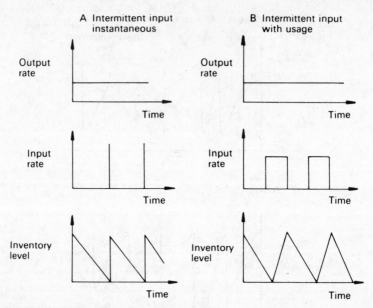

Figure 17.3 *Input control inventory: types of input flow. (Figures 17.2 and 17.3 from Wild, R. (1977) Concepts for Operations Management. New York: Wiley. Reproduced with permission.)*

by a fixed quantity. As a guide, the order level approach, i.e. the perpetual inventory control system, may be more appropriate where:

(a) the number of transactions (i.e. stock depletions) is low compared with the annual usage;
(b) the processing cost of transactions is low compared with the ordering cost;
(c) the unit price of items is high;
(d) the required service level or degree of protection against stock-outs is high;
(e) sales fluctuations are high and difficult to predict;
(f) inventory carrying costs are high;
(g) the use of a computer-based system permits frequent stock level updating (e.g. after every transaction), thus minimizing the disadvantage of the high operating cost of 'perpetual' inventory control.

Table 17.3 *'Periodic' (order interval) v. 'perpetual' (order quantity) inventory control systems*

(Probable) merits of 'periodic' system	(Probable) merits of 'perpetual' system
1. Less cost to operate system (i.e. less checking, recording, etc.)	1. Less buffer stock required for protection against stock-outs
2. Administratively easier in multi-item situations, i.e. easier to place order for each item at same time	2. Fewer stock-outs when demand is unusually high
	3. No need to determine order quantity for each replenishment
	4. Inventory carrying costs lower than for periodic system

Where demand is constant and replenishment is instantaneous or where the replenishment lead time is known, the fixed input level approach will resemble the fixed input interval approach. Only where either replenishment lead time or demand is uncertain will the adoption of each approach lead in practice to different inventory behaviour (e.g. Figure 17.2, in which the diagrams show the effect of each policy against the same demand patterns). Virtually all inventory control quantitative models deal with intermittent flow and input control, i.e. batch ordering, and in most cases the objective is cost minimization, i.e. the minimization of the total of holding and inventory change costs (see Figure 17.4). Most such models are deterministic, i.e. they assume a known constant demand and either known input rate with no lead time or instantaneous input and known lead time. In such deterministic situations (which rarely, if ever, occur) there will be no need for provision of buffer or safety stocks. Such stocks will be provided only to protect against uncertain demand and/or lead time (see below). Probabilistic models are available, as are models aimed at profit maximization, etc. Figure 17.5 provides a taxonomy of intermittent flow inventory models. (Models B, C and D are not discussed in the text).

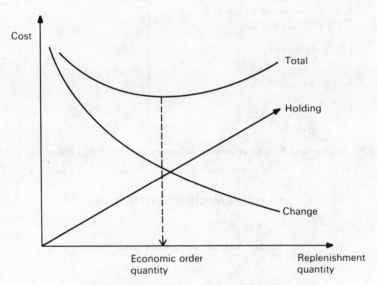

Figure 17.4 *Costs in determining order quantities.*

Although deterministic models make certain, unrealistic assumptions, they are nevertheless of use in practice. Providing the uncertainties to be accommodated (e.g. demand uncertainties) are not too great, they can be dealt with through the provision of buffer stocks. So in practice the models discussed below may often be used to determine the order quantity or interval for use in conjunction with the type of approach developed in the section on probabilistic situations.

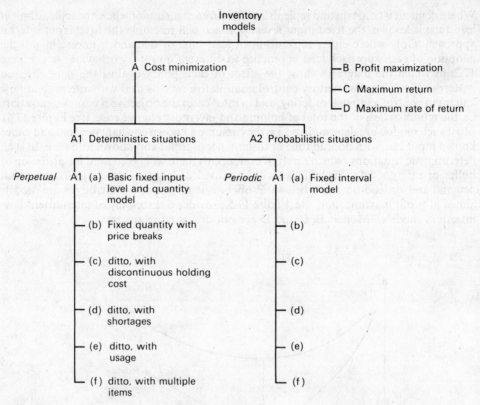

Figure 17.5 *Intermittent flow/input control, inventory models. NB: Letters, etc. refer to text.*

A1 DETERMINISTIC SITUATIONS

Perpetual control: the input level method

In this (the perpetual) inventory control method, two decisions must be made:

1. What fixed input quantity will be used to replenish stocks?
2. At what stock level will this replenishment order be made?

We shall first deal with the *order quantity* decisions.

Order quantities

The act of replenishing inventories is often expensive. Such replenishment costs are normally proportionate only to the number of orders placed and not to the size of the orders.

The ordering cost is equivalent to the set-up cost considered during our discussion of batch quantities in Chapter 14.

The order quantity decision involves the determination of the most economical order quantity—the quantity which minimizes total variable costs. In graphical terms the problem is one of establishing the order or batch quantity corresponding to the lowest point on a total cost curve such as that shown in Figure 17.4. Various economic order quantity (EOQ) models have been developed over the past fifty years so that now not only formulae but also tables, graphs, charts, etc., are available for calculating optimum order sizes in a variety of situations. The following are those commonly adopted and of most value.

Perpetual model A1(a)

1. Known constant demand.
2. Complete deliveries.
3. No shortages.

The derivation of the economic order quantity formula for this model is unnecessary since it was presented in Chapter 14 (see p. 412). The notation adopted is:

Q = Optimal order quantity
C_s = Ordering cost/order
C_1 = Holding cost/item/unit of time
r = Usage rate
p = Direct cost per unit (price or manufacturing cost)

EOQ =
$$Q^* = \sqrt{\frac{2C_s r}{C_1}}$$

Order cycle
$$t^* = \frac{Q^*}{r} = \sqrt{\frac{2C_s}{rC_1}}$$

Total ordering and
holding cost per unit time
$$C^* = \sqrt{2C_s r C_1}$$

Perpetual model A1(b)

As Model A1(a), *with price breaks*, i.e. bulk discounts on purchase price or reductions in cost of processing resulting from the use of different equipment for larger order sizes.

To take advantage of such discounts we are encouraged to order a quantity larger than the economic order quantity.

Previously the total cost equation for C included only holding and ordering costs, since only these varied with order quantity. Now the price of the item, or its direct processing cost, p, is a function of order quantity and this must therefore be included in the cost equation, which is now as follows:

$$C^1 = \frac{C_s r}{Q} + C_1\left(\frac{Q}{2}\right) + rp$$

The problem is to find the order quantity Q which leads to the minimization of this total cost C^1.

The item price, p, is a constant within each quantity range, e.g. let price $= p_i$ apply for quantities q where:

$$q_i \leqslant q < q_{i+1}$$

i.e. the price structure will be as follows:

$$
\begin{array}{lll}
p_1 & \text{for quantities } q_1 & \leqslant q < q_2 \\
p_2 & \text{for quantities } q_2 & \leqslant q < q_3 \\
p_3 & \text{for quantities } q_3 & \leqslant q < q_4 \\
p_{n-1} & \text{for quantities } q_{n-1} & \leqslant q < q_n \\
p_n & \text{for quantities} & q \geqslant q_n
\end{array}
$$

A total cost function, C^1, for a system with price breaks is shown in Figure 17.6. Clearly, our problem is to find the minimum (lowest) point on such a curve. This will occur at *either* the lower end of one of the price/quantity ranges *or* at the point at which the continuous part of the curve is minimum.

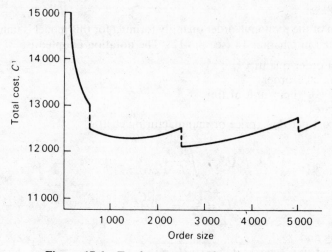

Figure 17.6 *Total cost curve with price breaks.*

EXAMPLE: A WINE RETAILER

The retailer sells large quantities of bottles of a chateau-bottled Bordeaux wine. His purchase prices are shown below.

Order quantity.	100–499	500–2499	2500–4999	5000 and over
Price per bottle	£5	£4.75	£4.6	£4.5

Find the economic order quantity, given that the constant sales rate is 2500 units per year, the holding cost, expressed as a percentage of unit price, is 10 per cent per unit per year, and the ordering cost is £100.

To determine the optimum order quantity we must first calculate the total cost associated with order quantities at the bottom of each price/quantity range, since one of these points may be the lowest on the curve, i.e.

Range 100–499 ($p = 5$)

$$C^1 = \frac{C_s r}{Q} + C_1\left(\frac{Q}{2}\right) + rp$$

$$= \frac{100 \times 2500}{100} + \frac{0.1\,(5)\,100}{2} + 2500\,(5)$$

| Ordering | Holding | Item |
| cost/year | cost/year | cost/year |

$$= £15\,025 \text{ per year}$$

Similarly

Range 500–2499 ($p = 4.75$):

$$C^1 = £12\,494$$

Range 2500–4999 ($p = 4.6$):

$$C^1 = £12\,175$$

Range 5000 and over ($p = 4.5$):

$$C^1 = £12\,425$$

Now we must look for the lowest point of the continuous part of the curve. This can be found by using the formula for economic order quantity:

$$Q = \sqrt{\frac{2C_s r}{C_1}}$$

but, since C_1 is now a function of item cost, we must calculate Q for each price/quantity range, i.e.

Range 100–499 ($p = 5$)

$$Q = \sqrt{\frac{2 \times 100 \times 2500}{0.1\,(5)}} = 1000$$

Range 500–2499 ($p = 4.75$)

$$Q = \sqrt{\frac{2 \times 100 \times 2500}{0.1\,(4.75)}} = 1026$$

Range 2500–4999 ($p = 4.6$)

$$Q = \sqrt{\frac{2 \times 100 \times 2500}{0.1\,(4.6)}} = 1043$$

Range 5000 and over ($p = 4.5$)

$$Q = \sqrt{\frac{2 \times 100 \times 2500}{0.1\,(4.5)}} = 1054$$

Notice that only one of these values of Q falls on the total cost curve, since there is only one minimum point to such a curve. The point in question is $Q = 1026$, which is within the quantity range 500–2499. We must now calculate the total cost for this ordering policy and compare it with the minimum previously obtained.

For $Q^* = 1026$

$$C^1 = \frac{C_s r}{Q} + C_1 \left(\frac{Q}{2}\right) + rp$$

$$= \frac{100 \times 2500}{1026} + \frac{0.1\,(4.75)\,1026}{2} + 4.75\,(2500)$$

$$= 244 + 243 + 11\,875$$

$$= 12\,362$$

This value is greater than the previous minimum of $C^1 = £12\,175$; consequently, in this case it is economically beneficial to take advantage of the quantity discount and order a quantity higher than might otherwise have been the case, i.e. $Q^* = 2500$ bottles.[1]

The total cost curve shown in Figure 17.6 is plotted from the costs calculated above.

Perpetual model A1(c)

As Model A1(a), *plus holding costs*, a proportion of which vary with the order quantity.

We have so far taken the unit holding cost, C_1, as being a constant with respect to the order quantity, but there may be occasions where this relationship is untrue. For example, we have considered the holding cost (in the previous example) as being related to the price or value of the item being stored, but since the price is perhaps dependent on order quantity we ought logically to consider the case in which holding cost is a function of order quantity. Two such functions will be investigated, first the case where holding cost varies continuously and second the discontinuous variation of holding cost.

1.   *Continuous variation.* Notation as before, plus:

C_{11} = The fixed portion of C_1 which is unrelated to order quantity.
C_{12} = The variable portion of C_1 which is a function of order quantity.

Total cost of holding and ordering = C

$$= \frac{C_s r}{Q} + C_{11} \left(\frac{Q}{2}\right) + C_{12} Q$$

Ordering   Fixed holding   Variable holding
cost/unit time   cost/unit time   cost/unit time

Differentiating with respect to Q:

$$\frac{dC}{dQ} = -\frac{C_s r}{Q^2} + \frac{C_{11}}{2} + C_{12}$$

Equating this to zero to obtain the minimum cost gives:

$$Q^* = \sqrt{\frac{2C_s r}{C_{11} + 2C_{12}}}$$

---

[1] This approach to determining order quantities is adequate where no safety stocks are held. Where safety stock exists the costs of carrying that stock must be considered. This will further encourage the use of order quantities sufficient to enable price discounts to be obtained.

Ancamp, D. C. (1981) A caveat on the inventory price-break model, *International Journal of Operations and Production Management*, **2** (2), pp. 30–31.

2. *Discontinuous variation of holding costs.* When storage space is rented it is frequently possible to obtain space only in fixed increments. For example, if a company that rents space in a warehouse finds that more space is required because of its new stock-holding policy, it may be offered the use of another floor or department rather than the exact additional space required. In such cases the cost of holding varies discontinuously with order quantity, as shown in Figure 17.7. A similar situation may apply where a company finds it necessary to build additional storage space, since again only certain increments can be added rather than the exact requirements. In the example shown in Figure 17.7, order quantities of size Q_2 or greater necessitate an increase in holding costs to level H_2. The same increase is necessitated for each increase in order quantity (Q_0).

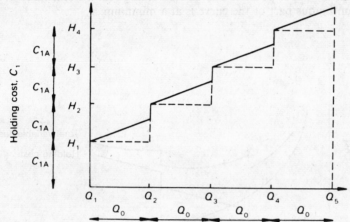

Figure 17.7 *Holding cost varying discontinuously with ordering quantity.*

If this variable holding cost associated with the cost per unit of time for renting one increment of storage is C_{1A}, while C_{11} is the holding cost per item per unit of time which does not vary with order quantity, then the total cost of storage per unit of time, neglecting buffer stock, is:

$$C_1 = C_{1A}\left\{\frac{Q}{Q_0}\right\} + C_{11}\frac{Q}{2}$$

where $\left\{\dfrac{Q}{Q_0}\right\} = $ is the next integer larger than Q/Q_0

EXAMPLE: A WINE IMPORTER

The company imports cases of wine from France. If storage space is available in increments each sufficient for 500 cases, the cost per year for each increment being £400, and if the fixed cost of holding is £1 per case per year, what is the total annual holding cost if the order quantity is 750 cases? There is no buffer stock.

$$C_1 = C_{1A}\left\{\frac{Q}{Q_0}\right\} + C_{11}\frac{Q}{2}$$

$$= 400\left\{\frac{750}{500}\right\} + 1\frac{750}{2}$$

$$= 400\,(2) + \frac{750}{2} = £1175 \text{ p.a.}$$

In such cases the total cost of holding and ordering (C):

$$C = \frac{C_s r}{Q} + C_{1A}\left\{\frac{Q}{Q_0}\right\} + C_{11}\left(\frac{Q}{2}\right)$$

$$\underset{\substack{\text{Ordering}\\\text{cost}}}{\uparrow} \qquad \underset{\substack{\text{Variable}\\\text{holding cost}}}{\uparrow} \qquad \underset{\substack{\text{Fixed}\\\text{holding cost}}}{\uparrow}$$

A curve for total variable cost (C) is shown in Figure 17.8. The economic order quantity can be determined in a similar manner to that used previously for price breaks. In this case the economic order quantity (i.e. the minimum point of the total variable cost curve) will occur *either* at the upper point of one of the holding cost increments *or* at the point at which the continuous part of the curve is at a minimum.

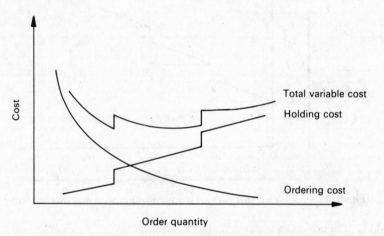

Figure 17.8   *Total variable cost with variable holding costs.*

Perpetual model A1(d)

As Model A1(a) *except shortages allowed* (see Figure 14.4). Notation as before, plus:

C_2 = Shortage or stock-out cost per item per unit of time
S = Stock level after replenishment

The derivation of Q^* and C^* for this model is given in Chapter 14 (see p. 414).

$$\text{EOQ} = Q^* = \sqrt{\frac{2rC_s}{C_1}}\sqrt{\frac{C_1 + C_2}{C_2}}$$

The total variable cost associated with this ordering policy is:

$$C^* = \sqrt{2rC_1 C_s}\sqrt{\frac{C_2}{C_1 + C_2}}$$

Perpetual model A1(e) for fixed quantity with usage

1. Known constant demand.
2. Delivery of order at a known and constant rate.
3. No shortages.
4. Buffer stock.

Notation:

Q = Order quantity
C_s = Ordering cost
C_1 = Holding cost/item/unit of time
q = Delivery or production rate
r = Usage or consumption rate

The derivation of Q^* and C^* for this model is given in Chapter 14 (see p. 416).

$$\text{EOQ} = Q^* = \sqrt{\dfrac{2C_s r}{C_1\left[1-\left(\dfrac{r}{q}\right)\right]}}$$

The total variable cost associated with this ordering policy is:

$$C^* = \sqrt{2C_s r C_1}\,\sqrt{1-\left(\dfrac{r}{q}\right)}$$

EXAMPLE: A HOSPITAL STERILE SUPPLY STORE

A hospital which uses a maximum–minimum stock ordering policy orders 2500 of purchased item A at a time. They wish to determine what annual saving might be made by ordering this item in different quantities. An examination of previous stock records indicates that the annual usage of these items is constant at 7000. They further find that the cost of placing an order, which is independent of the order size, is £10. The purchase price of the items is £0.5 and the cost of holding stock is 7 per cent of item price per item per year. The supplier undertakes to deliver the items at a constant rate of 50 per day.

q = 50 × 250/year (assuming that there are 250 working days per year)
r = 7000/year
C_s = £10
C_1 = 0.07(0.5) = £0.035/item/year

$$\text{EOQ} = Q^* = \sqrt{\dfrac{2\times 10\times 7000}{0.07(0.5)\times\left(1-\dfrac{7000}{12\,500}\right)}}$$

$$Q^* = 3015 \text{ units}$$

Total annual variable cost associated with this policy C^*:

$$= \sqrt{2\times 7000\times 10\times 0.07\,(0.5)}\,\sqrt{1-\dfrac{7000}{12\,500}}$$

$$= £46.4 \text{ p.a.}$$

Total annual variable cost associated with present policy:

$$= \frac{C_1 Q}{2}\left[1 - \left(\frac{r}{q}\right)\right] + \frac{C_s r}{Q}$$

$$= \frac{0.035 \times 2500}{2}(0.44) + 10 \times \frac{7000}{2500}$$

$$= \pounds 47.25 \text{ p.a.}$$

Potential annual saving on item A = £0.85.

Perpetual model A1(f) for multiple items

Our previous models have related to the ordering of a quantity of a *single* product, but in practice there are many occasions when our ordering decision and our ordering cost cover quantities of more than one type of product. If, for example, the ordering cost consists mainly of the cost of transport of items by road from the suppliers, then the cost of ordering could be independent of both quantity of items and the number of different types of product (except, of course, that larger quantities may necessitate more journeys).

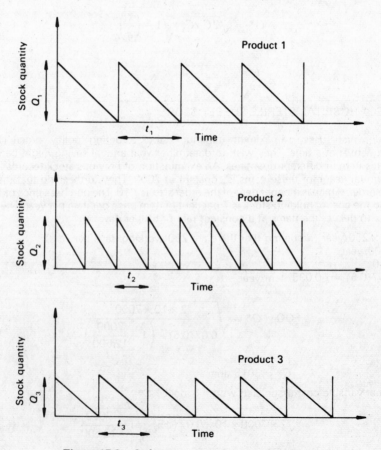

Figure 17.9   *Ordering systems for several products.*

Consider such a situation in which there are N different types of product to be ordered, where:

C_s = Ordering cost
Q_1 = Order size for product i ($i = 1, 2, 3, \ldots N$)
r_i = Usage or consumption rate for product i
C_{1i} = Holding cost/item i/unit of time
t_i = Re-order cycle for item i

Since ordering cost is independent of the number of items ordered, our objective, in order to attempt to minimize costs, must be to arrange the ordering policy so that as few orders as possible are made.

Referring to Figure 17.9, the longest order cycle is for product $1(t_1)$ and the shortest is for product $2(t_2)$. If the order cycle for product 1 is reduced then the average stock is also reduced from the present level, $Q_1/2$. This in itself results in a reduction in the holding cost. Normally such savings would be offset to some extent by an increase in the costs of ordering due to the increase in the number of orders placed over a given period. However, in this case, if the order cycle is reduced so that it coincides with the order cycle for one of the other products, say $t_1 = t_2$, then since ordering cost is independent of order size and since no more orders are being placed than previously, ordering costs are *not* increased and total costs are decreased.

It follows, then, that for an optimum ordering policy, all ordering cycles should be of equal length and orders for different products should be made at the same time.

Now the order size for each product Q_i $\qquad = r_i t$

Ordering cost/unit of time $\qquad = \dfrac{C_s}{t}$

Holding cost per unit of time $\qquad = \sum_{i=1}^{N} \left(C_{1i} \dfrac{Q_i}{2} \right) = \sum_{i=1}^{N} \left(\dfrac{C_{1i} r_i t}{2} \right)$

$\therefore$ Total ordering and holding cost/unit of time $C = \sum_{i=1}^{N} \left(\dfrac{C_{1i} r_i t}{2} \right) + \dfrac{C_s}{t}$

Differentiating with respect to t:

$$\frac{dC}{dt} = \sum_{i=1}^{N} \left(\frac{C_{1i} r_i}{2} \right) - \frac{C_s}{t^2}$$

Equating to zero gives:

$$\text{Optimum order cycle} = t^* = \sqrt{\frac{2C_s}{\sum\limits_{i=1}^{N} C_{1i} r_i}}$$

by substituting for t in the first equation above

$$\text{EOQ} = Q_i^* = r_i \sqrt{\frac{2C_s}{\sum\limits_{i=1}^{N} C_{1i} r_i}}$$

Notice that when N (the number of different products) = 1, the equation for Q^* reduces to EOQ equation for the basic model—A1(a).

EXAMPLE: A SUPERMARKET

The table below gives data relating to three types of product which a supermarket purchases from a company.

Purchased product	Annual sales (r_i)	Holding cost/item/year (C_{1i})
A	5000	0.5
B	3250	1.0
C	2900	0.75

The cost of ordering is £125 per order irrespective of its content. Items of each product are delivered to the shop by the supplier in complete orders. Neglecting buffer stock, what is the economic order size for each product and consequently the total order size? What is the order interval?

$$Q_i^* = r_i \sqrt{\frac{2C_s}{\sum\limits_{i=1}^{N} C_{1i} r_i}}$$

Product	$C_{1i} r_i$
A	2500
B	3250
C	2175

$$\sum_{i=1}^{N} C_{1i} r_i = 7925$$

$$Q^*_A = 5000 \sqrt{\frac{2(125)}{7925}} = 888 \qquad Q^*_B = 3250 \sqrt{\frac{2(125)}{7925}} = 577$$

$$Q^*_C = 2900 \sqrt{\frac{2(125)}{7925}} = 515 \qquad \text{Total } Q^* = 1980 \text{ order size}$$

$$\text{Order interval } t^* = \frac{Q_i^*}{r_i} = \frac{888}{5000} = 0.178 \text{ year}$$

The re-order level

We decided earlier that in the fixed quantity (two-bin or order quantity) ordering system two questions must be answered: what is the fixed order quantity (Q) and what is the re-order level (Q_1)? We have decided how, in a few typical situations, the fixed order quantity can be determined and we must now look at the problem of re-order levels.

If the usage or consumption of items is perfectly constant and accurately known and if stock replenishment time is zero, then the stock order level may be zero and orders for stock replenishments can be placed when stock falls to this level. Thus in a deterministic situation the order-level decision is easily made.

Unfortunately such an ideal situation rarely, if ever, exists. In practice two complications can arise. First, the usage rate may not be absolutely constant and consequently there is the risk that stock may be prematurely exhausted. Even so, if replenishment of stock is instantaneous, no problems arise because exhausted stock can immediately be replaced. The second complication concerns replenishment. If this is not immediate, it becomes necessary to place orders some time before the items are needed and replenishment times may fluctuate. The occurrence of both these complications necessitates the maintenance of buffer or safety stocks.

If both these complications arise in any magnitude then we cannot reasonably use any of the ordering models discussed in the previous section, since all of those assume a static and deterministic state. However, if these fluctuations are not excessive then these models can be used, since only a slight, and usually tolerable, error is introduced.

To summarize, then, the need to consider order levels other than zero arises because of uncertainty, i.e. the probabilistic nature of demand and/or replenishment lead time. Such uncertainty is alien to the ordering models we have discussed but they can nevertheless be used, with only minor error, provided demand and lead time vary only marginally. The approaches which might be employed are outlined in a discussion of probabilistic models later in this chapter.

Periodic control: the fixed input interval method

If, to begin with, we again assume that usage or demand is constant and known, then this system of ordering is, in both practice and theory, identical to the maximum–minimum or order quantity system. In the maximum–minimum system, when stocks fall to a predetermined level (which can be zero if order delivery is instantaneous), a further predetermined quantity of items is ordered. In the order cycle system, at predetermined intervals, a quantity of goods sufficient to restore stock to a given level is ordered. In the ideal conditions we have assumed both the order quantity and the order cycle would be the same, irrespective of the system we adopt. Consequently, for such cases the answers to our two basic questions—when to order and how much to order—can be found in the previous section, i.e.

$$\text{Order interval} = \frac{\text{Order quantity}}{\text{Usage rate}}$$

$$\text{Optimum order interval} = \frac{\text{EOQ}}{\text{Usage rate}}$$

$$\text{i.e. } t^* = \frac{Q^*}{r}$$

For the models we examined in the previous section the optimum order intervals are given by the following formulae.

Periodic model A1(a):

$$t^* = \sqrt{\frac{2C_s}{rC_1}}$$

Periodic model A1(b):

$$t^* = \frac{Q^*}{r}$$

Periodic model A1(c):

$$t^* = \sqrt{\frac{2C_s}{r(C_{11} + 2C_{12})}}$$

Periodic model A1(d):

$$t^* = \sqrt{\frac{2C_s}{rC_1}} \sqrt{\frac{C_1 + C_2}{C_2}}$$

Periodic model A1(e):

$$t^* = \sqrt{\frac{2C_s}{rC_1\left[1 - \left(\dfrac{r}{q}\right)\right]}}$$

Periodic model A1(f) multiple items:

$$t^* = \sqrt{\frac{2C_s}{\displaystyle\sum_{i=1}^{N} C_{1i}r_i}}$$

It is only during conditions of uncertainty that these two methods of ordering differ. The fundamental characteristic of the order cycle system is that the stock status of each item is examined at regular and fixed intervals, at which time the following questions are asked:

1. Should an order be placed to replenish stock now?
2. If so, how many units must be ordered?

A2 PROBABILISTIC SITUATIONS

All of the preceding discussion has assumed deterministic situations. The assumption has been made that demand, and the time required to replenish stocks, are known and constant, thus problems of managing inventory have been minimized. In this section we shall deal with the more realistic situation in which there is some uncertainty to be accommodated. We shall deal with both the order quantity and the order interval approaches outlined above, and show how these two approaches can be adapted for use in circumstances where there is some degree of uncertainty.

Where there is some uncertainty in demand and/or in the time between the placing of an order and the receipt of that order to replenish inventories, it becomes necessary to use some safety or buffer stocks to try to prevent a stock-out situation. Figure 17.10 refers to an order quantity method of inventory control and shows how variations in demand or usage rate, and/or replenishment lead time, might, unless buffer stock is used, result in a stock-out situation. The first case describes a situation in which the demand or usage rate is fixed but the replenishment lead time is variable. Here the ideal situation will occur where an order is placed at such time that items are received for replenishment stock when the constant rate of demand has depleted stocks to zero. However, it is possible that because lead time is greater than expected, the constant rate of demand has in fact reduced stocks to zero and a stock-out situation thus exists before items are obtained to replenish stock. The second situation concerns a variable demand or usage rate and fixed replenishment lead time. Here again there is a possible stock-out situation since, even though the lead time is fixed, demand during that period may be greater than expected, thus reducing stock to zero before replenishment. In the final situation both demand or usage and replenishment lead time are variable, so a stock-out siuation may occur because of the combination of the two situations described above.

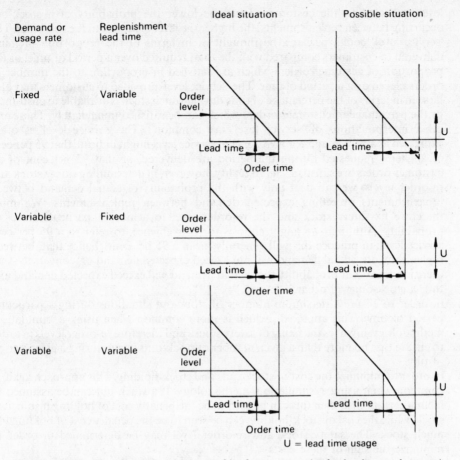

Figure 17.10 *The effect of uncertainty of lead time usage (order level control system).*

All three examples are in fact describing a situation in which usage or demand during the re-order lead time is uncertain. Uncertainty on lead time usage necessitates the use of buffer stocks, i.e. the placing of a replenishment order earlier, or at a higher level of stock, than would have been necessary in a deterministic situation. In these circumstances the order level can be calculated as follows:

$$\text{Re-order level} = \text{Average lead time usage} + \text{Safety stock}$$

Service levels and safety stock

The safety stock employed will be determined by the level of protection required against uncertainties in lead time usage. The required safety stock can be determined as follows:

1. In order to provide a given risk of a stock-out situation occurring, i.e. to provide a given risk that the actual demand between two replenishment orders will be greater than that expected, and thus that a stock-out situation will occur before replenishment stocks arrive. This probability of stock-out is often expressed in terms of the 'service

level' provided to the customer. Thus the lower the probability of a stock-out occurring between replenishments, the higher the level of service to the customer. The 'service level' could, perhaps, be thought of in terms of the proportion of items delivered to customers compared with the total required over a period of time, or the proportion of customer orders which are satisfied in proportion to the number of orders placed over a period of time. The 'service level' provided to customers may also be seen in terms of the percentage of time during which stock is available to customers or the percentage of customer orders which can be satisfied immediately. These and other interpretations of 'service level' are common.[2] The 'service level' is often expressed as a percentage, e.g. a 95 per cent service level might indicate that 95 per cent of all items requested during the period are delivered, or that 95 per cent of all customer orders are satisfied, etc. In reality, however, in determining safety stock and re-order levels, we can deal only with the probability of actual demand between replenishments exceeding expected demand between replenishments. We must therefore fix safety stock and the re-order level to achieve a particular level of probability. Although we might choose, for convenience, to refer to a 95 per cent service level, in practice this will generally mean a 95 per cent chance that, between replenishments, actual demand will not exceed expected demand or, conversely, that there is a 5 per cent probability that actual demand will exceed expected demand and thus a stock-out will occur.

2. In order to ensure a maximum number of stock-out situations during a particular period of time. This approach, which is more common when using a 'simulation' methodology, involves the fixing of safety stocks and therefore re-order levels in order to ensure that no more than a given number of stock-outs occur during a given period of time.

3. In order to minimize the cost of stock-outs and stock-holding. This approach again is common when using a 'simulation' methodology. If a stock-out can be assumed to incur a certain cost, then this can be seen to be the penalty cost of holding insufficient stock, while the cost of stock-holding can be seen to be the penalty cost of holding too much stock. The safety stock and re-order level may be determined in order to minimize the sum of these costs.

4. In order to minimize the cost of stock-outs, where the cost is taken also to be a function of the number of items short during the stock-out period, plus the cost of stock-holding.

The way in which the safety stock and re-order level is determined will to some extent depend on the information which is available. If, for example, uncertainties in demand or lead time, or both, can be expressed by probability distributions then a statistical approach can be employed, and in such cases the objective will be as described in (1) above, and will normally be expressed in terms of 'service level'. If, however, the uncertainties cannot be expressed by probability distributions, then an alternative approach will be employed. In these circumstances a 'simulation' methodology may be appropriate, as referred to above.

Both the statistical and the simulation methodology will be described below, where our discussion deals first with order quantity inventory control systems.

The order quantity method with uncertainty

The three examples below show how the three types of situation described in Figure 17.10 might be accommodated in those circumstances where demand, lead time usage, or the

[2] For a discussion see Ronen, D. (1983) Inventory service levels, *International Journal of Operations and Production Management*, **3** (2), pp. 37–45.

lead time period can be shown, or assumed, to be distributed Normally. The examples show how a re-order level can be calculated and, where appropriate, used in conjunction with a re-order quantity determined by use of one of the models described in the preceding sections (except model Al(d)). The first example deals with lead time variation,the second with demand variation during a known lead time, and the third directly with lead time and demand variations. In all cases service level is represented as a probability of actual demand between replenishments ≤ expected demand.

EXAMPLE: A GARAGE SELLING ACCESSORIES FOR CARS

Demand rate for car batteries	= 4500/month (constant)
Ordering cost	= £150/replenishment order
Stock-holding cost	= £3.75/item/year

Average stock replenishment lead time from supplier (assumed Normally distributed) = 1 month
Standard deviation of replenishment lead time (from study of past data) = 0.2 months
Service level required = 95 per cent

Determine:

1. Re-order quantity
2. Re-order level

Solution:

1. $Q^* = \sqrt{\dfrac{2 \times 150 \times 4500}{3.75/12}}$

    $Q^* = 2078$ items

2. Re-order level (R) = Average lead time demand + Safety stock
    NB: Safety stock = 1.64 × Standard deviation of lead time demand since for the Normal probability distribution, 1.64 standard deviations above the mean excludes 5 per cent of the distribution, i.e. equivalent to 95 per cent service level.
    Standard deviation of lead time demand = 0.2 (4500). Hence:

    $$R = 4500(1) + 1.64 (0.2 \times 4500)$$

    $$R = 5976 \text{ batteries}$$

EXAMPLE: A GARDEN CENTRE SELLING SACKS OF FERTILIZER

Average demand = 10 sacks/day
Standard deviation of daily demand = 3 (assumed Normally distributed)
Stock replenishment interval = 15 days (constant)
Service level required = 95 per cent

Determine re-order level (R)

$R = 10(15) + 1.64$ (standard deviation of usage during replenishment lead time)
Standard deviation of lead time usage

$$= \sqrt{\sum_{i=1}^{n} \sigma d_i^2} \text{ (where each day's demand is independent)}$$

where $\sigma d_i^2 =$ Variance of daily demand for $i = 1$ to n days $(n = 15)$

$$= \sqrt{15(3^2)}$$

$$= 11.6$$

Hence $R = 10(15) + 1.64 (11.6)$
        $= 169$ sacks

EXAMPLE: A COMPANY MANUFACTURING FERTILIZER

Customer service required = 95 per cent
Average manufacturing lead time to replenish stocks = 20 days
Average daily demand = 100 sacks
Standard deviation of demand during lead time = 200

Determine Re-order level (R)

Re-order level (R) = Average lead time usage + Safety stock
                    $= 20(100) + 1.64 (200)$
$R = 2000 + 328$
  $= 2328$ sacks

The above examples assume that it was appropriate to use the Normal probability distribution to describe the various uncertainties which were to be accommodated. The use of the Normal probability distribution is often appropriate where we are dealing with output or work-in-progress stocks in a manufacturing system. The use of a Poisson distribution is often more appropriate for retail stocks. The negative exponential distribution is often used for wholesale or retail stocks. In each of these cases statistical procedures similar to those described above can be used. Often, however, there will be no evidence to suggest that any probability distribution can or should be used, so in these cases it will be necessary to take a different approach. Such an approach is used in the following examples, in which historical lead time usage data are employed. The three examples show how the re-order level can be calculated to give:

(a) maximum number of stock-outs/period of time;
(b) minimum cost of stock-out + stock-holding;
(c) minimum cost of stock-outs (where cost is a function of the number of items short during a stock-out) + stock-holding.

EXAMPLE: A RESTAURANT

The annual usage rate of a purchased product is 5000. The cost of the product is 25 p each, the cost of placing the order is £1.25 and the cost of holding stock is 10 per cent of item price per year per item. Complete orders are delivered by the supplier.

An examination of the stock records indicates that lead time usage (U) varies from 32 to 40 as shown in the following table. Stock-outs are permitted, but no more than one per year should occur.

What is to be the re-order level?

U	$P(U)$	P(actual usage $> U$)
32	0.02	0.98
33	0.07	0.91
34	0.12	0.79
35	0.16	0.63
36	0.20	0.43
37	0.17	0.26
38	0.13	0.13
39	0.10	0.03
40	0.03	0.00

Using EOQ formula A1(a):

$$Q^* = 707$$

Hence number of orders per year is:

$$\frac{r}{Q} = \frac{5000}{707} = 7.07$$

Now buffer stock (B) can be defined as the difference between the re-order level (R) and the average lead time usage (U). Hence, if in this case the re-order level is set at 37:

$$B = R - \bar{U}$$
$$= 37 - 36$$
$$= 1$$
$$\text{etc.}$$

Now we can present all the information necessary for a solution in the form of a table:

Re-order level, R	36	37	38	39	40
Buffer stock, B	0	1	2	3	4
Holding cost p.a.					
(10 per cent $\times B \times$ 25 p p.a.)	0	2.5 p	5 p	7.5 p	10 p
Stock-outs					
Probability per order	0.43	0.26	0.13	0.03	0.00
Expected no. per year	3.04	1.83	0.92	0.21	0.00
(Probability $\times$ 7.07)					

Clearly from this table a re-order level of 38 must be used if no more than one stock-out per year is to occur.

EXAMPLE

As for the previous example but, instead of determining the re-order level to provide not more than one stock-out per year, determine the re-order level to minimize total cost. An analysis of past records has shown that stock-outs of this product lead to a fixed cost of 50 p per stock-out period. Alternative re-order levels are examined in the following table.

Since the stock-out costs dominate the holding cost of buffer stock, in order to minimize total cost it is clearly beneficial in this case to adopt a re-order level of 40, which corresponds, of course, to the maximum lead time usage.

Re-order level, R	36	37	38	39	40
Buffer stock, B	0	1	2	3	4
Holding cost p.a. (1)					
(10 per cent $\times B \times$ 25 p p.a.)	0 p	2.5 p	5 p	7.5 p	10 p
Stock-outs					
Number per year	3.04	1.83	0.92	0.21	0.00
Cost per year (2)					
(at 50 p each)	152 p	91.5p	46 p	10.5 p	0 p
Total cost per annum					
(1) + (2)	152 p	94 p	49 p	18 p	10 p

EXAMPLE

As for the first example, but in this case it has been found that the stock-out costs depend not only on the number of times stock-outs occur but also on the number of units short or required during the stock-out periods. It has been found from records that the stock-out cost is 5 p per item.

To determine the re-order level which provides minimum cost we must calculate not only the number of stock-outs per year at each re-order level but also the average number of units short during the stock-out periods, i.e.

$$\text{Average stock-out quantity} =$$

$$\frac{\text{Average stock-out per order during stock-out periods}}{\text{Probability of stock-out occurring}}$$

For re-order level $R = 36$, the relevant data and calculations are shown in the following table.

Actual usage (U)	Stock-out quantity $(U-R)$	Probability $P(U)$	$P(U) \times (U-R)$
37	1	0.17	0.17
38	2	0.13	0.26
39	3	0.10	0.30
40	4	0.03	0.12
		0.43	0.85

$$\text{Average stock-out quantity} = \frac{0.85}{0.43} = 1.98$$

Similarly:

For $R = 37$, Average stock-out quantity = 1.62
For $R = 38$, Average stock-out quantity = 1.23
For $R = 39$, Average stock-out quantity = 1.00
For $R = 40$, Average stock-out quantity = 0.00

Now all the data necessary to compare the merits of different re-order levels can be presented in tabular form, as in the following table.

These figures indicate that the minimum cost re-order level is 39, which results in an average of 0.21 stock-outs per year.

Re-order level, R	36	37	38	39	40
Average stock-out quantity per stock-out period	1.98	1.62	1.23	1.00	0.00
Buffer stock, B	0	1	2	3	4
Holding cost p.a. (1)	0 p	2.5 p	5 p	7.5 p	10 p
Stock-outs Number per year	3.04	1.83	0.92	0.21	0.00
Cost (number × quantity × 5 p) (2)	30.1 p	5 p	5.7 p	1 p	0 p
Total cost per annum (1) + (2)	30.1 p	17.5 p	10.7 p	8.5 p	10 p

The order interval method with uncertainty

Under conditions of uncertainty in demand or order lead time, or both, a buffer stock must be maintained. But, unlike the order level system, buffer stocks in the order interval system must protect against not only changes in lead time demand but also variations in demand at all other times. For example, consider the situation shown in Figure 17–11. The fixed order cycle is t while lead time is constant at l. Usage during lead time l_2 conforms exactly to expectations; consequently an order for the fixed replenishment quantity Q at this time eventually results in the replenishment of stock to the desired level Q_2. Usage remains constant during the following period and during the order lead time l_3 and again stock is replenished to the desired level. However, during the next lead time usage is greater than normal and consequently some of the buffer stock is consumed before replenishment can take place; therefore, unless a larger quantity is ordered, stock is replenished to a level less than Q_2. Usage during the entire next period is again greater than normal and further buffer stock is consumed. Again, unless a larger quantity of the product is ordered, the maximum stock level will fall since buffer stock must, as shown here, accommodate usage fluctuations throughout the entire period rather than just during lead time.

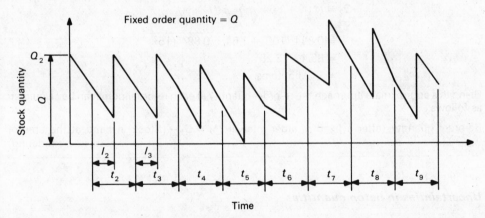

Figure 17.11　*The effect of usage uncertainty in an interval stock ordering system (using a fixed order quantity)*

The following example will give some indication of the manner in which this type of problem can be tackled. It deals with the fixed order interval system where the order quantity is variable, which is the more common approach. The procedure adopted involves first establishing the fixed re-order interval based on economic re-order quantity calculations and then determining, at each order time, the quantity to be ordered to protect against demand fluctuations over the next period. It will be appreciated that the first part of this solution assumes constant demand rate, whereas the second part is explicitly concerned with dealing with varying demand rate. This might seem contradictory, but the approach *might* be appropriate where demand rate varies about an established mean rather than where substantial trends are evident.

EXAMPLE: A BOOK PUBLISHER

Retailer demand for a book averages 100 books/week. There is no noticeable trend in demand, and the standard deviation of weekly demand has been found to be 15 books.

The stock-holding cost is £0.5/book/week and the re-order cost is £20 per batch.

It is intended to reprint the book, to replenish stock, in appropriately equal-sized batches at fixed intervals, and to do so in such a way as to try to ensure a 95 per cent service level. Calculate the re-order interval and show how the re-order quantity might be determined.

Solution:

A fixed re-order interval equal to the theoretical optimum re-order interval will be used, i.e.

$$t^* = \sqrt{\frac{2 \times 20}{100 \times 0.5}}$$

$$= 0.894 \text{ weeks}$$

The theoretical economic re-order quantity Q^* for constant demand situation $= t^*(r) = 89.4$ books, but this takes no account of demand uncertainty. If this quantity is ordered on every replenishment, a situation like that shown in Figure 17.11 may result. To protect against this it will be appropriate to determine the re-order quantity at the time of each replenishment.

If we assume that stock replenishment takes place, on average, at time intervals equal to the re-order interval t^*, then we must ensure that after each replenishment the stock in hand (Q_2) is sufficient to meet 95 per cent of customers' orders during the following period t^*, i.e.

$$Q_2 = t^*(r) + 1.64 \sqrt{\sum_{i=1}^{t^*} \sigma d_i^2}$$

$$= 0.894 (100) + 1.64 \sqrt{0.894 (15^2)}$$

$$= 89.4 + 23.25$$

$$= 112.65 \text{ items}$$

Using this approximate approach the re-order quantity at each re-order point can be calculated as follows:

Re-order quantity (after a fixed re-order interval t^*) = Q_2 − (Stock in hand at the time of ordering)

Uncertainties in batch quantities

Our discussion above has dealt with the situation where there is uncertainty about demand rate or lead time, or both. A third possible source of uncertainty is the delivered batch quantity. For example, in a purchasing situation it is possible that even though a particular batch quantity is ordered to replenish stock, a different batch quantity may eventually be received into stock. Where, for example, there are losses during delivery, there is a risk that a quantity less than the ordered batch quantity may be received to replenish stock. This uncertainty is not a major problem with the re-order level (perpetual) inventory control system, since the delivery of a quantity which is smaller than required will simply mean that the re-order level is reached more quickly than might have been expected, while the delivery of a larger batch than is expected results in the next order being placed later than might otherwise be expected. However, in the order interval system, since orders are placed to replenish stock to a particular level, the delivery of a quantity different from that which was ordered can increase the risk of a stock-out before the next replenishment is received. If there is enough information on likely variation in delivered batch quantity, this risk can be taken into account when establishing the re-order quantity in the manner described above. In other circumstances it will be possible only to estimate the likely shortfall in delivered quantity and add that to the re-order quantity determined in the manner described above.

CONTINUOUS FLOW/INPUT CONTROL

Conventional inventory control theory largely ignores the case of continuous, as opposed to intermittent, input flow, although a queuing theory approach may have some relevance. Assuming input control as a means of managing inventory to satisfy expected output needs, one problem for inventory management is the determination of an input rate (or average rate). Other problems will generally relate to the determination of average, minimum or safety inventory levels, and inventory capacity. Given deterministic output (or full control of output) and full control of input, input rate can be matched to output and inventory problems are obviated. Here, therefore, we must deal with problems deriving from probabilistic output and/or incomplete control of input.

The problem can be considered to be one of matching two probability distributions (i.e. for input and output rates). A mismatch may give rise to:

(a) *output starving*, i.e. depletion of stock due to excess of demand over input (i.e. shortage, etc.);
(b) (i) *input blocking*, i.e. insufficient space or capacity for inputs due to excess of input over output; or
     (ii) *excess stock-holding*, if inventory capacity is not limited.

The required average inventory capacity will be influenced by input and output rate variability (mean input rate must equal mean output rate). The higher the variability, the greater the stock capacity required to accommodate short-term differences in input and output sales. Hence as a general rule of thumb, the greater the possible short-term difference between rates (i.e. assuming symmetrical distributions, the upper end of one distribution minus the lower end of the other), the greater the stock capacity required. For a given (known or forecast) output rate distribution, inventory levels can be determined for alternative input rate distributions, and vice versa. Simulation techniques will normally be employed.

A similar problem is encountered in the design of flow processing systems, where inventory must exist between successive stages in the system (e.g. buffer stocks between the stations on a flow line) (see Chapter 15).

MATERIALS REQUIREMENTS PLANNING (MRP) *(see also Chapters 12 and 16)*

MRP was described in Chapter 12. It was seen there to involve the scheduling of activities and to impinge upon the control of inventories. MRP will normally be used in a situation where demand is dependent (see Chapter 12) and where activity scheduling is to be externally oriented. In such situations the end product demand may be known and thus it will be possible, by 'exploding' demand, to calculate with certainty the parts/components requirements to satisfy that demand. Where this certainty exists the MRP procedure can be used as the principal approach to activity scheduling, and the inventory control problem can be seen as a secondary problem. Thus at any one time the parts/components requirements of a system, the activities which are to be undertaken by the system, are known with certainty and any inventories which are maintained are simply inventories of work-in-progress. Used in this 'pure' fashion the impact of a materials requirements planning system on the management of inventory will be as shown in Figure 17.12.

In some circumstances, the end product demand will be forecast, and this forecast requirement will be exploded in order to estimate, for a given period, the parts/

Inventory Decisions	Type of Inventory Control System		MRP*
	Order Level System ('Perpetual')	Order Interval System ('Periodic')	
Order Quantity	Fixed	Variable	Variable
Re-order Level	Fixed	Variable	Variable
Re-order Interval	Variable	Fixed	Variable
Buffer Stock	Low	High	None

* The use of MRP as the principal/sole means for the scheduling of activities and the management of inventories (i.e. without the use of economic batching procedures, buffer stocks, etc.) (see text).

Figure 17.12 *Comparison of inventory decisions for inventory control system and MRP.*

components requirements for the system. In these cases, i.e. when there is some degree of uncertainty, it will be appropriate to maintain inventories of parts/components and/or end products. Additionally it may be appropriate to maintain such inventories where there is some need to manufacture and/or purchase parts or components in economic batches. In these circumstances the gross requirements determined from the MRP procedure can be interpreted to a scheduling/inventory requirement as follows:

Parts/components to be provided for a given period = Gross parts/components requirement for period – Opening inventory + Required closing inventory

Our discussion in Chapter 12 indicated the way in which an economic batch size approach and the use of buffer or safety stocks can be used alongside materials requirements planning. In this type of approach, therefore, MRP will be used alongside an inventory management procedure which might be developed in the way discussed above.

COMPUTERS IN INVENTORY MANAGEMENT

Table 17.4 lists some of the computer software packages which have been written, in whole or in part, to deal with inventory management. The rates of introduction of new packages and modification of existing packages are high, so the details in the table are only indicative and the discussion below provides only an outline of the types of packages available.

The packages listed in the first part of the table are mainly derivatives of earlier software and are designed for implementation on mainframe computers. For example 'MAPICS' from IBM is derived from 'INVEN' and other programs. In general these packages offer a wide range of facilities, in addition to inventory management. Such commercially available mainframe packages often provide planning and control routines, purchase order processing, etc., as well as inventory management. Those designed for the manufacturing industries provide for full production/inventory management. Some of these programs

Table 17.4 *Some computer software for inventory management*

Name	Supplier	References
OMAC	ICL	—
PCS	Burroughs	*Journal of Industrial Engineering*, March 1977, **9** (3)
MAPICS	IBM	—
IMS/66	Honeywell	*Journal of Industrial Engineering*, January 1977, **9** (1)
CYBER	Control Data	*Journal of Industrial Engineering*, December 1977, **9** (12)
Industrial Management System 201	Mod Comp Business System	*Journal of Industrial Engineering*, February 1977, **9** (2)
GIPSI	Aston University (UK)	*International Journal of Production Research* 1980, **18**, pp. 73–82
Inventory Control and Replenishment System	Data Systems for Industry	*Journal of Industrial Engineering*, August 1977, **9** (8)
PACS/VS	PA Computers and Telecommunications	Bailey, P. and Farmer, D. H. (1982) *Materials Management Handbook*. Aldershot: Gower.
MICROSS	Kewill Systems (Amida Systems)	—
INSYS and EOQ	—	Harris, R. D. and Maggard, M. J. (1977) *Computer Models in Operations Management*. London: Harper and Row.
(No name)	—	Nicholson, T. A. J. and Pullin, R. D. (1974) *Computers in Production Management Decisions*. London: Pitman.
Microfact	CMG (Computer Management Group)	—
Commodore Stock Controller	Anagram Systems (for PET Micro-computers)	—
Diamond 7	Data Recall Ltd	—
Powerstock	Omicron Business Systems	—
Tabs	Tabs Ltd	—
QUIBS	Quantum Computer Systems	—
ALPHACONTROLER	Derwent Data Systems	—
IPCON	Stavely Computing	—
(Several names)	Program listings in →	Atkinson, C. (1982) *Inventory Management for Small Computers*. dilithium.

(e.g. MAPICS) are built largely around MRP procedures. Some developed for distribution offer purchasing, warehousing, distribution and retail stocks control.

The packages towards the end of the list are a selection of the many available for implementation on micro-computers. These are likely to be of more interest in smaller organizations, or in the management of inventory in parts of larger organizations. Many of these packages are designed only as 'stock reporting' procedures, i.e. they provide for the recording, and handling of stock transactions, e.g. as a means of maintaining a 'perpetual' stock record, and identify ordering requirements. Some are more comprehensive and can be used for determining re-order levels and quantities, but in few cases can demand and/or order lead time uncertainties be accommodated. There is, however, a move towards the development of micro-computer-based yet comprehensive inventory management packages which provide not only for stock record keeping but also for decision-making in uncertain conditions against required service levels, etc. (The Diamond and Powerstock programs are of this type.)

CHECKLIST FOR CHAPTER 17

Single- and multi-stage inventories
Purpose and role of inventories
Different types of inventory
   Consumed/non-consumed
   Output
   Input resource
   Customer queues
Decision parameters for different situations
Inventory management strategies
Costs in inventory management
   Inventory costs
   Customer service costs
ABC/Pareto analysis
Inventory management systems
   Intermittent flow/input control system
     Fixed input level (perpetual control)
     Fixed input interval (periodic control)
Merits of 'periodic' and 'perpetual' systems
Different inventory models
A1: Deterministic models
   Input level method
     Order quantities
       (a) Constant demand/complete deliveries
       (b) As (a) with price breaks
       (c) As(a) with discontinuous holding costs
       (d) As(a) with shortages

       (e) Constant demand with usage
     Multiple items—otherwise as(a)
     Re-order level problem
   Input interval method
     (a) As above
     (b) As above
     (c) As above
     (d) As above
     (e) As above
     Multiple items
A2: Probabilistic situations
   Lead time and demand uncertainties
   Safety or buffer stocks
   'Service' level
   Order quantity and level method, with uncertainty
     Constant demand/variable lead time
     Constant lead time/variable demand
     Variable lead time demand
   Order interval method with uncertainty
     Uncertainties in batch quantities
Continuous flow/input control system
   Decisions
Materials requirement planning
Computers in inventory management

FURTHER READING

Computer applications are covered in the following book, and mentioned in some of those below (see also Table 17.4).

Atkinson, C. (1982) *Inventory Management for Small Computers*. dilithium.

Sandilya, M. S. and Gopalakrishnan, P. (1981) *Inventory Management, Text and Cases*. Macmillan/South Asia Books.

Thomas, A. B. (1980) *Stock Control in Manufacturing Industries* (2nd ed.). Aldershot: Gower.

Van Hees, R. N. and Monhemius, W. (1972) *An Introduction to Production and Inventory Control*. London: Macmillan.

Van Hees, R. N. and Monhemius, W. (1972) *Production and Inventory Control—Theory and Practice*. London: Macmillan.

Together the two books above provide a comprehensive treatment of inventory management, with a quantitative emphasis throughout.

QUESTIONS

17.1   Describe the principles of maximum–minimum and order cycle systems of stock control. In what circumstances is the use of each of these types of system appropriate?

      In what circumstances would the use of either system give rise to basically the same stock control system (i.e. the same ordering decision)?

17.2   In a certain situation, demand for goods is both known and stable. The goods are ordered from an 'outside' supplier, they are delivered in complete batches and no quantity discount arrangements apply. No buffer stock is to be maintained. Determine:

(a)   the economic order quantity, given:

ordering cost per order	= 20
holding cost per item per annum	= £0.05
demand per annum	= 10 000
price per item	= £15

(b)   the economic order quantity, given:

ordering cost per order	= £20
holding cost per item per annum	= 5 per cent of item price
demand per annum	= 10 000
price per item	= £15

(c)   the regular economic ordering interval, given:

ordering cost per order	= £50
holding cost per item per annum	= 5 per cent of item price
demand per annum	= 15 000
price per item	= £25

17.3   Determine the economic order quantity for the following:

(a)
C_s (ordering cost)	= £20
C_1 (holding cost per item)	= £0.07/year
r (demand)	= 12 000/year
p (price)	= £25

(b) $C_s = £20$
$C_1 = £0.07$
$r = 12\,000$
Purchase discounts as follows:

Order quantity	0–500	500–999	1000–2500	Over 2500
Price per item	£25	£22	£20	£19.5

(c) $C_s = £20$
$C_1 = 10$ per cent of price/year
$r = 10\,000$/year
Purchase discounts as follows:

Order quantity	0–500	500–999	1000–2500	Over 2500
Price per item	£25	£22	£20	£19.5

17.4   Determine the economic order quantity, given the following situation:

$$C_s = £100$$
$$r = 10\,000/\text{year}$$

Holding cost per item per annum, a portion of which is fixed and unrelated to the order quantity, i.e. £0.05, and a variable portion which is related to the order qantity, i.e. £0.07.

17.5   Determine the cost of storage and ordering per annum for order quantities of: (a) 1000; (b) 2000; and (c) 3000 items, given the following:

$$C_s = £150$$
$$r = 12\,000/\text{year}$$

Also, storage space is available in increments each sufficient for storing 1000 items. The cost per annum for each of these increments is £500 and the fixed cost of storage irrespective of quantity is £0.5 per annum. No buffer stock is required.

17.6   (a)   Derive the formula used to determine economic order quantities in the following circumstances:

Stock-outs permitted
Delivery of complete batches of ordered items
Deterministic and stable demand

(b)   What is the EOQ given the following:
Ordering cost = £125
Annual demand = 7500 items
Shortage or stock-out cost per item per month = £5
Stock-holding cost per item per annum = 10 per cent of price
Price of each item = £50

17.7   A company uses 75 000 components of a certain type each year, which it purchases from an outside supplier under the following terms:

Order size units	Price per unit (£)
1 to 999	0.60
1000 to 9999	0.54
10 000 upwards	0.45

Each time an order is placed, clerical and handling costs of £5 and transport costs of £15 are incurred. The cost of storage, interest and deterioration is £0.08 per unit stored per year. No safety stock is held. If the components are used at a uniform rate calculate the economic order size and the total annual cost to the company.

17.8   (a)   The assembly section of a factory uses a certain component part at a rate of 40 units per day. The machine shop within the factory can produce the component at a rate of 200 per day. The associated set-up cost is £100, the manufacturing cost is £5, and the inventory holding cost is £0.1 per unit per day.

   If management is prepared to tolerate an increase of up to 1 per cent in the minimum total cost per unit, what flexibility does this give in the choice of batch quantities and what is the total cost per unit of the cheapest solution if, for technical reasons, production batches are restricted to multiples of 50 units?

(b)   The component part can be purchased in any quantity from an outside source, the terms depending on the quantity supplies as shown below:

Order quantity (number of units)	Price per unit (£)
0 to 249	5.5
250 to 499	5.2
500 or more	5

If the ordering costs are £15 per order, what is the economic order quantity in this case? Is it cheaper to manufacture the component in the factory or purchase it from the outside supplier?

17.9   Quick Start Ltd are the 'manufacturers' of automobile batteries. They purchase four types of second-hand battery from a local company, which, after rebuilding, they sell to local dealers. Sales of each type of battery are stable. The cost of storage and the annual demand for the batteries are shown in the following table.

   Quick Start Ltd like to order all four types of second-hand battery from their suppliers simultaneously. The cost of ordering is £175. They do not believe in maintaining buffer stocks of batteries.

(a)   What are the economic order quantities for each type of battery?

Type of battery	Annual demand	Stock-holding cost of item per annum
Startrite	5000	£0.5
Quickfire	7000	£0.7
Longlife	3500	£0.7
Highpower	2750	£0.4

(b)   What is the order interval?

17.10   A shoe shop takes delivery of Phrayle shoes once every three months. The shoes cost about £2 per pair and retail at £4. What recommendations on stocks would you make for the various sizes and fittings?

17.11   The Universal Manufacturing Co. purchase plastic 'U' bends from a local company. They use the bends at a fairly constant rate of 2500 per year. The cost of placing an order for the bends is £15 and the stock-holding cost per bend per year is £0.10 /year.

Unfortunately, the supplier of the 'U' bends is a little unreliable and, consequently, the lead time on orders (which are always delivered complete) varies. In fact, a study of the purchase and production records reveals that lead time varies from two to four days and that the usage of bends during the lead time varies from 15 to 25 with the probabilities shown below.

Lead time usage of bends	Probability of usage
15	0.02
16	0.05
17	0.07
18	0.10
19	0.16
20	0.20
21	0.17
22	0.14
23	0.06
24	0.02
25	0.01

The Universal Manufacturing Co. insist that on no more than one occasion per year should there be stock-outs of 'U' bends.

(a)   What should the order quantity and re-order level be?

(b)   If the cost per stock-out is found to be £0.25, what re-order level provides the minimum cost?

17.12   Calculate the order quantity and the re-order level, to minimize costs, given the following information:

Annual usage	= 3000
Ordering cost	= £150
Price per item	= £50
Stock-holding cost/item per annum	= 20 per cent of item per annum
Fixed cost of stock-out	= £1
Maximum number of stock-outs allowed per annum	= 1

Lead time usage	Frequency
20	5
21	15
22	22
23	32
24	40
25	32
26	22
27	15
28	5

17.13 Referring to the previous question, it has recently been discovered that the cost of stock-outs depends not only on the frequency of stock-outs but also on the number of items short during stock-outs. The stock-out cost has been found to be £1 per item short during the stock-out period. Using the information provided in the previous question, determine the re-order level and order quantity which minimizes costs.

17.14 A hospital store stocks an item for which the annual average demand is 250. The demand during the lead time is normally distributed (15, 4).
The item sells at £32.5 and is bought at:

> £20   (if up to 39 are bought)
> £18.5 (if between 40 and 99 are bought)
> £16.5 (if 100 or more are bought in any order)

Inventory cost per year is taken as 20 per cent of stock value. The goodwill loss for each item not supplied against customer demand is taken as £10 and the cost of an order to the suppliers as £1.5.
If a lot size/re-order point system is used, determine the best order quantity, re-order point, safety stock and the annual cost.

17.15

Order quantity	< 500	500–2500	2500
Price per unit (p)	£5	£4.75	£4.6

$r = 2500$ per year (constant)
$c_s = £100$
$c_1 = 0.1$ p/unit/year

Average replenishment lead time	= 0.1 year
Standard deviation of lead time	= 0.02 year
Service level required	= 90 per cent

Determine:
(a) re-order quantity;
(b) re-order level.

17.16 The demand for an item held by a retailer is 150/week on average. Demand is not seasonal and has not changed from this average for the past two years. From a study of two years' data it has been found that the standard deviation of weekly demand is 20 items.
The stock-holding cost is £0.4/item/week and the re-order cost is £17/order irrespective of quantity. A 90 per cent service level is to be provided.
Design a 'periodic' stock control procedure and explain any assumptions or simplifications you make.

PART 8

THE CONTROL OF OPERATING SYSTEMS

INTRODUCTION TO PART 8

This section deals with control. The principal topics covered are: the control of the quality of the goods or services provided by the operating systems and the reliability of those goods and services; the maintenance and/or replacement of the system, and its constituent parts; and the control of the system through performance monitoring.

The introductory chapter sets the scene for chapters on the three principal topics. These topics are interrelated as well as having relationships with topics dealt with in other sections of the book, in particular Capacity Management (Part 5), Operations Scheduling (Part 6) and Materials Management (Part 7).

CHAPTER 18

The Nature of Operations Control

In Chapter 11 we distinguished between operations planning and operations control and chose to deal with the two aspects separately. Part 6 considered planning problems. In this chapter we shall consider operations control in a general manner before considering particular aspects of the control of operating systems in the remaining chapters in this section.

Few systems will operate continuously and effectively without the exercise of a certain amount of external control. The Government, as well as planning, must also exercise control in order to maintain a healthy national economy; within the economy, managements must exercise control to maintain or improve the performance of their companies, and within such companies control must be exercised over the various functions and systems.

Rarely within organizations will there be operations control departments. Normally the control function will be invested in departments alongside responsibilities for planning operations. For example, those responsible for inventory management decisions will be concerned with and responsible for both planning and control. Financial control will be exercised within most organizations; however, again, those involved will be responsible for financial planning and budgeting as well as financial and cost control.

We have noted (in Chapter 11) that the general purpose of control is to ensure, as far as possible, the implementation of plans. Thus those involved in control, and those procedures established for the purposes of control, will, in general, seek to monitor activities with a view to ensuring that these activities correspond to some intended situation or state. Control derives from this process of monitoring activities and the comparison of actual and intended states. The need for the exercise of control derives from the fact that rarely is it possible to ensure in advance that certain things will happen in a particular way at a particular time, etc. Control is necessary because of the existence of uncertainties. A purely deterministic situation is unlikely to necessitate control since, in such circumstances, planning in itself is sufficient. In practice such deterministic situations will rarely exist and thus control is an essential link in the circle or cycle which begins with planning and involves monitoring, action and correction, and possibly revision of planning for future events.

CONTROL OF OPERATING SYSTEMS

The relative *emphasis* on planning and control in operations management will, to a large extent, be determined by the nature of the operating system. Consider, for example, the following contrasting case examples, which are discussed below.

Case 1 This is the big 'one-off' planning project in a highly uncertain situation. Here planning cannot be perfect, and there will be little opportunity to replan. The emphasis, therefore, will be on the controls involved in using a given set of resources efficiently for different purposes. (Similar situations will exist in managing most one-off 'project' type situations, e.g. in the construction industry, hospital accident wards, expeditions, military operations.)

Case 2 This is the repetitive situation where the (annual) requirements of the operating system(s) are known and where planning can therefore be accurate and certain. Here considerable effort will be put into establishing the system, and the subsequent problems of control will be minimized. If the system is properly planned there will be little need for decision-making in control, since there will be few exceptions to the norm. (Similar situations exist in managing most repetitive/process-type operating systems, e.g. mass production, regular/scheduled transport systems, customer banking services, routine medical and surgery services.)

The way in which planning and control are organized will depend on the emphasis which must be placed on the relative difficulty and frequency of occurrence of problems of planning and control. Where the emphasis is on planning, responsibility may be more centralized. Where the emphasis is on control, responsibility may be more decentralized. (Some of these issues are discussed in connection with organization structure in Chapter 3.)

CASE 1: ESTABLISHING AND MANAGING EMERGENCY SERVICES IN A NEW TOWN

Objective

The operations manager must establish a comprehensive, integrated emergency service comprising ambulance, fire, health, evacuation, accommodation facilities, etc., for a new town. It must be able to cope with most conceivable local emergencies and disasters (e.g. major transport accidents, fires, floods, epidemics). The operations manager is then required to run the system.

Planning problems

The design and planning of a system to deal with a largely unknown demand is complex. The operations manager cannot know exactly what is required, and therefore must estimate and forecast, and try to establish a system which will cope with most needs for most of the time. Excess resources should be obtained if possible.

Control problems

The effectiveness of such a system, when established, will depend largely on the manner in which it is utilized. There will be flexibility in the system—alternative ways of deploying resources. The manner in which the system is used will differ on each occasion. No two emergencies will be the same. Thus effective control is paramount and the recurrent problem will be that of control, since the system cannot be redesigned frequently.

CASE 2: A COLLEGE STUDENT ACCOMMODATION UNIT

Objective

The accommodation manager in a large college is required to provide on-campus accommodation (study bedrooms) for all first-year students. The number of students entering the college is subject to an upper limit, and all places are expected to be filled each year for the conceivable future period.

Planning problems

The required number of study bedrooms must be provided. The exact number is known. Support staff, e.g. cleaners, wardens, must be provided. Students from each college department must be allocated to each set of rooms. A small number of rooms must be provided with special facilities, e.g. ground-floor rooms for some disabled students. Some rooms must be kept in reserve in case others become unusuable during the academic year.

Control problems

Apart from regular cleaning, the provision of security, the handling of occasional complaints and routine maintenance, there are few tasks which must be performed during the academic year. The nature of these tasks is similar each year.

Most control actions are '*information dependent*' in that they derive from the acquisition and use of information on the nature or state of the operating system. In Chapter 1 we modelled operating system(s) entirely in terms of physical flow. We should now note, however, that such systems are in effect 'covered' by links so that, together, there is adequate information available for the control of activities and events at all stages in the system. For example the control of physical flows in operating systems is exercised through a combination of activity scheduling and inventory control decisions. This situation can best be illustrated in the manner shown in Figure 18.1. The diagrams in this

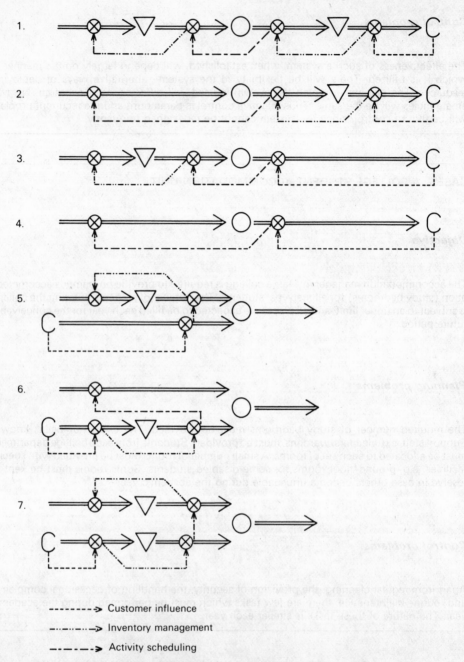

-------→ Customer influence

-·-·-·-→ Inventory management

-··-··-→ Activity scheduling

Figure 18.1 *Operations control relationships. From Wild, R. (1977) Concepts for Operations Management. New York: Wiley. Reproduced with permission.*

figure show the principal points in the system at which control of flow is exercised and the decision loops associated with such control. Thus in a 'function from stock to stock system', information in terms of order or delivery requirements goes from the customer to a point equivalent to inventory output. Flow at this stage is monitored and information, through the inventory management system, passes to the flow control point on inventory input, from where, through the activity scheduling system, information passes to a flow control point on function input, and so on through to resource supply. A similar chain of information loops and a similar series of control points exist for all systems. For example, in a 'function from stock from customer queue' system, the customer influences the input to customer queues, which are monitored in order to ensure that appropriate decisions are made in respect of flow from customer queues through to the system. The flow into the system is monitored through the activity scheduling system so that the flow of resources to the system is appropriate. The flow in turn is monitored through the inventory management system in order to ensure that flow into (i.e. replenishment of) resource stocks is appropriate.

Flow control is an essential responsibility of operations management. Such flow control is associated with the inventory management system(s) and the activity scheduling system. Supplementing this flow control there will be a need to consider the *nature* of the items or customers which are flowing in the system, in order to ensure, for example, that intended quality levels are maintained and resources are utilized in the intended fashion. Chapter 17 dealt with control decisions relating to inventory management. In this part we shall consider control associated with activity schedules and quality control and also controls associated with resource utilization, i.e. with resource maintenance, replacement and repair. Finally we shall take a broader approach and consider performance measurement, i.e. the way in which the performance of the whole operating system might be monitored for both planning and control purposes.

CONTROL CONCEPTS

Diagrammatically a control system may be represented in the manner shown in Figure 18.2. (This is an 'output' control system where output is monitored in order to assess the performance of the operation. In some situations it will be appropriate to employ a 'behaviour' control system where the behaviour of the operation itself is monitored; see Chapter 3). It will be seen that there are four components:

(a) a means of sensing output;
(b) a means of comparing actual output with intended output;

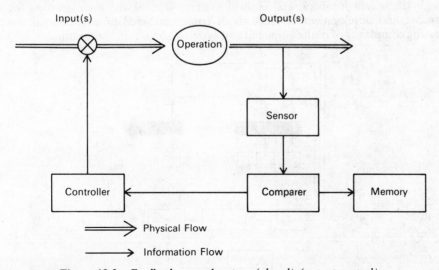

Figure 18.2 *Feedback control system (closed) (output control).*

(c)   a means of recording intended output (memory);
(d)   a means of exercising control.

A *closed system*, as shown in Figure 18.2, is directly influenced by its own past behaviour. Its own outputs are monitored or observed in order that some purposeful control might be exercised over its inputs. The operation of the system is dependent on direct feedback of information. The normal domestic central heating system is an example of such control, since the thermostat monitors room temperature and controls the boiler to maintain a given room temperature.

In contrast, an *open system* exists where outputs have no direct influence over earlier parts of the system. In other words an open system does not react to its own performance. Its past actions have no influence over current or future actions. There is no feedback of information on its outputs for the control of its outputs. The simple clock is an example of such an open system.

In practice most operations control will be of the closed system type, although the mechanism by which systems are closed will differ and will vary in their degree of sophistication. For example, in process control, i.e. the control of flow processes such as chemical processes using computers, several types of application exist, their principal differences being the manner in which information is fed back and control is exercised. Figure 18.3, for example, shows a simple data logging system. A computer is used here to scan very rapidly and frequently the information displayed by numerous instruments connected to the process, e.g. flow meters, transducers, thermometers, etc., this information being recorded, printed out and often used to calculate performance indices or guides which subsequently might be used by those concerned with the manual control of the process. Alarm systems are often incorporated, so the computer will signal the occurrence of faults or other unusual conditions in the process and also carry out simple diagnostic procedures using the input data to determine and indicate the cause of such conditions. Data logging systems are often the first stage in the application of computer control to operating systems. They are concerned both with monitoring and, indirectly, with control. The feedback loop, however, comprises both electronic and manual elements. The electronic monitoring of the condition of patients in hospital intensive-care units is an example of such control, since the medical staff responsible for the patient must, of necessity, take any remedial action.

In contrast, supervisory control systems provide for the application of computers through the whole feedback and control system. One of the main reasons for the emergence and development of methods of computer-based process control was the increasing complexity of both equipment and systems, so that efficient manual control was

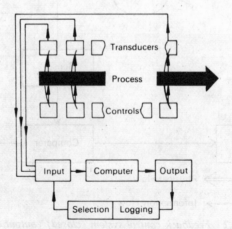

Figure 18.3 *A data logging system.*

increasingly difficult to achieve. Furthermore, in complex and expensive installations, penalties for inferior or poor performance are considerable, so expensive control systems are readily justifiable. Sequentially dependent processes such as those found in the chemical industries depend entirely for their efficient operation on the near optimum control and the stable operation of their parts, since any disturbance in any part will be reflected and perhaps amplified in subsequent parts of the process. Conditions such as these militate against manual control and necessitate some form of automatic monitoring and control system capable of monitoring performance and compensating for changes in operations. Figure 18.4 represents such a supervisory control system. The efficiency of supervisory systems depends on their being fed with the correct information, i.e. efficient data logging, and on the speed with which the control system works. Such systems must be carefully designed to accord with the characteristics of the process. The nature of the inputs must correspond to known and foreseeable disturbances of the process and the speed of the computer to the nature of the process, since there is little point in installing a control system whose reaction time is greatly in excess of the erection time of the process being controlled.

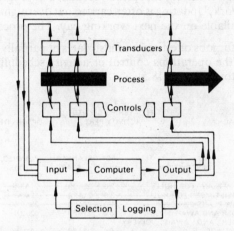

Figure 18.4   *A supervisory control system.*

It is inappropriate here to enter into a detailed discussion of control theory: however, it is worth noting that in the development of feedback control systems, whether manual, automatic or mixed, it is essential that the feedback mechanism be matched to the characteristics and capability of the process. It is essential also that control be exercised at appropriate stages within the process and that each of the important variables be monitored for control purposes. In practice, therefore, control systems will often be complex, multi-stage and multi-level.

ACTIVITY CONTROLS

The control of activities associated with activity scheduling is one aspect of flow control within a system. Inventory control, the complementary aspect of flow control, has been dealt with in Chapter 17. Here, therefore, we shall deal briefly with the elements of activity control. Essentially there are three steps necessary in achieving control of activities: (a) monitoring and recording flows or activities; (b) analysing flows and/or progress by comparison with plans or schedules; and (c) control, that is, modification of plans or a rearrangement of schedules in order to conform as nearly as possible to original targets.

To some extent the manner in which these steps are accomplished will depend on the nature and manner of activity scheduling and the nature of the activity schedules. Thus if schedules have been developed in order to achieve a particular flow or particular state at certain points in the system at particular times, then performance will be recorded and monitored by reference to these same points. The manner in which plans and schedules have been expressed and drawn up will influence the way in which step (b) above is achieved, i.e. the analysis of progress by comparison with plans and schedules. The extent and nature of control will of course depend on the variance identified between actual progress or flows and intended progress or flows. The manner in which this control will be achieved will depend to some extent on the nature of the system and the opportunities for the exercise of control. Thus, for example, if a particular procedure has been established for scheduling purposes then control will be linked to the use of the same procedure. If bar charts have been used then progress and monitoring will utilize such charts. If network analysis has been used then similar calculations and procedures will be employed for purposes of control. The latter application will be developed in a little more detail here by way of illustration.

When network analysis is employed, periodic feedback of progress information will be used to update the network. Updating is often carried out overnight or at weekends so that new information is available on the next working day. The procedure is as follows:

1. Actual finish dates for jobs or estimated finish dates of partially completed jobs will be supplied to either the operations control or activity scheduling department on the departmental printout (Figure 18.5).

FLOATSHIP + CO. LTD

CONSTRUCTION OF A MOTOR YACHT — ACTIVITY PERT — ORDER: DEPT — PAGE 1
RUN NUMBER: 2 — BY PLANNED START
REPORT DATE: 15MAR — BY TOTAL FLOAT

DEPT	PROJECT	DESCRIPTION	ACT DUR	PLANNED START	PLANNED FINISH	ACTUAL FINISH	ESTIMATED FINISH
OFFICE	MYO39	DRAW PLANS FOR HULL	2.0	05APR	21APR	18 April	
OFFICE	MYO39	ORDER TIMBER FOR HULL	3.0	21APR	12MAY	12 May	
OFFICE	MYO39	DRAW PLANS FOR DECK	1.0	21APR	20APR	28 April	
OFFICE	MYO39	ORDER AND AWAIT ENGINE	6.0	21APR	02JUN		11 June
OFFICE	MYO39	ORDER AND AWAIT JOINERY FITTINGS	6.0	28APR	10JUN		18 June
OFFICE	MYO39	ORDER TIMBER FOR DECK	1.0	28APR	05MAY	5 May	
OFFICE	MYO39	ORDER AND AWAIT PAINT + VARNISH	4.0	28APR	26MAY		28 May

FLOATSHIP + CO. LTD

CONSTRUCTION OF A MOTOR YACHT — ACTIVITY PERT — ORDER: DEPT — PAGE 1
RUN NUMBER: 2 — BY PLANNED START
REPORT DATE: 15MAR — BY TOTAL FLOAT

DEPT	PROJECT	DESCRIPTION	ACT DUR	PLANNED START	PLANNED FINISH	ACTUAL FINISH	REMARKS
YARD	MYO39	MAKE TEMPLATE FOR HULL	2.0	21APR	05MAY	5 May	
YARD	MYO39	MAKE JOINERY UNITS	3.0	05MAY	26MAY	21 May	
YARD	MYO39	CUT TIMBER FOR DECK	4.0	05MAY	02JUN	4 June	
YARD	MYO39	CUT TIMBER FOR HULL	4.0	12MAY	10JUN	11 June	
YARD	MYO39	PREPARE ENGINE	2.0	02JUN	17JUN		
YARD	MYO39	CONSTRUCT HULL	4.0	10JUN	08JUL		
YARD	MYO39	ASSEMBLE JOINERY UNITS + FITTINGS	3.0	10JUN	01JUL		
YARD	MYO39	INSTALL FITTINGS + JOINERY	2.0	08JUL	22JUL		
YARD	MYO39	INSTALL ENGINE	1.0	08JUL	15JUL		
YARD	MYO39	CLEAN OFF HULL	1.0	08JUL	15JUL		
YARD	MYO39	CONSTRUCT DECK + CLEAN OFF	3.0	22JUL	12AUG		
YARD	MYO39	PAINT + VARNISH	4.0	12AUG	23SEP		
YARD	MYO39	FINAL FIT OUT	2.0	23SEP	07OCT		

Figure 18.5 *Feedback of progress information via network analysis schedules.*

2. All such information will be fed into the computer. (It is usually necessary to input only amendments or additions rather than the complete network, since the information from the previous run is normally stored on magnetic tape.)
3. These dates will then be used as a basis for a complete set of calculations for the remainder of the network.
4. An updated set of figures will be printed out in the same format as before and distributed before the beginning of the next working week or shift (Figure 18.6).

```
                                      FLOATSHIP + CO. LTD.
CONSTRUCTION OF A MOTOR YACHT           ACTIVITY PERT            ORDER: DEPT                    PAGE 1
    RUN NUMBER:  3                                                   BY PLANNED START
    REPORT DATE:  14MAY                                              BY TOTAL FLOAT


                                            ACT   PLANNED    PLANNED    ACTUAL    REMARKS
   DEPT      PROJECT      DESCRIPTION        DUR   START      FINISH     FINISH

  OFFICE     MYO39    ORDER AND AWAIT ENGINE  4.0            11JUN
  OFFICE     MYO39    ORDER AND  AWAIT  JOINERY
                          FITTINGS            5.0            18JUN
  OFFICE     MYO39    ORDER AND AWAIT
                          PAINT + VARNISH     2.0            28MAY

                                      FLOATSHIP + CO. LTD
CONSTRUCTION OF A MOTOR YACHT           ACTIVITY PERT            ORDER: DEPT                    PAGE 1
    RUN NUMBER:                                                     BY PLANNED START
    REPORT DATE:                                                    BY TOTAL FLOAT


                                            ACT   PLANNED    PLANNED    ACTUAL    REMARKS.
   DEPT      PROJECT      DESCRIPTION        DUR   START      FINISH     FINISH

  YARD       MYO39    MAKE JOINERY UNITS      1.0            21MAY
  YARD       MYO39    CUT TIMBER FOR DECK     3.0            4JUN
  YARD       MYO39    CUT TIMBER FOR HULL     4.0            11JUN

  YARD       MYO39    CONSTRUCT HULL          4.0   11JUN    9JUL

  YARD       MYO39    PREPARE ENGINE          2.0   11JUN    25JUN
  YARD       MYO39    ASSEMBLE JOINERY
                          UNITS + FITTINGS    3.0   18JUN    9JUL
  YARD       MYO39    INSTALL FITTINGS + JOINERY  2.0  9JUL  23JUL
  YARD       MYO39    INSTALL ENGINE          1.0   9JUL     16JUL
  YARD       MYO39    CLEAN OFF HULL          1.0   9JUL     16JUL

  YARD       MYO39    CONSTRUCT DECK + CLEAN OFF  3.0  23JUL  3AUG
  YARD       MYO39    PAINT + VARNISH         4.0   13AUG    10SEP
  YARD       MYO39    FINAL FIT OUT           2.0   10SEP    24SEP
```

Figure 18.6 *Updated printouts.*

OTHER OPERATIONS CONTROLS

Although the relative emphasis will vary, where any form of planning is employed, there must logically also be some form of control. For example when setting business objectives it will be necessary to determine also the controls which will be employed to ensure that such objectives are achieved. It follows that wherever in this book we discuss planning we should also discuss control. In fact in most chapters both topics are implicitly covered, but in some cases separate chapters are devoted to one or other aspect. As a checklist Table 18.1 identifies some of the controls which will be of relevance to the operations manager, and gives cross-references to the relevant chapter in the book.

Table 18.1 *Some operations planning and control tasks*

Area	Planning task	Control task	See:
Operations policy	Selection/formulation of objectives Selection/choice of system structure Selection/formulation of strategies	Monitor effective operation of system and achievement of objectives	Performance Audit, Chapter 21 Cost Controls, Chapter 4
Design/specification of product/service	Contribute to design/specification of product/service	Monitor effectiveness of provision of product/service in order to ensure that specification and operating system are matched, i.e. that the system is capable of providing the product/service effectively	Chapter 21
Facilities location	Make/contribute to decision on location of facilities	Monitor effectiveness of location through, e.g. transport cost changes, effectiveness of communications, etc.	Chapter 21
Facilities layout	Plan layout of all facilities	Monitor effectiveness of layout and control its use, e.g. through changes in routeing, traffic flows, etc., where traffic patterns/demand change	Chapter 6
Work and job design	Design work methods, establish work standards, design workplaces, etc.	Monitor effectiveness of work, e.g. through measurement of output, labour costs, work performance, as well as indirect measures, e.g. labour turnover, absenteeism, etc.	Chapters 7, 8, 9 and 10
Capacity management	Determine capacity required and plan for its utilization	Monitor capacity utilization to ensure that appropriate capacity has been provided and appropriate strategies are being employed. Control capacity utilization through decisions on subcontracting, capacity changes, inventory levels, scheduling decisions, etc.	Chapter 11 and Chapters 12 to 16
Scheduling	Determine what activities are to be performed at what time, in what order and at what place	Check completion of activities against scheduled dates to establish whether there is any lateness, excess queuing, excess congestion, work in progress, etc. Control activities through schedule changes, changes in priority rules, etc.	Chapters 12 to 15
Inventory management	Determine locations of inventories, inventory levels, replenishment procedures, etc.	Control inventory through checks on inventory turnover rates, stock level changes, cost of obsolescence, deterioration, wastage and loss, etc.	Chapters 16 and 21
Purchasing and supply	Determine sources of supply, purchase procedures, quantities, goods receiving procedures, etc.	Check on effectiveness of purchasing and supply through delivery performance, vendor rating, etc.	Chapter 17
Quality and reliability	Determine quality levels and reliability standards	Establish quality control procedures, e.g. acceptance sampling, control charts, and establish procedures for monitoring reliability and product/service performance	Chapter 19

Area	Planning task	Control task	See:
Maintenance and replacement	Determine preventive maintenance and break-down (repair) mainten-ance policies to include policies/schedules for in-spection, preventive maintenance, etc. Establish replacement policies through life-cycle costing, etc.	Check effectiveness of maintenance through monitoring facilities avail-ability, facilities downtime, or maintenance costs. Check effective-ness of replacement policy through investment cost analysis etc.	Chapter 20

CHECKLIST FOR CHAPTER 18

Distinction: planning and control
The nature of control
Control of operating systems: emphasis on plan-ning and on control
Control 'links' in operating systems
Control relationships in operating systems
Control concepts
  Output and behaviour control
  Open and closed control
  Data logging
  Supervisory control
Activity controls
  In network analysis

Other operations controls
  In operations policy
  Design/specification
  Location of facility
  Layout of facilities
  Work and job design
  Capacity management
  Scheduling
  Inventory management
  Purchasing and supply
  Quality and reliability
  Maintenance and replacement

FURTHER READING

Cleland, D. I. and King, W. R. (1972) *Management: A Systems Approach*. New York: McGraw-Hill. A management text emphasizing the 'systems' view, with organizations and planning, but with some treatment of management control and management information systems (Chapters 16 and 17).

Eilon, S. (1971) *Management Control*. London: Macmillan. A study of management systems and control with emphasis on information processing and control theory.

Mize, J. H., White, C. R. and Brooks, S. G. H. (1971) *Operations Planning and Control*. Englewood Cliffs, NJ: Prentice-Hall. A detailed treatment of operations inventory systems, planning and control. Brief treatments of control system design and control system concepts (Chapters 8 and 9).

QUESTIONS

18.1 Show diagrammatically, in the manner of Figure 18.1, the principal control 'loops which will be used for the control of flows through the following systems:
  (a) a small 'jobbing' engineering production works;

(b)   a restaurant;
(c)   a specialist retail delicatessen store.

18.2   Explain the main features of, and identify the difference between, a closed and an open loop feedback control system.

18.3   Consider one of the scheduling procedures outlined in the chapters in Part 6 and show how a related control system might work.

CHAPTER 19

Quality Management and Reliability

NOTATION USED IN THIS CHAPTER

AOQL	Average outgoing quality level (as percentage defective)
AQL	Average outgoing quality level (as percentage defective)
σ	Standard deviation of individuals
$\sigma\bar{p}$	Standard deviation of proportions
σx	Standard deviation of a sample
$\sigma\bar{x}$	Standard deviation of a sample means
$\bar{\sigma}x$	Mean standard deviation of several samples
C	Acceptable number of defectives in a sample
c	Number of defective items in a sample
$\bar{c}$	Average number of defectives in several samples
LR	Lot rating
LSL	Lower specification limit
LTPD	Lot tolerance percentage defective
N	Batch or lot size
N_m	Number of lots submitted during a given month
n	Sample size
p	Proportion of defective items in a sample
$\bar{p}$	Average proportion of defective items in several samples
P	Probability
P(a)	Probability of accepting a batch
PD	Actual percentage defective in batch or process
USL	Upper specification limit
w_x	Range of a sample
$\bar{w}_x$	Mean range of several samples
$\bar{x}$	Mean of a sample
$\bar{\bar{x}}$	Mean of sample means
X	Dimension for an individual
$\bar{X}$	Mean dimension for individuals

We tend to think of quality from a customer's viewpoint. Taking such a view we can identify some of the factors which give rise to the provision of items or services which are judged by customers to be of an acceptable quality.

As consumers of *products* we expect our supplier (e.g. retailer) to provide only those goods which we find acceptable. This in turn requires suppliers to try to ensure that they themselves receive from manufacturers only goods or items which are acceptable, and that these items do not deteriorate or get damaged while being held by the supplier. Manufacturers in turn must ensure that they receive and use only materials and items which are of an acceptable quality, and that their manufacturing processes are used in such a way as to ensure that the goods that they produce are of a quality that is acceptable to their customers.

As consumers of *services and transports* we are again concerned with quality. For example, if we want to be transported by an organization we expect to be taken from an agreed place to an agreed destination, possibly by an agreed route, with an agreed duration. In being treated by a service system we expect the quality of the service to be acceptable. For example, in seeking accommodation in a hotel we expect to wait for only a relatively short period of time before being provided with a room of acceptable proportions with appropriate furniture, etc., and to be provided with facilities elsewhere in the hotel which are of an acceptable standard. Thus both transport and service organizations must ensure that they use items and products which are of an acceptable quality and that their operations conform to some acceptable standards so that we, the customers, when leaving the system, will express some satisfaction with the treatment that we have received there.

Thus as customers we will have some expectation of the quality of the goods or services with which we are to be provided. There will be an agreed *specification*. Agreement on this specification will have been reached with the organization. They will have accepted the specification which we have laid down, or we will have accepted the specification which the organization has offered, or there will be agreement from discussion and compromise. Given an agreed or acceptable specification we will expect the product or service which is provided to *conform* to that specification.

These two factors—specification which is to do with the 'design quality' of an item, and conformity, which is to do with the manufacture or process quality which is achieved—are of particular importance to customers. Ultimately they are the two factors which determine the quality levels provided by an organization to its customers. These two factors, however, are themselves determined by other factors, as shown in Figure 19.1. Consider first the specification. This will have been determined as a result of an organization's product or service policy, which in turn will result from decisions on its market policy, which in turn will result from its consideration of the market or customer needs and requirements, and the activities of competitors. This is the process of *designing quality* into the product or service.

The degree to which the product or service conforms to the technical specification will be influenced by the capability of the conversion process. If the conversion process is incapable of producing products or services at the level required by the specification then it must follow that the products or services provided to customers will in some way be inferior. However, the fact that a conversion process is inherently capable of producing or providing products/services according to a specification will not in itself ensure that all products or services are of an acceptable standard, for some management control will be required to ensure that the conversion process is used in the appropriate fashion in order to ensure that the product/service specification is achieved. This is all to do with the *management of process quality*.

In this chapter we shall deal primarily with the *management of process quality*, i.e.

(a) management's quality control and assurance procedures;
(b) capability of the process.

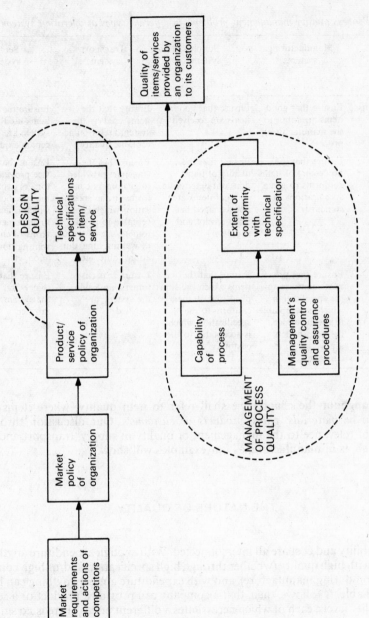

Figure 19.1 *Factors influencing the quality of items/services, as provided to customers.*

We have seen that the management of process quality is concerned with the management of inputs to systems, the conversion system itself, and outputs from systems. The problem areas and decisions required in this respect are outlined, for the four types of operating system, in Table 19.1.

Table 19.1 *Process quality management problems in different types of operating system*

Process quality management problem areas	Manufacturing systems	Supply systems	Transport systems	Service systems
Inputs to systems	Ensure that good items are input to the manufacturing process	Ensure that good items are received	Ensure that the items used by the system are of an acceptable quality	Ensure that the items used by the system are of an acceptable quality
The conversion system	Ensure that the processing of items conforms to given specifications or standards	Ensure that the quality of items does not deteriorate, e.g. that items are not damaged between receipt and supply	Ensure that the transport provided to customers conforms to the specification which is acceptable to to customers, e.g. in terms of waiting time, duration, route, etc.	Ensure that the service provided to customers conforms to the specification which is acceptable to customers, e.g. in terms of customer waiting time, duration, etc.
Outputs from system	Ensure that products conform to the specification which is acceptable to the customer before products are passed to the customer	Ensure that the items which are supplied to customers conform to the specification which is acceptable to the customer	Ensure that customers, on leaving the system, are satisfied	Ensure that customers, on leaving the system, are satisfied

Note: Throughout the chapter we shall refer to item quality, where items will be considered to be *materials, parts, products or customers*. Our discussion throughout, therefore, is of relevance to the management of quality in supply, transport and service systems as well as in manufacture, as our examples will show.

THE NATURE OF QUALITY

Quality, reliability and cost are all interconnected. With enough expenditure anything can be endowed with high quality (whether through high specification and/or high conformity to specification during manufacture), and with expenditure almost anything can be made to be very reliable. It follows, then, that a company can provide a product or a service at different quality levels, each of which necessitates a different price. There is no single level of quality; nor is there an absolute quality level. Nothing will be perfect, no matter how much it costs. Figure 19.2 shows the general relationship of cost and quality. In general, costs rise steeply for increasing quality, but beyond a certain level value to the customers increases more slowly. Thus it is possible to identify, notionally at least, a point at which the difference of value and cost is maximized. Figure 19.3 shows the general relationship of cost to reliability. Again, notionally, it is possible to identify a point of minimum total cost.

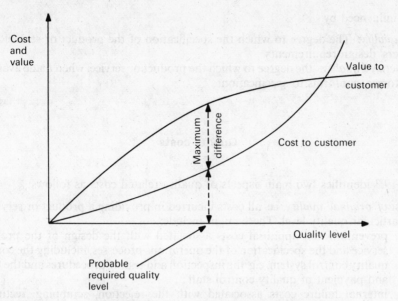

Figure 19.2 *The cost and value of quality.*

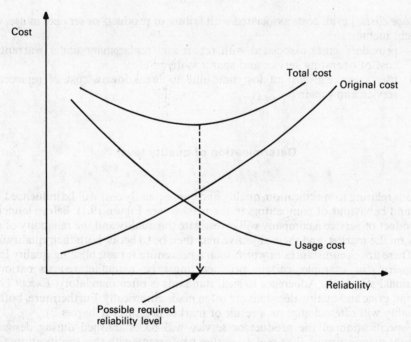

Figure 19.3 *Cost v. reliability.*

Definitions

From the above we can develop simple definitions as follows:

Quality: The quality of a product or service is the degree to which it satisfies customers' requirements.

This is influenced by:

Design quality: The degree to which the specification of the product or service satisfies customers' design requirements.

Manufactured quality: the degree to which the product or service, when made available to the customer, conforms to specifications.

Quality costs

Figure 19.3 identifies two main aspects of quality-related costs as follows:

1. *Cost of 'original' quality*, i.e. all costs incurred in providing a product or service with a particular quality level. These might include:
    (a) prevention and appraisal costs associated with the design of the product or service and the specification of the operations processes, including the cost of the quality control system, e.g. the inspection and testing procedures and the training and payment of quality control staff;
    (b) internal failure costs associated with the rejection, scrapping, rectification, etc., of items found to be defective before being offered to the customer.

2. *Usage costs*, i.e. all costs associated with failure of products or services in use, which might include:
    (a) providers' costs associated with repair and replacement under warranty, the cost of operating service and spares systems, etc.;
    (b) user costs, e.g. cost of lost time due to breakdowns, cost of replacements, service and repair.

Determination of quality level

Decisions relating to specification, quality and consequently cost will be influenced by the policy and behaviour of competitors in the market (see Figure 19.1). Before launching a new product or service a company will investigate the quality and the reliability of others already on the market, and their objective may then be to better both their quality and/or price. There are circumstances in which such a procedure for establishing quality levels is unnecessary; for example, certain products must be manufactured to national or international standards. Adherence to such standards is often mandatory. Except on such occasions, price and quality decisions are often made empirically. Furthermore, both price and quality will often change as a result of market pressures (Chapter 3).

The specification of the product or service will be established during design. The operations manager must then seek to ensure conformity with this specification. Clearly process capabilities should influence design decisions, since there is little point in specifying something that cannot be achieved. Process capability is therefore of importance in determining quality levels. Similarly, the feasibility and cost of ensuring conformity with design specifications must be taken into account.

QUALITY CONTROL AND ASSURANCE

We shall assume that item specifications have been established and that an appropriate process is available. Hence it is now our task to ensure conformity to the specifications.

To achieve this objective three stages can be defined. We must first ensure that only materials and parts which conform to the given specifications are accepted from suppliers. Second, we must implement control procedures to attempt to ensure that during the conversion of these items only products which conform to the specifications are produced. And finally, we must ensure that only those items which conform to the specifications are offered to the customers. These procedures are outlined diagrammatically in Figure 19.4 and are discussed below.

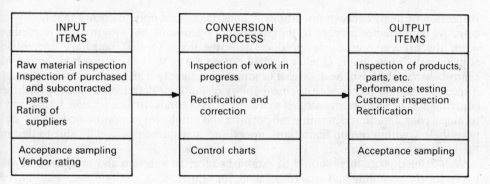

Figure 19.4 *The stages, processes and procedures of quality control and assurance.*

Control of inputs

An organization may adopt one or (usually) both of the following procedures in an attempt to ensure that it uses only items which fully conform to the required specifications and standards.

1. Items used by the organization will be inspected. The items which are supplied to the firm will normally have been subjected by the supplier to some form of quality control. The purchasing firm will institute its own procedure, carried out in the receiving department on its own premises, and/or monitor the quality controls conducted by the supplier. It may ask to be supplied with regular information about the quality of the items as they are prepared, ask for copies of all the final inspection documents to be supplied, or ask a third party (e.g. an insurance company) to ensure that the items conform to the required minimum quality. However, despite such precautionary steps, inspection of purchased items will normally be conducted on receipt, and before use. One or both of the following procedures will normally be adopted:
   (a) exhaustive inspection of every item received;
   (b) an inspection of a sample of the items received—this procedure, which is commonly adopted, is referred to as *acceptance sampling* and is discussed in some detail later in the chapter.
2. The organization will purchase only from those suppliers which are known to be likely to provide acceptable items. To ensure this the purchaser may undertake some form of

vendor rating, (VR) i.e. a comparative rating of suppliers taking into account quality-related factors such as:

(a) percentage of acceptable items received in the past;
(b) quality of packaging;
(c) price;
(d) percentage of warranty claims which can be traced to defective items provided by the vendor.

The commonest VR procedures will be discussed below.

Control of process

Inspection of items between operations is undertaken, not only to ensure that faulty or defective items do not proceed to the subsequent operations, but also in order to predict when the process is likely to produce defective items so that necessary preventive adjustments can be made. Quality control during the process often involves the use of *control charts*, which will be discussed in some detail shortly. The number and location of inspections should reflect both the probability of faults or defectives occurring and the consequences of such occurrences, as well as the cost of conducting inspection. Frequently, technical considerations determine the position and number of inspection operations, but nevertheless, within certain limitations, operations management is usually able to design the inspection procedure.

Well-defined procedures should be established for the selection and inspection of the items, for the recording and analysis of data, for reprocessing, rectifying or scrapping of defectives, and for the feedback of information. We have tended to assume that a group of people attached to a separate department within the organization is involved in these quality control procedures, but two other alternatives exist. First, automatic 'on-line' inspection or gauging could be used. Such procedures are increasingly used for automatic inspection and checking of variables (dimensions); often the equipment involves a 'feedback' to the machine, which is self-correcting. A second alternative is for workers to be responsible for checking and inspecting their own work. In such cases appropriate time allowances must be provided.

Control of outputs

Quality inspection of output items is essential because unless defective output is identified by the producer it will be passed on to the consumer. Final inspection is unfortunate, since the purpose of all previous inspection has been to ensure that defective or faulty output is not produced. However, it is not a reflection on the ineffectiveness of earlier inspection, since items can be damaged at any time during the entire process.

Final inspection may involve only a sampling procedure, or exhaustive checks. Suitable procedures must be designed for the collection and retention of inspection data, for the correction, replacement or further examination of faulty items and, if necessary, for the adjustment or modification of either previous inspection or processing operations to ensure that faulty items do not continue to be produced—at least not for the same reasons

Inspection of output is normally conducted in a similar manner to the inspection of input items, the procedures being referred to as *acceptance sampling*.

Control of inspection

Quality control and inspection procedures almost invariably involve the use of equipment. If output is to be satisfactory, we must ensure that the means by which it is checked is adequate. A periodic examination and recalibration of all instruments should be undertaken.

The economics of quality control

As more effort is made to control the quality, fewer defective items pass by unnoticed. Any increase in quality control effort will, of course, cost more and there is therefore a point at which the total variable cost of quality control is minimized (see Figure 19.5). Any increase in effort beyond this level, while reducing the number of defective items passing undetected, will also increase total cost, and less effort will also increase cost because of the greater number of defective items allowed to pass.

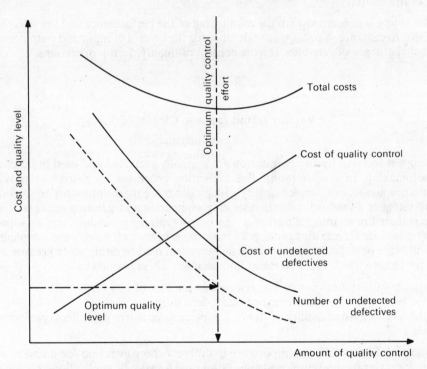

Figure 19.5 *Optimum quality level and amount of quality control.*

In practice, the amount of quality control effort made by an organization, and consequently the actual quality level obtained, are determined by experiment and experience. The actual or average quality level may be high if the subsequent cost of defective items, in terms of loss of future orders, rectification costs, cost of wasted subsequent processing, etc., is high, and vice versa. The average quality level obtained will be determined to a large extent by the various 'pressures for quality' or the known consequences of providing inferior output.

QUALITY CONTROL PROCEDURES

We have identified three basic stages in quality control (Figure 19.4), i.e.

1. Control of quality of input items.
2. Control of quality during operations.
3. Control of quality of output items.

These three stages are complementary. Inadequate control at one stage will necessitate greater effort at subsequent stages. In the remainder of this chapter we shall focus on quality control procedures, and shall discuss three procedures:

1. Vendor rating ⎫
2. Acceptance sampling ⎬ involving the *inspection* of items.
3. Control charts ⎭

Vendor rating is concerned with the monitoring of the performance and the selection of suppliers. Acceptance sampling is of relevance for the control of input and output quality. Control charts are of relevance for the control of quality during operations.

Vendor rating *(see also Chapter 16)*

The supplies received by an organization are normally evaluated and used in purchasing decision-making. In vendor rating, this evaluation process is formalized to provide a quantitative measure of 'vendor quality'. Such ratings are meant primarily to provide an overall rating of a vendor for use in reviewing, comparing and selecting vendors. Vendor rating is therefore an integral part of a rigorous purchasing procedure, and an aspect of quality assurance for use alongside, or in some cases instead of, acceptance sampling.

It will often be difficult to create a single numerical quality/rating score because of the different factors which must be taken into account. These may include:

(a) the lot quality (number of lots rejected or number of lots inspected);
(b) the parts qualities (percentage of items defective);
(c) the 'characteristic' quality of items (e.g. percentage active ingredient, performance, etc.).

Because such factors differ in importance in different companies and for different items, the vendor rating method employed must be tailored for specific applications. However, in general such methods will fall into one of the following four categories:

1. Categorical plan: a non-quantitative system in which those responsible for buying hold a periodic meeting to discuss vendors and rate each one, usually only as 'plus', 'minus' or 'neutral'.
2. Weighted point plan: each vendor is scored on quality, price and service. These factors are weighted and a composite rating is then calculated for each vendor. An example is shown in Table 19.2.

Table 19.2 *Example of a 'weighted point' vendor rating plan. A hospital purchases sterile supplies from three companies. Data are collected over a one-year period so that the three suppliers can be compared.*

	Supplier A	Supplier B	Supplier C
1. Lots received [a]	60	60	20
2. Lots accepted [a]	54	56	16
3. Percentage accepted [b]	90.0	93.3	80.0
4. Quality rating $((3) \times 0.4)$ [b]	36	37.3	32
5. Net price [a]	0.93	1.12	1.23
6. $\dfrac{\text{Lowest price}}{\text{Net price}} \times 100$ [b]	100	83	75.6
7. Price rating $((6) \times 0.35)$ [b]	35	29	26.5
8. Delivery promises kept [a]	90%	95%	100%
9. Service rating $((8) \times 0.25)$ [b]	22.5	23.8	25
10. Total rating $(4)+(7)+(9)$ [b]	93.5	90.1	83.5

[a] Data
[b] Calculations
Note. Here the relative importances of quality, price and service have been judged to be 0.4, 0.35 and 0.25.

3. Cost ratio plan: compares vendors on the *total* cost involved for a specific purchase. This will include:
   (a) price quotation;
   (b) quality costs (e.g. repair, return or replacement of defectives);
   (c) delivery costs.
4. Quality only rating plans: the first three types of plans above recognize item quality in the rating of vendors but in no case is the rating restricted to quality alone. In the fourth type of plan *only* quality is taken into account. An example of a formula based only on quality is the Bendix vendor rating plan. The formula for the Bendix system is:

$$\text{Quality rating} = 70 + \left[\frac{\sum^{N} \text{LR}}{N_m} - 70 \right] \sqrt{N_m}$$

where N_m = number of lots submitted during a given month and

$$\text{LR} = 70 - 10 \left[\frac{p - \text{AQL}}{\sqrt{\text{AQL}(100 - \text{AQL})/n}} \right]$$

where p = percentage defective of the sample quantity inspected from a lot
LR $\quad$ = lot rating
AQL $\quad$ = acceptable quality level (%)
n $\qquad$ = sample size
   With such a system each vendor starts out with a score which is considered to be average (in this case 70). Points are then added or subtracted to this to yield quality rating. The specific number of points added or subtracted in the formula is dependent on:

(a) comparison of the percentage defective;
(b) the number of lots submitted.

Hence 90 = quality significantly better than the AQL
50–90 = quality acceptable
50 = quality significantly worse than the AQL
The following is an example of the use of a vendor rating plan based only on quality.

EXAMPLE: DOMESTIC APPLIANCES

The following vendor rating and grading system is used for all suppliers of piece parts to an electrical company.
Vendor rating is based on points obtained covering five deliveries.
Grade is dependent on vendor rating achieved covering five deliveries.
Vendor rating and grading are reappraised every fifth consecutive delivery. Factors involved are as follows:

(a) total number of samples inspected over five deliveries;
(b) total number of rejects observed during sample inspection over five deliveries;
(c) total number of batches accepted over five deliveries;
(d) total number of batches received—five normally, but the system allows for more should the fifth delivery be overlooked, and in this instance the total number of batches involved becomes the common denominator.

The system is divided into two sections:

Section *one* carries a maximum of 60 points.
Section *two* carries a maximum of 40 points.
Total = 100 *points maximum*

How vendor rating and grading are calculated
Vendor rating:
Section *one*

$$\frac{\text{Total number of rejects}}{\text{Total number of samples}} \times 60 = Z$$

$$\text{Therefore } 60 - Z = A$$

Section *two*

$$\frac{\text{Total number of batches accepted}}{\text{Total number of batches received}} \times 40 = B$$

$$\text{Therefore } A + B = \text{Total points obtained}$$

Grading is based on total points obtained as follows:

Grade A = 100 down to 90 points—Quality level acceptable
Grade B = 89 down to 70 points—Quality level requires some improvement
Grade C = 69 down to 40 points—Quality level requires considerable improvement
Grade D = 39 down to 0 points—Quality level requires immediate improvement or
supplies terminated

How the system operates between the company and the supplier
Suppliers falling into grades B, C or D on components supplied are notified by the company and requested to improve their quality level.
Any supplier falling into grade D and remaining there for more than ten deliveries is dropped.
Notification is given when improvement in quality results in *upgrading*.
Suppliers are vendor rated and graded on each component manufactured and supplied to the company.
No notification will be given while supplier remains in grade A.

Many such vendor rating systems exist. In selecting a system for a particular situation, a basic decision must be whether the rating will be based solely on quality performance or on additional considerations such as cost and delivery.

True vendor ratings (for the purpose of making decisions on retaining or dropping vendors) are published infrequently. These ratings are not to be confused with monthly publications of 'vendor performance', which serve mainly as product rating rather than vendor rating.

It is important that vendor ratings be used as an *aid*, and not as the sole criterion in vendor decision-making. It should be remembered that:

1. A single index will often hide important detail.
2. The specific purpose of the rating should be kept in mind.

Most vendor rating plans involve some degree of subjectivity and guesswork. The mathematical treatment of data in the plans often tends to obscure the fact that the results are no more accurate than the assumptions on which the quantitative data are based. In the final analysis, therefore, supplier evaluation must represent a combined appraisal of facts, quantitative computations and value judgements. In most cases vendor rating will be used along with an acceptance sampling plan.

Vendor rating is an important defect prevention device if it is used in an atmosphere of interdependence between vendor and customer. This means that the customer must:

(a) make the investment of time, effort and special skills to help the poor vendors to improve;
(b) be willing to change the specifications when warranted (in some companies 20 to 40 per cent of rejected purchases can be used without any quality compromise).

Finally, in cases of consistently poor vendors who cannot respond to help, the vendor rating highlights them as candidates to be dropped as vendors.

Inspection

In this section we shall consider both acceptance sampling and control chart procedures. Both procedures will involve the *inspection* of items so that a decision can be made on whether an item, or the batch from which a sample of items is drawn, is acceptable or not. The planning of inspection may involve deciding *where* to inspect. These problems will be considered before we look at acceptance sampling and control chart techniques.

The location of inspection

There will normally be some choice of the location of quality inspection points in operating systems. For example, we may choose to locate inspection before or after the inventories which exist in operating systems, or between an operation and its supplier, and its customer. This will provide a wide choice of locations, as shown in Figure 19.6, but, additionally, since most businesses are multi-stage, it will usually be necessary to decide where to inspect within a sequence of operations. Rarely will items be inspected formally after every stage in the system, since to do so would be expensive. The problem, therefore, is

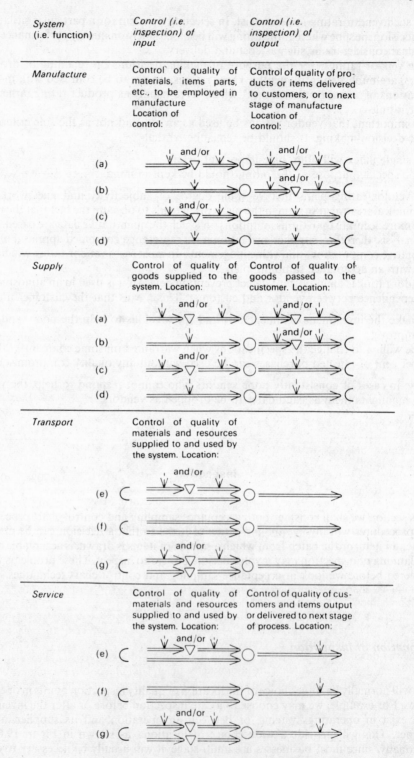

Figure 19.6 *Locations for control, i.e. inspection, in operating systems (control shown by a dotted arrow).*

to locate inspection operations, taking into account of the cost of inspection and the benefits of inspecting (or the risks of not inspecting).

In practice such decisions are often based on empirical and quantitative rules. For example, good 'rules of thumb' are:

1. Inspect before costly operations in order to avoid high processing costs for defective items.
2. Inspect before any series of operations during which inspection will be difficult and/or costly.
3. Inspect after operations which generally result in a high rate of defectives.
4. Inspect before operations which would conceal defects previously caused.
5. Inspect before a 'point of no return', i.e. after which any rectification is impossible.
6. Inspect before points at which potential damage may be caused, i.e. before the use of equipment which would be damaged through the processing of faulty items.
7. Inspect before a change in quality responsibility, e.g. between departments.

A simple approach to the location of inspection stations is illustrated by means of the following example.

EXAMPLE: FOOD PROCESSING

Consider a six-operation confectionery-making process where the expected proportion of defective items created at each operation and the processing cost per item for each operation are given in the following table.

Operation number (j)	1	2	3	4	5	6
Proportion of defective items created at operation	0.010	0.015	0.005	0.010	0.002	0.005
Number of defective items per 10 000 items	100	150	50	100	20	50
Processing cost/item for station ($£$)	1.00	0.50	1.00	1.00	0.60	1.10

The next table shows the processing cost of the defective items created at an operation through subsequent operations. For example, processing the 100 defective items created at operation 4 through operations 5 and 6 incurs a cost of $£0.60 \times 100 + £1.10 \times 100$, i.e. $£60$ for operation 5 and $£110$ for operation 6, a total of $£170$. Thus if an inspection station capable of identifying all passing defective items were located after operation 4, it would lead to the saving of this $£170$ and, in addition, it would save the remaining processing costs for defective items created at earlier operations, i.e. a total saving of $£680$.

Thus the processing cost saving given by the location of a single inspection station after operation j is given by the total of the figures in the column for operation $j+1$ in the table. If we know the cost of inspection, we can use this method to assist in determining the location of inspection stations. For example, the best location of two inspection stations is after operations 2 and 4, i.e.

$£$

Inspection after operation 2 saves = 925
Inspection after operation 4 saves $£680 - (170 + 255)$ = 255
_____
$£1180$

Operation number (*j*)	Number of defective items	Cost of processing defective items created at operation *j* through subsequent operations (£)				
1	100	420	370	270	170	110
2	150		555	405	255	165
3	50			135	85	55
4	100					170	110
5	20					22
6	50					
	Column sums (£)	420	925	810	680	462

This method of analysis relies on two basic assumptions. First, it is assumed that 100 per cent inspection is used and all defective items are identified. Second, no account is taken of the accumulation of defects in items, for example, it is assumed that the 150 defective items created at operation 2 do not include any of the 100 created at operation I and thus that the total number of defective items produced by the system is equal to the sum of those produced at each operation. This is unlikely to happen in practice. The technique can be modified to take account of this fact, but the distortion of the results occasioned by this assumption is unlikely to be high, unless the proportion of defects produced at the operations is high.

Acceptance sampling

Inspection of each critical feature of every item may be undertaken so that no defective items would pass unnoticed, except by a mistake or error in the inspection procedure. There are, however, several reasons why such a procedure may be uneconomical or even impossible:

1. Inspection may cause damage or even complete destruction of the items.
2. The accuracy of inspection may be diminished after frequent repetition.
3. Handling of the item may result in deterioration, or items may naturally deteriorate and lengthy inspection procedures may be undesirable.
4. Inspection may be particularly expensive.
5. Inspection may be a hazardous, even dangerous procedure.

For these reasons, some form of *sampling inspection* is often required. In acceptance sampling, decisions about the quality of batches of items are made after inspection of only a portion of those items. If the sample of items conforms to the required quality levels then the whole batch from which it came is accepted. If the sample does not conform to the required quality level, then the whole batch is rejected or subjected to further inspection. Adopting this procedure, decisions about the quality levels of items can be made fairly quickly and cheaply. However, a certain amount of risk is involved, since there is the possibility that the sample taken will not be of the same quality as the batch from which it came. A greater proportion of defectives in the sample will lead us erroneously to attribute a lower quality level to the batch and vice versa.

Several types of acceptance sampling plan may be used. Some necessitate taking a *single* sample from a batch, upon which a quality decision is made. Others may necessitate the use of *multiple* samples. Plans will also vary in the types of measurement that are involved. The most common, and simplest, type of inspection decision involves classifying items as acceptable or unacceptable. This is referred to as acceptance sampling by *attributes*. Less often, acceptance sampling by *variables* is utilized, in which the purpose of inspection is to obtain exact measurements for dimensions. We shall concentrate on the more usual procedure, which is *single acceptance sampling* by *attributes*.

Acceptance sampling by attributes is not only suitable for items whose critical features cannot easily be measured, but may also be used where inspection is concerned with dimensions, since such dimensions ultimately are either acceptable or not.

Customers would ideally like 100 per cent of their items to be acceptable but this, as we have pointed out previously, is impractical. Therefore some lower quality level must, of necessity, be agreed. Even so, only by 100 per cent inspection (and even then, only if there are no errors during inspection) can we be absolutely certain that a batch conforms to this agreed standard. In Figure 19.7, 100 per cent inspection has been used, so we can be 100 per cent certain that batches do, or do not, conform to the agreed quality level, which is a maximum of 20 per cent defectives per batch (again assuming no mistakes during inspection).

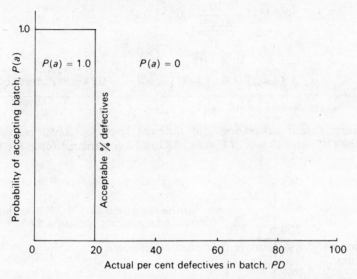

Figure 19.7 *The probability of accepting batches, with 100 per cent inspection (acceptable per cent defectives, 20 per cent or less).*

A shape such as this is known as an *operating characteristic* curve and shows the probability of accepting batches with various percentage defectives. Operating characteristic (OC) curves can be calculated and drawn for any sampling plan if we specify:

(a)   the sample size, n;
(b)   the acceptance number, i.e. the allowance number of defects in the sample, C.

If the batches are large compared with the size of the sample, the construction of such curves is based on the use of the *binomial* probability expression, from which we can calculate the probability that a given number of defectives will be found when a sample of given size is drawn from a batch with a given proportion of defectives, i.e.[1]

$$P(r) = \frac{n!}{r!(n-r)!} \left(\frac{PD}{100} \right)^r \left(1 - \frac{PD}{100} \right)^{(n-r)}$$

---

[1] $n! = n \times (n-1) \times (n-2) \ldots \times (n - (n-1))$
O! is taken to be 1.

where r = number of defectives found
       n = sample size
     PD = percentage of defectives in batch
   $P(r)$ = probability of finding r defectives

EXAMPLE: PROOFREADING

A sampling inspection procedure is used as a final check of the printing of a large encyclopedia. Ten pages are selected at random and checked for printing errors. The whole book is accepted if only one or zero pages with errors are found by the sample, which is probability of acceptance.
Sample size $n = 10$
Acceptable number of mistakes $C = 1$ or less
   If actual percentage of mistakes in a book = 10 per cent:

$$P(1) = \frac{10!}{1! \;\; 9!} \times 0.1^1 \times 0.9^9 \;\; = 0.39$$

$$P(0) = \frac{10!}{0! \;\; 10!} \times 0.1^0 \times 0.9^{10} = 0.35$$

$$\therefore \;\; P(\leqslant 1) = P(0) + P(1) \qquad\qquad = 0.74 = \text{Probability of acceptance}$$

By performing similar calculations for different levels of actual percentage batch defectives, the OC curve shown in Figure 19.8 can be constructed for $n = 10$ and $C \leqslant 1$.

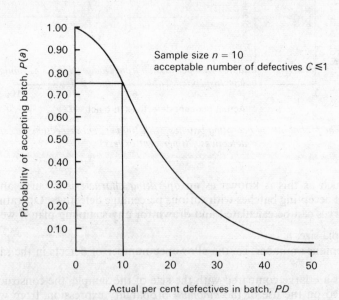

Figure 19.8 *Operating characteristic curve (n = 10; C ≤ 1).*

Where the value of n (sample size) is large, the use of this method of calculation becomes laborious, and it is fortunate therefore that in most cases it is possible to use an approximate yet adequate method of determining probabilities. It can be shown that when the expected number of defectives is small relative to the lot size, the *Poisson* distribution can be used as an adequate approximation to the binomial.[2] To simplify matters further in such circumstances the calculations may be performed with the assistance of the *Thorndike chart*. This chart, as shown in Figure 19.9, is in fact a set of cumulative Poisson probability curves from which the probability of C or less defectives ($P(a)$ on the vertical axis) for given values of $PD \times n/100$ (on the horizontal axis) can be determined, where PD = actual percent defectives in a batch or lot and n = sample size.

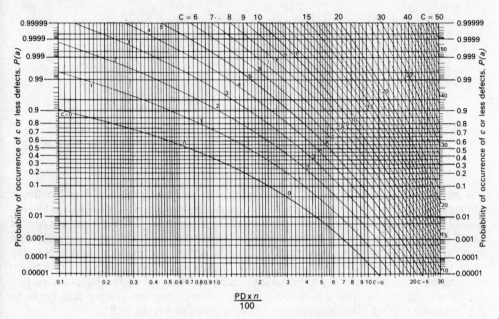

Figure 19.9 *Thorndike chart. Adapted with permission from Dodge, H. F. and Romig, H. G. (1959) Sampling Inspection Tables. London: Wiley.*

EXAMPLE: A RESTAURANT

A restaurant owner wishes to monitor the quality of the frozen beefburgers which are supplied in large quantities daily. Use the Thorndike chart to construct an operating characteristic curve for:

Sample size, $n = 100$/day
Allowable number of defective (e.g. misshapen) items per sample, $C = 3$

---

[2] It is generally accepted that the Poisson distribution may be used where N is large, where N is over five times the sample size n and where the proportion of defects, PD, is less than 10 per cent. In cases where the batch or lot size is small, neither the Poisson nor the binomial distribution is satisfactory and use should be made of the hypergeometric distribution.

For both large N and large n and when PD is greater than 10 per cent use of the Normal distribution is satisfactory.

Answer:	Actual percentage of defectives in batch (*PD*)	$\dfrac{PD \times n}{100}$	*P(a)*
	1	1	0.98
	2	2	0.86
	3	3	0.65
	4	4	0.44
	5	5	0.26
	6	6	0.15
	7	7	0.08
	8	8	0.04
	9	9	0.02
	10	10	0.01

These figures can now be used to plot an OC curve of the type shown previously.

The ability of a sampling procedure to distinguish between good and bad batches is primarily a function of the sample size. If three sampling processes are designed to test the quality level of batches of components for which the acceptable quality level is 1 per cent or less of defectives, then the procedure using the largest sample will be more accurate than those using smaller samples, particularly where the actual percentage of defectives in the batch is high. Figure 19.10 shows three such OC curves, each of which is fairly accurate up to a percentage defective level just below the acceptable level, but above that point, *curve* 3 *is superior*. As the sample size is increased, the curves become steeper and begin to approach the perfectly discriminating OC curve given in Figure 19.8.

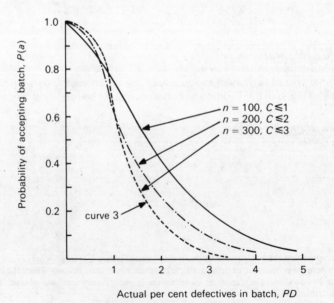

Figure 19.10 *Operating characteristic curves.*

The design of single acceptance sampling plans

The merit of any sampling plan depends on the relationship of sampling cost to risk. As the cost of inspection decreases and the cost of accepting defective items increases, then the merit of inspection increases and the more willing we are to use larger samples. The OC curve shows, for any plan, both the probability of accepting batches with more than the acceptable number of defectives and the probability of rejecting batches with less than the acceptable number of defectives.

It is the consumer's desire to reduce the probability of accepting batches including too many defectives and the producer's desire to minimize the probability of rejecting batches including an acceptable number of defectives. These are called respectively the *consumer's risk* (β) and the *producer's risk* (α). These two values are used to design acceptance sampling plans and, in addition, two further points are used:

1. *Acceptable quality level* (*AQL*)—the desired quality level, at which probability of acceptance should be high
2. *Lot tolerance per cent defective* (*LTPD*)—a quality level below which batches are considered unacceptable, and a level at which probability of acceptance should be low.

These four values are shown on the OC curve in Figure 19.11. The consumer's risk (β) is usually specified at about 10 per cent and the producer's risk (α) at approximately 5 per cent. Acceptable quality level is often around 2 per cent and lot tolerance per cent defective around 10 per cent. These four figures are specified in designing the sampling plan; all that then remains is to construct an OC curve which passes through the two points (AQL; α)

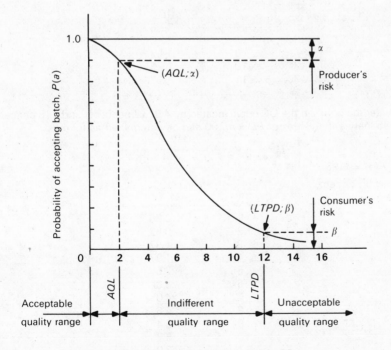

Figure 19.11 *Operating characteristic curve and points specifying a sampling plan.*

and ($LTPD$; β). This can be done by trial and error, selecting various values for the sample size (n) and acceptable number of defectives (C) and substituting into the binomial probability formula until an acceptable curve is obtained, or by use of the Thorndike chart.

EXAMPLE: SILICON CHIP MANUFACTURE

Use the Thorndike chart to construct an OC curve which as nearly as possible satisfies the following requirements, which have been agreed by the manufacturer and its major customer.

$$LTPD = 5 \text{ per cent} \qquad \beta = 10 \text{ per cent}$$
$$AQL = 2 \text{ per cent} \qquad \alpha = 5 \text{ per cent}$$

To specify the OC curve we must establish a value for n and for C. Consider first of all the point on the OC curve located by $LTPD$ (5 per cent) and β (10 per cent). Here the probability of acceptance, or $P(a)$, on the Thorndike chart is 0.1. Reading along the $P(a) = 0.1$ ordinate, we can determine the value on the other axis, $PD \times n/100$, for each value of C, i.e.

when $P(a) = 0.1$ ($\beta = 10$ per cent)	C	$\dfrac{PD \times n}{100}$
	1	3.9
	2	5.3
	3	6.7
	4	8.0
	5	9.3
	6	10.5
	7	11.8
	8	13.0
	9	14.2
	10	15.5
	11	16.7

Now consider the point on the OC curve located by AQL (2 per cent) and α (5 per cent). Here $P(a) = 0.95$, hence the values of $PD \times n/100$ can be determined as follows:

when $P(a) = 0.95$ ($\alpha = 5$ per cent)	C	$\dfrac{PD \times n}{100}$
	1	0.36
	2	0.82
	3	1.37
	4	1.97
	5	2.6
	6	3.3
	7	4.0
	8	4.6
	9	5.4
	10	6.2
	11	7.0

Now, in order to determine which OC curve best fits our requirements, we must use the two sets of $PD \times n/100$ values. In the first set ($P(a) = 0.1$ or $\beta = 10$ per cent) we require a $PD \times n/100$ value equivalent to the $LTPD$ of 5 per cent, while in the last set we require a $PD \times n/100$ value equivalent to $AQL = 2$ per cent. If we divide the pairs of $PD \times n/100$ values for each value of C we have in fact determined the value of $LTPD/AQL$, i.e.

C	$\dfrac{PD \times n}{100}$ for $\beta = 10$ per cent	$\dfrac{PD \times n}{100}$ for $\alpha = 5$ per cent	$\dfrac{PD \times n/100 \text{ for } \beta = 10}{PD \times n/100 \text{ for } \alpha = 5} = \dfrac{LTPD}{AQL}$
1	3.9	0.36	10.8
2	5.3	0.82	6.46
3	6.7	1.37	4.89
4	8.0	1.97	4.06
5	9.3	2.6	3.58
6	10.5	3.3	3.18
7	11.8	4.0	2.95
8	13.0	4.6	2.83
9	14.2	5.4	2.63
10	15.5	6.2	2.50
11	16.7	7.0	2.39

In fact the ratio for $LTPD/AQL$ specified in the question is $5/2 = 2.5$, which corresponds to the ratio obtained for $C = 10$. It now remains only to determine n, which can be found as follows:

where $C = 10$ for $\beta = 10$ per cent

$$\frac{PD \times n}{100} = \frac{LTPD \times n}{100} = 15.5$$

$$\therefore \quad n = \frac{15.5 \times 100}{LTPD}$$

$$= \frac{15.5 \times 100}{5}$$

$$= 310$$

Our OC curve is therefore specified by $C = 10$ and $n = 310$.

Defective items found in the *samples* will always be either rectified or replaced. If, during inspection, samples are drawn from the batch which include more than the acceptable number of defectives, then two alternatives are available:

1. Reject and scrap the complete *batch*.
2. Subject the complete *batch* to 100 per cent inspection and replace or rectify all faulty items found in it.

The choice of alternative (1) or (2) will depend on the value of the items concerned and the cost of replacing or rectifying them, but often, in order to obtain a high-quality level for batches with a minimum of inspection, the second alternative is adopted. In such a case we can represent our acceptance sampling procedure diagrammatically as shown in Figure 19.12. Referring to this diagrammatic representation, a random sample of n items is taken from the batch of N items. The sample is inspected and c defectives are found, which

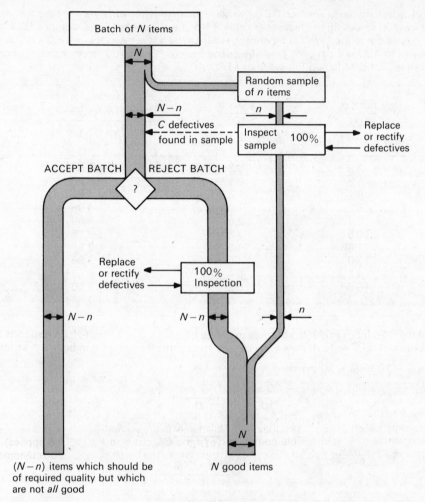

Figure 19.12 *The operation of a sampling procedure in which rejected batches are subject to 100 per cent inspection.*

are then replaced or rectified. Depending on whether c is greater than C (the acceptable number of defects) the entire batch is either accepted or rejected. If the batch is rejected ($c > C$), the remaining $(N - n)$ items in the batch are all inspected, defective items being either rectified or replaced. In this case we can be certain (subject to inspection error) that we are left with N good items. If, on the other hand, the batch is accepted because $c \leqslant C$ then we can be certain that the sample contains all good items, but of course some of the remaining $(N - n)$ items will be defective.

The *average outgoing quality* (*AOQ*) is the overall proportion of defective items in a large number of batches, when all batches are assumed to have the same actual percentage of defectives (*PD*) and when all batches are subjected to the type of inspection procedure described above. The *AOQ* percentage, which must be less than *PD*, can be found as follows:

$$AOQ \text{ per cent} = \frac{\text{Number of defectives remaining}}{\text{Total number of items}} \times 100$$

$$= \frac{\text{Number of defective items in accepted batches each of size } N - n}{\text{Total number of items}} \times 100$$

$$\therefore AOQ \text{ per cent} = \frac{P(a)(PD)(N-n)k}{Nk}$$

where $P(a)$ = probability of accepting batch (from OC curve)
$\quad PD$ = actual per cent defectives in all batches
$\quad N$ = batch sizes
$\quad n$ = sample sizes
$\quad k$ = large number of batches

$$\text{i.e. } AOQ \text{ per cent} = \frac{P(a)(PD)(N-n)}{N}$$

Curves showing the average outgoing quality level for any actual per cent defectives can be calculated quite simply.

EXAMPLE: A HOTEL

A hotel is anxious to check the attitudes of its residents when they leave. They take a sample of ten customers each day and ask if they were satisfied with the service. No action is taken if one or fewer customers in each sample complain (i.e. if the OC curve in Figure 19.8 applies).

Construct the *AOQ* curve for this sampling plan where the batch size N = 200 customers per day.

$$AOQ \text{ per cent} = P(a) (PD) \frac{N-n}{N}$$

$$= P(a) (PD) 0.95$$

$P(a)$ (from OC curve)[a]	PD per cent	AOQ per cent
0.90	5	4.3
0.77	10	7.3
0.55	15	7.8
0.37	20	7.0
0.22	25	5.2
0.13	30	3.7
0.08	35	2.7
0.06	40	2.3

[a] See Figure 19.8

This *AOQ* curve is shown in Figure 19.13.

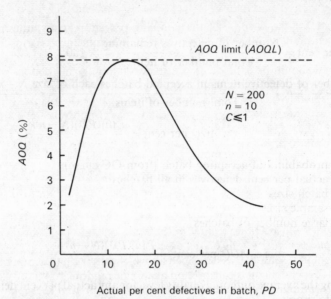

Figure 19.13 *AOQ curve.*

Using such a sampling procedure, not only is the *AOQ* better than the specified acceptable quality level, but also a 'built-in' *limit* for the proportion of defectives—the average outgoing quality limit—exists. This limit represents the worst average quality which, over a large number of batches, we may expect to pass either to the customer or to the next production stage. Acceptance sampling plans may also be designed to provide a given *AOQL*.

Summary of the design of single acceptance sampling plans for attributes

Sampling plans may be designed to provide:

(a)   an average outgoing quality limit (*AOQL*);
(b)   a given consumer or producer risk (*LTPD* and *AQL*).

AOQL plans are usually adopted where interest centres on the average quality level after inspection, whereas LTPD and/or *AQL* plans are used where a certain given level of risk is to be satisfied.

The basic steps involved in the design and use of an acceptance sampling procedure are as follows:

1.   Decide what features or characteristics of the items will be inspected.
     (a)   If necessary, treat different characteristics with separate sampling procedures; but
     (b)   wherever possible combine all characteristics which are the subject of the same kind of inspection (e.g. all characteristics necessitating visual inspection) and treat them all with the same acceptance sampling plan.

2. Decide what, for the purpose of the sampling procedure, constitutes a batch, i.e.
   (a) A batch should, as far as possible, consist of homogeneous items from the same source.
   (b) Batches should be as large as possible to minimize inspection.
3. Choose the type of sampling plan to be used, i.e. *AOQL* or *AQL/LTPD* plans, and determine suitable quality or risk figures to be used in the plan.
4. Select a random sample from the batch and inspect appropriate characteristics on each item.
5. As a result of the quality level of the sample, accept or reject the batch.

Double and multiple sampling

The total amount of inspection required to obtain a certain output quality level can be reduced if *double* or *multiple sampling* is used.

In single acceptance sampling as described above, the decision to accept or to reject the batch of items is dependent on the inspection of a single random sample of size n from that batch. In *double* sampling there is the possibility of delaying that decision until a second sample has been taken. A random sample of n items is drawn from the batch, each item is inspected and the number of defectives (c) is counted. If this number is less than or equal to a given acceptance number $(C1)$ then the batch is accepted. Alternatively, if it is greater than a larger given acceptance number $(C2)$ the batch is rejected. If, however, the number of defectives in the sample falls between these two levels, then the result is inconclusive and a second sample is drawn from the same batch. Again, the number of defectives is counted and this number is added to the number of defectives found in the first sample. If the total number is less than $C2$, the batch is accepted, but if the total number is greater than $C2$ the batch is rejected.

Multiple sampling is a similar procedure, but here there is the possibility of taking more than two samples from the same batch. An initial sample is drawn from the batch and, depending on the number of defectives found, the batch is either accepted $(c \leqslant C1)$ or rejected $(c > C2)$, or a decision is deferred $(C1 < c < C2)$. The number of defectives in the second sample is added to the number found in the first and the total is compared with two further acceptance numbers, the batch being accepted or rejected or the decision deferred as before. This procedure is repeated until a decision can be made. A multiple sampling plan is depicted diagrammatically in Figure 19.14.

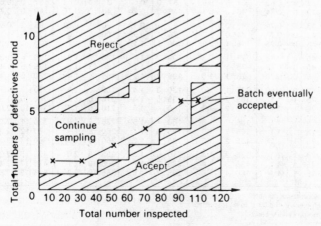

Figure 19.14 *Multiple sampling plan (for batch sizes of 500 to 799 for 3 per cent AQL).*

Sequential sampling is a similar procedure but involves taking one at a time from the batch and basing acceptance or rejection decisions on the number of defectives accumulated.

Double or multiple sampling permits smaller-sized samples to be taken. Consequently, on the occasions when the items or material inspected are well within, or well beyond, acceptable quality levels, fewer items need be inspected. In such cases double or multiple sampling is more economical than single acceptance sampling.

Acceptance sampling tables

In practice people responsible for the design and use of acceptance sampling rarely establish their sampling plans from first principles. More often one or more of the numerous sets of published charts or tables is used. For example, a widely used *AQL* scheme acceptance sampling for variables was devised jointly in the USA, Canada and the UK, and is published in British Standard BS 6001 and in the USA as MIL–STD–105D. The UK Military Standard Attributes AS Scheme is covered by Standard DEF–131–A, while in the USA an AS for variables is given in MIL–STD–414. Another widely used set of tables was developed by Dodge and Romig at the Bell Telephone Laboratories.

The Dodge and Romig tables are of four types. Each is concerned with attributes.

1. Single sampling lot tolerance tables (see Figure 19.15).
2. Single sampling *AOQL* tables (see Figure 19.16).
3. Double sampling lot tolerance tables (see Figure 19.17).
4. Double sampling *AOQL* tables (see Figure 19.18).

The *LTPD* tables provide values of n and c for a consumer's risk of 10 per cent and for *LTPD*s from 0.5 per cent to 10.0 per cent. To use the tables the batch or lot size and the

Lot Size	Process Average 0 to 0.05%			Process Average 0.06 to 0.50%			Process Average 0.51 to 1.00%			Process Average 1.01 to 1.50%			Process Average 1.51 to 2.00%			Process Average 2.01 to 2.50%		
	n	C	AOQL %	n	C	AOQL %	n	C	AOQL %	n	C	AOQL %	n	C	AOQL %	n	C	AOQL %
1 30	All	0	0	All	0	0	All	0	0	All	0	0	All	0	0	All	0	0
31 50	30	0	0.49	30	0	0.49	30	0	0.49	30	0	0.49	30	0	0.49	30	0	0.49
51 100	37	0	0.63	37	0	0.63	37	0	0.63	37	0	0.63	37	0	0.63	37	0	0.63
101 200	40	0	0.74	40	0	0.74	40	0	0.74	40	0	0.74	40	0	0.74	40	0	0.71
201 300	43	0	0.74	43	0	0.74	70	1	0.92	70	1	0.92	95	2	0.99	95	2	0.99
301 400	44	0	0.74	44	0	0.74	70	1	0.99	100	2	1.0	120	3	1.1	145	4	1.1
401 500	45	0	0.75	75	1	0.95	100	2	1.1	100	2	1.1	125	3	1.2	150	4	1.2
501 600	45	0	0.76	75	1	0.98	100	2	1.1	125	3	1.2	150	4	1.3	175	5	1.3
601 800	45	0	0.77	75	1	1.0	100	2	1.2	130	3	1.2	175	5	1.4	200	6	1.4
801 1000	45	0	0.78	75	1	1.0	105	2	1.2	155	4	1.4	180	5	1.4	225	7	1.5
1001 2000	45	0	0.80	75	1	1.0	130	3	1.4	180	5	1.6	230	7	1.7	280	9	1.8
2001 3000	75	1	1.1	105	2	1.3	135	3	1.4	210	6	1.7	280	9	1.9	370	13	2.1
3001 4000	75	1	1.1	105	2	1.3	160	4	1.5	210	6	1.7	305	10	2.0	420	15	2.2
4001 5000	75	1	1.1	105	2	1.3	160	4	1.5	235	7	1.8	330	11	2.0	440	16	2.2
5001 7000	75	1	1.1	105	2	1.3	185	5	1.7	260	8	1.9	350	12	2.2	490	18	2.4
7001 10,000	75	1	1.1	105	2	1.3	185	5	1.7	260	8	1.9	380	13	2.2	535	20	2.5
10,001 20,000	75	1	1.1	135	3	1.4	210	6	1.8	285	9	2.0	425	15	2.3	610	23	2.6
20,001 50,000	75	1	1.1	135	3	1.4	235	7	1.9	305	10	2.1	470	17	2.4	700	27	2.7
50,001 100,000	75	1	1.1	160	4	1.6	235	7	1.9	355	12	2.2	515	19	2.5	770	30	2.8

n = sample size; C = acceptance number
'All' indicates that each piece in the lot is to be inspected
AOQL = Average Outgoing Quality Limit

Figure 19.15 *Single sampling table for lot tolerance per cent defective (LTPD) = 5.0 per cent.*

Lot Size	Process Average 0 to 0.05%			Process Average 0.06 to 0.50%			Process Average 0.51 to 1.00%			Process Average 1.01 to 1.50%			Process Average 1.51 to 2.00%			Process Average 2.01 to 2.50%		
	n	C	p_t%	n	C	p_t%	n	C	p_t%	n	C	p_t%	n	C	p_t%	n	C	p_t%
1–10	All	0	–	All	0	–	All	0	–	All	0	–	All	0	–	All	0	–
11–50	11	0	17.6	11	0	17.6	11	0	17.6	11	0	17.6	11	0	17.6	11	0	17.6
51–100	13	0	15.3	13	0	15.3	13	0	15.3	13	0	15.3	13	0	15.3	13	0	15.3
101–200	14	0	14.7	14	0	14.7	14	0	14.7	29	1	12.9	29	1	12.9	29	1	12.9
201–300	14	0	14.9	14	0	14.9	30	1	12.7	30	1	12.7	30	1	12.7	30	1	12.7
301–400	14	0	15.0	14	0	15.0	31	1	12.3	31	1	12.3	31	1	12.3	48	2	10.7
401–500	14	0	15.0	14	0	15.0	32	1	12.0	32	1	12.0	49	2	10.6	49	2	10.6
501–600	14	0	15.1	32	1	12.0	32	1	12.0	50	2	10.4	50	2	10.4	70	3	9.3
601–800	14	0	15.1	32	1	12.0	32	1	12.0	50	2	10.5	50	2	10.5	70	3	9.4
801–1000	15	0	14.2	33	1	11.7	33	1	11.7	50	2	10.6	70	3	9.4	90	4	8.5
1001–2000	15	0	14.2	33	1	11.7	55	2	9.3	75	3	8.8	95	4	8.0	120	5	7.6
2001–3000	15	0	14.2	33	1	11.8	55	2	9.4	75	3	8.8	120	5	7.6	145	6	7.2
3001–4000	15	0	14.3	33	1	11.8	55	2	9.5	100	4	7.9	125	5	7.4	195	8	6.6
4001–5000	15	0	14.3	33	1	11.8	75	3	8.9	100	4	7.9	150	6	7.0	225	9	6.3
5001–7000	33	1	11.8	55	2	9.7	75	3	8.9	125	5	7.4	175	7	6.7	250	10	6.1
7001–10,000	34	1	11.4	55	2	9.7	75	3	8.9	125	5	7.4	200	8	6.4	310	12	5.8
10,001–20,000	34	1	11.4	55	2	9.7	100	4	8.0	150	6	7.0	260	10	6.0	425	16	5.3
20,001–50,000	34	1	11.4	55	2	9.7	100	4	8.0	180	7	6.7	345	13	5.5	640	23	4.8
50,001–100,000	34	1	11.4	80	3	8.4	125	5	7.4	235	9	6.1	435	16	5.2	800	28	4.5

n = sample size; C = acceptance number
'All' indicates that each piece in the lot is to be inspected
p_t = lot tolerance per cent defective with a Consumer's Risk (P_C) of 0.10

Figure 19.16 *Single sample table for average outgoing quality limit (AOQL) = 2.5 per cent.*

actual process average percentage defective must be known. The latter will usually be obtained from a pilot study. The *LTPD* tables also show in each case the *AOQL* which would result if rejected batches were subject to 100 per cent inspection.

The *AOQL* tables provide values of *n* and *c* for a consumer's risk of 10 per cent and for *AOQL*s from 0.1 to 10.0 per cent. Again, to use these tables the batch size and the process average percentage defective must be known. The tables also give the *LTPD* which will result from each sampling plan.

Lot Size	Process Average 0 to 0.05%				Process Average 0.06 to 0.50%				Process Average 0.51 to 1.00%			
	Trial 1	Trial 2		AOQL in %	Trial 1	Trial 2		AOQL in %	Trial 1	Trial 2		AOQL in %
	n_1, C_1	n_2	n_1+n_2 C_2		n_1, C_1	n_2	n_1+n_2 C_2		n_1, C_1	n_2	n_1+n_2 C_2	
1–30	All 0	–	– –	0	All 0	–	– –	0	All 0	–	– –	0
31–50	30 0	–	– –	0.49	30 0	–	– –	0.49	30 0	–	– –	0.49
51–75	38 0	–	– –	0.59	38 0	–	– –	0.59	38 0	–	– –	0.59
76–100	44 0	21	65 1	0.64	44 0	21	65 1	0.64	44 0	21	65 1	0.64
101–200	49 0	26	75 1	0.84	49 0	26	75 1	0.84	49 0	26	75 1	0.84
201–300	50 0	30	80 1	0.91	50 0	30	80 1	0.91	50 0	55	105 2	1.0
301–400	55 0	30	85 1	0.92	55 0	55	110 2	1.1	55 0	55	110 2	1.1
401–500	55 0	30	85 ·1	0.93	55 0	55	110 2	1.1	55 0	80	135 3	1.2
501–600	55 0	30	85 1	0.94	55 0	60	115 2	1.1	55 0	85	140 3	1.2
601–800	55 0	35	90 1	0.95	55 0	65	120 2	1.1	55 0	85	140 3	1.3
801–1000	55 0	35	90 1	0.96	55 0	65	120 2	1.1	55 0	115	170 4	1.4
1001–2000	55 0	35	90 1	0.98	55 0	95	150 3	1.3	55 0	120	175 4	1.4
2001–3000	55 0	65	120 2	1.2	55 0	95	150 3	1.3	55 0	150	205 5	1.5
3001–4000	55 0	65	120 2	1.2	55 0	95	150 3	1.3	90 1	140	230 6	1.6
4001–5000	55 0	65	120 2	1.2	55 0	95	150 3	1.4	90 1	165	255 7	1.8
5001–7000	55 0'	65	120 2	1.2	55 0	95	150 3	1.4	90 1	165	255 7	1.8
7001–10,000	55 0	65	120 2	1.2	55 0	120	175 4	1.5	90 1	190	280 8	1.9
10,001–20,000	55 0	65	120 2	1.2	55 0	120	175 4	1.5	90 1	190	280 8	1.9
20,001–50,000	55 0	65	120 2	1.2	55 0	150	205 5	1.7	90 1	215	305 9	2.0
50,001–100,000	55 0	65	120 2	1.2	55 0	150	205 5	1.7	90 1	240	330 10	2.1

Figure 19.17 *(contd.)*

Lot Size	Process Average 1.01 to 1.50%						Process Average 1.51 to 2.00%						Process Average 2.01 to 2.50%					
	Trial 1		Trial 2			AOQL in %	Trial 1		Trial 2			AOQL in %	Trial 1		Trial 2			AOQL in %
	n_1	C_1	n_2	n_1+n_2	C_2		n_1	C_1	n_2	n_1+n_2	C_2		n_1	C_1	n_2	n_1+n_2	C_2	
1–30	All	0				0	All	0				0	All	0				0
31–50	30	0				0.49	30	0				0.49	30	0				0.49
51–75	38	0				0.59	38	0				0.59	38	0				0.59
76–100	44	0	21	65	1	0.64	44	0	21	65	1	0.64	44	0	21	65	1	0.64
101–200	49	0	51	100	2	0.91	49	0	51	100	2	0.91	49	0	51	100	2	0.91
201–300	50	0	55	105	2	1.0	50	0	80	130	3	1.1	50	0	100	150	4	1.1
301–400	55	0	80	135	3	1.1	55	0	100	155	4	1.2	85	1	105	190	6	1.3
401–500	55	0	105	160	4	1.3	85	1	120	205	6	1.4	85	1	140	225	7	1.4
501–600	55	0	110	165	4	1.3	85	1	145	230	7	1.4	85	1	165	250	8	1.5
601–800	90	1	125	215	6	1.5	90	1	170	260	8	1.5	120	2	185	305	10	1.6
801–1000	90	1	150	240	7	1.5	90	1	200	290	9	1.6	120	2	210	330	11	1.7
1001–2000	90	1	185	275	8	1.7	120	2	225	345	11	1.9	175	4	260	435	15	2.0
2001–3000	120	2	180	300	9	1.9	150	3	270	420	14	2.1	205	5	375	580	21	2.3
3001–4000	120	2	210	330	10	2.0	150	3	295	445	15	2.3	230	6	420	650	24	2.4
4001–5000	120	2	255	375	12	2.1	150	3	345	495	17	2.3	255	7	445	700	26	2.5
5001–7000	120	2	260	380	12	2.1	150	3	370	520	18	2.3	255	7	495	750	28	2.6
7001–10,000	120	2	285	405	13	2.1	175	4	370	545	19	2.4	280	8	540	820	31	2.7
10,001–20,000	120	2	310	430	14	2.2	175	4	420	595	21	2.4	280	8	660	940	36	2.8
20,001–50,000	120	2	335	455	15	2.2	205	5	485	690	25	2.5	305	9	745	1050	41	2.9
50,001–100,000	120	2	360	480	16	2.3	205	5	555	760	28	2.6	330	10	810	1140	45	3.0

Trial 1: n_1 = first sample size C_1 = acceptance number for first sample
'All' indicates that each piece in the lot is to be inspected
Trial 2: n_2 = second sample size; C_2 = acceptance number for first and second samples combined
AOQL = Average Outgoing Quality Limit

Figure 19.17 *Double sampling table for lot tolerance per cent defective (LTPD)* = 5.0 *per cent.*

Control charts

Acceptance sampling is a method of quality control which is used to ensure that defective items are not accepted by the firm and to ensure that defectives are not offered to the customer. It is concerned with both ends of the quality function but not (*at least not in this form*) with the middle. It is not concerned with controlling quality during the process. This problem, however, is particularly important, since it is during the process that steps may be taken to *prevent* the output of defective and sub-standard items. In fact, we can regard this as being the *quality assurance* function, as opposed to the *quality control* exercised by acceptance sampling. The procedure used during quality assurance is the *control chart*, which is a special application of statistical sampling techniques.

Irrespective of the capability of the process, the items produced will inevitably be subject to some variation. Not only *variables* such as length, weight etc. will vary, but also other *attributes* which will be subject to some variations. These variations might be caused by several factors, which can be classified into two categories:

(a) *usual or chance* variations, which are likely to occur in a random manner and about which comparatively little can be done;
(b) *unusual or assignable* variations, which occur less frequently and can normally be traced to some 'external' causes.

'Usual' variations are normally smaller than 'unusual' variations and, since they result from some inherent process variability, they occur randomly and can be described by the Normal probability distribution. Quality controllers define *limits* within which variations are acceptable and beyond which they are either unacceptable or necessitate some

Lot Size	Process Average 0 to 0.05% Trial 1 n_1 C_1	Trial 2 n_2	n_1+n_2	C_2	p_t %	Process Average 0.06 to 0.50% Trial 1 n_1 C_1	Trial 2 n_2	n_1+n_2	C_2	p_t %	Process Average 0.51 to 1.00% Trial 1 n_1 C_1	Trial 2 n_2	n_1+n_2	C_2	p_t %
1 10	All 0	-	-	-	-	All 0	-	-	-	-	All 0	-	-	-	-
11 50	11 0	-	-	-	17.6	11 0	-	-	-	17.6	11 0	-	-	-	17.6
51 100	18 0	10	28	1	14.1	18 0	10	28	1	14.1	18 0	10	28	1	14.1
101 200	20 0	11	31	1	13.7	20 0	11	31	1	13.7	23 0	25	48	2	11.7
201 300	21 0	13	34	1	13.0	21 0	13	34	1	13.0	24 0	25	49	2	11.4
301 400	21 0	14	35	1	12.8	24 0	26	50	2	11.3	24 0	26	50	2	11.3
401 500	22 0	13	35	1	12.7	25 0	25	50	2	11.1	28 0	47	75	3	9.8
501 600	22 0	14	36	1	12.5	25 0	30	55	2	10.9	28 0	47	75	3	9.8
601 800	22 0	14	36	1	12.5	26 0	29	55	2	10.8	28 0	47	75	3	9.8
801 1000	26 0	29	55	2	10.8	26 0	29	55	2	10.8	29 0	46	75	3	9.6
1001 2000	27 0	33	60	2	10.5	27 0	33	60	2	10.5	33 0	72	105	4	8.3
2001 3000	27 0	33	60	2	10.5	30 0	50	80	3	9.3	33 0	72	105	4	8.3
3001 4000	27 0	33	60	2	10.5	31 0	49	80	3	9.1	33 0	77	110	4	8.2
4001 5000	27 0	33	60	2	10.5	31 0	49	80	3	9.1	36 0	94	130	5	7.6
5001 7000	28 0	32	60	2	10.3	31 0	49	80	3	9.1	36 0	94	130	5	7.7
7001 10,000	28 0	32	60	2	10.3	31 0	49	80	3	9.2	36 0	94	130	5	7.7
10,001 20,000	28 0	32	60	2	10.3	31 0	49	80	3	9.2	36 0	94	130	5	7.8
20,001 50,000	28 0	32	60	2	10.3	33 0	87	120	4	7.7	70 1	145	215	8	6.6
50,001 100,000	28 0	37	65	2	10.2	33 0	92	125	4	7.6	70 1	170	240	9	6.4

Lot Size	Process Average 1.01 to 1.50% Trial 1 n_1 C_1	Trial 2 n_2	n_1+n_2	C_2	p_t %	Process Average 1.51 to 2.00% Trial 1 n_1 C_1	Trial 2 n_2	n_1+n_2	C_2	p_t %	Process Average 2.01 to 2.50% Trial 1 n_1 C_1	Trial 2 n_2	n_1+n_2	C_2	p_t %
1 10	All 0	-	-	-	-	All 0	-	-	-	-	All 0	-	-	-	-
11 50	11 0	-	-	-	17.6	11 0	-	-	-	17.6	11 0	-	-	-	17.6
51 100	18 0	10	28	1	14.1	20 0	20	40	2	13.0	20 0	20	40	2	13.0
101 200	23 0	25	48	2	11.7	23 0	25	48	2	11.7	25 0	35	60	3	10.8
201 300	26 0	44	70	3	10.3	26 0	44	70	3	10.3	28 0	57	85	4	9.5
301 400	27 0	43	70	3	9.9	29 0	61	90	4	9.3	49 1	71	120	6	8.8
401 500	28 0	47	75	3	9.8	30 0	60	90	4	9.2	50 1	80	130	6	8.4
501 600	30 0	65	95	4	9.1	30 0	65	95	4	9.1	55 1	95	150	7	8.0
601 800	31 0	69	100	4	8.8	55 1	85	140	6	8.0	60 1	115	175	8	7.6
801 1000	32 0	68	100	4	8.7	60 1	100	160	7	7.8	85 2	120	205	9	7.2
1001 2000	60 1	90	150	6	7.6	65 1	150	215	9	7.0	95 2	210	305	13	6.5
2001 3000	65 1	115	180	7	7.2	90 2	170	260	11	6.8	125 3	265	390	16	6.0
3001 4000	65 1	140	205	8	6.8	95 2	205	300	12	6.4	185 5	350	535	21	5.5
4001 5000	70 1	160	230	9	6.5	100 2	255	355	14	6.0	220 6	410	630	24	5.2
5001 7000	75 1	190	265	10	6.2	130 3	265	395	15	5.7	255 7	495	750	28	5.0
7001 10,000	100 2	195	295	11	6.0	140 3	355	495	18	5.3	325 9	665	990	36	4.7
10,001 20,000	105 2	215	320	12	5.9	170 4	380	550	20	5.2	360 10	830	1190	43	4.6
20,001 50,000	105 2	245	350	13	5.8	205 5	485	690	25	5.0	415 11	1145	1560	54	4.3
50,001 100,000	110 2	295	405	15	5.6	245 6	610	855	30	4.7	510 14	1370	1880	65	4.2

Trial 1: n_1 = first sample size; C_1 = acceptance number for first sample
'All' indicates that each piece in the lot is to be inspected
Trial 2: n_2 = second sample size; C_2 = acceptance number for first and second samples combined
p_t = lot tolerance per cent defective with a Consumer's Risk (P_C) of 0.10

Figure 19.18 *Double sampling table for average outgoing quality limit (AOQL) = 2.5. (Figures 19.15 to 19.18 from Dodge, H. F. and Romig, H. G. (1959) Sampling Inspection Tables. London: Wiley. Reproduced with permission.)*

examination. Such limits are called *control limits*. For example, for a Normal probability distribution, 99.73 per cent of all chance or usual variations would be expected to occur within limits placed three standard deviations larger, and smaller, than the mean value of a variable. Therefore any variation occurring beyond such limits would probably have resulted from some other unusual or assignable cause and would merit some investigation.

For example, after a pilot investigation of the length of rods produced by an automatic

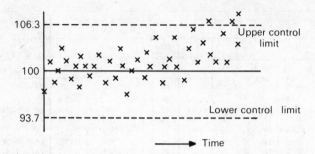

Figure 19.19 *A simple control chart for the lengths of rods.*

guillotine, we discover that the mean length ($\overline{X}$) is 100 cm, and that after excluding the faulty rods that were produced when the setting was accidentally altered, the standard deviation[3] (σ), which is a measure of the variability of the rods produced, was 2.1 cm. We could then set up a control chart with a mean of 100 and control limits of plus and minus three standard deviations. Such a chart (Figure 19.19) might then be used to test the quality of rods then produced. Rather than examine every rod, we take a sample rod every hour and examine it, then plot our result on the control chart, and by so doing we are able to discover that the process, though initially 'in control', is now running 'out of control' and often producing rods which are too long.

A process is considered to be statistically 'under control' or 'in control' if it regularly produces items whose attributes or variables fall within the acceptable or tolerable range, whereas a process is said to be 'out of control' if items are produced whose attributes or variables are beyond the acceptable or tolerable range. In this case (Figure 19.19) the process appears to have gone out of control because of a change in the mean value ($\overline{X}$).

This is only one of the three possible types of change which might occur in a process, i.e. in Figure 19.20 (1) has resulted from a change in the value of mean, (2) has resulted from a change in the standard deviation, and (3) has resulted from a change in both of these characteristics. Each of these changes or disturbances in the process might lead to the production of defective items, but in each case the use of a control chart to monitor output will enable such items to be observed and action to be taken to prevent the production of defective items.

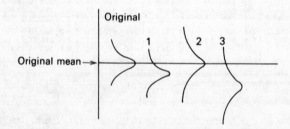

Figure 19.20 *Frequency distributions showing types of change which might occur in a process.*

---

[3] The standard deviation (σ) is calculated using the formula:

$$\sigma = \sqrt{\frac{\Sigma(\overline{X} - X^2)}{N}}$$

where X = length of individual bar
$\overline{X}$ = mean length of all bars
N = number of bars

Control charts would therefore be used as follows:

Step 1   Decide which characteristics of the items are to be controlled.

Step 2   Conduct a pilot study of the process to determine the mean and the standard deviation of the characteristics.

Step 3   Design the control chart(s) using these data.

Step 4   Check these control limits to ensure that they are economically feasible and realistic.

Step 5   Take samples of the process output and plot the characteristics on the control charts.

Step 6   Whenever points fall beyond the control limits:
     (a) investigate causes;
     (b) take corrective action;
     (c) inspect remainder of batch if necessary.

Control charts for variables

Control charts for variables are usually based on the normal probability distribution and are usually designed to test the *means* of samples rather than individual measurements. The main reason why means are used is that, even when the actual distribution of a variable resulting from a process does not conform to the normal distribution, sample means will tend to be distributed Normally. This is known as the central limit theorem of statistics. In practice, therefore, the dimensions of individual components are not plotted separately on control charts; only the *mean*, or average value of the dimensions in the sample, is plotted. Because we are now concerned with a distribution of means, the standard deviation ($\sigma_{\bar{x}}$) is calculated by a different formula, as follows:

$$\sigma_{\bar{x}} = \frac{\sigma}{\sqrt{n}}$$

where $\sigma_{\bar{x}}$ = standard deviation of mean values of samples
      σ = standard deviation of individuals
      n = sample size

Two upper and two lower control limits are normally used, these being referred to as the *upper and lower warning limit* and the *upper and lower action limit*. If points fall beyond the warning limits, this is taken to indicate that the process may be going out of control and that careful observation or additional sampling is required. Points falling beyond the action limits indicate the need to take immediate steps to establish and to eliminate the causes. Action limits are normally set so as to exclude only 0.2 per cent of the points through usual or random variations. Warning limits are set so as to exclude 5 per cent of the points through usual or random variation, i.e.

$$\text{Upper action lmit} \;\; = \bar{X} + 3.09\sigma/\sqrt{n}$$
$$\text{Upper warning limit} = \bar{X} + 1.96\sigma/\sqrt{n}$$
$$\text{Centre} = \bar{X}$$
$$\text{Lower warning limit} = \bar{X} - 1.96\sigma/\sqrt{n}$$
$$\text{Lower action limit} = \bar{X} - 3.09\sigma/\sqrt{n}$$

where $\bar{X}$ = overall process mean value

In practice it is a little tiresome to calculate standard deviations for samples, particularly under the conditions which often exist in practice, and consequently the *range* is usually used as a measure of variability in place of the standard deviation. The *range* is merely the difference between the largest dimension and the smallest, and for small samples it has been shown that:

$$\sigma = \frac{\bar{w}_x}{d_n}$$

where σ = standard deviation of individual items

$\bar{w}_x$ = mean range of several samples

d_n = a constant depending on the sample size

Consequently, our control limits are now calculated as follows:

Upper action limit $\qquad = \bar{X} + \dfrac{3.09(\bar{w}_x/d_n)}{\sqrt{n}}$

Upper warning limit $\qquad = \bar{X} + \dfrac{1.96(\bar{w}_x/d_n)}{\sqrt{n}}$

Centre (= process mean) $\quad = \bar{X}$

Lower warning limit $\qquad = \bar{X} - \dfrac{1.96(\bar{w}_x/d_n)}{\sqrt{n}}$

Lower action limit $\qquad = \bar{X} - \dfrac{3.09(\bar{w}_x/d_n)}{\sqrt{n}}$

To simplify such calculations even further, tables for $3.09/\sqrt{n}\,d_n$ and $1.96/\sqrt{n}\,d_n$ can be used (see Table 19.3).

Table 19.3 *Factors for calculating control limits for control charts for means*

Sample size n	Constant d_n	Factors (m) for warning limits $= \dfrac{1.96}{\sqrt{n}\,d_n}$	Factors (m) for action limits $= \dfrac{3.09}{\sqrt{n}\,d_n}$
2	1.128	1.23	1.94
3	1.693	0.67	1.05
4	2.059	0.48	0.75
5	2.236	0.38	0.59
6	2.334	0.32	0.50
7	2.704	0.27	0.43
8	2.847	0.24	0.38
9	2.970	0.22	0.35
10	3.078	0.20	0.32

Note: To calculate control limits, multiply $\bar{w}_x$ by factor (m) and add or subtract from $\bar{X}$.

Even though the mean value is constant, we have seen how the process might produce defective items by an increase in variability (Figure 19.20). Consequently, a process cannot be said to be fully under control unless *both* mean and standard deviation are under control. We should, therefore, also construct a control chart on which to plot standard deviations but, for the same reasons as before, it is found to be easier to use the range as a measure of variability. In much the same way as for control limits for means, factors can be calculated from which control limits for ranges can be established. These are shown in Table 19.4.

Table 19.4 *Factors for calculating control limits for control charts for ranges*

Sample size n	Factor (R) for warning limits		Factor (R) for action limits	
	Upper	Lower	Upper	Lower
2	2.81	0.04	4.12	0.00
3	2.17	0.18	2.98	0.04
4	1.93	0.29	2.57	0.10
5	1.81	0.37	2.34	0.16
6	1.72	0.42	2.21	0.21
7	1.66	0.46	2.11	0.26
8	1.62	0.50	2.04	0.29
9	1.58	0.52	1.99	0.32
10	1.56	0.54	1.94	0.35

Note: To calculate control limit, multiply $\bar{w}_x$ by the appropriate factor (R).

EXAMPLE: BOTTLING LIQUEUR

A process is used to fill bottles. Each bottle should contain 12 cl.

A random sample of five bottles is taken each hour, and for each sample the mean and range are calculated, i.e.

Sample (size $n = 5$)	Sample mean ($\bar{x}$)	Sample range (w_x)
9.00 a.m.	12.005	0.007
10.00 a.m.	12.001	0.008
11.00 a.m.	11.993	0.010
12.00	11.991	0.003
1.00 p.m.	12.001	0.006
2.00 p.m.	12.003	0.015
3.00 p.m.	11.995	0.011
4.00 p.m.	12.004	0.008
5.00 p.m.	12.003	0.009
6.00 p.m.	12.000	0.010
7.00 p.m.	11.999	0.006
8.00 p.m.	11.997	0.013
9.00 p.m.	11.999	0.011
10.00 p.m.	12.000	0.010
Total	167.991	0.127

From an *earlier* pilot study the overall mean ($\bar{X}$) and the average range ($\bar{w}$) have been found to be:

$$\bar{X} = 11.9994; \qquad \bar{w} = 0.0091$$

Now, using the factors from Tables 19.3 and 19.4, control limits for means and ranges can be calculated.

$$
\text{Mean}\begin{cases}
\text{UAL} & = 11.9994 + 0.59(0.0091) = 12.0048 \\
\text{UWL} & = 11.9994 + 0.38(0.0091) = 12.0029 \\
\text{Centre} & = 11.9994 \\
\text{LWL} & = 11.9994 - 0.38(0.0091) = 11.9959 \\
\text{LAL} & = 11.9994 - 0.59(0.0091) = 11.9940
\end{cases}
$$

$$
\text{Range}\begin{cases}
\text{UAL} & = 0.0091 \times 2.34 & = 0.0213 \\
\text{UWL} & = 0.0091 \times 1.81 & = 0.0165 \\
\text{Centre} & = 0.0091 \\
\text{LWL} & = 0.0091 \times 0.37 & = 0.0034 \\
\text{LAL} & = 0.0091 \times 0.16 & = 0.0015
\end{cases}
$$

The control charts can now be constructed using these figures and the individual sample means and ranges plotted (Figure 19.21). The charts indicate that the process is beginning to settle down. The means from early samples were probably unacceptable (see 'Control Limits and Design Limits' below) but towards the end of the day the process was under better control.

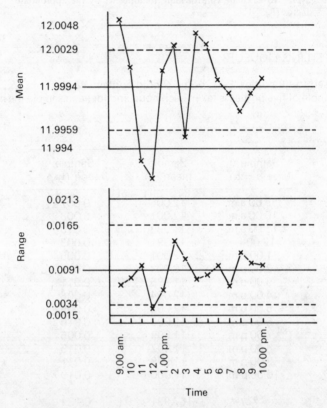

Figure 19.21   *Control chart for means and for range.*

Control charts for attributes

Often, as was the case in acceptance sampling, it is possible after inspecting items to classify them only as 'good' or 'bad', as 'acceptable' or 'not acceptable', and it is for reasons such as these that control charts for attributes have been devised. Such charts are developed in much the same way as were control charts for variables.

Two types of chart are most popular:

1. Control chart for *proportion* or *per cent* defective.
2. Control chart for *number* of defects.

The method of using the charts is similar to that outlined previously, except that in this case, rather than calculate the mean and range of all the items in each random sample, only the number or the percentage of defective items in the sample is calculated.

Control charts for *proportion* or *per cent defective* are known as *p-charts*. Control limits are constructed after a pilot investigation and if, during production, the proportion of defectives in a sample falls within these limits the process is considered to be 'under control', whereas if the proportion of defectives in a sample falls beyond these limits this is taken to be a good indication that the process is, for some reason, out of control and that some investigation and corrective action are required.

An estimate of the proportion of defectives produced by the process is obtained after a pilot study consisting of several samples, i.e.

$$\bar{p} = \frac{\text{Total number of defectives in 10 to 20 samples}}{\text{Total number inspected}}$$

0.2 per cent (and less frequently 5 per cent) control limits are set in the usual way, i.e.

$$\text{Action limits} = \bar{p} \pm 3.09\sigma_{\bar{p}}$$

where $\bar{p}$ = proportion of defectives produced by the process

$\sigma_{\bar{p}}$ = standard deviation of this distribution

The statistical theory of the binomial probability distribution is used, by which it can be shown that:

$$\sigma_{\bar{p}} = \sqrt{\frac{\bar{p}(1-\bar{p})}{n}}$$

Consequently, the action limits are set at:

$$\text{Upper:} \quad \bar{p} + 3.09\sqrt{\frac{\bar{p}(1-\bar{p})}{n}} \qquad (\text{where } \bar{p} < 0.1)$$

$$\text{Lower:} \quad \bar{p} - 3.09\sqrt{\frac{\bar{p}(1-\bar{p})}{n}}$$

where n = sample size

EXAMPLE: MAIL SORTING

An automatic machine sorts letters in a large post office. A manual check is kept on the machine. About 200 letters are checked each hour to see if they have been sorted correctly. The data from one day's work are given below. Construct a *p*-chart and examine the data.

Throughput for previous week $\qquad\qquad$ = 10 000

Number of defectives included in that throughput $\quad$ = 370

The proportion of defectives produced by the machine can in this case be estimated from the

Time of sample	Sample size (n)	Numbers of defectives in sample	p
9.00 a.m.	205	12	0.0585
10.00 a.m.	206	14	0.07
11.00 a.m.	195	12	0.0615
12.00	200	15	0.075
1.00 p.m.	210	14	0.0665
2.00 p.m.	195	12	0.0615
3.00 p.m.	200	15	0.075
4.00 p.m.	200	16	0.080
5.00 p.m.	205	13	0.0635
6.00 p.m.	195	14	0.0715
7.00 p.m.	200	15	0.075
8.00 p.m.	195	14	0.0715

figures given for the previous week's throughput, i.e.

$$\bar{p} = \frac{370}{10\,000} = 0.037$$

Therefore upper action limit is:

$$\bar{p} + 3.09 \sqrt{\frac{\bar{p}(1-\bar{p})}{n}}$$

$$= 0.037 + 3.09 \sqrt{\frac{0.037(0.963)}{200}}$$

$$= 0.0785$$

This action limit is shown on the *p*-chart given as Figure 19.22. The proportion of defectives in each of the 12 samples is plotted on the chart, from which it can be seen that, compared with the previous week's throughput, the proportion of defectives in the batches has increased, and the process is almost 'out of control'.

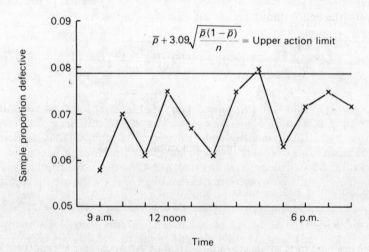

Figure 19.22 *p-chart*.

Since the control limits for a *p*-chart are a function of *n* (the sample size), when the sample size changes the control limits must also change (e.g. Figure 19.23). In the above example, the sample size was nearly constant, hence a mean *n* = 200 was taken.

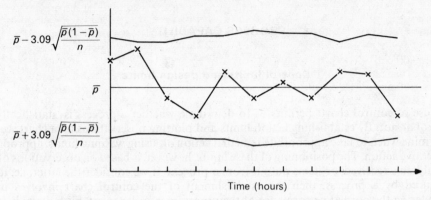

Figure 19.23 *A proportion defective control chart (p-chart) in which the sample size, n, has changed.*

Control charts for *number* of defects are known as *c*-charts and are of particular value for controlling the number of defects in, or on, a particular unit, i.e. a single item, a group of items, or a part of an item. For example, the *c*-chart might be used to control the quality of cloth by counting the number of defects in a roll, to control the quality of a riveted structure by counting the number of faulty rivets. etc. Conditions such as these enable the Poisson distribution to be used. The symbol $\bar{c}$ is the average number of defects per unit obtained after a pilot investigation over several samples. The standard deviation of the Poisson distribution is given by $\sqrt{\bar{c}}$; consequently, the control limits are set at:

$$\text{Upper action} = \bar{c} + 3.09\sqrt{\bar{c}} \qquad \text{(where } \bar{c} < 15\text{)}$$
$$\text{Lower action} = \bar{c} - 3.09\sqrt{\bar{c}}$$

The manner in which *c*-charts are constructed and used is very similar to the construction and use of *p*-charts.

Cumulative sum techniques in quality control

The control chart is a useful and convenient method of recording successive readings, and it provides a clear presentation of historical data. The action limits are a convenient device for prompting corrective action, but unfortunately it is often difficult to detect small changes in the mean value of observations. In fact the control chart is basically a means of studing observations independently, rather than a method of studying trends in a series of observations. This insensitivity is to some extent overcome by the use of warning limits, but even so it is often desirable in quality control to use a procedure which is more sensitive to small changes in mean values.

The principal advantage of the *cumulative sum (CUSUM) chart*[4] is its ability to show such changes; indeed the CUSUM chart actually emphasizes changes in such mean values. Cumulative sum charts can also be constructed for ranges and number or proportion defectives. Their use, in the manner outlined above, maximizes the value of the data

---

[4] See Appendix II.

collected, since, unlike control charts, which concentrate attention on the latest figures. CUSUM charts promote an examination of long sequences of data.

PROCESS CAPABILITY

Control limits and design limits

The use of control charts permits us to determine whether a process is 'statistically' in control or not. By establishing action limits and plotting observations on a chart we can determine when to take appropriate remedial action or, using warning limits, appropriate preventive action. The positioning of these limits, however, is based on observations of the actual items received, or items output from a process. If we consider the latter, i.e. items produced by a process, then the establishment of the control chart involves us in considering the normal performance of the processes in order to establish limits beyond which output can be considered to be abnormal for those same circumstances. Thus if a process is highly reliable and extremely accurate, the control chart limits will be set relatively close to the mean. If, perhaps many years later, the same process becomes unreliable, the equipment worn, etc., then the normal variability in, for example, the dimensions of an item produced by the process will be greater, and thus the action and warning limits will be set further away from the overall mean.

It should be noted, therefore, that the limits set on control charts bear no direct relationship to the limits set in the specification for items. If a process is capable of producing items with considerable accuracy and extremely reliably, but the design specification for those items is very 'loose', then it is possible that, by using control charts designed in the manner described above, we will reject items which are acceptable under the original design specification. Conversely, if a process is not consistently capable of producing items to fine tolerances, yet the design tolerances for the item are very narrow, then it is possible, in using a control chart, to accept items which are not acceptable against the original design specification.

For these reasons we must consider the relationship between control chart limits and design or specification limits, and in doing so we must consider the question of *process capability*.

The use of the mean and range charts shows us whether a process is in statistical control or not, but does not necessarily give any adequate indication of whether individual items are acceptable within specification limits. Organizations are concerned primarily with ensuring that items are within the intended specification tolerance rather than being under 'statistical' control overall.

It will be recalled that in discussing the design of control charts for items we chose to use charts for mean values for reasons of convenience. Ideally we would have liked to set up control charts for individual observations in the manner shown below:

$$UAL_{individuals} = \text{Overall mean} + 3.09\sigma$$
$$LAL_{individuals} = \text{Overall mean} - 3.09\sigma$$

We chose instead to set up a control chart for mean values as follows:

$$UAL_{means} = \text{Overall mean} + 3.09\frac{\sigma}{\sqrt{n}}$$
$$LAL_{means} = \text{Overall mean} - 3.09\frac{\sigma}{\sqrt{n}}$$

In fact the action limits for a control chart based on mean values are somewhat narrower than those that would be established for the same population of individuals. It follows, therefore, that if in using control charts based on mean values we are to be sure that individual items conform to design specifications, the design limits must be placed well beyond the action limits of a mean control chart. This relationship is shown in Figure 19.24. If the design limits are within the action limits for the mean chart, or even just beyond those limits, then it is possible that, using the means chart, individual items will be accepted which do not conform to the specification limits.

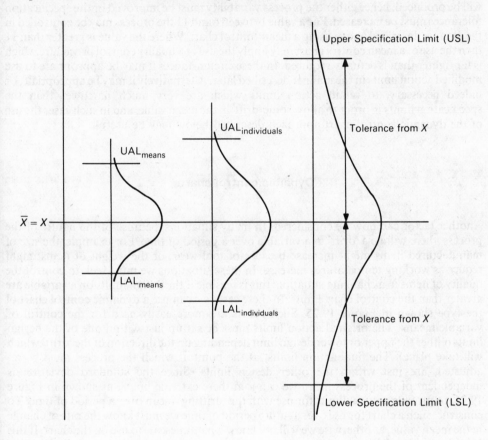

where X = specified dimension
X = overall process mean dimension

Figure 19.24 *Comparison of action limits and possible specification limits.*

Process capability measurement

In studying process capability we shall be concerned with the extent to which a process is capable of processing items which correspond to the design specification limits.

A measure of process capability can be obtained as follows:

$$PC = \frac{USL - LSL}{\sigma}$$

where   PC = Process capability
       USL = Upper specification limit
       LSL = Lower specification limit
        σ = Standard deviation of individual items

Strictly, this measure of process capability applies only where the specification tolerances are distributed symmetrically about the intended dimension, and where the overall mean dimension produced by a process is the same as the intended dimension. In these circumstances, where the value of PC is less than 6, more than 2 per cent of defective items will be produced, hence either the process variability must be improved or the specification tolerances must be increased. For a value between 6 and 11 the process may be controlled in the manner described above using a mean control chart. Where the value is greater than 11 then the use of a mean control chart may imply the use of a quality control procedure which is far tighter than is actually required. In these circumstances it may be appropriate to use modified action limits in the manner described later. Alternatively it may be appropriate, or indeed necessary, to retain action limits which are very much narrower than the specification limits in order to allow some 'drift' in the mean value, and in such cases the use of the dynamic control chart approach described below may be useful.

Dynamic control charts

Another factor can now be considered. In many situations, because of the nature of the process, there will be a 'drift' in a variable over a period of time. For example, the size of manufactured items might increase because of tool wear, or the weight of items might reduce as working temperatures increase. In these situations we must seek to control the quality of items in a changing situation: this is feasible if the design limits on a variable are greater than the control chart limits. In these cases we can use a dynamic control chart of the type shown in Figure 19.25. Such charts are more easily used for the control of variable means. The original action limits must be set up just within one of the design limits (either the upper or lower design limit depending on the direction of the 'drift' which will take place). The final action limits, at the point at which the process must be re-adjusted, are just within the other design limits. Since the standard deviation is independent of the process mean we can join these extreme limits, as shown in Figure 19.25, to provide control limits for use with the 'drifting' mean over a period of time. To construct such a chart for use over a future period of time we must know the rate of change in the mean value, as otherwise we will not know what timescale to use on the chart. If this is not known it will be necessary to construct the chart step by step, by calculating the new mean value from time to time. (This in turn may result in a 'stepped' chart.)

Modified action limits

Where a process is inherently capable of producing items very consistently with very small variation in dimension, it may be possible to modify the control to provide wider action limits than would otherwise have been employed. This approach may be appropriate, since it can be unnecessarily expensive to try to maintain the process in statistical control if in fact items which fall beyond the control limits are still acceptable within broader specification limits. In these cases modified action limits can be established

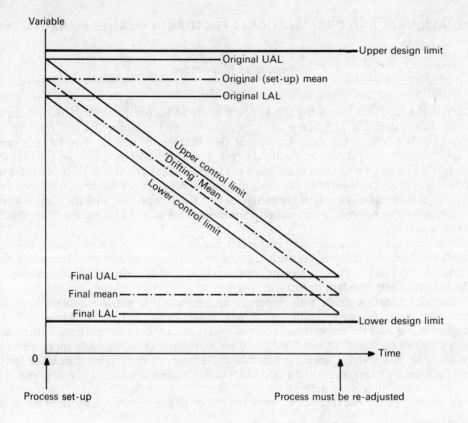

Figure 19.25 *'Dynamic' control chart for mean.*

as follows:

$$\text{Modified UAL}_{\text{means}} = \text{USL} - 3.09\sigma + 3.09\frac{\sigma}{\sqrt{n}}$$

$$\text{Modified LAL}_{\text{means}} = \text{LSL} + 3.09\sigma - 3.09\frac{\sigma}{\sqrt{n}}$$

The use of such an approach again permits the process mean to change providing the sample mean values are within the modified action limits. The approach therefore is similar to that shown in Figure 19.25, except in this case the establishment of these broader, modified action control limits permits the process mean to 'wander' whereas the 'dynamic control chart' is designed specifically to deal with the situation in which the mean drifts in a known direction.

BEHAVIOURAL AND ORGANIZATIONAL FACTORS IN QUALITY MANAGEMENT

People as inspectors

Despite the fact that increasing use is being made of automatic devices, the principal method of inspection, and hence of quality control and assurance, is still the human inspector. We have taken care throughout this chapter to indicate that 100 per cent inspection does not necessarily ensure the complete absence of defects from the output, because inspectors, being human, are liable to make mistakes. It will now be appropriate to look briefly at the problem of error during inspection. What sort of decisions are inspectors asked to make? Essentially, there are two types: first, those connected with the inspection of variables (i.e. measurement); and second, those connected with the inspection of attributes (i.e. assessment).

In measurement, an inspector compares a characteristic of the item with a defined standard. Often this involves the use of a gauge or instrument against or within which the item is placed. Greater opportunity for error or mistake exists as the ease of comparison of characteristic and standard decreases.

A similar situation exists with respect to assessment. It is not too difficult to make decisions about the acceptability of certain noise levels, and of attributes such as brightness, because the inspector, conceptually at least, is able to compare such attributes with a known standard. In fact these could be considered as only slightly more difficult problems of *measurement* since it is possible to use decibel meters to measure noise levels and light meters to measure light levels. More difficult is the assessment of colour quality, since it is more difficult to define colour standards. The assessment of smell and taste is even more difficult because such characteristic standards are virtually impossible to define.

The more remote and ill-defined the standard the more difficult the comparison of characteristic and standard and, consequently, the more difficult and the more equivocal the decision. It should be clear, therefore, that in order to ensure adequate and consistent inspection procedures, instruments should be used which ensure easy and accurate comparison of characteristic and standard. Furthermore, standards for which instruments cannot be used should be clearly defined, e.g. colour shade cards might be used and inspectors could be trained and retrained to recognize standard noise levels, brightness levels, etc., in much the same way that time study practitioners are trained to recognize a notional concept of standard performance. Workplaces should be designed to permit and, preferably, emphasize the comparison of characteristic and standard.

The following notes will illustrate how the equipment and the situation might be designed to facilitate accurate and consistent inspection.

1. Ideally the standard itself should be used during the inspection process as, for example, in the physical comparison of dimensions while using Go/No go gauges.
2. The standard, if not used during inspection, should be prominently displayed so that comparison of characteristic and standard is easy or, alternatively, so that inspectors might regularly refer to the standard in order to 'recalibrate their perception'.
3. Where possible, inspection procedures might be 'reconstructed' as pattern recognition procedures. For example, in the design of instrument displays, dials are often arranged so that when each instrument is reading correctly all pointers appear horizontal or vertical. Consequently, when one instrument shows an unusual or wrong reading, the pattern is disrupted and recognition of the fact is made easier. In such a case the acceptable standard has been redefined, acceptability now being associated with consistency of appearance.

4. Wherever possible the workplace conditions should be arranged to emphasize the characteristic being measured or assessed. For example, lighting might be arranged to emphasize irregularities or roughness of surfaces.

'Zero defects' programmes

The original 'zero defects' programme was established by the Martin-Marietta Corporation in the USA around 1962. It was introduced to augment the established statistical quality control programme in order to try to improve product quality beyond that level which might economically be achieved by the statistical procedures. The programme was in large part a 'motivational' device which sought to organize and motivate direct and indirect workers to achieve higher levels of quality in their work. The slogan 'zero defects' was an important part of this motivational exercise.

This original zero defects programme was considered to be highly successful, and the company was able to demonstrate significant improvements in product quality as a result of its introduction. This in turn led other companies in similar industries, e.g. defence and aerospace, to adopt this motivational/organizational approach to quality assurance and, in time, 'zero defects' programmes became well established. It has been suggested that the principal features of such programmes were as follows:[5]

'1. A motivational package aimed at reducing individual operator controlled defects. The contents of this package were such things as the 'Big Meeting Rally', 'Pledge Cards', 'Posters', 'Attention getters', 'Scoreboards' etc.
2. A prevention package aimed at reducing management controlled defects. This package centred around 'error cause removal' (ECR) suggestions to be made by employers for subsequent analysis and action by supervisors. These suggestions were submitted to the supervisor on ECR forms which defined the probable error cause and proposed action.
3. Procedures to provide for prompt feedback to the worker.'

Basic behavioural science principles and practices are the basis of 'zero defects' programmes. Such programmes are based on efforts to motivate workers, and the approaches employed, e.g. providing clear objectives, participation in decision-making and positive feedback on performance, are established principles which have widespread use in other applications. Thus the development of 'zero defects' programmes demonstrates a sensible application of established theories in a relatively new field.

Effective ZD programmes would probably involve the following:

(a) some method of establishing agreement on the quality problems, or quality goals to be achieved, or the reasons behind these problems and/or goals;
(b) the use of a well-structured approach to establishing a motivational programme aimed at solving these problems and/or achieving these goals;
(c) the participation of all those involved, i.e. all those who might in some way contribute to the solving of quality problems/achievement of quality objectives, in both the establishment and running of the programme;
(d) the setting of clear targets against which to measure improvements;
(e) the establishment of formalized, regular, simple procedures for reporting achievement on goals;
(f) the establishment of procedures for reinforcing effort in connection with the above;
(g) the organization of jobs, e.g. of workers, quality controllers, supervisors, management, etc., in such a way as to facilitate the above.

---

[5] Juran, J. M. and Gryna, F. M. (1970) *Product Planning and Analysis*. Maidenhead: McGraw-Hill.

'Quality circles'[6]

The quality circle approach to quality assurance was widely established in Japan before being adopted in Europe and North America. Wherever employed the QC approach rests upon the motivation of individuals and the organization of efforts to improve quality through error reduction, etc., and as such the procedure is designed to supplement conventional quality control procedure as previously discussed in this chapter.

A quality circle comprises a group of workers and supervisors in a single area or department within an organization, which meets regularly to study ways of improving quality and to monitor progress towards such goals. Thus it is a participative device, perhaps fundamentally more in tune with Japanese culture than with Western culture. A company will seek to establish quality circles largely on a voluntary basis. Those volunteering will often be up to half of the direct and indirect workers involved in the activities of a particular department. They are offered training in the analysis and identification of quality problems and problem-solving procedures. Once this training is completed the circle is formed and is invited to tackle particular quality problems nominated by management or identified by the circle itself. Each quality circle will normally tackle a series of projects, one at a time, identifying quality problems and means of eliminating such problems and establishing targets (often financial targets) to be achieved through quality improvement.

There will be numerous quality circles within an organization and their work will be monitored and co-ordinated by company management, who will be responsible for establishing overall objectives and monitoring the progress towards the achievement of these objectives. Thus the quality control effort within the organization is diffused through all levels rather than being seen as the responsibility of managers and indirect, often specialist, staff.

The *original* concept of QC may be of relevance only in a Japanese type of culture. For example, originally most of the training for those involved in QC and the meetings of the circles themselves took place out of working hours and on a voluntary and often unpaid basis. Normally there was no financial incentive in the improvement of quality except that obtained indirectly through improvements in the performance and financial status of the organization as a whole. The only major incentive was that of obtaining further training and of recognition within the organization. This analysis, however, conceals the fundamental nature of the programme, i.e. that of motivating individuals through participation in decision-making and reinforcing by positive feedback of results. Fundamentally such an approach is 'culture free' and can possibly be employed with benefit in other situations where quality performance is largely a function of individual effort and attention.[7] Certainly the use of QC in Europe and North America does not follow exactly the pattern established in Japan, and interest in this type of approach to quality 'assurance' is increasing.

Quality circles have some similarity to ZD programmes; however, the former is essentially a group approach and the latter individual. The QC methodology (which is almost a ritualistic approach in Japan) probably requires considerable effort to establish and sustain, and it is perhaps for this reason that those companies which have adopted the approach, especially in Japan, have tended to concentrate on this one concept, rather than trying to sustain several different types of programme or campaign.

---

[6] Originally, in Japan, referred to as 'quality control circles' but now generally abbreviated to 'quality circles' or QC in the West.

[7] One should not, however, underestimate the effort required to make such an approach successful. When importing QC, may companies in the West were initially unsuccessful, often because of insufficient attention to training. (See, for example, Goodfellow, M. (1981) Quality control circle programs—what works and what doesn't?, *Quality Progress*, August, pp. 30–33.)

COMPUTERS IN QUALITY CONTROL

Computer software 'packages' are available for use in the broadly defined area of quality management, but few are of direct relevance to the topics discussed in this chapter. If quality management is 'the function which must be performed throughout an organization in order to achieve quality objectives' then computers will have relevance in tasks such as the following:

(a) *data accumulation*, on item and process properties, i.e. the collection, organization and filing of data on quality levels, reject ratios, breakdown rates, customer complaints, etc., for use in decision-making on design, equipment replacement, pricing, etc.;
(b) *data reduction*, analysis and reporting, i.e. deriving from the above the analysis of data for presentation in, for example, graphical form;
(c) *real time process control*, i.e. direct process monitoring and control to ensure the achievement of given quality requirements;
(d) *automated inspection and testing*, perhaps associated with (c) above, but also to replace the manual monitoring of incoming or outgoing items;
(e) *statistical analysis* of data, e.g. of sample data to construct control charts and to make accept/reject decisions.

Item (e) above is of direct relevance to this chapter. Certainly computer programs are available for the analysis of statistical data, e.g. for the calculation of means, standard deviations, etc., but few programs have been developed and are *commercially available* specifically for use in quality control.

RELIABILITY OF ITEMS

The reliability of items was considered above in connection with the specification and achievement of quality. We have seen that quality, reliability and cost are linked, higher quality being associated with higher reliability and normally higher cost. In Chapter 20 we shall consider the maintenance and replacement of facilities. There again, consideration of reliability is relevant, since the higher the reliability the less the need for replacement and maintenance. We shall also have cause to mention reliability in a slightly different context in discussing performance measurement in Chapter 21.

Clearly, therefore, the reliability of items, products and facilities is an important consideration in design. It is of relevance to the user, and is a factor to consider in quality management and in maintenance and replacement. It merits some further consideration at this point.

Failure

We tend to think of unreliability in terms of failure. An item which is prone to frequent failure will be considered to be unreliable. A reliable item would be one which is expected to operate for long periods of time without failure. However, we should not overlook the fact that the ways in which items fail may differ. Some items may suddenly cease to operate, while others may operate poorly or partially.

Failure is the termination of the ability of an item to perform its required function. We can consider failure in four classes, as follows:

1. As to cause:
    (a) misuse failure;
    (b) inherent weakness failure.
2. As to suddenness:
    (a) sudden failure;
    (b) gradual failure.
3. As to extent:
    (a) partial failure (i.e. deviation from specified characteristics but not enough to cause total loss of function);
    (b) complete failure.

Hence:
4. Catastrophic failure = 2(a) + 3(b)
    Degradation failure = 2(b) + 3(a)

Clearly the cause, nature, manner and consequences of failure will vary. Thus in seeking to examine or in some way measure reliability of any item or process we must first be clear about what constitutes reliable operation and what constitutes a failure. Only having defined these terms, for our particular circumstances, can we then set out to study and/or measure reliability.

Reliability characteristics and measures

The curves shown in Figure 19.26 are reliability distributions. They are different ways of illustrating the classic component reliability pattern which is found for some types of equipment. Each curve is in fact a different type of measure of reliability. The terms used in Figure 19.26 are defined in Table 19.5 and discussed below. The example on pp. 610–11 shows how the various reliability measures can be calculated. This example (and the descriptions below) concern a situation in which a test has begun on a given number of items at time $t = 0$. In this test the number of items failing in each time period is counted, and from these data the various reliability measures can be calculated.

Failure probability (f(t))

This gives, at any instant in time, the probability of the failure of an item which was working satisfactorily at time $t = 0$.

The curve shown in Figure 19.26 (a) shows high probability of item failure in early life, falling for a period only to begin to rise again as items begin to wear out. The peak in the latter part of the curve (3–4) represents the mean 'wear-out' life of items. After this point we are left only with the more reliable items in operation.

Cumulative failure probability (F(t))

This is the cumulative measure of the probability of failure. It is in effect the probability of all items having failed after a given time (Figure 19.26(b)).

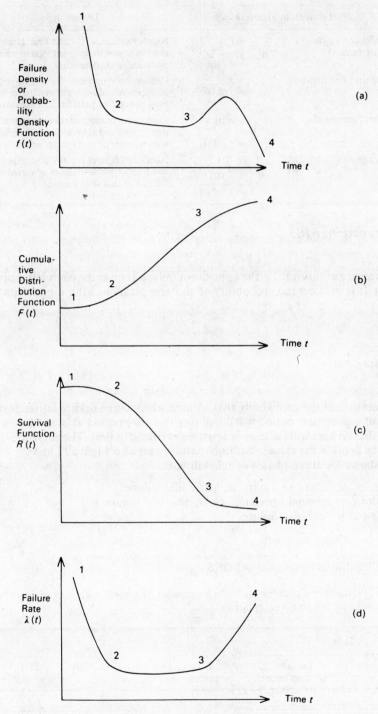

Figure 19.26 *Reliability distributions.*

Table 19.5 *Reliability distribution terminology*

Terms from Figure 19.26		Definition
Probability distribution (Failure density)	$= f(t)$	Number of failures per unit time, expressed as a fraction of the original total number of parts under examination
Cumulative distribution	$= F(t)$ $= \int f(t)\,dt$	Cumulative number of failures up to any time t, expressed as a fraction of the original total number of parts under examination
Survival function	$= R(t)$ $= 1 - F(t)$	Cumulative number of survivors up to any time t, expressed as a fraction of the original total number of parts under examination
Failure rate	$= \lambda(t)$ $= \dfrac{f(t)}{1 - F(t)}$	Number of failures per unit time, expressed as a fraction of the number of survivors at the end of that time interval

Survival function (R (t))

This is a measure of survival, i.e. the opposite of failure. It gives the cumulative probability of survival. It is in effect the probability of all items surviving after a given time (Figure 19.26(c)).

Failure rate (λ (t))

This is a measure of the probability that an item which was working satisfactorily at the beginning of a given time period will fail during that time period. It is, in effect, a measure of the risk that an item will fail during a particular period of time. The curve for $\lambda(t)$ shown in Figure 19.26(d) is the classic 'bathtub' pattern (see also Figure 11.8).
It clearly shows the three phases of reliability, i.e.

1–2 'burn-in' or 'infant mortality' or 'early life' failure;
2–3 'random' or 'normal operating' or 'middle life' failure;
3–4 'wear-out or 'old age' failure.

EXAMPLE: RELIABILITY CALCULATIONS

There were 100 items in use at the start of a test period. The items are checked every hour. $f(t)$, $F(t)$, $R(t)$ and $\lambda(t)$ are to be calculated.

Data						
Time elapsed (h)	Failures (in past hour)	Cumulative failures	$f(t)$	$F(t)$	$R(t)$	$\lambda(t)$
1	10	10	0.1	0.1	0.9	0.11
2	8	18	0.08	0.18	0.82	0.09
3	6	24	0.06	0.24	0.76	0.08
4	5	29	0.05	0.29	0.71	0.07
5	4	33	0.04	0.33	0.67	0.06

Time elapsed (h)	Failures (in past hour)	Cumulative failures	$f(t)$	$F(t)$	$R(t)$	(t)
	Data					
6	5	38	0.05	0.38	0.62	0.08
7	3	41	0.03	0.41	0.59	0.05
8	2	43	0.02	0.43	0.57	0.04
9	1	44	0.01	0.44	0.56	0.02
10	0	44	0.00	0.44	0.56	—.
11	0	44	0.00	0.44	0.56	—
12	1	45	0.01	0.45	0.55	0.02
13	3	48	0.03	0.48	0.52	0.06
14	4	52	0.04	0.52	0.48	0.08
15	7	59	0.07	0.59	0.41	0.17
16	6	65	0.06	0.65	0.35	0.17
17	7	72	0.07	0.72	0.28	0.25
18	6	78	0.06	0.78	0.22	0.27
19	5	83	0.05	0.83	0.17	0.29
20	4	87	0.04	0.87	0,13	0.31

Two other measures of component or item reliability will often be encountered. The mean time between failures (MTBF) is the measure of the operating life of items between failures. The mean time to failure (MTTF) is, strictly, a measure of the operating life of an item up to its first failure. Strictly speaking these two measures are different. The MTBF should be used for items which are repaired on failure whereas the MTTF should be used for items which are replaced rather than repaired on failure. In practice the two terms have become confused and there is a tendency to use the MTBF measure for both repaired and replaced items. There is a tendency to use MTBF as a measure of reliability when the failure rate is approximately constant. However, strictly, MTBF is a function of time, particularly when we are concerned with the system which is dependent on the operation of many components. When the system is first operated with all new components the MTBF will be high. After that the mean time between failures may fluctuate until, after several failures and replacements, it will stabilize at a lower value, given by the following equation, which shows the relationship between MTBF and MTTF for a system comprising many components.

$$\frac{1}{\text{MTBF}} = \sum_{j=1}^{m} \frac{1}{\bar{T}_j}$$

where the system has m components of different ages, each of which is replaced immediately following failure, and where $\bar{T}_j$ is the MTTF of the jth component.

In analysing item reliability we must consider each of the three phases of the reliability distributions shown in Figure 19.26. Following a period of decreasing failure rate during the 'infant mortality' period, the failure rate would be expected to remain relatively constant during 'middle age' and then to increase again during the old age period. Analysis of reliability during these periods necessitates the use of appropriate formulae to describe these three essentially different curves. The Weibull distribution is often used for this purpose. It is, in effect, a generalization of the exponential distribution and can be expressed, for the survival function, as follows:

$$R(t) = \exp\left[\frac{-(t-\gamma)^\beta}{\alpha}\right]$$

where γ is the 'locating constant on the time axis (origin of the distribution)

α is a 'scaling' constant ('characteristic life')

β is a 'shaping' constant (Weibull slope)

Suitable choice of these three constants enables the Weibull distribution to be used to fit or simulate each of the three phases of the reliability curve.

Reliability estimation

The Weibull formulation above may be used to estimate the reliability of items and products in service. Such estimates will be of value in design and in determining maintenance policies, etc.

First the three distribution constants α, β and γ must be determined. This is most easily done by the use of Weibull probability graph paper, which has logarithmic scales. When γ is zero, the cumulative percentage failures plotted on the graph will fall in a straight line,[8] the slope of which gives the value β, which in turn gives the shape of the failure distribution, which indicates whether failures are occurring during 'infant', 'middle age' or 'old age' periods.

If from such a plot β is found to be less than 1, the failure pattern is likely to represent 'infant mortality'. If $\beta = 1$, the failure rate is constant, i.e. equivalent to 'middle age'. If β is greater than 1, the failure rate is equivalent to 'old age' or wear-out.

A simple example will illustrate this and show how various other reliability measures can be estimated.

EXAMPLE: DOMESTIC APPLIANCE TESTING BY A CONSUMERS' ASSOCIATION

To estimate the reliability of a cooker, 25 products are chosen at random and tested. The following results were obtained:

Failure number	Cumulative percentage frequency	Number of cycles in operation ($\times 10^4$)
1	4	2.0
2	8	3.1
3	12	4.0
4	16	4.9
5	20	5.9
6	24	7.0
7	28	8.1
8	32	8.9
9	36	10.0
10	40	10.9
11	44	11.6
12	48	12.7
13	52	13.6
14	56	14.3
15	60	15.0

10 products still operating at 15×10^4 operating cycles

---

[8] If, in plotting points, a straight line does not result, $\gamma \neq 0$. The value of γ must then be determined and the points replotted against a new time axis. For details of the procedure see Caplan (1978) in Further Reading.

The results are plotted on Weibull probability paper in Figure 19.27. They follow a straight line, from which β is obtained by constructing a line perpendicular to the plot to meet the 'estimation point' marked on the graph paper. This line crosses the auxiliary scale, β, to give the value for β, i.e. in this case 1.45, suggesting that the failure pattern for the product corresponds to 'old age'.

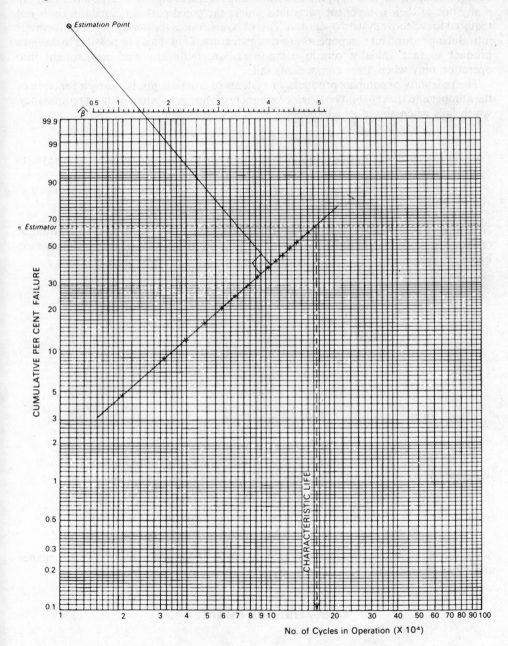

Figure 19.27 *Weibull probability plot of failure date.*

The *characteristic life, η*, is the time after which 36.8 per cent of products will be expected to have survived, i.e. 63.2 per cent failed. In this case the characteristic life is at *16.5× 10⁴ cycles*.

System reliability

The characteristics and the estimation procedure discussed above apply both to single items or components and to products comprising several components. The latter may fail if any one of their component parts fails unless the failed part is redundant, i.e. is not required for effective system operation. This of course raises the possibility of deliberately introducing redundant components as a design feature. Thus it may be possible to design a product so that, initially, certain components are redundant and are brought into operation only when other components fail.

The reliability of complex products, or systems of components, is clearly a function of the number and the reliability of their components. Thus in a system without redundancy, which fails when any of its components A, B, C and D, fail:

$$R_{\text{SYSTEM}} = R_A \times R_B \times R_C \times R_D$$

For example, in a system comprising 10 components, each essential for satisfactory system operation (i.e. without redundancy), if component reliability is 0.99:

$$R_{\text{SYSTEM}} = 0.99^{10}$$
$$= 0.904 \text{ approximately}$$

Now if in this example, because of built-in redundancy, five of the components would be replaced instantly by parallel components if they fail, the system might be shown as in Figure 19.28.

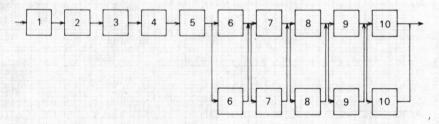

Figure 19.28 *Diagrammatic representation of a ten-component system with redundancy.*

The reliability of components 1–5 = 0.99; the reliability of components 6–10 = 0.99; but since these are each arranged in parallel, the reliability of each pair is:

$$1 - (1 - R_{6,7 \text{ etc}})^2$$
$$\text{Thus } R_{\text{SYSTEM}} = 0.99^5 \times (1 - (1 - 0.99)^2)^5$$
$$= 0.950$$

Such system reliability considerations are relevant in design and in planning maintenance and replacement.

CHECKLIST FOR CHAPTER 19

Customer perceptions of quality
Factors influencing quality
Management of process quality

Examples in manufacturing, supply, transport, service
Product quality

FURTHER READING

British Standard BS4778 (1979) *Glossary of General Terms used in Quality Assurance*. London: HMSO. Also contained, with further information, in Quality Assurance, BSI Handbook No. 22.

Cadwgan, P. G. (1981) Quality circles, *Management Services*, January pp. 6–9. A straightforward description of QC.

Caplan, R. H. (1978) *A Practical Approach to Reliability*, 3rd edition. London: Business Books. A comprehensive and comparatively easy-to-read treatment of reliability theory and management.

Guenther, W. C. (1977) *Sampling Inspection and Quality Control*. New York: Griffin. A detailed book on the statistics of quality control.

Jardine, A. K. S., Macfarlane, J. D. and Greensted, C. S. (1975) *Statistical Methods for Quality Control*. London: Heinemann. Acceptance sampling and control charts together with the statistics of sampling, probability, significance testing, etc.

Juran, J. M. (1981) Product quality—a prescription for the West, *Management Review*, **70** (7), July, pp. 57–61.

Kirkpatrick, E. G. (1970) *Quality Control for Managers and Engineers*. New York: Wiley. A detailed treatment covering all topics in this chapter.

National Association of Purchasing Agents (1964) *Evaluation of Supplier Performance*. New York. Vendor rating systems and similar procedures for the monitoring of the quality of items and suppliers.

Nixon, F. (1971) *Managing to Achieve Quality and Reliability*. New York: McGraw-Hill. A largely descriptive account also dealing with rudiments of reliability.

Robson, M. (1982) *Quality Circles—A Practical Guide*. Aldershot: Gower. A straightforward introductory book; also part of a training 'package'.

QUESTIONS

19.1   (a)   What is the purpose of acceptance sampling?

          (b)   What is an operating characteristic curve?

(c) Use the binomial probability expression to calculate the probability of finding two or fewer defectives in a sample of size 12, if the actual percentage defectives in the batch from which the sample was drawn is 20 per cent.

19.2 Construct an operating characteristic curve to show the probability of accepting batches of varying percentage actual defective levels if sample sizes of 80 items are drawn from the batches and if batches are accepted when two or fewer defectives are found in the samples.

19.3 Use the Thorndike or cumulative Poisson probability chart to specify an OC curve which can be used in a single acceptance sampling plan specified as follows:

Lot tolerance percentage defective   6 per cent   Producer's risk   6 per cent
Acceptable quality level   3 per cent   Consumer's risk   12 per cent

19.4 Construct an average outgoing quality curve and determine the average outgoing quality limit for the operating characteristic curve for $n = 200$, $c \leqslant 2$ shown in Figure 19.10 and batch size of $N = 2500$.

19.5 An office machine processes 2000 items every day. From every lot processed a random sample of 100 is subjected to a visual quality check.

The defectives found in the samples are rectified or replaced and if more than one defective is found in a sample of 100 the entire lot produced is subjected to a quality inspection, during which all defectives are either rectified or replaced. If only one or no defectives are found in the sample the entire lot is accepted without further inspection.

Figure Q19.5 is the OC curve for the sampling plan. It has been calculated using binomial probabilities.

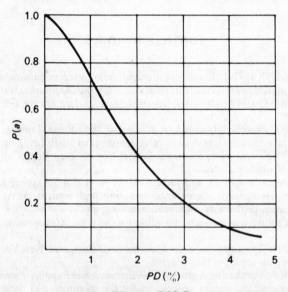

Figure Q19.5

(a) What is the average outgoing quality limit for this quality control procedure?

(b) Under what circumstances can the Poisson probability distribution be used to design the sampling plan? Note:

Poisson probability $P(c) = \dfrac{e^{-pn}(pn)^c}{c!}$ where c = number of defectives in sample

n = sample size
p = actual percentage defective in lot

(c) Using the cumulative Poisson probability chart, design a single acceptance sampling plan to satisfy the following requirements.

Producer's risk		= 0.050
Consumer's risk		= 0.100
Acceptance quality level		= 0.022
Lowest tolerance defective		= 0.090

19.6 (a) Consider the output of a service system. Distinguish between and describe the use of double acceptance sampling and multiple acceptance sampling in this situation.

(b) Using the tables provided in the chapter (Figures 19.17 and 19.18) specify the sample size and the maximum acceptable number of defectives in the sample for:

Double acceptance sampling	
Lot tolerance percentage defective	= 5 per cent
Batch sizes	= 1500
Actual process percentage defective	= 0.5–1.0 per cent

(c) Using the tables provided, what is the average outgoing quality limit, given:

Single acceptance sampling	
Lot tolerance percentage defective	= 5 per cent
Batch sizes	= 2000
Actual process percentage defective	= 0.5–1.0 per cent

What is the lot tolerance percentage defective, given:

Single acceptance sampling	
Average outgoing quality limit	= 2.5 per cent
Batch sizes	= 750
Actual process percentage defective	= 0.5–1.0 per cent
Consumer's risk	= 10 per cent

19.7 Consider two single acceptance sampling plans specified as follows:

1. Sample size 50. Acceptable number of defects 1.
2. Sample size 100. Acceptable number of defects 2.

For each plan determine:

(a) the producer's risk for an acceptable quality level of 2 per cent;
(b) the consumer's risk for a lot tolerance percentage defective of 5 per cent.

Which of these two plans would be considered preferable by:

(i) the producer;
(ii) the consumer?

What is the average outgoing quality limit for each plan if in each case the batch sizes are equal to 1000? State the statistical assumptions you have made in arriving at your answers.

19.8 Refer throughout to supply, service or transport systems.
(a) Distinguish between quality assurance and quality control.
(b) Distinguish between quality control as regards the 'attributes' of items and the 'variables' of items.
(c) Distinguish between design limits and control limits.
(d) Distinguish between usual or chance variation and unusual or assignable variation in respect of quality control.
(e) Distinguish between warning limits and action limits in respect of control charts.

19.9 (a) A machine produces components at a rate of 100 per hour. Every hour a random sample of five components is taken and their lengths measured. After ten hours the data given below have been collected. Use these data to design control charts for the sample mean and range of the dimension concerned.

Sample number	Measurements (cm)				
1	9.00	9.10	9.00	9.05	8.95
2	9.10	9.10	9.00	9.05	9.05
3	9.00	9.05	9.00	9.05	9.00
4	9.00	9.00	8.95	9.00	9.05
5	9.00	9.05	9.05	9.05	9.00
6	9.00	9.10	9.10	9.05	9.00
7	9.00	9.10	9.05	9.15	9.05
8	9.00	9.10	9.10	9.00	9.05
9	9.00	9.00	8.95	9.00	9.00
10	9.00	9.05	9.00	9.10	8.95

(b) Following the construction of the charts, the same sampling procedure is followed and the data shown below are obtained. Plot these data on the control charts and comment on the quality 'performance' of the process.

Sample number	Mean length (cm)	Range	Sample number	Mean length (cm)	Range
1	9.020	0.100	11	9.040	0.150
2	9.030	0.100	12	9.040	0.125
3	9.025	0.050	13	9.035	0.100
4	9.030	0.100	14	9.040	0.055
5	9.035	0.025	15	9.030	0.100
6	9.040	0.105	16	9.025	0.050
7	9.020	0.050	17	9.030	0.125
8	9.030	0.100	18	9.025	0.100
9	9.040	0.050	19	9.025	0.150
10	9.035	0.065	20	9.030	0.150

19.10 Using the data given in the first table below, which have resulted from a study over a period of one week, construct a control chart and, on that control chart, plot the data given in the second table below. Comment on the results.

Target throughput of items for period = 6250
Throughput of good-quality items = 5620
Total number of defective items = 99

$$\text{Percentage performance} = \frac{\text{Acceptable output}}{\text{Target}} \times 100 = 90 \text{ per cent}$$

Sample	Output	Sample	Numbers defective in sample
Mon. a.m.	575	60	1
Mon. p.m.	600	60	2
Tues. a.m.	550	60	2
Tues. p.m.	550	60	1
Wed. a.m.	600	60	2
Wed. p.m.	650	65	2
Thurs. a.m.	625	65	1
Thurs. p.m.	590	70	2
Fri. a.m.	625	75	2
Fri. p.m.	490	60	1
Sat. a.m.	565	60	1

19.11 Phragyle Products Ltd supply imitation glass decanters to the hotel trade. Because of the nature of the items, each decanter is expected to have some minor blemishes, most of which are completely invisible to the naked eye. These very minor blemishes may occur almost anywhere on the product and are not usually sufficient to lead to the rejection of the item. Nevertheless, the sales manager of Phragyle Products is anxious to investigate the effects of recent efforts that the manufacturers claim to have made to improve the manufacturing process and the quality of the products supplied to Phragyle.

Prior to the modifications to the process, each decanter had an average of five almost imperceptible blemishes. The table below shows the number of blemishes on every fifth decanter for a short period after the claimed improvement in manufacture. Comment on the success of the supposed adjustments to the manufacturing process.

Number of blemishes per product: 6, 7, 6, 5, 6, 7, 7, 6, 8, 7, 7, 7, 6, 8, 9, 8, 7, 8, 9, 8, 8, 7

19.12 (a) 'Even if 100 per cent acceptance sampling is adopted, it is likely that a certain number of defective items will be accepted.' Discuss.

(b) What measures can be taken, and in what circumstances, to decrease the error of human inspectors?

19.13 Referring to Question 19.9 above, plot a cumulative-sum chart of the 'mean' values given in the second table. Comment on the resulting chart and compare the results obtained with those obtained from the control chart previously constructed.

19.14 Three phases are often evident in the reliability of items. Describe them and explain the reasons for their existence. Use examples.

19.15 In order to estimate the reliability of an item, 20 items are taken at random and tested. The following results are obtained:

Failure number	Percentage failures	Number of cycles in operation ($\times 10^4$)
1	5	3.0
2	10	4.2
3	15	5.5
4	20	6.4
5	25	6.7
6	30	7.4
7	35	8.3
8	40	9.0
9	45	9.3
10	50	10.3
11	55	10.9
12	60	12.0
13	65	13.0
14	70	14.0
15	75	14.7

Five items were still operative after 14.7×10^4 cycles

(a) Determine β and comment on the result.
(b) Calculate the 'characteristic life' of the item.

CHAPTER 20

Maintenance and Replacement

NOTATION USED IN THIS CHAPTER

C_m	Cost/unit time of preventive maintenance
C_s	Cost/unit time of repair
E_n	Expenditure for year n
G	Value of the output of a facility ($£$/unit time)
i	Annual rate of interest
I_n	Income for year n
k	Constant
K	Number of machines allocated to one maintenance team
L	Life of equipment
M	Number of maintenance teams
N	Number of inspections/facility/unit time
NPV	Net present value
S_L	Sale or scrap value at end of life, i.e. at year L
T_a	Average operating life without breakdowns
t_I	Time for an inspection
T_m	Average time for a preventive maintenance operation
T_p	Preventive maintenance interval
T_s	Average time for a repair
t_s	Time for a repair
T_T	Total downtime

Our discussion of quality in the previous chapter led us to consider the question of reliability. We noted that quality and reliability were related: in general, higher-quality items were likely to be more reliable. We noticed also that quality level and cost were related, higher quality often being associated with higher costs. Since few purchases are made irrespective of cost, most products or items in use will have less than perfect reliability. At some time most items will cease to function satisfactorily. On such occasions

620

they will have to be repaired or replaced. To some extent, however, the need for repair or replacement may be reduced through effective servicing and maintenance. Thus:

1. Most items will be *inspected* regularly, in order to detect any signs of reduced effectiveness or impending failure. And additionally
2. Items will normally be *serviced* regularly, e.g. readjusted, lubricated, etc., also to try to ensure continued effective operation.
3. *Preventive maintenance* will often be provided on a regular basis and/or as seen to be required in order to try to sustain satisfactory operation of items or equipment. During preventive maintenance, components which are liable to failure may be changed prior to the end of their working life. But nevertheless
4. *Breakdown maintenance* (*i.e. repair*) will normally be required so that items and equipment might be returned to satisfactory operation. And eventually
5. *Replacement* of items and equipment will occur when they are no longer capable of satisfactory operation and are beyond economic repair.

The relationship of these five activities is outlined in Figure 20.1: 1 to 4 above can be seen to be part of the maintenance function, while 5 is concerned with replacement. Initially in this chapter we shall consider maintenance, and then the problem of replacement.

THE MAINTENANCE FUNCTION

Equipment of whatever type, however complex or simple, however cheap or expensive, is liable to breakdown. Thus in manufacture, supply, transport and service not only must procedures exist for equipment maintenance, but also the inevitability of breakdowns and disruption of operation must be considered during capacity planning and activity scheduling. The effective operation of any system is dependent on the maintenance of all parts of the system, e.g. machines, buildings, services. In this chapter we shall be concerned only with the maintenance of mechanical rather than human facilities, although, in concept at least, the maintenance requirement also applies to workers. Indeed, company welfare or personnel practice may be designed partly as a maintenance activity, e.g. training and retraining to maintain the availability of appropriate skills, medical facilities to maintain human capacity, counselling to maintain interest and motivation.

A UK Government Report[1] has shown that manufacturing industry wastes large sums of money each year because of ineffective and badly organized maintenance. The report indicated that although the loss to manufacturing industry directly attributable to poor performance was estimated at £550 million, the total loss to British industry deriving from similar causes was probably several times this figure. The report recognized that improvements in performance could be achieved only by the co-ordinated application of several disciplines which had not previously been brought together in such a way, and because no existing word adequately described this multi-disciplinary approach to the specification, design, installation, commissioning, use and disposal of facilities, equipment and buildings, the name 'terotechnology' was chosen. Terotechnology is a combination of management, financial, engineering and other practices applied to physical assets in pursuit of economic life-cycle costs. In practice it is concerned with the selection and provision of permanent physical resources used for the provision of goods and services, for the care of the resources, and for their co-ordination and improvement. Thus terotechnology comprises the practice of design, maintenance, replacement and repair. It

---

[1] Department of Industry's Report on Maintenance Engineering, HMSO, London, 1970.

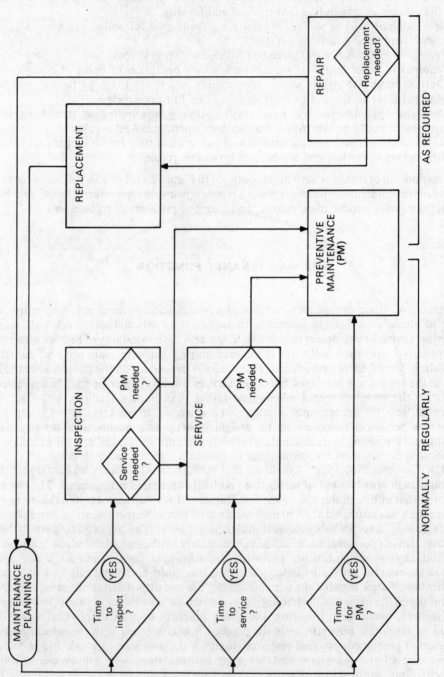

Figure 20.1 *Maintenance and replacement activities.*

is therefore a somewhat broader concept than discussed in this chapter; however, some consideration of this function will provide an adequate background for our discussion.

Figure 20.2 shows a typical life-cycle for a facility. The diagram indicates those activities required in conceiving, creating, providing, operating, maintaining and disposing of a physical facility. Taking maintenance from this set, it will be seen that many decisions and activities will affect the nature and amount of maintenance required. The design of the facility, both with regard to its design 'for function' and its design 'for maintainability and reliability', will influence operation, as will its installation and commissioning. The effectiveness of maintenance will influence the time available for and the time spent in operation. Thus the need for maintenance and the nature of the maintenance required are determined by a variety of factors. The maintenance function within an organization is therefore influenced by many other activities within the organization.

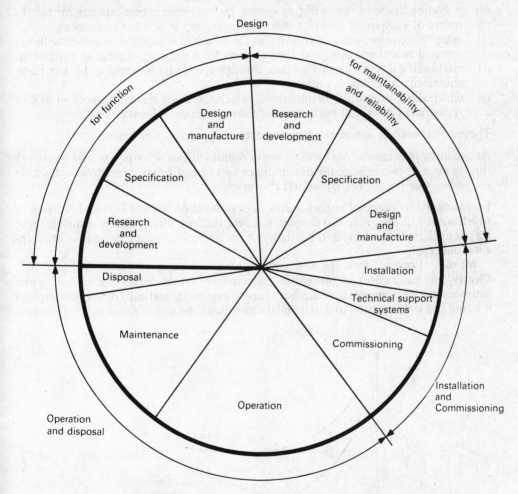

Figure 20.2 *The operating life-cycle of a facility.*

The objectives of maintenance

The purpose of maintenance is to attempt to maximize the performance of production equipment by ensuring that such equipment performs regularly and efficiently, by attempting to prevent breakdowns or failures, and by minimizing the production loss resulting from breakdowns or failures. In fact it is the objective of the maintenance function to maintain or increase the reliability of the operating system as a whole.

Many steps can be taken to ensure that such an objective is achieved, but only a few of these are normally considered to be the responsibility of the maintenance department. For example, each of the following will contribute to the reliability of the operating system:

(a) improvement of the quality of equipment and components through improved design and or 'tighter' manufacturing standards;

(b) improvements in the design of equipment to facilitate the replacement of broken items and inspection and routine maintenance work;

(c) improvements in the layout of equipment to facilitate maintenance work, i.e. providing space around or underneath equipment;

(d) providing 'slack' in the operating system, i.e. providing excess capacity so that the failure of equipment does not affect the performance of other equipment;

(e) using 'work-in-progress' to ensure that the failure of equipment is not immediately reflected in a shortage of materials or parts for a subsequent piece of equipment;

(f) establishing a repair facility so that, through speedy replacement of broken parts, equipment downtime is reduced;

(g) undertaking preventive maintenance, which, through regular inspection and/or replacement of critical parts, reduces the occurrence of breakdowns.

These points may be summarized in two overall objectives, which are:

(a) to attempt to ensure that breakdowns or failures do not occur (see (a) and (g) above);

(b) to attempt to minimize the disruption or loss caused by the breakdowns which do occur (see (b), (c), (d), (e) and (f) above).

Excluding the influence of improvements in equipment design and layout, discussion of which is not appropriate to this chapter, it is clear that two distinct facets of maintenance may contribute to the increased reliability of the operating system: preventive maintenance and repair.

We can, of course, draw the now familiar total cost curve as shown in Figure 20.3. Clearly, increased effort in preventive maintenance should reduce the cost of repair maintenance. Were we able to define both these curves mathematically or graphically, then it would be a simple matter to determine the minimum cost maintenance policy. However,

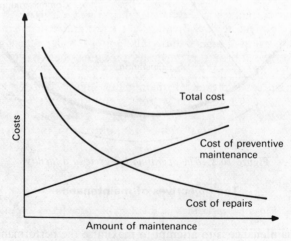

Figure 20.3 *Maintenance costs.*

as might be expected, the problem is not as simple as this, and consequently maintenance policy is substantially more difficult to determine.

MAINTENANCE DECISIONS

It will be seen from the above that several decisions are required in the establishment of a comprehensive maintenance policy for any set of facilities. We can consider the establishment of a maintenance policy as comprising three necessary and interdependent decisions:

1. Which items, facilities, etc., are to be maintained?
2. What kind of maintenance will be applied in each case?
3. How is this maintenance work to be organized?

What is to be maintained?

Any maintenance activity incurs some cost. Inspection is costly in that it involves someone devoting some time to looking at an item or a facility, and that may mean that the operation of that facility has to be interrupted. Service work will be expensive and will not normally be possible while the facility is operating. Preventive maintenance will normally be undertaken while the facility is out of operation. To some extent all this work can be planned to take place at a time when the disruption caused by the inoperation of the facility is minimized, but of course breakdown maintenance can occur at any time and can be very disruptive, and can therefore be expensive in terms of both the direct effort involved and the time lost while the facility is repaired. If the cost of any of this maintenance exceeds the cost benefits obtained, then it may be cheaper simply to dispose of items when they eventually break down. Indeed in some situations the way in which the items work and the conditions in which they are employed necessitate such an approach. There will, therefore, be situations in which it will be decided that some items will not be maintained, except perhaps through regular inspection and service to avoid safety and health hazards. Furthermore, the manner in which items break down or are subject to failure may make it difficult to develop an effective preventive maintenance strategy. For example if the cost per unit of time of undertaking preventive maintenance is greater than the cost per unit of time of breakdown maintenance, then there will be a tendency to rely on the latter.

Although in some cases preventive maintenance may be inappropriate, and even breakdown maintenance, i.e. repair, may not be employed, in most cases facilities will require one or both of these approaches in addition to inspection and service. In these situations we must decide on the size of 'unit' to be maintained. Here there are three possible approaches:

1. A large system comprising several interdependent facilities can be considered as one 'unit' for maintenance purposes.
2. Single facilities can be considered to be the 'unit'.
3. Parts or subsections of a particular facility can be considered to be the 'unit' for which maintenance must be planned.

For example, in a manufacturing situation an entire system may comprise all the interdependent and interlinked machines on an assembly line, whereas the single-facility approach may involve the development of a maintenance plan for each of the separate machine tools and/or facilities in that system. The third approach would involve the planning of maintenance for appropriate parts of these separate facilities, e.g. electric motors. As a non-manufacturing example, a complete computer installation can be considered as a 'unit' for maintenance, or alternatively each device in that system, e.g. the central processor, terminals, printers, can be seen as a 'unit' for the development of separate maintenance plans, or a maintenance policy can be developed for the components, e.g. the printer circuit boards, within certain facilities. An entire hospital operating theatre can be considered as a 'unit' for manufacture, but if more appropriate a maintenance plan can be developed for the separate facilities within that system or for components within those facilities.

The extent to which the facilities within a larger system are interdependent, i.e. the extent to which the breakdown of one can cause disruption of the others, will influence the approach which will be employed. A system comprising similar facilities all installed at around the same time would perhaps be treated as an entire unit for maintenance purposes, whereas a system in which items, although linked together in some inter-dependent way, were installed at different times and have quite different reliability characteristics might encourage us to adopt the second approach. If an entire configur-ation of facilities operates continuously, then the entire system must be stopped when any part requires maintenance, and again there will be a tendency to see the entire system as the 'unit' for maintenance. On the other hand, where facilities operate intermittently, different facilities being idle at different times, then there will be a tendency to see each facility as a 'unit' for maintenance, since this provides the greatest opportunity for scheduling maintenance work. Where a system comprises several facilities, and where each facility has similar component parts, e.g. electric motors, and where the reliability and/or breakdown characteristics of these parts are known, the third approach above may be appropriate.

Types of maintenance

Inspection

Facilities will normally be inspected at intervals in order to determine whether service and/or preventive maintenance is required or is likely to be required in the near future. Such work may involve visual inspection or the measurement of certain of the physical characteristics of a facility. Inspection may involve the whole facility or simply those parts which are known to be liable to failure. One of the problems in planning inspection is to decide on the *inspection interval*. This problem will be tackled in the next section.

Service

This will involve the routine readjustment of equipment, lubrication, cleaning, etc. Such work will often be undertaken, if seen to be required, alongside inspection.

Preventive maintenance

Preventive maintenance is precautionary and is undertaken to try to prevent or delay breakdowns, and therefore the need for repair. Such preventive action may be undertaken according to a predetermined and regular schedule or when required. A regular schedule can be established for items which have known and fairly predictable reliability or breakdown characteristics. Preventive maintenance can be undertaken as and when required in circumstances where there is some evidence of deteriorating efficiency or impending breakdown. One of the problems, therefore, in planning preventive mainten-ance is to identify the type of approach which will be suitable in particular circumstances.

Repair

Breakdown maintenance or repair is remedial, taking place after an item has ceased to operate. The need for repair is not necessarily the result of inefficient or insufficient inspection, service and preventive maintenance, since in some cases the cost of repairs will be less than the accumulated cost of preventive work. One of the major problems in planning repair work is to decide on the amount of resources to be made available, since the larger the repair 'team' the shorter the repair time, but also the larger the amount of repair team idle time.

The organization of maintenance

Maintenance work can be performed by:

(a) the personnel who normally use the equipment;
(b) staff employed in a maintenance department by and within the organization;
(c) external maintenance personnel, e.g. under certain service contracts from equipment suppliers.

The first approach will often be employed for inspection and sometimes for service work. It may also be an appropriate approach where preventive maintenance activities are relatively straightforward and are undertaken as and when required, i.e. where some urgent preventive action is required without prior warning. It may be employed for repair work where the facility operator has specialist skills and knowledge, perhaps acquired through the use of the facility, which are not available to other personnel.

More often an organization will maintain a specialist 'maintenance department'. The staff and resources of this department will be employed in inspection, service, preventive maintenance and repair work, some of which can be undertaken on a scheduled basis. The main problems in organizing maintenance in this way are to decide on the size of the maintenance 'crew', the range of skills required, the amount of stocks to be held, the amount of standby equipment to be held in stock, etc.

Maintenance will be the responsibility of an external organization either where specialist equipment is involved or where a service or maintenance contract has been provided as a compulsory or normal part of the purchase contract for that equipment. Such situations are normal for computer installations, etc. The approach may also be appropriate where maintenance work is highly specialized or hazardous, but infrequent, e.g. the maintenance of complex installations or underwater installations.

The planning of effective maintenance, however undertaken, will require collection and maintenance of certain data. For example, a complete list of all facilities in use, their date of purchase and their maintenance history to date will normally be maintained. Statistics on operating life between failures, the time required to perform repair operations, etc., will be maintained so that decisions can be made about the scheduling of preventive work and the merits of preventive compared with repair maintenance.

The 'data base' of information on each facility will be updated regularly so that appropriate statistics, etc., can be extracted. Often such data will be held on a computer-based system, such a system being used to schedule maintenance, allocate maintenance resources, etc. (These will be discussed towards the end of this chapter.)

INSPECTION

Facilities will normally be inspected at intervals to determine whether maintenance is required or likely to be required in the near future. Often such inspection is disruptive, e.g. the operation of facilities may have to be halted while inspection is undertaken. On the other hand inspection might reasonably be expected to reduce the amount of time lost (downtime) through breakdowns. One problem, therefore, is to decide how much time to devote to inspection so that total downtime is minimized.

$$If\ T_T = \text{total downtime per unit time}$$
$$t_I = \text{downtime per inspection}$$
$$t_S = \text{downtime per breakdown}$$
$$N = \text{number of inspections per facility per unit time}$$
$$k = \text{a constant for a particular facility}$$

If the total time lost through inspection is a function of t_I and N, and if we assume that the total time lost through breakdowns is a function of t_S and inversely related to N, then:

$$T_T = t_I N + t_S \frac{k}{N}$$

Differentiating this equation with respect to N and equating to zero will give the optimum value of N. If t_I and t_S are constants:

$$N \text{ to minimize } T_T = \sqrt{t_S \times \frac{k}{t_I}}$$

EXAMPLE

$$t_S = 0.9 \text{ weeks}$$
$$t_1 = 0.2 \text{ weeks}$$

From experience it has been found that $k = 2$. Hence:

$$N_{opt} = \sqrt{0.9 \times \frac{2}{0.2}} = 3 \text{ per week}$$

PREVENTIVE MAINTENANCE

Although preventive maintenance is clearly an important means of increasing the reliability of equipment, it is not necessarily generally applicable.

We want to perform the minimum amount of preventive maintenance, since maintenance even of this type will be expensive in terms of labour and material costs, and possible costs of disrupting production. Ideally, therefore, we would like to perform our preventive maintenance of equipment just before it would otherwise have broken down. Such a policy is possible only if either, because of the nature of the equipment, we receive some advance warning of impending failure or if failure of equipment is perfectly predictable. Rarely is warning of impending failure of value in practice, since either the warning is insufficiently in advance of failure (e.g. a bearing smoking before seizing up) or the warning is itself associated with some loss of efficiency or capacity in the equipment. Optimum preventive maintenance, therefore, depends on a situation such as that shown by a in Figure 20.4 in which the operating life of equipment between breakdowns is perfectly constant. Rarely, however, will such a situation exist; indeed, it is more likely that one of the other curves shown in this figure will result, i.e.:

Curve b Random operating life, normally distributed about mean T_a.
Curve c Large probability of failure immediately after repair.

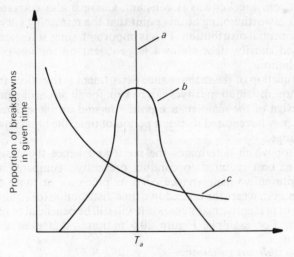

Operating life since last breakdown

Figure 20.4   *Operating life curves.*

The design of maintenance programmes depends to a large extent on the operating life characteristics of the equipment, a thorough investigation of which should be made by equipment manufacturers, trade associations or users prior to the determination of maintenance procedures. For convenience, such data are normally presented in the manner shown in Figure 20.5, such curves being referred to as *breakdown time distributions*. Obviously the nearer the actual breakdown time distribution approaches to the ideal distribution, a, the more appropriate and effective preventive maintenance will be.

In Figure 20.5 curve a corresponds to curve a of Figure 20.4, i.e. a situation in which the

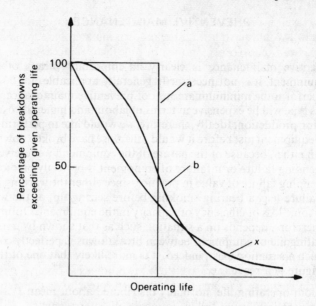

Figure 20.5   *Breakdown time distributions.*

operating life between breakdowns is constant. Curve b also corresponds to *b* in the previous figure. It is worth noting at this point that the remaining curve, *x*, corresponds closely to the exponential distribution. This is important, since statistical queuing theory, which will be used shortly, depends to a large extent on the use of the exponential probability distribution.

An important function of the maintenance department is to collect and record data so that breakdown time distribution curves can be kept for all pieces of equipment. Not only will the initial design of the maintenance policy depend on these data, but subsequent changes in policy may be required if, over a period of time, the breakdown characteristics of equipment change.

One other factor which determines the merit and hence the design of preventive maintenance is the cost required to conduct preventive, compared with breakdown, maintenance. If preventive maintenance costs as much as, or more than, breakdown maintenance, then, even where the breakdown time distribution for equipment permits the efficient adoption of preventive maintenance, it will still be beneficial to rely on breakdown maintenance only. For example, Figure 20.6 indicates that even though preventive

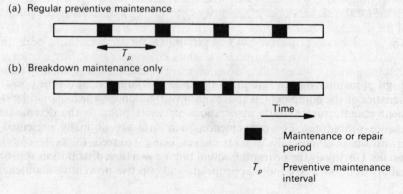

Figure 20.6   *The effect of maintenance durations.*

maintenance may result in fewer downtime periods, the total downtime and hence the cost are greater than they would have been if breakdown maintenance alone had been used.

It is not enough, however, to consider only the time factor, since even though preventive maintenance operations may be comparatively time-consuming, they may be scheduled to occur at convenient times, such as during holidays, weekends, or periods during which the load on equipment is low. We should, therefore, compare the costs of maintenance in order to evaluate the benefit of preventive maintenance.

Having established the conditions in which preventive maintenance is likely to be beneficial, let us now look more closely at the subject.

The scheduling of preventive maintenance for a single machine

One of the best treatments of this problem was developed by Morse.[2] If the breakdown time distribution approaches the ideal one, then, if preventive maintenance is used effectively, one would expect comparatively few breakdowns to occur. On the other hand, if the distribution is more variable, then, even if preventive maintenance is used, breakdowns may still occur, i.e. a breakdown may occur before the next preventive maintenance operation is due. If we let

T_p = fixed preventive maintenance interval, i.e. the time period between successive preventive maintenance operations on the same item of equipment
T_m = average time required to perform a preventive maintenance operation
T_s = average time required to perform a repair
T_a = average operating life without breakdowns;

and if we further assume that maintenance on a piece of equipment, whether it is preventive maintenance or repair maintenance, is equally effective in that both leave the equipment with the same probable operating life, then it has been shown by Morse that the operating efficiency of equipment, in terms of the percentage of time spent running, is a function of the ratio of the preventive maintenance interval to the average operating life, i.e. T_p/T_a.

Using this relationship, curves can be drawn like those in Figure 20.7. Notice that where the preventive maintenance interval is short in comparison with the average operating life, the operating efficiency of the equipment is low because a large proportion of the time is spent in preventive maintenance. On the other hand, as the preventive maintenance period is increased in comparison with the average operating life, then a larger number of breakdowns will occur. Notice also that where the breakdown time distribution *does not* approach the ideal situation, operating efficiency continues to increase as the comparative length of the preventive maintenance interval increases, whereas in the situation shown by curve *b*, in which the operating life has low variability, the curve reaches a peak. In other words, the use of preventive maintenance enables equipment operating efficiency to be maximized only when the variability on equipment operating life is small. We can, as a general rule, consider that preventive maintenance leads to an optimal policy for breakdown time distributions which have variability less than the exponential distribution (curve *x*).

It has been mentioned previously that the merit of preventive maintenance also depends on the relative time required for preventive maintenance operations. Figure 20.8 shows how an increase in the size of T_m (the time required for preventive maintenance) relative to

[2] Morse, P. M. (1958) *Queues, Inventories and Maintenance*. London: Wiley.

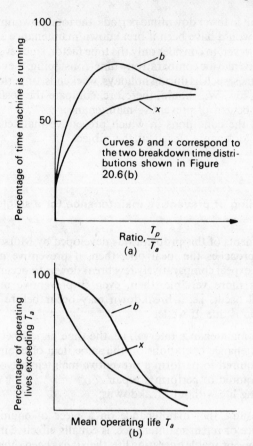

Curves *b* and *x* correspond to
the two breakdown time distributions shown in Figure
20.6(b)

Ratio, $\dfrac{T_p}{T_a}$

(a)

Mean operating life T_a

(b)

Figure 20.7   *Breakdown time distributions.*

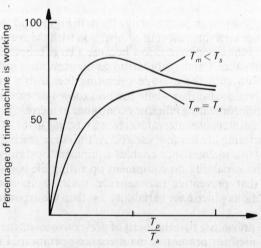

$T_m < T_s$

$T_m = T_s$

N B   Both of these curves correspond to breakdown
time distributions with low variability, i.e. curve *b* in
Figure 20.7

Figure 20.8

T_s (the time required for repair) reduces or eliminates the advantages previously offered by the preventive maintenance policy.

Clearly, if the breakdown time distribution for equipment is known, or can be obtained from records, then, using the method developed by Morse, the merits of a preventive maintenance policy, and the optimum preventive maintenance interval, can be established.

This is clearly not an appropriate place in which to study statistical queuing theory, since it can be a complex subject. It is, however, necessary to touch briefly upon the subject in order to deal more satisfactorily with preventive maintenance.

We have pointed out above that only where breakdown time distributions show comparatively little variability will preventive maintenance produce an optimal result. We should, therefore, discuss only those cases in which variability is less than that of the exponential distribution (curve x in Figure 20.9). The solution of the preventive maintenance planning problem depends on the use of queuing theory, and it so happens that useful queuing theory formulae have been developed for two types of situation which occur frequently in practice. The first deals with the exponential case mentioned above and the second deals with the case where the *Erlang* distribution applies. The precise nature of this distribution need not concern us here, and it is sufficient to say that the Erlang distribution covers those distributions which show variability equal to or less than the exponential. For example, curve x in Figure 20.9 as well as being an exponential distribution, is also one of a family of Erlang distributions, as are the remaining curves in this figure. (The parameter l is the only parameter which determines the variability of the distribution.)

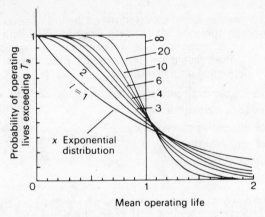

Figure 20.9 *Erlang breakdown time distributions (Figures 20.9 and 20.10 adapted with permission from Morse, P. M. (1958) Queues, Inventories and Maintenance. New York: Wiley.)*

If we adopt the following further notation:

G = Value of the output of the machine (£/unit of time)
C_m = Cost per unit time of preventive maintenance
C_s = Cost per unit time of repair

then the optimal value of T_p—the preventive maintenance interval—can be obtained from the curves shown in Figure 20.10. To use these curves, the appropriate value of l is found by comparing the breakdown time distribution with the Erlang distribution. The factor on the y axis is calculated from known values of T_m, T_s, C_m, C_s and G, and hence the ratio T_p/T_a is obtained. From this, since T_a is known, T_p can be calculated.

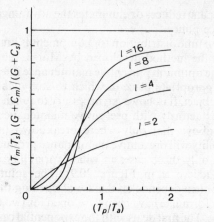

Figure 20.10 *Curves for determining the optimum period, T_p, for preventive maintenance for different degrees of variability of breakdown time distribution (see Figure 20.9) and for different values of the ratio $T_m (G + C_m)/T_s (G + C_s)$ (explained in the text).*

EXAMPLE

From data concerning a capstan lathe, collected over a period of several years, it has been established that the average operating life between breakdowns is four weeks and that the breakdown time distribution corresponds approximately to an Erlang distribution with $l = 4$. Given the following information, determine the optimum regular interval at which preventive maintenance should be performed on this machine.

Average time for preventive maintenance operation on lathe	= 2 hours
Average time for a repair to lathe	= 4 hours
Cost/hour of preventive maintenance	= £3
Cost/hour of repair work	= £6
Value of output of this lathe	= £25/hour

Answer:

$$\left(\frac{T_m}{T_s}\right)\left(\frac{G + C_m}{G + C_s}\right) = \left(\frac{2}{4}\right)\left(\frac{25 + 3}{25 + 6}\right) = 0.452$$

From Figure 20.10, for $l = 4$:

$$\frac{T_p}{T_a} = 0.9$$

Since $T_a = 4$ weeks, preventive maintenance interval, $T_p = 3.6$ weeks.

What would be the effect on the optimum preventive maintenance interval if:

(a) the average time for a repair was equal to the average time for a preventive maintenance operation;
(b) the breakdown time distribution for the lathe corresponded to an Erlang distribution with $l = 1$?

Answer: (a)

$$\left(\frac{T_m}{T_s}\right)\left(\frac{G + C_m}{G + C_s}\right) = 0.901$$

hence for $l = 4$ there is no solution for T_p/T_a. In other words, in such circumstances there is no benefit in preventive maintenance.

(b) There is also no solution for T_p/T_a for $l = 1$, i.e. because the breakdown variance is large (no better than the exponential distribution), preventive maintenance is not appropriate.

Scheduling preventive maintenance for several machines

The foregoing discussion has dealt only with the planning, i.e. the scheduling, of preventive maintenance for single machines.

We should, of course, also look at the scheduling of preventive maintenance for multi-machine systems, but to do so would necessitate a prior detour through rather complex statistical theory which would be inappropriate in this book. Multi-machine systems differ from single-machine systems in that machine idle time may result if a machine breaks down while the maintenance team are engaged in the repair of another machine. Such a situation is, therefore, similar to the multi-machine assignment problem in which interference may occur (see Chapter 12). Indeed, were we concerned only with the repair of machines rather than repair *and* preventive maintenance, the two situations would be analogous. In the present context, however, we are concerned with the possibility of using regular preventive maintenance to reduce the occurrence of breakdowns. This, of course, adds considerably to the complexity of the situation. Readers may wish to note that a good treatment of this problem, using a Markov chain approach, has been presented by Bovaird.[3] In the next section we shall consider the 'repair only' maintenance policy for several machines.

REPAIRS

Consider now the situation in which several machines of the same type are to be maintained. Furthermore, let us consider a policy which provides only for repair maintenance and not for preventive maintenance (a policy which might have been adopted because of large variability in breakdown time distributions).

Providing appropriate assumptions are made about the nature of breakdowns and repair time, the design of a maintenance system for such a situation can be accomplished by using conventional queuing theory.

Clearly, machine idle time caused by waiting for service by a maintenance team currently engaged on another machine can be reduced if the time needed to repair machines is reduced. Reduction in machine repair time, T_s, can normally be achieved by devoting more resources to maintenance, i.e. by increasing the size of the maintenance team. Such action, however, will increase costs; consequently the problem is one of achieving an acceptable balance between, on the one hand, the cost incurred by machine idle time due to breakdowns, and on the other hand the cost of the maintenance facility.

Let us first consider the case in which only *one maintenance team* looks after several identical machines. If we consider the breakdown time distribution to be exponential with

[3] Bovaird, R. L. (1961) Characteristics of optimal maintenance policies, *Management Science*, 7 (3) pp. 238–254.

average operating life $= T_a$, then it is reasonable that our maintenance policy should rely only on repairs, since preventive maintenance is unlikely to reduce costs. Let us further consider that the repair time is also exponentially distributed with an average of T_s. Such assumptions, which often correspond quite closely with reality, enable statistical queuing theory to be adopted. Using this approach Figure 20.11 can be calculated (see Morse, 1958). This shows the average number of machines running as a function of the ratio T_a/T_s where K is the number of machines allocated to one maintenance team.

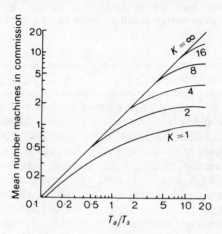

Figure 20.11 *Mean number of machines working: for K machines and for the exponential breakdown distribution.*

An examination of this figure shows that for large values of T_a/T_s the number of machines running differs only slightly from the total number of machines, K. For example, if $T_a/T_s = 10$, then if the system contains four machines ($K = 4$) the average number running over a period of time is approximately 3.5. If, however, the ratio of T_a/T_s falls, because of either reduced reliability of the machines or increased average repair times (T_s) then, naturally, the efficiency of the whole system falls. In fact it seems that, in order to maintain a reasonably efficient system, $T_a/T_s \geqslant K$.

This figure enables us to assess the cost of machine idle time due to breakdowns and time spent waiting for repair.

To assess the cost of the maintenance team, Figure 20.12 may be used. This shows the proportion of time that the maintenance team is busy, as a function of KT_s/T_a.

EXAMPLE

A single maintenance team is to be responsible for repairs to eight identical machine tools. It has been found from experience that the breakdown time distribution for the machines corresponds to the exponential distribution, as does that for the repair times. Because of a high and stable demand from customers, the operation planning department has scheduled operations making the assumption that the average number of machines that will be running is six. If the average operating life of the machines is seven five-day weeks, what average repair time should the maintenance department aim at providing, and how busy will the team be?

From Figure 20.11 the ratio T_a/T_s corresponding to $K = 8$ and 6 on the y axis is 7, i.e.

$$\frac{T_a}{T_s} = 7$$

$$T_s = \frac{7 \times 5}{7}$$

$$T_s = 5 \text{ days}$$

$$K\frac{T_s}{T_a} = \frac{8 \times 5}{7 \times 5} = 1.14$$

Therefore percentage of time team is occupied = 82 per cent (from Figure 20.12).

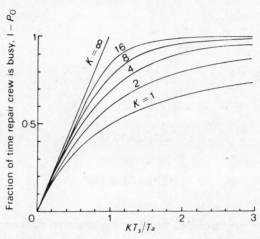

Figure 20.12 *Mean fraction of time the repair team is busy: for K machines and for the exponential breakdown distribution. (Figures 20.11 and 20.12 from Morse, P. M. (1958) Queues, Inventories and Maintenance. New York: Wiley. Reproduced with permission.)*

Now let us consider a situation in which there is more than one maintenance team responsible for the repair of a set of identical machines. Let us assume again both exponential breakdown characteristics and exponential service times for all maintenance teams. If the breakdowns are attended to on a 'first come, first served' basis, then curves such as those shown in Figure 20.13 can be constructed. One interesting point is evident from these curves. It can be seen that the use of one maintenance team performing the repair work twice as quickly as each of two teams is superior to the use of the two slower teams. For example, consider a situation in which there are four machines, where $T_a = 4$ days. Suppose that there is a choice of using one quite large maintenance team which is capable of an average repair time of $\frac{1}{2}$ day *or* two smaller teams each capable of average repair times of 1 day, then in both cases $MT_a/T_s = 8$, but it can be seen from Figure 20.13 that the use of one team ($M = 1$) results in an average number of approximately 3.7 machines working, whereas the use of two teams results in an average of 3.5 machines working.

Clearly, if our objective is the reduction in machine idle time, then it is better, where possible, to use a single fast maintenance team rather than two or more slower ones.

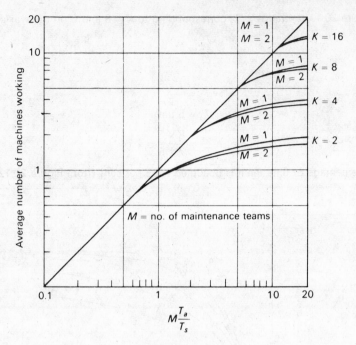

Figure 20.13

REPLACEMENT

Replacement policies for items subject to sudden failure

When a machine stops because of the failure of one component, then the maintenance team may simply go along to the machine and effect a repair by replacing the broken component. An alternative strategy is to replace not only the broken component but also all similar components, on the assumption that since they have all been in service for some length of time, because one has already failed the others are also likely to fail in the near future. Or a third strategy might be adopted: the replacement of the broken component and *certain* of the similar components.

As an example, consider the problem faced by someone whose job is to replace, when necessary, the bulbs in the lights of every room of a multi-storey building. The replacement strategies may be as follows:

1. Replace only those bulbs that fail. Such a strategy may involve an excessive amount of work, since replacing a bulb takes an average of 30 minutes erecting a ladder, obtaining new bulbs from stores, etc. Because of the difference between the comparatively low cost of a new bulb and the comparatively high cost of replacement, an alternative strategy may be preferred.
2. When one bulb fails, replace *all* bulbs in that room or on that floor.
3. Alternatively, as a compromise, replace the bulb that has failed *and* a proportion of other bulbs, perhaps those that have been in use for longer than six months, in other words those that are expected to fail fairly soon.

The problem then is to decide which of these strategies to adopt, a decision which must, of course, be made on the basis of cost considerations. The cost involved in replacement is dependent on the probability of component failure. In the case of strategy 1 the probable total cost of maintenance over, say, a year is given by the following:

$$\text{Cost of making a single replacement} \times \text{Probable number of failures during year}$$

In the case of strategy 2, the total cost is determined by the number of components replaced each time and the number of 'first failures' during the period. In the final strategy, 3, the cost would depend on the number of 'first failures' and the number of components at every replacement period which have been in use longer than a given time.

Although it is possible to develop formulae for the replacement problem in which items are subject to sudden failure, such formulae are often inadequate for the practical situation; consequently the choice of replacement strategy is often made with the aid of a simulation exercise, a procedure which will be adopted here.

It should be noted that, although we have spoken of the problem as being one of repair, similar considerations might apply during preventive maintenance. For example, if during the inspection of a machine for preventive maintenance purposes a component is seen to be likely to fail if left in service, then it must be decided whether or not to replace this component only, or some or all of the similar components. The logic behind the latter strategy is that, while some components do not yet show signs of impending failure, they are nevertheless likely to fail before the next scheduled maintenance period.

Simulation of replacement policies

Before using a simple example to illustrate this technique it is perhaps appropriate to consider the merits and purpose of simulation.

Very often it is impractical to contemplate manipulation or experiment in an industrial situation. It is inconceivable, for example, that we should determine an optimum stock control policy deliberately by trial and error, since to do so may incur considerable financial loss before a satisfactory solution is achieved. In such a situation we might solve our problems by recourse to theory, i.e. by using mathematical expressions which are known to be an adequate description of the situation concerned. Often, however, this is not possible, since in complex situations adequate formulae and equations cannot be obtained. In this type of situation simulation is invaluable, since it enables us to experiment with and manipulate a situation *on paper* and thus develop satisfactory solutions or procedures.

A type of simulation much used is the Monte Carlo method, which essentially involves the use of random sampling from distributions of variables. You will recall that on several occasions throughout this book we have made assumptions about the nature of distributions, often considering them to be normal, exponential, Poisson, etc., thus enabling us to develop statistical decision rules. When distributions of variables do not conform to one of these types then a simulation procedure must be adopted, often the Monte Carlo method in which use is made of the *actual* distribution of the variable rather than a convenient approximation to it.

EXAMPLE

Consider the case of one machine which has four identical bearings, each subject to the same operating conditions.

The manufacturer is able to provide us with a probability distribution for the life of these bearings (Table 20.1), which does not, however, conform to any of the conventional types of statistical probability distribution.

Our own maintenance and costing departments are able to tell us, from an analysis of past work sheets:

(a) that the time required to replace these bearings is as follows:
    (i)   to replace one bearing = 2 work hours;
    (ii) to replace two bearings = 4 work hours;
    (iii) to replace three bearings = 5 work hours;
    (iv) to replace four bearings = 7 work hours;
(b) that the relevant maintenance costs are as follows:
    (i)   cost of bearing   = £3 each;
    (ii) direct labour cost of maintenance = £2/worker/hour;
    (iii) cost of idle or machine downtime = £15/hour/machine.

We have to decide which of the three repair strategies to adopt for this particular machine.

First, we must construct a cumulative probability curve from the data given in Table 20.1. This is shown in Figure 20.14. Now we can use this figure to simulate the failure of bearings and to test the three repair strategies. To do this we also need random number tables.[4]

Table 20.1 *Probability of bearings failure*

Bearing life (hours)	Number of failures	Cumulative number of failures	Cumulative percentage of failures
0—49	0	0	0
50—99	1	1	1
100—149	3	4	4
150—199	5	9	9
200—249	9	18	18
250—299	16	34	34
300—349	24	58	58
350—399	20	78	78
400—449	13	91	91
450—499	6	97	97
500—549	2	99	99
550—599	1	100	100
	100		

The simulation is performed by first drawing any series of random numbers from random number tables, which are then used to enable us to take a random sample from the cumulative probability distribution in order to determine the simulated bearing operating life.

For example, consider bearing no. 1. If the first random number taken from four-figure random number tables is 2251, since we wish to sample from a scale of 0 to 100, we consider this to represent 22.5 per cent on the *y* axis of Figure 20.14. A horizontal line from this point cuts the cumulative probability curve at a point corresponding to 238 on the *x* axis, hence the life of the first no. 1 bearing is taken to be 238 hours.

Similarly the life of the first ten no. 1 bearings might be found to be:

Random (number)	Operating life (hours)
2251	238
7459	363
9380	450

---

[4] Tables of random numbers or digits are available in most testbooks on statistics.

Random (number)	Operating Life (hours)
2212	235
9237	440
3975	285
3278	270
1621	215
0413	125
3249	270

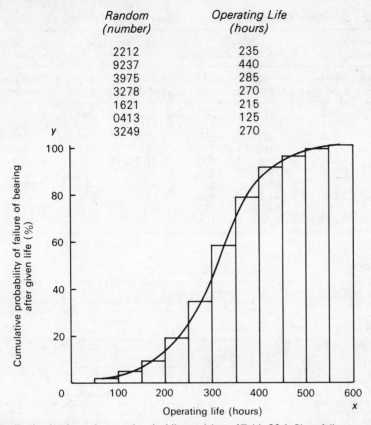

N.B. This distribution has been drawn using the 'discrete' data of Table 20.1. Since failure may occur at any time, probability of failure is a 'continuous' function, hence the continuous curve is used in the simulation.

Figure 20.14 *Cumulative probability of failure of bearings*

By drawing more random numbers, the probable life of several of all four bearings can be determined, as shown in Table 20.2. These figures can now be used in the simulation of the three repair strategies:

1. Replace bearings individually on failure
2. Replace all bearings together whenever one of them fails.
3. Replace the bearing that fails and at the same time replace those that have been in service for over 335 hours (the average operating life).

The simulation is shown by bar charts in Figure 20.15. For the first strategy the simulation merely consists of the operating life figures for the bearings taken from Table 20.2 arranged sequentially on a common timescale.[5] For the second strategy each replacement is occasioned by the failure of only one bearing (shown by a solid line), the other three being replaced at the same time as a matter of policy (shown by dotted lines). The simulation for the third strategy is more involved. Initially bearings are replaced one at a time because, when each failure occurs, none of the others has been in service for more than the specified time (335 hours), and hence do not require replacing. However, on the fourth replacement of bearing no. 4 it is found that bearing no. 1 has already been in service for a period in excess of 335 hours. Consequently it is replaced.[6] A similar situation occurs on four other occasions (shown by dotted lines).

---

[5] Notice that, for reasons of simplicity, we have not attempted to include the comparatively short periods of time required for replacement on any of these charts.

[6] In fact at this time bearing no. 1 has been in service for 379 hours, i.e. $(325 + 175 + 240 + 240) - (238 + 363)$.

Table 20.2 *Simulated operative life for ten of each of four bearings*

Bearing no. 1		Bearing no. 2		Bearing no. 3		Bearing no. 4	
Random number	Life	Random number	Life	Random number	Life	Random number	Life
2251	238	3711	280	2235	240	5761	325
7459	363	0347	115	0212	100	0983	175
9380	450	5034	310	3768	280	2236	240
2212	235	7816	375	6889	350	2250	240
9237	440	1385	200	2782	255	3053	265
3975	285	7823	375	3316	275	9938	550
3278	270	9942	550	8733	410	9360	450
1621	215	9019	430	1994	230	4558	300
0413	125	6307	335	6254	340	8015	380
3249	270	1873	225	0630	150	6104	330

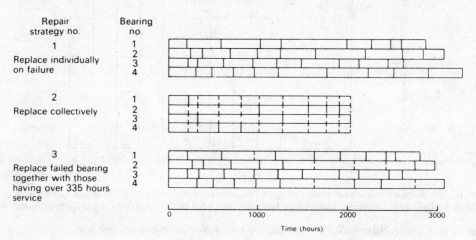

Figure 20.15

Now let us consider the maintenance cost incurred by each of these strategies. Let us consider a 2000-hour period and look first at strategy 1:

Number of replacements	= 24
Maintenance cost	= 24 × 2 hours × £2
	= £96
Cost of machine idle time	= 24 × 2 hours × £15
	= £720
Cost of bearings	= 24 × 3
	= £72
	Total cost = £888

Now consider strategy 2:

Number of replacements	= 9 (each involving 4 bearings)
Maintenance cost	= 9 × 7 × 2
	= £126
Cost of machine idle time	= 9 × 7 × 15
	= £945
Cost of bearings	= 36 × 3
	= £108
	Total cost = £1179

Now consider strategy 3:

Number of replacements	= 20 of 1 bearing
	1 of 2 bearings
	1 of 3 bearings
Maintenance cost	$= 20 \times 2 \times 2 = 80$
	$+1 \times 4 \times 2 = 8$
	$+1 \times 5 \times 2 = 10$
	$= £98$
Cost of machine idle time	$= 20 \times 2 \times 15 = 600$
	$+1 \times 4 \times 15 = 60$
	$+1 \times 5 \times 15 = 75$
	$= £735$
Cost of bearings	$= 25 \times 3$
	$= £75$
Total cost	$= £908$

The results of this simulation show that, considered over a 2000-hour operating period, it is economically advisable to adopt replacement strategy 1, since this incurs less cost than strategy 3 and substantially less cost than strategy 2.

In practice such a simulation would be conducted over a considerably longer period than the 2000 hours used here, since it is essential to ensure that the simulated situation has stabilized itself. By using the comparatively short period adopted here we run the risk of selecting a replacement policy which in the longer term may not be optimal. Furthermore, in practice such a simulation would be conducted with the aid of a computer, since manual simulation for a long time-period would be very tedious and time-consuming. (In this example, simulation of strategy 3 over a period much longer than 2000 hours would be extremely laborious.)

Replacement policies for items which deteriorate

The cost of operating equipment and machinery normally increases with the increasing age of the equipment. Such increasing cost may be caused by: (a) the increasing cost of the maintenance necessary to obtain continuing reliability of the equipment; and (b) the obsolescence of the equipment, making its continued operation comparatively more costly when compared with the equipment which might be used to replace it. There comes a time, therefore, when it is not only economically justifiable to replace the present ageing equipment, but economically beneficial in order to obtain equipment which has greater output, reliability, etc.

Our present problem, then is to decide at what time such equipment should be replaced. Such a decision must obviously be made on economic grounds, by a comparison of the net economic benefit of retaining present equipment and the net economic benefit of replacing present equipment.

As regards *present* equipment we must consider the following:

(a) its life;
(b) its current and future salvage or sale value;
(c) the revenue produced throughout the rest of its life;
(d) the expenditure incurred throughout the rest of its life.

As regards the *proposed* replacement equipment we must consider:

(a) the purchase price of the equipment;
(b) its life;
(c) the salvage or sale value at various times in its life;
(d) the revenue produced by the equipment;
(e) the expenditure incurred throughout its life.

In considering the replacement of equipment it is important to remember that money has a time value. For example, £100 is of more value to us now than it would be next year. The evaluation of the economic worth of equipment, therefore, depends on both its earning potential and time considerations. We must therefore make our replacement decisions by considering the *present value* of the net revenue associated with its use.

If i = annual rate of interest, then £100 now is worth

$$\frac{100}{(1+i)^n} \text{ in } n \text{ years' time}$$

e.g. £100 is worth $100/1.1^2 = £82.6$ in two years' time.

Suppose that the investment of £10 000 in a new piece of equipment results in a net income of £5000 for each of the following three years. If we assume that the 'cost of capital' or the rate of interest which might have been achieved had the £10 000 been invested is 10 per cent, then the *present value* of this income is £12 434, i.e.

$$\frac{5000}{(1.1)} + \frac{5000}{(1.1)^2} + \frac{5000}{(1.1)^3}$$

$$= £12 434$$

The calculation of present values in this way, by *discounting* future sums of money at a given rate, is the basis of the *discounted cash flow* technique for investment appraisal.

When concerned with equipment replacement, this discounting procedure can be expressed by the following equation:

$$NPV = \left(\sum_{n=1}^{L} \frac{I_n - E_n}{(1+i)^n} \right) + \frac{S_L}{(1+i)^L}$$

Where NPV = net present value
I_n = income for year n
E_n = expenditure for year n
i = discount rate
L = life of equipment or number of years being considered
S_L = sale or scrap value at end of life, i.e. year N

Clearly, to be economically beneficial the net present value (NPV) must be equal to or greater than zero.

To assist discounted cash flow calculations, tables for $1/(1+i)^n$ have been prepared (see Table 20.3).

The replacement decision normally takes the following form: whether to replace existing equipment now, or at a later date, up to and including the last year in the life of the existing equipment. The problem then is one of comparing, at *present value*, the cash flows associated with the use of the present and the proposed equipment over the common period from the present time to the end of the life of the present equipment. Naturally cash flows that have already occurred do not enter into the decision—for example, past operating costs of present equipment. We are concerned only with the cash flows that will result from the decision to retain the equipment and the decision to replace it, i.e. the operating costs, the revenues and the changes in disposal values.

Table 20.3 *Compound interest table* $(1/(1+i)^n)$

n	i = 1%	2	3	4	5	6	7	8	9	10
1	0.9901	0.9804	0.9709	0.9615	0.9524	0.9434	0.9346	0.9259	0.9174	0.9091
2	0.9803	0.9612	0.9426	0.9246	0.9070	0.8900	0.8734	0.8573	0.8417	0.8264
3	0.9706	0.9423	0.9151	0.8890	0.8638	0.8396	0.8163	0.7938	0.7722	0.7513
4	0.9610	0.9238	0.8885	0.8548	0.8227	0.7921	0.7629	0.7350	0.7084	0.6830
5	0.9515	0.9057	0.8626	0.8219	0.7835	0.7473	0.7130	0.6806	0.6499	0.6209
6	0.9420	0.8880	0.8375	0.7903	0.7462	0.7050	0.6663	0.6302	0.5963	0.5645
7	0.9327	0.8706	0.8131	0.7599	0.7107	0.6651	0.6227	0.5835	0.5470	0.5132
8	0.9235	0.8535	0.7894	0.7307	0.6768	0.6274	0.5820	0.5403	0.5019	0.4665
9	0.9143	0.8368	0.7664	0.7026	0.6446	0.5919	0.5439	0.5002	0.4604	0.4241
10	0.9053	0.8302	0.7441	0.6756	0.6139	0.5584	0.5083	0.4632	0.4224	0.3588
11	0.8963	0.8043	0.7224	0.6496	0.5847	0.5268	0.4751	0.4289	0.3875	0.3505
12	0.8874	0.7885	0.7014	0.6246	0.5568	0.4970	0.4440	0.3971	0.3555	0.3186
13	0.8787	0.7730	0.6810	0.6006	0.5303	0.4688	0.4150	0.3677	0.3262	0.2897
14	0.8700	0.7579	0.6611	0.5775	0.5051	0.4423	0.3878	0.3405	0.2992	0.2633
15	0.8613	0.7430	0.6419	0.5553	0.4810	0.4173	0.3624	0.3152	0.2745	0.2394
16	0.8528	0.7284	0.6232	0.5339	0.4581	0.3936	0.3387	0.2919	0.2519	0.2176
17	0.8444	0.7142	0.6050	0.5134	0.4363	0.3714	0.3166	0.2703	0.2311	0.1978
18	0.8360	0.7002	0.5874	0.4936	0.4155	0.3503	0.2959	0.2502	0.2120	0.1799
19	0.8277	0.6864	0.5703	0.4746	0.3957	0.3305	0.2765	0.2317	0.1945	0.1635
20	0.8195	0.6730	0.5537	0.4564	0.3769	0.3118	0.2584	0.2145	0.1784	0.1486
21	0.8114	0.6598	0.5375	0.4388	0.3589	0.2942	0.2415	0.1987	0.1637	0.1351
22	0.8034	0.6468	0.5219	0.4220	0.3418	0.2775	0.2257	0.1839	0.1502	0.1228
23	0.7954	0.6432	0.5067	0.4057	0.3256	0.2618	0.2109	0.1703	0.1378	0.1117
24	0.7876	0.6217	0.4919	0.3901	0.3101	0.2470	0.1971	0.1577	0.1264	0.1015
25	0.7798	0.6095	0.4776	0.3751	0.2953	0.2330	0.1842	0.1460	0.1160	0.0923
26	0.7720	0.5976	0.4637	0.3607	0.2812	0.2198	0.1722	0.1352	0.1064	0.0839
27	0.7644	0.5859	0.4502	0.3468	0.2678	0.2074	0.1696	0.1252	0.0976	0.0763
28	0.7568	0.5744	0.4371	0.3335	0.2551	0.1956	0.1504	0.1159	0.0895	0.0693
29	0.7493	0.5631	0.4243	0.3207	0.2429	0.1846	0.1406	0.1073	0.0822	0.0630
30	0.7419	0.5521	0.4120	0.3083	0.2314	0.1741	0.1314	0.0994	0.0754	0.0573

where i = annual interest rate
n = number of years

EXAMPLE: REPLACEMENT OF A PHOTOCOPIER

The management of a company is anxious to determine whether or not to replace an existing photocopier with a new one of the latest type. The present machine has many years of useful service life left, but nevertheless it is thought that it may be better to obtain the new machine, which is known to have lower operating costs.

The cost of the new machine is £10 000 and its anticipated life is 20 years. The present machine is known to have a current disposal value of £5000 and an anticipated life of 16 years.

If the new machine is purchased an overhaul costing £2000 will be necessary after it has been in service for 10 years, and its disposal value after 16 and 20 years of service will be £500 and £200 respectively. If the present machine is retained, two overhauls will be required at 6 and 12 years, costing £2500 and £1500 respectively. Its disposal value after 16 years will be £150.

The net income (revenue less operating costs) which is expected to result from the use of the machines is shown in Table 20.4 along with the above data.

The net present value (using a discount rate of 10 per cent per annum) of the cash flows over the 16 years for each machine is also calculated in Table 20.4. The *NPV* of the cash flow associated with decision 1 (replace present machine) is £2278. The *NPV* of the cash flow associated with decision 2 is £4061. Clearly, therefore, it is in the company's interest to retain the present machine rather than replace it.

Table 20.4

Year	$\dfrac{1}{(1+i)^n}$	(1) Machine is replaced				(2) Machine is *not* replaced			
		Outlays (£)	Net income (£)	Net cash flow	PV	Outlays (£)	Net income (£)	Net cash flow	PV
0	1.000	10 000	5000	−5000	−5000				
1	0.909		1500	1500	1365		1000	1000	909
2	0.826		1400	1400	1155		1000	1000	826
3	0.751		1300	1300	980		1000	1000	751
4	0.683		1200	1200	820		900	900	615
5	0.620		1100	1100	685		800	800	498
6	0.564		1000	1000	565	2500	700	−1800	−1015
7	0.513		900	900	460		700	700	360
8	0.466		800	800	374		700	700	327
9	0.424		700	700	297		700	700	297
10	0.385	2000	600	−1400	−540		600	600	232
11	0.350		600	600	211		500	500	175
12	0.318		600	600	191	1500	400	−1100	−351
13	0.289		600	600	174		400	400	116
14	0.263		600	600	158		400	400	105
15	0.239		600	600	144		400	400	96
16	0.217		600 + 500	1100	239		400 + 150	550	120

$$NPV = \left(\sum_{n=1}^{16} \frac{I_n - E_n}{(1.1)^n} \right) + \frac{S_{16}}{(1.1)^{16}} = 2278 \qquad NPV = \left(\sum_{n=1}^{16} \frac{I_n - E_n}{(1.1)^n} \right) + \frac{S_{16}}{(1.1)^{16}} \qquad 4061$$

It should be remembered, of course, that the discounted cash flow technique takes no account of the following, all of which may influence the replacement decision:

(a) risk, i.e. the uncertainty of factors such as operating life, repair costs, disposal values, etc.;
(b) inflation;
(c) the timing of the cash flows in relation to opportunities for the use of the money elsewhere;
(d) the difficulty of raising money for the outlays;
(e) policy after the period considered;
(f) possible future development of improved equipment.

Despite these omissions, the discounted cash flow technique is undoubtedly of considerable value; however, as regards replacement policy, perhaps the major obstacle to its adoption is the difficulty of predicting future cash flows accurately. This difficulty is particularly acute in this case, since, when considering capital equipment such as machine tools, anticipated life is often quite long. Estimation of cash flows ten or more years ahead is often pure speculation; indeed, estimation of the life of equipment is often a hazardous procedure. Consequently it would be of considerable advantage to have available a rational decision-making procedure which depends on more immediate events, one which could be applied quickly and repeatedly if necessary, without the need for a major costing or forecasting exercise.

Such a system was developed by the Machinery and Allied Products Institute (MAPI) in America. Several versions of the MAPI system have existed since it was first developed in

1949;[7] however, each of these has been conceptually alike in that the objective of each version of the MAPI system has been the calculation of an *urgency rating*, which is a measure of the economic benefit associated with the replacement of equipment. In other words, the urgency rating is a measure of the urgency of making an investment as compared with delaying the investment for a period of time. In earlier MAPI systems the urgency rating was calculated by comparing, *for the next year only*, the relative economic merits of replacing equipment and retaining it; however, the current systems permits comparisons for periods longer than one year.

In the current system[8] the urgency rating is, in fact, a measure of the rate of return on the investment after tax, i.e.

$$\frac{\text{Operating advantage} - \text{Capital consumption}}{\text{Net investment}} \times 100$$

The calculation of this after-tax rate of return on investment is accomplished quite easily using the MAPI forms and charts shown in Figures 20.16 and 20.17.

PROJECT NO   SHEET 1

MAPI SUMMARY FORM
(AVERAGING SHORTCUT)

PROJECT **AUTOMATIC LATHE**
ALTERNATIVE **RETAIN EXISTING MANUAL LATHE**
COMPARISON PERIOD (YEARS)   (P)   **1**
ASSUMED OPERATING RATE OF PROJECT (HOURS PER YEAR)   **1500**

I. OPERATING ADVANTAGE
(NEXT-YEAR FOR A 1-YEAR COMPARISON PERIOD * ANNUAL AVERAGES FOR LONGER PERIODS)

A. EFFECT OF PROJECT ON REVENUE

		INCREASE	DECREASE	
1	FROM CHANGE IN QUALITY OF PRODUCTS	S	S	1
2	FROM CHANGE IN VOLUME OF OUTPUT	1000		2
3	TOTAL	S 1000 X	S Y	3

B. EFFECT ON OPERATING COSTS

		INCREASE	DECREASE	
4	DIRECT LABOR	S	S 750	4
5	INDIRECT LABOR	150		5
6	FRINGE BENEFITS			6
7	MAINTENANCE		200	7
8	TOOLING		500	8
9	MATERIALS AND SUPPLIES			9
10	INSPECTION		150	10
11	ASSEMBLY			11
12	SCRAP AND REWORK		100	12
13	DOWN TIME			13
14	POWER	100		14
15	FLOOR SPACE			15
16	PROPERTY TAXES AND INSURANCE			16
17	SUBCONTRACTING			17
18	INVENTORY			18
19	SAFETY			19
20	FLEXIBILITY			20
21	OTHER	175		21
22	TOTAL	S 425 Y	S 1700 X	22

C. COMBINED EFFECT

23	NET INCREASE IN REVENUE (3X – 3Y)	S 1000	23
24	NET DECREASE IN OPERATING COSTS (22X – 22Y)	S 1275	24
25	ANNUAL OPERATING ADVANTAGE (23 + 24)	S 2275	25

* Next year means the first year of project operation. For projects with a significant break-in period, use performance after break-in.

Figure 20.16

[7] Terborgh, G. (1949) *Dynamic Equipment Policy*. New York: McGraw-Hill.
[8] Terborgh, G. (1967) *Business Investment Management*. Washington DC: Machinery and Allied Products Institute.

II. INVESTMENT AND RETURN

A. INITIAL INVESTMENT

26	INSTALLED COST OF PROJECT MINUS INITIAL TAX BENEFIT OF	$ _____ $ _____ (Net Cost)	$ **9000**	26
27	INVESTMENT IN ALTERNATIVE CAPITAL ADDITIONS MINUS INITIAL TAX BENEFIT PLUS: DISPOSAL VALUE OF ASSETS RETIRED BY PROJECT*	$ _____ $ **500**	$ **500**	27
28	INITIAL NET INVESTMENT (26 27)		$ **8500**	28

B. TERMINAL INVESTMENT

29 RETENTION VALUE OF PROJECT AT END OF COMPARISON PERIOD
(ESTIMATE FOR ASSETS, IF ANY, THAT CANNOT BE DEPRECIATED OR EXPENSED. FOR OTHERS, ESTIMATE OR USE MAPI CHARTS.)

Item or Group	Installed Cost, Minus Initial Tax Benefit (Net Cost) A	Service Life (Years) B	Disposal Value, End of Life (Percent of Net Cost) C	MAPI Chart Number D	Chart Percentage E	Retention Value $\left(\dfrac{A \times E}{100}\right)$ F
Automatic Lathe	$ **9000**	**8**	**20**%	**1A**	**85**%	$ **7650**

	ESTIMATED FROM CHARTS (TOTAL OF COL. F) PLUS: OTHERWISE ESTIMATED	$ _____ $ _____	$ **7650**	29
30	DISPOSAL VALUE OF ALTERNATIVE AT END OF PERIOD*		$ **500**	30
31	TERMINAL NET INVESTMENT (29 30)		$ **7150**	31

C. RETURN

32	AVERAGE NET CAPITAL CONSUMPTION $\left(\dfrac{28-31}{P}\right)$	$ **1350**	32
33	AVERAGE NET INVESTMENT $\left(\dfrac{28+31}{2}\right)$	$ **7825.**	33
34	BEFORE TAX RETURN $\left(\dfrac{25-32}{33} \times 100\right)$	% **11.9**	34
35	INCREASE IN DEPRECIATION AND INTEREST DEDUCTIONS	$ **1000**	35
36	TAXABLE OPERATING ADVANTAGE (25-35)	$ **1275**	36
37	INCREASE IN INCOME TAX (36 × TAX RATE)	$ **510**	37
38	AFTER-TAX OPERATING ADVANTAGE (25 - 37)	$ **1765**	38
39	AVAILABLE FOR RETURN ON INVESTMENT (38 - 32)	$ **415**	39
40	AFTER-TAX RETURN $\left(\dfrac{39}{33} \times 100\right)$	% **5.3**	40

* After terminal tax adjustments.

Figure 20.17

EXAMPLE

Project: To evaluate the benefit of replacing an existing manual lathe by an automatic lathe.

Automatic lathe: cost   = £9000 (after adjustment for tax grant, etc.)
                 service life   = 8 years
                 disposal value after service = £1800
Existing lathe: present disposal value   = £500

Estimated savings for one year associated with replacement of existing lathe:

(a) increased output   £1000
(b) on direct labour   £750
(c) on maintenance   £200
(d) on tools and jigs   £500
(e) on acceptance inspection £150
(f) on scrap   £100

MAPI CHART No. 1A

(ONE-YEAR COMPARISON PERIOD AND SUM-OF-DIGITS TAX DEPRECIATION)

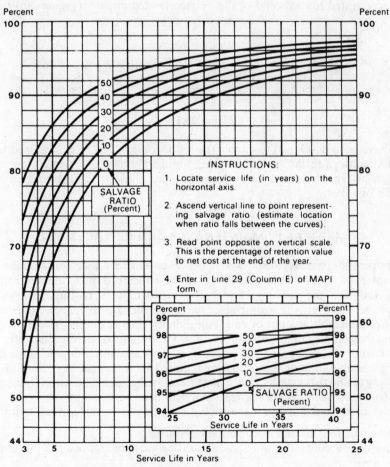

INSTRUCTIONS:

1. Locate service life (in years) on the horizontal axis.

2. Ascend vertical line to point representing salvage ratio (estimate location when ratio falls between the curves).

3. Read point opposite on vertical scale. This is the percentage of retention value to net cost at the end of the year.

4. Enter in Line 29 (Column E) of MAPI form.

Figure 20.18

Estimated added costs for one year associated with replacement of existing lathe:

(a) on indirect labour   £150
(b) on power   £100
(c) for conveyers and pallets £175
(d) increase in depreciation £1000

Tax rate = 40 per cent

The evaluation of this investment for a one-year period is undertaken by means of the standard MAPI forms (Figures 20.16 and 20.17). Chart No. 1A (Figure 20.18) has been used to estimate the retention value of the equipment at the end of the comparison period. It has been found that the after-tax return on the investment is only 5.3 per cent, thus indicating the low urgency of the project.

Perhaps the principal benefit of the MAPI system is the ease with which it can be used. The forms permit ready calculation of the 'operating advantage' and the capital consumption. Three methods are available for calculating the reduction in the value of the new equipment depending on whether depreciation is: (a) of the standard straight-line type; (b) accelerated towards end of life; (c) accelerated initially (Figure 20.19).

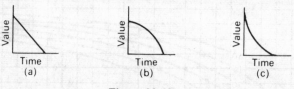

Figure 20.19

Charts have been developed to enable the reduction in value to be obtained without recourse to the use of formulae. For example, the chart shown in Figure 20.18 applies to depreciation of type (b) above. Likewise, charts are available for comparison periods longer than one year.

COMPUTERS IN MAINTENANCE AND REPLACEMENT

Few other operations management responsibilities cover such a wide area as maintenance management. The maintenance manager will be concerned with the acquisition of equipment and parts, the planning of work, the control of work, costing, quality control, etc. To operate effectively the maintenance manager will need to collect, store and have access to a considerable amount of data. Additionally complex decisions will have to be made about the planning of inspection, service work, preventive maintenance, etc., as well as the organization of repair and the planning of replacement. Given this range of tasks and the considerable amount of information required for the execution of these tasks, it is not surprising to find that maintenance departments are becoming increasingly committed to computer-based maintenance management systems.

Computer-based maintenance management systems can be categorized as follows:[9]

(a)   maintenance records and documentation systems;
(b)   maintenance records, documentation, decision-making and planning systems.

---

[9] Here we are ignoring the simpler application of computers for the solution of specific problems, such as the comparison of alternative replacement policies through simulation e.g. the BEARISM program in Harris, R.D. and Maggard, M.J. (1972) *Computer Models in Operations Management*. London: Harper and Row.

Many proprietary systems are available for use on micro- and mini-computers to provide (a) above. They offer the opportunity of storing data on equipment and inventories, producing work schedules and requirements, analysing plant history, labour costs, etc. They are essentially data processing systems rather than decision-making systems. One such system will be described below. The approach involved for (b) above involves such data processing but also provides for some decision-making. The use of such systems will enable preventive maintenance and inspection to be planned, replacement intervals to be determined, etc. This latter approach is, of course, more sophisticated and as yet there are relatively few examples of the use of such computer-based maintenance management systems, except in highly specialized areas.

Maintenance record/information systems

The use of small and relatively cheap micro-computers with floppy discs and line printers permits the development and use of computer-based maintenance records and information systems within the maintenance department. An alternative approach involves the use of a VDU terminal in the maintenance department to provide access to a larger mini-computer or mainframe computer elsewhere in the organization. The low cost of the micro-based systems is encouraging the development of this type of approach. The example below involves the use of a 32K storage micro-computer with twin floppy disc drives and a line printer. The system is employed in a considerable number of different types of organization and is available at low cost. The system comprises a number of programs packaged in modular form to allow progressive introduction and further development with minimal effort. The manner in which maintenance personnel interact with the computer is outlined in Figure 20.20. The various modules are described below.

The asset register

This module records details of the plant and equipment together with date of purchase, equipment code, expected life, supplier's name, installed cost, etc. Its prime purpose is to provide an inventory of the plant to be maintained. The register is organized into maintenance areas so that sections of plant can be added as time is found to complete the inventory. The search program provided enables the user to extract information in accordance with the criteria specified, e.g. 'list all electric motors older than five years'. The depreciated cost of plant may be listed using either a straight line or reducing balance method.

Maintenance planning

The planning module enables the maintenance manager to specify when and where the maintenance work is to be executed. Any number of routines can be assigned to a particular piece of plant and provision is made to store and display the routine , the job title, the planned hours, week planned, interval between visits, contract or direct labour, a financial reference and the trade(s) required. The module allows capital projects and major installations to be scheduled into the overall plan.

Each week the computer will search the plan and print a list of all work due, giving

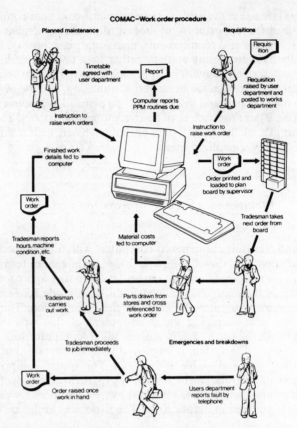

Figure 20.20   *A micro-computer based maintenance records system (COMAC III). Reproduced with the permission of Comac Systems UK.*

number of hours required and trade(s) by area and in total. Work overdue is indicated by an asterisk. This listing is used by the maintenance manager to agree the schedule of work with the user departments and to ensure that enough labour and materials are available. If plant cannot be made available or the workload is too great, there is provision for rescheduling the routines. Once the schedule is agreed the computer is instructed to raise the necessary work orders. The details are transferred to the orders module and the planned week is rolled forward in accordance with the routine interval. At any time the maintenance manager can order a projection of forward workload. This is a printout of the number of hours required in the next twelve months. It indicates peaks and troughs in the workload and aids the development of a smoothed plan.

Work order management

The computer keeps track of jobs available for issue, currently in progress, interrupted for any reason, or recently finished. The flow chart in Figure 20.20 shows how the work order information is collected and how the details are fed back to the computer. Such a procedure might be impractical if the computer were not continually available to the maintenance department. The micro-computer has the great advantage of being cheap enough to be dedicated solely to works department activities.

Orders for planned work are raised automatically and orders for breakdowns or requisitions are created by typing the details straight into the computer. The orders are sorted by the computer and are printed in trade sequence so that they can be passed directly to the supervisor concerned, and the computer keeps a copy, so one less piece of paper is needed for every work order issued. A full search facility exists which enables the engineer to interrogate the work order file for information on the status or cost of any particular work order or project.

The labour module

Because labour cost is often the most significant expense on the maintenance budget, the system provides comprehensive labour analysis and reporting facilities.

A reconciliation program checks that the hours worked by each worker equal the hours claimed on work orders. It is not uncommon to find differences of between 10 and 30 per cent. The program will also list a summary of every job performed by each worker together with the performance against each job, which enables estimated time to be compared with actual time.

Summaries of attendance and lost time can be printed, as can a performance analysis. The latter reports achievement against planned times for each individual and in total. Where a bonus scheme is in operation, each individual's bonus and basic pay are calculated and presented in a labour cost analysis.

The control statistics summary provides the manager with indices on lost time, unmeasured work, amount of overtime, proportion of unplanned absence and the cost per standard hour of work done.

Plant history

At the end of each week a program searches the work order file for finished jobs, extracts the job details and transfers them to plant history discs. Between 4000 and 6000 history records can be stored on a single disc, depending on the amount of information required. There is no limit to the number of discs that can be used.

The plant history files can be searched and information extracted as needed. The cost of all breakdowns could be extracted, as could the cost of contract labour between any two dates.

An incident report allows monitoring of maintenance and breakdown trends and helps the manager to decide on the optimum maintenance frequency. It also reports the average work hours and material costs expended per week, thus allowing comparison of two different pieces of plant.

Stock record

A stock control module is available. This module stores the costs and quantities of each item in the maintenance stores. As parts are issued the stock record will be updated and the costs of each work order issued will be extracted. It will also be possible to check parts availability against a given maintenance routine.

'Complete' computer-based maintenance management systems

The provision of facilities similar to those described above, *together* with decision-making and planning procedures, requires a more sophisticated approach. In most cases a mainframe computer will be needed, possibly with the provision of on-line access through

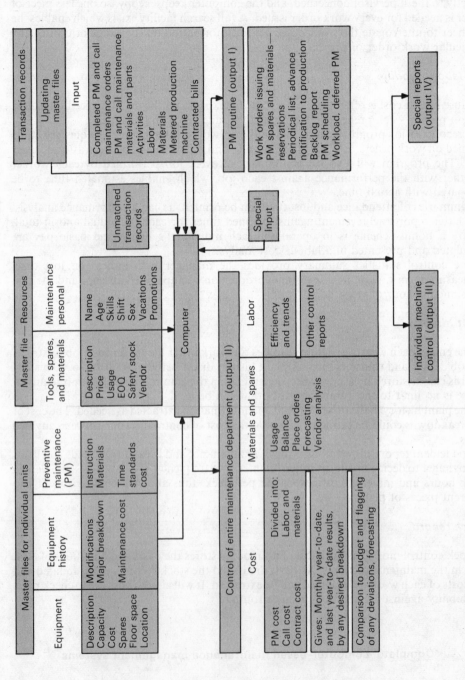

Figure 20.21 *A complete computer-based maintenance management system. From Turban, E. (1969) The complete computerized maintenance system, Industrial Engineering, March, p. 20. Reproduced with permission.*

the use of a VDU terminal in the maintenance department. As yet there are few examples of the use of a comprehensive computer-based maintenance management system of this type. The system outlined in Figure 20.21 was conceived some time ago but can still be seen as a model for a complete computer-based maintenance management system.

CHECKLIST FOR CHAPTER 20

The need for maintenance and repair
Types of maintenance activity and their interrelationships
The maintenance function
Terotechnology and life-cycle costing
Objectives of maintenance
Maintenance decisions
  What is to be maintained?
  Types of maintenance
  Organization of maintenance
Inspection
Preventive maintenance
  Nature
  Operating life curves
  Breakdown time distributions
  Preventive maintenance for a single machine

Preventive maintenance for several machines
Repair
  Nature
  Repair teams (crews)
  Allocation/size of repair teams
Replacement
  Nature
  Replacement policies
    Items subject to sudden failure
    Simulation method
    Items which deteriorate
    Discounted cash flow methods
    MAPI method
Computers in maintenance
  Maintenance records and information systems
  'Complete' maintenance management systems

FURTHER READING

Corder, A. (1976) *Maintenance Management Techniques*. New York: McGraw-Hill. Chapters on maintenance, organization, costing, planning and control, preparation, and operation and materials control, with case studies.

Hewgill, J. C. and Parkes, D. (1979) Terotechnology—philosophy and concept, *Terotechnica*, **1**, pp. 3–8.

Husband, T. M. (1976) *Maintenance Management and Terotechnology*. London: Saxon House.

Jardine, A. K. S. (1973) *Maintenance Replacement and Reliability*. London: Pitman. A largely quantitative treatment of maintenance, replacement and reliability.

Kelly, A. and Harris, M. J. (1978) *Management of Industrial Maintenance*. London: Newnes-Butterworth. An introductory descriptive treatment.

Stuedel, H. J. and Kirchman, D. G. (1981) Planning equipment purchases, overhauls, based on usage, sales, deterioration, *Industrial Engineering*, October, pp. 66–72. A system for machine tool replacement planning taking into account deterioration, capacity requirements and usage rates.

UK Department of Industry (1975) *Terotechnology—An Introduction to the Management of Physical resources*. London: HMSO.

UK Department of Industry (1975) *Terotechnology—Case Histories*. London: HMSO. Simple descriptions and examples of terotechnology, principles and practices.

Wilkinson, J. J. (1968) How to manage maintenance, *Harvard Business Review*, March/April.

QUESTIONS

20.1 Define and differentiate between preventive maintenance and repair. What are the objectives of maintenance? In what circumstances is preventive maintenance particularly appropriate?

20.2 An examination of the machine operating history together with statistical information provided by the manufacturer has revealed that the breakdown time distribution approximates to an Erlang distribution with parameter $l = 2$. It has also been established that the average trouble-free life between breakdowns is 175 hours.

The maintenance manager estimates that the average time for repairs is 4.6 hours, and a study of the maintenance and service instructions for the machine indicates that the average time for preventive maintenance is 2.5 hours.

It has further been estimated that the costs of maintenance and repair are as follows:

> Preventive maintenance £5/h
> Repair   £10/h

The average value of the output of the machine is £74.6/h.
(a)   Determine the optimum preventive maintenance schedule.
(b)   How would this schedule change if:
   (i) the cost of repairs decreased to £5/h;
   (ii) the average running life between breakdowns decreased to 75 h?

20.3 Referring to the previous question, i.e.

Breakdown time distribution	= Erlang, $l = 2$
Average life between breakdowns	= 175 h
Time for repair	= 4.6 h
Time per preventive maintenance	= 2.5 h
Cost of preventive maintenance	= £5/h
Cost of repair	= 10/h

(a)   Because of a change in the use of the machine the value of the hourly output changes. (All other figures above remain the same.) It is calculated that in the new situation the optimum preventive maintenance interval is 262 hours. What is the value of the hourly machine output?

(b)   A work study team is engaged to study work methods during preventive maintenance, with the object of reducing the average time required for such maintenance.

For the data given initially, an average trouble-free life between breakdowns of 175 hours and an output value of £74.6 per hour, what is the optimum preventive maintenance interval if:
   (i)   both the cost and average duration for preventive maintenance are reduced by 25 per cent?
   (ii) the average duration of preventive maintenance is reduced by 50 per cent but cost is increased by 25 per cent?

20.4 If the average operating life, without breakdowns, of four similar machines is four weeks, and if the average time to repair a machine which has broken down six weeks, what is the average number of machines working at any time? State what statistical assumptions you have made in arriving at your answer?

If one repair team is allocated to the repair of the above machines, what proportion of the time will this team be occupied? State what statistical assumption you have made in arriving at your answer.

20.5 (a)   A single maintenance team is expected to effect repairs to several identical machines as and when necessary. Because of other, less important duties (which can be interrupted if necessary), the team can devote only 80 per cent of their time to the repair of the machines. It is known that the breakdown distribution of the machines approximates closely to the exponential distribution and that the average time between breakdown is 75 hours.
   (i)   How many machines can the team attend if the repair time is exponentially distributed with mean $= 15$ hours?

(ii) What is the average number of machines in service at any time?

(b) An unlikely situation has arisen and a maintenance manager has a choice of allocating a repair team to look after one of three different groups of machines. The details of each group of machines are as follows:

Group of 'A' type machines:
Number   = 8
Average time between breakdowns   = 50 h
Average time to make repair   = 5 h

Group of 'B' type machines:
Number   = 6
Average time between breakdowns   = 40 h
Average time to make repair   = 6 h

Group of 'C' type machines:
Number   = 10
Average time between breakdowns   = 20 h
Average time to make a repair   = 2 h

Assuming that the breakdown time distribution and the repair time distribution are exponential:

(i) Other things being equal, which group of machines would keep the repair team busiest?

(ii) Which group should the repair team be allocated to if the criterion is the maximization of the average percentage of the total number of machines in service at any time?

20.6 Describe briefly how you would collect and analyse data in order to assist in the determination of a maintenance policy for a large computer installation in a bank.

Having determined the policy, what data would you collect regularly in order to ensure that the maintenance procedures were adjusted to conform to changes in the characteristics of the equipment?

20.7 (a) Determine the maximum average time required to perform a repair if two maintenance teams are to attend to two identical machines and if, on average, a minimum of one machine should be in service at any time. The repair time and the machine breakdown time are both exponentially distributed, and the average operating life of machines between breakdowns is 40 hours.

(b) What is the maximum average repair time if one maintenance team is to ensure the same performance of the machines?

20.8 A machine has three identical and rather complex mechanisms, each of which

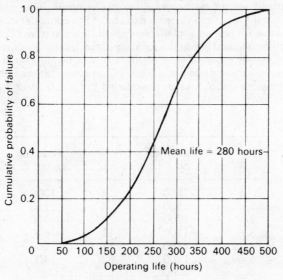

Figure Q20.8

occasionally fails to operate satisfactorily. The cumulative probability of failure of a mechanism is given in the graph. It has been found from experience that the replacement of one mechanism takes 1 hour, while the replacement of two together takes 1.75 hours and the replacement of all three takes 2.5 hours. The costs associated with this operation are given below.

Direct labour cost	$= £8/h$
Cost of replacement mechanism	$= £10$
Downtime cost of machine	$= £75/h$

Three replacement strategies are available:
(a) Replace each mechanism individually when it fails.
(b) Replace all three mechanisms every time one mechanism fails.
(c) Replace each mechanism when it fails and, *at the same time*, replace all other mechanisms that have been in service for longer than the known average operating life of the mechanism.
Using a simulation approach determine the minimum cost replacement strategy.

20.9 Profit Makers Ltd are considering the purchase of a computer to replace an ageing existing machine. The new computer would cost £6000 and is expected to have a life of fifteen years during which it would earn revenue as follows:

Year	Revenue £	Year	Revenue £
This year	1500	8	1800
1	2000	9	1600
2	2000	10	1500
3	2000	11	1500
4	2000	12	1000
5	2000	13	700
6	2000	14	500
7	2000	15	500

One major overhaul would be necessary in five years' time, costing £3750, and a second overhaul would be necessary in twelve years' time, costing £2500. It is anticipated that the realizable value on disposal of this computer would be £2500 at any time after the twelfth year and £5000 between the tenth and twelfth years inclusive. The existing machine is sound but technologically dated. Nevertheless, it has an expected life of a further twelve years. If it is retained it will be necessary to conduct minor maintenance work this year, at a cost of £1500, and every fifth year thereafter at a cost of £500 each time. Its disposal value is expected to be £500 and it is expected to earn revenue as follows:

Year	Revenue £	Year	Revenue £
This year	1500	7	1000
1	1500	8	750
2	1200	9	750
3	1200	10	600
4	1100	11	500
5	1100	12	400
6	1000		

The company is in the habit of evaluating future investment and revenues at present value, by means of a 10 per cent 'discount' rate.

(a) Should Profit Makers Ltd replace the existing computer?

(b) What is the cost difference at present value between the two alternative strategies?

CHAPTER 21

Performance Measurements

NOTATION USED IN THIS CHAPTER

AV	Added value or net output
C	Operations cost
Cx	Indirect external expenses
F	Total factorial costs
H	Net earnings
K	Capital charges
L	Employment or labour charges
M	Materials throughput
N	Non-labour factorial cost
P	Profits
R	Internal expenses
S	Sales revenue or gross output
T	Total earnings
X	Total external purchases

In this chapter we shall consider briefly some aspects of performance measurement. This section of the book is concerned with control, and in Chapter 18 we noted that the measurement of operating system performance provides for control through the use of a feedback mechanism. Thus actual system performance might be compared with planned or intended performance, any resulting difference being used in determining appropriate action aimed at securing performance more closely corresponding to that intended. Performance measurement will of course have other uses, often associated with and resulting from its use for control. For example, present performance may be measured so that incentives, objectives and targets may be set or modified.

Two basic objectives for operating systems and operations management were identified in Chapter 1, i.e. the provision of customer service and resource productivity. If operating systems are intended to achieve certain objectives in respect of both customer service and resource productivity, it is appropriate that system performance should be measured in respect of both objectives. Performance measurement in respect of resource productivity is common in operations management, but the measurement of performance in respect of customer service is less common.

Here we shall again consider the nature of both customer service and resource productivity and the manner in which objectives in each area are established and performance against them is measured.

CUSTOMER SERVICE PERFORMANCE *(see also Chapter 1)*

Recapping briefly on Chapter 1, the function of operating systems is the satisfaction of customer wants. This, therefore, is an objective of operations management. The items, movement or treatment provided by the operating system must match customers' needs if these customers are to be satisfied. The provision of customer service and the creation of customer satisfaction is a multi-dimensional problem, three principal factors having been identified in Chapter 1 as follows:

(a) *specification*, i.e. the provision of goods, movement or treatment as requested or specified by the customer, *or* to a standard but acceptable specification;
(b) *cost*, i.e. the provision of goods, movement or treatment at a requested cost *or* at a standard but acceptable cost;
(c) *timing*, i.e. (i) the provision of goods, movement or treatment at a requested time *or* at a standard but acceptable time, and or at an acceptable delay, and (ii) in the case of movement or transport the provision of movement or transport having a requested duration *or* requiring a standard but acceptable duration.

An organization will seek to create customer satisfaction through the provision of adequate customer service by pursuing appropriate objectives in these three areas, hence ultimately the effectiveness of the operating system can be assessed by considering the extent to which intended specification, cost and timing objectives are met.

The measures of customer service

These three customer service factors are general factors only; they each comprise several dimensions and in most cases it will be more practical and appropriate to assess or measure performance on these narrower dimensions.

1. The *specification* of goods may be considered in terms of their design features and performance characteristics. Together these dimensions define what the item is and how it is intended to perform its purpose. Similarly, the specification of a transport may be expressed in terms of its 'design' and performance. In this context design, i.e. the nature of the transport movement, may be expressed in terms of the origin, destination and route of movement. The performance can be considered synonymous with 'means', i.e. the means or method by which the movement is achieved. A service treatment may be defined in similar terms. The nature of the treatment can be considered to be the design characteristic or dimension, and the means by which the treatment is provided can be considered to be the performance characteristic. Two

main dimensions can therefore be identified for the specification of items, movement or treatment. They are the 'what' and 'how' dimensions. In designing an item, a movement or a treatment an organization will define these two characteristics. In assessing the performance of an organization the customer will again consider these two dimensions. They are summarized in Table 21.1.

Table 21.1 *The specifications of items, movement and treatment*

Dimensions for specification	Items	Movement	Treatment
Design, i.e. *what* is the item movement/ treatment?	e.g. comprising *Appearance* and dimensions *Material* specifications Design and manufacture quality	e.g. comprising *Source*, *destination* and *route*	e.g. comprising *Nature* of treatment
Performance, i.e. *how* is the purpose achieved?—the means or method employed	e.g. comprising *Operating* characteristics or performance characteristics, or *operating* principles or means	e.g. comprising *Means* of transport	e.g. comprising Means of treatment or *procedures* employed, or *form* of treatment

2. The general dimension of *cost* identified above may similarly be broken down into important components. The customer—theoretically at least—will evaluate an item of a given specification in terms of its total expected costs, i.e. acquisition price plus any necessary additional expenses associated with an item, e.g. installation, running and maintenance costs, all discounted to the present time in order to take into account cash flows over a period of time. Similarly the cost of a transport movement or service may be expressed in terms of the original price of acquisition plus any additional and necessary costs or expenses. We can therefore distinguish, for our purposes, two aspects of costs, i.e. price and expenses. In seeking to provide customer service an organization will consider these two dimensions. In evaluating an organization customers will consider or respond to these two dimensions. These cost dimensions of customer service are summarized in Table 21.2.

Table 21.2 *The cost of items, movement and treatment*

Dimensions for *cost*	Items	Movement	Treatment
Price, i.e. intended or quoted cost	e.g. comprising *Purchase price*, or initial cost of good	e.g. comprising *Cost of journey or fare*	e.g. comprising *Cost of treatment or charge*
Expenses, i.e. expected additional costs	e.g. comprising Cost of installation Cost of maintenance and replacement Running costs	e.g. comprising Additional costs such as insurance, etc.	e.g. comprising Additional costs such as insurance, etc.

3. The third factor identified above—*timing*—may also be subdivided. Consider first the cost of goods. Customers will take into account the delay or wait between their expression of a want and the subsequent satisfaction of that want. This delay or wait will normally be evident as the period of time between placing an order and receiving

the goods. This is clearly an important dimension of customer service, since delay greatly in excess of that which is acceptable will give rise to reduced overall customer satisfaction and loss of customers. Again this is a dimension which is, to some extent, within the control of the organization. It can, for example, set out deliberately to provide goods virtually on demand, or alternatively might choose to provide goods for which customers are expected to wait, perhaps for some considerable time. This delay dimension is also relevant in the provision of both transport and service. However, a further dimension is also important in these two functions. Both transport (i.e. movement) and service (i.e. treatment) are time consuming. In both cases, therefore, the customers will consider their likely duration or the time required for their performance, i.e. to move from source to destination, or to be treated or accommodated. In assessing an organization the customer will therefore consider this dimension, and equally, in seeking to achieve customer service, an organization will seek to provide an appropriate or acceptable duration for its transport or service. The timing factor can therefore be subdivided into the dimensions of delay and duration, summarized in Table 21.3.

Table 21.3 *The timing of the provision of items, movement and treatment*

Dimensions for *timing*	Items	Movement	Treatment
Delay	e.g. comprising	e.g. comprising	e.g. comprising
i.e intended or quoted delay or waiting time	*Delivery time* or waiting time for delivery of goods	Time spent waiting for transport	Time spent waiting for treatment
Duration		e.g. comprising	e.g. comprising
i.e. intended or quoted duration		Travel time or duration of journey	Treatment time or duration of treatment

Table 21.1 to 21.4 from Wild, R. (1979) *Operations Management—A Policy Framework*. Oxford: Pergamon. Reproduced with permission.

Customers, in appraising the specification of an item, will be aware that it may perform differently in practice from the way intended at design. Design and performance characteristics may therefore be seen as intended features. There will be some probability that items will perform unsatisfactorily. An item may fail to function as intended, i.e. to achieve its intended purpose. It may function for some time and then fail, i.e. break down. It may break down regularly. It may function, but not at a desired level of performance. The customer must therefore consider the probability of an item satisfactorily achieving its intended purpose or continuing to achieve that purpose, i.e. its reliability. An organization must recognize this as a dimension of customer service and a characteristic of the product. The manner in which this reliability might be measured will depend on the nature of the item. It could, for example, be measured in terms of mean time between failures, or average operating life, or simply the probability that it will work at all. Similarly, in the specification of transport or service, it is necessary to consider reliability, the probability of the required destination being reached and the probability of the movement being achieved as intended. The cost factor will also be seen in terms of its reliability. Price and expenses, as outlined above, can be considered to be quoted or intended costs. In practice actual costs may differ, hence the probability of such changes will be an important customer service dimension and characteristic.

In considering the timing of goods, transport and service it is necessary to consider reliability issues. Both delay and duration, as discussed above, can be considered as intended times. The customer must consider the likelihood of the quoted or intended delay occurring and the likelihood of the quoted or intended duration occurring. In many cases in the provision of goods a delivery time is quoted, but both parties realize that there is a probability that in practice a longer delay will occur. Similarly, in the provision of transport, both parties will realize that while the normal intended or quoted duration for a journey may be X hours, due to a variety of factors the actual duration may be greatly in excess of X hours. In this case, therefore, it is necessary again to consider reliability, i.e. the probability that the intended or quoted duration will in fact be achieved and the probability that the intended delay will in fact occur.

These three reliability dimensions (reliability of specification, cost and timing) are of major concern to operations management. The reliability of intended specification, cost and timing will depend to a considerable extent on the effectiveness of operations management. Inadequate management of capacity and inventories and poor scheduling may give rise to cost, timing and specification changes. Poor resource utilization will add to costs, bring delays, and increase durations. Inadequate execution of design intentions may give rise to poor performance. Since the responsibility for achieving customer service in these three areas is primarily the responsibility of operations management, operations management must have a major influence on the formulation of objectives on these three reliability dimensions.

Nine basic customer service dimensions can therefore be identified (Table 21.4). The intended specification, cost and timing of goods, transports and services will be largely determined by policy decisions within the organization. In some cases organizations will seek to maximize customer service on each of the six main dimensions, but in most cases different importance will be attached to each of these six dimensions. For this reason there can be no valid absolute measure of the performance of operations on design, performance, price, expenses, delay and duration. It is relevant only to measure the extent to which intended objectives are achieved, i.e. specification, cost and timing reliability.

Table 21.4 *The principal dimensions of customer service*

Factors	Dimensions	
Specifications	i.e.	
of goods, movement	1. *Design*	7. *Specification reliability*
or treatment	2. *Performance*	
Cost	i.e.	
of goods, movement	3. *Price*	8. *Cost reliability*
or treatment	4. *Expenses*	
Timing	i.e.	
of goods, movement	5. *Delay*	9. *Timing reliability*
or treatment	6. *Duration*	

Table 21.5 identifies some of the means of measuring and/or assessing operating system performance against these three customer service dimensions.

RESOURCE PRODUCTIVITY PERFORMANCE

Here we are on more familiar ground, for in most situations the intensity of the utilization of resources will be accepted as a legitimate measure of the performance of the operating system.

Table 21.5 *Measures of customer service performance*

Customer service dimensions	Measures
Specification reliability	Degree of conformity of goods, transport or service with specifications on design and performance (e.g. manufacture quality) Number or proportion of goods, transports or services conforming to given and or acceptable standards of design and performance.
Cost reliability	Variance of goods, transport or service on price and expense specification. Number or proportion of goods, transports or services within given and or acceptable price and expense range.
Timing reliability	Variance of goods, transport or service on delay or duration specification. Number or proportion of goods, transports or services within given and, or acceptable delay and duration range (e.g. delivery performance).

A useful approach to the discussion of resource productivity as a concept is the identification of the manner in which various interested parties might apply measurement. From the engineer's standpoint, productivity and efficiency are synonymous and efficiency is the measure of the amount of energy supplies converted into useful work. Productivity would be seen as the quotient obtained by dividing output by a factor of production, whether capital or raw material. Input generates output, and in a physical sense at least the quotient cannot exceed unity, although in a financial sense it must do so if the business is to secure a profit to survive.

An economist might take a different approach and might emphasize labour rather than capital productivity. Emphasis on the former encourages one to express inputs in terms of labour or labour equivalent, with attendant risks of estimation, averaging, etc. In an attempt to overcome this, the United Kingdom Department of Trade and Industry developed the idea of net output per employee as a productivity measure, i.e.

$$\text{Net output per employee} = \frac{\text{Added value per annum}}{\text{Total number of employees}}$$

'Added value' represents the value added to materials by the process of production and from which wages, salaries, rent, rates, tax reserves and dividends, selling distribution, and advertising costs have to be met.

An accountant might take yet another view. Many contemporary productivity measures are financially oriented because many firms evaluate the worth and effectiveness of their enterprise by using 'financial ratio analysis'. A variety of ratios might be developed, but it is essential that those adopted are seen to be useful and relevant. The following are among those commonly employed.

(a) profit/capital employed;
(b) profit/sales;
(c) sales/capital employed;
(d) sales/fixed assets;
(e) sales/stocks;
(f) sales/employee;
(g) profits/employee.

In such an approach, an emphasis is placed on sales revenue and profit; however, it is possible that both are affected by market supply and demand factors as well as being influenced by the efficiency of operations.

Integrated productivity measurement

Each of these approaches to the measurement of productivity may be seen as parts of a composite or integrated productivity model. Such a model has been developed and presented by Norman and Bahiri (see 'Further Reading'). Figure 21.1 presents an integrated productivity model through which can be identified various means of measuring the productivity of operating systems. The notation is given in Table 21.6. All inputs and outputs are measured in financial units, and though the model is particularly relevant in the measurement of resource productivity in conversion or creation systems, it can be modified for use in service and even non-profit systems. Referring back to the above, the engineer's measure of efficiency might be seen to be equivalent to a measure of total earnings productivity, i.e. $\dfrac{T}{C}$ in Figure 21.1. The economist's measure may be seen to be equivalent to added value productivity, i.e. $\dfrac{AV}{R}$, while the accountant's measure of productivity may be seen to be equivalent to the measure of gross efficiency shown in Figure 21.1, i.e. $\dfrac{S}{F}$.

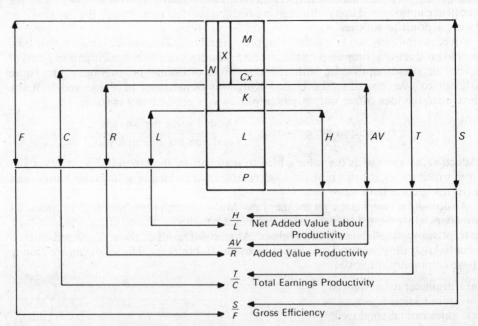

Figure 21.1 *Integrated productivity measurement model. Adapted with permission from Norman, R. G. and Bahiri, S. (1972) Productivity Measurement and Incentives. London: Butterworth.*

The 'physical' dimensions of resource productivity

The above integrated approach takes a largely financial approach to resource productivity measurement. Returning, however, to the operations management objectives developed in Chapter 1, we might alternatively logically consider three dimensions of resource

Table 21.6 *Notation for integrated productivity measurement model. Adapted with permission from Norman, R. G. and Bahiri, S. Productivity Measurement and Incentives. London: Butterworth.*

S = Sales revenue or gross output
T = Total earnings
AV = Added value or net output
H = Net earnings

M = Materials throughput
Cx = Indirect external expenses
X = Total external purchase
K = Capital charges
N = Non-labour factorial cost
L = Employment or labour charges
P = Profits

C = Operations costs
F = Total factorial inputs
R = Internal expenses

---

productivity, and in so doing take a largely 'physical' approach to the measurement of productivity. In Chapter 1 we identified three principal types of operating system resource: machines, labour and materials. We shall now consider these dimensions of productivity measurement. They offer another means of productivity measurement. Capital or money will often be considered, as above, although since all resources can be measured and expressed in financial terms it may sometimes be logical to consider money as a common denominator resource, and as a unit for the measurement of productivity for each resource and overall productivity.

Each of our three main physical resources must be used effectively, so we must consider productivity on each of these three 'dimensions'. Table 21.7 outlines some objectives for each resource and some means of measuring productivity against these objectives. In each case the achievement of high productivity can be considered in terms of maximizing resource utilization or, of course, minimizing loss or waste. The precise objectives and hence also the performance standards employed will depend on the nature of the resource in each area, as will also the amount of detail necessary in both stating and measuring the achievement of objectives in these areas.

OTHER PERFORMANCE MEASURES *(see also Chapters 5–17, 19 and 20)*

Finally in this chapter it is worth reminding ourselves that we have in previous chapters dealt both directly and indirectly with the measurement of system performance-related factors and dimensions. In fact in most decision areas of operations management there will be means of either indirect or direct assessment of outcomes, and thus for the measurement not only of system performance in particular respects, but also of the effectiveness of operations management decisions. Table 21.8 reminds us of some of the performance measures which might be used in relation to each of the operations management decision areas.

Table 21.7 *Resource productivity and measurement*

Resource	Productivity objectives	Productivity measures
Machines i.e. all physical items, e.g. equipment, tools, buildings, space, directly and indirectly used by the system.	e.g. *Maximize* Output/distance/throughput/ machine hour Proportion of total available time utilized Effectiveness of utilization (e.g. capacity utilized) Occupancy/space utilization	Output/distance/throughput/ machine hour Time(s) used or percentage Capacity used or percentage Occupancy/space utilization or percentage
	Minimize Idle time and downtime Under-utilized/unoccupied space Machine cost content	Idle time and/or downtime or percentage Percentage utilized/occupied space Machine cost content or percentage
Labour i.e. those people who directly or indirectly necessarily provide or contribute to the operation of the system, e.g. manual labour, supervision.	e.g. *Maximize* Output/distance/throughput/ work hour Proportion of total available time utilized Effectiveness of utilization (e.g. capacity utilized)	Output/distance/throughput/ work hour Time(s) used or percentage Capacity used or percentage
	Minimize Idle and ineffective time Labour cost content	Idle and/or ineffective time or percentage Labour cost content or percentage
Materials i.e. those physical items directly or indirectly consumed or converted by the system.	e.g. *Maximize* Yield (i.e. output/distance/ throughput) per unit weight/ volume, etc. *Minimize* Wastage, losses or scrap Material cost content	Yield quantity, weight, etc. Wastage, losses or scrap quantity or percentage Rework/rectification quantity or percentage Material cost content or percentage

PERFORMANCE MEASUREMENT AND MANAGEMENT CONTROL

In Chapter 3 we noted that in seeking to exercise control over the parts of an organization, top management will use certain performance measurements. We identified two forms of measurement which might be employed in exercising management control of the operations function:

(a)   the use of behaviour controls, in which the actual *behaviour of the system is measured* and compared with a required standard as a means of providing the management with control;

Table 21.8 *Some measures of operations performance*

Operations decision area	Some typical performance measures
The location of facilities (see Chapter 5)	Transport costs
The layout of facilities (see Chapter 6)	Transport/movement costs Physical throughput/unit of space (or value of turnover/unit of space
Work methods and work standards (see Chapters 7, 8, 9 and 10)	Value added/work hour Staffing required/unit throughput or output Accident rates (Labour absenteeism/turnover/rates and dispute levels)
Capacity management (see Chapter 11)	Percentage of full capacity normally available Utilization of available capacity Overtime, subcontract costs
Activity scheduling and planning (see Chapters 12, 13, 14 and 15)	Percentage work/jobs/customer delivered or dealt with on time (or conversely percentage late) Percentage utilization of available capacity Levels of work in progress Average customer or input queue length or waiting time
Materials management and inventory management (see Chapters 16 and 17)	Inventory turnover rates Rate of change of inventory levels Capital tied up in stock Occurrence/frequency of disruptions/delays in supply Delivery performance Customer queuing times
Quality management and reliability (see Chapter 19)	Reject rates Rate of return of goods from customers/warranty claim Rate of customer complaints on services Percentage rejected batches Rework/reject costs
Maintenance and replacement (see Chapter 20)	Facilities downtime or availability Utilization of maintenance personnel Operating life of equipment between breakdowns Life-cycle cost of equipment

EXAMPLE: COMPUTER 'SOFTWARE' COMPANY

A small company develops, tests and sells software (i.e. programs) for a range of micro-computers. The principal resources are the systems and programming staff, who use the company's micro-computers to develop either standard program packages or software for specific customer requirements. The software is normally sold as discs, together with printed instructions, etc. for the use of the discs. The following provisional data are available for the company for the financial year just ended:

L	Total labour costs	$= £50\,000$
K	'Straight line' depreciation charge against all capital items including equipment	$= £30\,000$
M	Cost of all materials consumed and sold to customers (including costs of discs)	$= £10\,000$
S	Total sales revenue	$= £140\,000$
C	Total operations cost	$= £95\,000$

Company management use certain performance measures to monitor the performance of the company. Figures are available for the previous financial year. How does performance for the year just ended compare with that for the previous year?

	Previous year	Year just ended
Profits for year	£25 000	140 000 − (95 000 + 10 000) = £35 000
Gross efficiency	1.24	140 000 ÷ (95 000 + 10 000) = 1.33
Net added value		(50 000 + 35 000) ÷ 50 000
Labour productivity	1.8	= 1.7

Comments on performance for year just ended: Increased profits and gross efficiency, but drop in VA labour productivity, suggests an increase in labour costs, possibly partly offset by improvements elsewhere, e.g. increased profits from higher margins on product prices.[1]

(b)   the use of output control, in which the *output of the system is measured* and compared with a standard so that the system can be controlled.

We noted that in some cases the use of either form of measurement is sufficient to provide full control of the operating system, but in some situations because of the nature of the system and the manner in which it is managed, it will be necessary to use both types of control in order to ensure that the operations function achieves both its customer service and resource utilization objectives.

It is worth returning to this distinction at this stage so that we might be reminded that many of the performance measures discussed previously in this chapter will provide a basis for behaviour or output control. In general when the operating system is not 'buffered' from its customers by the existence of output stocks or input customer queues, where the scheduling of the activities of the system is entirely 'externally' oriented (i.e. where scheduling takes direct account of individual customers' timing requirements (see Chapter 12)) and where the capacity management strategy does not require customer queuing, etc., in order to avoid capacity adjustment, then either an output or a behaviour performance measure will be sufficient to ensure conformity to both customer service and resource productivity objectives. However, where these circumstances do not apply then, by definition, the operating system is insulated or buffered from individual customer demands, hence a behaviour measure concentrating on the actual internal behaviour of the operating system will be sufficient to monitor resource productivity performance, but an output measure will be required to investigate customer service performance adequately.

Operations managers must ensure that the performance measures which are used by top management to monitor the performance of the operations function are adequate to measure performance against *both* objectives. The use of performance measures which emphasize only resource productivity will lead ultimately to a distortion in the operations managers' behaviour, so that the resource productivity objective is emphasized at the expense of the customer service objective. Equally, any performance measure which emphasizes customer service will lead ultimately to the pursuit of that objective at the

---

[1] Detailed figures for previous year were:

Total labour cost	=	£30K
Depreciation	=	£30K
Materials	=	£10K
Sales	=	£130K
Operations costs	=	£95K

expense of resource utilization. A balance must be achieved and it must be obtained between the two objectives, and the performance measures used must reflect and reinforce the balance. The two case examples which follow will illustrate this point.

EXAMPLE: PUBLIC SERVICES LTD MOTEL

Public Services Ltd owns several small companies specializing in service activities. One company recently acquired runs a small motel located in a 'prime' site adjacent to a major highway. The motel has 15 bedrooms, each of which has the usual facilities. Apart from a reception area, car parking, and a limited number of vending machines, the motel offers no other facilities. It is managed entirely by a residential manager who is responsible for bookings, reception and the maintenance of the motel and who is assisted by one part-time person who does all the cleaning. There is no pre-booking arrangement for the motel, which depends entirely on trade from 'passing' customers. There is little repeat custom. Customers pay on entry, i.e. before occupying their bedroom. Public Services Ltd wish to introduce certain performance measures to ensure that the motel operates efficiently. It is their intention to give the manager considerable discretion and local responsibility, and to monitor his performance only through the performance measures. The following performance measures were proposed by the manager. The reasons for his proposals are given below.

Resource utilization.
1. Bedroom occupancy rate, i.e. percentage of total bedrooms occupied each month. (The manager considers this to be a sufficient measure of resource utilization since the labour cost is low and the principal resources are the bedrooms.)

Customer service.
2. The manager proposes to place in each room a *questionnaire* to be completed by residents and handed in before leaving. The questionnaire is designed only to establish whether customers are satisfied with the level of service provided at the cost charged. (The manager feels that this will be a sufficient measure of customer service since he is not concerned with those customers who do not register in the motel (e.g. on the few occasions when the motel is full) or with customers' attitude to price, since he believes that people use the motel only if the price is acceptable to them. There are few delays in registering in the motel, so he believes that the principal consideration should be the quality of service provided at the cost charged.)

The manager believes that in this service system these two 'internal' measures of performance (i.e. 'behaviour measures') will be sufficient to ensure control of the motel against the twin objectives of resource utilization and customer service. However, the parent organization, while accepting these measures, has also asked for the addition of a third measure so that the relative profitability of the motel might be evaluated against that of the other businesses run by the company:

3. *Gross efficiency* = total revenue ÷ total operating cost, measured monthly.

EXAMPLE: PUBLIC SERVICES LTD, A PRIVATE HOSPITAL (see also Example in Chapter 3)

Public Services Ltd own and run a small private hospital. It has 30 beds in small wards, an operating theatre, a radiology and X-ray department, and a lounge. The hospital manager is responsible for a senior nurse and four assistant nurses. There is a resident doctor, and the hospital has a contract for up to 25 per cent of the time of each of four medical/surgical specialists, and up to 50 per cent of the time of an anaesthetist and a radiologist.

The hospital admits patients referred by a group of local doctors. The patients are all subscribers to a private hospital insurance scheme which meets the costs of treatment. The hospital has a waiting list for admissions and patients are admitted from the list as appropriate facilities become available. In many cases they are selected for admission by a form of 'batch processing', e.g. a set of patients are admitted, all of whom are thought to require the services of a particular surgeon. This facilitates scheduling in the hospital and makes better use of facilities.

Public Services Ltd currently monitor the performance of the hospital through use of the following statistics, which are collected monthly:

1. *Bed occupancy.* In an average month 900 bed days are assumed to be available. Returns show the actual bed occupancy as a percentage of this 900 bed day capacity.
2. *Length of patient stay.* The average length of patient stay in the hospital is calculated each month.
3. *Patient bed days/member of staff.* The number of patient bed days is compared with the number of staff (nursing and medical) days worked each month.
4. *Gross efficiency*/month $= \dfrac{\text{Total revenue}}{\text{Total operating cost}}$

Recently the hospital manager was able to demonstrate the inadequacy of this set of performance measures. She pointed out that the hospital's activities were largely 'internally' scheduled, that a queue of customers always existed, and that the capacity of the hospital was not adjusted to match changes in demand. She pointed out that the hospital had two sets of customers, and that because of the above factors internal (i.e. 'behaviour') controls could not be used to control the performance of the hospital in respect of the provision of adequate customer service. She persuaded the company that the following performance measures were also required:

5. *Average time on waiting list,* i.e. the average time customers spend waiting for admission (calculated monthly for patients admitted during the month).
6. *Doctors' attitudes to the service provided by the hospital.* A monthly sample survey of doctors' attitudes to the hospital, together with a monthly check on the number of referrals from each doctor.

A PERFORMANCE AUDIT

The emphasis above is on performance measurement. The measurement of performance provides the opportunity to monitor achievements.

If the measurements are quite specific (as for example some of those in Table 21.8) then where performance is seen to be inadequate the type of remedial action required will be fairly clear. But where broader measurements are employed the specific causes of inadequate performance may be hidden, so it may not be clear how best to rectify the situation. For this reason it will often be appropriate also to employ a more diagnostic approach aimed at identifying the causes of inadequate performance and appropriate remedial actions. One broad-based diagnostic procedure, presented in the form of an 'audit', is described in Figure 21.2. It is derived from the type of approach introduced in this book and provides a simple but comprehensive tool.

1. MARKETS AND THE CUSTOMER INTERFACE

Questions	*Comments*
(a) What are the products? (What is included? Excluded?) What is the market? (What is included? Excluded?) Who are the customers? (Why them?)	Productive systems exist to satisfy a demand. Analysis *must* begin by identifying the source and nature of that demand. **Figure 21.2**

Questions	*Comments*
(b) How do the customers get involved? In particular, do they merely place an order, or do they need to supply a significant input to the production operation—either themselves or their property?	If the customers merely order the product, we are dealing with a manufacturing or supply operation. If they must supply a significant input, we have a service or transport operation with special problems related to the quality, reliability and timeliness of the supply, all of which are outside our control, but which we must be capable of handling efficiently and effectively.
(c) Is there any record of problems or complaints from the market?	Known problems may be 'swept under the carpet', but may provide very strong leads for change.

2. . OPERATIONS STRUCTURE

(a) If manufacture or supply:
What type of production system is indicated—flow, mass, batch or jobbing? Why that? What else?

Object here is to identify the basic structure or 'shape' of the operation. Production typing (flow, mass, batch, jobbing) is widely understood. But why is this type chosen here? (Flow and mass may be more efficient than batch or jobbing but are much less flexible—rethink the nature of customer demand.)

(b) Can we stock the inputs in advance? Or must we obtain them specially, or accept them when available without the option of deferral?

There are four possible structures for manufacure and supply:

$$\longrightarrow \triangle \longrightarrow 0 \longrightarrow \triangle \longrightarrow C$$

Buffered both ends.

$$\rightarrow\triangle \longrightarrow 0 \relbar\joinrel\relbar\joinrel\relbar C$$

Make-to-order but from stocked resources.

$$\relbar\joinrel\relbar\joinrel\relbar 0 \rightarrow\triangle \rightarrow C$$

Direct input but making to stock.

$$\relbar\joinrel\relbar\joinrel\relbar 0 \relbar\joinrel\relbar\joinrel\relbar C$$

Special orders needing special resources.
Is the chosen structure logical? What alternatives?

(c) If service or transport:
Will the customers wait or must they be served immediately, on demand?
Can we expect to stock the resources needed to satisfy them, or must we obtain them specially?

As for (b), object is to define structure or 'shape'. There are three possible structures:

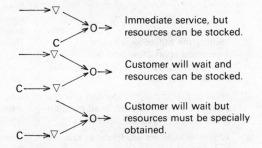

Immediate service, but resources can be stocked.

Customer will wait and resources can be stocked.

Customer will wait but resources must be specially obtained.

(Defining structure identifies some significant features: where strategic stock control is needed, where queue disciplines must be established, what scheduling objectives are important, where immediate supply lines are needed. Note that there may be several, or many, structures in one firm.)

Figure 21.2 *(contd.)*

(d)   What are the major influences on the structures identified in (b) and/or (c)? Under what circumstances might they change?

Usual problem is change in the supply/demand relationship—stocks may form or be depleted, queues may form or disappear. Can we handle that?

(e)   Define the aspect of productivity which emerges as being the more important— efficiency, or customer service, i.e. just what are the productivity objectives?

Where stocks/queues exist, we have the luxury of planning for efficient operation. Otherwise, customer service (e.g. date required) will override and force lower efficiencies.

3.   CAPACITY MANAGEMENT

(a)   Obtain monthly/weekly output figures for at least one, probably two years. Graph them. Look for growth/decline; is it straight-line or is there a market growth curve?

Do it separately for products or product groups if appropriate.

Overall capacity level is fundamental to productivity. Too much means low efficiency. Too little means poor customer service. Question 3(a) shows how the balance between them is changing.

(b)   Identify seasonal peaks and troughs. What strategies have been used to cope?

A key issue. If marked peaks and troughs occur, two basic strategies are possible:

(i)   adjust capacity to match—subcontract, buy in, defer maintenance, work overtime, rearrange shifts, employ more/less staff, use temporary staff, transfer labour, seek counter-seasonal products or counter-seasonal markets (export?);

(ii)   eliminate the need to adjust—use stocks to buffer the peaks, maintain excess capacity in troughs, alter prices in peaks, queue or lose customers in peaks.

(Choice is mainly by markets, customers, structure and productivity objectives.)

4.   OVERALL PERFORMANCE AND MODUS OPERANDI

(a)   Analyse whatever overall performance data exist: balance sheet, income statement, cost summaries, added value ratios. Match with all facts collected above and interpret.

Where is the money spent? Where is it stocked? Does that agree with above analyses or is it incongruous? What is changing? Especially, look for coincidental changes in two or more variables. Check what changes when volume increases or decreases.

(b)   Identify resource dependence and intensity.

Cost accounts will reveal which resource (labour, capital, materials) is most expensive.

Observation will show whether operation is labour or capital dependent in each area within the plant. (Key: can you increase output by increasing labour? If so, operation is labour dependent.) Thus, where is systematic work study best directed—at labour or machine efficiency?

(c)   Identify the objectives of current production scheduling and control systems. Do they try to optimize labour or machine utilization?

Does this agree with 4(b)?

(d)   What is the underlying logic of physical layout—process, product, fixed position or site layout? (See standard texts.)

Does this match the operating system structure and production type? (2(a), (b), (c))? Does it match the resource dependencies (4(b))?

(e)   What methods are used to plan raw materials inventory? Maintain stock for random draw-off? (How are re-order points and quantities determined?) Or purchase to a specific production plan? (Does it work?)

Does this match with structure (2(a), (b), (c))? With overall performance (4(a))? Inventory can be a key tactical issue: objective is not always to minimize it.

Note: At this point in the audit, the principal issues affecting productivity should have been identified, and in particular any incongruities or mis-matches should be laid bare. Sections 5 and 6 below depend on this having been done.

Figure 21.2 (*contd.*)

5. DESIGN OF CHANGES NEEDED

(a) In each selected 'sensitive area' identified, dig for detailed performance data: material yields or scrap, labour performance, machine utilization, stockout frequency, late deliveries, labour turnover, absenteeism, quality performance, breakdown frequency, etc. Note that data will be in physical units, not financial.

Look for trends, patterns, coincident changes.

Note especially what is *not* available. If these really are key areas, why not?

Shortlist the main opportunities for change. They may be in new technology (plant, methods, layout, etc.), planning and control systems (capacity strategies, inventory and scheduling systems, quality control, labour or machine performance control, etc.), or organizational changes (new shift systems, supervisory structure, selection and training, financial rewards, etc.).

(b) For each shortlisted change, think out what else it will affect and identify compensating changes that will be needed.

It is not possible to make a single, isolated change in a productive system. If compensating changes are not identified now they will emerge as crises later.

6. DETAILED DESIGN OF CHANGES

The purpose of the productivity audit is to identify current trends, strengths and weaknesses. At this point we re-enter the conventional disciplines of work study and industrial engineering, production engineering, cost and management accounting, organizational behaviour and perhaps marketing. The range of possible changes is vast, and no general discussion here could do justice to it.

Figure 21.2   *A performance audit framework. Reproduced, with minor changes only, with the permission of B. Melville, University of Waikato, Hamilton, New Zealand.*

CHECKLIST FOR CHAPTER 21

The objectives of operations measurement
   Customer service
   Resource utilization
Customer service performance
   Measures of customer service
     Specification
     Cost
     Timing
   Measures of customer service performance
Resource productivity performance
   Performance rates
   Integrated productivity measurement
   The 'physical' dimensions of resource productivity
     Machines: objectives and measures
     Labour: objectives and measures
     Materials: objectives and measures
Other performance measures, e.g. relevant to:
   Location of facilities

Layout of facilities
Work methods and standards
Capacity management
Scheduling and planning
Inventory management, purchasing and supply
Quality management and reliability
Maintenance and replacement
Management controls and performance
  measurement
   'Behaviour'-type performance measures
   'Output'-type performance measures

A performance audit
   Markets and customers
   Operations structure
   Capacity
   Overall performance and modus operandi
   Design of changes needed
   Detailed design of changes

FURTHER READING

Bailey, D. and Hubert, T. (ed.) (1981) *Productivity Measurement*. Aldershot: Gower. An international review of concepts, techniques and problems.

Craig, C. F. and Harris, R. C. (1973) Total productivity measurement at the firm level, *Sloan*

Management Review, Spring, pp. 13–29. The authors develop a comprehensive concept of and approach to, measuring productivity at the level of the firm.

Eilon, S. (1976) *Applied Productivity Analysis for Industry*. Oxford: Pergamon.

James, G. (1980) Total productivity measurement, *Management Services*, December, pp. 6–12.

Norman, R. G. and Bahiri, S. (1972) *Productivity Measurement and Incentives*. London: Butterworth. A detailed treatment of productivity measurement techniques and procedures. A comparative productivity study and a discussion of productivity bargaining and incentives.

QUESTIONS

21.1 Describe and compare the customer service objectives which might be expected to influence the operation of the following systems:

  (a) a small bespoke (i.e. 'made to measure') gents' manufacturing tailor;
  (b) a dentist's practice;
  (c) a city bus service.

  How might system performance in respect of these objectives be measured in each case?

21.2 Show how (a) added value productivity, (b) gross efficiency and (c) total earnings productivity would be measured in a small batch production to stock manufacturing organization.

21.3 Compare the notion of reliability introduced in this chapter with that discussed in Chapter 20. How might measures of item performance reliability and techniques for maintenance management be of value in performance measurement?

21.4 Identify and explain the types of performance measurement that might be employed in order to achieve adequate management control in the following types of operation:
  (a) a dentist (see Example in Chapter 4);
  (b) fire service (see Example in Chapter 11).

APPENDICES

APPENDIX I

Linear Programming

NOTATION USED IN APPENDIX I

a_i	Capacity for source i
b_j	Requirement of destination j
i	Source ($i = 1$ to m)
j	Destination ($j = 1$ to n)
x_{ij}	Volume 'transported' from source i to destination j

Consider the problem facing a firm making a range of different products. Each product is made in a different way, and for each product there exists a best or optimal method of manufacture. Unfortunately, there are insufficient resources to make each product in the best possible way, hence the problem is to decide which products to make, and in what proportions, in order to maximize profits, or minimize costs.

This is an *allocation* problem. Such problems arise whenever there are several activities to perform, but limitations on resources prevent the performance of each activity in *its* best way. For example, a manufacturer makes two types of product, A and B. Each product A requires one hour of machining, five hours of fabrication and three hours of assembly. Each product B requires two hours of machining, four hours of fabrication and one hour of assembly. In a given period of time there are only 720 hours of machining, 1800 hours of fabrication and 900 hours of assembly time available. How should the manufacturer use this capacity in order to maximize profit if the profit on each product A is £80 and on B £100?

Allocation problems such as this can be solved by means of linear programming, provided:

(a) the objective to be achieved can be expressed as a linear function in terms of the various activities;

(b) the limiting constraints can also be expressed in linear form.

678

THE SIMPLEX ALGORITHM

The Simplex algorithm is best described by means of an example (based on the above manufacturing example).

EXAMPLE I.1 MAXIMIZING

Two products, A and B. Manufacturing time required is shown in Figure I.1.

	Machining	Fabrication	Assembly	Profit on product
A	1 hour	5 hours	3 hours	£80
B	2 hours	4 hours	1 hour	£100
Total capacity available	720 hours	1800 hours	900 hours	

Figure I.1

Our *objective* in this case is to maximize profits. If W = profit obtained, we wish to maximize W where $W = 80A + 100B$.

Our *constraints* are as follows:

Machining capacity $A + 2B \leqslant 720$ (Total machining hours used cannot exceed 720)
Fabrication capacity $5A + 4B \leqslant 1800$
Assembly capacity $3A + B \leqslant 900$

We must express these constraints as equations rather than as the inequalities shown above. This can be done by introducing further variables (called *slack variables*) as follows:

$$A + 2B + p = 720 \tag{1}$$
$$5A + 4B + q = 1800 \tag{2}$$
$$3A + B + r = 900 \tag{3}$$

These slack variables (p, q, r) will, of course, represent either zero or positive figures.

The Simplex method is a procedure for solving a set of such equations simultaneously. The first step is to set down the data in a *tableau* or table form, as in Figure I.2.

The first three rows of figures represent equations (1) (2) and (3). P_o is the figure on the right-hand side of the equation, and p, q and r appear in the first column to indicate that they also

	A	B	p	q	r	P_o
p	1	2	1	0	0	720
q	5	4	0	1	0	1800
r	3	1	0	0	1	900
W	−80	−100	0	0	0	0

Figure I.2

feature in the equations. The fourth row is the objective function, but written in negative form.

The procedure by which the solution is achieved is known as the Gauss Jordan Complete Elimination Procedure.[1]

The steps in the procedure for obtaining an optimum solution are as follows:

1.   Select the largest negative figure in the W row. In our case this is 100 in column B.
2.   Find the figure in *this column* which gives the smallest positive figure when divided into P_o. In our case this is 2 in the first row, since 720/2 is smaller than either 1800/4 or 900/1.
3.   Divide *this row* by *this figure*; enter the results as the equivalent row of a new tableau under W, and replace the slack variable letter on the left with the variable of the column concerned, as in Figure I.3.

	A	B	p	q	r	P_o
→ p	1	②	1	0	0	720
q	5	4	0	1	0	1800
r	3	1	0	0	1	900
W	−80	−100	0	0	0	0
→ B	$\frac{1}{2}$	1	$\frac{1}{2}$	0	0	360

Figure I.3

4.   Eliminate this variable from each of the other rows by multiplying the new row in turn by the negative values of the figures in the column and adding the result to the row concerned.
      Consider the second row. The negative of the figure in the second column is −4. Multiply all of the new row by −4 and add the result to the original second row, as in Figure I.4.
      Consider the third row. The negative of the figure in the second columns is −1. Multiply all of the first row in the new tableau by −1 and add the result to the original third row.
      Do the same for the original W row, i.e. multiply the first row in new tableau by 100 (the negative of −100), then add to original W row, as in Figure I.5.
5.   Repeat the same procedure for the new tableau, i.e. largest negative in last row is − 30. Select 3 in this column. Divide this row by 3 and write the new row into the third tableau, as in Figure I.6.

	A	B	p	q	r	P_o
p	1	②	1	0	0	720
→ q	5	4	0	1	0	1800
r	3	1	0	0	1	900
W	− 80	−100	0	0	0	0
B	$\frac{1}{2}$	1	$\frac{1}{2}$	0	0	360
→ q	3	0	−2	1	0	360

Figure I.4

---

[1] We shall use the procedure and show that an optimum answer results. The basis and development of the procedure and of the Simplex algorithm can be found in most operational research textbooks (see 'Further Reading' at the end of this appendix).

	A	B	p	q	r	P_0
p	1	②	1	0	0	720
q	5	4	0	1	0	1800
→ r	3	1	0	0	1	900
→ W	−80	−100	0	0	0	0
B	$\frac{1}{2}$	1	$\frac{1}{2}$	0	0	360
q	3	0	−2	1	0	360
→ r	$\frac{5}{2}$	0	$-\frac{1}{2}$	0	1	540
→ W	−30	0	50	0	0	36000

Figure I.5

	A	B	p	q	r	P_0
p	1	2	1	0	0	720
q	5	4	0	1	0	1800
r	3	1	0	0	1	900
W	−80	−100	0	0	0	0
B	$\frac{1}{2}$	1	$\frac{1}{2}$	0	0	360
q	③	0	−2	1	0	360
r	$\frac{5}{2}$	0	$-\frac{1}{2}$	0	1	540
W	−30	0	50	0	0	36000
—	—	—	—	—	—	—
A	1	0	$-\frac{2}{3}$	$\frac{1}{3}$	0	120

Figure I.6

Eliminate this variable from each of the other rows by multiplying in turn the new row by the negative value of the figure in the column and adding the result to the row concerned, i.e. for first row in new tableau multiply by $-\frac{1}{2}$ and add, etc. (Figure I.7).

6. Repeat until there are no further negative values in row *W*. Then the optimal solution has been obtained. In this case there are no further negative values in last row, so this last tableau represents the optimal solution.

The solution is interpreted as follows.

The letters on the left of the tableau represent the variables which feature in the solution, i.e. in this case, variables B, A and *r*. In other words *p* and *q* have been lost, hence our three equations are now as follows:

$$A + 2B \qquad = 720$$
$$5A + 4B \qquad = 1800$$
$$3A + B + r = 900$$

	A	B	p	q	r	P_o
p	1	2	1	0	0	720
q	5	4	0	1	0	1800
r	3	1	0	0	1	900
W	−80	−100	0	0	0	0
B	$\frac{1}{2}$	1	$\frac{1}{2}$	0	0	360
q	③	0	−2	1	0	360
r	$\frac{5}{2}$	0	$-\frac{1}{2}$	0	1	540
W	−30	0	50	0	0	36000
B	0	1	$\frac{5}{6}$	$-\frac{1}{6}$	0	300
A	1	0	$-\frac{2}{3}$	$\frac{1}{3}$	0	120
r	0	0	$\frac{7}{6}$	$-\frac{5}{6}$	1	240
W	0	0	30	10	0	39600

Figure I.7

From these equations the values of A and B can be found. Alternatively, they can be read straight from the final tableau, i.e.

$$B = 300 \ (P_o)$$
$$A = 120 \ (P_o)$$
$$\text{The profit } W = 80 \ (120) + 100 \ (300)$$
$$= £39\,600$$

EXAMPLE I.2   MINIMIZING

It is often necessary to minimize a function such as cost. Minimization of an objective function can be achieved quite easily, since the objective *Min. W = x + y* is equivalent to *Max. (− W) = −x − y*. Consequently a Simplex solution can be obtained in exactly the same manner as previously.

Minimize the following objective function: $W = 4A - 6B$ subject to the following constraints:

$$-A + 2B \leqslant 8$$
$$-3A + 4B \leqslant 12$$

The equivalent of minimizing W is *Max. (− W)*, i.e.

$$\text{Objective} = Max. \ (-W) = -4A + 6B$$

The constraints can be expressed as equalities as follows:

$$-A + 2B + p = 8$$
$$-3A + 4B + q = 12$$

The initial tableau is shown in Figure I.8.

	A	B	p	q	P_0
p	−1	2	1	0	8
q	−3	4	0	1	12
(−W)	4	−6	0	0	0

Figure I.8

A solution is obtained as follows:

1. Select largest negative figure in $(-W)$ row, i.e. −6.
2. Find the figure in this column which gives the smallest positive figure when divided by P_0, i.e. 4.
3. Divide this row by this figure, enter the result as the equivalent row of a new tableau, and replace slack variable on left, as in Figure I.9.

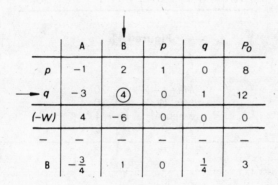

	A	B	p	q	P_0
p	−1	2	1	0	8
q	−3	④	0	1	12
(−W)	4	−6	0	0	0
—	—	—	—	—	—
B	$-\frac{3}{4}$	1	0	$\frac{1}{4}$	3

Figure I.9

4. Eliminate this variable from each of the other rows by multiplying the new row in turn by the negative value of the figure in the column, and adding the result to the row concerned, as in Figure I.10.
5. Repeat this procedure for the new tableau until there are no more negative values in the $(-W)$ row (Figure I.11).

	A	B	p	q	P_0
p	−1	2	1	0	8
q	−3	4	0	1	12
(−W)	4	−6	0	0	0
p	$\frac{1}{2}$	0	1	$-\frac{1}{2}$	2
B	$-\frac{3}{4}$	1	0	$\frac{1}{4}$	3
(−W)	$-\frac{1}{2}$	0	0	$1\frac{1}{2}$	18

Figure I.10

	A	B	p	q	P_o
p	-1	2	1	0	8
q	-3	4	0	1	12
$(-W)$	4	6	0	0	0
p	$\frac{1}{2}$	0	1	$-\frac{1}{2}$	2
B	$-\frac{3}{4}$	1	0	$\frac{1}{4}$	3
$(-W)$	$-\frac{1}{2}$	0	0	$1\frac{1}{2}$	18
A	1	0	2	-1	4
B	0	1	$1\frac{1}{2}$	$-\frac{1}{2}$	6
$(-W)$	0	0	1	1	20

Figure I.11

The solution is:

$$
\begin{aligned}
\text{Max. } (-W) &= 20 \\
\text{Min. } W &= -20 \\
\text{when A} &= 4 \\
\text{B} &= 6
\end{aligned}
$$

Inequalities of the form $x-y \geqslant N$

Suppose the constraints in a linear programming problem were as follows:

$$3x + y \geqslant 3$$
$$4x + 3y \geqslant 6$$

Then introducing slack variables gives:

$$3x + y - p = 3$$
$$4x + 3y - q = 6$$

where p and q are positive values or zero.

It is not possible, however, to use the Simplex procedure to solve equations such as these, since, using this method, only slack variables with positive signs are allowed. However, a solution can be achieved by introducing a further set of variables called artificial variables, as follows:

$$3x + y - p + s = 3$$
$$4x + 3y - q + t = 6$$

Although we do not propose to describe the procedure, the Simplex method can now be used to obtain an optimum solution in a manner very similar to that described above.

Equations

A similar situation to the above arises when constraints must be expressed as equations rather than inequalities. If, in our original example, it was essential that *all* of the machining capacity were used, our constraints would be:

$$A + 2B = 720$$
$$5A + 4B = 1800$$
$$3A + B = 900$$

Such a situation again necessitates the use of *artificial variables*, and a solution can again be obtained using the Simplex method.

THE TRANSPORTATION ALGORITHM

The transportation algorithm is a special case of linear programming and is applicable to the special type of allocation problem in which both requirements and resources are expressed in terms of one type of unit. It can be used, for example, to minimize the total cost of distributing goods from n dispatch point to m receiving points, providing the following conditions are satisfied:

1. The number of items to be dispatched from, and the number to be received at, each point is known.
2. The cost of transportation between each pair of points is known.

Again the technique is best illustrated by means of a simple example.

EXAMPLE I.3

Three steel mills produce steel at rate of:

$$A = 60 \text{ tonnes/h}$$
$$B = 100 \text{ tonnes/h}$$
$$C = 150 \text{ tonnes/h}$$

Three factories require steel at rates of:

$$1 = 140 \text{ tonnes/h}$$
$$2 = 120 \text{ tonnes/h}$$
$$3 = 50 \text{ tonnes/h}$$

The costs of transportation between steel mills and factories are given by the values in the cells in the matrix in Figure I.12.

Using all of this information we can construct our first transportation tableau or this allocation problem, where x_{ij} is the amount of steel transported or allocated from mill i to factory j (Figure I.13).

The objective is to allocate steel to factories so as to minimize total transportation costs.

It is possible to obtain a solution to the problem by using what is known as the *North West Corner* rule, which gives rise to the following procedure:

1. Start at the NW (i.e. top left-hand) cell.
2. If $a_i < b_j$, set $x_{ij} = a_i$ and proceed vertically.
3. If $a_i > b_j$, set $x_{ij} = b_j$ and proceed horizontally.

Factories

		1	2	3
	A	6	8	4
Steel mills	B	4	9	3
	C	1	2	6

Figure I.12

Mill $(i=A,B,C)$ \ Factory $(j=1,2,3)$	1	2	3	Output per mill per hour (a_i)
A	x_{ij} 6	x_{ij} 8	x_{ij} 4	$a_A = 60$
B	x_{ij} 4	x_{ij} 9	x_{ij} 3	$a_B = 100$
C	x_{ij} 1	x_{ij} 2	x_{ij} 6	$a_C = 150$
Requirements per factory per hour (b_j)	$b_1=140$	$b_2=120$	$b_3=50$	

Figure I.13

4. If $a_i = b_j$, set $x_{ij} = a_i = b_j$ and proceed diagonally.
5. Repeat until SE (i.e. bottom right-hand) cell is reached.

Adopting this North West Corner rule and referring to our example, as in Figure I.14, the steps we would take are as follows:

	1	2	3	a_i
A	60 6	8	4	$a_A = 60$
B	80 4	20 9	3	$a_B = 100$
C	1	100 2	50 6	$a_C = 150$
b_j	$b_1=140$	$b_2=120$	$b_3=50$	

Figure I.14

1. Start in cell A1 (the NW corner).
2. Since $a_i < b_j$ (i.e. $60 < 140$), set $x_{ij} = 60$ and proceed vertically to B1.
3. At B1, $a_i = 100$ and $b_j = (140 - 60) = 80$ (i.e. factory 1 required 140, but it has now been allowed 60 from steel mill A and therefore still requires 80). Set B1 = 80 and proceed horizontally.

4. At B2, b_j is now 20 and $a_i = 120$. Set B2 $= 20$ and proceed vertically.
5. At C2, $a_i < b_j$ (100 < 150). Set C2 $= 100$ and proceed horizontally.
6. Finally set C3 $= 50$.

This procedure gives us our first solution to this allocation problem, but this solution is unlikely to be the optimal solution and we must now try to improve on it.

In an attempt to improve on the solution we introduce the concept of *dispatch* and *receiving* costs. The dispatch cost plus the receiving cost will equal the transportation cost for the route in question.

To set the dispatch and receiving costs for mills and factories respectively, let us begin with steel mill A. If the dispatch cost here is 0 then the receiving cost for factory 1 must be 6, since the transportation cost for the route is 6.

Proceeding in an identical manner and using only the cells used in the first solution, we can now determine both dispatch and receiving costs for all the routes used by the first solution (Figure I.15).

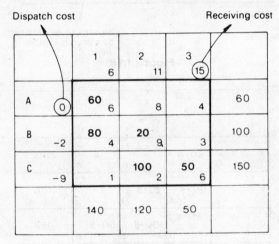

Figure I.15

After setting the two costs for route A to 1, the receiving cost at 1 can be used to set the dispatch cost for B. This must be -2, so the total cost for the route will equal 4. This cost can now be used to set the receiving cost at 2, by considering route B2, etc.

Now let us look at the routes which were *not* used by the first solution. The 'costs' for these routes are the sum of the appropriate dispatch and receiving costs, e.g. for route A2 the cost is $0 + 11 = 11$. Now the difference between the *actual* cost for that route (i.e. 8) and the cost just calculated (i.e. 11) represents the saving which might be obtained by introducing this route into the solution (Figure I.16).

In our case the maximum saving will result from the use of route A3, so let us try to introduce this route into the solution.

Let us imagine that the quantity θ is allocated to that route. The total quantity transported by the other routes must be reduced by θ in order to balance out the allocation. The problem then is merely *to place* $-\theta$ *and* $+\theta$ *on the routes in use, so that the* θs *for both columns and rows cancel out* (see Figure I.17).

From this tableau it can be seen that, in practice, the maximum value that θ can take is 20, since any quantity larger than this would result in the quantity for route B2 becoming negative, which is of course impossible. We will therefore replace θ by 20, its maximum value, to produce a new tableau which represents an improved solution (Figure I.17).

Again we are not certain that it is the optimal solution, so we must once more attempt to improve on it by calculating dispatch and receiving costs to determine whether any of the other routes represent a cost saving (Figure I.18). Route C1 would result in a cost saving of 7; we must

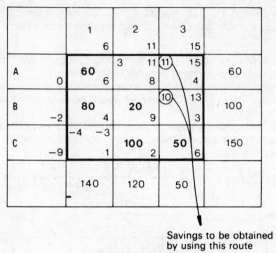

Savings to be obtained
by using this route

Figure I.16

	1 (6)	2 (11)	3 (15)	Supply
A (0)	60−θ [6]	[3 11] [8]	⑪ θ [15 / 4]	60
B (−2)	80+θ [4]	20−θ [9]	[10 13] [3]	100
C (−9)	[−4 3] [1]	100+θ [2]	50−θ [6]	150
Demand	140	120	50	

Figure I.17

	1 (6)	2 (0)	3 (4)	Supply
A (0)	40 [6]	−8 0 [8]	20 [4]	60
B (−2)	100 [4]	−11 −2 [9]	−1 2 [3]	100
C (2)	⑦ 8 [1]	120 [2]	30 [6]	50
Demand	140	120	50	

Figure I.18

therefore introduce this into the solution by allocating θ to that cell and then balancing out as before (Figure I.19).

	1 6	2 0	3 4	
A 0	**40−θ** **6**	−8 0 8	**20+θ** 4	60
B −2	**100** **4**	−11 −2 9	−1 2 3	100
C 2	⑦ 8 θ 1	**120** 2	**30−θ** 6	150
	140	120	50	

Figure I.19

The maximum value for θ is 30, hence we can obtain a third solution. Again, we can attempt to improve on this solution, but since none of the figures in the unused cells is positive no saving can be made, and an optimal allocation has been found (Figure I.20).

	1 6	2 7	3 4	
A 0	10 6	−1 7 8	50 4	60
B −2	100 4	−4 5 9	−1 2 3	100
C −5	30 1	120 2	−7 −1 6	150
	140	120	50	

Figure I.20

The minimum total cost associated with this allocation is:

$$10(6) + 100(4) + 30(1) + 120(2) + 50(4) = 930$$

Complications

Maximizing

Often the objective is to maximize rather than minimize a function. In such cases basically the same procedure is adopted. The first solution is obtained using the North West Corner rule, but improvements are sought from routes not in use by selecting the cell with the largest *negative* value in the top left-hand corner. For example, had we been minimizing in the previous case, an improvement to the first solution would be sought by introducing cell C1.

Unequal supply and demand

In the above example the output from the three steel mills was equal to the requirements of the three factories. However, occasions may arise where such an equality does not exist, in which case a modified procedure is required:

1. If total supply exceeds total demand an additional or 'dummy' column must be added to the matrix in order to accommodate this excess supply.
2. If total demand exceeds total supply a 'dummy' row must be introduced in order to satisfy this excess demand.

In either case a solution is obtained in exactly the same manner as described previously, but in the case of (1) (supply in excess of demand) the allocations determined for the 'dummy' column (the imaginary consumer) represent the supply or production capacity not utilized, and in the case of (2) (demand in excess of supply), the allocations determined for the 'dummy' row represent the demands which are not satisfied.

Degeneracy

When, as in the above example, a transportation solution, either intermediate or final, utilizes at least $m + n - 1$ routes or cells, it is possible to determine all 'dispatch' and 'receiving' costs (where m = number of rows and n = number of columns). However, if less than this number of cells are in use it is impossible to determine these costs by the procedure outlined above. Such a situation is said to be *degenerate* and this type of problem requires a slightly different procedure, a description of which can be found in the book given in 'Further Reading'.

THE ASSIGNMENT ALGORITHM

The assignment problem is a special case of the transportation problem.[2] It can be described as follows.

Given μ customers and μ facilities for processing those customers, and given the effectiveness of each facility for each customer, the problem is to allocate each customer to one facility so that a given measure of effectiveness is optimized.

In other words, in the assignment problem we are concerned with the allocation of one item only from each source and the assignment of one item only to each location. The measure of effectiveness of each job for each machine can be represented as before by means of a matrix (Figure I.21).

_____

[2] The assignment problem is the completely *degenerate* form of the transportation problem.

Customers

	A	B	C	D	E
1	10	5	9	18	11
2	13	19	6	12	14
3	3	2	4	4	5
4	18	9	12	17	15
5	11	6	14	19	10

Facilities (rows 1–5)

Figure I.21

For example, the above matrix gives the cost associated with the processing of each of five customers (A–E) on each of five facilities (1–5). The problem therefore is to assign one customer to each facility so that the measure of effectiveness (total cost) is optimized. The problem therefore is a *minimization* one.

The minimization problem

A solution to this type of problem can be obtained by means of the simple routine described below:

1. Take out the *minimum* figures from each row, as in Figure I.22.

	A	B	C	D	E	Minimums
1	10	5	9	18	11	5
2	13	19	6	12	14	6
3	3	2	4	4	5	2
4	18	9	12	17	15	9
5	11	6	14	19	10	6

Figure I.22

2. Deduct each minimum figure from the figures in that row, as in Figure I.23.

	A	B	C	D	E
1	5	0	4	13	6
2	7	13	0	6	8
3	1	0	2	2	3
4	9	0	3	8	6
5	5	0	8	13	4

Figure I.23

3. Determine the least number of vertical and/or horizontal lines required to cover all zeros in the new matrix, as in Figure I.24.

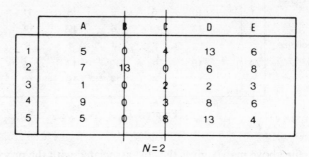

$N = 2$

Figure I.24

4. If the number of lines is less than the number of columns or rows (i.e. since $N = 2 < 5$) proceed to the next step.
5. Take out the minimum figures from each of the new columns, as in Figure I.25.

	A	B	C	D	E
1	5	0	4	13	6
2	7	13	0	6	8
3	1	0	2	2	3
4	9	0	3	8	6
5	5	0	8	13	4
Minimums	1	0	0	2	3

Figure I.25

6. Deduct each minimum figure from the figures in that column, as in Figure I.26.

	A	B	C	D	E
1	4	0	4	11	3
2	6	13	0	4	5
3	0	0	2	0	0
4	3	0	3	6	3
5	4	0	8	11	1

Figure I.26

7. Determine the least number of vertical and/or horizontal lines required to cover all zeros in the new matrix, as in Figure I.27.
8. If the number of lines is less than the number of columns or rows (i.e. since $N = 3 < 5$), proceed to next step.

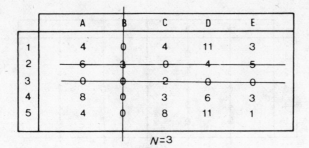

$$N=3$$

Figure I.27

9. Identify *minimum uncovered element* in the new matrix, i.e. Min. = 1 (at E5).
10. (a) Subtract this number from all uncovered elements in the new matrix.
    (b) Add this number to those elements covered by two lines.
    (c) Do not change those elements covered by one line.
    (See Figure I.28)

	A	B	C	D	E
1	3	0	3	10	2
2	6	4	0	4	5
3	0	1	2	0	0
4	7	0	2	5	2
5	3	0	7	10	0

Figure I.28

11. Determine the least number of lines to cover all zeros, as in Figure I.29.

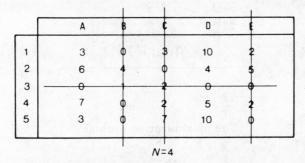

$$N=4$$

Figure I.29

12. If the number of lines is less than the number of columns or rows, repeat steps 9, 10 and 11 until the number of lines is equal to the number of columns or rows, i.e. repeating step 9, Min. = 3 (at A5); repeating steps 10 and 11 gives Figure I.30.
13. The optimal assignment is obtained when the number of lines equals the number of columns or rows. The assignment of customers to facilities is given by the zeros in the matrix, as in Figure I.31.

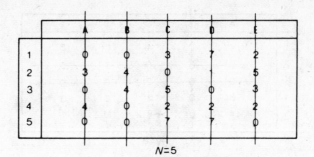

Figure I.30

	A	B	C	D	E
1	[0]	0	3	7	2
2	3	4	[0]	1	5
3	0	4	5	[0]	3
4	4	[0]	2	2	2
5	0	0	7	7	[0]

Figure I.31

14. The cost associated with the optimal assignment may be calculated as follows:

Assignment	Cost (from initial matrix)
1–A	10
2–C	6
3–D	4
4–B	9
5–E	10
	Total = 39

The maximization problem

The procedure for maximizing is identical to that described for minimizing, except for:

Step 1   The maximum figures for each row are extracted.

Step 2   Each of the figures in each row is subtracted from its respective maximum to produce the second matrix.

Thereafter the maximizing procedure follows that described above, i.e. the new matrix is modified by first subtracting the minimum figure for each row from the figures in that row, etc.

FURTHER READING

An adequate treatment of the Simplex and transportation and assignment methods of linear programming can be found in most books on operations research, e.g.
Buffa, E. S. and Dyer, J. S. (1977) *Management Science/Operations Research*. New York: Wiley.

QUESTIONS

I.1 Given the following constraints, determine the values of x, y and z which minimize W, where $W = x - 3y + 2z$

$$3x - y + 2z \leqslant 7$$
$$-2x + 4y \leqslant 12$$
$$-4x + 3y + 8z \leqslant 10$$

I.2 A health 'retreat' is engaged in the treatment of two types of customers: type X and type Y. The retreat is capable of treating either 400 of type X or 800 of type Y per month but, because of a shortage of staff, it is restricted to treating at most 500 customers per month.

Each customer of type X requires four hours of 'infra-red' treatment, while each of type Y of any type requires only half as many. There are only 500 hours of this treatment available each month. The merit of providing treatment for a type X customer is judged to be equivalent to an addition of £7 to the profit of the 'retreat', whereas that for type Y is rated as only £5. How many of each type of customer should be treated if 'merit', as defined here, is to be maximized?

I.3 A chemical company manufactures three types of fertilizer: *Grow*, *Quick Grow* and *Rapid Grow*. Each fertilizer contains the same maximum number of three ingredients, i.e. potash, peat and lime, but in different proportions as shown below:

	Potash per cent	Peat per cent	Lime per cent
Grow	40	40	20
Quick Grow	60	20	20
Rapid Grow	80	0	20

Each week up to 6000 kg of potash can be used in the manufacture of fertilizer and up to 3000 kg of peat is available, but there is no restriction on the lime that may be used.
The fertilizer is sold in 5 kg bags, the profit on each type being as follows:

Grow (G)	1p
Quick Grow (Q)	1.5p
Rapid Grow (R)	2p

How many bags of each type must be produced per week if profit is to be maximized and the maximum total output per week is 10 000 kg?

I.4 Solve the following minimization problem using the transportation algorithm.

		Customer A	B	C	D	E	Hotel capacity
Hotel	1	23	27	32	30	43	115
	2	15	15	20	16	35	65
	3	14	19	25	21	37	100
	4	35	44	47	45	60	35
Customer requirements		25	100	70	65	45	

Figure QI.4

I.5 The costs shown in the cells of the matrix given below relate to the cost of transporting one product between one of three factories (A, B, C) and one of three warehouses (X, Y, Z). Warehouses X, Y and Z must receive a total of 25, 5 and 35 products respectively from the factories A, B and C, which have capacities of 20, 15 and 30 products respectively.

    Allocate the output of the factories to the warehouses in such a way that total transportation costs are minimized.

	X	Y	Z
A	£9	£8	£6
B	£3	£2	£5
C	£10	£7	£11

Figure QI.5

I.6 A large garage wishes to buy four types of accessories in the following quantities:

Standard	25
De luxe	15
Super	10
Super de luxe	5

Quotations are received from three distributors who undertake to supply the garage with each of these accessories. The maximum quantities that the three distributors will supply are as follows:

    A: 30 of all types combined
    B: 30 of all types combined
    C: 15 of all types combined

From the quotations, the financial manager of the garage calculates that the profit ($£$) on each accessory from each distributor is as follows:

	Standard	De luxe	Super	Super de luxe
A	10	11	12	15
B	9	12	15	15
C	5	7	13	20

Figure QI.6

    The manager is confident that he can sell all accessories. How should he buy them, i.e. how many of each type from which distributors?

I.7 Each of five distribution depots is to supply one item to one customer. The costs involved in supplying customers are given in the matrix below. Find the 'assignment' of depot to customer which minimizes the total cost of supplying all five customers.

	Customers				
	A	B	C	D	E
1	2	5	4	3	7
2	2	6	5	4	6
Depots 3	5	6	5	3	7
4	3	4	7	2	4
5	7	5	6	2	1

Figure QI.7

I.8 A transport and general haulage company must send trucks to four cities in England. At the time in question there are six trucks vacant in different parts of the country. The matrix below indicates the costs associated with sending each of the available trucks to each of the four cities. If the company is to minimize the cost associated with redirecting these trucks, which two trucks will not be redirected, and where will the trucks presently at A and B be sent to?

		City			
		1	2	3	4
	A	3	8	2	6
	B	7	1	4	5
Present location of truck	C	3	8	5	8
	D	6	4	3	6
	E	5	2	5	3
	F	5	7	6	2

Figure QI.8

APPENDIX II

Forecasting Techniques[1]

NOTATION USED IN APPENDIX II

α	Exponential smoothing constant
a	Constant (intercept value) for linear regression line
b	Constant in linear regression
CUSUM	Cumulative sum
h	Decision interval in CUSUM technique
n	Number of observations/values
N	Number of periods in a moving average forecast
r	Pearson product moment correlation coefficient
S	Standard error of estimate of Y and X
$\bar{x}$	Mean value of individual x values
$\bar{y}$	Mean value of individual y values

FORECASTING BY PAST AVERAGE

If our objective is to forecast or predict the sales of an item for the next sales period, then using this method:

Forecasted sales for next period = Average sales for previous periods

---

[1] Although our discussion of forecasting will focus on sales figures, the procedures considered are equally relevant for other applications.

EXAMPLE II.I

Period	Sales
1	6
2	4
3	8
4	7
5	4
6	7

Forecasted sales for period $7 = (6+4+8+7+4+7) \div 6 = 6$.

Using this technique we might obtain data as shown in the following table. Clearly our forecast for period 7 was very accurate, as sales prior to this period had remained at much the same average level. But when sales began to increase in later periods, the accuracy of our forecast was reduced because the forecast was influenced too much by the early sales figures and consequently was unable to rise quickly enough to keep up with actual sales.

Period	Actual sales	Forecast sales	Error in forecast
1	6		
2	4		
3	8		
4	7		
5	4		
6	7		
7	6	6.	0.
8	8	6.	−2.
9	9	6.25	−2.75
10	10	6.55	−3.45
11	12	6.9	−5.10
12	13	7.35	−5.65

FORECAST FROM LAST PERIOD'S SALES

One obvious method of overcoming this is to eliminate the influence of old data and base the forecast only on the sales of the previous period. Had this technique been adopted, our forecasts would have been as in Table II.1. Now our forecast is less accurate during the early period because of the fluctuating sales, whereas in the later period the forecast is more accurate because of the *steady* rising sales.

FORECASTING BY MOVING AVERAGE

This method represents a compromise between the two previous methods, in that neither is the forecast influenced by very old data, nor does it solely reflect the figure for the previous period. Consider the historical sales figures shown in Table II.2, which are to be used to

Table II.1

Period	Actual sales	Forecast sales	Error in forecast
1	6		
2	4	6	+2
3	8	4	−4
4	7	8	+1
5	4	7	+3
6	7	4	−3
7	6	7	+1
8	8	6	−2
9	9	8	−1
10	10	9	−1
11	12	10	−2
12	13	12	−1

Table II.2

Year	Period	Sales	Four-period moving average forecast
1974	1	50	
	2	60	
	3	50	
	4	40	
1975	1	50	50
	2	55	50
	3	40	48.75
	4	30	46.25
1976	1	35	43.75
	2	45	40
	3	35	37.5
	4	25	36.25
1977	1	35	35
	2	45	35
	3	35	35
	4	30	36.25

construct a sales forecast for the next year. We must use a four-period moving average in this case, because it is clear from the graph (Figure II.1) that sales fluctuate on an approximate four-period cycle.

Seasonal variations

The moving average forecast sales for the example in Table II.2 are compared with actual sales in Figure II.1. Clearly the effect of the moving average is to smooth the sales pattern, and it is therefore of more value in establishing trends. In this case, in order to make a useful forecast of sales, the seasonal variations must be taken into account. For example, for the four periods of 1974 the average sales were:

$$\frac{50 + 60 + 50 + 40}{4} = 50$$

The sales during periods 1 and 3 conformed to the average figure, but the sales during

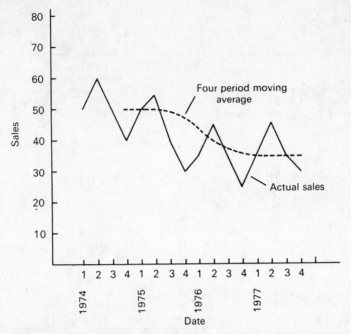

Figure II.1 *Comparison of moving average forecast sales (Table II.4) with actual sales.*

period 2 were high (20 per cent high), while those during period 4 were low (only 80 per cent of the mean for the year).

The percentage variation from the annual mean can be calculated for each period, as shown in Table II.3.

Table II.3 *Percentage variations calculated from annual means*

	(Values in brackets indicate the mean for the year)				Average variation percentage
Period	1974(50)	1975(43.75)	1976(35)	1977(36.25)	
1	100	114.2	100	96.6	102.7
2	120	125.7	128.5	124.0	124.6
3	100	91.5	100	96.6	97.0
4	80	68.7	71.4	82.8	75.7

The average percentage variation from the mean for each period can now be used to modify the moving average forecast sales. For example, the forecast for 1977 period 1 would be 35 (moving average) × 102.7 per cent (average percentage variation) = 35.95. Of course this method of obtaining the average percentage variation can be justified only if, as in this example, the annual figures for each period do not differ substantially.

Secular trends

A secular trend is one which causes sales steadily to increase or decrease. The use of simple moving averages is an adequate method of forecasting, providing sales are subject to neither seasonal variation (as we have seen in Table II.3) nor marked secular trends.

Consider, for example, the sales figures in Table II.4, for which a five-period moving

Table II.4

Period	(a) Actual sales	(b) Five-period moving average	(c) Trend between successive moving averages	(d) Forecast moving average +3 (trend)
0	50			
1	50			
2	50			
3	50			
4	50			
5	55	50		
6	60	51	+1	54
7	65	53	+2	59
8	70	56	+3	65
9	75	60	+4	72
10	80	65	+5	80
11	85	70	+5	85
12	90	75	+5	90
13	90	80	+5	95
14	90	84	+4	96
15	90	87	+3	96
16	90	89	+2	95
17	90	90	+1	93
		90	0	90

average has been calculated (column (b)). Both actual sales and moving average forecast sales are plotted in Figure II.2—curves *a* and *b* respectively—from which it can be seen that the forecast curve lags behind the actual curve. In fact the extent of the time lag is given

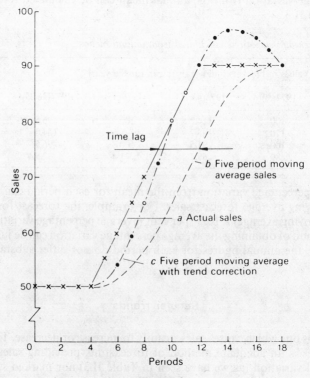

Figure II.2

by:
$$\text{Time lag} = \frac{\text{Time span or number of periods of moving average} - 1}{2}$$

But since the moving average is used as the forecast for the *next* period, the time lag is increased by one period, i.e.

$$\text{Actual time lag} = \left(\frac{\text{Time span} - 1}{2}\right) + 1$$

In this case the time lag of the forecast is three periods. In order to overcome this disadvantage it is necessary to apply a *trend correction* to the moving average forecast. The difference between pairs of moving averages is a measure of the secular trend over one period (assuming that there is no seasonal variation in the data), hence the correction factor should equal this figure multiplied by the time lag, which in this case is three periods. The corrected forecast is given in column (d) of Table II.4.

Curve *c* in Figure II.2 shows how the corrected sales 'catch up' with actual sales after a brief lag period, then settle down to the new constant level after a brief overshoot period.

FORECASTING BY EXPONENTIAL SMOOTHING

The main disadvantages of the moving average method are:

(a) the lengthy calculations involved;
(b) the need to keep quantities of historical data;
(c) the fact that the normal moving average method places equal weight on each of the historical figures used (equal weight on five figures in the above case);
(d) the age of the data, which increases with the number of periods used.

All these disadvantages are overcome by the exponential smoothing technique. Using this technique it is necessary only to retain the previous forecast figure and to know the latest actual sales figure. The technique works by modifying the old forecast in the light of the new sales figure, i.e.

$$\text{New forecast} = \alpha \,(\text{latest sales figure}) + (1 - \alpha) \,(\text{old forecast})$$

where α is known as the smoothing constant.

EXAMPLE II.2

Forecast sales for last period	$= 22$
Actual sales for last period	$= 20$
∴ Forecast sales for next period	$= \alpha(20) + (1 - \alpha)\,22$
Let smoothing constant α	$= 0.1$
∴ Forecast sales for next period	$= 0.1\,(20) + (0.9)\,22$
	$= 2 + 19.8$
	$= 21.8$

The use of this technique permits the forecast to respond to recent actual events but at the same time retain a certain amount of stability. The amount by which the new forecast responds to the latest sales figure, or the extent to which it is 'damped' by the previous forecast, is, of course, determined by the size of the smoothing constant, α. The size of α should be carefully chosen in the light of the stability or variability of actual sales, and is normally from 0.1 to 0.4.

The smoothing constant, α, that gives the equivalent of an N-period moving average can be calculated as follows:

$$\alpha = \frac{2}{N+1}$$

For example, if we wish to adopt an exponential smoothing technique equivalent to a nine-period moving average, α can be found as follows:

$$\alpha = \frac{2}{9+1} = 0.2$$

EXAMPLE II.3

Week	Sales	Four-period moving average forecast	Error	Exponential smoothing forecast ($\alpha = 0.4$)	Error
1	10				
2	12				
3	8				
4	9				
5	10	9.75	0.25	9.45	0.55
6	14	9.75	4.25	9.67	4.33
7	15	10.25	4.75	11.00	4.00
8	14	12.00	2.00	12.60	2.40
9	10	13.25	3.25	13.25	3.25
10	8	13.25	5.25	11.95	3.95
11	6	11.75	5.75	10.37	4.37
12	10	9.50	0.50	8.62	1.38
13	12	8.50	3.50	9.17	2.83
14	8	9.00	1.00	10.30	2.30
15	15	9.00	4.00	9.38	5.62
		11.25		11.63	

Secular trends and seasonal variations

When a secular trend is present the forecast sales obtained by the normal exponential smoothing method will lag behind actual sales, in just the same way as the moving average forecast did. As before, if we are able to estimate the magnitude of the trend in the data, we can apply a trend correction to the forecast to overcome the time lag.

Let us again estimate the trend by comparing successive pairs of forecast figures. In the example in Table II.5 any overall secular trend in the data is obscured by seasonal variations; consequently, in such cases, rather than just taking the difference between successive sales figures as an indication of trends, we must use an estimating procedure. In fact we can use the exponential smoothing method to estimate future trend, i.e.

Forecast trend over next period = α (latest trend figure) + $(1 - \alpha)$ (old trend forecast)

The forecast trend can then be used as a correction factor by adding it to the exponential smoothing forecast in just the same way as the trend correction was added to the moving average forecast in the previous section. Hence:

Final forecast of sales = Normal exponential smoothing forecast
                         + [(Time lag) × Exponential smoothing forecast of trend]

Table II.5

Period	Sales	Exponential smoothing forecast	Trend in actual sales
7	15	11.00	
8	14	12.60	−1
9	10	13.25	−4
10	8	11.95	−2
11	6	10.37	−2
12	10	8.62	+4
13	12	9.17	+2
14	8	10.30	−4
15	15	9.38	+7

Adoptive forecasting

In employing the exponential smoothing technique in forecasting we must choose an appropriate value for α. A large value of α will give considerable weighting to the latest actual values, and will be appropriate where a significant trend exists. While a small value of α will give more weighting to older data, and will therefore provide more smoothing in the forecast, the correct value of α will depend on the nature of the data. Ideally we should monitor the data and the forecast to check the errors in the forecast, and thus be able to modify the value of α. This is the essence of adoptive forecasting, for which several well-established techniques are available, perhaps the best known being that derived by Trigg–Leach.[2]

THE USE OF THE CUMULATIVE SUM TECHNIQUE

The cumulative sum method of examining data is of comparatively recent origin. It is conceptually extremely simple and has found widespread application, particularly in quality control and in forecasting. The cumulative sum chart is simply a plot of the cumulative total of a series of data, or a plot of the cumulative difference between each of the individual readings and a given constant quantity.

For example, consider the monthly sales figures shown in Figure II.3(a). From this figure it appears that sales over the 26 periods have fluctuated about a mean of 11. If, therefore, we consider 11 to be the mean or target value for these data, and subtract this amount from each of the months' sales, plotting the difference cumulatively, the CUSUM chart shown in Figure II.3(b) is obtained.

Notice that while the average value of the data is near to the target value, some of the differences between actual and target values will be positive and some negative, and hence the cumulative sum (CUSUM) chart will be more or less horizontal, but if the average value of the data rises then more of the differences between actual and target values will be positive and the CUSUM graph will rise. Referring to the data in Figure II.3(a) and (b), while a change in the average sales is barely perceptible in Figure II.3(a), it is very noticeable in the CUSUM chart, which rises markedly from about period 15. Had the average sales fallen, this would have been reflected in a noticeable negative (downward) slope of the CUSUM graph.

The great advantage of the CUSUM chart, therefore, is its ability to reveal clearly

---

[2] Trigg, D. W. and Leach, D. H. (1967) Exponential smoothing with an adoptive response rate, *Operational Research Quarterly*, **18**, pp. 53–59.

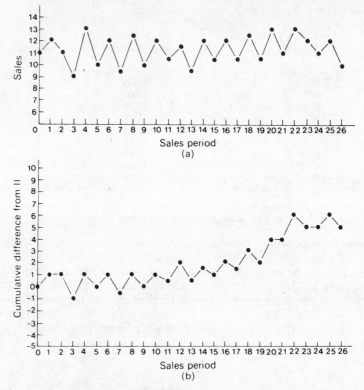

Figure II.3

changes in the average level of data. The chart is interpreted solely on the basis of its slope, a horizontal graph indicating stability in the data, a positive slope indicating an increase in the data average, and a negative slope a decrease in the data average.

Target or reference value and scale sizes

If the target value chosen is less than the average value of the data, the CUSUM graph will rise steadily, and vice versa. Should this happen, the chart can be restarted at zero, this time adopting a higher target value. Similarly, it is of value to restart at zero charts which have previously risen because of a change in the average value of the data. Unless this is done any subsequent change in average value may be less evident from the chart.

The choice of both the horizontal and vertical scales of the CUSUM chart is important, since the scale factors will influence the slope of the graph and hence its ability to show up changes in mean values. It has been suggested[3] that, considering the distance between successive readings on the *x* axis as 1 point, a similar distance on the *y* axis should equal 2σ units, where σ is the standard deviation about the mean of the data in the short term. This scale factor enables significant variations in the data means to be deducted while random variations appear quite small.

[3] Woodward, R. H. and Goldsmith, P. L. (1964) *Cumulative Sum Techniques*, ICI Monograph No. 3. Edinburgh: Oliver and Boyd.

Using cumulative sum charts

Cumulative sum charts are not appropriate for use against data which exhibit a steady trend, or data which exhibit a marked seasonal variation. Their main value, as has already been illustrated, is in determining the nature and extent of changes in mean values. The use of CUSUM charts, therefore, centres around a study of slopes, and in particular the decision of whether or not changes in slope are significant.

There are basically two methods of examining the slope of CUSUM charts in search of significant changes:

1. *The decision interval method.* This method can be usefully adopted where the problem is one of studying either increases or decreases in slope, but not both. A significant increase in slope, necessitating corrective action, is considered to have occurred if the latest point of the chart is more than a given amount (*h*) below (or above) the highest (or lowest) point which has occurred on the chart since the last decision. The amount *h* is termed the 'decision interval' (Figure II.4). This method is therefore analogous to the use of control limits in quality control.

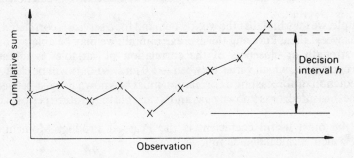

Figure II.4 *The decision interval method.*

2. *The masking method.* This method is useful where the problem is one of examining simultaneously increases and decreases in slope. A V-shaped mask is made and superimposed on the CUSUM chart in such a way that if any of the points on the chart lie beyond the limits of the 'V' then it is considered that a significant change in slope has occurred (Figure II.5).

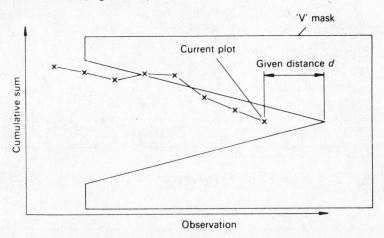

Figure II.5 *Reduction in process mean.*

Methods of calculating decision intervals and constructing masks are given in the 'Further Reading' references listed at the end of this appendix.

The cumulative sum technique is of considerable value in both quality control and forecasting. It is invaluable as a means of detecting errors in forecasts, assessing the influence of price changes on demand, and so on.

ASSOCIATIVE PREDICTIONS OR ECONOMIC INDICATORS

Calculation of correlation coefficients

A correlation coefficient is a measure of the extent to which two variables are associated. In other words, a correlation coefficient is an indication of the extent to which knowledge of the value of one variable is useful for the prediction of the value of the other. This is the basis of a method of forecasting variously known as associative predictions or economic indicators.

For example, we may find that the weekly demand for a service is correlated to rainfall in the previous week; then, knowing the average rainfall, we may be able to forecast future sales. The strength or closeness of the correlation of variables is measured by the correlation coefficient, which varies between -1.0 and $+1.0$. It will be clear that to be of value in prediction or forecasting a correlation must be known to exist between a variable which can be measured, or is known *now*, and a variable for a future period; i.e. there must be a time lag.

Perhaps the most useful coefficient is the Pearson Product Moment Correlation Coefficient, which is calculated as follows:

$$\text{Coefficient, } r, \text{ for two variables X and Y} = \frac{\Sigma(x - \bar{x})(y - \bar{y})}{\sqrt{\Sigma(x - \bar{x})^2 \Sigma(y - \bar{y})^2}}$$

where $\bar{x}$ is the mean value of all the individual x values

$\bar{y}$ is the mean value of all the individual y values.

This formula measures linear correlation (Figure II.6).

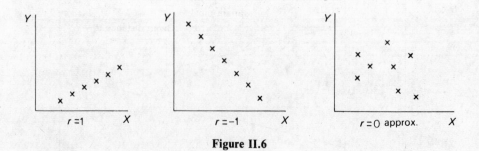

Figure II.6

EXAMPLE II.4

Observation of two variables, x and y, yields the following data. Calculate the linear correlation coefficient of X and Y.

$$x \ 1, 3, 5, 7, 11; \ y \ 2, 4, 8, 9, 10$$

x	$(x-\bar{x})$	$(x-\bar{x})^2$	y	$(y-\bar{y})$	$(y-\bar{y})^2$	$(x-\bar{x})(y-\bar{y})$
1	-4.4	19.4	2	-4.6	21.2	20.2
3	-2.4	5.8	4	-2.6	6.8	6.2
5	-0.4	1.6	8	$+1.4$	2.0	-0.6
7	$+1.6$	2.6	9	$+2.4$	5.8	3.8
11	$+5.6$	31.4	10	$+3.4$	11.6	19.0
$\Sigma x = 27$		60.8	$\Sigma y = 33$		47.4	48.6

$$\bar{x} = \frac{27}{5} = 5.4$$

$$\bar{y} = \frac{33}{5} = 6.6$$

$$r = \frac{\Sigma(x-\bar{x})(y-\bar{y})}{\sqrt{\Sigma(x-\bar{x})^2\Sigma(y-\bar{y})^2}}$$

$$= \frac{48.6}{\sqrt{60.8 \times 47.4}} = 0.91$$

EXAMPLE II.5

A comparison of the monthly sales of an expensive item against the total number of visits made by sales representatives during the *previous* month yields the data shown in the table below. Is the correlation of the two variables good enough to enable the number of sales during a month to be adopted as an efficient indicator of sales during the next month?

Month	Sales (x)	Visits made (y)	$(x-\bar{x})$	$(x-\bar{x})^2$	$(y-\bar{y})$	$(y-\bar{y})^2$	$(x-\bar{x})(y-\bar{y})$
1	11	605	-1.46	2.132	-52.7	2777.3	76.9
2	13	640	$+0.54$	0.292	-17.7	313.3	-9.6
3	12	625	-0.46	0.212	-32.7	1069.3	15.0
4	12	630	-0.46	0.212	-27.7	767.3	12.7
5	10	630	-2.46	6.05	-27.7	767.3	68.1
6	12	645	-0.46	0.212	-12.7	161.3	5.8
7	13	655	$+0.54$	0.292	-2.7	7.3	-1.5
8	14	680	$+1.54$	2.37	$+22.3$	497.3	34.3
9	12	660	-0.46	0.212	$+2.3$	5.3	-1.1
10	14	680	$+1.54$	2.37	$+22.3$	497.3	34.3
11	11	675	$+1.46$	2.132	$+17.3$	299.3	-25.3
12	11	670	-1.46	2.132	$+12.3$	151.3	-18.0
13	13	670	$+0.54$	0.292	$+12.3$	151.3	6.6
14	14	690	$+1.54$	2.37	$+32.3$	1043.3	49.7
15	15	710	$+2.54$	6.45	$+52.3$	2735.3	132.8
	$\Sigma x = 187$	$\Sigma y = 9865$		27.730		11243.5	380.7

$\bar{x} = 12.46$ $\bar{y} = 657.7$

$$r = \frac{380.7}{\sqrt{(27.73)(11\,243.5)}} = 0.681$$

The correlation between the number of visits during the previous month and the number of sales is 0.681, which is perhaps insufficient to justify its possible use as a method of short-term sales forecasting.

Linear regression[4]

We have seen that a linear relationship between two variables, X and Y, is indicated by a high value of the correlation coefficient. However, this coefficient does not indicate the true relationship, hence we are unable to estimate either a value of X for a given value of Y, or vice versa. To do this a regression equation must be calculated, as in Figure II.7.

The regression line for Y on X is the best line for calculating values of Y, and is obtained by minimizing the sum of the squares of the errors of estimation, i.e. the *y* values in Figure II.7(a).

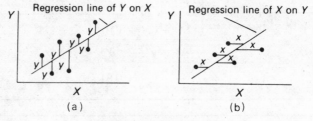

Figure II.7

The regression line for X on Y is the best line for calculating values of X, and is obtained by minimizing the sum of the squares of the errors of estimation, i.e. the *x* values in Figure II.7(b). The general equation for the regression line of Y on X is given by:

$$Y = a + bX$$

where *a* and *b* are two constants. The values of these two constants are obtained by the following formula:

$$b = \frac{n\Sigma xy - (\Sigma x)(\Sigma y)}{n(\Sigma x^2) - (\Sigma x)^2}$$

$$a = \frac{\Sigma y - b\Sigma x}{n}$$

Similarly the general equation for the linear regression of X on Y is:

$$X = a + bY$$

---

[4] We shall deal exclusively with linear regression equations, whereas in fact our data may be of a curvilinear form. A similar procedure to the one described here may be used to derive formulae for calculating non-linear regression equations. Furthermore, we shall be concerned only with the regression of two variables, whereas in practice two or more variables may be involved. In such cases a similar, if longer, procedure to that described here can be adopted. Description of multiple and non-linear regression can be found in the books in 'Further Reading'.

where

$$b = \frac{n\Sigma xy - (\Sigma x)(\Sigma y)}{n(\Sigma y^2) - (\Sigma y)^2}$$

$$a = \frac{\Sigma x - b\Sigma y}{n}$$

EXAMPLE II.6

The data in the following table relate to the weight of an item at a period of time and its growth at a future period. Find the regression line for predicting 'growth' and calculate the growth for a weight value of 52.

Let growth be variable Y
Let weight be variable X

$$b = \frac{7(1632) - (210)(51)}{7(7308) - (210)^2}$$

$$= \frac{714}{7056}$$

$$= 0.101$$

Weight (x)	Growth (y)	x^2	xy
12	5.5	144	66
18	5.9	324	106
24	6.5	576	156
30	7.4	900	222
36	8.2	1296	295.2
42	8.9	1764	373.8
48	8.6	2304	412.8
$\Sigma x = 210$	$\Sigma y = 51.0$	$\Sigma x^2 = 7308$	$\Sigma xy = 1632.0$

$$a = \frac{(51) - 0.101(210)}{7}$$

$$= \frac{29.79}{7}$$

$$= 4.26$$
$$x = 52$$
$$\therefore y = 4.26 + 0.101(52)$$
$$= 4.26 + 5.25$$
$$y = 9.51$$

The regression line provides only an estimate of the value of Y on X. The uncertainty or accuracy of the estimate can be assessed by calculating the 'standard error' of the estimate of Y on X ($S_{Y,X}$):

$$S_{Y,X} = \sqrt{\frac{\Sigma(y - y^1)^2}{n - 2}}$$

where y = actual value

y^1 = value calculated from regression equation

The standard error of the estimate of X on Y is given similarly by:

$$S_{X.Y} = \sqrt{\frac{\Sigma(x - x^1)^2}{n - 2}}$$

For example, in the above case:

y	y^1	$= 4.26 + 0.101(x)$	$(y - y^1)$	$(y - y^1)^2$
5.5	5.47		0.03	0.0009
5.9	6.08		−0.18	0.0324
6.5	6.68		−0.18	0.0324
7.4	7.29		0.11	0.0121
8.2	7.90		0.30	0.0900
8.9	8.50		0.40	0.1600
8.6	9.11		−0.51	0.2601
			$\Sigma(y - y^1)^2 =$	0.5879

$$S_{Y.X} = \sqrt{\frac{0.5879}{5}}$$

$$S_{Y.X} = 0.343$$

$S_{Y.X}$ or $S_{X.Y}$ provides a measure of the 'closeness' of the relationship between the two variables. The smaller the figure, the closer the values are to the regression line and hence the more accurate the regression equation is for predictive purposes.

FURTHER READING

Anderson, O. D. (1976) *Time Series Analysis and Forecasting*. London: Butterworth. A rather more specialist book concerned largely with the 'Box–Jenkins' approach for dealing with time series of data which are not independent but serially correlated (not covered in Appendix II).

Chisholm, R. K. and Whitaker, G. R. (1971) *Forecasting Methods*. Homewood, Illinois: Irwin. A fairly comprehensive and simple coverage of forecasting methods including a brief treatment of moving averages and exponential smoothing and a detailed treatment of regression methods.

Woodward, R. H. and Goldsmith, P. L. (1964) *Cumulative Sum Techniques*, ICI Monograph No. 3. Edinburgh: Oliver and Boyd.

QUESTIONS

II.1 The table below gives the monthly sales of a particular product over a 20-month period. Use (a) forecasting by previous average, and (b) forecasting from last period's sales, to forecast sales for period 4 onwards. Compare the accuracy of the two forecasts and comment on the practical implications of adopting these two simple methods of forecasting.

Period	Sales
1	20
2	18
3	17
4	21
5	22
6	21
7	20
8	18
9	19
10	21
11	24
12	28
13	34
14	36
15	35
16	30
17	28
18	26
19	30
20	31

II.2 Plot the four years' sales figures shown in the tables below, along with the appropriate moving average sales figure.

Year	Sales
1976	250
	275
	300
	230
1977	260
	280
	300
	240
1978	260
	295
	320
	245
1979	245
	290
	315
	230

How does the moving average sales graph compare with the actual sales, and what refinements are necessary before the moving average method can be used as an accurate technique for forecasting sales of this type?

II.3 Calculate the seasonally adjusted four-period moving average sales for the data given below:

Year	Period	Sales ('000)
1976	1	50
	2	60
	3	50
	4	44
1977	1	50
	2	64
	3	56
	4	50
1978	1	54
	2	70
	3	56
	4	50
1979	1	54
	2	60
	3	52
	4	50

II.4 Use the moving average technique with secular trend correction and seasonal adjustment to forecast quarterly sales of product X. The actual sales of product X over a five-year period are shown below. Calculate the forecasted sales over as much of this period as possible, and compare the forecasted sales with the actual.

Year	Quarter	Actual Sales ('000)
1965	S	20
	S	15
	A	30
	W	25
1966	S	20
	S	20
	A	35
	W	30
1967	S	25
	S	20
	A	40
	W	35
1968	S	30
	S	25
	A	45
	W	35
1969	S	30
	S	25
	A	50
	W	40

II.5 The figures below show the actual sales of product Y which have occurred on each of 20 successive periods. Calculate the appropriate simple moving average sales (without seasonal adjustment) for as much of this period as possible and compare the difference between actual and moving average with the difference between actual and an exponentially smoothed demand equivalent to the moving average. Comment on the nature of your results.

Period	Actual sales
1	10
2	12
3	12
4	10
5	8
6	10
7	13
8	12
9	9
10	8
11	10
12	13
13	14
14	12
15	9
16	10
17	13
18	14
19	11
20	10

II.6 Historical data for product Z indicate that there are both seasonal variations and a continuously increasing trend in sales. How can the simple exponential smoothing technique be modified to provide acceptable forecasts in such a situation?

Illustrate your answer by means of simple numerical examples of your own construction.

II.7 (a) Use the cumulative sum technique to examine the following sales data for any changes in average monthly sales.

Month	1977	1978	1979
1	10	10	9
2	11	9	12
3	10	10	11
4	12	11	13
5	8	10	12
6	10	12	11
7	12	13	10
8	9	12	11
9	12	10	10
10	7	9	9
11	9	11	10
12	10	12	11

(b) Comment on the value of this technique. How is its value affected by the choice of (i) the reference value and (ii) the scale factor?

II.8 Explain the meaning of (a) the decision interval and (b) the 'masking' method in the context of the cumulative sum technique.

II.9 Calculate the Pearson Product Moment Correlation Coefficient (r):
(a) of variables X and Y;
(b) of a setting x and a reading y

X	Y		x	y
15	0		1	5
16	2		2	6
17	4		3	—
18	6		4	12
19	8		5	11
20	10		6	13
21	12		7	16
22	14		8	16
23	16		9	—
24	18		10	19
			11	23
			12	22

II.10　Calculate the linear regression of Y and X and, using the equation, calculate Y for the following values of X:
(a)　137;
(b)　95.

Y	X
2	20
5	45
4	30
3	30
5	45
6	65
7	65
6	60
8	70
9	85
10	105
12	115
13	120

II.11　(a)　Calculate the linear regression line for determining consumption from the gross national product.

GNP (£) in year	Consumption for following year
20 200	13 900
20 800	14 500
21 200	14 600
21 600	14 900
21 700	15 300
22 500	16 000
23 600	16 600
24 400	17 000
24 600	17 300
25 500	18 000

(b)　It is estimated that the GNP three years hence will equal £30 000. What is consumption likely to be four years hence?

Answers to Odd-numbered Analytical Questions

Chapter 4

4.5

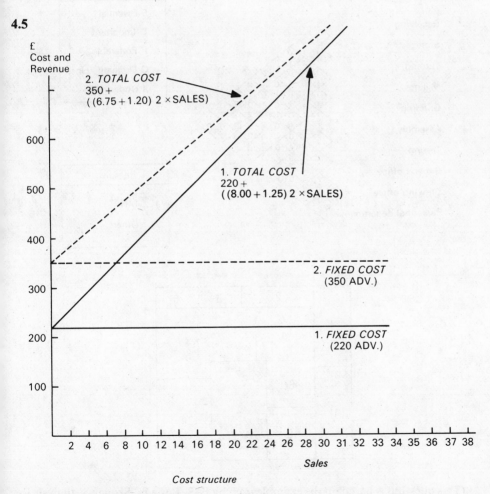

£
Cost and
Revenue

2. *TOTAL COST*
350 +
((6.75 + 1.20) 2 × SALES)

1. *TOTAL COST*
220 +
((8.00 + 1.25) 2 × SALES)

2. *FIXED COST*
(350 ADV.)

1. *FIXED COST*
(220 ADV.)

Sales

Cost structure

(Employ option 1 for sales of 30.)

Chapter 5

5.3 About 95 km north east of Birmingham.

5.5 Sunderland.

5.7 Additional factory should be established at location D.
Total cost for ABD = £16990/month.
Total cost for ABC = £17240/month (assuming cost of excess capacity is zero).

5.9 (a) Yes.
(b) Store at B.

Chapter 6

6.1

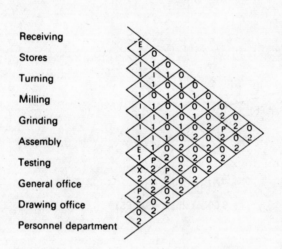

Closeness
E Essential
I Important
P Preferable
O Ordinarily close
X Undesirable

Reason	
1	MH
2	Others

6.3

(This question is based on the example used by E. S. Buffa in 'Sequence analysis for functional layouts', *Journal of Industrial Engineering*, March/April, pp. 12–25 (1955).)

Chapter 7

7.3

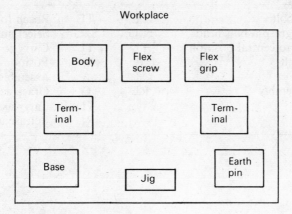

Workplace

N.B. Screwdriver suspended over jig.

Left hand		Right hand	
Reach for base piece	⇨	Reach for earth pin	⇨
Grasp base	O	Grasp pin	O
Carry to jig/orient in fingers	⇨	Carry to jig/orient in fingers	⇨
Place in jig	O	Position in base	O
Reach to terminal	⇨	Reach to terminal	⇨
Grasp/orient	O	Grasp/orient	O
Carry to base	⇨	Carry to base	⇨
Place in base	O	Place in base	O
Reach to body top	⇨	Reach to flex grip	⇨
Grasp	O	Grasp/orient	O
Carry to jig	⇨	Carry to jig	⇨
		Place in base	O
Place in jig	O	Reach to body screw	⇨
Grasp assembly	O	Grasp/orient	O
Remove from jig	O	Carry to assembly/orient	⇨
Place inverted on bench	O	Place screw in hole	O
Hold	O	Reach to flex screws	⇨
I		Grasp two screws	O
I		Carry	⇨
I		Place one screw in hole	O
I		Place second screw in hole	O
I		Reach for screwdriver	⇨
I		Grasp	O
I		Carry to assembly	O
I		Tighten body screw	O
I		Tighten one flex screw	O
Grasp plug	O	Tighten second flex screw	O
Carry to bin	⇨	Return screwdriver	⇨
Release	O	Release screwdriver	O

7.5

Left hand	Therblig	Therblig	Right hand
Reach for bolt	TE	TE	Reach for nut
Select and grasp a bolt head	S, G	S, G	Select and grasp nut
Carry bolt to central position	TL	TL	Carry to central position
Position bolt	P	P	Position nut
Hold head	H	A	Assemble nut onto bolt
Release assembly	RL	G	Grasp assembly
Idle		TL	Carry assembly to box
Idle		RL	Release assembly into box

Chapter 8

8.1 $N^1 = 9$, therefore sufficient observations have been made.

8.3 2262 pieces.

8.5 Output per shift at standard performance = 200.
Production cost per piece = 9 p.

8.7 10.2 SM

8.11 Worker A El 1 BM = 0.09 ⎱ 0.23/item
El 2 BM = 0.14 ⎰
Worker B El 3 BM = 0.15 ⎱ 0.20/item
El 4 BM = 0.05 ⎰
Worker C El 5 BM = 0.20   0.20/item

(This question is based on an example given in Chapter 6 of Graham, C. F. (1965) *Work Measurement and Cost Control*. Oxford: Pergamon. This excellent little book gives a good description of the uses of rated systematic sampling.)

Chapter 9

9.7 (a)   45.9 hours
(b)   51.2 hours
(c)   16

Chapter 10

10.1 2530 p

10.3 (a) 13 500 p
(b) 18 000 p
(c) 12 150 p
(d) 14 000 p

Chapter 11

11.1 The production plan is given by the following matrix:

Week number		26	27	28	29
26	Stock	31	4		
27	Normal shift		35		
	Night shift		4	11	
28	Normal shift			35	
	Night shift			9	6
29	Normal shift				33
	Night shift				

11.3 Total cost associated with this plan = £1501.

Month	Shift	May			June			July			August			Stock			Available capacity (work hours)
		I	II	III	I	II	III	I	II	III	I	II	III	I	II	III	
May	1	5	6	4	5·5	6·6	4·5	6·0	7·2	5·0	6·5	7·8	5·5	7·0	8·6	6·0	150
	2	7	8	6	7·5	8·6	6·5	8·0	9·2	7·0	8·5	9·8	7·5	9·0	10·6	8·0	.200
	3	7	8	6	7·5	8·6	6·5	8·0	9·2	7·0	8·5	9·8	7·5	9·0	10·6	8·0	200
June	1				5	6	4	5·5	6·6	4·5	6·0	7·2	5·0	6·5	7·8	5·5	200
	2				7	8	6	7·5	8·6	6·5	8·0	9·2	7·0	8·5	9·8	7·5	300
	3				7	8	6	7·5	8·6	6·5	8·0	9·2	7·0	8·5	9·8	7·5	350
July	1							5	6	4	5·5	6·6	4·5	6·0	7·2	5·0	250
	2							7	8	6	7·5	8·6	6·5	8·0	9·2	7·0	300
	3							7	8	6	7·5	8·6	6·5	8·0	9·2	7·0	300
August	1										6	7	5	6·5	7·6	5·5	300
	2										8	9	7	8·5	9·6	7·5	250
	3										8	9	7	8·5	9·6	7·5	250
Total demand numbers		20	50	30	40	65	25	25	75	50	40	72	32				3 050
work hours		100	350	150	200	455	125	125	525	250	200	504	140	3 144			

Since total demand in work hours exceeds total capacity, work will have to be subcontracted. For example, unless work is subcontracted, insufficient sub-assembly IIs will be available in May.

Chapter 12

12.1

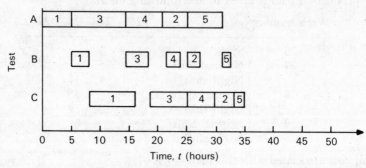

12.3   (a) Sequence   = 3, 6, 2, 4, 7, 1, 5
                            or 3, 6, 2, 7, 4, 1, 5
       (b) Sequence X = 3, 2, 5, 6, 1
                    Y = 4, 3, 2, 5, 6
       (c) Several sequences give T (throughput time) = 22   e.g. 3, 1, 4, 2;   2, 3, 4, 1;
           1, 3, 2, 4;   2, 1, 3, 4;   3, 2, 4, 1 (obtained empirically since the special case of
           Johnson's rule does *not* apply)

12.5   (a)   (b)

Job	Priority rule									Job	Priority rule (+ FCFS)								
	1	2	3	4	5	6	7	8	9		1	2	3	4	5	6	7	8	9
1	4	4	3	7	4	3	7	1		1	4	4	3	7	4	3	7	1	
2	1	1	5	3	1	1	4	10		2	1	2	1	8	6	1	1	4	10
3	5	4	8	3	7	5	3	9	2	3	5	5	8	4	8	5	4	9	2
4	2	1	2	9	2	2	2	6	4	4	2	1	2	9	2	2	2	6	4
5	3	3	3	1	9	3	6	3	9	5	3	3	3	2	10	3	6	3	9
6	10	8	9	5	3	10	8	7	3	6	10	8	9	5	3	10	8	8	3
7	8	7	10	1	9	8	3	10	5	7	8	7	10	1	9	8	5	10	5
8	5	6	4	10	1	5	9	2	8	8	7	6	5	10	1	7	9	2	8
9	5	8	7	5	3	5	7	4	6	9	6	9	7	6	4	6	7	5	6
10	8	10	6	5	3	8	10	1	7	10	9	10	6	7	5	9	10	1	7

12.7

Order number	Number of products	Machine					
		A		B		C	
		I	Hours	I	Hours	I	Hours
1	50	0.33		0.67		0	150
2	75	0.5		0	150	1.0	
3	25	0.67		0.33	100	0	
4	80	0	160	1.5		1.0	
			175 (91%)		275 (91%)		175 (86%)

12.9   Minimize C = $2(4Q_{1,A} + 3Q_{2,A} + 5Q_{3,A} + 2Q_{4,A})$
$+ 3(5Q_{1,B} + 2Q_{2,B} + 4Q_{3,B} + 5Q_{4,B})$
$+ 2.5(3Q_{1,C} + 4Q_{2,C} + 3Q_{3,C} + 4Q_{4,C})$

Subject to the following constraints:

$$Q_{1,A} + Q_{1,B} + Q_{1,C} = 50$$
$$Q_{2,A} + Q_{2,B} + Q_{2,C} = 75$$
$$Q_{3,A} + Q_{3,B} + Q_{3,C} = 25$$
$$Q_{4,A} + Q_{4,B} + Q_{4,C} = 80$$
$$Q_{ij} \geqslant 0 \text{ where } i = 1, 2, 3, 4$$
$$j = A, B, C$$

where Q_{ij} = Quantity of order i allocated to machine j

12.11   The production plan is shown below, assuming production during one month may be used to satisfy demand in the same month.

			May A units	May B units	June A units	June B units
May	Factory 1	Normal	100	50		
		Overtime		20		
	Factory 2	Normal		80	90	
		Overtime			20	20
June	Factory 1	Normal				100
		Overtime				5
	Factory 2	Normal				65
		Overtime				

Total cost = £2770 (assuming excess capacity has zero cost)

12.13   (a) 67 per cent
(b) Two lines
(c) (i) The probability of a line requiring service by the telephonist is independent of the time it has been used hitherto.
(ii) All service times are constant.
(iii) There is no priority system for answering calls on a line.
(iv) All lines have similar operational characteristics.

Chapter 13

13.1

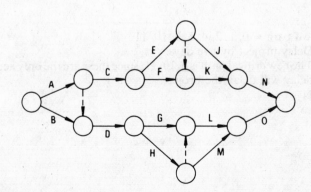

13.3

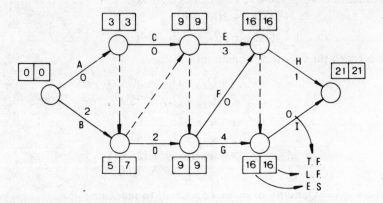

Critical path = A, C, F, I

13.5   Critical path = A, B, F, H, for which $t = 28$ and $\sigma^2 = 7.23$. From tables $P = 2$ per cent, i.e. considering critical path only, probably of finishing on or before 22.5 days = 2 per cent. *But* minimum duration for path A, C, D, G $= 2 + 9 + 5 + 7 = 23$. Therefore actual probability = 0.

13.7   (a)

Activity	TF
0–1	0
1–2	0
1–3	1
2–4	0
3–5	1
4–5	0
4–6	3
5–7	9
5–8	7
5–9	0
6–10	3
7–10	9
8–10	3
9–10	0
10–11	0

Critical path = 0, 1, 2, 4, 5, 9, 10, 11
   (b) (i) Delay project by five days.
        (ii) The new critical path is 6, 10, 11, since these are the only activities in which delay will delay the project.

13.11   (a) 31 days

(b)

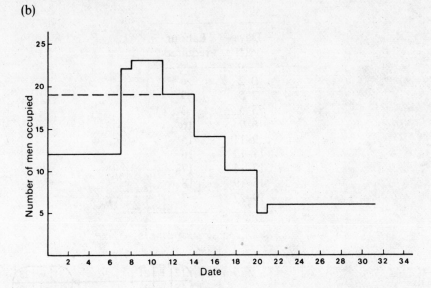

(c)

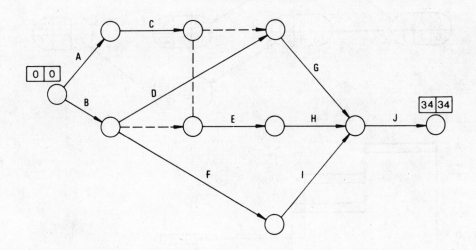

(d) Three days

13.13

(a) Earliest completion = 27 days.
   Critical path = A, B, E, H, J.
   Total float: A = 0, B = 0, C = 5, D = 4, E = 0, F = 4, G = 4, H = 0,
   I = 4, J = 0, K = 8.

(b)

Days	Labour required
0–2	4
2–5	9
5–6	3
6–9	16
9–11	15
11–12	16
12–15	17
15–19	18
19–27	7

13.15

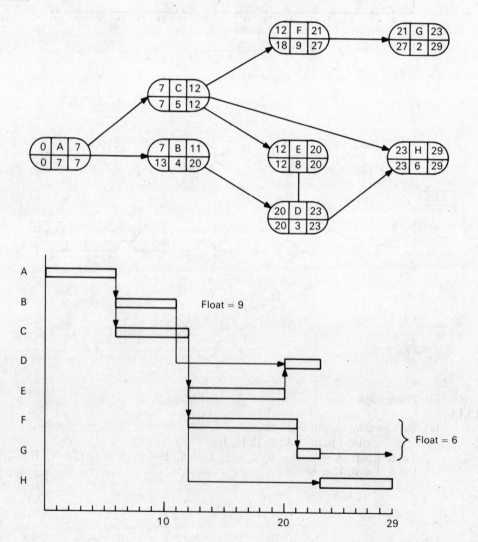

Chapter 14

14.3 21 000 litres (equivalent)
14.5 14 100 to 31 200 litres (equivalent)
14.7 (a) 1.2 months
       (b) 1.22 months
       (c) 1.26 months
14.9 $Q_E = 4670$
       $Q_V = 6670$
       $Q_G = 10\,000$
       $Q_M = 3330$
       $N = 1.5$

Chapter 15

15.1 $n_{min.} = 28$
       $C = 0.4$ minutes
15.3 Cycle time = 20 minutes

Station	Work elements	Station time
1	0, 1, 2, 4	20 min
2	3, 5, 7, 8	20 min
3	6, 9, 10, 11	20 min

Balancing loss = zero

15.5

	Station					
	1	2	3	4	5	6
4.61 per hour $C = 13$ minutes	0, 1, 2,	3, 4	5, 6	7	8, 10	9

Balancing loss = 25.7 per cent
5 per hour $C = 12$ minutes
Balancing loss = 19.6 per cent

	0, 1, 2	3, 4	5, 6,	7	8, 10	9

15.9 (a) 1
       (b) 2
15.11 A, E, D, B, C
       £320
15.13 Using the method described at the end of the chapter:
       Fixed launching interval, $\gamma = 0.47$ minutes
       Models must be launched in cycles as follows: A C A BA CC A CC
       In other words, proportions of each model produced are as follows:

$$A = 0.40$$
$$B = 0.10$$
$$C = 0.50$$
$$D = 0.00$$

Except in special circumstances this method will not provide a complete solution to the problem.

15.15   Cost of present arrangement $= £323$
Cost of Alternative 1 (mixed-model) $= £224$
Cost of Alternative 2 (multi-model) $= £270$
Use Alternative 1

Chapter 17

17.3   (a) 2620
(b) 2620
(c) 2500
17.5   (a) $£2550$
(b) $£2400$
(c) $£2850$
$Q = 10\,000$
$C = £34\,300$
17.9   (a) Startrite $=$ 890
Quickfire $= 1246$
Longlife $=$ 622
Highpower $=$ 490
(b) 2.14 months
17.11   (a) $Q^* = 862$
Re-order level = 21 items
(b) Re-order level = 21 items
17.13   Re-order level = 24 items
Order quantity = 300 items

Chapter 18

18.1

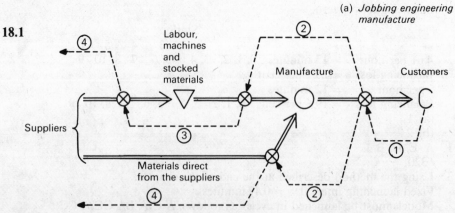

(a) *Jobbing engineering manufacture*

Controls: ① Information on each customer's requirements:
controls the flow out of the function

② Activity scheduling and control: controls the
flow through the function or process in the system

③ Inventory control: controls inventory
levels and inventory inputs

④ Purchasing control: controls input of
resources from suppliers

(b) *A restaurant*

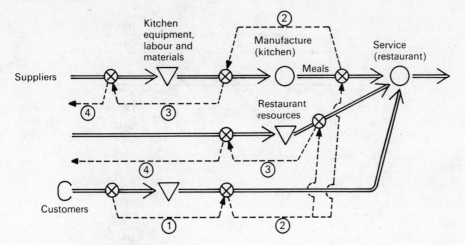

Controls: As for (a); however, the control
of inventories③ here
involves the control of
input stocks (through the
control of levels and stock inputs),
and also customer input
queues (through the control
of levels and queue outputs)

(c) *A delicatessen*

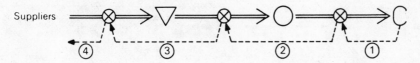

Controls: As for (a)

Chapter 19

19.1 (c) 0.56
19.3 $C = 14$
  $n = 317$
19.5 (a) Approximately 0.82
  (c) $n = 89$
    $c = 4$
19.7 (a) 1, $\alpha = 26$ per cent 2. $\alpha = 33$ per cent
  (b) 1. $\beta = 29$ per cent 2. $\beta = 12$ per cent
  (i) Plan 1
  (ii) Plan 2
  Average outgoing quality limit:
  Plan 1 = 1.7 approximately
  Plan 2 = 1.2 approximately

19.9

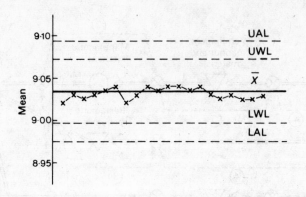

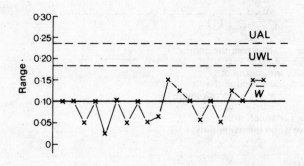

19.11

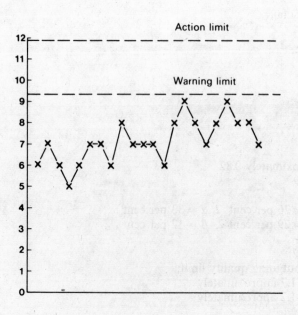

19.13

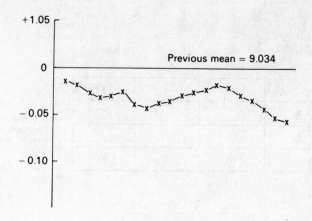

19.15 (a) 2.2
(b) 12.4×10^4

Chapter 20

20.3 (a) £2.20/hour
(b) (i) 280 hours
(ii) 157 hours
20.5 (a) (i) 6
(ii) 3.5
(b) (i) Group C
(ii) Group A
20.7 (a) 47 hours
(b) 29 hours
20.9 (a) Yes
(b) £18

Appendix I

I.1 $x = 4$
$y = 5$
$z = 10$
Min. $W = -11$
I.3 Constraints:

$$2G + Q \qquad + p = \quad 3000$$
$$2G + 3Q + 4R + q = \quad 6000$$
$$G + \quad Q + \quad R + r = 10\,000$$
$$\text{Max. } W = G + 3/2Q + 2R$$

Solution: $R = 1500$
Profit: $W = 3000$ p

I.5

	X	Y	Z
A			20
B	15		
C	10	5	15

Minimum
transportation
cost = £465

I.6

	Standard	De luxe	Super	Super de luxe
A	25			
B		15	10	
C				5

Profit = £633

I.7

	A	B	C	D	E
1			1		
2	1				
3				1	
4		1			
5					1

Minimum cost
= 14

Appendix II

II.1

Period	Actual sales	Forecast (a)	Error	Forecast (b)	Error
1	20				
2	18				
3	17				
4	21	18.3	−2.7	17	−4.0
5	22	19.0	−3.0	21	−1.0
6	21	19.6	−1.4	22	+1.0
7	20	19.8	−0.2	21	+1.0
8	18	19.9	+1.9	20	+2.0
9	19	19.6	+0.6	18	−1.0
10	21	19.6	−1.4	19	−2.0
11	24	19.7	−4.3	21	−3.0
12	28	20.0	−8.0	24	−4.0
13	34	20.7	−13.3	28	−6.0
14	36	21.7	−14.3	34	−2.0
15	35	22.8	−13.2	36	+1.0
16	30	23.6	−6.4	35	+5.0
17	28	24.0	−4.0	30	+2.0
18	26	24.3	−1.7	28	+2.0
19	30	24.4	−5.6	26	−4.0
20	31	24.6	−6.4	30	−1.0
		25.0		31	

	(a)	(b)
Average error (neglecting sign) periods 4–20	5.20	2.47
Average error (neglecting sign) periods 4–10	1.6	1.71
Average error (neglecting sign) periods 11–20	7.72	3.00

II.3

Year	Period	Sales ('000)	Four-period moving average	Seasonally adjusted four-period moving average
1976	1	50		
	2	60		
	3	50		
	4	44		
1977	1	50	51.0	48.5
	2	64	51.0	60.8
	3	56	52.0	51.0
	4	50	53.5	47.0
1978	1	54	55.0	52.5
	2	70	56.0	66.7
	3	56	57.5	56.2
	4	50	57.5	50.8
1979	1	54	57.5	54.7
	2	66	57.5	68.2
	3	52	56.5	55.3
	4	50	55.5	49.0
			55.5	52.8

II.5

Period	Actual sales	Five-period moving average	Error	Exponential smoothing $\alpha = 0.33$	Error
1	10				
2	12				
3	12				
4	10				
5	8				
6	10	10.4	+0.4	10.4	+0.4
7	13	10.4	−2.6	10.3	−2.7
8	12	10.6	−1.4	11.2	−0.8
9	9	10.6	+1.6	11.4	+2.4
10	8	10.4	+2.4	10.7	+2.7
11	10	10.4	+0.4	9.8	+0.2
12	13	10.4	−2.6	9.9	−3.1
13	14	10.4	−3.6	10.9	−3.1
14	12	10.8	−1.2	11.9	−0.1
15	9	11.4	+2.4	12.0	+3.0
16	10	11.6	+1.6	11.0	+1.0
17	13	11.6	−1.4	10.8	−2.2
18	14	11.6	−2.4	11.5	−2.5
19	11	11.6	+0.6	12.3	+1.3
20	10	11.4	+1.4	11.9	+1.9
		11.6		11.3	
Average error (neglecting sign)			1.73		1.83

(taking period 6 exponential forecast as equal to period 6 moving average forecast)

II.7

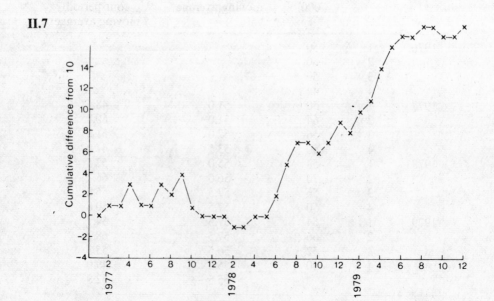

II.9   (a) $r = 1.0$
      (b) $r = 0.97$

II.11 (a) $y = -1330 + 0.757x$
         where $y = $ consumption
               $x = $ GNP
      (b) 20 670

Author Index

Subject Index